The
TIME MACHINE
and the
DOMAINE

Origins and Functions of
Imaginative Literature

for Michèle of long ago
(d'autrefois)
" Fit audience, though few."
Richard Bevis

RICHARD W. BEVIS

 FriesenPress

One Printers Way
Altona, MB R0G0B0,
Canada

www.friesenpress.com

ISBN
978-1-03-912490-5 (Hardcover)
978-1-03-912489-9 (Paperback)
978-1-03-912491-2 (eBook)

1. *Literary Criticism, Semiotics & Theory*

Distributed to the trade by The Ingram Book Company

In Loving Memory of Vivian Leamer Bevis

My *Domaine perdu*

Table of Contents

PART THREE: BROADENING

INTRODUCTION

MOST SOCIETIES IN MOST TIMES and places have (often after a long period of oral expression) produced something called "literature," and still do. The following chapters ask *why*, from what motives, they did and we do so. What uses, roles, or benefits are foreseen, such that highly disparate peoples generate some type of literary expression? What needs, of writers and of readers, does literature meet, and how does it function within the context of those needs? In short, what is literature's *economy*, its system of production, consumption, and use (from the Greek word for 'steward' or 'manager')? This question has piqued me since the early 1990s, but I was slow to formulate these particular queries, let alone answer them. Knowing that my own responses were merely personal opinions, I began to canvass books and other people for their views.

Colleagues and friends offered several answers, but also posed counter-questions. *What do you mean by "literature"?* was the most common, and a reasonable comeback. I mean "the smaller tent," what is usually called imaginative or "creative" writing – fiction, poetry, drama – rather than the broader root sense of *litterae*: writing of all kinds. We do not need to query the function of utilitarian writing such as a laundry list – unless it crops up in a Jane Austen novel. *There are different answers for different kinds of literature in different places and periods* was another popular (and fair) response. It may be true, but that does not prevent me from seeking what universal or archetypal motives may underlie literary expression. I also "read around" in critical theory and literary criticism, hoping to find a secondary text for a possible seminar, but came across little that addressed my questions in a sustained way. (Some partial answers that did crop up are discussed below.) This paucity of theorizing about the psychic bases of imaginative literature by scholars in the humanities baffled me. They seemed to be taking a foundational point for granted. Why would serious commentators on literature *not* investigate such central issues as its origins and *raison d'être?*

I waded through Hazard Adams and Leroy Searle's *Critical Theory Since 1965* (1986; they treat the tribute to Northrop Frye at the 1965 English Institute meeting as the founding event of a new era). While some of their theorists struck me as bores or even charlatans, others made sense and, I thought, might prove useful: Geoffrey Hartman, Wolfgang Iser, Meyer Abrams, Charles Altieri, Edward Said, Max Horkheimer, Georg Lukács, Claude Lévi-Strauss. I also came across works critiquing critical theory by writers with credentials in the field; they included Said's "Secular Criticism" in *The World, the Text, and the Critic*, and Christopher Norris' *What's Wrong with Postmodernism*. These protests grew as veterans of the culture wars came to assess the social and intellectual costs of "theory" (Graham Good), while some scientists complained about its hegemonic use of the term *theory*, as if other disciplines had none.

My interest in literature's deepest, widest function(s), and puzzlement at how few theorists shared that interest, continued. Why *problematize* so many inherited assumptions about writing and not the very idea of literature? My list of writings with any bearing on my topic in Adams and Searle's 872-page tome was as follows:

1) Martin Heidegger's essay on "Hölderlin and the Essence of Poetry" quotes the poet as saying that language is "given to man... so that he may affirm what he is" (759). Heidegger himself states that poetry establishes Being "by means of the word" (762).

2) Georg Lukács writes that for Marx, Engels, and Lenin, literature's purpose is to serve ideology ("the active social function, the propaganda effect of the genuine work of art" [798]).

3) Maurice Blanchot distinguishes between a journal, which roots writing in time, and literature, which is the "fascinating domain of the absence of time" (829).

4) Hans-Georg Gadamer derives literature from a "will to permanence" or a "will to hand on" (848, 850).

5) Co-editor Leroy Searle adds in an Afterword that poetry can function as an "antidote to alienation" (862).

Still, there were leads to be investigated among these few authors, particularly when reinforced or developed by other voices. Ernst Bloch (*The Utopian Function of Art and Literature*, 1988), for example, offered another Marxist analysis, but I could find no reason to follow him there. Heidegger's *dictum* that poetry establishes Being appeared not long after Jean-Paul Sartre wrote that creative art seeks the "recovery of the totality of being" (1965, 51). While this concept, popular with postwar existentialist philosophers, is not crucial in Sartre's *What Is Literature?*, several ideas in *Critical Theory Since 1965* – especially regarding time, permanence, and alienation – proved useful.

Widening my net to include library catalogues and online searches caught some germane material, though never as much as I had hoped for and still half-expected to find. Some help came from literary critics and historians, though David Margolies' book on *The Function of Literature* (1969) was just *A Study of Christopher Caudwell's Aesthetics*, Caudwell being "the most important English Marxist critic" (7). It tended to confirm Lukacs' observation that Marxist-Leninists know from the start that the function of literature is socio-economic, but Margolies also notes that Caudwell saw literature as one way we try to "moderate the conflict" between our desires and the world, our instincts and our experience (54, 68). That sounded like another case of the alienation that many were discussing then. In *Fictional Realities: The Uses of Literary Imagination* (1993), J.J.A. Mooij says that "poetry and art" can reconcile "nature and the human mind" (27). This would obviously be an important function, once we know exactly what needs reconciling, and how literature does that. Could it actually resolve such fundamental polarities as desires (or mind) and the natural world into one? I wondered if Robert Graves had the same polarity in mind when he wrote that poetry records the struggles between our "various pairs of Jekyll and Hyde" (or "the deliberate and the unwitting") and our attempts to square those antinomies (2000, 34-35).

The fullest presentation of the "alienation motive" behind literature I found was Northrop Frye's – not in *Anatomy of Criticism*, but in a public, almost popular venue: six radio talks based on a lecture series, published by the CBC as *The Educated Imagination* (1963). His prime question – "What good is the study of literature?" – is not the same as mine, but our answers were bound to overlap, since he could not argue for the study of literature without having a concept of its origin and function. His premise is that literature arises from our imagination's attempts to bridge the gaps between world and self, intellect and emotions. By crossing this bridge we hope to "recapture...that original lost sense of identity with our surroundings" (Frye 1963, 9). If this sounds like paradise lost, it is: for Frye (who studied theology and was an ordained minister before becoming a professor), literature carries us back to a Biblical Eden or classical Golden Age, and the feeling of belonging we suppose we would have had there (20-21). Although I was wary of Frye the theologian and schematizer, he seemed to be onto something in his emphasis on time and loss. In a later work, *Spiritus Mundi* (1976), he returned to this idea, arguing that literature is part of our attempt to give the non-human world human meaning ("The Rising of the Moon"; 1976, 245). Another essay in the same collection endorses the classical idea that the function of poetry is to provide "verbal imaginative models for human civilization" (Frye 1976, 89).

I searched for *patterns* in the various commentators' ideas, but alienation was almost the only one. Mostly they were isolated gestures, discrete efforts to find coherence in the flux. Murray Krieger's eloquent appeal for common sense and the general reader against theoretical abstractions – "we must...take seriously the aesthetic need for closure, a hunger for form and for verbal presence that accounts for the human quest for poetry" (in Strelka 389) – seemed to be a serious attempt to identify the needs of the human spirit that give rise to literature. One might think that such an obvious response to my query as "It meets some of our aesthetic needs" would have lots of company, but most looked elsewhere. In *The Winter Sun. Notes on a Vocation*, Susan Howe suggests that through literature we can achieve a kind of trans-dimensional tuning: "Why write if it is not to align yourself with time and space?" she asks (quoted Mlinko 36). The contributors to Monroe Engel's *Uses of Literature* (1973) advance other distinct theses. Clara Claiborne Park argues that literature teaches us about life, reality, people, and ourselves; Adrienne Rich believes that reading and writing liberate us from some of the constraints of existence; Philip Fisher suggests that literature exists to show us the deadening effects of habit, and to create or record escapes from it (possibly one of Rich's "liberations").

One writer in the volume *Aesthetic Transgressions. Modernity, Liberalism, and the Function of Literature* (2006) insists that the functions of literature are many and varied because they change with history and culture (Nünning 130, 120): a warning against attempts (like mine) to formulate a single *über*-purpose.

Marching to a different drummer, Robert Graves had written in *On English Poetry* (1922) that poetry stirs wonder by creating the illusion of life from lifeless materials (2000, 4), which does at least suggest a role for it in our spiritual life. His idea is seconded by J. Hillis Miller, who twice calls poetry's *illusion of life* a "virtual reality" (21, 113), though Miller seems unsure whether literature *creates* or *discovers* a world (16-20, 77-79). And it is not clear that either of them puts forward this "illusion" as poetry's *function*, its purpose and benefit.

In 2008 Rita Felski made a major and welcome effort to pull together her own and our predecessors' thinking on the *Uses of Literature*. After a sceptical survey of the current state of "theory," she joins those who believe that "aesthetic value is inseparable from use"(8), then stakes out her own territory. Reading literature, Felski proposes, brings us recognition, enchantment, knowledge, and/or shock – remnants ("shadows") of older aesthetic terms: respectively *anagnorisis* [recognition], beauty, mimesis, and sublimity (14-15). Most of her book analyses these terms and some examples of them. She eventually concludes that the four modes or uses she identifies are "indissolubly intertwined" (133), a conclusion with which I agree. Felski gives substantial space in each chapter to refuting critical theory hostile to her argument, which rather muddies the water, but her book is a valuable contribution to scholarship on this subject.

And perhaps this is, after all, as much help as one who ventures into *terra incognita* should ever have expected to receive from critics, scholars, or theorists; at some point you have to stop consuming and produce. Edward Said called attention to Erich Auerbach's acknowledgement that it was his library-challenged wartime years in Istanbul that forced him to sit down and actually write *Mimesis* (Said 1983, 5-7). There are (interrogative) leads here, in Frye and others, that can be pursued and developed. What "aesthetic needs" can literature meet? Alienation was fashionable in the 'sixties, almost a designer malady for western culture, but what sort of alienation is so universal as to evoke literature globally in every age? How can a novel or poem help align us with time and space? Are we indeed liberated – not held – by a poem? Do the literary arts simply recreate and transmit experience, or do they rather heighten and intensify it? Why would we *want* an illusion of life or a virtual reality (if we do)? The practitioners of *Funktiongeschichte* – the study of literature's changing uses – maintain that *all* of these ideas may be valid for some time and place.

I seek more explicit answers to my original question about literature's *raison d'être*, answers based not on *a priori* assumptions about it or its producers, but on analyses of a fair range of texts leading to insights about how they function to satisfy our needs. I do not claim to have reached the bottom of the question or the end of the answers; one must always leave open the possibility, even the likelihood, that other scholars studying these or other works will draw different conclusions. The stance I hope to maintain is the agnostic one of Montaigne's famous motto: "*Que sais-je?*" What do I know? What *can* I know?

The chapters that follow present material in support of the two most widespread functions of literature I have found thus far, and essay tentative answers to the questions posed at the outset. Part One addresses the universal human experience of living in *time*, feeling its passage, seeing its effects on ourselves and others, fearing it; and the role that literature can play in expressing our reactions to all that. Part Two concerns a sense, almost as universal, that once upon a time, when we – individuals, tribes, nations, or species – were younger, life felt different for a while: more moving, either terribly or wonderfully, perhaps briefly ideal, somewhere else, somewhere Other. This idea has been imaged as childhood, nature, a golden age, a garden, an island, a party, or an estate. I follow John Fowles in calling that sense of heightened experience in a special place the *domaine* – the castle or manor and grounds of the *ancien régime* (see Part II, Prologue and Ch. 5). One of literature's recurrent roles has been to describe encounters with such *domaines*, our changing verdicts on them, our loss of them and the effects thereof. Each of these uses has its variants. The evidence I put forward is suggestive, not exhaustive, but it does represent a number of different styles, places, periods, and degrees of importance. If my hypotheses are valid, these two functions, at least, may be archetypal and hence found to operate widely. Of course additional roles may emerge: if not from my mind, then from others'.

ACKNOWLEDGMENTS

ANY RESEARCHER ACCUMULATES LARGE DEBTS to the work of earlier authors and scholars on which he or she builds. Those listed in "Works Cited" are only the tip of the iceberg, the ones mentioned in the final text. In addition I am grateful to the friends and associates who heard my story and made suggestions ranging from brilliant to sardonic, or both. Special thanks are due to four teachers who assiduously read and commented on the manuscript: Prof. William Bevis, Prof. Donald K. Frye, Peter Johnson, and Prof. Lee Whitehead. I owe them a great deal, but since I subsequently revised the entire work myself, they cannot be held responsible for mistakes or infelicities.

PART ONE:

THE TIME MACHINE

CHAPTER 1:

It's About Time

But at my back I always hear
Time's wingéd chariot hurrying near.
ANDREW MARVELL

WHY DO WE HAVE LITERATURE, and how do we use it? What is the seed, in writer and reader (or speaker and audience) of the desire to write and read (or speak and hear) imaginative fictions? Or are there various seeds and impulses? Some of the earliest answers given have come to seem more likely, and are more widely confirmed, than others. In the fifth century BCE, Herodotus, "the father of history" (with a high imaginative content), wrote that he hoped his *Histories* would "preserve the memory of the past," and thus "prevent the traces of human events from being erased by time" (quoted Dirda 13, 8; trans. Sélincourt). We all live within the bounds of time, though we do not know exactly where the boundaries lie, and as the years pass we become more conscious of their constraints. "There is a time": for birth, for social relations, for death, for everything; time is in our begetting, in our work and play, in our music and art, in our flesh and bones. We calibrate it, regret or treasure our memories, anticipate or fear the future, speculate about a release from our present in time travel. For all those reasons – and others, no doubt – some form or aspect of time has figured as a major subject in (at least) western literature over the ages. Part One is devoted to examining some of the many variations on this theme.

Before discussing the treatment of time *in literature*, however, let me provide some context by acknowledging some of the broader issues that arise when time is examined. The subject has many facets, which have been and still are debated by physicists, cosmologists, psychologists and philosophers – the likes of Henri Bergson, Albert Einstein, and Stephen Hawking – as well as by literary critics and theorists. Are we talking about absolute time or subjective time? Do we admit the possibility of time travel? Is relativity an issue? And what place does literature occupy in all of this?

Tenseless in Spacetime: Physics and Cosmology

Time travel is an open question . . .
debates among physicists continue . . . .
PAUL NAHIN

Time's power to limit and otherwise affect our lives naturally fascinates practitioners of both the arts and the sciences, that power being part of our universal experience of ageing. This is not to say that poets and physicists have approached the problem of time from the same angle. Poets have typically asked whether (or explained how) art can somehow manipulate, fix, or otherwise "do something about" the seemingly inexorable flux of time, and have considered how we can or should behave under that dispensation. Science and philosophy have tended to discuss the nature of time, its measurement, its "arrows," and the possibility of time travel.

Yet there has come to be a good deal of interdisciplinary overlap, with humanists and scientists taking cognizance of efforts on both sides of the line to a degree unusual in most areas of joint inquiry. Hans Meyerhoff, in *Time in Literature* (1955), tried to limit himself to psychological aspects of time that are important in literature, but felt obliged to bring in the "objective time" of physics in order to make some needed distinctions. Joost Meerloo's *Along the Fourth Dimension* (1970) ranges from Heidegger to Heisenberg to Robert Heinlein and science-fiction films. The breadth of Paul Nahin's *Time Machines* (1993) is indicated by his subtitle: *Time Travel in Physics, Metaphysics, and Science Fiction*. Works of science fiction have often drawn on cosmological speculation or physical theories about time. Physicist and cosmologist Stephen Hawking, delighted to visit the set of *Star Trek: The Next Generation*, sat beaming in Captain Picard's chair.

I admit to a fondness for books about time by mature authors: often serious, highly educated people who set down their thoughts as they "get on." In *The Challenge of the Passing Years. My Encounter with Time* (1962), R.M. MacIver was seeking "freedom under time" – which he must have known would be gravely limited (xxiv). Meerloo, scouting *Along the Fourth Dimension*, admitted to "forty years of struggling with the subjective approach to time" (ix). Meyerhoff, after examining the role of time in literature, concluded that "What is man?" and "What is time?" are at bottom the same question (2). Time's irreversibility, he concluded, was its "most significant aspect...in human experience" (66). Most authors of books on time care deeply enough about the subject to read widely, report exhaustively on their research, and present others' views deferentially. The subject does have its eccentrics: J.W. Dunne's *An Experiment with Time* (1927 *et seq.*) is an attempt to understand how the author and some friends can have anticipatory dreams, previsions of coming events. Part philosopher, part mystic, he presents diagrams and charts as mysterious as his text. But in most cases the arguments of time's veteran students are reasonable and weighty.

Their individual concerns within and among the different kinds of temporal speculation vary considerably. J.T. Fraser's *The Genesis and Evolution of Time* (1982) provides a history of ideas about a range of chronological issues. *The Problem of Time* (1929), by J. Alexander Gunn, is a learned, useful survey of speculation about time from the pre-Socratics to Henri Bergson. Peter Hughes titled his meditation on a philosophy of history *Spots of Time* (1969), a nod to Wordsworth, and decided that "art offers the best way for us to comprehend time and memory" (71). MacIver's *Challenge of the Passing Years*, which distinguishes four modes of existence through time (duration, continuity, succession, and recurrence), also grants the arts a role in redeeming time and seeking immortality. That point is also made by Meerloo, who notes that we yearn "to override time's boundary lines and pass into the world of immortality" (10): Yeats's "Byzantium." One way of "capturing time and making it endure," he writes, is "artistic effort"; you could say that "creativity is eternization" (11). Working in the same area, Meyerhoff asserts that "very little poetry...is not concerned with preserving the timeless" (55; I would say "preserving the evanescent"). Stephen Toulmin and June Goodfield's *The Discovery of Time* (1965) deals with the development of history-writing and of a sense of history, while Charles Nordmann's *The Tyranny of Time. Einstein or*

Bergson? (1925) discusses the "modalities" of relative and absolute time.

The idea of "time travel" on a "time machine," which has fascinated a wide public ever since H.G. Wells, is a relatively minor concern of these writers, most of whom treat the topic dismissively if they bring it up at all. Meerloo, for example, considers the manipulation of time in most science fiction infantile (146.) Physicist Paul Nahin, however, puts it at the centre of his book, published by the American Institute of Physics: thus a scientific Establishment comment on the idea. Nahin, in summarizing the status of the debate in the early '90s, leaves open a slim theoretical possibility of such travel, but describes the problems associated with actually building a time machine as "staggering" (245). Most practicing physicists, he says, believe that time travel, if it can be achieved at all, will be enormously difficult, terribly costly, and very limited in duration, direction, or both. Travellers may require a lightning-fast rocket or an "infinitely long" rotating cylinder to achieve even a minimal version of "chronomotion" (62). Mission planners will have to make the right choices among differing theories (general or special relativity?) and theorists (Hawking? Kip Thorne?), and perhaps none of these will prove to be correct. Black holes could present a problem. And what would it mean to move along Gödel's "closed timelike world lines," anyway? (11) Will this turn out to be what we humans were seeking?

And that is only to commence the journey. If we actually manage to arrive somewhen else, we may run the risk of interfering with history by creating anachronisms, "causal loops," or backwards causation. If I happen to kill my grandfather or marry my grandmother, what would be the effect on spacetime, and on me? Would we even *survive* time travel, and if so will we have any control over what happens when we arrive, or be able to return to the present? Perhaps we can visit only the past, or only the future, or move in only one direction, or cannot know our destination. Time may have arrows we have not imagined; there could be temporal equivalents of pollution and climate change. Problems, perils, and unknowables would be legion. Why not just give up and admit that the task is impossible, then? Our deep need to resist the "tyranny of time," that's why, so the speculation and the interest will continue. Nahin evokes an exciting but surreal world in which perhaps only a cosmologist would be comfortable: "With the four-dimensional block-universe concept, all world lines lie tenseless in spacetime" (208).

The phrase is resonant, stirring the imagination, but that is not where its author wants to go. Nahin declares at the outset that *imaginative* journeys through time and "mind travel" (by drugs or dreams) are irrelevant to his study, which treats of "real," rational time machines that heed Einstein's theories and can move in space (5, 8, 14). Yet in this connection he pays tribute to Herbert George Wells's science-fiction classic *The Time Machine* (1895), which "pioneered time travel as we think of it in this book," though its time travel is as imaginary as that of any other piece of science fiction (98). Growing up in the heady early days of modern science, Wells studied at the Royal College of Science with, among others, Thomas Henry Huxley, Darwin's best publicist: credentials that impress even Nahin. Wells's original contribution to his subject, he writes, is a "science-based rationale" for a time machine (35).

This is true, as far as it goes. During the after-dinner conversation that opens the novel and precedes his demonstration of the machine, the "Time Traveller" explains the theoretical bases of his experiments in a general way to prepare his listeners – friends, educated men – for what will follow. Predictably, he presents time as the fourth dimension, "only a kind of space … except that our consciousness moves along it" (Wells 1961, 195, 194). He hints at a "four-dimension geometry," adducing a series of portraits of a man at different ages, and a barometric graph, as examples of time represented in two dimensions. And he has a working model to show the diners, as well as the full-scale time machine: vaguely described contraptions of nickel, ivory, rock crystal and quartz that provide a marginal plausibility for the thing, allowing scientific readers to suspend disbelief if they wish. Still, his guests – like most present-day scientists – remain sceptical.

Absent-Minded

But Nahin misses something, giving only a partial account of Wells's "rationale" for time travel, and what he leaves out is vital here. Wells, more open and liberal in his views, recognizes another type of time travel, and in doing so presents an idea worth exploring: mental or psychic movement in time. (His was also an age of excitement about psychology.) When one friend objects that we "cannot move about in Time" as we do in space, the host counters that *imaginative* travel in fact provides a conceptual basis for his work:

...you are wrong to say that we cannot move about in Time. For instance, if I am recalling an incident very vividly I go back to the first instance of its occurrence: I become absent-minded, as you say. I jump back for a moment. Of course we have no means of staying back for any length of Time... (1961, 196).

Nahin rules imagination and mind travel irrelevant, and as the Traveller goes on to present his model and full-scale time machines, "absent-mindedness" is forgotten. But this passage about *mental* travel deserves closer attention. If your mind is "absent" (from here), where is it present? And where are *you* when your mind is "absent": here or there? During vivid recall, says Wells, "I jump back for a moment" – back to the incident. Is this psychological phenomenon not only the root of the idea of time travel, its basis in our make-up, but the one kind we have so far achieved?

The Traveller's description of what the mind can *do* in the fourth dimension is very limited: "if I am recalling an incident ... I become absent-minded." But in addition to recollected experience, our imaginations can be prompted by our wills or by literature, a fact that Wells (just starting his career as a novelist in 1895) would have realized. We can imagine how the past might have been, or project our minds "forward" to imagine the future, or let literature help us in either direction. In this respect, Wells's *The Time Machine* (like many modern literary artifacts) is about itself. He describes the mental process by which we can temporarily abandon our everyday selves and enter another world: an 1890s drawing room, for example, or a lawn in the year 802,701, or a desolate beach at the end of the world, when "the sun had ceased to set," and "the work of the tidal drag was done. The earth had come to rest with one face to the sun," and such life as survived in the rarefied air existed in "a perpetual twilight" (266-67). In other words, Wells's book *The Time Machine* is a time machine. But then the penny drops: so are other novels, poems, plays, paintings (as the Time Traveller points out), films, and even music.

What Wells alludes to here, briefly and almost casually, may be an archetypal function of literature and art in general: to rise above time by letting artist and audience stop or move about in the dimension that life presents as a relentlessly unidirectional flow. The frescoes and pottery designs of Minoan Crete seem as fresh as if they had been made yesterday instead of in the third millennium BCE; Shakespeare can transport us to the night before the battle of Agincourt in 1415, two centuries before his own time:

From camp to camp through the foul womb of night
The hum of either army stilly sounds,
That the fixed sentinels almost receive
The secret whispers of each other's watch.
Fire answers fire, and through their paly flames,
Each battle sees the other's umbered face.
Steed threatens steed, in high and boastful neighs
Piercing the night's dull ear. And from the tents
The armorers, accomplishing the knights,
With busy hammers closing rivets up
Give dreadful note of preparation. (Henry V, 4.4-14)

Or – if you need a less archaic passage to achieve the degree of self-forgetful-ness required to board this time machine – let Charles Dickens take you back to his own time: Victorian England, fall 1850.

London. Michaelmas Term lately over, and the Lord Chancellor
sitting in Lincoln's Inn Hall. Implacable November weather. As much
mud in the streets, as if the waters had but newly retired from the face
of the earth, and it would not be wonderful to meet a Megalosaurus,
forty feet long or so, waddling like an elephantine lizard up Holborn
Hill. Smoke lowering down from chimney-pots, making a soft black
drizzle, with flakes of soot in it as big as full-grown snow-flakes - gone
into mourning, one might imagine, for the death of the sun. Dogs,
indistinguishable in mire. Horses, scarcely better; splashed to their
very blinkers. Foot-passengers, jostling one another's umbrellas, in
a general infection of ill-temper, and losing their foothold at street-
corners, where tens of thousands of other foot passengers have been
slipping and sliding since the day broke (if this day ever broke),
adding new deposits to the crusts upon crusts of mud, sticking at those
points tenaciously to the pavement, and accumulating at compound
interest. (Bleak House, p. 1).

Neither passage is a simple word-picture; rather, they are more nearly paintings, conveying mood, attitude, emotion. And, for my purposes, neither could be any shorter: it takes a while for the effect to coalesce. The mind does not immediately relinquish a consciousness of its surroundings and launch off elsewhere or else-when. But when such passages work, when they are well-executed and we allow them to seduce us, we are *then and there* while reading them. We forget ourselves.

Let's Pretend: Sci Fi and Psy Fi

Science fiction books and films about time travel can be rather crude examples of artistic expression. While they provide metaphors for the relationship of art to time, they may be relatively superficial: the tip of an iceberg, most of which floats in deeper water. The Caspak novels of Edgar Rice Burroughs are "potboil-ers," operating at the level of young readers' literature, but they operate quite effectively, and probably impress more readers than care to admit it later. What gives time fiction by Burroughs (or Wells or Jules Verne) its power, its *élan vital*, is the energy of one imagination acting on another via art, crude or sophisticated: *that* is the "warp drive" we developed long ago to leap across the abysses of time and space.

There are a number of ways in which this artistic/imaginative force can be generated and applied, corresponding roughly to different kinds or "levels" of art. The simplest of these (a good starting place) are fiction and drama that openly take time travel as their subject, i.e. that "foreground" their temporal manipula-tion. Wells's *The Time Machine* seems to have founded the modern genre, as Nahin says; and since 1895 many other science-fiction books, stories, films, television programs, series, and re-runs – including *Doctor Who*, the whole *Star Trek* con-stellation, and several *Back to the Futures* – have followed his lead, using time "machines" and time shifts as a major or minor premise in their plots.

Still, other approaches have been tried; purpose-built technology is not the only way to go. Jules Verne's *Journey to the Center of the Earth* (1864) is also a journey into the deep past, which turns out to be alive beneath the floor of the Atlantic Ocean, the British Isles, and Europe. What sends his team of time travel-lers off is their research into mediaeval manuscripts, which convince them that the planet's core may be (and perhaps has been) reached through the crater of the dormant Snaefells volcano in Iceland. So naturally they walk down into it, car-rying flashlights and knapsacks with food, ropes, and dynamite. Identifying the various rock strata, these learned adventurers realize that they are passing through several geological periods, which is confirmed by giant ferns, fossils, mastodons, and primeval sea monsters in an ocean miles beneath Scotland. It turns out that not *all* the dinosaurs perished in the wake of an asteroid strike. Verne waters down the "scientific" aspect of his fiction toward the end. Following a long voyage on their raft, and more walking, the team (still hoping to reach the earth's core) blow up a boulder blocking the entrance to a tunnel, whereupon they and the sea go rushing down it at great speed – and then up. The water turns to lava (which one might think could be inconvenient) and they are spewed out a side crater of the Stromboli island-volcano north of Sicily. A bit ruffled but basically unharmed, and still scholars, they go on to publish their findings.

Burroughs uses the same basic formula: marginally credible travel in space that proves to be travel in time as well. The three novelettes of his "Caspak Trilogy" (*The Land That Time Forgot, The People That Time Forgot,* and *Out of Time's Abyss*) tell tall tales of a 1916 submarine voyage by a motley crew of British, Americans, and Germans to the Antarctic island of Caprona and up a subterranean river into the land of Caspak: not only a prehistoric but an evolutionary place, exhibiting every stage of earthly life from first to the present. Though he draws on popular nineteenth-century stories about warm regions at the poles (also used by Edgar Allen Poe), Burroughs works at being more specific than Verne. When the U-33 first surfaces in the Caspak river within the barrier cliffs, the crew find themselves in "an unknown world" with "flora and fauna as strange and wonderful to us as that of a distant planet," but also curiously familiar: "giant arboraceous ferns" two hundred feet high; a huge lizard-like creature with "batlike wings" as "large as a large whale"; enormous humming insects; and a river monster that attacks the ship, shrugs off gunfire, and devours one of the Germans (Burroughs 39). It was "sixteen or eighteen feet" long, estimates Bowen Tyler, Jr, the designer and commander *pro tem* of the sub, who evidently keeps up on popular science. He remarks that the river beast "closely resembled pictures I had seen of restored plesiosaurs of the lower Jurassic." It sounds rather like an activated museum diorama.

These first impressions are systematically developed. The passengers eat steaks and broth from a plesiosaurus, "a creature that should, by all the laws of paleontology, have been extinct for several million years" (Burroughs 42), feel separated by "eons of time" from their past lives (46), and meet a humanoid with "a close resemblance to the so-called Neanderthal man of La Chapelle-aux-Saints" (50). In the second tale, Billings (searching for Tyler) and his Caspakian girlfriend Ajor are saved when a saber-tooth tiger and a huge bear, both eager to devour them, fight each other to their deaths. Later they meet some Band-lu people, "analogous to the so-called Cro-Magnon race of the Upper Paleolithic" (106). In one of several nods to Darwin, the final story, "Out of Time's Abyss," explains the workings of evolution in Caspak, whose lack of children has puzzled the visitors. Bradley (split off from Tyler's party) learns "why the women of each tribe immersed themselves for an hour or more in the warm pools" near their caves each morning: in order to deposit fertilized eggs that will develop into tadpoles. (199).

> *Down the warm stream from the pool floated the countless billions of*
> *eggs and tadpoles, developing as they drifted slowly toward the sea.*
> *Some became tadpoles in the pool, some in the sluggish stream and*
> *some [in] the great inland sea. In the next stage they became fishes*
> *or reptiles. ...some of them evolved into amphibians. Few indeed were*
> *those that eventually developed into baboons and then apes.... From*
> *the egg, then, the individual developed slowly into a higher form, just*
> *as the frog's egg develops.* (199)

Bradley – strong and sensible, a man for all seasons – finds it "not difficult to believe in the possibility of such a scheme," since "there was nothing new in it" (199). He can say this because he is familiar with Darwin and contemporary biology. A few of the apes will develop into forms more nearly *homo sapiens*; both Bradley and Billings eventually take Galu women (the highest stage) as wives. Bradley observes that the "countless millions of other eggs" dropped in the pools to float down to the great central lake "go through a similar process of evolution outside the womb as develops our own young within," and considers the Caspakian way simpler and "much more inclusive, for it combines not only individual development, but the evolution of species and genera," a point developed at length (199). Though it makes his head whirl, he decides that the scheme is "less difficult to comprehend than that with which he is familiar" (200).

Why Burroughs chose to go into all this becomes clear a few pages later, when Bradley climbs down a long ladder in a dark artificial pit to a ledge formed of vast numbers of human skulls above a subterranean river. From this and other evidence, he concludes that "the infancy of Caspak dated doubtlessly back into remote ages, far beyond what the outer world considered the beginning of earthly time" (203): another example of Burroughs's interest in Darwin. The age of the earth had been a controversial topic in the nineteenth century, and was still being debated in 1918 (as it is today). The evolutionary geology of Charles Lyell and the evolutionary biology of Charles Darwin required a long time-span. The traditional six thousand years of Christian conservatives (since Bishop Ussher in the seventeenth century) would not suffice, and scientists had shown that to be a laughably low estimate; Lyell and Darwin argued for a figure in the millions. In the Caspak trilogy Burroughs supports the position of evolutionary scientists for a popular audience. Claude C. Albritton titled his history of the battle over the earth's antiquity *The Abyss of Time* (1980), possibly a nod to Burroughs.

These three magazine stories, first published as monthly installments in the fall of 1918, are permeated with the anti-German jingoism of the period. Even apart from the idea that a warm, wet, fecund land exists near Antarctica, whose true nature Scott, Amundsen, and Shackleton had described before 1918, much of the trilogy is highly improbable – e.g. the Americans and British learning the utterly foreign Caspak language so well so quickly – and parts of it are careless, rushed, or perfunctory. "Caprona" was named by the "early Italian navigator" Caproni, who "followed Cook about 1721" (Burroughs 32). Cook's voyages occurred in the second half of the eighteenth century. But such shortcomings seem to have made little difference to the effect of Burroughs's vividly imagined tableaux on many twentieth-century readers.

In any case, whatever their limitations, the progeny of early science fiction writers – Verne, Wells, and Burroughs particularly – are still legion, in the visual arts as well as in imaginative literature. Their major works involving time transport were all made into movies, in some cases more than once. I treat cinema and television as "imaginative literature" because they usually work from written texts, and often derive from literary sources.

ONE OF THE ABIDING SUCCESSES of American commercial television, often re-run, has been *The Twilight Zone*, a recurrent dramatic series (1959-64; 1985-89; 2002-03, 2019) with strong science-fiction leanings and a fair number of time journeys. In season two of the early, black-and-white program, a pioneer emigrant in the western desert walks over a sand dune and through a mysterious portal from 1847 into 1961, where he obtains penicillin for his son's pneumonia, and learns that his son will become a doctor in California. He returns through the portal with the medicine and his son survives, presumably to treat some pneumonia cases. The "time-loop" plotting is neat, but "science" is absent. The nature of this time-portal, and the reason why it appears there and then, are not explained; is there a benevolent Providence at work? But then this is, a voice intones, "the Twilight Zone" (Episode 59, "A Hundred Yards Over the Rim," 1961, written by Rod Serling).

Star Trek, a successful franchise and a popular cult, also has instances of time travel. The original television series ran from 1966 to 1969, and begot a string of sequels or prequels: *The Next Generation, Deep Space Nine, Voyager, Enterprise,* and *Discovery*, besides an animated series. There have been, in addition, over a dozen feature films, stretching from 1979 to (at least) 2016, plus assorted novels, comics, and games. Time travel is not a regular feature of the series or a capability of the earthly spaceships, but the crews do encounter time travellers with machines (some of which are deployed against them), and nature sometimes provides an example. Most time travel here is mechanical and scientific, or at least "scientified."

Time travel programs burgeoned on television as special effects became more sophisticated, and by the 'nineties viewers could expect to be offered at least a patina of scientific explanation for most time shifts. In *Quantum Leap* (NBC, 1989-93), Scott Bakula played a quantum physicist conducting time travel experiments who at one point enters the "Quantum Leap Accelerator" himself. It works as a time machine, but proves to have uncontrollable side effects, causing Bakula to leap to a new time and situation each week. Similar but with some differences was *Sliders* (1995-2000), in which a team of four jumps ("slides") to a new time and reality each week. They make use of a "wormhole" to move between parallel universes: a bow to the interest in theoretical physicists and cosmologists such as Stephen Hawking.

Other programs, however, were still casual about the mechanism of time travel, often obscured by the glare and flash of a quick cut. In the television mini-series *Timecop* (ABC, 1997; based on the 1994 film of the same name), police working for the Time Enforcement Commission regularly dispatch officers to other periods to solve problems: mainly unauthorized time travellers altering the past and disturbing history or "timelines." Little effort was expended on describing how this was done; the shifts were a given. In the Canadian drama *Being Erica* (CBC,

2009-2011), the heroine's therapist has the power to send her back to revisit various episodes in her troubled life: time travel as therapy, though they could also be psychotic episodes. *Stargate*, another sci-fi franchise, comprises several films, television series, books, comics, an animated series, and video games. It was an efficient revenue machine, but was it a time machine? The Stargate device allows a team to travel light years through a wormhole instantly, but light years commonly measure *distance*; it is not clear whether the teams are also moving in time.

POSTWAR CINEMA ALSO TOOK AN interest in science fiction, including time travel; it too displays a spectrum of approaches, from vague to technical. In *World Without End* (1956), a spaceship bound for Mars returns to earth in the 26th century: having broken the "time barrier," the crew have become victims of "time dilation." In a variation of Wells's novel, they encounter "mutates," though here the rough, primitive types occupy the surface, while the soft sophisticates live underground. *The Time Machine* itself was filmed in 1960, with H.G. Wells as the time traveller. He makes several frightening stops in the 20th century before fleeing its wars to the year 802,701. A new version, set in New York City and with added material, was made in 2002. Both films show a time machine in general accord with Wells's minimal description. In *The Time Travelers* (1964), scientists studying time travel contrive to use their "time-viewing screen" as a portal to the future. We are not told how that works, but it does: they visit the year 2071, return to the present, and then leap a hundred thousand years into the hereafter.

The *Planet of the Apes* is yet another "franchise." It consist of seven films (so far), two television series, and comic books. The original film of that name (1968), based on Pierre Boulle's novel *La Planète des singes* (1963), tells the story of three astronauts who leave earth in a spaceship and travel for about 2600 years, but age only 18 months. They ditch in a lake on an unknown planet; their chronometer registers the year 3978. After various adventures, they encounter a society run by English-speaking simians, ruling over debased humans. At the end, Charleton Heston discovers the head of the Statue of Liberty on an empty beach and realizes that this is post-nuclear holocaust Earth. The plot twist resembles *The Twilight Zone*, which is not surprising, since Rod Serling wrote the original script. Clearly the idea touched a nerve: besides the 2001 remake, *The Planet of the Apes* has spawned *Beneath the...* (1970), *Escape from...* (1971), *Conquest of...* (1972), *Battle for...* (1973), *Rise of...* (2011), *Dawn of...* (2014), and *War for...* (2017). Will the line stretch out to the crack o' doom? Its theme appears to be a warning about the future of the earth under our stewardship.

A banner decade for time-travel films began in 1979 with *Time After Time*, in which H.G. Wells's friend John Stevenson – aka Jack the Ripper – steals Wells's time machine and leaps to 1960s San Francisco, where he is hardly noticed. Fortunately he does not know that unless the machine's "non-return key" is operated, it shoots back to its starting point, 1893. When it re-materializes in Wells's home, he figures out what has happened and follows Stevenson into the future to check him. The mechanism for time travel looks like the Victorian contraption of the book and the first film, but it can travel in space, too.

Somewhere in Time (1980) was adapted from the novel *Bid Time Return* (1975) by its author, Richard Matheson. Here the means of temporal shift is self-hypnosis. An elderly Jane Seymour approaches young Christopher Reeve, says "Come back to me," and dies soon after. Fascinated, he learns more about her and tries to will himself back to 1912. He fails, but finding that he actually signed the guest book that year strengthens his resolve (and allays our suspicion that he dreamed it all), and on his second try he wakes up in 1912 to enjoy a delicious few days with the youthful Jane. The honeymoon ends when he chances upon a 1979 penny in his trousers pocket, and is sucked back through a time vortex to 1980. The film's plot parallels the reading experience described by Wells (1961, 196): so long as we are caught up in a book or a memory we can be "absent-minded" and *there*, but as soon as our concentration breaks we lose that other world and return to our quotidian selves.

The Final Countdown, starring Kirk Douglas as a naval captain and Martin Sheen as a civilian consultant, also appeared in 1980. Here a US aircraft carrier is caught in a time-warp storm, emerges on December 6, 1941, and almost interferes with the Japanese attack on Pearl Harbor before a second such storm returns it to the present. A couple left on an island in 1941 reappear as senior citizens in 1980 Pearl Harbor, linking the two poles of the story and closing the temporal loop. While the ship is in 1941 and its jets are in contact with Japanese fighters, a confrontation occurs on the bridge. Sheen wants to disrupt the air raid and use modern technology to change history, but Douglas instead recalls his planes as the second storm approaches. The film's discussions of time mention Einstein's theories and the might-kill-your-grandfather paradox.

By now readers will have noticed that time-travel plots are falling into two broad types: those in which the shift occurs because of an external, (super)natural force – as in *The Final Countdown* – and those of the Wellsian kind in which a human machine is involved, and sometimes misfires (the "Frankenstein variant"). *The Philadelphia Experiment* (1984) is an instance of the latter. It tells of a 1943 attempt to make a naval warship invisible (to radar) in Philadelphia harbor. Something goes wrong in the electrical department; the ship disappears; and two men who jump overboard pass through a space/time vortex and emerge in 1984 Nevada, near a small town that also disappears. Jim dies in a burst of electric energy, but David soldiers on, trying to find out what happened. Eventually he finds the scientist who masterminded the experiment, and whose work made the town disappear. Evidently a vortex remains open in hyperspace, endangering the earth, so David is sent back through it to the ship and smashes the generator, causing the ship (and the town) to reappear. He then dives over the side, but later resurfaces in the reborn town. The film was successful enough to call forth *The Philadelphia Experiment II* (1993) – in which a time-displaced sailor has to head off an alternate reality where the Nazis won the war – and another sequel in 2012.

Back to the Future began life in 1985. The hugely popular film, which jumps between 1985 and 1955, was followed by Part II (which travels ahead to 2015) in 1989, and Part III (back to 1885) in 1990. In all the trilogy earned well over 400 million dollars, not including what the animated TV series, the theme-park rides, or the video game brought in. The time machine here is made as specific as such things can be: it is a sporty DeLorean automobile with a plutonium-fuelled, 1.21 gigawatt flux capacitor. You could look it up.

The film *Peggy Sue Got Married* (1986), on the other hand, takes an offhand approach to time travel: no scientists, no machines. The titular heroine, unhappily separated from her husband Charlie, faints when she is named Queen of her 25th high school reunion, and wakes up back in 1960. Readjusting to high school, she falls for Michael (to whom she was attracted back then) and spends the night with him. Then her future husband courts her ardently, but as she and Charlie start to make love, she reawakens in 1985. At the end it looks as if she and Charlie may reconcile. So was it all a fainting dream, albeit one that cleared her head? No: she finds a book written by Michael, dedicated to herself and their night together.

So she *was* there! But where, exactly? On an alternative timeline in a multiverse where things happened differently? Director Francis Ford Coppola leaves many questions unanswered.

This decade also gave us *Time Trackers* (1989), in which a mad or evil scientist steals his colleague's time machine in 2033. Three "trackers" (the colleague's daughter and two men) then pursue the scientist back to the twelfth century and attempt to stop him from changing history. In the same year, *Millennium* disclosed why time travellers snatched away some airline passengers moments before a crash. Based on John Varley's 1977 story "Air Raid" and his 1983 novel *Millennium*, the film reveals the plight of a future society (a millennium from now) that is polluted and sterile. In bad health and rocked by earthquake-like time anomalies, they regularly send squads back to earlier times (though that activity seems to cause quakes) in quest of healthy bodies to improve the stock. Their time machine is called "the Gate."

I do not claim that all or even most science fiction is dominated by the theme of time, but it is common in that genre. *Star Trek, Planet of the Apes, Back to the Future* and other franchises remain popular, time travel plots often appear in television re-runs, and more such films continue to be made. In *The Time Traveler's Wife* (2009, based on Audrey Niffenegger's 2003 novel of the same title), a librarian with a "rare genetic disorder" jumps around randomly in time, particularly when under stress. Here time travel seems to be an illness, but since his daughter time-travels too, and reports that she has gained some control over the shifts, it appears that this gene is accessible to rational control. A novel approach! The subject is well-worn by now, and may at times appear shop-worn as well, but evidently originality is still possible.

Poetry, Fame, and the Fountain of Youth

Creativity is eternization.

JOOST MEERLOO

Viewed as "science fiction," not as powerful subconscious impulses, these "jumps," "slides," or movements in time are just staged wish-fulfillment dreams (which also treat time very freely). We wish we could, but cannot, so we resort to fiction, only half convinced but willing to go along for the ride. It is important to remember, however, that not all efforts to address our time-*Angst* directly are either philosophy or science fiction; time is a subject that myth, art, and imaginative literature have treated seriously from as far back as we can see. In a well-known Greek myth, the god Chronos devours his children – an episode unforgettably rendered in Goya's famous painting, one of his *pinturas negras*. Chronos is, of course, the God of Time.

The third-millennium BCE Sumerian epic *Gilgamesh* – considered by many the beginning of Western literature, 1500 or so years before "Homer" – has at its centre the protagonist's anguished realization that he is, after all, mortal. The hero Gilgamesh, created two-thirds god, is still one-third man, and that dooms him to death: a fact he spends much of the poem resisting. At the height of his powers, adventuring with his wild friend Enkidu, he can strike the heroic note: "All living creatures born of the flesh shall sit at last in the boat of the West...but we shall go forward..." (*Gilgamesh* 79). But Enkidu's death produces an existential crisis that sends Gilgamesh in search of Utnapishtim: the only mortal whom the Sumerian gods had made immortal ("on his [Enkidu's] account I have come, for the common lot of man has taken him": 95).

In the garden of the gods, the sun god Shamash warns him, "You will never find the life for which you are searching" (*Gilgamesh* 97). The hero responds, "Although I am no better than a dead man, still let me see the light of the sun." Siduri, goddess of the vine, urges him to make his peace with mortality, but Gilgamesh asks, "How can I be silent, how can I rest, when Enkidu whom I love is dust, and I too shall die and be laid in the earth for ever?" (99). He finds Utnapishtim and hears the story of the Flood, but receives no encouragement. The Immortal One proposes a test: if Gilgamesh can stay awake for seven nights, then perhaps.... But the hero soon nods off, and *sleeps* for seven days instead. Awakened, he despairs: "the thief in the night has hold of my limbs, death inhabits my room"(112). On the way home, though, Urshanabi the ferryman tells him of a thorny plant that grows underwater: if plucked, it can restore youth. Long before Ponce de Leon, Gilgamesh finds the plant, which he names "The old men are young again," and decides to take it back to Uruk to eat and give the elders. But en route he stops to bathe in a pool, where a serpent snatches it away and dives. In effect, as in *Genesis*, the serpent brings death. Finally Gilgamesh accepts that he is doomed and returns to Uruk to await his end, but meanwhile he "engraved on a stone the whole story" (59 and 115), i.e. he writes *Gilgamesh*. What he feared in death was oblivion, but the stone telling his story will outlive him. This is a primordial literary impulse, then: to use art and imagination to preserve the spirit, which otherwise time devours.

Penguin's translator, N.K. Sandars, notes that through the epic's theme of a quest for immortality "runs a single idea, like the refrain of the mediaeval poet, '*Timor mortis conturbat me*'" (*Gilgamesh* 22-23): 'the fear of death disturbs me.' It is a valid observation; the later mood of Gilgamesh and that often found in European religious poetry of the late Middle Ages are close kin. *Contemptus mundi* ('contempt of the world'), a common refrain in monastic writing of the period, was a natural response to and psychological defence against fears of early death. Many passages in the Bible, especially in the New Testament, can be used to support the idea that "All flesh is grass." An anonymous mediaeval poem expresses *contemptus mundi* in a famous rhetorical question, "*Ubi sunt?*" 'Where are they' (now), those who came and went before us? "*Où sont les neiges d'antan?*" asked François Villon in the fifteenth century: "Where are the snows of yester-year?" as Dante Gabriel Rossetti deftly translated it in "The Ballad of Dead Ladies"(1869). But though the poets of Villon's age had strong feelings about the ravages of time and the evanescence of mortal life, they did not suggest that their work could do any more about the thorns of the human condition than make us more fully aware of them.

In English, the claim that art might exercise some kind of power over time dates from Elizabethan sonnets, which often acknowledge time's power over us. The idea of using poetry to counter time is embryonic in the period's first major sonnet sequence, Sir Philip Sidney's *Astrophel and Stella* (written ca. 1580). In the "Fourth Song" accompanying the sonnets, the sixth stanza of "Only Joy, now here you are" begins

> *Niggard Time threats, if we miss*
> *This large offer of our bliss,*
> *Long stay ere he grant the same: (Rollins 329)*

It sounds ominous, but is not meant (or taken) seriously, nor does the speaker claim that poetry can oppose these "threats." Perhaps because Sidney died young (age 32, in battle), or because "Stella" married as he wrote, he did not defy time in his love poetry.

Several of Samuel Daniel's *Sonnets to Delia* (1592) feature temporal themes. The speaker of #34 seems almost to look forward to the day when Delia's "golden hairs shall change to silver wire," freeing him from her spell, for "Then Beauty... / Must yield up all to tyrant Time's desire" (Rollins 404). Yet his motive, he says, is benevolent. If in future it pains her to look in a mirror,

> *Go you, my verse, go tell her what she was,*
> *For what she was she best shall find in you.*
> *Your fiery heat lets not her glory pass,*
> *But, phoenix-like, shall make her live anew.*

The tone is self-important, even triumphant. The poet is fascinated by his power to deploy a time machine: a notion so pleasing that Sonnet #38 replays it. Again, when gold has turned to silver, she will yet be able to view "the gifts that God and Nature lent thee" in the "lasting monument" of his poems. "*These* colors" (my italics) will not fade when she does:

> *These may remain when thou and I shall perish.*
> *If they remain, then thou shalt live thereby;*
> *They will remain, and so thou canst not die.*

The speaker's self-confidence grows by the moment: "If they remain...They *will* remain" (my italics). The "phoenix-like" rebirth of #34 becomes in #38 the immortality of "thou canst not die." Sonnet #50 dresses this idea differently; here poems are "arks" and "trophies" to "fortify thy name against old age." We do not mistake Daniel's verse for Spenser's or Shakespeare's, but they were not above mining his ideas. Before cameras were invented, poetry had a near-monopoly on the "preservation-of-youthful-beauty" angle, most poets being too poor to commission a painting.

The connection between poetic art and time also figures in Michael Drayton's *Idea* poems. "Amour #7" of *Idea's Mirror. Amours in Quartorzains* (1594) is a fresh departure. It does not ply a lady, but addresses a personified Time directly: "Stay, stay, sweet Time!" (Rollins 426). A fruitless injunction, surely, with Time moving on "From world to world," but the poet has a hook: the mirror that ladies were often warned to fear is here imaged as a heavenly one.

Nay, look thee, Time, in this celestial glass,
And thy youth past in this fair mirror see;
Behold world's Beauty in her infancy...

Time too had a youth, and as it goes on to "after-worlds," the poet urges it to "Tell truly...what in thy time hath been." Thus the lady may learn about ageing from her mirror, but must go to poetry to revisit her youth. Then, characteristically, Drayton takes a new tack in the closing couplet: "Here make a period, Time, and say for me, / "She was, the like that never was nor never more shall be." The shift from ten to fourteen syllables in the last line reflects the fluctuating message to Time, which is first to stay, then go on, then stay. The only "she" mentioned has been the "world's Beauty in her infancy," though there is little to stop a mortal lady from seeing herself in that, or a reader from taking "this celestial glass" and "this fair mirror" as the poem. Poetry is a (magic) mirror in other sonnets. Drayton is anything but conventional and predictable here.

The sixth sonnet of *Idea. In Sixty-Three Sonnets* (1619) is quite another matter; it echoes earlier verse and would itself be imitated later. The speaker contrasts the too made-up ladies of the day, destined for oblivion, with his inamorata, who will live on, "for I to thee eternity shall give / When nothing else remaineth of these days," and "So shalt thou fly above the vulgar throng / Still to survive in my immortal song" (Rollins 427). This is a breathtaking claim, hubristic in scope and as fanciful as any science fiction writer's time machine, yet by 1619 it was becoming a convention of English verse, and a claim that some poets could make good on. If the ladies commemorated in the sonnets had only known, they might have requested that their right names be used.

The next poet to take up this theme after Drayton's 1594 *Idea's Mirror* was Edmund Spenser. In sonnet LXX of his *Amoretti* (1595; "little love poems"), the speaker asks Spring, the season of love, to visit his "careless" lady, still "not well awake," and (in modernized spelling)

Tell her the joyous time will not be stayed
Unless she do him by the forelock take.
Bid her therefore herself soon ready make,
To wait on love... (Spenser 574)

To "take time by the forelock" is the characteristic advice of Roman love poets (*carpe diem*, 'seize the day'), of seventeenth-century Cavalier poets, and of seducers in general. In the closing couplet, the speaker addresses his lady directly: "Make haste therefore sweet love, whilst it is prime, / For none can call again the passèd time." From this point of view, time – unstoppable, irrecoverable – is seen as a problem whose only solution is to yield to the speaker's desire. But only a few sonnets later, Spenser reveals that there is another way out of time's prison.

> *One day I wrote her name upon the strand,*
> *But came the waves and washèd it away*
> *Again I wrote it with a second hand,*
> *But came the tide, and made my pains his prey. (LXXV,*
> *Spenser 575)*

This has more resonance if we recall that "tide" can mean 'time, season,' as in *Yuletide* (the expression "Time and tide wait for no man" also plays on the double meaning). This first effort, however, is critiqued by no less than his lady, who is at the seashore with him.

> *Vain man, said she, that dost in vain essay*
> *A mortal thing so to immortalize,*
> *For I myself shall like to this decay,*
> *And eek my name be wipèd out likewise.*

Clearly conversant with the tradition that casts time as the Great Destroyer, she poses its challenge to the "vain man" (both 'proud' and 'futile'). But at this critical juncture (the "turn" in the sonnet) he is prepared, and devotes the sestet to refuting the conventional position she has taken:

> *Not so (quoth I); let baser things devise*
> *To die in dust: but you shall live by fame*
> *My verse your virtues rare shall eternize,*
> *And in the heavens write your glorious name.*
> *Where whenas Death shall all the world subdue,*
> *Our love shall live, and later life renew. (LXXV)*

The idea that poetry can confer *eternal* fame is an important development, which soon became an Elizabethan convention and has lasted remarkably. The claim that a poet can "eternize" a subject underlies Joost Meerloo's assertion that "Creativity is eternization." With this preservative, says Spenser's speaker, you need not fear being forgotten...nor has she been; the poem has acted as a time capsule. Yes, in the final couplet the speaker goes over the top: how will their story "live, and later life renew" *after* Death has subdued "all the world"? But the main point – for our purposes, and perhaps for the speaker's – seems to have been carried.

When Spenser published the final installment of *The Faerie Queene* in 1596, "Two Cantos of *Mutabilitie*, Which...appear to be parcell of some following Booke of the *Faerie Queene*" were appended to it. (Oxford's *Spenser. Poetical Works* calls them Cantos VI and VII, plus two stanzas of Canto VIII, meant for Book VII.) The title page adds, "Under the legend of *Constancie*," the virtue that was to be represented allegorically in Book VII. All we have, however, are these cantos on Mutability, i.e. the opposite of Constancy. This concern is more typical of the Middle Ages than of the Renaissance, as in the "O Fortuna" song in the *Carmina Burana*, and the image of the Wheel of Fortune (turning as inexorably as time flows), which appears in the first line of Canto VI as the "ever-whirling wheele / Of *Change*." In the fragment, the Titaness Mutability rises in an assembly of Greek gods and calls on "great dame Nature" to acknowledge her as the supreme deity, pointing to the manifold changes of the natural world: the elements, the seasons, day and night, life and death, etc. Jove agrees that Time changes all, but says that *he* rules Time. Mutability denies this, asserts that even the gods are subject to change, and appeals to Dame Nature. After a pause, she pronounces judgment: the plaintiff's suit is rejected, because, though all things *do* change,

> *They are not changed from their first estate [state, essence];*
> *But by their change their being do dilate*
> *And turning to themselves at length again,*
> *Do work their own perfection so by fate. (Canto VII, stanza 58, ll.*
> *4-7, spelling modernized)*

Nature seems to have studied law and philosophy. Things only *appear* to change, but retain their essences as they "dilate," and eventually come back to themselves, having worked their own "perfection" (completion). Thus Change does not rule over them; *they* rule over Change. While Mutability is mulling that over, the assembly is dissolved and Nature vanishes.

In the first stanza of the fragment of Canto VIII, however, Spenser's persona records his own reaction to Mutability's long speech, which dominates Canto VII:

Me seems, that though she all unworthy were
Of the Heavens Rule; yet very sooth to say,
In all things else she bears the greatest sway. (VIII.1.3-5)

Mutability is not *identical* with Time, but there are similarities. During her speech, Mutability presents a masque of phenomena that change with time and are often used to mark its passage: tides, seasons, months, hours. At its conclusion, she asks, "who sees not, that *Time* on all doth prey? / But *Times* do change and move continually" (VII.47.5-6). Jove adopts this view, acknowledging that all things on earth "Are changed of *Time*" (VII.48.3). They agree, then, that mutability occurs through the action of time. The persona goes even farther as he reviews the debate: "Short *Time* shall soon cut down with his consuming sickle" our entire "state of life" (VIII.1.9,6). His position is Mutability's, though his feelings as a *victim* of Time are naturally stronger, almost mediaeval in their gloomy resignation. He does not claim that poetry can relieve any of this darkness, but the need for that relief is made clear. Spenser's grim *Mutability Cantos* bear the same relation to his optimistic *Amoretti* that Keats's "Ode on Melancholy" has to his "Ode on a Grecian Urn," discussed in Chapter 2: they depict a problem addressed elsewhere.

Spenser's younger contemporary William Shakespeare treated the theme of time, and poetry's relation to it, extensively in his sonnets (1609). In the earlier poems, his stance is the interested one of the lover, keen to demoralize the reluctant virgin with the bogeyman of Time. "Look in thy glass, and tell the face thou viewest / Now is the time that face should form another," he advises the lady at the beginning of sonnet #3 (Harrison 1595). In the sestet he returns to the mirror image and develops it as a metaphor of the generations.

Thou art thy mother's glass, and she in thee
Calls back the lovely April of her prime.
So thou through windows of thine age shalt see,
Despite of wrinkles, this thy golden time.
But if thou live, remembered not to be,
Die single, and thine image dies with thee.

Here the main intent is to affright the lady, and recommend reproduction (with the speaker), not poetry, as the best defence against time's depredations.

Similarly in #12, the speaker enumerates all the signs and slaves of time that he has been observing – clocks, nightfall, fading flowers, white hair, falling leaves, changing seasons – and ventures to point a moral to his lady. "Then of thy beauty do I question make, / That thou among the wastes of time must go," which is too bad, of course, but fortunately he knows a remedy, and is entirely at her service in this matter: "And nothing 'gainst Time's scythe can make defense / Save breed, to brave him when he takes thee hence" (Harrison 1597). And this jaunty blade has nothing else to suggest, no *poetic* alternative to procreation. Yet a few sonnets later, in #18, Shakespeare offers some of his best-known lines in defense of poetry as a weapon against oblivion. "Shall I compare thee to a summer's day?" he asks rhetorically (Harrison 1598). No, for that would be no contest, he writes. Summer days can be windy, or too hot, or cloudy, and in any case British summers are notoriously short, whereas

> ...thy eternal summer shall not fade,
> Nor lose possession of that fair thou owest; [have]
> Nor shall Death brag thou wander'st in his shade
> When in eternal lines to time thou grow'st
> So long as men can breathe, or eyes can see,
> So long lives this, and this gives life to thee.

These are crucial assertions. The poet's "eternal lines" will defy time, enduring to the crack o' doom; the poem will live as long as humanity itself, and she along with it. Nor need she grant any favours not to her liking: her passport to fame is granted freely, without barter or payment. As she reads, it is already given, and is still valid as we read.

The zenith of this conception of poetry's capabilities in Shakespeare is Sonnet #55. "Not marble, nor the gilded monuments / Of princes, shall outlive this powerful rhyme," it begins proudly (Harrison 1605). Again a speaker is addressing someone, but the "you" is not particularized to any degree, although the mention of "lovers" in the last line suggests a romantic or erotic relationship of some kind. The point is that the poem constitutes a "living record of your memory": it will have a life of its own.

> 'Gainst death and all-oblivious enmity
> Shall you pace forth. Your praise shall still find room
> Even in the eyes of all posterity

That wear this world out to the ending doom.
So, till the judgment that yourself arise,
You live in this, and dwell in lovers' eyes.

Yes, this poet has a very high opinion of his own ability, proclaiming, like Spenser, that his poem will be proof against the ravages of time. He does not, however, follow Spenser and fancy that his sonnet will *outlast* Time, the Second Coming, and the End of Things. What he does assert is bold enough, though: that the poem – and by inference good literature – will last as long as humanity does. His poetry is death-defying, and if not quite eternal, is immortal.

THERE WAS A LATER SEVENTEENTH-CENTURY coda to these Tudor and Stuart developments among the poets generally called "Cavalier," some of them – adherents of the *"Now, baby, now!"* school of gender relations – clearly a debasement of the Elizabethans. Others played more lightly with the idea that the spectre of the Grim Reaper might be used to speed the transition from maiden to mother. Robert Herrick, a follower of Ben Jonson (and a vicar until displaced by the Puritans), is one of the latter: a merry voice, but humane and civilized. In "The Argument" to his book of poems, *Hesperides* (1648), he lists his subjects, mainly nature and rural life, among which "I write of *Youth*, of *Love*, and have Accesse / By these, to sing of cleanly-*Wantonnesse*": a seeming oxymoron, difficult to achieve (White 233). He does have a serious side, warning Dianeme, "Sweet, be not proud" of your beauty, for beauty must fade (White 239); but his specialty is a smooth, lyrical *carpe diem*, which he combines with *tempus fugit*: 'Times flies, (therefore) seize the day.' "Corinna's Going a Maying" certainly leers at what it may mean to "go a-Maying" with comely young members of the opposite sex, but Herrick controls the term's studied ambiguity, and comes down on the "cleanly" side (White 240):

Come, let us goe, while we are in our prime;
And take the harmlesse follie of the time.
We shall grow old apace, and die
Before we know our Liberty.
Our life is short..../
..../

> Then while time serves, and we are but decaying;
> Come, my Corinna, come, let's goe a Maying.

The 'folly' proposed is to be 'harmless': the vicar votes for innocence. This is ostensibly a May Day rise-and-shine to the speaker's "sweet-Slug-a-bed," whose laziness may cause her to miss the fun that others are having. But there are moments when he hints at something more, as when Corinna is enjoined to "be briefe in praying / Few Beads are best, when once we goe a Maying." Why is that, Parson, and why the jests about "betraying" keys and picked locks? The poem is delicately balanced between "cleanly" and "wantonness," between "decaying" and "Maying."

Herrick's best-known effort along these lines is "To the Virgins, to Make much of Time," an English classic of its type. It begins, famously,

> Gather ye Rose-buds while ye may,
> Old Time is still a flying
> And this same flower that smiles today,
> To morrow will be dying. (White 244)

Classic and conventional: the line of argument is well-worn and well-oiled. Herrick develops it for two more stanzas, shifting the images and hailing youth as the best time of life, before drawing his conclusion:

> Then be not coy, but use your time;
> And while ye may, goe marry
> For having lost but once your prime,
> You may for ever tarry.

Again the lubricious possibilities are directed into wedlock; the speaker is not a seducer but a marriage counsellor. *Hesperides* appeared a year after the Puritans ejected Herrick from his cure of souls, and he may have enjoyed waving these stimulating images in front of them, then explaining what they really meant. His young love poems are fertility rituals, like classical comedy: endorsements of the life force that perpetuates the species. In the context of this study, these poems are notable for dramatizing the ravages caused by the swift, relentless passage of time and recommending a course of action, without making the claims of some Elizabethans that poetry itself can give relief or solve the problem.

Chapter 1: It's About Time   37

Andrew Marvell was also a religious man. The son of an Anglican preacher with Puritan leanings, he was influenced by the Jesuits in his youth, but grew to become a sound Church of England man who believed deeply in reason and toleration. His *Miscellaneous Poems* (1681) exhibit both Metaphysical and Cavalier impulses. Like Herrick, he was a good Latinist. "To His Coy Mistress" is another example of the *tempus fugit* so *carpe diem* school in England. Its three verse paragraphs could be an oration in a handbook on classical rhetoric. In the *introductio*, Marvell sets out for his (evidently cool) lady love the world as they might wish it: "Had we but World enough, and Time, / This coyness Lady were no crime" (White 460). They could stroll the globe at their leisure, perambulate from India to Britain; his love might begin before the Flood, and she might put him off, if she pleased,

> *Till the Conversion of the Jews.*
> *My vegetable Love should grow*
> *Vaster than Empires, and more slow.*

He would devote years, decades, centuries to praising each item in the Petrarchan catalogue of her beauties: "An Age at least to every part, / And the last Age should show your Heart." If only there were "world enough"! For this is what she deserves, and what he would wish. It is a delightful send-up and *reductio ad absurdum* of the rituals of courtly love. There is just one problem, familiar by now, which he rolls out in the second verse paragraph, the *expositio*:

> *But at my back I alwaies hear*
> *Times winged Chariot hurrying near*
> *And yonder all before us lye*
> *Desarts of vast Eternity.*

In this huge, barren, frightening perspective, Mutability reigns; the grave, worms, and dust await them both. "The Grave's a fine and private place, / But none I think do there embrace," he remarks drily. This brings the speaker to his inevitable, logical *conclusio* or *peroratio*: the final paragraph. "Now therefore," while we are young, lusty, and beautiful, "let us sport us while we may," devouring Time when it thinks to devour us. "Thus, though we cannot make our Sun / Stand still, yet we will make him run."

What the poet disclaims here, in a dependent clause – "though we cannot make our Sun / Stand still" – is a major concession, a reversal of Elizabethan momentum.

That is exactly what Daniel, Drayton, Spenser, and Shakespeare claimed their verse *could* do: stop time's juggernaut, immortalize or "eternize" the lady's beauty. But a civil (and religious) war and a regicide intervened between Shakespeare and Marvell, and such things take their toll on belief and self-confidence. Marvell cannot bring himself to offer to stop time for her, only to make it pass quickly so that it will not hang heavy on their hands. He hopes she will not despise that.

The later, more dissolute "Cavaliers" seldom venture on such a weighty subject as time except to wield it as a weapon in sexual skirmishes. *Their* formative events were the Restoration and subsequent reign of the Merry Monarch, Charles II, whose morals trickled down to his courtiers. A "Song" by John Wilmot, Earl of Rochester – the *notorious* Earl of Rochester – is a fair sample of the tone their verse adopts with uncooperative women:

> *Phillis, be gentler, I advise;*
> *Make up for time mispent.*
> *When Beauty on its Death-bed lyes,*
> *'Tis high time to repent. (Pinto 26)*

He begins with this insult to her deteriorating looks and spirals down from there. A malicious fate has made her old prematurely, and if she insists on remaining stand-offish, Time will only ladle out more in the "fading Beauties" department.

> *Then if, to make your ruine more,*
> *You'l peevishly be coy,*
> *Dye with the Scandal of a Whore,*
> *And never know the Joy. (Pinto 27)*

The joy of a whore? The cruelty of this is its most impressive feature (just ahead of ignorance), and the unlucky use of the word "coy" invites comparison with Marvell's infinitely more thoughtful and graceful treatment of female reticence. Sir George Etherege, another of the period's poetic rakes (and a successful playwright), is marginally gentler, or at least suaver, in replying "To a Lady, Asking him how Long He Would Love Her." But Celia, what a question!

> *It is not, Celia, in our power*
> *To say how long our love will last;*

It may be we within this hour
May lose those joys we now do taste: (Pinto 32)

Only the immortals are free from changeability in amorous affairs, he avers (dubiously). The rest of us, Celia, are subjects of the tyrant time, and so the question is how we may best live under that absolute dictatorship. To this he has a typical Cavalier answer:

Then, since we mortal Lovers are,
Ask not how long our love will last;
But while it does, let us take care
Each minute be with pleasure past.

This is certainly hedonistic, but so is the last verse paragraph of "To His Coy Mistress," bowling the pleasure ball through the iron gates of time-bound life. And Etherege avoids the nastiness of Rochester's "Song." He simply thinks that it would be mad not "To live, because we're sure to die," and strategically equates living with having affairs. Neither he nor Rochester nor Marvell suggests that a poem will enshrine a lady for the ages: to go there requires more respect for poetry, and for a lady love, than Cavaliers are willing to show.

DESPITE THIS LATE SEVENTEENTH-CENTURY FALLING-OFF from the higher seriousness with which some Elizabethan sonneteers treated the problem of time, the earlier part of the century laid a foundation for positions held or developed by major British poets well into the twentieth century. And it was not only Drayton's "immortal song" and Shakespeare's "eternal lines" that would aspire to challenge or throw off the bonds of time, but literature, music, and art generally, as a variety of artists would eventually assert.

CHAPTER 2:

And Time Shall Be No More

Some Later British Poets
Spots of Time

The concerns of the major English Romantic poets included time's human meaning. They often wrote about it, though not in a monolithic or predictable way. Their dean, William Wordsworth, neither a champion of the powers of verse to immortalize nor a seducer, addressed the issue with his characteristic sobriety. A famous passage in the final version of *The Prelude* (1850, but almost identical in the 1805-06 version) explains his mature outlook, and sheds some light on earlier poems:

> *There are in our existence spots of time,*
> *That with distinct pre-eminence retain*
> *A renovating virtue, whence...*
>
> ....
>
> *...our minds*
> *Are nourished and invisibly repaired;*
> *A virtue by which pleasure is enhanced... (Bk XII.208-10, 214-16;*
> *Maxwell 479)*

These moments, retained from our past, possess the power ("virtue," Italian *virtù*) of nourishing, repairing, and "renovating" (1850; "vivifying" in 1805-06) us. Just *how* they go about renewing minds and enhancing pleasure is not spelled out here, which is typical of Wordsworth's broader, more philosophical passages. Nor does he specify *literature's* role in this process, though that might be inferred. Many of his best-known poems focus on the meaning of his own *spots of time*, which are "scattered everywhere, taking their date / From our first childhood" (XII.223-24). His "Lines" on Tintern Abbey and the Wye River valley (1798) are a sustained meditation on two visits there (1793 and 1798) and the relationship between them: not only his memories, but what he was then, what he is now, and what connects those selves. As in the passage from *The Prelude* quoted above (and several lyrics), he asserts a vital continuity:

> These beauteous forms,
> Through a long absence, have not been to me
> As is a landscape to a blind man's eye
> But oft, in lonely rooms, and 'mid the din
> Of towns and cities, I have owed to them,
> In hours of weariness, sensations sweet,
> Felt in the blood, and felt along the heart,
> And passing even into my purer mind,
> With tranquil restoration:... (ll. 23-30; Stillinger 108)

Here he is more specific about the process than in *The Prelude*: the " restoration" operates at the levels of sensations, of feelings, and of thought. The year 1793 is long gone, but the images and emotions of that visit endure in his body, have become a part of him that time has *not* taken. What is more, he now has reason to hope that this will happen again, so that the 1798 tour will become as much a part of the future William Wordsworth as 1793 is of his present self (ll. 64-65).

We have been set up, however, and here comes the bad news. Whereas *then* he "bounded o'er the mountains" with "glad animal movements," a creature for whom nature was "all in all," much has subsequently "changed" within him, changed utterly (ll. 68, 74, 75, 66).

> That time is past,
> And all its aching joys are now no more,
> And all its dizzy raptures. (ll. 83-85; Stillinger 110)

There has been an undeniable loss, then, a loss of at least one kind of joy. But – and this part is controversial, some critics questioning whether Wordsworth was being totally honest with himself and us – the poet tells us that the wisdom he has since gained amounts to "abundant recompense" for his losses (l. 88).

For I have learned
To look on nature, not as in the hour
Of thoughtless youth; but hearing oftentimes
The still, sad music of humanity... (ll. 88-91)

"Thoughtless" *may* have been implicit in the "glad animal movements" of his youth, but *saying* it puts them in a harsher light. Do we believe that the 23-year-old Wordsworth was "thoughtless"? And it is difficult to paraphrase the passage that follows in a way satisfactory to everyone; many readers feel that murky clouds roll in here. Is it a religious passage, and if so, of what kind? Should the "presence" that "disturbs" him with "the joy / Of elevated thoughts" and gives him a "sense sublime" of itself be taken as a version of the commonly-received western notion of God, or does it belong to a private, or perhaps an eastern, religion? (ll. 94-95) This *presence* dwells in sunlight, air, ocean, "and in the mind of man" (l. 99). Is that pantheism? Nature worship? Or is the passage really psychological, or aesthetic? I never taught a class that could agree on its nature or message. Readers tend to see reflections of themselves in it.

In his closing peroration Wordsworth does what he can to dispel the clouds. He has "long" been "A worshipper of Nature," and remains "Unwearied in that service"; feels, in fact, a "warmer love," a "deeper zeal / Of holier love" than in his youth (ll. 151-55). Perhaps he was wise to leave it there: holiness can take many forms. What is clear and unarguable, I think, is that this is a poet who feels deeply the influence of time on our lives, both what it gives and what it takes. He will not try to fool himself, or push the idea that literature can affect this process. He has no time machine, but neither does he ask us to pretend, to suspend disbelief while he indulges a fantasy. He may not be entertaining, but he is credible, and has a heaviness, a *gravitas*, reminiscent of Gilgamesh wrestling with Enkidu, or with his mortality.

Wordsworth returned to the existential conundrum of "Tintern Abbey" in his "Ode. Intimations of Immortality from Recollections of Early Childhood" (begun 1802, published 1807). This long gestation, and Wordsworth's revisions, gave it depth and complexity. It revisits the issues raised in "Tintern Abbey," but using a different structure. Whereas the earlier poem opens in a positive, 'glad-to-be-back' mood, praising the beauty of the Wye valley for sixty-odd lines before introducing change and darkening the mood, "Intimations" hits us at once with the sadness of loss owing to the action of time: a difficult mood to lighten. "There was a time," it begins sonorously, when all of nature was "Apparelled in celestial light" for the speaker, *but* "It is not now as it has been of yore"; wherever he turns, "The things which I have seen I now can see no more" (ll. 1, 4, 6, 9). Verse paragraph II enlarges the complaint: rainbows, roses, and moonlight are lovely, "But yet I know, where'er I go, / That there hath past away a glory from the earth" (ll. 17-18) – that is, for him. In III, he tries to rouse himself, chiding his "thought of grief" in May, when "all the earth is gay" (ll. 22, 29), an effort carried over into the earlier lines of IV. This upward thrust is soon exhausted, however, and he falls back into his first despondency:

> - But there's a Tree, of many, one,
> A single Field which I have looked upon,
> Both of them speak of something that is gone
> The Pansy at my feet
> Doth the same tale repeat
> Whither is fled the visionary gleam?
> Where is it now, the glory and the dream? (ll. 51-57; Stillinger 187)

"Where is it now?" *Ubi sunt?*: the cry of the mediaeval monk or poet that all flesh is grass and this life is transient. But it is neither the vanity of human wishes nor fear of death that disturbs Wordsworth; it is his fear that he has lost the freshness of his youthful vision, his religion of nature, perhaps irretrievably. Here he seems to draw not strength or a sense of renewal from the past, as in "Tintern Abbey," but sadness, even despair.

At this point Wordsworth put aside the ode for about two years. What follows, from paragraph V onwards, looks like a fresh start in quest of consolation for all that time takes from us. That involves a reinterpretation of childhood. In "Tintern Abbey," he wrote of the "coarser pleasures" of "boyish days" or "thoughtless youth"; his "elevated thoughts" came subsequently (ll. 73, 90, 95). The Child of the "Intimations Ode" is quite another being ("trailing clouds of glory do we come / From God, who is our home": ll. 64-65), and the poet's exalted thoughts of immortality spring from his "Recollections of Early Childhood."

> *Our birth is but a sleep and a forgetting*
> *The Soul that rises with us, our life's Star,*
> *Hath had elsewhere its setting,*
> *And cometh from afar.... (ll. 58-61)*

In his own day, some of Wordsworth's more pious readers wondered whether this part of the ode was 'tainted' by alien notions of metempsychosis or transmigration of souls. He is careful to use terms and phrases from the Christian tradition, "God" and "Heaven," yet several of his metaphors – he insisted that was all they were, not beliefs – are consistent with other religions wherein the sun (or sunlight) is an image of God. The Child, "Nature's Priest," comes from the east, attended by a "vision splendid," but "At length the Man perceives it die away, / And fade into the light of common day" (ll. 72-76). The verse paragraphs that follow, hailing the quasi-divine child as our "best Philosopher," "Mighty Prophet! Seer blest!" (ll. 110, 114), have raised many questions and some eyebrows. Wordsworth's friend, fellow poet, and (in *Lyrical Ballads*) collaborator, Samuel Taylor Coleridge, described parts of VIII as "*mental* bombast" (*Biographia Litteraria*, ch. XXII; bombast was cotton wadding stuffed into Elizabethan theatrical costumes to make the top actors look bigger). In any case, the force and logic of the "light from the East" image carry over into the years that "bring the inevitable yoke" and the soul's burden of "earthly freight" (ll. 124, 126).

Then in IX the poet declares that "The thought of our past years in me doth breed / Perpetual benediction" (ll. 133-34). It is difficult to see where this blessing comes from. An editor of Wordsworth's poems (among others) notes the Ode's "seeming instability of tone, the obscurity of what is lost..., and the tenuousness of the connection made in stanza IX between idealism and immortality" (Stillinger 538). The shift of mood in IX can be explained, I think, as the poet turning from what we inevitably lose to his conviction about what we did, after all, once have. Those vague but "obstinate questionings / Of sense and outward things," those "shadowy recollections" of our infancy and youth (ll. 141-42, 149), are, he believes, "intimations of immortality," and he pulls all this together in a splendid metaphor that justifies some earlier floundering:

> *Hence in a season of calm weather*
> *Though inland far we be,*

Our souls have sight of that immortal sea
Which brought us hither,
Can in a moment travel thither,
And see the Children sport upon the shore,
And hear the mighty waters rolling evermore. (ll.161-67;
Stillinger 190)

A poet will not have many moments like this in a career, when the work done and
the tumbles taken enable such a triumph. What though he has shifted our origins
from the sun to the ocean? The biologists agree. And the metrical freedom of the
classical ode allows him to represent the everlasting roll of the "mighty waters"
onshore in a six-beat alexandrine.

In the final two verse paragraphs, Wordsworth takes stock of profit and loss. He
is evidently determined to be positive about the balance, but refuses to suppress
the darker shades from the early part of the poem. They will out:

What though the radiance which was once so bright
Be now for ever taken from my sight,
Though nothing can bring back the hour
Of splendour in the grass, of glory in the flower;
We will grieve not, rather find
Strength in what remains behind;
In the primal sympathy
Which having been must ever be;
In the soothing thoughts that spring
Out of human suffering;
In the faith that looks through death,
In years that bring the philosophic mind. (ll. 175-86)

Wordsworth has not been able to convince all his readers with this audit, either;
to put it plainly, some believe that he was cooking the books. Some of the deduc-
tions he claims look shaky. That the "primal sympathy" (of the Youth with Nature)
"having been must ever be" is only an assumption, and the thoughts that arise
from "human suffering" often test faith and are anything but "soothing." We
cannot be strengthened by a "faith that looks through death" unless we believe
in an afterlife of some kind; the years that *may* bring "the philosophic mind" can

also bring bitterness, dementia, or loss of faith. It is an optimistic wish-list – Here's what we *need* to believe to endure – rather than a sober reckoning, and the closing paragraph, theistic and personal, is even less persuasive.

Nevertheless, Wordsworth does not deserve to be indicted for fraud, because he does not suppress evidence. The feelings of his darkest moments are admitted at the end as at the beginning, and placed alongside his proposed mitigations. If we find his consolations weaker than his heartfelt losses, that may be us, or the *lacrimae rerum*. As John Milton and readers of *Paradise Lost* found, it is easier to make a dark, active evil interesting than to make a rather passive and abstract good likable. Perhaps that is the tide that Wordsworth is swimming against in both the "Lines" and the "Ode." It is worth noting that in his latest statement, the final *Prelude*, he did not withdraw his claims for the "renovating" powers of those youthful "spots of time" that he had celebrated: i.e., for him, time cut both ways. Finally, he retains his credibility and his right to speak on this subject.

She Cannot Fade

In discussing H.G. Wells, I suggested that art and literature may allow us to "stop or move about" in time. Besides being able to give us the illusion of temporal movement, the artistic imagination possesses the power to dam the river of Heraclitian time, to "fix" an experience, to capture the moment and "seize the day." A Minoan vase or *Bleak House* may seem to transport *us* in time, but from the standpoint of the original artists what they did was halt time's flow or flight, and preserve an otherwise fleeting scene indefinitely.

One of the best and best-known literary examples of this effect is John Keats's "Ode on a Grecian Urn," whose figures are posed in a tableau of Beauty Desired. But to feel the force of the claim he makes there we need to look first at his "Ode on Melancholy," where the problem is stated. Both poems were composed in May 1819, during Keats's *annus mirabilis*. In its finished form (without the original first stanza that Keats discarded), the "Ode on Melancholy" begins by rejecting the usual accoutrements of eighteenth-century English poetic melancholy, as given in Thomas Gray's "Elegy in a Country Churchyard": gravestones, yew trees, nightshade, owls, "death-moths," etc. The rejection is based on psychological and aesthetic grounds. Gray's poem is all in one key, and so lacks the contrast required to generate the shock and deep feeling that Keats wants: "For shade to shade will come too drowsily, / And drown the wakeful anguish of the soul" (ll. 9-10; Thorpe 354).

No, if you really want to feel your sadness keenly "when the melancholy fit shall fall / ...like a weeping cloud," Keats insists that you should concentrate on the transience of earthly life. It is *perishable delights* that bring time's penalties home.

> *Then glut thy sorrow on a morning rose,*
> *Or on the rainbow of the salt sand-wave,*
> *Or on the wealth of globéd peonies.... (ll. 15-17)*

Ah, but the richest of all sources of melancholy will of course be a fellow human, so take the hand of your beloved and look deep into her incomparable eyes. Actually, he writes "feed deep, deep upon her peerless eyes," as if to consume them while they are still beautiful. For there you will find true sadness, and it is this: "She dwells with Beauty – Beauty that must die," with Joy, which is always saying goodbye, and with Pleasure,

> *Turning to Poison while the bee-mouth sips,*
> *Ay, in the very temple of Delight*
> *Veil'd Melancholy has her sovran shrine.... (ll. 24-26)*

Here we reach the inner sanctum, the final dark secret, which is, not surprisingly, the human condition, wherein the inevitable ravages of time play a leading role. Keats does not attempt to "solve the problem" of sadness here, or to jolly you out of your depression. This ode is for when you feel the melancholy mood descending, and want to feel that "wakeful anguish" *more intensely* – want to know it all, as a Romantic poet would.

In the "Ode on a Grecian Urn," though, he *does* present a consolation; the two poems are related as problem and resolution, like the octave and sestet of a sonnet. "Melancholy" states the problem: life blooms, declines, and perishes; from this iron law there can be no appeal, no reprieve. What "Grecian Urn" shows, however, is that we *do* have a way to hold time *at a point of our choosing*, and that way is art – not just literature, but art in general, for Keats's poem is about an ancient Greek vase decorated with scenes from myth and legend (such as he had been examining in the British Museum), and they depict musicians piping "to the spirit ditties of no tone" (l. 14; Thorpe 353). While the "sensual ear" (l. 13) must perish, the spirit survives. These scenes – and the urn's endurance – pique his curiosity: "What men or gods are these? What maidens loth? / What mad pursuit? What struggle to escape?" (ll. 8-9)

The urn may depict Apollo and Daphne, or be an imaginary composite: it does not matter. The point, for Keats, is that the ancient artist managed to "freeze" time (as cinematographers say) at a propitious moment, perhaps the best moment for the actors in the urn's drama. This realization moves the poet to address the urn, and particularly the pursuer, directly:

> Fair youth, beneath the trees, thou canst not leave
> Thy song, nor ever can those trees be bare;
> Bold Lover, never, never canst thou kiss,
> Though winning near the goal – yet, do not grieve;
> She cannot fade, though thou hast not thy bliss,
> For ever wilt thou love, and she be fair! (ll. 15-20)

Keats's realization of art's power to "eternize" one second stuns him into exclamation. Though the "Fair youth" will never have his kiss, yet "She cannot fade," but will remain always fair – just as the trees will never lose their leaves in this eternal spring, and the "happy melodist" will never cease piping "songs for ever new"(24). If we object that what art has done here is stop the course of natural human life, Keats has thought of that: the figures on the vase are

> All breathing human passion far above,
> That leaves a heart high-sorrowful and cloy'd,
> A burning forehead, and a parching tongue. (ll. 28-30)

Admittedly Keats expresses here a deep pessimism about the arc of human emotions from which some readers will dissent, and these lines lead into the darker and more ambiguous fourth stanza (the sacrifice). But in the fifth he returns to the affirmative, wondering mood of the second and third ("O Attic shape!"), and spells out his claim for art: "Thou, silent form, dost tease us out of thought / As doth eternity" (44-45). This, surely, is his central claim, and a large one: that the artistic product resembles eternity, which is "the end of time." The old gospel song "When the Roll Is Called Up Yonder" contains the striking lines,

When the trumpets of the Lord shall sound
And time shall be no more,
And the morning breaks eternal bright and fair....

It is startling to find ourselves in the world of *The Book of Revelation*, but that is where the "Cold Pastoral" (45) of the urn operates: in a timeless realm from which it delivers its famous message, "Beauty is truth, truth beauty," whose meaning generations of readers, critics, teachers, and students have pondered.

In Keats, then, we find (in the "Ode on Melancholy") as keen a sense of inevitable loss over time as in the novels of Arnold Bennett, but also a strong conviction that art can serve as a link between remote ages. The point driven home by the "Ode on a Grecian Urn" about the relation of the artistic imagination to the wasting action of time had been made, as we have seen, by several Elizabethan sonneteers and seventeenth-century poets, with various emphases. Keats lived and wrote at roughly the halfway point between them and us.

An Artifice of Eternity

The idea that literature can step off the wheel of time into a kind of immortality was, then, well established in British verse by the early nineteenth century, though Wordsworth begged to be excused. A century later, William Butler Yeats elaborated on the claims of Spenser, Shakespeare, Keats, and others for the "eternizing" powers of art. The earlier Yeats can sound like a follower of Wordsworth: "The Wild Swans at Coole" (1919) dwells on the changes (mostly within the poet) during the years since he first saw them; its structure and mood are reminiscent of "Tintern Abbey." But "Sailing to Byzantium" (1927) counterpoises the image of "an aged man," just "a paltry thing, / A tattered coat upon a stick," to that of art as an ageless, golden realm (ll. 9-10; Yeats 191). There is no Wordsworthian vacillating, debit and credit; in four *ottava rima* stanzas, Yeats lays out his two thought-landscapes crisply and clearly.

"That is no country for old men," it begins. "That" is *not* Ireland (as a notorious footnote in one anthology proposed), but much of the planet: i.e. all lands and realms or places where "The young" may be found "In one another's arms," birds sing in the trees, fish crowd the rivers and seas, etc. "Those dying generations," the poet calls them: doomed to death, with a play on the Elizabethan usage of "dying" as sexual climax. And here is the problem with them for an old man (Yeats was then in his 60s) and an artist.

> Fish, flesh, or fowl, commend all summer long
> Whatever is begotten, born, and dies.
> Caught in that sensual music all neglect
> Monuments of unageing intellect. (ll. 5-8)

This central claim comes in the first stanza, and is slipped in almost casually, adjectivally: unlike the dying generations, "intellect" is "unageing," timeless, immortal. That makes the correct course for an old man clear. He is all but finished, used up, turfed out, in *that* country – "unless / Soul clap its hands and sing" (ll. 10-11). Poets traditionally referred to verse as "singing," though here it stands for all creative art. Fortunately there are "singing schools" that do not live only in the present of the senses, but have a feeling for history, and every one of them studies

> Monuments of its own magnificence;
> And therefore I have sailed the seas and come
> To the holy city of Byzantium. (ll. 14-16)

This is no more a travel journal than *that country* was Ireland; the sea that Yeats sails here is the one that Keats traverses to visit "realms of gold" in "On First Reading Chapman's Homer." And the "holy city" Yeats reaches is not Turkish Istanbul, or Byzantine Constantinople, but Greek Byzantium, which predated them both: like the singing schools, the speaker respects and lives in cultural history. Thus he addresses himself to the "sages, standing in God's holy fire / As in the gold mosaic of a wall" such as Byzantine artists made, which have survived in Istanbul and in some Greek and Italian churches (ll. 17-18). The saints and apostles depicted on those walls might not encourage his art-eternity concept, but the makers of the mosaics would, and he beseeches those artists and craftsmen to "Come from the holy fire, perne in a gyre": step back into history and be his "singing-masters" so that he can learn to transcend time (ll. 19-20). This is paradoxical – they are asked to re-enter history in order to help him rise above it – and that is not the last paradox:

Consume my heart away; sick with desire
And fastened to a dying animal
It knows not what it is: and gather me
Into the artifice of eternity. (ll. 21-24)

This is not a death-wish: his body, subject to time, will die in accordance with the laws of nature. What he wants is a school for his soul and his imagination, which are not subject to time, but capable of induction into "the artifice of eternity." That piquant phrase – which challenges every reader – *may* suggest that the concept of eternity is an artifice, a human construct, but my interest is in what sort of artifice could be "of eternity." That is the subject of the entire final stanza, dominated by an image drawn from tales of rare gifts given to Byzantine emperors.

Once out of nature I shall never take
My bodily form from any natural thing,
But such a form as Grecian goldsmiths make
Of hammered gold and gold enamelling
To keep a drowsy Emperor awake
Or set upon a golden bough to sing
To lords and ladies of Byzantium
Of what is past, or passing, or to come. (ll. 25-32; Yeats 192)

Once "out of nature" and *that country*, his soul will want an appropriate form, and Yeats finds that in the old story of Greek artisans presenting the emperor with a mechanical singing bird. His emphasis is on the metal that we prize largely for its permanence. Gold appears four times in as many lines: goldsmiths make the bird of "hammered gold and gold enamelling" and set it on "a golden bough," unchanged as the "dying generations" come and go.

And what will it *do*? Yeats formulates the Artistic Paradox. The art-object's voice comes from outside nature, yet addresses itself to mortal audiences – "lords and ladies of Byzantium," aristocratic consumers of art but also "dying generations" – and its theme is human history ("what is past, or passing, or to come"). It is a human arti-fact, a device, and though it will last, being gold, it sings of the perishing existence that mortals know. This is the condition of the undying soul "fastened to a dying animal": the part of Yeats and each of us that belongs to the transient historical world. Art is both of time and out of time – an "artifice of eternity."

Whereas popular treatments of time (such as science fiction dramas) can be and often are facile, serious art tends to treat the subject tragically, acknowledging inevitable losses while seeking and sometimes finding compensation, as Wordsworth did. He and Keats operate far above the sixteenth- and seventeenth-century poetic seducers for whom "time's arrow" was merely one more in their rakish quiver, and they knew the work of some Tudor sonneteers who hailed the immortalizing powers of verse. Yeats, well aware of these earlier traditions, presents perhaps the clearest statement of the way in which art must operate, keeping a foot in each world – though Gilgamesh might have said, "I told you so."

IF THIS CHAPTER HAS SEEMED to suggest that art's case against Time was pleaded solely in Britain, that was not so; even a brief glance across the Channel reveals that it had Continental advocates as well. Théophile Gautier is one of the French poets who moved beyond François Villon's lament for *"les neiges d'antan"* to the position that art can capture the moment, can be a rock in the stream of time. In the prefatory sonnet to *Émaux et Camées* (*Enamels and Cameos*, 1857, 1872) Gautier identifies with poets such as Hafiz and Goethe who kept working through whatever worldly storms were raging, convinced that art, not events, would endure. He returns to the point at the end of the volume in "L'Art," though with a novel twist. The artist must, he says, choose a *medium* that will last: not an easy, pliable one, but a form that is *rebelle*, "obstinate," and so requires intense application. His examples are onyx, marble, enamel, and verse. Sculptor, he exhorts, reject the soft clay that your thumb can shape. Instead, struggle with durable Carrara or Parian marble; borrow the bronze of Syracuse; work Apollo's profile in agate. Painter, he urges, lay aside your watercolours and fix your "too-frail" colours in the enamelist's kiln. But why these stern injunctions? Towards the end, Gautier explains:

Tout passe. – L'art robuste	All passes. – Only strong art
Seul a l'éternité.	Passes to eternity.
Le buste	The bust
Survit à la cité.	Survives the city.
Et la médaille austère	And the austere coin
Que trouve un laboureur	That a workman finds

Sous terre	Underground
Révèle un empereur.	Reveals an emperor.

We note that poor art and superior art will not fare equally well in these sweep-stakes. Like Shakespeare and Spenser, who specify that *their* poems, not just anyone's, will survive ("*My* verse," "*this* powerful rime"), Gautier, a spare, almost minimal poet here, has protected himself with one word: "*robuste*," which means in French what it does in English. And in the next quatrain he sums up the claim he is making in terms we should recognize:

Les dieux eux-mêmes meurent.	The gods themselves die.
Mais les vers souverains	But poetry, sovereign,
Demeurent	Remains
Plus forts que les airains.	Stronger than bronze.

"Not marble, nor the gilded monuments / Of princes, shall outlive this powerful rime," wrote Shakespeare (Sonnet #55). Gautier endorses the central idea, while adding a nice touch. In the end poetry proves "sovereign," an epithet often applied to earthly emperors and heavenly gods. *La lutte* – the one against Time – *continue.*

CHAPTER 3:

Modern Times

THE IDEA OF USING ART to counter the depredations of time in some way – halt, modify, examine, recover, "eternize" – was not, then, the private preserve of any one nation or language. It recurs in ancient Mesopotamia, in Tudor, Stuart, and Romantic poetry in England, in French poetry, in Yeats. The subchapter on Science Fiction suggests how widely dispersed the fascination with exploring and manipulating time has been in films and television programs, many of which are based on books. European novelists and (less often) essayists were weighing in on the whole subject – the problems of having to find a *modus vivendi* under time's sway – by the beginning of the twentieth century.

Everything Came to That

No one interested in extended treatments of the operation of time on human souls and bodies can afford to overlook the novels of Arnold Bennett (1867-1931), considered a major novelist in his day. Though his reputation has faded, his meticulous workmanship and psychological insight still compel respect, and time was his overriding, almost obsessive theme. The British novelist Alan Sillitoe writes that "The tragic theme of many of Bennett's novels is 'the passing of time'... it is a deadly hunter who pursues you into all sorts of swamps, dreadful situations, and sunny valleys, but which corners you in the end" (Bennett 9).

In *The Old Wives' Tale* (1908), one of his most highly regarded books, "the passing of time" serves as both thought and protagonist, rather as landscape does in Thomas Hardy. We are shown – relentlessly – the sudden or gradual alteration in faces, fashions, fortunes, relationships, and material things over four decades.

Bennett, inspired by Guy de Maupassant's *Une Vie*, "revolted against the absurd youthfulness, the unfading youthfulness of the average heroine," when really "the change from the young girl to the stout ageing woman is made up of an infinite number of infinitesimal changes, each unperceived by her" (Bennett 22). They do *not* go "unperceived" by him. Historical events come and go (America's Civil War, the advent of motorized transport in England, the Franco-Prussian War, the Paris Commune, the Federation plan for the Five Towns of Staffordshire, etc.), while characters visibly age and a good many die. Bennett occasionally notes the year, or at least gives readers means to calculate it. Book Two, "Constance," narrates events from 1867 to 1893; Book Three backs up to account for Sophia ca. 1870.

The novel could have been called "Sense and Sensibility," or (since that had been taken) "A Tale of Two Sisters." Constance the Constant and elder is plain, steady, conservative; Sophia is beautiful, daring, irresponsible: her name ('Wisdom') long seems ironic. Early on, Bennett contrasts her with her mother as they sit by the fire at afternoon tea: the "monumental matron" in her widow's weeds, face "creased and wrinkled" by the seemingly "countless years of joy and disillusion," and "the young, slim girl, so fresh, so virginal, so ignorant, with all the pathos of an unsuspecting victim about to be sacrificed to the minotaur of Time!" (Bennett 133-34). Readers who missed Sillitoe's warning about a "deadly hunter" may wonder what this nightmare from a Cretan labyrinth is doing in a respectable English draper's parlour. But Bennett means it, and readers who bear with him for another few hundred pages will realize that the allusion was not overwrought. Sophia will elope with a worthless travelling salesman, Gerald Scales, go with him to Paris, be deserted by him there and left to make her own way. Tougher than she looks, Sophia never considers crawling back to her family or England; she learns French, marshals her resources, rents out rooms, and eventually acquires ownership of a successful *pension* popular with English visitors. Decades pass in unremitting work before a chance meeting with a friend of a nephew she has never seen pitches her headlong into depression and harsh self-scrutiny:

> *Undoubtedly she should have communicated with her family. It was silly not to have done so.... She had been proud. She was criminally proud. That was her vice.... She was ageing, and she was alone in the world.... She was the most solitary person on earth. She had heard*

> *no word of Gerald, no word of anybody.... It was appalling - the*
> *passage of years; and the passage of years would grow more appall-*
> *ing. Ten years hence, where would she be? She pictured herself dying.*
> *Horrible!* (446-47)

Nothing in her situation has changed; her circumstances are comfortable, the *pension* is thriving. This is a mental movement, a hard look at her life occasioned by an accidental encounter, and she cannot escape her own candour. She knows that her "reputation for sagacity" in business is "enormous," yet she has "been guilty of the capital folly of cutting herself off from her family" (446-47). That situation too has not changed, only her view of it, and the minotaur now appears in the form of the "appalling...passage of years," which she extrapolates to her death. Though her soul recoils from the idea, it would be good to have a family.

The penultimate Book, "End of Sophia," is mostly about time, here very much the Grim Reaper as Sophy reacts to seeing the remains of her long-estranged husband Gerald laid out on his deathbed. It is only

> *...the face of an aged man peeping out from under a white sheet on a*
> *naked mattress.... In her mind she had not pictured Gerald as a very*
> *old man. ... This face on the bed was painfully, pitiably old. A with-*
> *ered face, with the shiny skin all drawn into wrinkles!* (Bennett 536)

I pass over the rest of the passage, which continues describing Gerald's corpse and Sophia's horrified reaction for many lines: it is too much like viewing a friend's body. As Dr Johnson said of the final scene in *Othello*, "I am glad that I have ended my revisal [re-examination] of this dreadful scene. It is not to be endured." Time has brought mechanical progress, but it is felt here (and in many other passages) as a heavy burden borne by everyone. Sophia has long since ceased to love Gerald, or even to like him, but that is not the issue.

> *What affected her was that he had once been young, and that he had*
> *grown old, and was now dead. That was all. Youth and vigour had*
> *come to that. Youth and vigour always came to that. Everything came*
> *to that.* (536)

There is a problem here, a danger for the novelist and his readers. Time seems to have no redeeming qualities, to be an all-negating condition of mortal life. Does an artist, or anyone, have a right to do this to us? We are *not* told that literature has the power to help, although we might postulate that Bennett wrote to help himself or us in some way. Perhaps this novel is his voyage to Byzantium, a timeless realm. But can this truth set us free, or lighten our burden?

A single passage shortly after the one just quoted may hint at mitigation. Sophia is deeply depressed after seeing Gerald's body. "My life has been too terrible!" she thinks. "I wish I was dead" (Bennett 537). The narrator does not comment, but Sophia hears a discreet knock at the door: the admirably tactful Mr. Till Boldero, inviting her to tea: "'Come in,' she said, in a calm, resigned, cheerful voice. The sound had recalled her with the swiftness of a miracle to the unconquerable dignity of human pride" (538).

We wonder where cheerfulness could possibly come from at such a moment, but an answer is immediately provided: society calls, and it is show time. Psychologically Bennett is subtle, quite capable of rounding his characters, especially Sophia, who finds that "dignity" is what we have, maybe all we have, in the face of inevitable defeat. The exercise of that "unconquerable" quality when defeat is certain may suggest tragic stature, as when Macbeth realizes he has been fooled and still roars, "Lay on, Macduff, / And damned be him that first cries 'Hold, enough!'" But this is the "dignity of human *pride*": the Cardinal Sin, the sin of Satan. Sophia has admitted to being proud. Bennett may want to remind us that pride is double-edged, being also an attribute of heroes – none of whom, however, except Gilgamesh, ever faced an opponent as powerful as Time.

The Paradise We Have Lost

Marcel Proust's famous super-novel or series of novels *A la Recherche du temps perdu* (1913-28; usually translated *Remembrance of Things Past*, from Shakespeare's sonnet #30) is an expedition 'in search of lost time,' but not in Burroughs's sense. What is to be rediscovered and in a sense recovered here is the narrator / author's youth. The nature of time, and what can be done about or with its passage, is at least as central to this *magnum opus* as it is to Wordsworth's longer poems. The *Oxford Companion to English Literature* offers an admirably concise summary of Proust's "metaphysical attitude" throughout the fifteen novels:

> *...the conception of the unreality and reversibility of time, the power*
> *of sensation rather than intellectual memory to recover 'the past',*
> *and the subject's consequent power to cheat time and death....* (3rd
> ed., 641)

The first clause needs qualification – time also appears as real and non-reversible in the work – but the second and third clauses are accurate (the third is already familiar).

The seed of the whole vast project is the scene at the end of the "Overture" section of *Du Côté de chez Swann* (1913, rev. 1918; trans. as *Swann's Way*) where the narrator's memories of his childhood in Combray are awakened. This does not come about easily; at first he blunders as in a maze, following false leads. So "for a long time," says the narrator (also named Marcel), "when I lay awake at night and revived old memories of Combray, I saw no more of it than [a] sort of luminous panel" (Proust 1928, 60). The trouble, he realizes, is that a direct "exercise of the will" produces only an "intellectual memory," and "the pictures which that kind of memory shews us of the past preserve nothing of the past itself" (61). Therefore "To me it was in reality all dead." Meditating on Celtic beliefs, he concludes that

> *...all the efforts of our intellect must prove futile. The past is hidden*
> *somewhere outside the realm, beyond the reach of intellect, in some*
> *material object...it depends on chance whether we come upon it or not*
> *before we ourselves must die.* (61)

"...some material object...." Light is vouchsafed on a cold winter day when his mother offers him tea and one of those "plump little cakes called 'petite madeleines.'" And then, unaware that this is the road to Damascus, that his life is about to change and his mission be given,

> *...mechanically, weary after a dull day with the prospect of a depress-*
> *ing morrow, I raised to my lips a spoonful of the tea in which I had*
> *soaked a morsel of the cake....a shudder ran through my whole body....*
> *An exquisite pleasure had invaded my senses...this new sensation*
> *having had on me the effect which love has.... Whence could it have*
> *come to me, this all-powerful joy?...What did it signify?* (62)

Repeated sips give similar (though less orgasmic) effects. Marcel decides that "the object of my quest, the truth, lies not in the cup but in myself," so the task is to "examine my own mind," to "ask myself what it could have been" (62-63). This approach is not immediately successful, however: working to "make it reappear," shutting out his environment, and giving his fatigued mind the relief of distraction are all ineffectual (63). But when he again focuses on his first taste of the tea impregnated with cake crumbs, he does feel

> ...something start within me, something that leaves its resting-place and attempts to rise, something that has been embedded like an anchor at a great depth; I can feel it mounting slowly.... (64)

Proust – who seems to have thought as long and as deeply about remembrance as any writer before him – gives "Marcel" no doubts about what that "something" is. It "must be the image, the visual memory which, being linked to that taste, has tried to follow it into my conscious mind," but cannot yet do so. He knows that the image-memory has to do with "the taste of cake soaked in tea," but for now it has "gone down again into its darkness" and he feels nothing. "Ten times over" he "must lean down over the abyss," vainly trying to recapture it. Then

> ...suddenly the memory returns. The taste was that of the little crumb of madeleine which on Sunday mornings at Combray...my aunt Léonie used to give me, dipping it first in her own cup of real or of lime-flower tea. (65)

Thus is the memory that he has been seeking – genesis of the super-novel – recovered, but for Proust that is only a mid-point from which to launch upon a more intensive analysis of the experience in its immediate and applied dimensions:

> ...when from a long-dead past nothing subsists, after the people are dead,...still, alone, more fragile, but with more vitality, more unsubstantial, more persistent, more faithful, the smell and taste of things remain poised a long time, like souls, ready to remind us, waiting and hoping for their moment,...and bear unfaltering, in the tiny and almost impalpable drop of their essence, the vast structure of recollection. (65)

It is an admirably acute analysis of an evanescent phenomenon that many people have had, but that none has examined so minutely. Proust would have been an avid follower of modern brain research, which suggests that the reason our sense of smell is so evocative of the past is that the olfactory function is located in the brainstem, the oldest part of the brain. At a much earlier stage, smell was a vital function for *homo sapiens,* a survival skill, not just an aesthetic pleasure (or displeasure). It has not entirely lost its intensity and power as its sensitivity has diminished.

But Proust has not finished with this crucial scene. He wants to show us the full meaning of his statement that a sense memory contains and can release a "vast structure of recollection."

> *...immediately the old grey house upon the street...rose up like the scenery of a theatre...and with the house the town, ...the Square..., the streets..., the country roads.... ...in that moment all the flowers in our garden and in M. Swann's park, and the water-lilies on the Vivonne and the good folk of the village and their little dwellings and the parish church and the whole of Combray and its surroundings, taking their proper shapes and growing solid, sprang into being, town and gardens alike, from my cup of tea.* (65-66)

Proust's excitement at this discovery and his eagerness to describe Combray's revivification are embedded in the breathless quality of this passage as it piles up details, outruns the use of commas, and even repeats itself. It may occur to us that, by the time all this reaches us, it is neither taste nor smell but literary imagination that has preserved the memory – or we may be so caught up in Proust's rapture that it does not occur.

This section has been said to contain the whole *Temps perdu* project in miniature. One corollary of that architecture is that Marcel cannot very well make steady progress throughout the fifteen novels. He still takes wrong turns, as he did prior to his epiphany, and at times seems to lose track of the wisdom – the insight into the nature of memory – that he gained in the "Overture," or at least cannot tell what he should do with it. At the end of *Swann's Way* he tries to return physically to the scene of his memories, this time of Paris, and discovers for himself what can happen when you try to go home again.

> *"Oh, horrible!" I exclaimed to myself. "Does anyone really imagine that these motor-cars are as smart as the old carriage-and-pair? I*

dare say, I am too old now – but I was not intended for a world in
which women shackle themselves in garments that are not even made
of cloth." (608)

Most people of a certain age who have revisited youthful haunts will have had comparable reactions, but Proust, as we would expect, pursues this first disillusion to a deeper level: that of the humanity to be found in the *Bois de Boulogne*, then and now.

To what purpose shall I walk among these trees if there is nothing left
now of the assembly that used to meet beneath the delicate tracery
of reddening leaves.... Oh, horrible! My consolation is to think of the
women whom I have known, in the past, now that there is no stan-
dard left of elegance. (609)

Still, despite his overall disappointment that he "had not managed to discover the pleasures for which I longed" (610), the experience is not without psychological interest, and provides further insight into the object of his *recherche*:

Because of the solidarity that binds together the different parts of
a general impression, parts that our memory keeps in a balanced
whole,...I should have liked to be able to pass the rest of the day with
one of those women, over a cup of tea.... (609-10)

This wish is of course futile, since "I should have required also that they were the same women," which is impossible without a time machine (610). Ah, but reality is an ironist, and has not yet finished with the education of M. Proust and his narrator.

Alas! In the acacia-avenue – the myrtle-alley – I did see some of them
again, grown old, no more now than grim spectres of what once they
had been, wandering to and fro, in desperate search of heaven knew
what, through the Virgilian groves. (610)

Marcel stands "vainly questioning the deserted paths," a pale shadow of the Roman poet who let his Aeneas visit Hades and himself escorted Dante through Purgatory. He admits that any notion of the *Bois* as "the Elysian Garden of Woman" has evaporated, but the experience has helped him "understand how paradoxical it is to seek in reality for the pictures that are stored in one's memory....

The reality that I had known no longer existed" (611). Yet not everything is lost, for now he has a firm grasp of the truth that he glimpsed earlier, which concludes *Swann's Way*:

> The places that we have known belong now only to the little world
> of space on which we map them for our own convenience. ...remem-
> brance of a particular form is but regret for a particular moment;
> and houses, roads, avenues are as fugitive, alas, as the years. (611)

Some readers may be inclined to say, It needs no ghost come from the grave to tell us this, but they probably have not gone and struggled where Marcel and his creator have, thus earning the right to reach this conclusion.

At the far end of his sprawling project, in *Le Temps retrouvé* (1927; *The Past Recaptured*, 1932), Proust/Marcel is still finding new images for the operation of time. Exploring the mysteries of mental association, "watching how the nimble shuttles of the years weave threads between memories that seemed most unre-lated," he achieves a fuller understanding of the ways in which diverse relics of the past can give us further access to it (Proust 1932, 169). The taste of a piece of tea-soaked *petite madeleine* brought the revelation in *Swann's Way*, but hearing a word may also suffice. For example, the name "Guermantes"

> brought up from the depths of my memory a cross section of the
> past associated with that name, together with all the accompany-
> ing mental pictures of manorial forests or tall flowers, and it once
> more assumed the charm and significance it used to have for me in
> Combray.... (179)

Or a sensation associated with the past but felt again *can* act as a time machine to lift him out of his immediate surroundings; his associative memory may contra-dict his present physical reality. Taking a carriage to the Princesse de Guermantes' reception, Marcel remembers when he used to visit the Guermantes in their former mansion, and what he felt then, before they built a magnificent new place on the *Avenue du Bois*. His carriage passes along

> streets leading to the Champs-Elysées. They were very badly paved
> at that time, but from the very moment we entered them, I was nev-
> ertheless recalled from my deep thought by a sensation of extreme

smoothness; the carriage seemed to run more easily, more softly and noiselessly, as when the gates of an estate open and you glide over roads covered with fine sand or fallen leaves. Nothing of the sort had actually occurred, but I felt at once the removal of external obstacles.... (181)

This experience seems to combine recollected visits to the Guermantes in their previous place with his realization that these streets had earlier been "the long-forgotten paths I formerly used to follow" when walking with Françoise. In any case the effect is uncanny, almost preternatural, though no longer unprecedented. He is flying in time now.

And, like an aviator who has been laboriously rolling along the ground and then suddenly takes off, I rose slowly toward the silent heights of memories past. ... I was not passing through the same streets as the strollers who were abroad that day, but through a past that glided softly, sad and sweet. (181-82)

This is not just a vivid recollection, he maintains; the past has actually survived intact: "the most insignificant gesture, the simplest act remain enclosed, as it were, in a thousand sealed jars" – jars that he has learned how to open (195). To Proust, the kind of time travel represented by such recovery of the past is vitally important, "for the only true paradise is always the paradise we have lost" (195). I envisage Proust and Milton discussing this point in the afterlife.

By no means are all the manifestations of Proust's enhanced consciousness of time so lyrical or exalting, however. In the middle of the novel Marcel attends "a social gathering" that will mark his "return to society life" after an unspecified absence (Proust 1932, 250). He is looking forward to it, both as a change from his usual solitude and as a source of stimulation for the work he has decided to undertake – a book about time and memory – but as he reaches the foot of the stairs leading down into the drawing room he finds himself "...in the midst of a fête...very different from those I had formerly attended..." (253).

...the moment I entered the drawing-room,...a coup de théâtre occurred.... ...I could not immediately recognise the master of the house and the guests, who seemed to have "made themselves up,"

> *usually with powdered hair...that completely changed their appear-*
> *ance.* (253)

No one had told him that this was a costume party, he grouses. His old friend
the Prince has a white beard and may represent one of the last of the Seven Ages
of Man. The Duc de Châtellerault's hoary mustache makes him look so old that
Marcel almost compliments him on his wonderful make-up job. But the most
remarkable get-up is that of his old enemy M. d'Argencourt, who "had turned
himself into an old beggar" or maybe a "senile old-clothes dealer"; "his limbs
shook and the flaccid features of his usually haughty face smirked continually with
a stupidly beatific expression" (255). Carried this far, Marcel reflects, a disguise is
really a transformation.

> *I burst into a laugh at the sight of this remarkable old dotard, as*
> *sottish in his friendly caricature of himself as was in a tragic sense M.*
> *de Charlus, paralysed and yet polite...in his King Lear rôle....* (255)

Apart from this laugh, Marcel refrains from expressing his admiration of the costumes, realizing just in time – as the reader probably has – that his friends have
simply aged since he last saw them. *This is how they look now.* And he has another
epiphany, from which he can generalize:

> *every social gathering which one attends after a long absence from*
> *such affairs...produces the effect of a masquerade fête...one at which*
> *we are..."puzzled" by the other guests, but...the strange faces they have*
> *been unintentionally developing for a long time cannot be removed*
> *with a little soap and water.... Puzzled by other guests? Alas, we*
> *puzzle them quite as much....* (256-57)

This is the equivalent of the court jester's *tu quoque*: 'You too [are a fool, though
I wear the motley']. His own mirror and his old friends are all jesters. There is
nothing that Marcel can say or observe about the guests that they could not retort
upon him in full measure. If his friends and enemies now resemble a "Punch and
Judy show of...puppets personifying Time," he is part of the show (257-58). While
cocooned in his solitary existence he was insulated from such effects, but now he
is presented with "'an optical view'...of the years," the more dramatic for his long
absence (259). Meeting a younger friend again,

I was astonished to note on his face some of the signs that are char-
acteristic rather of old men. I then understood that it was because he
really was old and that it is out of young men who last long enough
that life makes its old men. (263)

This wisdom is, of course, acquired by most of those "who last long enough." The
irony is that Marcel/Proust, after his lone Cartesian meditation on time, must
come back to society to recognize the most fundamental truth about his subject.

I was discovering this destructive action of Time at the very moment
when I was about to undertake to make clear and to intellectualise
in a literary work some realities that had no relation whatsoever to
Time. (265)

For a few pages Proust sounds rather like Arnold Bennett on this matter, except
that the French author makes his persona a principal object of the research, while
the Englishman displaces ageing onto his characters. Proust marvels at "the power
of complete reconstruction possessed by Time," which has altered him and his
friends, generally for the worse; he prefers the earlier images stored in memory,
before "the artist Time" went to work (271).

The novel ends on a more positive note: the memory of a tinkling bell gives
Marcel a final revelation about the time-continuum, and he moves to emulate his
creator by starting the work that Proust is just finishing. In a typically modernist
gesture, the book becomes about itself, especially its own origins. At a fête he is
remembering how, as a child, having been sent up to bed, he would go sit by the
window, waiting for the company to leave so that his mother would come to give
him the good-night kiss he wanted.

I heard the door open, the bell tinkle and the door shut again. Even at
this moment, in the mansion of the Prince de Guermantes, I heard the
sound of my parents' footsteps as they accompanied M. Swann and
the reverberating, ferruginous, interminable, sharp, jangling tinkle
of the little bell which announced to me that at last M. Swann had
gone and Mamma was going to come upstairs – I heard these sounds
again, the very identical sounds themselves, although situated so far
back in the past. (400)

The two strata of time are clear: the reception at the Guermantes', and long-ago Combray. The five specific adjectives modifying "tinkle" prove that this is not just any old bell ringing, but a clear recollection of a single bell. "Of many, one."

> I was startled at the thought that it was, indeed, this bell which was still tinkling within me and that I could in no wise change its sharp janglings, since, having forgotten just how they died away, to recapture it and hear it distinctly, I was forced to close my ears to the sound of the conversations the masks were carrying on around me. ...I had to descend again into my own consciousness. (400)

If Marcel is startled by the discovery that this old sense-memory was in fact ("indeed") alive within him, the reader is surprised to be reminded that this intense introspection is transpiring in the middle of a masquerade. The narrator's reaction is not to rejoin the party, but – like his creator – to shut out the conversations of *le beau monde*, dive back into his own consciousness, and try to understand this phenomenon better.

> It must be, then, that this tinkling was still there and also, between it and the present moment, all the infinitely unrolling past which I had been unconsciously carrying within me. ...there must have been no break of continuity,...since this distant moment still clung to me and I could recapture it, go back to it, merely by descending more deeply within myself. (400)

To Marcel this comes as the existential equivalent of a scientific breakthrough and a vision: we ourselves are time machines, limited but effective. He will devote his book to "this conception of time as incarnate." We carry around the past carnally; it lives inside as our "very self," and once unlocked is a real presence, as in the mystery of transubstantiation (401). Thus there is "no break of continuity" – "The child is father to the man," as Wordsworth said – and the "long stretch of time... uninterruptedly lived" that we remember really *is ourselves*, is our identity (401). St Augustine wrote, in the *Confessions*, "Great is the power of memory, a fearful thing...; and this thing is the mind, and this am I myself."

The effect of this latest realization on the narrator is almost as powerful as his rediscovery of the taste of tea with *petite madeleine*.

> *The date when I heard the sound – so distant and yet so deep within*
> *me – of the little bell in the garden at Combray was a landmark I did*
> *not know I had available in this enormous dimension of Time. My*
> *head swam to see so many years below me, and yet within me, as if I*
> *were thousands of leagues in height.* (401)

But beyond the dizziness lies, for him, a new and grander conception of *la condition humaine* in its temporal context, "the understanding of which was this day so forcibly impressing itself upon me" – the progressive form of the verb telling us that the experience is both immediate and enduring (402). Seen in this light, the subject will require that a different approach be taken in his book. He will need to describe men as

> *...occupying in Time a place far more considerable than the so*
> *restricted one allotted them in space, a place...extending boundlessly*
> *since, giant-like, reaching far back into the years, they touch simulta-*
> *neously epochs of their lives – with countless intervening days between*
> *– so widely separated from one another in Time.* (402)

Thus ends *Le Temps retrouvé* and the entire *A la Recherche du temps perdu* project. Only at this point can we say with certainty that Proust was *not*, like Arnold Bennett, a grim chronicler of the ravages of time, but rather a profound analyst who found greatness in the human condition within its mortal bonds. The rhetorical move made here is similar to Charles Lyell's strategy in a famous lecture series delivered in London in the 1830s. Defending his controversial *Principles of Geology*, Lyell argued that its estimate of the age of the earth – much greater than that traditionally derived from the Bible – did *not* undermine Holy Scripture, but rather conveyed a more august conception of the Creator by vastly enlarging the scale of Creation. Similarly, Proust finally lifts *homo sapiens* out of the category of a body crushed by time – without denying the physical facts – to that of a contemplative mind that can transcend bodily decay and range over long vistas of time. No literary writer has taken the investigation of Chronos deeper or farther than he.

Proust's line of thought here is mainly psychological and philosophical, but we note that what he used to convey all this to us was literature. The art of writing serves as the fixing agent or handmaid to his memory, to all memory, which is seen as one way in which we defend against time's depredations, and a significant component of art.

Imposing Order on Experience

Aldous Huxley makes the case for art as a bulwark against time from a different angle in his essay "Usually Destroyed" (in *Adonis and the Alphabet*, 1956). Wandering around Jerusalem in the early 1950s, Huxley was sorry for and impressed by his guide, "a young Christian refugee from the other side of the wall" – i.e. a Palestinian Arab.

> *He was a sad, embittered young man – and well he might be. His prospects had been blighted, his family reduced from comparative wealth to the most abject penury, their house and land taken away from them, their bank account frozen and devaluated.* (Huxley 204)

Huxley found Jerusalem "profoundly depressing," albeit strangely beautiful. His guide spoke English well, he says, but had a habit of inserting "into almost every sentence" the word "usually" (205). At first it seemed just a meaningless verbal tic, yet it "had a fascinating way of making a kind of sense." In the examples Huxley gives, it accompanies a past-tense verb, often in the passive mood – houses and whole areas were "usually destroyed" in 529 and 1948, the Temple was "usually demolished" by Nebuchadnezzar, etc. – so it sounds like a form of the imperfect, which the guide had probably been taught is used when something happens repeatedly. Huxley soon feels "overwhelmed" by the accumulating list of objects "Usually destroyed and then usually rebuilt, in order, of course, to be destroyed again and then rebuilt" (206). "Usually" comes to sum up history at its most futile: all of those people "alternately building and destroying, killing and being killed, indefinitely" (207). This is time and history as they appear in Bennett's *The Old Wives' Tale*: eroding, wasting, defeating. "Everything came to that," as Sophia says beside Gerald's deathbed.

A Catholic friend of mine, horrified by his first visit to Jerusalem, remarked that "The Church is the cross that Christ had to bear," but the grounds for melancholy are much more broadly based than that, and Huxley knows most of them. Consider the Mongols, those "aesthetes of militarism" and devotees of "gratuitous massacre" (209) – yet the ancients could not destroy lives on our modern scale, he remarks. After all, how many Hebrews does the Bible claim were exiled to Babylon? Jeremiah says 4600; *II Kings* makes it ten thousand.

> *Compared with the forced migrations of our time, the Exile was*
> *the most trivial affair. How many millions were uprooted by Hitler*
> *and the Communists? How many more millions were driven out of*
> *Pakistan into India, out of India into Pakistan? How many hundreds*
> *of thousands had to flee, with our young guide, from their homes in*
> *Israel? By the waters of Babylon ten thousand at the most sat down*
> *and wept. In the single refugee camp at Bethlehem there are more*
> *exiles than that. And Bethlehem's is only one of dozens of such camps*
> *scattered far and wide over the Near East.* (210)

His sadness and bitterness build to pessimism about the future, based on what we know or can estimate about the rising curves of hunger, birth rates and population pressures, erosion, deforestation, political and social unrest, attacks on individual liberties. And terrorism, chemical warfare, desertification and climate change do not even make his 'fifties agenda. So "here we were in Jerusalem, looking at the usually destroyed antiquities...the usually poverty-stricken inhabitants, the usually superstitious pilgrims," having a wonderful time, wish you were here (214). Almost the "only oasis of cheerfulness" in sight is the Armenian church of St James which, with its numerous paintings and coloured tiles, "glowed like a dim religious merry-go-round." And then there is an unexpected aural bonus: passing through the courtyard before the church, "we heard a strange and wonderful sound" (215).

> *High up, in one of the houses surrounding the court, someone was*
> *playing the opening Fantasia of Bach's Partita in A minor – playing*
> *it, what was more, remarkably well. From out of the open window, up*
> *there on the third floor, the ordered torrent of bright pure notes went*
> *streaming out over the city's immemorial squalor.*

"Immemorial squalor" – not a phrase that the Jerusalem Chamber of Commerce would want to quote – is used as a foil to the human achievement of the Fantasia's composition and performance. Wandering as he has been, from darkness to darkness, oppressed by the wanton destructiveness of human beings and the prospect of greater miseries to come, Huxley has bowed under a crushing sense of Time as destroyer, of history as endless, meaningless cycles of violence. Then, when most needed, come the lights of St James's and the disembodied eighteenth-century music. They enable Huxley to start thinking about what should be put on the other side of the ledger: the forces that can be marshalled against chaos and cruelty.

> *Art and religion, philosophy and science, morals and politics – these*
> *are the instruments by means of which men have tried to discover a*
> *coherence in the flux of events, to impose an order on the chaos of*
> *experience. The most intractable of our experiences is the experience*
> *of Time – the intuition of duration, combined with the thought of*
> *perpetual perishing. Music is a device for working directly upon the*
> *experience of Time. The composer takes a piece of raw, undifferenti-*
> *ated duration and extracts from it, as the sculptor extracts the statue*
> *from his marble, a complex pattern of tones and silences, of harmonic*
> *sequences and contrapuntal interweavings. For the number of minutes*
> *it takes to play or listen to his composition, duration is transformed*
> *into something intrinsically significant, something held together by*
> *the internal logics of style and temperament, of personal feelings*
> *interacting with an artistic tradition, of creative insights expressing*
> *themselves within and beyond some given technical convention. This*
> *Fantasia, for example - with what a tireless persistence it drills its way*
> *through time!* (215-16)

Today we may cringe or laugh or cry or protest at hearing politics named along-side philosophy and science as ways in which humans seek to reveal coherence or impose order. But Huxley is right: ours is a debased version of a system *intended* to regulate communal interactions and mitigate conflict. In 1956, with the creation of the United Nations and a Universal Declaration of Human Rights recently achieved, it would have seemed reasonable (as it did to Aristotle) to list politics among the constructions we have devised for the betterment and governing of our lives. Still, Huxley's list begins with art and religion. Note that, although he uses music as an example, it is "art" in general that he proposes as one of the ways in which we strive to organize the raw chronological stuff of existence. Literature, painting, sculpture, architecture: these too can drill their way through time, if we let them.

Huxley does not conceal the weakness of this effect: its evanescence. "For the number of minutes it takes to play" the Fantasia, duration becomes significant and coherent. Time the Destroyer becomes Time the Creator – the hopeful, "usually rebuilt" part of the cycle – *for a few minutes*. Then the "fantasy" stops and time floods back in, as powerful a tide as ever, claiming us all. Nor is brevity the only problem with Huxley's consolation: the audience must be attentive, receptive, perhaps even educated or cultured, to gain these minutes of respite. Another visitor might have walked on through the courtyard, head down, grim-faced, barely noticing the music, failing to recognize Bach, or cursing the noisemaker. If we are tired, boorish, ignorant, or distracted, this time machine does not work.

> *"...the silent artillery of time..."*
> ABRAHAM LINCOLN, "LYCEUM ADDRESS," 1838

A Timely Coda: Portals to the Past

Poems, novels, essays and visual media that self-consciously define or explore our relationship with time make up only a small portion of the full spectrum of literature and the arts. Most imaginative creations treat other aspects of existence, and while they may exert some power over time for some people some of the time, they do not *discuss* that function as such. Before moving on from the temporal aspect of the literary arts to another of their roles or uses, we ought at least to acknowledge the rest of the spectrum, whose occupants (like dark energy and dark matter) make up the bulk of their cosmos without being known for what they are.

To start with a sector lying on the boundary: patently historical plays, novels, and films – Shakespeare's *Henry V*, Bulwer-Lytton's *The Last Days of Pompeii*, Thackeray's *Barry Lyndon*, Hawthorne's *The Scarlet Letter*, Dickens's *A Tale of Two Cities*, Reade's *The Cloister and the Hearth*, Mitchell's *Gone With the Wind* – inhabit a middle ground between the works discussed in earlier chapters and the greater mass of literature not ostensibly concerned with delving into quandaries associated with time. Historical works generally try to pique our interest by transporting our imaginations to a specific past, and there are many ways to do that. The physical and cultural details of the past may be gathered casually or carefully, recreated elaborately or sketchily. Shakespeare's Roman and British history plays, which borrow plots, characters, and some details from standard sources such as Plutarch or Hall and Holinshed, bear only passing resemblance to the painstakingly researched works produced by most historical writers from the nineteenth century onward; modern readers generally expect a higher standard of accuracy and verisimilitude than did the "groundlings" in the Globe Theatre. But whether these "transportations" of the reader are chilling (*les tricoteuses*, the ladies who knit as the guillotine falls in Paris) or spectacular (the great eruption of Vesuvius), bloody battlefields or quiet drawing-rooms, they seek to create an atmosphere well removed from the world we know, "other," yet credible. As with Huxley and the Fantasia, though, attention is required. Readers who can avoid distraction and concentrate on the book may enter the imagined world for a time via the Word; those who fall short in this regard will be left cold, and probably blame the author. "Historicals" are not automatic, guaranteed time machines.

The "historical" category is highly Protean, open to debate and revision. Many books set or "framed" in their authors' present contain flashbacks, and operate in the historical arena for some part of the work. At the beginning of Evelyn Waugh's *Brideshead Revisited*, the sight of an old manor house during the Second World War triggers Charles Ryder's memories of holidays spent there in the 1920s, and of all that followed from his acquaintance with the family. The re-creation of that bygone world – Oxford, Brideshead, Venice, Morocco, ocean voyages, etc. – occupies much of the novel. And while we do not ordinarily think of *Paradise Lost* as an "historical poem," one of Milton's aims was to take us back to the Biblical Garden of Eden, bring it to life with vivid description, and make us relive the Fall. In the early books he describes Eden as Satan first saw it (with grudging admiration), and makes us voyeurs of Adam and Eve's innocent, ignorant bliss. By the time the Fall occurs, we can feel the loss keenly. Both of these are works to which we will return, under different rubrics, in the second part of this study.

A familiar (and hugely popular) kind of historical art is "the Western," which exports us, usually, to a slice of American pioneer life spanning about twenty years in the late nineteenth century west of the Mississippi. Some film classics of the genre focus on bringing to life a specific, often violent moment: *High Noon*, *The Gunfight at the O.K. Corral*, *Bad Day at Black Rock*. Others try for a broader view of "what is past, and passing, and to come." The television mini-series *Lonesome Dove* (1989, from Larry McMurtry's 1985 novel) is a detailed re-creation of the Old West of Texas Rangers, horse thieves, and cattle drives that eventually manages to convey a sense of historical change underlying individual struggles. The eager young journalist who interviews a veteran Texas Ranger near the end of the series belongs to the next era, beyond the Ranger's – and the western's – day. That strikes an elegiac note: this time machine is curving back home to our world. Micro or macro, fiction, cinema, or television, westerns have enabled many readers and viewers to visit a period and a region that still fascinate us.

Yet "historical" poems, novels, films, and paintings are still only one of the ways that art can interface with time. Most older works of literature function in a quasi-historical way for us, even though set more or less in the author's own time. This is true of *Moll Flanders*, *Bleak House*, *Huckleberry Finn*, *Portrait of the Artist as a Young Man*, and *The Sun Also Rises*, the list lengthening relentlessly as the decades pass. The passage from *Bleak House* quoted in Chapter 1 plops us into the "implacable November weather" of Victorian London, where Dickens would not have been surprised to see a dinosaur waddle up Holborn Hill. Defoe's wealth of detail about seventeenth-century England helped shape the English realist novel, and Twain pleased American readers with descriptions of Mississippi Valley landscapes that he knew well. Similarly with Joyce in turn-of-the-century Dublin and Hemingway in post-World War I France and Spain – yet all seem exotic and "other" now. In the twenty-first century, films and books about the Second World War, the Vietnam war, and Wall Street in the 'eighties involve time travel – especially for younger readers – affording poignant glimpses of (as the 1973 film and song put it) "The Way We Were." H.G. Wells's time traveller says that a series of paintings of an individual done years apart (such as Rembrandt's self-portraits), though "contemporary" when painted, creates a portrait of time. Probably almost everyone over the age of ten has had a simple version of this experience while looking at snapshots of his or her impossibly young self.

It is worth recalling how the 1980 film *Somewhere in Time* dramatized the limitations inherent in purely mental time travel. Reeve moves to the early twentieth century (to meet a young Jane Seymour) by going to the Grand Hotel where she stayed, taking a room, dressing in period costume and entering a trance. He "jumps back," it seems successfully – until he notices the date on a coin accidentally left in his pocket: *1979*. Rudely awakened to his real place in time, he cannot sustain his vision, and is unceremoniously whisked back to 1980. Wells had warned that the effect of "absent-mindedness" with regard to time is tenuous and only "for a moment." We must be entirely lost in the illusion; as soon as we think of it *as* an illusion that we are observing from outside, it evaporates, unable to survive analysis or self-consciousness.

At this point, however, we need to distinguish between the characters in a fiction, its creator, and its consumers: ourselves as audience. While watching the film, we may be aware of the flimsiness of the illusion, the improbability of the whole idea, and the possibility that it was all just a dream (though having Reeve find his signature in an old guest register suggests that it reaslly happened). But once outside the theatre, we realize that the artist has created something that endures as Reeve's illusion cannot, and we can relive his creation as often as we can re-enter the fiction and accept his imaginative artifact. Reeve's character is the fragile, theorized time traveller of science fiction (albeit his "machine" is only his will), while *our* time machine is that of art and imagination: the one we have, the one we've always had, the one that works. (Today's viewers may know about Christopher Reeve's subsequent riding accident, paralysis, and early death; and can see pictures of an older Jane Seymour: ironic perspectives not originally available.)

If, as Blake wrote ("Proverbs of Hell" in *The Marriage of Heaven and Hell*), "What is now proved was once only imagin'd," it follows that what we can now imagine may someday be proved. *May* be proved. When and if the physicists, engineers, and cosmologists do come up with a time machine that can transport me to other periods of my choosing *and* bring me back alive – not just change my rate of ageing – I will sign up. But if London in 1850 or 802,701 CE is no more appealing than Dickens or Wells suggested, I want to be able to shift into reverse and return to the present as easily as I would close a book.

> *There is no Frigate like a Book*
> *To take us Lands away*
> *This Traverse may the poorest take*
> *Without oppress of Toll –*
> *How frugal is the Chariot*
> *That bears the Human Soul.*
>
> EMILY DICKINSON

> *Imagination is more important than knowledge. Knowledge*
> *is limited. Imagination encircles the world.*
>
> ALBERT EINSTEIN

PART TWO:

THE DOMAINE

PROLOGUE:

Defining 'Domaine'

DISCUSSING TIME AND TIME MACHINES was the easy part, however. Despite the difficulties and elusiveness of its nature, most of us experience the effects of time in *roughly* the same fashion, and have a general understanding of what others mean when they say "Time flies," "Time will tell," or "Time out." If we are not always on the same page, we are nearby. But a "domaine"? What's that? Have *I* had a domaine? Why have I not heard about it before? Is he even spelling it right?

English and North American dictionaries tend to define the word "domain" primarily in legal terms: a property that you rule or own, as in "eminent domain." (The Oxford dictionary does allow "estate" as a principal meaning.) In French dictionaries, a *domaine* is above all an estate: a manorial house or castle and the lands appertaining thereunto. It is this sense that I mean to draw on and develop, hence the (italicized) French spelling. Middle English *demesne*, found as late as Keats, links the two, but is too archaic to use. A literary *domaine*, however, is not only a physical estate (buildings and grounds), but also a state of mind and nerves produced by a place where characters had extraordinary experiences that altered them, changing their previous sense of the world and themselves, and thus are remembered while they live.

Defining terms has been compared to surveying boundaries, but it is more like writing instructions for surveyors. Frontiers are inherently prone to dispute, this one crosses unfamiliar terrain, and I have not been given the authority to define *domaine* prescriptively, *a priori*. If I *had* to do so, I would stage a party at a large, carefully prepared house, preferably on a private island, and invite you and people you do not know. You could not reliably distinguish fellow guests from actors playing roles, nor tell when the party was over, but interesting, even unforgettable things would happen, and you would leave knowing as much as I do about what a *domaine* is.

Preparing a seminar on this subject, I wrote a brief description for prospective students: "The idea of the *Domaine* or enchanted place, rarely obtained and easily lost, recurs throughout our literature in works that try to recapture the impact of magical spaces on impressionable minds, and in the process become themselves new Domaines." When the seminar convened, the students just wanted to use my definition, not explore the concept. I argued that texts must be allowed to define the term, and admitted that my own definition was oversimplified. Not every *domaine* seems "magical" at first; that may creep up on the visitor later. Some of them are not "easily lost": they sink hooks into you that cannot readily be thrown. And what was "our literature," anyway? I led them through a small woodland park to a rough facsimile of a sacred grove. It looked like a setting for a *domaine*, but there was no enchantment, no magic. Had I been expecting that?

Some writers who have created *domaines* also help define the concept. The man chiefly responsible for giving the idea such modern currency as it has was the late British novelist John Fowles. In *The Magus* (1965), he crafted a powerful island-*domaine* for his "Magus," Maurice Conchis, who applies the term to his property. In *The Ebony Tower* (1974), Henry Breasley lives on a literal French *domaine*, the *Manoir de Coëtminais* and its surrounding wood, a remnant of the forest of mediaeval Brittany, home of Celtic legends. Fowles included in that volume "A Personal Note" that names sources for both books. Behind *The Magus*, he says, lies Henri Alain-Fournier's novel *Le Grand Meaulnes* (1913), and behind *The Ebony Tower*, the twelfth-century romance writer Marie de France, of whose *Eliduc* he provides a translation; both writers are discussed in chapter 5. In his "Foreword" to the Revised Edition of *The Magus* (1978), Fowles adds two more influences on that novel: Dickens's *Great Expectations* and Richard Jefferies's *Bevis* (1882), another *domaine*-book (chapter 6). Fowles did not claim to have *originated* this idea, then, but rather to be working in a tradition.

Knowing these sources helps to clarify the meaning of a *domaine*. In *Le Grand Meaulnes*, the protagonist chances on a remote chateau that is hosting a *fête*; he is so moved by this, and the people there, that his life is altered. The romances of Marie de France cycle from castle through forest to *chateau* and back: all *domaines* where magical things can happen, and characters be tested and known. In her

Eliduc, a slandered knight is exiled from Brittany. In England he falls for a young woman, and is subsequently torn between her and his wife (like David Williams in "The Ebony Tower"). Jefferies's *Bevis* tells of two Victorian boys whose imaginations transform the Wiltshire downs into a world of great adventure for a few months. In *Great Expectations,* Miss Havisham's house and garden provide a kind of *domaine* for Pip while his infatuation with Estella lasts, though Dickens suggests almost from the beginning some darker aspects, what could be called an anti-*domaine* for its unpleasantness. Most *domaines* have a dark side, but it is usually recognized after the fact.

Not that Fowles is merely derivative, rehashing earlier ideas and effects. Conchis's Villa Bourani on a Greek island may be a shrewd rewrite of Marie's castles and manors in a different key, but his interest in *domaines* originated in personal experience. In "Behind *The Magus*" (1994), he revealed that when he went to Spetsai (the model for Conchis's island) to teach, he kept a journal, which he retained. In 1993 he came across a forgotten passage: "The School & the Island: 1952." Written within days of his arrival, it describes an exploratory walk inland, to the top of the central ridge, where he sat down on the edge of a cliff with the sun-drenched Mediterranean world spread out beneath him:

> *...for a few minutes I felt incomprehensibly excited, as if I were expe-*
> *riencing something infinitely rare. ...I have never seen so beautiful a*
> *landscape...exquisitely blue sky, brilliant sunlight, miles of rock and*
> *pine, and the sea. All the elements, at such a pitch of purity that I*
> *was spellbound. ... A sort of supreme level of awareness of existence,*
> *an all-embracing euphoria. ... the impact and the uplifting had made*
> *me lose myself. I was suspended in bright air, timeless, motionless....*
> (Fowles 1996, 64).

Various terms have been used for what he describes here: ecstasy (Greek for 'standing outside oneself'), a "peak experience," being "in the moment." This kind of language, recalling a scene and a time when life seemed so dramatically heightened that even in long retrospect it stands out – set apart, enchanted – occurs again and again in the texts discussed below. Ecstatic language is so characteristic of encounters with *domaines* that it helps us recognize the experience and define the term.

Authors who create *domaines* rarely do more than imply a definition, but these few hints may suffice if we read flexibly. *Domaines* do not always take the same form, signaling their presence with a castle, *chateau*, or mansion, as in Marie de France, Alain-Fournier, or *The Great Gatsby*. Their settings are many and various; an island will do. The core element is a special place where at some point events of great import happened to a character, who keeps harking back to them as a revelation, a crux, a touchstone of existential meaning. When Sophia, in Alice Munro's story "Too Much Happiness" (2009), recalls that "She had written the recollections of her life at Palibino in a glow of love for everything lost, things once despaired of as well as things once treasured. She had written it far from home when that home and her sister were gone," she is alluding to a *domaine*, and describing what one is (Munro 281).

Films are a powerful way of presenting *domaines*: audiences sitting in a darkened theatre are highly susceptible to the combined sensory input of visual images, the spoken word, and sometimes a musical score. A few examples of "*domaine* films" (many of which use time travel as well) may bring the idea into sharper focus. Their *paterfamilias* is Frank Capra's *Lost Horizon* (1937), based on James Hilton's novel, which introduced Shangri-La to the world as a happy place in a remote Asian mountain range, whose long-lived residents are guided by gentle lamas (ancient Tibetan scriptures are said to mention several such retreats). The visitors find it attractive, and two remain. The name Shangri-La has since been given to gardens, estates, resorts, and an aircraft carrier. In *Brigadoon*, by Alan J. Lerner and Frederic Loewe (stage play 1947, film 1954), two rambling Americans stumble on a remote Scottish village that appears for only one day every century; naturally one of them falls in love with a Brigadoonian lass. This was a Celtic legend, and similar myths have been found in other countries. And *Orfeo Negro* (*Black Orpheus*, 1959), set in Rio de Janiero during Carnival, makes Mardi Gras a kind of *domaine*. Two lovers pursued by Death through festive streets become Orpheus and Eurydice in Hades. This Orpheus plays guitar and sings the haunting music of Carlos Jobim and Joao Gilberto; at the end he is gone, but his young acolyte strums the sun's rise on the maestro's guitar. The party is over, but the world will go on.

In *Butch Cassidy and the Sundance Kid* (1969), Paul Newman and Robert Redford's first big duet, the *domaine* is reached technically: as a honky-tonk piano plays western-era music, a sepia-toned photograph of the outlaws melts into a colour film about their salad days. When Pinkerton lawmen make Wyoming too hot, they decamp to Bolivia, where their fortunes decline further. At the end they charge out of hiding, guns blazing, into a fusillade from Bolivian *federales*, the freeze-frame of their hopeless bravado becomes another sepia photo, and the piano reprises the plaintive theme. This *domaine* has two levels: for the duo, a few months of successful robberies; for us, it is the whole film, including the sepia transitions, which frame our time travel. Redford carried over this feeling for charmed moments of the past into *A River Runs Through It* (1992, based on Norman Maclean's novel), which he directed and narrated in voiceover. The film is a nostalgic lament for the golden times when a preacher and his two sons fly-fished Montana's pristine rivers, before the younger brother fell from grace. The film treats these outings lyrically, as *domaines*.

Other examples are quite diverse. Tom Hanks starred in *Big* (1988), wherein an unplugged amusement-park machine fortune teller, Zoltar, grants a twelve-year-old boy's wish to grow big (age 30) *now*. That time machine propels him into a *domaine* of exciting young adulthood in New York City – until he misses his family and carefree youth. There is usually a catch to the magic, a price to pay or a "best-before" date. He has to find Zoltar again to reverse the spell. *Groundhog Day* (1993) features time loops, but at the end, by practicing February 2nd until he gets it right, Bill Murray reaches a *domaine* of love and self-improvement. *Eyes Wide Shut* (1999), based on Arthur Schnitzler's novel *Traumnovelle*, is a party and estate *domaine*. After his wife admits that she *contemplated* an affair with a man a year earlier, Bill Harford goes to an all-night orgy of masked guests at a secret and rather sinister society's secluded manor. An old friend plays the piano there, blindfolded so that he will not know the identities of the guests. This *Traum* (dream) teeters on the edge of nightmare. At the end the couple start to "work on their marriage," but the orgy dominates the film (directed by Stanley Kubrick) and will haunt Bill and the viewer.

2011 was a banner year for such films. The romantic couples in *The Adjustment Bureau* and *Source Code* have to struggle through terrible difficulties before achieving their love *domaines*, but the pick of that year's crop was Woody Allen's *Midnight in Paris*, in which a young American screenwriter, Gil, who is working on a novel, is nightly taken from the back streets of present-day Paris in an old taxi to...the 1920s, where he sees or meets Salvador Dali, Hemingway, Fitzgerald, Jean Cocteau, Cole Porter, Josephine Baker, Gertrude Stein, etc. But it is a slippery *domaine*: returning to his hotel means returning to 2010 and his odious fiancée. He goes on to meet Picasso, Luis Buñuel and other surrealists, and falls for Picasso's lover Adriana. A horse carriage takes them to...the 1890s, where they meet Toulouse-Lautrec, Gauguin, and Degas. Adriana chooses to stay there, but Gil returns to 2010, breaks his engagement, decides to stay in Paris, and walks off with the winsome young antique dealer Gabrielle, preferring a possible love *domaine* now to more time shifting.

It would be easy to multiply illustrations, but we have enough films to establish the type. (Some other classic *domaine* films are discussed in Chapters 7 and 8.) Television provides additional examples, which is not surprising, since it too works from imaginative literature: scripts. An early instance occurs in *Wagon Train*, the popular western series said to have inspired *Star Trek*. In "The Princess of a Lost Tribe" (1960), a solemn, beautiful young woman escorts four men from the train (looking for the father of one) to an "Aztec" Shangri-La tucked away in a mountain fastness. Her father is King Montezuma. The lost father is there, but refuses to leave: they do not emigrate. This *domaine* is radically ambiguous; the inhabitants are pagan polytheists who practice human sacrifice, and the princess is to be next. The wagon train men persuade the king to liberalize, to open to the world, but the people revolt and kill him. In the end the wagoneers leave, carrying only vivid memories, but the princess stays, her fate uncertain.

Another way to grasp the concept of a *domaine* is via analogy. Mircea Eliade's *The Myth of the Eternal Return* (1949, 1954) provides a close one as he "examines the fundamental concepts of archaic societies" (ix). What "especially struck" him, Eliade writes, was their "disregard" of our sense of "historical time" in favour of a ritualized "nostalgia for a periodical return to the mythical time of the beginning of things, to the 'Great Time.'" Among his multicultural examples is the myth of the end of the world (or of an historical cycle) by fire, a purifying cosmic flame that destroys evil and spares good, renewing the world and conferring "beatitude" (124). This is experience and language of a sort often found in reports of encounters with *domaines* – the sense of returning to what is primordial or basic, of a "Great Time" during which one is purged and renewed. The chief difference is that Eliade is describing a communal ritual, in many cases repeated annually or regularly, whereas *domaines* tend to be unique and unforeseen. But as an analogue to the emotional impact of a *domaine*, Eliade's "eternal return" to archaic fundamentals is helpful.

Domaines occur in various models, as the following chapters will show. Some of our earliest were gardens, of which Eden is the best known, though not the first. In ancient Persia, a walled garden like the Hanging Gardens of Babylon was called a *paradise*. For Bible-reading cultures, however, Eden was the archetype, and many a later literary garden alludes to it, subtly or openly. But from the period called "Romantic" onwards, it occurred to some authors that wild nature is an unwalled garden, and might be another type of *domaine*. Wordsworth treats unspoiled English nature in this way, and W.H. Hudson describes a South American jungle similarly in *Green Mansions*. For other authors, the stimulus is not so much wild nature (though it may be present) as a culture that was once rich and vital but is now threatened or moribund. Margaret Mitchell's title, *Gone With the Wind*, could serve for most of them. Karen Blixen / Isak Dinesen's *Out of Africa* also works this vein. Of course every culture inhabits a place, and often that place is part of the magic.

Some writers have treated youth itself as a *domaine*, one that we all visit but have to leave, making it one of the most accessible types. Wordsworth is the great apostle of the halo-encircled childhood, especially in *The Prelude* and the "Immortality Ode," and James Agee recreated the world according to his five-year-old mind (*A Death in the Family*). Evelyn Waugh sanctified a first year at Oxford in *Brideshead Revisited*. All admit darkness in the form of the *domaine's* vulnerability to internal and external threats, including time. Youth is of course a time, not a place, but since childhood, like culture, must occur somewhere, the two intertwine here as well.

A great party or festival can also be felt or remembered as a *domaine*: usually one that is soon lost, and cannot be revisited. F. Scott Fitzgerald's novels and stories provide several instances; Christopher Ames's study of him is titled *The Life of the Party*. This (relatively small) category specializes in highlighting the ambiguity and fragility of *domaines*. We wish we knew more about the house party that William Beckford arranged in 1781, but his guests kept quiet, which fueled speculation about wild goings-on. The Woodstock music festival (1969) provided a good example of an extra-literary *domaine*. When the CBC interviewed three attendees twenty years later, "Country Joe" McDonald recalled it as a love-in shared with four hundred thousand people, giving a sense of community that he yearned to feel again – which sounds like the "oceanic feeling" described by Freud in *Civilization and Its Discontents*. Others must have felt similarly, because anniversaries have been observed every five or ten years.

Woodstock illustrates the permeability and interpenetration of the various kinds of *domaine* sketched here. They are not mutually exclusive; a work or event may belong to several at once, so they may be considered *aspects* rather than discrete types. Joni Mitchell, who could not make it to the concerts, watched them on television and was moved to write her anthem-like "Woodstock," which became a part of the gathering's legacy. But does it celebrate a party, a culture, nature ("I'm going to camp out on the land"), or a garden? The refrain is:

> We are stardust
> We are golden
> And we've got to get ourselves
> Back to the garden

This can hardly escape being read as an allusion to the Garden of Eden, though hippies also prized gardens that fed communes, and their own liberated youth culture, with its various parties, celebrations, and observances. "Woodstock" evokes them all.

Instances of multifaceted or permeable *domaines* abound. Guy Pocock, in introducing the Everyman edition of Jefferies's *Bevis*, calls it the "epic" of "things that do not change": boyhood and nature (Jefferies xi-xii). They *do* change, of course, but their archetypes recur, with variations. In my terms, *Bevis* creates a *domaine* composed of youth and nature; Wordsworth's major poems also blend those two reverences. And does Isak Dinesen's *Out of Africa* present a *domaine* of nature or of Ngong culture? Both, clearly – and so it goes. Although I have devised these labels, partly to structure the discussion of individual works, we need to keep in mind that all such classifications are artifices whose limitations must be admitted if they are not to encumber us.

It is possible to distill a working definition from the scattered remarks above. A literary *domaine* presents a place, usually removed from "the world," where characters have extraordinary experiences that seem magical or surrealistic, lifting them for a time out of their ordinary lives, and prove unforgettable. These transformational occasions are revelations or touchstones, often understood by the characters and the author as testing or defining them. The themes of alienation and identity that Northrop Frye discusses in *The Educated Imagination* often occur in *domaines*. Their language is typically ecstatic and rapturous. The setting may be an estate, castle, or manor house, but can take other forms, or be a certain time at a certain place. A *domaine* is definitely not a funhouse, a simply wonderful location or function, though it may appear so at first. Most *domaines* have a dark side to be uncovered: a hidden agenda, or a vulnerability to inner or outer threats. It is important to realize the ambiguity and transience, the unsustainability, of the *domaine*, which is destined to be lost at some point, and cannot (or should not) be recovered.

This said, I pass to a series of chapters examining particular *domaines* in their full complexity, intended to flesh out the general definition. It has seemed more intelligible to present these examples by type than chronologically.

CHAPTER 4:

Garden Domaines

PROBABLY THE OLDEST *DOMAINES* THAT we can recognize as such are some gardens of Asian or legendary antiquity. The Garden of Eden in Genesis is one of them, but it has ancestors. In the desert-bounded civilizations of the first- and second-millennium BCE Middle East, where water was scarce, the verdure it made possible was of course highly prized; a garden – often walled and royal – was a planned oasis. The Hanging Gardens of Babylon are a good example, and a perfect setting for a literary *domaine*. *Paradise* comes to us (via Greek) from the ancient Persian word *pairidaēza*, meaning 'surrounded by a sticky mass': i.e. a pleasure garden within a clay wall (Geertz 92). The gods were imagined as living in such a place (no desert, all oasis for them), but there could be an earthly paradise as well. In reading the Zoroastrian *Avesta* – the Persian Book of Knowledge and Wisdom – says Will Durant,

> ...one comes across passages of ancient Babylonian provenance, such as the creation of the world in six periods..., the descent of all men from two first parents, the establishment of an earthly paradise, the discontent of the Creator with his Creation, and his resolve to destroy all but a remnant of it by a flood. ...the world is conceived... as the stage of a conflict... between the god Ahura-Mazda and the devil Ahriman....

> ...Ahriman, Prince of Darkness and ruler of the nether world, prototype of that busy Satan whom the Jews appear to have adopted from Persia...created serpents, vermin, locusts, ants, winter, darkness, crime, sodomy, menstruation, and the other plagues of life; and...

> *these inventions of the Devil...ruined the Paradise in which Ahura-*
> *Mazda had placed the first progenitors of the human race.* (Durant
> 1935, 366-67)

For our purposes, what is important here is the assertion by a pre-biblical source
that a garden paradise was set aside for the first humans, and that it had problems.
The "discontent of the Creator with his creation," his decision to destroy most of
it, and the presence of the Devil who "ruined the Paradise" are all there. In other
words, there was "trouble in Paradise" from the beginning – a point to keep in
mind as we look at later *domaines*.

The Eden of Genesis familiar to western readers is no simpler than the *Avesta's*
paradise. A composite of several sources embodying variant traditions, it was
compiled by unknown hands over, probably, centuries, and often plays on Hebrew
words (Durant 219, 329; Geertz 90-91). Eden has evoked conflicting analyses,
spawned imitations, and made to serve other writers' agendas. Students of the
domaine might hope to stay clear of haggling over sources, influences, dates, loca-
tions, etc., but it is a faint hope. Just ask what "Eden" meant and the waters become
turbid. *Baker's Pocket Bible Concordance,* from a religious publishing house, says it
is the Hebrew word for 'delight,' keeping a tight biblical focus. But the liberal Jesuit
scholar John L. Mackenzie's *Dictionary of the Bible* suggests that it derives from
the ancient Akkadian word *edinu,* meaning 'a plain'; and notes that Eden sounds
like a Mesopotamian, not a Palestinian, garden (296), placing it in an older, wider
Middle Eastern context. (*Edinu* also supports those who argue that Eden was on
flat land rather than on a mountain top, as in Milton.)

The text that presented Eden to the world was Genesis 2-3. In the King James
translation, after the seven days of creation narrated by the P (Priestly) source
have been completed, the J (Jehovist) source describes the creation of man from
"the dust of the ground" (*adamah,* Gen. 2:7; the P source gives a different version
in Gen. 1:27, see below):

> 8 And the LORD God planted a garden eastward in Eden; and
> there he put the man whom he had formed.
>
> 9 And out of the ground made the LORD God to grow every
> tree that is pleasant to the sight, and good for food; the tree of

life also in the midst of the garden, and the tree of knowledge of good and evil.

10 And a river went out of Eden to water the garden....

It divides into four streams. One is the Euphrates, and Hiddekel, which "goeth toward the east of Assyria," may be the Tigris, giving a Mesopotamian basis, but Gihon flows through Ethiopia, and Pison is thought to be imaginary, so the drainage is large and vague.

And for whom was the garden made? In the J source, the LORD God installs man as Eden's gardener, warns him not to eat the fruit of the tree of knowledge on pain of death, creates the animals, has Adam name them, puts him to sleep, and creates Eve from his rib. In the P source, however, "God created man in his own image, in the image of God created he him; male and female created he them" *before* planting the garden (Gen. 1:27). This hermaphroditic or androgynous creation is repeated in Gen. 5:2, also from the P source: "Male and female created he them; and blessed them, and called their name Adam." So the Garden of Eden was planted either for the man-woman AdamEve, or just for Adam, with Eve being created there. In any case it is "the garden of God" (or "LORD God") in several books of the Bible. Most Middle Eastern gardens in those days *were* gardens of a lord.

Eden had two trees of special interest: the tree "of life," and that "of knowledge of good and evil." Their identities are made to intertwine. The LORD God's warning clearly refers to the latter, which He makes the tree of death ("in the day that thou eatest thereof thou shalt surely die": Gen. 2:17b). But when the subtle serpent appears in Gen. 3:1 and interrogates Eve, she explains that they may eat anything except "the fruit of the tree which is in the midst of the garden" (Gen. 3:3). She does not specify which tree, though both are "in the midst of the garden" (Gen. 2:9). The serpent, later identified with Satan, denies that they would die from eating the fruit, and supplies a reason: "For God doth know that in the day ye eat thereof, then your eyes shall be opened, and ye shall be as gods, knowing good and evil" (Gen. 3:5). The last phrase clearly alludes to the Tree of Knowledge, but if Adam and Eve will be "as gods" after eating it, they will *not* die, gods being immortal. In effect, the serpent has conflated the properties of the Tree of Life and the Tree of Knowledge. Confusing? Remember that "the Father of Lies" is speaking.

WHAT FOLLOWS DOES NOT SOLVE all the puzzles. Having eaten the fruit, Adam and Eve grow ashamed of their nakedness, don fig leaves, and meet "the LORD God walking in the garden in the cool of the day" (Gen. 3:8). Seeing what has happened, He announces penalties to all three, including death, and clothes the humans in "coats of skins." Animal skins?! Then He is said to have a thought reminiscent of the serpent's temptation of Eve: "Behold, the man is become as one of us [yes, plural], to know good and evil: and now, lest he put forth his hand, and take also of the tree of life, and eat, and live for ever" (Gen. 3:22), I will send them forth. For Him also, the two trees are related, though not confused; He sees cause and effect. With their new-found knowledge, Adam and Eve might decide to eat the fruit of the tree of life, which they have not been forbidden to do, and which could obviate the penalty that has just been imposed. So they are expelled from Eden, and an armed guard is set over the garden with its Tree of Life.

Interpretations of what all this means have been legion, from Gnostics and Hermetics to modern theologians, Freud, and Jung. The range of views is summarized by Frank and Fritzie Manuel in their "Sketch for a Natural History of Paradise" (in Geertz, 83-128). Some early writers proposed that Eden was an allegory of the soul, or of the church, while the Gnostics likened it to the womb from which we were all born. Jung treated Eden as "the positive aspect of the archetypal mother" (Geertz, 99). The meaning of the serpent, since Freud, has been only too obvious: "The snake...is doubtless a phallic symbol, representing sex as the origin of evil" (Durant, 61). Yet the first mention of carnal knowledge (Gen. 4.1) postdates the Fall and expulsion, and the first sin ("the origin of evil") was disobedience, not intercourse. Other writers have emphasized connections between the Eden story and the myth of the "Golden Age" that was widespread in the Graeco-Roman Mediterranean and Middle East (Geertz 87).

The aftermath of the Fall has also generated diverse interpretations on multiple levels. Though Christian theology believed that Adam and Eve sinned and their punishment was just, it espoused the idea of the "Fortunate Fall" (*felix culpa*, 'happy guilt') to explain why an omniscient, omnipotent God let this happen. Because the Fall brought Jesus (known as "the second Adam") into human history, it was ultimately "fortunate"; also, God wanted free choice, not blind obedience. In time a secular version of the Fortunate Fall developed along several fronts: moral, psychological, and emotional. We *needed* to grow up as moral beings, ran the argument, *wanted* knowledge of good and evil. "God's daughter Eve," writes Joseph Campbell, was "ripe to depart from the idyl of the Garden" (1968, 52). Sexual maturation is often the subtext – what the Manuels call the "underthought" (Geertz 97) – of later gardens. The Song of Solomon makes the walled garden a metaphor of the beloved's body: "A garden inclosed is my sister, my spouse" (SS 4:12); "I am come into my garden, my sister, my spouse" (SS 5:1).

This whole line of thought – the necessary, if not entirely fortunate, Fall from the womb – is related to my chief interest here. The Manuels' introduction to their "History of Paradise" shows the similarity between paradise and the idea of a *domaine*.

> In visions of paradise terrestrial and celestial, men have been disclos-
> ing their innermost desires, whether they thrust them backward into
> the past, projected them forward into the future on earth, or raised
> them beyond the bounds of this sphere. As in dreams, men displaced
> themselves in time and space and compressed their manifold wishes
> into an all-embracing metaphor.... (Geertz 83)

This also describes the impulses behind many mythic and literary *domaines*, and Eden is one of the Manuels' prime examples. Its importance is obvious: Eden comes early in the western literary tradition, is central to Judaeo-Christian thought, and has been tremendously influential through its wide diffusion. It has most of the qualities that define a *domaine*: an isolated, spiritually intense place where protagonists undergo searching trials of their core values, making it life-changing, and which they must then leave. Power, apartness, testing, and transience: all are there. The serpent appears in most *domaines* in one form or another: tempter, seducer, Lord of the Flies, Father Time, bringer of death, Father of Lies. He may have worked on Eve because (according to the J source) she was not present when "the LORD God commanded the man" to avoid the forbidden fruit (Gen. 2:16); she heard the prohibition only at second-hand, from Adam. *Domaines* require vigilance; expect the unexpected. Referees warn boxers to protect themselves at all times *in the ring*, but no ropes set the limits of the ring in a *domaine*. Adam and Eve probably trusted God to tell them all they needed to know, but, lacking knowledge of good and evil, they were unacquainted with serpentine guile. Protect yourself at all times, period.

John Milton's Eden

The most famous and prolonged version of the Garden of Eden in English literature is John Milton's *Paradise Lost* (10 books, 1667; 12 books, 1674). I follow the later text, which is fuller, better known, and gives the poet's final words. In terms of *gravitas*, at least, it is the *Ur*-text for Anglophone study of *domaines*. "Puritans" such as Milton supposedly wanted to go back to the beginnings, and for him Eden would have been the first paradise. But his treatment of the story is hardly "pure," admitting much material from later sources: theological interpretations ranging from Church Fathers to seventeenth-century writers; angelology; scientific speculation about the structure of the universe; literary adornment from classical and later sources, etc. Far from being a bare Dissenters' chapel, *Paradise Lost* is a cathedral full of statuary and stained glass. Its learned commentators, anxious to 'justify the ways of Milton to man', have also gone outside the epic and the Bible in trying to explain what he really meant. I will concentrate on the garden *domaine* in *Paradise Lost* itself. Though Milton created a number of theological, scientific, social, and aesthetic problems for himself by attempting to serve the various gods of religion, art, and science, the parts of the poem that concern us here are among the most satisfactory in that regard.

Given his decision to "sing" the epic

> *Of Man's First Disobedience, and the Fruit*
> *Of that Forbidden Tree, whose mortal taste*
> *Brought Death into the World, and all our woe,*
> *With loss of Eden.... (PL I: 1-4)*

as well as to "justify the ways of God to men," Milton's presentation of Eden is clearly central to his purpose. The paradise that the Creator made for the First Parents, a place where they would be delightfully accommodated and walk with Him, is also the place which they lost, entailing sweat, pain, and death on humanity. C.S. Lewis pointed out that Milton works both obviously and subliminally. As he *tells* us about Eden in Book IV, he works to make us *feel* "the paradisal idea as it exists in our minds," i.e. the archetype of 'paradiseness' (Lewis 1942; 1960, 48). Milton does this first by emphasizing its height, which means taking sides in the dispute over whether Eden was in a desert or on a mountain. By choosing the latter, he could give a stronger sense of its remoteness from the world. Moreover, he shows Eden through Satan's fresh but fallen eyes on his first approach (IV: 205ff.). Milton may have noticed in Shakespeare's *Antony and Cleopatra* how impressive praise of Cleopatra's beauty sounds coming from a cynic like Enobarbus.

> *So on he fares, and to the border comes*
> *Of Eden, where delicious Paradise,*
> *Now nearer, Crowns with her enclosure green,*
> *As with a rural mound the champain head*
> *Of a steep wilderness, whose hairy sides*
> *With thicket overgrown, grotesque and wild,*
> *Access deni'd; and over head up grew*
> *Insuperable highth of loftiest shade,*
> *Cedar, and Pine, and Fir, and branching Palm,*
> *A Silvan Scene, and as the ranks ascend*
> *Shade above shade, a woody Theatre*
> *Of stateliest view. Yet higher than thir tops*
> *The verdurous wall of Paradise up sprung:*
> *Which to our general Sire gave prospect large*
> *Into his nether Empire neighboring round.*
> *And higher than that Wall a circling row*
> *Of goodliest Trees loaden with fairest Fruit...* (IV 131-47)

It would be difficult to overstate how skillfully Milton accomplishes the task he set himself here: impressing Satan with the "Insuperable" altitude of Eden. One level rises above another as in a Renaissance "Tower of Babel" painting. Even to the ruler of Hell is "Access denied" into the "steep wilderness," and that is still low down. For "over head up grew" a lofty forest, and above that "the ranks ascend / Shade above shade"; "Yet higher than thir tops" the "verdurous wall of Paradise up sprung," and even "higher than that Wall" are the fruit-laden trees. Height o'ertops height, with many a curious detail en route. That Paradise is "delicious" brings to mind eating, an association reinforced by the "fairest Fruit" of the "goodliest Trees" (l. 147); knowing what one of those trees is makes the passage ironic. "Champaign" is an English version of Italian *campagna*: the lush plain south of Rome. The "hairy sides" of the wilderness show how Latinate Milton was: he is probably thinking of *horridus*, 'bristling,' one of Virgil's favourite adjectives for thick woods. "Grotesque" meant like a grotto, such as the "umbrageous Grots" in Eden (IV: 257). Milton was interested in Italian ideas about landscape gardening, including artificial grottoes. He makes Eden a walled garden, which Genesis does not, though it is a "verdurous" rather than an artificial wall.

But a *domaine* – besides being out of this world – must also be highly attractive to characters and readers to work its magic, and Milton, rising to the challenge, deploys all his descriptive powers to make it so. Wylie Sypher calls the poem "baroque" in its "plenitude" (193).

> *...from that Sapphire Fount the crisped Brooks,*
> *Rolling on Orient Pearl and sands of Gold,*
> *With mazy error under pendant shades*
> *Ran Nectar, visiting each plant, and fed*
> *Flow'rs worthy of Paradise which not nice Art*
> *In Beds and curious Knots, but Nature boon*
> *Pour'd forth profuse on Hill and Dale and Plain,*
> *Both where the morning Sun first warmly smote*
> *The open field, and where the unpierc't shade*
> *Imbrown'd the noontide Bow'rs....* (IV: 237-46)

Again there is much to admire here, from the bejewelled palette and the brooks' "nectar" feeding the plants to the declaration of the poet's taste in gardening: "not nice Art /...but Nature." While interested in formal gardens, he preferred the wilder, more nearly natural style. "Mazy error" may sound odd applied to Eden's watercourses, but *error* in Latin meant 'wandering' as well as 'mistake,' so it both describes meandering brooks and foreshadows the Fall. Also, mazes were a popular feature of seventeenth-century gardens. Though his primary concern here is theological, Milton increased the popularity of landscape poetry. There is little doubt that he envisioned Eden as the prototype of England's and Europe's country estates, with their planned gardens, groves, "wilds," falls, streams, and lakes. The First Garden was

> *A happy rural seat of various view:*
> *Groves whose rich Trees wept odorous Gums and Balm,*
> *Others whose fruit burnisht with Golden Rind*

Hung amiable, Hesperian fables true,
If true, here only, and of delicious taste:
Betwixt them Lawns, or level Downs, and Flocks
Grazing the tender herb, were interpos'd,
Or palmy hillock, or the flow'ry lap
Of some irriguous valley spread her store,
Flow'rs of all hue, and without Thorn the Rose…. (IV: 247-56)

As a genre-conscious writer of (secondary) epic, Milton tried to bring in everything, including classical fables that Puritans distrusted, such as the "golden apples" of the Hesperides, another famous garden of antiquity. They must know their place, however; only the *rind* was "golden," and even if that was so, it was "here only." Eden also had grazing flocks of sheep – an important part of pastoral poetry *and* of England's economy – and roses "without Thorn." Prelapsarian Eden being perfect, thorns must have grown *after* the Fall, as the earth's axis tilted, producing seasons instead of "Eternal Spring" (IV: 268). It was a splendid place for a honeymoon: grapes and other fruit hung ripe for the picking, birds provided music, fields and groves smelled sweet, the landscape pleased the eye, and old Pan from Greek myth led the Graces and Hours in dances. Human society was limited, but exotic characters and novelty made Eden magical.

Yet Milton's Eden is full of irony, and hits some dubious notes. He could have a near-certainty that his readers would be familiar with his plot, which made dramatic irony possible. When you know that the "fairest Fruit" in the garden (IV: 147) includes the Forbidden Fruit that Eve will eat, you have your *frisson* early. This irony can be felt by re-reading Genesis 2-3; the Biblical Eden, fair and seemingly innocent, already contains the prince and principle of evil. But Milton chooses to go beyond Scripture, letting Satan into the Garden the night before the Fall, where (disguised as a toad) he squats at Eve's ear and gives her dreams (IV: 800ff.). In the crucial one (recounted in V: 30-95), she eats the Forbidden Fruit and is *not* punished, instead rising with an angelic guide into the heavens – just the effect that the serpent later promises Eve. This compounds the theological difficulties of Gen. 2-3: an omnipotent, omniscient God not only allows Satan into Eden, but permits him to enter Eve's naive unconscious the night before the Fall and give her a false preview of what eating the fruit would entail. Questions

of fairness may seem naive or irrelevant to theologians, but among common folk
they will arise: for *this* offence we all deserved endless sweat, pain, the subjugation
of women, and death?

The question of misogyny in Genesis itself has occasioned many debates. A
great deal depends on whether you focus on 1:27, where the P source has God
create "man in his own image," "male and female created he them," i.e. both sexes
at the same time (see also 5:2); or rather on 2:22-23, where the J source's LORD
God takes a rib from Adam and creates Eve from it – and what you make of that.
Is Eve an afterthought, or the capstone of creation? It is she who is approached
by the serpent, eats the forbidden fruit, and gives it to Adam: does that mean that
woman's weakness caused the Fall, or does it argue for the education of women?
Eve is not present when the LORD God forbids the eating of the fruit; she presumably heard about the prohibition from Adam.

Milton enters this controversy, too. Even before the Fall, when Satan first sees
Adam and Eve, they are characterized and differentiated in a tendentious way.

> *Though both*
> *Not equal, as thir sex not equal seem'd;*
> *For contemplation hee and valor form'd,*
> *For softness shee and sweet attractive Grace,*
> *Hee for God only, shee for God in him.... (IV: 295-99)*

Whereas Adam's "fair large Front [forehead] and Eye sublime declar'd / Absolute
rule," and his "manly" hair hung only to his shoulders (IV: 300-303), Eve's waist-
length hair

> *in wanton ringlets wav'd*
> *As the Vine curls her tendrils, which impli'd*
> *Subjection, but requir'd with gentle sway*
> *And by her yielded, by him best receiv'd,*
> *Yielded with coy submission, modest pride,*
> *And sweet reluctant amorous delay. (IV: 306-11)*

Miltonists and feminists have clashed over this and some similar passages. Does
the "gentle sway" required of Adam mitigate his "Absolute rule" and take the edge
off Eve's "subjection" (apparently deduced from her naturally curly hair)? Adam's
primacy in creation (in the J source) seems to extend into other areas. Is Eve

represented as his inferior? Later, after admiring her own image reflected in a pool, Narcissus-like, she is made to say that when Adam first took her by the hand,

> *I yielded, and from that time see*
> *How beauty is excelled by manly grace*
> *And wisdom, which alone is truly fair. (IV: 489-91)*

"Yielded" again! As she leans on Adam in "meek surrender," and "half her swelling Breast / Naked met his under the flowing Gold / Of her loose tresses hid" – prurient lines that border on soft pornography –

> *hee in delight*
> *Both of her Beauty and submissive Charms*
> *Smil'd with superior Love.... (IV: 497-99)*

It is difficult to avoid a suspicion that Adam's smile of *superior* love is also Milton's. And if Adam is "superior," who but "yielding," "meek," "submissive" Eve is inferior? I would not dwell on this point if relations between the sexes, especially men's attitudes toward and treatment of women, were not so often important in *domaine* narratives by Marie de France, Chrétien de Troyes, Henri Alain-Fournier, John Fowles and others. The topic can be a touchstone of values, both for the author's view of some characters and for our view of the author.

Other aspects of Milton's influential epic also reappear in later works. An *undermining* of some kind is common in *domaines*, and may be considered symptomatic. They may be beautiful places, but are inherently fragile, unstable, or deceptive. A fundamental danger exists somewhere; if you don't see it, better keep looking. Alain-Fournier's *domaine perdu* is built on sand; Fowles's estate houses and some mediaeval *domaines* are ruled by evil or autocratic masters with their own agendas. Milton's Adam and Eve are caught between a prohibiting God, his "subtil" Adversary, and the author's own values. The warning issued in Graeco-Roman pastoral, *Et in Arcadia ego* ('I too [am] in Arcadia,' with 'I' understood to be Death), applies fully in *Paradise Lost*.

And how are we meant to feel about the First Couple's ejection from Eden? The action and their experiences are complex and ambiguous. The epic's official theological position is that of *felix culpa*, the Fortunate Fall, which Adam is given to enunciate near the end:

O goodness infinite, goodness immense!
That all this good of evil shall produce,
And evil turn to good.... (XII: 469-71)

He even wonders "Whether I should repent me now of sin /...or rejoice /...that much more good thereof shall spring..." (XII: 474-76) – a turn of thought that seems logical within the framework of this doctrine. Yet they are expelled from the Garden for disobeying God's command not to eat the fruit of the tree of knowledge of good and evil: i.e. the acquisition of a moral sense caused their banishment. But would we have *wanted* to live in total innocence, lacking a conscience? Is that not a definition of childhood, a time when we do not know enough to be held responsible for our transgressions? ("Oh, he doesn't know any better"; "She's too young to punish.") So was it perhaps a Fortunate Fall in that regard, too?

Whatever our feelings about these questions, it hurts to leave all the beauty that Milton has devised for our imaginations. He packs a great deal of emotional ambivalence into the last lines, after the angel has escorted them out the gate and down towards the "subjected Plain" as the temperate climate begins to parch:

They looking back, all th' Eastern side beheld
Of Paradise, so late thir happy seat,
Wav'd over by that flaming Brand, the Gate
With dreadful Faces throng'd and fiery Arms
Some natural tears they dropp'd, but wip'd them soon;
The World was all before them, where to choose
Thir place of rest, and Providence thir guide
They hand in hand with wand'ring steps and slow,
Through Eden took thir solitary way. (XII: 641-49)

Despite the awful view back to the lost paradise, perhaps the most striking line here is "The world was all before them, where to choose." Yes! In front of them lies the uncharted world in which they will raise their children, have *choices* and no prohibitions (except the Garden), only consequences: *that* is the way forward, and perhaps it will be fortunate. No more freeloading or talks with God, but they still have Providence, and, as the saying goes, they will have each other. Just watch out for serpents.

Paradise Lost and the Garden of Eden are touchstones, conceptual bases for this study; some version of "sadder but wiser" is heard in most *domaine* narratives. In Wordsworth's "Immortality Ode," for example, the speaker looks back to youthful "splendour in the grass" and asks himself what compensations we find in later life for losing it. Northrop Frye writes that literature and art try to re-establish contact with a 'world we have lost,' a time in a place of union and happiness. Though we may feel alienated from the world around us, we vaguely remember feeling closely connected to it once, and desire to feel that way again.

> *That's a dim, misty outline of a story that's told so often, of how man once lived in a golden age or a garden of Eden or the Hesperides, or a happy island kingdom in the Atlantic, how that world was lost, and how some day we may be able to get it back again. ...a feeling of lost identity....* (Frye 1963, 20)

Poetry, Frye argues, tries to recover the lost time / garden / world by leading the imagination back to what I call the *domaine* and some psychoanalysts call the womb. He believes that the "story of the loss and regaining of identity [is] the framework of all literature" (1963, 21; I prefer "regaining of *the feeling of* identity), and locates the "monomyth" of Joseph Campbell's *The Hero With a Thousand Faces* inside that framework as well.

In leaving Eden we should review what this central story says about *domaines*. We have noted its fragility, and the ironic stance that comes with foreknowledge of the outcome. Duration is often an issue, too. How long did Adam and Eve enjoy their innocent bliss? There is no way to tell in Genesis. Modern *domaines* are apt to be more precise about time, which is usually short. How long were Alain-Fournier's and Fowles's protagonists enchanted? Not long. As soon as we are consciously happy in such a place, it seems, we must leave, and (Thomas Wolfe insisted) *You Can't Go Home Again*. Also, *domaines* are often constructed within difficult, hostile contexts. Being "set apart" comes at a price. Eden's Garden is surrounded by an unpeopled world (a desert in the old sense), then by raw, uncaring Chaos, a hostile Hell, and a watchful, lawgiving Heaven. In later *domaines* we may see a modern, earthly version of this cosmos: the magical, seemingly timeless place fenced off from the modern world by geography, law, economics, culture, time, or design. In "Sailing to Byzantium," Yeats refers to the "artifice of eternity." A *domaine* may also be an artifice – but of what, exactly? That is the question.

Romancing the Rose

Pagan "paradises" predated the Judaeo-Christian one, and as well-known as Eden was in Europe, it never wholly monopolized the field of garden *domaines*. They often had an erotic aspect (like The Song of Solomon), i.e. an interest in the social relations of men and women, with their sexual potential. For later "Latinate" civilization – the European Middle Ages and Renaissance – the walled private garden (*hortus inclusus* or *conclusus*) might be a Garden of Love or of Pleasure. You would not meet God there, but you might encounter other lords, other tests, other beasts. Christian readers, of course, would not *completely* forget Eden as they read secular romances set in gardens, but they did not necessarily say, "Oh, he's *really* talking about Eden."

The great mediaeval exemplar of a garden *domaine* was the *Roman de la Rose*, a long French verse romance in two discrete parts. Guillaume de Lorris wrote the original and more admired poem, a four-thousand-line allegory of a young courtier's quest for the "rose" of his lady's love, in the early thirteenth century. Evidently unfinished, it breaks off with the lover in disfavour, kept at a distance, his fate uncertain. Several decades later, Jean de Meun(g) added ca. 18,000 lines – radically different in content and tone – to finish it. His "continuation" shows little interest in allegory or courtly love while ranging widely over satirical attacks (including some on women), learned references, and various digressions. In the end, Venus helps the lover obtain the rose. Readers saw that the two parts were fundamentally at war with each other ("la querelle du *Roman de la Rose*"), and the poem figured in the debate about the value of women for the next century or two. I ignore de Meun's counterattack and follow de Lorris.

The importance of the *Roman* is generally conceded. In the standard American *Literary History of England*, Albert C. Baugh called it "the most popular and influential of all French poems in the Middle Ages," one which "set a fashion in courtly poetry for two centuries in western Europe" (252). Chaucer wrote that he translated it (though the Middle English *Romaunt of the Rose* is not *all* by him); other poets also wrote versions of the *Roman*. Chaucer's editor, F.N. Robinson, believed that the first part of the poem "probably exerted on Chaucer a more lasting and more important influence than any other work in the vernacular literature of either France or England" (564).

Enjoying it today is, of course, a different issue. The problem is not only the difficulty of understanding mediaeval French or Middle English, but also the oddity of allegorical narratives using personified characters with names like Fair Welcome, Frankness, and Danger. Who can help us enjoy reading such a thing? Perhaps C.S. Lewis can. In *The Allegory of Love* (1936) he briefed modern readers on allegory and personification in general, and on the *Roman de la Rose*. Allegory, he argues, was the means that de Lorris chose to bring "the subjective" (psychological and emotional elements) into his poem (1958, 113). His personifications are not external abstractions, but dramatic representations of a character's "inner world" (113, 115). The *Roman* is "a story of real life," with personifications showing "moods or aspects" of real people (116, 118). Lewis leads a tour of the scenes and characters, explaining what they mean and how they work.

Many conventions of mediaeval European literature appear in the *Roman*. It is a dream-vision, set in some space apart from ordinary life. (While *we* tend to respect dreams as messages from the unconscious, de Lorris feels a need to review the literature attacking them as fables and lies.) And it opens conventionally on a May morning, the "tyme of love and jolite" (l. 52 of the Middle English *Romaunt*, in Robinson's edition of Chaucer); "Hard is the hert that loveth nought / In May" (ll. 85-86). The dreamer – not a hero, only an *ingenu* with a lot to learn – walks happily beside a clear river, listening to birdsong, until he sees an enclosed garden whose high wall is decorated with statues and paintings. Translation: a young man (in the "spring" or "morning" of life) comes to court, the principal *domaine* of courtly love, for the first time. Images on the wall around the garden depict characteristics and conditions that are excluded from the society within. These include both moral failings, some of them sins (*Coveitise, Avarice, Envye*), and lamentable circumstances: *Sorowe, Elde* [Age], and *Povert*. The author expresses sympathy for these unfortunates, especially the aged (forty-odd lines on the ravages of time). Nevertheless, these misfortunes disqualify one from courtly society as effectively as vices do.

The dreamer circumambulates the wall until he finds a small wicket-gate, which he knocks on. It is opened by a young blonde, fair of face and form, who gives her name as *Ydelnesse*. And indeed, he remarks drily, to judge by her clothes and appearance "She was not wont [used] to gret travayle": l. 576). He asks if he may see the garden, and she promptly welcomes him in:

In at the wiket went I tho, [then]
That Ydelnesse had opened me,
Into that gardyn fair to see. (642-44)

Obviously idleness is a requirement for admission to this society; *Pressinge Bisynesse* could be another portrait on the Wall of Disqualification. He is now in the antechamber of the *domaine*, which seems to him a "paradys erthly," "a place espirituel," as good as *the* paradise (648-54), and devotes dozens of lines to the splendid birdsong. Then I saw clearly, he remarks, "That Ydelnesse me served well" (696). Within the garden he finds what anyone entering a new social milieu would hope for: mirth, gladness, and courtesy – except that he meets characters named *Sir Myrthe* (who decorated the wall), *Gladnesse*, and *Curtesie*, who invites him to join the "daunce," i.e. enter courtly society. Of course he accepts: this is exactly what he craves!

Ogling the beautiful people ("fair folk and so fresh": 737), the dreamer describes their elegant dance. Besides the previously named characters there are the God of Love, accompanied by a "bacheler" named *Swete-Lokyng*, whom bows and arrows identify as Cupid; *Beaute* (the name of one of Cupid's arrows); the lady *Richesse*, whom all serve, since she can both "helpe and hyndre," dressed in royal purple and a golden circlet; the lady *Largesse*, who loves giving more than Avarice loves hoarding, escorted by a young knight fresh from a joust; *Fraunchise* (generosity), "debonaire of herte" (1220); and *Youthe*, "not yit twelve yeer of age," being kissed by her partner in plain sight (1283). 'She meant no harm,' the narrator confides, 'but you know young people think of little except their play' and "make no force of pryvete" [privacy] (1294).

Afterwards many couples stroll under the trees while the dreamer visits a beautiful garden, especially its rose bushes (court ladies). Watched by Love and Cupid, he plays the field at first ("Wente up and doun full many a wey": 1345), wanting to see them all. Then he rests beside a well and reads an inscription on it: 'Narcissus died here' (1468). The myth of Echo and Narcissus is related in detail. Why? Is the dreamer guilty of narcissism? No charge is made against him, so perhaps courtiers were considered inherently narcissistic. The dreamer recoils at first, but cannot tear himself away. Leaning over, he looks down through clear water to the bottom, and sees there "Two cristall stonys" (1568) that reflect the entire garden when sunlight enters the well. The crystal stones are a lady's eyes, which (in Petrarchan and courtly poetry) show us the whole world, and the well is "the mirrour peril-ous" (1601) in which we *must* love what we see, as Narcissus did. Cupid rules this "Welle of Love" (1627) and sets snares there.

Now the dreamer says that it was a "sory houre" (1639) when he gazed into the well, ignorant of its power. He has been *"entriked"* (1642) by his curiosity! But the God of Love remarks that love has both highs and lows, rewards and pains, and the crystal eyes in the well "shewide me full openly / A thousand thinges" (1637-38). This is the epiphanic moment when the *Romaunt* comes nearest to Eden's forbidden Tree of Knowledge. The dreamer sees a rosebush in bloom, inside a hedge: an enclosure enclosed. Drawn by the fragrance, he goes toward the rose-bush, where he is much taken by the fresh rose*buds* ("knoppes," 1685). These are the younger ladies, of whom one especially appeals to him: "Among the knoppes I ches [chose] oon" (1691).

At this point Fragment A of the Middle English *Romaunt* (where Chaucer's hand is most likely) ends, but Fragment B continues de Lorris' allegory. As the dreamer approaches the *knoppe*, the God of Love shoots five arrows into him. They are called *Beaute*, *Symplesse* (simplicity), *Curtesie*, *Company*; and *Faire-Semblant*, 'fair appearance': all attributes of Lady Rosebud. *Company* (who can make ladies merciful) connotes sociability (1863-64). Several arrows enter through the eye, but all reach the heart: he can draw out the shaft, but the barbed point stays in. All this accords with the physiology of love given by Petrarch, Andreas Cappelanus, and Ovid. The God of Love now says "Yield!" and the weary dreamer replies, "Gladly." He kneels, is accepted as a courtly lover, and saluted by Love, who then asks a "hostage" as security for his submission. The dreamer says, "Make a key for my heart," and Love produces "A litel keye"

> *With which anoon he touchide me*
> *Undir the side full softily,*
> *That he myn herte sodeynly*
> *Withouten anoy hadde spered...(2096-99)*

Now the allegory appears to falter. We know that the narrator is smitten, but the next section, after he asks Love to enumerate the "comaundementis" he must keep, is problematical. Love complies for almost two hundred lines: Avoid *"Vilanye"* (churlishness), ribaldry, and pride; be as courteous as Sir Gawain; honour women; live within your means; mind your dress and hygiene; be generous and merry; expect both good and bad from love; cultivate arms and the arts. In sum,

> *Whoso with Love wole goon or ride,*
> *He mot be curteis, and voide of pride,*
> *Mery, and full of jolite,*
> *And of largesse alosed [praised] be. (2351-54)*

Love also warns the dreamer to make sure his love is durable and for one woman only, adding hundreds of lines about the pains of love, gift-giving, etc. Our *ingenu* asks how lovers endure their pains, evoking two hundred more lines listing the rewards: Hope, "Swete-Thought," "Swete Speche," and "Swete-Lokyng." In case we have lost track of time, the narrator notes that Love "al the day / Had taught me," after which the god has the decency to vanish (2951-53).

What are we to make of this? Is it a comic or pedantic interlude? It is not allegorical, and whence does it come? Not from the lady, still a remote figure, and the young lover does not know this much. He might by now have friends at court, yet the character named *Freend* will not appear for another four hundred lines. The author seems to have inserted into the plot a manual on the proper conduct of a courtly love affair in the manner of Andreas Capellanus' *De Arte Honeste Amandi*. But if the God of Love's long discourse meshes awkwardly with de Lorris' allegory, it fits my interest very well. Almost every *domaine* has rules governing visitors, but usually they are not written down or spoken in time; most novices discover them only belatedly, to their discomfiture. In that regard the narrator can consider himself lucky: an authority figure told him how things ought to be done at a fairly early stage. As we know from the Genesis Eden, however, "ought to" is not always a sufficient wave to carry you over the shoals.

Once the God of Love disappears, psychological allegory returns. The lover yearns to approach the rosebud, and is granted audience by her *Bialacoil*, a warm or at least forthright welcome: a courtesy she would extend to any gentleman at court. But the lady has other qualities that take a dimmer view of men. Her *Daunger* (wariness, readiness to take offence) is hiding nearby, and with him are *Wykked-Tongue* (gossip) and *Shame*. Shame is the keeper of the rosebush, and Chastity its chatelaine. Nevertheless, Bialacoil allows the dreamer to approach and touch the rosebush, even giving him a green leaf. Encouraged, the dreamer then babbles to Bialacoil about his devotion, his arrow-wounds, and his "peynes gret" that will never cease until "ye the bouton graunte me": 'give me the bud' of love (3109).

This is asking far too much way too soon, showing the lover's naïveté. All hell breaks loose, starting with Bialacoil, who is "affrayed all": 'totally frightened'.

> *What? Wolde ye shende [disgrace] me in this wise?*
> *A mochel [great] fool thanne I were,*
> *If I suffride you awey to bere*
> *The freesh botoun so faire of sight. (3116-19)*

I.e. 'Do you think I was born yesterday?' But Bialacoil's unkindest cut is, "Ye are not *curteys* (courteous, courtly) to ask it" (3123). You have broken rules, violated the code, palmed a card, skied out of bounds. And "With that sterte oute anoon Daunger" (3130). The lady's wariness comes forth, looking churlish: "Full gret he was and blak of hewe / Sturdy and hidous" (3133-34). His eyes blaze and he yells like a madman, first at Bialacoil, then at the dreamer. 'What do you think you're doing?! And *you!* Get out of here before I lose my temper!' The lady is torn, but with Bialacoil on the defensive, no longer supporting the lover, her sense of outraged virtue prevails; Daunger chases the cowering young lover back out through the hedge.

Now the allegorical action moves inside the narrator, who stands regretting his "high foly" and feeling his banishment keenly (3171). After a "A long while," Lady Resoun appears, i.e. he begins to reflect rationally on his situation (3189). Resoun is represented as

> *neither yong ne hoor [hoar, white-haired]*
> *Ne high ne lowe, ne fat ne lene,*
> *But best, as it were in a mene [mean]. (3196-98)*

This Goddess of the Middle Way's first move is to fire a broadside at "Foly and childhood," and the bad influences that have brought the dreamer to this pass (3220). For her, his whole venture into the realm of courtly love has been a huge mistake. No friend of *carpe diem*, she observes caustically, "Thou hast bought deere the tyme of May" (3222).

> *In yvel tyme thou wentist to see*
> *The gardyn, whereof Ydilnesse*
> *Bar the keye, and was maistresse, (3224-26)*

and you *danced* with her whose "aqueyntaunce is perilous." In brief, "She hath [thee] trasshed" (3229, 3231). So much for his tour of the rose garden! Leave off your folly, commands Resoun. Stop taking bad advice! Mend your ways! Above all, "I counseile thee... / The God of Love hoolly foryet": he is the source of all your pain (3244-45). *Your loving is the problem.* She continues attacking love for another thirty lines before pausing for breath.

But the dreamer's reflective moment passes quickly; like Lady Rosebud he is at war with himself, and rounds on Resoun. As if he could throw off love just like that! You "waste" your words "in idilnesse" (3223) – redirecting her attack on the gatekeeper. He does not *refute* her arguments, merely dismisses them with "All that ye seyn is but in veyne" (3325). And by the way, "Who that me chastisith, I hym hate" (3331). This rebuke is administered not by a personified emotion, but by the "whole" narrator. Now Love and Reason have both had their say, and Love is victorious. Resoun, too rational to bandy or waste words, leaves in silence.

Since Love advised him to consult a friend, the dreamer turns to "a felowe faste [close] by" whose name is *Freend* (3344). When told the situation, Freend says calm down, for "Mysilf I knowe full well Daunger" (3371) – he's been around, knows the ropes. He prescribes an apology, some flattery, and a plea for mercy. The lover approaches Daunger, kneels, asks forgiveness, blames Love for his trespass, and pledges not to re-offend. He has just one request: "That I may love" (3427). His closing is bold, though, shifting from request to defiance:

> *And ye may not letten [prevent] me,*
> *For wel wot [know]ye that love is free,*
> *And I shall loven, sith that I will,*
> *Who ever like it well or ill.... (3431-34)*

This might seem a bridge too far, but Daunger takes it in his stride, agreeing – up to a point: 'Love where you like, but *stay away from my roses!*' The love that he cannot prevent is merely an internal state. The dreamer reports to Freend, who ignores the exclusionary proviso and says, 'Well done! He's your friend now'. As if spellbound, the narrator stands by the hedge, whence he can see the rosebud, lamenting his lot while Daunger watches closely.

At this juncture two more qualities of the lady make their first appearance: *Fraunchise* and *Pite*. C.S. Lewis calls them Bialacoil's "chief allies," glossing Fraunchise ('frankness') as "the innocent security of a great lady" (1958, 123). They take the dreamer's side, telling Daunger that he acts out of love. Don't be discourteous, they urge: recall Bialacoil! Daunger relents. Fraunchise chides Bialacoil for having been rude to a respectable suitor, who should be restored to favour. Bialacoil agrees, goes to the dreamer with the same pleasant mien as at first, and escorts him through the hedge: "Fro helle unto paradys," says the narrator (Robinson 3622). Finding the rose larger and higher – time has passed – he feels more firmly caught in love's snare than ever.

Forces within the lady are turning in the dreamer's favour, then, but again he overplays his hand, asking Bialacoil for "a kyssynge precious / Of the goodly fresshe Rose" (3658-59). This triggers more alarm. Bialacoil is afraid of *Chastyte*, who opposes kissing on the grounds that he who attains that much will want the rest. This disheartens the lover, but now *Venus* herself rises as his advocate: the lady, Lewis writes, discovers that she has "senses of her own" (1958, 133). Venus is carrying a torch – as many a lover has done since – and the dreamer describes her as "wondirfull of apparayle," with a good figure; anyone can see that "She was not of religioun" (Robinson 3712, 3715). Venus assures Bialacoil that a kiss is but a kiss, the dreamer is "Loves servaunt," and being "yong, lusty, and fair," with sweet breath and clean teeth, he is "Worthy of love" (3732-38). Let him have a kiss! Bialacoil the Flexible forthwith grants permission. The dreamer kisses the rose, and pain gives way to "joye and blisse" (3765).

But the kiss evokes a spate of old adages about the transience of earthly pleasure: "Aftir the calm the trouble sone / Mot [must] folowe," etc. (3777-78). *Wikkid-Tunge* berates Bialacoil and the lover, awakening *Jelousy*, who demands, 'Why are you so negligent? You should be locked up. And where is Shame, anyway!' This is not easy to explain: who is jealous of whom, and who is ashamed of what? Lewis suggests relatives, guardians, even a hitherto-unsuspected husband. After all, the rosebud is the lady's *love*, which in the courtly system was distinct from marriage, with its family alliances, property, and inheritance concerns. It is difficult to reconcile the customary associations of a fresh rosebud with a married woman, however, and this reading would mean that the psychological allegory has broken down again.

Bialacoil is stunned, the dreamer flees, and Shame appears, but, to our surprise, she insists that Jelousy *not* believe Wikkid-Tunge's lies. Bialacoil is basically a good fellow, she says; don't chastise him. But is that a line for *Shame* to take? And it only provokes Jelousy further. He launches a general attack on society's morals: "Overall regneth Lecchery"; chastity is an endangered virtue (3914). His speech is also personal: he can no longer trust Shame. He will enclose the rose garden in a "forteresse," in which will be a tower imprisoning Bialacoil (3942). 'Fair welcome' will be replaced by a chastity belt. When Jelousy leaves, *Drede* emerges to tell Shame that this is all just too much; they must ask Daunger to rein in Bialacoil.

They find Daunger lying under a hawthorn tree. Caught napping, he is berated by Shame for foolishness and villainy in letting Bialacoil bring the dreamer to kiss the rose. He will ruin them all! Repair the hedge and "Be like thi name!" (4040). Daunger is struck dumb. Drede warns him to do his job or Jelousy will be offended. At last Daunger stirs, roars 'No one else goes into the garden!' and plugs every gap in the hedge. All the dreamer can do is bewail his fall from paradise into hell. He blames Wikkid-Tunge's lies for his plight, but his aggressive requests to Bialacoil and his kissing of the bud also played a part in his fall from grace.

Here the narrative shifts into a quite different mode: military architecture (psychological division). Jelousy has a deep ditch dug and a sturdy wall built – a hundred fathoms on a side, with battlements and towers – right around the roses; its corners have larger towers and portcullis gateways. Within the wall is the tower where Bialacoil will be held. Another wall surrounds this tower, with roses planted between tower and wall. There is a "castell" provided with gunners, archers, and "Grete engynes" (4194); the gatekeepers are Daunger, Shame, Drede, and Wikked-Tunge. All this amounts to a formidable barrier against a would-be suitor, and runs directly counter to the usual associations of rose gardens.

The narrator ends this section with attacks on Wikked-Tunge (gendered male) and Jelousy: qualities not of the lady, but of those around her. Wikked-Tunge (slander) guards his own gate, visits the others, and walks on the wall at night, making atrocious sounds: "Discordaunt ever fro armonye / And distoned from melodie" (4247-48). He employs "hornepipes of Cornewaile" (apparently the worst kind) and ill-attuned flutes, and sings about faithless wives. *Evidence* of adultery does not concern him: their sinfulness is assumed. "He lieth, though they ben giltes" (4270). The Middle Ages had its share of misogynist texts, but here those views are given to Wikked-Tunge, who is cursed for harming innocents. God is also asked to thwart Jelousy, an "olde vekke" (hag), for building the tower, imprisoning Bialacoil, and serving the devil (4286). She is efficient, though: the prisoner can forget about escape, for "she knew all the olde daunce" (4300).

With those Parthian shots, the narrator takes stock. Love sold me his wares too dear, he concludes, and now, having ruined me, wants to make "a newe bargeyn" (4325). I'm like a farmer who sows seed, only to have his crop ruined by rain. He also likens his case to a favourite trope of the time: "It is of Love, as of Fortune, / That chaungeth ofte..." (4353-54). Smiling, then glowering, "Now freend, now foo," they swing us from pole to pole (4357). It is the mood of the song "*O fortuna!*" in Karl Orff's *Carmina Burana*. Love too can in "a twynklyng turneth hir wheel" (4358), dooming the lover to "change and revolucioun" (4366). Having lost his wager, the lover can only launch one last appeal to Bialacoil: 'Be true to me; pay no heed to their lies. You are all I have!' And with this final wail about the pains of love, de Lorris' *Roman de la Rose* ends, his last word being *wanhope*: 'faint hope'. The first line of Jean de Meun's continuation proclaims its stance by rejecting that word: "Allas, in wanhope? Nay, pardee!" (4433).

C.S. Lewis wrote that Guillaume de Lorris "deserves to be called the founder of the sentimental novel" (1958, 135). The postwar years – after *both* world wars – have been hard on the word "sentimental," now rarely used in serious writing with positive connotations. The "novel of feeling" (which is probably what Lewis meant) avoids this objection, as does "the psychological novel," though emotions are as important in the *Roman* as the psyche is.

In any case de Lorris's poem is a foundational text for treatments of *domaines* in post-classical European literature: an archetype or paradigm for later efforts. The definition of a *domaine* offered in the Introduction to Part Two – a magical setting with a dark side, away from the world, characters having extraordinary experiences that test them – describes the first part of the *Roman de la Rose* well. That it is allegorical is no bar to membership. The walled garden of high society on a May morning rich in birdsong is certainly felt by the young man as a *domaine*: fresh, attractive, enchanted. His experiences and reactions are at first lyrical, but the longer he stays, and the more he learns about the ways of this world, the more complex and uncomfortable it becomes. He is sucked into situations too tempting to resist, tripped by unfamiliar codes. There are moments of ecstasy, such as the kiss, but agony follows and lasts longer – as the old French court song warned:

> *Plaisirs d'amour*
> *Ne durent qu'un moment*
> *Chagrins d'amour*
> *Durent toute la vie.*

We notice, even when he does not, that among the *glitterati* lurk some dubious characters: Danger, Jealousy, Idleness, Shame. Even "Love" has a very pointed way of initiating the dreamer. They all have their uses, but there are tolls to pay and nightmares to endure. Whether this *domaine* can last is not clear, but it is definitely ambiguous and exacting.

We do not know where de Lorris intended to go with his plot. Would the dreamer eventually have been accepted at court? Or would he have withdrawn, or been expelled, sadder but wiser? The sudden breaking-off makes the *Roman* even more useful as a broadly defining example; later *domaines* would make different choices at this fork, some providing a favourable ending of some kind, more opting for failure, chastening, or unhappiness. Ironically, the poem that de Lorris bequeathed us nearly eight centuries ago feels modern when its protagonist is left dangling inconclusively, licking his wounds, somewhere between hope, *Angst*, and recuperation. Even de Meun gives an unconscious tribute to the power of de Lorris' *domaine* in his passionate, prolonged rejection of its despairing excuse for a conclusion. (I had a similar reaction to the later chapters of Fowles's *The Magus*, wishing there could be another way out.)

M. Rousseau's Gardens

One example of the lasting influence that the *Roman de la Rose* had on later European literature is given by Paul de Man in his discussion of Jean-Jacques Rousseau's epistolary novel *Julie, or the New Eloise* (*Julie; ou la nouvelle Héloïse*). *Letters of Two Lovers, Inhabitants of a Small Town at the Foot of the Alps* (1761). It was an enormously popular novel in its time, possibly the eighteenth century's best seller; both Byron and Shelley toured the Alps sixty years after its publication with copies of the book in hand. De Man believed that he knew one source of its power.

The close similarity between Julie's garden and the love garden of
Deduit [Myrthe in the Middle English *Romaunt*], *which appears*
in the first part of Guillaume de Lorris' poem, is obvious. There is
hardly a detail of Rousseau's description that does not find its coun-
terpart in the medieval text: the self-enclosed, isolating space of the
"asile"; the special privilege reserved to the happy few who possess a
key that unlocks the gate.... ...Rousseau has deliberately taken all the
details of his setting from the medieval literary source, one of the best-
known versions of the traditional topos of the erotic garden. ("The
Rhetoric of Temporality" [1969], in *Blindness and Insight*)

There *are* parallels between *Julie* and the *Roman* (as well as significant diver-
gences). An outsider aspires to a higher social level: Julie's father is the proud Baron
d'Étange, whereas her tutor Saint-Preux (who compares her to a "newly opened
rose") comes of an "inconsiderable bourgeois" family (Rousseau 39-41; Letters
VII, VIII). "In the country" with her family, Julie walks in a grove, fantasizes about
being there with him, and plots with her cousin Claire to surprise him in a delightful arbor (50; XIII). He visits, and at sunset they kiss there with "burning lips";
she faints, and he feels "destroyed" (52-53; XIV). Julie banishes Saint-Preux to the
mountainous Valais district, which he enjoys, particularly a place whence he can
look across Lake Geneva and see her house. Returning, he asks Julie to elope with
him. She refuses, but receives him in her room, where (as she sees it) he "ruins"
her, with help from her "pity" (77-78; XXIX). That is, her *Pité*.

The arbor and Julie's bedroom are (briefly) "love-*domaines*" for them. Saint-
Preux has a different *domaine* in the Valais, gateway to the Alps. Despite being
"exiled" from Julie there – or perhaps because of that – Saint-Preux feels his mind
and soul to be more "grand" and "serene" among those "savage," unknown landscapes, where Parisian society seems a "vast desert" (57; XVIII; 64-67; XXIII).
Thus *Julie* glances at three *domaines* early on, none developed descriptively. But is
it a *domaine* novel, and, if so, of what kind? That requires closer analysis.

Post coitum we have much moral agonizing; seeking pleasure, they lost virtue
and happiness. The narrative could easily be allegorized, as De Man saw: *Bialacoil*,
Pité, Daunger, Jelousy and *Resoun* all appear. The relationship of the lovers has
as many vicissitudes as in the *Roman*. Trysts are proposed but missed; Julie

reproaches Saint-Preux for using immodest language while tipsy (he swears off wine); and she makes him an assignation in her room, where he pens her a note as he waits. His English friend Lord Bomston angers Julie's father by offering part of his fortune to them if they are allowed to marry, and denigrating the importance of noble descent. This occasions a *fracas*: the Baron strikes his wife, knocks Julie down, and forbids any contact with Saint Preux. *He* has a husband for her! Then something happens to Julie. Pregnancy? A miscarriage? In fact, both. Claire urges Julie to dismiss Saint-Preux, and convinces him to leave, ending Part I.

In Part II, Rousseau (posing as the "editor") warns that henceforth "the two separated lovers do nothing but speak irrationally and deliriously" (159; Part II: I). Saint-Preux does beseech, rave, accuse, question and exclaim; Julie never loses her head. Bomston offers her his estate if she elopes with Saint-Preux, but she refuses: an only child, she will not abandon her parents. Writing Saint-Preux, she condemns his self-pitying letters and forbids him to write her. He replies to Claire. Julie welcomes his return to reason, but will never marry him without her father's consent – nor marry anyone without Saint-Preux's! The mood becomes increasingly renunciatory. Saint-Preux thinks that if she will not marry without his consent, then she is saving herself for him; *he* will never marry anyone else. Julie writes that they will be together in their hearts and souls, but, "Sensual man, will you never know how to love?" (198; XV). She approves of Claire's marriage to M. d'Orbe, but reclaims the love-letters Claire was holding: they cannot be such close confidantes now. When Julie sends him an amulet bearing her image, Saint-Preux is ecstatic, and she is pleased. So they still have a relationship, but her next letter begins, "All is ruined!" Her mother has found the love-letters. Julie will have to confess all. This thunderclap ends Part II.

Their love-*domaine*, already just a memory, soon becomes a bad one. Claire condemns Saint-Preux for making Julie and her mother miserable, and demands that he give her up. His reply encloses a note to Mme d'Étange, promising not to see or write Julie. Claire praises this action, and says that Madame was moved by his note. But Julie's next letter announces her mother's death, calls Saint-Preux a "matricide," and renounces him (III: V). Saint-Preux asks Claire if he really killed Julie's mother. No, she replies: pleurisy did, and her father is guiltier than you. The Baron then writes Saint-Preux, demanding an answer to Julie's enclosed note asking freedom to marry. He replies sharply, but sends the release. Her next, distraught notes to Saint-Preux and Claire mention illness, disfiguring, and dreaming of a visit from Saint-Preux. Claire tells her that after hearing of Julie's *smallpox*, he rushed to see her and caught it himself. Julie writes Saint-Preux that she will always love him, but must obey her father. He replies that he cannot give her up, and notes that it was only one night. (I count two: see letters I:XXIX and LV.)

Claire informs Saint-Preux that Julie has married her father's old friend Wolmar. Julie's note confirms this: he must confine himself to loving her soul, and she wants to confess to Wolmar. Saint-Preux urges her to be prudent and *not* confess. He asks if she is happy. Julie describes Wolmar as cool, even-tempered, and almost 50, so she has reason to be happy, and marriage does not need love; it is about the duties of civil society: the mediaeval view that begot courtly love. If Wolmar dies before me, I will not remarry, she writes, and ends the correspondence. Saint-Preux, despairing, talks of suicide. Bomston advises him to grow up and do something: he could sail around the world with Admiral George Anson (an historical figure) for a few years! Saint-Preux agrees, and writes to tell Claire, who informs him that Julie is now a mother. Part III stops there.

Four years pass. Julie writes Claire that, for her, "Love is extinguished forever" (274; IV: I). She has not heard from Saint-Preux, and still wants to confess to Wolmar. Claire's husband having died, she is welcome to come live with the Wolmars. Claire likes that idea, but urges Julie *not* to confess. Saint-Preux's ship has been seen in the Atlantic, homeward bound. He writes Claire when he lands, asking to see them. Claire's warm reply encloses a note from Wolmar and Julie (who *has* confessed), inviting him to visit them. Saint-Preux writes Bomston about his kind reception at the Wolmars'. Claire too wants to see Saint-Preux, who is soon dispatched to her. She reports to Julie that he is realistic about the present but soft on the past; he will not give back the amulet with Julie's image (as she asked), which he wears over his heart: "the only comfort I have left..." (299; IX). He describes for Bomston the Wolmars' "Elysium," an enclosed garden full of birdsong, like the one in de Lorris. This is de Man's "Julie's garden," for keyholders only. It is not erotic, not a trysting-place for lovers, but more nearly a *dis*pleasure garden, chaste and expiatory.

Wolmar leads Julie and Saint-Preux to the arbor where they first kissed, sits between them on a bench, takes their hands and says, "My children,...I know you both better than you know me. It is only fair to make things equal" (316; XII). His friendship with the Baron led to the offer of Julie's hand in marriage; Wolmar was to replace the Baron's dead son (imagine the couple's reaction). On a visit he fell in love with Julie, and married her despite knowing of her affair. He has their letters, which she thought had been burned! "This conduct was inexcusable," he admits (319). Yet the letters evoked his esteem, which has since been confirmed. "[S]tay as you are," he urges, insisting that they embrace each other. He is going away for a few days, leaving them together, and looks unhappy when Julie hesitates. She asks advice of Claire, who encourages her to trust herself, stay there with Saint-Preux but take precautions, and keep a journal for Wolmar.

On the road, Wolmar writes Claire about his plans. When she and Saint-Preux join their *ménage*, Saint-Preux will educate the boys, she will manage the household, and Julie will tutor Claire's daughter. A commune! Saint-Preux informs Bomston that Julie has a secret sorrow that poisons her happiness. Her note to Wolmar includes the expression "your conduct is not the most proper," but she does not explain (332; XVI). Saint-Preux writes Bomston that he and Julie had a scare while rowing on Lake Geneva. They went far out, the wind rose, waves damaged the boat, and they had to land on the far shore for repairs. He took Julie up to the crags where he had once sat and looked at her house, showing her where he had carved her initials on a rock. He became so emotional that she drew him away, but rowing back he wept, and thought of drowning them both in the lake! She told him that this would be "the last time that [we] will speak in this manner" (338; XVII). Saint-Preux calls it a "dangerous day" (339) as Part IV ends.

In Part V, Bomston rebukes Saint-Preux for his sentimental letters. Grow up, he urges; act your age (now 30). If Julie were not so strong, you would be an adulterer by now. Saint-Preux replies that "the crisis of my folly" is past; with Wolmar back home, he feels serene (344; V: II). And he discloses Julie's secret sorrow: Wolmar is an unbeliever. His next letter describes Claire's arrival at Clarens and the warm reunion of the cousins. Another reveals that, at Wolmar's urging, he was 'reconciled' with the Baron (who *joked* about the days of his courtship!). En route to Italy with Bomston, Saint-Preux thanks Wolmar for purifying his heart, hails him as a second father, and agrees to tutor the boys. From Milan, he informs Claire that a nightmare about Julie's death so terrified him that he returned to Clarens, but continued after hearing Julie's voice in the garden. Saint-Preux writes Wolmar from Rome about Bomston's untidy marriage negotiations involving two women, and his own advisory role. Julie writes Claire (in Geneva) to say that if she loves Saint-Preux, virtue requires that she declare her feelings.

In Part VI, Claire admits but downplays that attachment. Bomston informs Wolmar that one prospective bride withdrew to take the veil, and that Saint-Preux shone as a confidante. Bomston has decided not to marry, but to join the Clarens commune! Julie writes Saint-Preux that it is wonderful to be able to address him innocently – "a real triumph of virtue." "What a career of honor" we have had, she exclaims (393; VI: VI). But a servant writes Saint-Preux that on an excursion to Chillon, Julie's younger son fell into the water and she jumped in to save him. The boy has recovered, but Julie has not: "...she will not recover." Why not? "...the shock, the fall, the condition she was in" (395; IX). The next note (from Claire and Wolmar) announces Julie's death. Later Wolmar writes Saint-Preux a detailed account of her last days. Feverish, fainting but clear-minded, she said her good-byes and gave Wolmar a final epistle for Saint-Preux (which he encloses). Julie died in Claire's arms. We are entitled to wonder why Rousseau decided to kill off his heroine thus. Was she, after all, a fallen woman who must pay for her sin? Will there also be a penalty for Saint-Preux, the tutor who abused his trust and seduced his pupil?

Julie's dying note to Saint-Preux looks both forward and back. "All is changed" (again); resign yourself, as I have. Heaven is thus "preventing misfortune." I have been deluding myself, thinking that I was "cured of my love for you.... One day more, perhaps, and I might be guilty!" (405; XII). She recommends a "chaste union" with Claire (406; XII). This appears to open a door to happiness, which Rousseau quickly slams. The last letter is from Claire to Saint-Preux. Come home, she writes. "I have loved you, I confess. Perhaps I do yet...." Still, any man once loved by Julie who would then marry another woman is "unworthy and base"; I would not even have him as a friend, and no man who speaks to me of love will ever speak to me again (408; XIII). But do come to Clarens and take up your duties: educate the children and convert Wolmar.

This is Rousseau's last word on the "chaste union" Julie proposed. Has Claire taken an extreme position that time may moderate? Like de Lorris' *Roman de la Rose, Julie* leaves readers and protagonists dangling. We must accept a truncated plot, or speculate beyond it. Will Saint-Preux return to Clarens as tutor, or commit suicide, as he has threatened? He is never heard from, or of, after Julie's accident.

Wolmar's soul is left unsaved. Will he become a Christian? Do we want that for him? And what about the Baron, arguably the novel's moral villain? He is never called to account for his class pride and peremptory actions, even in his own mind. Devotees of happy endings, poetic justice, or neat wrap-ups are left treading water. It is difficult to think of another once-popular and influential European novel whose conclusion is so inconclusive.

Rousseau's pattern is to create a *domaine* and then discredit it. The arbor of the first kiss is not revisited until Wolmar leads the ex-lovers there for his disclosure. Afterwards "he said, laughing, 'Julie, fear that refuge no longer. It has just been profaned'" (322; IV: XII). And it is balanced by Julie's innocent, approved garden, the Elysium. Their other *domaine*, Julie's bedroom, is spoken of later with horror: by her, by Claire, and by Saint-Preux. His refuge in the Valais is divisive. He brings Julie there and tries to share his strong emotions, but she sees the threat and pulls him away. None of these places is treated as a lovers' shrine by both, only with revulsion or fear. Rousseau's handling of them is moralistic; they were way-stations to fornication. Conventional morality deems them sinful, paternal authority makes them disobedient, and the lovers cannot prevail against such opposition. Briefly it looks as if Claire and Saint-Preux may find their own *domaine*, but Claire's grief rejects that. She is too scarred by her part in her cousin's affair to contemplate a closer relationship with Saint-Preux. And there the author leaves it.

This is not to say that Rousseau is irrelevant to a study of *domaines*. His stance was not unique. We have already visited *domaines* where the plot eventually undermines the magical place by showing its weaknesses or dark side, and traces its loss or the waning of its influence. In the *Roman de la Rose*, de Lorris brings the prospective lovers together a couple of times, only to show how various forces within and without push or pull them apart. Where it breaks off they are separated and their prospects are dark, nor can we know what the author intended to do with them. If Rousseau did have the *Roman* in the back of his mind, as de Man suggests, he had a precedent for making the choice he did: De Lorris might have taken the same road. And a good many *domaines* and relationships have been left up in the air since *Julie*.

What distinguishes Rousseau here – besides his often bizarre sensibility and tortuous analysis of psychological and emotional states – is his determined rejection of a happy outcome for his principal lovers (and Claire). Saint-Preux and Julie have a few moments of ecstasy in Part I, but the novel has six parts, and they spend the last five paying for their early pleasure. Note that only the Baron's aristocratic pride stands between the lovers and the union they could have in a "state of nature." Rousseau's most famous *dictum* is that "Man was born free, and is everywhere in chains" (*The Social Contract*). Are not the Baron's social views his chains? But Rousseau treats his pride as a given, and the lovers jumped the gun, dooming them to guilt, renunciation, and atonement. The novel's morality is distinctly bourgeois. The most charitable reading consistent with Rousseau's general social thought is that this was a needless tragedy caused by the arrogance and narrowness of an entrenched upper class.

Child's Play

We might expect to find the purest exemplars of the garden *domaine* in children's literature. Children playing in gardens, finding wonder and magic there, appear in the tales of many lands and periods. Robert Louis Stevenson's title *A Child's Garden of Verses* (1885) could stand for a large array of international writings celebrating gardens, using them metaphorically, or both. *Beginning* this chapter with "Child's Play" would seem to present the idea of the *domaine* in its plainest, simplest form. But the adult approach to this phenomenon is to see through to its drawbacks, so that would have meant ending with a demolition by Rousseau or another modern. I have chosen to close the chapter with children's stories – though not because they are paragons of purity or simplicity. It is amazing how much tendentious ideological content the adult authors of children's books – of books that we use for children – will pour into young minds. Think of *Gulliver's Travels* (philosophical and political satire, 'savage indignation'), *Robinson Crusoe* (colonial mercantile capitalism), *The Wizard of Oz* (monetary policy), or C.S. Lewis's Narnia books (eschatological Christianity). One would think that indoctrination were one of their purposes. Some variant of "Give me the education of the young and I will give you the man / the nation" is variously attributed to the Jesuits, Lenin, and Hitler. Adam and Eve are the simple people of this chapter.

For my purposes, we cannot do better than the "secret garden" motif, descended from the walled "paradise" of the ancient Middle East and popular with English writers around the turn of the twentieth century. England loves its gardens, and the great houses of the day might have a whole reticulated network of walled gardens, some of which had lockable doors in high walls.

Frances Hodgson Burnett, an English author who settled in the United States, is best known for her children's books, especially *Little Lord Fauntleroy* (1886) and *The Secret Garden* (1911). The latter tells of Mary Lennox, who grew up in India, where – neglected by her busy father and mother, left with an *ayah* (nurse), almost friendless, considered ugly and nasty – she was of course unhappy. Then cholera killed her parents and *ayah*. After a stay with a clergyman's family, "Mistress Mary Quite Contrary" was sent at the age of ten to live with her uncle and guardian Mr Craven, whom she had never met, in a huge manor-house on the Yorkshire moors. Still unhappy there at first, disliked and largely neglected, she gradually makes friends with Martha, a young servant, who tells her about her own family and life on the moor. Mr Craven, at their one meeting, appears as unhappy as his niece; he misses his wife, who died young a decade earlier, and spends most of his time abroad. He wants nothing to do with Mary, but before leaving again gives her permission to wander through the house and gardens. This provides some diversion, particularly as she learns to use the skipping rope that Martha's mother sends her. A couple of times she thinks that she hears distant crying, but the servants say it is only the wind.

One day Mary (assisted by a friendly robin who seems to lead her to a half-buried key) examines a stretch of wall with no apparent ingress and discovers a door to a locked garden that Martha mentioned. It was Mrs Craven's pride and joy, a special place that only she and her husband tended: they would lock the door and spend hours in there (there is no erotic innuendo: this is a children's book). But one day the branch of an old *apple* tree that she liked to climb broke; she fell, and died of her injuries. Mr Craven, bitter and grieving, locked the garden door and buried the key. Mary unlocks it and enters, full of "excitement, and wonder, and delight" (Burnett 24). In late winter the trees and roses look dead, yet it is "the sweetest, most mysterious-looking place any one could imagine." Even bare and silent (apart from the spritely robin), it is "wonderful," and "she felt as if she had found a world all her own." Mary discovers many green shoots beneath the grass and weeds, so "It isn't a quite dead garden" (25). With a sharp piece of wood she begins to dig and weed, clearing space for the shoots. Already the garden is therapeutic: she is active and interested in something for the first time. Despite the shadow of the tragedy, the "secret garden" is immediately a *domaine* for Mary, as it seems to have been once for the Cravens.

Mary's life and the plot quicken from this point. She asks more questions, mostly of Martha and the old gardener, Ben Weatherstaff, and their answers create further interest. "She was beginning to like to be out of doors," and to "run faster, and longer, and...skip up to a hundred" (27). Most of all she loves to work in the garden (she has read about such in "fairy-story books"), where the bulbs, "astonished" at this activity, seem "very much alive." Her social circle widens, too. The questions she asks about Mary's brother Dickon, a wild nature-boy who talks to birds and keeps orphaned animals, lead to a meeting with him. Soon she takes him into the garden, which for him, too, is a *domaine*: "It's like as if a body was in a dream" (31). He shows Mary that the roses are not dead, but will bloom in spring. They begin to work there together in decent weather.

Her new vivacity prompts Mary to trace the crying she has heard to its source. One dark and stormy night, carrying a candle, she follows many a corridor and turning until she finds – not a madwoman in the attic, though the Brontës feel close here – but a sickly, whimpering, bed-ridden boy her own age: Colin, Mr Craven's spoiled, surly son, of whose very existence she has been unaware. Considered too frail to venture outdoors, he has heard his doctor say that he will not live long. As they become friends, he expresses interest in this "secret garden."

They reveal their friendship to the surprised caretakers and the pace accelerates again. Colin must be obeyed (Mary calls him Rajah), so when he requests that a footman wheel him around outside, the doctor agrees. After Mary brings Dickon and his menagerie to meet Colin, Dickon replaces the footman as wheeler-in-chief. As spring approaches, the garden *domaine* becomes even more enchanting, sending Dickon on Thoreauvian flights ("Th' world's all fair begun again this mornin'"), and making Mary "so happy I can scarcely breathe"(47). They decide to bring Colin to the garden. Mary describes it to him, admitting she has been there, and they make their plan: Dickon will wheel him on a long garden tour; gardeners are to stay clear. All this is granted, and the garden works its magic. Upon entering, "he gasped with delight," crying, "I shall get well! And I shall live forever...!" (63). The first prediction is soon realized as he gains strength. His colour and disposition improve, and trying to rise and walk seems to make him healthier. Evidently there was never much wrong with him physically except being kept in bed; he just needed to be outdoors. Ben Weatherstaff (who climbs a ladder to see what the noise is all about) is moved to tears when he sees Colin walk, and joins their group. The garden is therapeutic for him, too.

In Chapter XXIII, "Magic," the author has the children ask what makes the springtime garden so healthful. Colin exclaims, "There is Magic [always capitalized] in there" (69). And even if it isn't "real Magic," still, "Something is there – something!" This seems to include the force that through the green fuse drives the flower, its effect on humans, and their passionate response. Magic is also what makes the garden a *domaine*. When the party has gathered, Colin, inspired by the "fakirs and devotees" in his picture-books, suggests that they all sit cross-legged under a tree, "like...a sort of temple" (71). When they do, their circle feels so "majestic and mysterious" that Weatherstaff wonders if he's at "a prayer-meeting," and Mary is "solemnly enraptured" (71). Dickon sits down holding a rabbit, whereupon crow, fox, squirrels "and the lamb slowly drew near and made part of the circle," as if illustrating one of Isaiah's prophecies (71). Colin chants that sunshine, flowers, and living are all part of the Magic. The religious mood is strong, yet Colin, walking around the garden for the first time, decides to become "a Scientific Discoverer" (72). *Scientia* originally meant "knowledge" in general, and Burnett was influenced by the writings of Mary Baker Eddy, so *Christian* Science is on her agenda.

Physical workouts soon join Magic in the *domaine*, whose powers grow daily. Colin badly needs strengthening, as does Mary to a lesser extent, so Dickon shows them exercises taught by a local physical culturist. Soon all three are doing them regularly, and Colin takes up running as soon as walking is comfortable. All look healthier. Even the manor-house seems poised to join the *domaine* when Colin notes that a hundred unvisited rooms "sounds almost like a secret garden" (78). But this idea is not developed; the focus remains on the garden's vital properties, which increase throughout the spring. Colin gives lectures on Magic, plans a book on it, and pronounces himself cured: "I shall never stop making Magic. I'm well!" It makes him "want to shout out something – something thankful, joyful!" (79) Ben suggests the Doxology. Colin, who has never been to church, wants to hear it, so all doff their caps and Dickon sings the hymn. Hearing that each line begins with "Praise," Colin says, "Perhaps it means just what I mean when I want to shout

out that I am thankful to the Magic.... Perhaps they are both the same thing" (80).

They all sing it, and old Ben tears up. Then in through the open door – the garden seems less secret now – walks Dickon and Martha's mother, Susan Sowerby. Praised by everybody, she has sent gifts and picnic lunches to Mary and Colin, and been told of the garden. Her arrival in effect ratifies the presence of Christianity and confirms its relevance. She tours the garden and is told about the Magic. Asked if she believes in it, she says (in her broad Yorkshire) that she does indeed:

> I never knowed it by that name but what does th' name matter?...
> Th' same thing as set th' seeds swellin' an' th' sun shinin' made thee a
> well lad an' it's th' Good Thing.... The Big Good Thing doesn't stop to
> worrit.... It goes on makin' worlds by th' million.... Never stop believin'
> in th' Big Good Thing...th' world's full of it...call it what tha' likes.
> Tha' wert singin' to it when I come into th' garden. (81)

Here is the Rosetta stone: the Magic is the Big Good Thing is the God of the Doxology, and Susan joins the others in its worship. Unpacking her picnic basket, she spreads their communion meal, with attendant animals as at the Nativity. The scene ends with Colin declaring his desire to see his father, and Susan agreeing: "Thy father mun [must] come back to thee – he mun!" (82).

In the last chapter, the Magic cures every physical or psychological ill in sight, and also manifests itself in Switzerland. Archibald Craven is still wandering sadly, but one day, walking alone in a beautiful valley, gazing on birds and wildflowers, he suddenly feels a little better: "I almost feel as if – I were alive!" (83). That will prove to be the day Colin first entered the secret garden. Craven wanders on for a time, but now there are periods of relief. One evening he falls asleep on a waterside terrace and dreams that a voice, "sweet and clear and happy," calls "Archy!" (83). It is his dead wife. "Where are you?" he cries. The dream ends with her response: "In the garden!" (84). When he wakes it is morning, and a servant has brought his letters. Among them is a note from Susan that says, "I would come home if I was you." Craven no longer, he hastens home and finds Colin in the garden with his friends. "Mr. Craven's soul [shakes] with unbelieving joy" as Colin *runs* up to him, shows off the garden, and tells his tale of "Mystery and Magic and wild creatures" (86). The garden, healing and gladdening all, triumphs.

The Secret Garden sold well, and gained influence as it was adapted for stage, film, and television. The tale has many facets. Besides Christianity (and Christian Science), there is enough emphasis on "the power of positive thinking" to delight Norman Vincent Peale. It is also a paean to English customs and character – especially the sturdy independence and dignity of Yorkshire country people – and even to English weather, all of them contrasted favourably with Indian servility and India's enervating climate. Of course the British would have been welcome to leave anytime; they had not been invited. Thus imperialism and even de facto racism are part of the story's mix. It is also a remarkably pure example of a positive *domaine*, with its strong magic, efficacious for all visitors and unambiguous in its operations, promoting health and happiness. Its only stain was Mrs Craven's fatal accident – another tree and fall in a garden – but that was ten years ago, the biblical parallel is not developed, and the sadness is expiated through Mary, Colin, and Mr Craven. There is none of the disappointment that plagues most adult *domaines*. The plot goes from unhappy beginnings and a locked, neglected garden to joyous well-being in a open, well-tended paradise. There Burnett leaves us, at the very top and with no shadow in sight. If Mr Craven regrets missing his son's childhood, or Colin resents having been left with doctors, nurses, and servants, they keep it to themselves. The closing song is "Happily ever after."

Nothing shows the sunniness of Burnett's *domaine* more clearly than setting it beside H.G. Wells's short story "The Door in the Wall," also published in 1911 (in *The Door in the Wall and Other Stories*), wherein a man remembers all his life a strange walled garden that he entered as a child. One evening shortly before his death, Lionel Wallace revealed this secret to the narrator, Redmond, who explains that they were once schoolmates. Wallace was a brilliant student, and has since become an MP who seemed destined for a Cabinet post. Late one October afternoon when he was 5 or 6, Wallace said, he was "wandering" through the streets of urban West Kensington, which sounds odd, but his mother died when he was born, his father was always busy, and a governess had charge of him: much the same situation as Mary and Colin. When young Lionel saw a green door in a white wall covered with crimson Virginia creeper, he badly wanted to enter, and the door was unlocked, but he felt that it would be wrong to go in. After hesitating, however, he barged through the door and into "immortal realities," he says solemnly (Wells 1911).

The walled garden was a *domaine*, as magical as any we have visited. Its air was exhilarating, its colours were luminous, and at once he felt joyful. One of two gentle panthers playing there came to him, purring for a pet, as tame as Dickon's animals in Burnett's tale. It was "an enchanted garden," he said, and *huge*, stretching (in complete disregard of Kensington) to far-off hills: i.e. larger inside than outside, like some of C.S. Lewis's creations in the Narnia books. It felt "like coming home," so he promptly forgot about his home, the city, obedience, etc., and became a "wonder-happy little boy – in another world." A long path led between (weedless) flower beds; a tall girl kissed him, spoke sweetly, took his hand and led him along an avenue under old shade trees; a Capuchin monkey hopped on his shoulder. There were parakeets, a palace, fountains, "many people...beautiful and kind" to him, and, in a court with a sundial and many flowers, playmates. As a *domaine* it was perfect, unblemished, a child's garden of wonders.

Then came a "sombre dark woman" in a robe, carrying a book, to take him away, though his playmates seemed unhappy and shouted, "Come back!" She led him upstairs and showed him a book whose "living pictures" moved, telling his life story, and these too were "realities." She tried to stop him at the one that showed him outside the garden's green door, but he insisted on turning the page. When he did, it showed only a "long grey street" in West Kensington at dusk. Nor was it just a picture, for he was suddenly *there*, on the street, weeping for his loss. He could not describe what now seemed the "translucent unreality" of that garden, he said. At home he was "thrashed" for telling lies. He prayed that he might dream of the garden, and did so.

We recognize the shape of this plot: "The Door in the Wall" is another reworking of the Genesis Garden of Eden story. As in Milton, or Rousseau's *Julie*, the *domaine* appears too soon, and being young and unready, the characters lose it and cannot return. And though Wells's garden is wondrous, it has sinister touches. Why does this "sombre dark woman" come and take Wallace away? Why are the children there? They seem to have seen this show before. Could they leave if they wanted to? The scenario is ominous in familiar ways: more trouble in paradise.

Wells adds a twist, however. Young Lionel longed to see the garden again, and how many streets could there be in West Kensington? He did not search for it (because his father punished and schoolmates ridiculed him), but one day he saw the door again by chance. Being late for school, though, he went on by. Actually, he happened on it several more times in later years. Each time, however, he was too rushed or distracted – en route to an interview, going to see a woman, conversing with friends – to try the door. He recognized the pattern, swore that the next time he *would* go in, regardless, but when he did see it again (in a different place) he did not touch the door. Would it have been open if he had? What would have been inside this time? He never knew, not having tried. He came to believe that these repeated failures said something profoundly damning about his character, and was filled with futile regrets. In the end, Redmond reads in the paper that MP Wallace has been found dead: he went through a door (in the hoarding around a construction site) in the darkness and fell into a deep excavation. He was 39.

Burnett's *The Secret Garden* has almost the opposite shape. "In the beginning," more than ten years before the story opens, the garden *was* charmed, a source of happiness. Then came the fall, death, misery, anger: lock it up and bury the key! That past, however, is only gradually pieced together; in the story's present, Mary finds the key and enters the garden a quarter of the way through the book. Its healing powers are felt at once, starting with her own unhappiness. From there on, its efficacy grows and spreads, drawing in others, pleasing or curing them as needed. This ascent has no falling-off: you can read the ending to children at bedtime and know that it will not disturb their sleep. Craven and Weatherstaff, who saw the garden of old, know that a *domaine* can darken and wound, but they have also witnessed its renaissance, and are duly moved. If Mr Craven had refused the calls from his wife and Susan Sowerby, persisting in his miserable odyssey, he *could* have come to resemble Wallace. But that is not Burnett's brief: Craven heeds the summons, goes through the door – and that makes all the difference.

Joni Mitchell's lines on Woodstock seem relevant to both of these tales:

> We are stardust
> We are golden
> And we've got to get ourselves
> Back to the garden

This imperative addressed to her generation and her perceived community is also a general proposition that would be recognized by Wordsworth, among others. Wells's Wallace has a vague sense that the lines are true and apply to him, but cannot find the time or summon the resolve to act on that belief; he dies young, unhappy and unfulfilled. Mr Craven, after years of lonely misery during which he alienated himself from what his beloved wife left him (and deprived their son of a father), hears the call and goes "back to the garden," where he finds a fountain of youth, a kind of magic, and family ties in abundance. That is a *domaine* in its most nearly perfect state.

CHAPTER 5:

Castle and Estate Domaines

EUROPE'S EARLIEST CONTRIBUTION TO LITERARY *domaines* was to locate their magic in a mediaeval castle, and later at the manor house or estate of a wealthy family or powerful man. The name I use for this function of literature is borrowed from such *domaines*. In the late Middle Ages and Renaissance they were centres of power and social recreation where people and reputations might be made or unmade quickly and decisively. Later they were venues set apart from the world and not subject to its rules. A *domaine* usually belonged to a lord (Latin *dominus*, abbreviated *dom*), who might rule it absolutely if he wished. Often a literary *domaine* revolves around such a person, who wields arbitrary power that he may use to manipulate his guests or give them a controlled "*domaine* experience." This may have sinister aspects, though it can also be governed by a desire to test or enlighten, or simple curiosity. I discuss several examples of this popular, long-lived species below. They range from the Middle Ages to the twentieth century, and fall into several sub-types.

Marie and Chrétien

This branch of my subject begins with two members of "The Renaissance of the Twelfth Century": Marie de France and Chrétien de Troyes. Biographical information about them is sparse. Both were French, but Marie lived in England for part of her life. Her editors date her literary career from 1155 or 1160 to around 1215; Chrétien's ascribe his major work to the 1170s and 1180s. They were contemporaries, then, two generations before Guillaume de Lorris. There is some evidence that Chrétien knew Marie's prologue to her *Lais*, and none that she read him, so her work may have been prior. Early research by James G. Frazer (*The Golden Bough*, 1890-1915) and Jesse L. Weston (*From Ritual to Romance*, 1920) showed that her Breton *lais* and his Arthurian stories drew on folk legends, magic lore, and religious mystery cults. These sources helped shape later *domaines* as places where anything might happen: transformations, improbable reversals, natural oddities, and other wonders. As writers and stylists, they could hardly be more different. Marie's tales are compressed and sophisticated; she has a light touch. Chrétien's material is more familiar to us through later Arthurian literature, but he is episodic, inclined to digress or pontificate, and apt to pad his plot, as if to achieve a certain length. He is more massive, she a better ironist. Between them they defined castle *domaines* and influenced many later writers, including T.S. Eliot and John Fowles.

Marie creates *domaines* less often than Chrétien does. Several of her *lais* (poetic tales) do have happy endings suggesting that one develops later. In *Bisclavret*, the wife of the titular knight, who is a werewolf, betrays him. Captured by the king, he is kept as a pet. When the wife appears with her new husband, the usually placid Bisclavret bites him, arousing suspicion. Given back his clothes, Bisclavret becomes a human knight again. The wife and her husband are exiled. In *Equitan* a betrayal is avenged, but there the tale ends; the survivor is left to seek his own happiness. Marie often approaches a possible love-*domaine*, but turns aside. In *Chevrefoil* – an incident in the legend of Tristan and Isolde – the lovers no sooner meet in the Cornish forest than they part again. Even *Eliduc*, Marie's longest and probably best-known *lai*, in which a knight has a wife in Brittany and a mistress in England, never portrays a lovers' *domaine*. Both relationships are tainted and undermined by lies and guilt. The knight cannot enjoy either woman without hurting the other. In the end conjugal relations yield to religion; each renounces earthly love, turns to God, and makes "a very good end." That may qualify as a *domaine* for some, but it is offstage, and unknowable.

Marie does present some *domaines*; however, *Milun* works from a clandestine affair towards one. A Welsh knight (Milun) has trysts with a baron's daughter, producing a love-child (kept by her sister). Milun goes a-tourneying on the Continent and the baron marries his daughter to a rich lord. After a long train of the daunting difficulties, cunning contrivances, love-tokens and coincidences that define "romance," the lovers are reunited, married under the good offices of their grown son, and "they lived happily ever after" (Marie, l. 532). A fuller example is *Guigemar*. The title character is a fine knight, but indifferent to love. When he is wounded by an arrow – Cupid's weapon of choice – a deserted ship sails him to a woman imprisoned in a castle tower by her jealous husband. They become lovers, but he is discovered and sent home in the empty ship. Later she escapes and the same ship takes her to him. After various complications they are reunited. Their year and a half in the tower is a typically fragile love-*domaine*: she is guarded and watched. They must leave the tower and survive challenges to win the right to (presumably) lasting love. Marie's editors consider it "one of the most satisfying of all medieval short narratives" (Marie 59).

Yonec presents a similar situation. A beautiful young wife kept in a tower by her jealous husband ("a rich man, old...lord of the land") longs for a young lover. It is springtime. A hawk flies in at the window and becomes a man, Muldumarec, the answer to her prayers. They are happy for a time – another tower love-*domaine* ("she had him all to her pleasure") – but her husband learns of their trysts and installs iron spikes on the window, which wound the hawk fatally. Muldumarec tells her that she is pregnant, that their son Yonec will avenge them, and departs. She jumps out of the tower, follows the trail of blood, and finds him. He gives her a ring and a sword before dying. When Yonec grows up, he, his mother, and her husband travel to a feast and stay in the abbey where Muldumarec rests. The lady gives Yonec the sword, accuses her husband of murdering her lover, faints and dies. Yonec decapitates the old man and replaces him as "lord of the land."

Lanval, a long and unusual *lai*, provides two *domaines*. Lanval is an Arthurian knight whom "Arthur forgot" (l. 19): he has neither wife nor treasure. But one day when he is out riding, he meets a rich and beautiful lady who offers him every-thing a wealthy beauty can offer. He gladly accepts, and they are happy for some time: the first *domaine*. Then one day "the queen" – not named but presumably Guinevere – sees Lanval and propositions him. When he refuses, the queen insults him, and he replies in kind. She goes to "the king" and accuses Lanval of assault. Lanval, tried by the barons, is in deep trouble until his lady arrives, confirms his story, and carries him off to the legendary land of Avalon, the 'Blessed Isle' of the Celts, where they can enjoy *domaine* number two indefinitely. Among other anomalous features, this *lai* depicts King Arthur (also said to have been taken to Avalon) and his court in an unflattering light.

Most of Marie's tales are set in and around castles or great houses belonging to royals or aristocrats. In those venues she sometimes constructs a *domaine*; when she does, love is usually central to it. Her domestic plots present fewer *domaines* and marvels: magically heightened experiences flourished best in the rarefied air of castles, baronial tables, and knightly valor. It is a pattern to watch for as we proceed.

CHRÉTIEN'S ARTHURIAN ROMANCES, WHICH MAY be dated with some confidence, are set in royal and knightly circles. His style and subjects hardly vary: larger-than-life people, heroic or beautiful, moving in an aristocratic world, to and from *domaines*, through adventures perilous and improbable. Exploits are strung like beads on a necklace, whose number could be increased or decreased at will. Marie's *lais* are tight, focusing on small scenes; Chrétien's long poems are loose and rambling. Some of his subjects are familiar from later treatments of Arthurian figures, while others need introduction. I follow D.D.R. Owen's prose translations (Everyman).

In *Erec and Enide* (ca. 1170), earliest of his extant romances, the Arthurian knight Erec, a prince of Wales, woos and weds Enide, the daughter of a poor family, then retires to marital bliss. That does not suffice for romance, however: murmurs about his diminished fame spur Erec to new knightly exploits, which bring the couple even closer together. When his father dies, Erec is crowned in Brittany. While "on the road" he has more chivalric encounters than I could recount. Everything is high, idealized, "the best" or "the most." Each castle is a dazzling *domaine* of noble, courteous people. Enide's cousin is "more beautiful, more attractive and fairer than was Helen" (Chrétien 84). King Arthur's liberality is epic: at Nantes, he knights over four hundred "sons of counts and kings," and doles out cloaks of velvet and ermine, not "serge or rabbit fur or brown cloth." Alexander the Great "was poor and mean compared with him," for neither he nor Caesar "dared spend as much as was paid out at that court" (88). And so on.

Chrétien's next major work, *Cligés* (1176), bulges with two generations, two heroes, and two parts. In the first a Greek prince, Alexander, sails to Britain with a band of Greek warriors and rides to Camelot, askng to be knighted by King Arthur. Alexander excels as soldier and courtier, helping to put down a rebellion and marrying Soredamors, a lady-in-waiting. She bears him a son, Cligés. When

Alexander's father dies they return to Greece, but find that Alis, Alexander's brother, has taken the crown. Alexander lets him keep it, but he must not marry, so that Cligés will succeed him. In part two, Alexander and Soredamors die. Alis breaks his promise and sets off to marry a German princess, Fenice. She and Cligés, however, fall in love. The marriage proceeds, but Fenice's wily nurse Thessala gives Alis a potion that causes nightly wet dreams, which he mistakes for consummation! Cligés goes to Camelot and shines there. Once knighted by Arthur, he returns to Constantinople, where he and Fenice conspire with Thessala to fake Fenice's death. She lies still and silent on a bed, though Alis's sceptical doctors tear her flesh – seen as a "crucifixion trope" (Fenice means "phoenix"). She survives, and Cligés takes her to a tower with a garden, where they enjoy each other until discovered; then flee. Here Chrétien finally seems to tire: the couple hide until Alis dies, then emerge and are crowned emperor and empress.

Domaines take several forms here. One is Arthur's court, for both Alexander and his son; the relationship between Camelot and its visitors is ideal. When the Greeks appear, "All the nobles fell silent, very pleased at the sight of these handsome, well-mannered young men...good-looking and well built" (Chrétien 97). Alexander, "well schooled in wise and elegant speech," salutes Arthur grandly: "... since God created the first man there never was born a God-fearing king of your might. ...your widespread fame has brought me to your court to serve and honour you" (97). Arthur replies in kind. It is a classic meeting of the mediaeval liege lord and his faithful vassal.

Courtly *domaines* flourish wherever chivalry does. In the field, the Greeks and English defeat the forces of a rebel count, whom Alexander captures and presents to Arthur. "The king...praises and esteems Alexander highly," and "the others make much of him..." (122). Arthur rewards them well. Cligés lives by the same code. In Germany he is challenged to single combat by an aggrieved duke. Cligés begs Alis to allow him to fight the duke, and weeps for joy when his suit is granted. He defeats the duke, and the Greeks depart victorious. Reaching England, Cligés does not go straight to Arthur's court and reveal his identity, but enters a tournament incognito and defeats every opponent. His long combat with Gawain is halted by King Arthur, who calls it a stand-off and ends the tournament. Arriving at court, Cligés is acclaimed as the star of the tourney by everyone, and reveals his identity at the king's request. Gawain "embraces and welcomes him," Arthur "loves and honours him," and "everybody else behaves warmly towards him" (161).

After travelling and jousting in Britain and France, Cligés returns to Constantinople and shares a love-*domaine* with Fenice. Hidden in a tower, "they embrace and kiss each other"; "there is nothing that one of them wishes in which the other does not acquiesce" (178). This lasts for over a year. The next summer Fenice revels in their walled garden. Heavily treed, protected against the sun and prying eyes, it is all that she desires, a veritable Eden. "There Fenice goes for her pleasure, ...there they indulge their joy and delight." The author gives them (and us) a luxurious and extended love-*domaine*. "Now Fenice enjoys great comfort: ...she lacks nothing she wants...she is free to embrace her lover beneath the blossom and the leaves" (179). But one day a knight looking for his hawk climbs the wall and sees them; they have to flee. That *domaine* is adjourned. After Alis's death they marry, but continue to treat each other as lovers.

Lancelot, or the Knight of the Cart (1177) rests on the idea that riding in carts is dishonourable (because prisoners did so). Sir Lancelot of the Lake – one of the Round Table's best-known knights (for gallantry, knightly prowess, and love for Queen Guinevere) – is in disgrace because he briefly rode in a cart, but when Guinevere is abducted by Prince Meleagant, he goes in pursuit at once. After various improbable fights and tests, he defeats Meleagant, liberating the Queen, Kay (Arthur's seneschal), and many other captives, it being "the custom in that country that, once one person left it, all the others would leave" (Chrétien 237). This refers to foreign captives, but it is odd to call it a "custom," since (we are told) it has never happened before. Lancelot spends a night with Guinevere there, leaving blood on her sheets (he cut his hands pulling the iron bars out of her window), which makes Meleagant suspicious. But Lancelot conceals his injury, and Kay (whose sheets are bloody from his wounds) is accused instead, so Lancelot can fight Meleagant for her honour, and wins. The Queen returns to Camelot; Lancelot is captured by Meleagant's followers and held in a tower for a year or so. Finally Meleagant's sister finds and releases Lancelot (who had once done her a favour), enabling him to reach Camelot in time to accept Meleagant's challenge and kill him.

Lancelot is weak in motivation, causality, and logical sequence, but strong on wonders. Some actions can be read as religious allegory; others draw on Celtic folk tales that admit marvels, so the inexplicable is common. Strange people keep popping up with unlikely stories, and Lancelot (not named until halfway through) just has to play along. Oddities abound: the unhelpful (under)Water Bridge, the very unpleasant Sword Bridge, et cetera. But *domaines* are tolerant of surrealism, and in *Lancelot* almost every court and castle is wondrous, every knight a hero or a villain, and every lady at least beautiful. "Meleagant's castle" is actually his father's, good King Bademagu, who deplores most of his son's conduct and sympathizes with his captives. While he is ineffectual at stopping Meleagant's cruelty, the king does give us a sense that the *régime* is fundamentally just. Yet we are left with many questions. Why *didn't* he check his son? Why haven't other kingdoms invaded to free their captured subjects? And if all those captives – men, women, children – were brought there somehow, why did Lancelot have to come over the Sword Bridge? These, however, are not questions of the sort that a Chrétien romance feels obliged to answer.

Yvain, the Knight With the Lion (1177) is another long, digressive collection of adventures with magical episodes in castles, fields, and forests, but is worth examining as an example of Chrétien's mature work and a contribution to the historical development of the literary *domaine*. It opens at Carlisle, where King Arthur is holding court. The first note struck is the decline of courtly love: at the time of this story it was flourishing, but now it is debased. Queen Guinevere encourages the knight Calogrenant to recite his adventures in the forest of Brocéliande in Brittany. He says that a giant told him about a boiling spring whose water, if poured on a certain rock, produced thunderstorms. Calogrenant rode there, did as instructed, and caused a tempest. A knight appeared, complained of the damage, challenged Calogrenant to joust, and defeated him. Yvain promises to avenge him, but Kay the seneschal mocks Calogrenant, for which the queen rebukes him. King Arthur then arrives, hears Calogrenant's story retold, and vows to see the spring for himself. The whole court decides to accompany him.

Yvain goes on ahead, finds the spring and evokes the storm. A knight arrives to fight, but flees when Yvain wounds him. Chasing him across a drawbridge into a castle, Yvain barely escapes as the portcullis falls, slicing off the rear half of his horse. The knight disappears. Yvain is trapped, but a beautiful damsel comes to say that he was once good to her at court, so she will save him. Lending him a ring that confers invisibility, she leaves. Angry men enter, looking for their lord's murderer, but see no one. Then a *really* beautiful lady appears, weeping over her husband's corpse, borne in on a bier. His wounds bleed again (because they are in the presence of his murderer). The mob go to bury the body; the lady follows. The damsel places Yvain where he can watch the burial, warning him to keep quiet. Yvain is smitten with the wife of his victim and torn by love-agony and emotional conflicts. The damsel, finding Yvain lovesick, urges her lady to take a new husband / protector in this dangerous world. The lady resists at first, but overnight talks herself into Yvain, though she knows he killed her husband! Brought together by the damsel, they have a courtly-love conversation and are reconciled. The lady then presents him to her advisors, who concur. Yvain and the Lady Laudine of Landuc are wed immediately, their nuptials hastened by reports that King Arthur is approaching with a large retinue of knights. Their intentions are unknown, and Yvain is now the defender of Laudine's real property and assets.

As the Arthurians approach, Kay is heard disparaging Yvain. Arthur pours spring water on the slab, the heavens open, and Yvain gallops up, unrecognized in his helmet and armor. Kay asks for and is granted the combat; Yvain unhorses him at once. When Arthur asks his name, he gives it, delighting everyone but Kay. Yvain recounts his adventures and invites the court to his castle, where Laudine and the town welcome them with music, dancing, and ceremony. For a week there is joy and flirtation; Gawain (the "sun" of chivalry) and Lunete (the moon), who saved Yvain, hit it off splendidly. Gawain then convinces Yvain *not* to retire to wedded bliss, but to return to the knightly jousting circuit. Laudine grants him a one-year leave of absence. Oh, not *that* long, exclaims Yvain. Laudine gives him a magic ring that will protect any "true, loyal lover" (316). They part tenderly, and Yvain rides away from his (feudal and love) *domaine* with the court.

But the two knights make the round of tournaments for a year *plus six weeks* before Yvain notices that he has overstayed his leave. Then he sees Lunete riding toward them, sent by Laudine to denounce him as a "disloyal traitor, liar and deceiver" (317). She yanks the magic ring off his finger and departs. Stunned, Yvain goes off alone, knowing that "he has robbed himself of his own joy" (319). He becomes a different literary type, the "wild madman" of the woods – hunting game with bow and arrow, eating raw venison, accepting bread and water from a hermit – until the day two damsels and a lady find him asleep in the woods, naked. One damsel recognizes him by a facial scar, and observes that a healthy Yvain could help her mistress fight Count Alier. The lady produces an ointment (given her by Morgan le Fay) and says, Rub some on his temples. The zealous damsel proceeds to "anoint him all over," leaves him some fine clothes, and withdraws (321). When he awakes, no longer mad, and dons the clothes, she escorts him to their castle.

Chrétien then returns to heroic action. Count Alier and his force arrive, Yvain leads the defence, takes the count prisoner and presents him to the lady. She invites Yvain to remain as her lover or husband, but he, "deaf to all entreaties," declines that potential *domaine* and departs (326). Riding through the forest, he sees a dragon biting a lion and scorching it with flames. Killing the dragon earns him the lion's undying gratitude; they hunt deer and camp together. Reaching the magic spring again, however, Yvain recalls his trespass, faints, then wakes and wounds himself on his sword. Loud lamentations are heard in a nearby chapel, from a maiden who will be executed tomorrow for treason. Her crime? Helping Yvain and betraying her lady. It is Lunete! She says that Laudine's seneschal made the charge; her only hope is to have a champion fight for her against the seneschal and his two brothers by tomorrow. Yvain volunteers. But the castle where he stays that night is beset by a murderous giant. His host says that King Arthur and Gawain cannot help, being distracted by the queen's abduction (see *Lancelot*). Yvain promises to fight the giant early tomorrow morning, before his noon date with the three knights at the chapel!

Yvain and the lion manage to kill the giant (whose dwarf is sent to tell Gawain), then rush to the chapel and fight the three brothers. Laudine is among the spectators. Yvain wounds one, the lion kills one, and the other two surrender. All are bleeding. The defeated knights are burnt on the pyre they intended for Lunete. Chivalry hath its rules: they acted basely. Yvain, *not recognized by Laudine* in his armour, rides off carrying the wounded lion in an improvised litter on his shield (it must be a puma or cougar, not an African lion.) Both are healed by people at a nearby house.

Then the scene shifts. Two sisters, disputing the ownership of their deceased father's land, seek judgment from King Arthur and Gawain. The older claims it all; the younger goes in search of Yvain as her champion. When she falls ill, her servant continues the quest, and finds him and the lion. She makes her pitch: by helping to right a wrong you will have "increased your chivalry" (349). Yvain agrees that "No man can win fame by inactivity." So they start off, but the way is long and has

its distractions. Reaching the town of Pesme Avanture, Yvain enters, despite warnings, and sees three hundred damsels in rags, sewing – perhaps western literature's
first sweatshop. D.D.R. Owen, the translator, suggests that Chrétien was "protesting against the exploitation of female labour in the developing silk industry" in
France (Chrétien 519n. to l. 5188). Natives of the Isle of Maidens, the women are
held by two demons, who force their king to send thirty more women each year;
they will remain slaves until the demons are killed.

In the castle garden Yvain is welcomed by a gentleman, a lady, and their lovely
daughter. The two demons arrive and demand that Yvain shut up his lion before
they fight. In a deplorable fit of sportsmanship he complies, and is hard pressed
until the lion escapes confinement and mauls one demon; Yvain then kills the
other. Hailed as victor and liberator, he has the captives released, but declines the
gentleman's offer of his daughter in marriage: another possible *domaine* skirted.
Yvain leaves along with the grateful seamstresses, and after their ways part the
damsel conducts him to the disinherited sister, who is overjoyed to see him.

She, Yvain, and the lion travel to the castle where Arthur is staying. Arriving on
the eve of the day of judgment, they spend the night "in a small, cramped lodging
where nobody knew them" (360). Gawain appears at the castle the next morning
(also incognito), having agreed to be the older sister's champion. The dispute will
be settled by a combat between the two champions, neither of whom recognizes
the other (Chrétien foreshadows the tormented emotions of sentimental novels
and the extremes of melodrama). The spectators dislike the older sister, who
still demands all of the patrimony; the younger will accept the king's decision.
But Arthur *refuses* to decide ("he would never take the responsibility for making
peace": 364). Chrétien would rather show him as indecisive than give up his
combat. They fight all day to a draw; then stop to exchange compliments on each
other's prowess. Finally Gawain gives his name. Yvain, "utterly dumbfounded and
dismayed," throws down his weapons in "rage and anger," and tells *his* name (365).
Gawain is equally amazed. They dismount, make peace, and embrace, each declaring himself vanquished. Arthur then settles the dispute by declaring in favour
of the younger sister: the knights can adjourn the combat honourably. They are
disarmed and their wounds dressed.

Now at last the plot can be resolved. Yvain returns to his castle and Lady
Laudine. Lunete tricks her into accepting "the Knight with the Lion" as a protector,

then reveals that he is Yvain. Laudine is furious – "You'll have me love in spite of myself that man who neither loves nor respects me" – but will keep her word, "now that I *have* to be reconciled with him" (372; my italics). Yvain apologizes, promising never to wrong her again. Laudine takes him back halfheartedly ("I should perjure myself if I didn't": 373), but Chrétien says they lived happily ever after. It is, as D.D.R. Owen puts it, a "psychologically unsatisfying" conclusion (520n. to l. 6761).

Domaines are a vexed ideal in this romance. Yvain finds magic and love early, marrying Laudine and settling in the castle, but soon leaves to follow the jousting circuit with Gawain. Though chivalry can be a kind of *domaine*, it is an alternative, not an adjunct, to the love-in-a-castle type. During his knightly roaming, Yvain twice has (after Laudine casts him off) opportunities to marry other lovely ladies with castles. He gives these short shrift and resumes the role of the wandering paladin, until Fortune's wheel returns him to the lost *domaine* of Laudine's castle. Following a dubious reconciliation with his wife, Yvain again settles down with her – or does he? Do we believe that he will stay home this time, and not go off to seek glory with the next knight who teases him about *losing merit* or *dreaming his time away* in marriage (314-15)? Is that what we, the readers, want for him? It is not only in respect to Laudine's feelings that the end of *Yvain* is "psychologically unsatisfying." Can the hero of a chivalric romance plausibly morph into a good husband? Will that be 'happily ever after' for him?

Chrétien's earlier poems are between 6700 and 7100 lines long. *Perceval: The Story of the Grail* (1182) breaks off at 9234. Its plot is bifurcated: Chrétien begins by telling how Perceval, a crude Welsh youth crazy about knights and chivalry, left for Arthur's court as his mother collapsed and died (a desertion for which he is later blamed). He succeeds amazingly, winning every fight from the first without any training. Then we suddenly leave him to hear the exploits of Gawain. Later Chrétien returns to Perceval, then goes back to Gawain, but ends in the middle of a scene. Scholars suggest that *The Story of the Grail* is a collocation of two poems – one on each knight – neither finished at Chrétien's death, which is plausible (Owen, 524n. to l. 4741).

The convoluted structure accords with the motivation for many of the knights' adventures. Incidents hardly worth recounting pile up rapidly, often leaving unan-swered questions. Both knights behave inexplicably (especially their reticences) and fall into apparently hopeless predicaments, yet always eventually succeed. We soon stop worrying about them: these heroes are too big to fail. *Perceval* is like a dream after you realize that it is *only* a dream. That is not necessarily a flaw – *domaines* are often dreamlike – but readers expecting or hoping for some development of the religious symbols will be disappointed. By the end, the Grail (appearing in western literature for the first time), the Bleeding Lance, and the Fisher King are no closer – which is quite dreamlike – and have almost been forgotten: Gawain is busy trying to find his mother and sister.

Perceval offers a number of *domaines,* but never dwells in them. For both heroes, the chivalric ideal of errant adventure in the service of a noble king, distressed damsel, or nearly hopeless cause, in hope of fame and reputation, is The One Quest. Castles may provide rest and opportunities to be recognized, puzzled over, celebrated, and / or tested. Perceval sends the Haughty Knight of the Heath, whom he has defeated, to "Caerleon, where King Arthur was holding court, though on a very intimate scale, for only three thousand knights of repute were there!" (427). Chrétien's tone is veiled here: is he trying to impress us, or is the exclamation point a wink? Gawain has quite a different experience at a castle in the forest. Despite being warned about the Wondrous Bed, which "no knight ever sat on...and left it alive," Gawain sits on it – fully armed – and provokes a show worthy of an old carnival steam organ. The bed screeches, "all the bells ring," "all the windows open and the marvels are disclosed and the enchantments revealed" (477). These include "arrows, ...more than seven hundred" of which strike his shield and wound him before the windows close. Then a "churl" kicks in the door, admitting a "ravenous lion" that attacks the knight. Gawain decapitates it and his host enters, smiling, to assure him that "the marvels of the hall have ceased for ever": he can disarm now. This turns out to be true, although why Gawain would believe him is a mystery. Chrétien's descendants here include many a House of Horrors.

MARIE AND CHRÉTIEN LEFT A heterogeneous literary legacy. The romance was many things to mediaeval readers: epic, historical novel, melodrama, chronicle, pulp fiction, Harlequin romance. Much of what it put into the stream of time would sink or be rejected – "romance" became a term of opprobrium, indicating a rank below what "realists" wrote – but it was still a stratum. Part of that detritus was a tradition of bringing powerful or beautiful people together in great houses, castles, or towers for any number of reasons: exercise of power, social display, love, testing, verdict. These places might be wondrous, offering splendour, or magical, enchanted. And what happened there was important, owing to the high status or quality of the inhabitants and visitors; trials would be remembered and lives changed. In other words, they were *domaines*: an important part of Marie's and Chrétien's bequest to European literature. Even the British country-house drama ("I have brought you all here tonight for a particular reason") is a distant relative.

Gawain, Bertilak, and Morgan

The mediaeval chivalric romance that Marie and Chrétien popularized spread across Europe to intrigue other authors and audiences. Some two centuries after they flourished, "the *Pearl* poet" (after another poem in the same manuscript) composed *Sir Gawain and the Green Knight* (abbreviated *SGGK*) in Britain. Despite its difficult Northwest dialect of Middle English and use of old-fashioned alliterative verse, the poem has been judged "the finest Arthurian romance in English" and "quite in the spirit of French romance" (Baugh 236). But while *Sir Gawain* makes free use of the marvellous, it also employs a kind of realism rarely found in Marie or Chrétien. The *Gawain* poet lives in the world of Kafka's *Metamorphosis*: if you grant the absurd initial premise (a man wakes up as an insect, a decapitated knight picks up his head and resumes the conversation), then what follows seems almost reasonable. It *might* have unfolded that way! The frame is unbelievable ("romantic"), but the conduct of the action inside that frame is not. The poem focuses on two *domaines*, with a section that bridges the gap between them.

The opening bears traces of a seasonal vegetation myth. It is January 2nd, and the company – Arthur and Guinevere, knights of the Round Table, ladies and gentlemen – are feasting in Camelot. This is a *domaine* if there ever was one: the Arthurians at their peak, joyous, confident, famous. But *domaines* are fragile, and when a strange knight rides his horse *into the banqueting hall*, the chatter stops. Man and horse are green, with gold trim. The knight is a big one, "Half a giant," yet seemly in his bearing, with fair features (*SGGK*, l. 140). With a sprig of holly in one hand and a large axe in the other, he offers to trade strokes with any knight.

That is, he will take one today, and return it in one year. Gawain rises to claim that honour, and all agree that he should be chosen. The Green Knight kneels and bares his neck. Gawain cuts off his head with one stroke of the axe. There is nothing vague or formulaic about the beheading: blood gushes from the body, the head rolls around on the floor and under the table, so that "Many...found it at their feet" (l. 428). The body, however, rises, picks up the head, mounts his horse and points the head toward the high table. The eyes open and the mouth speaks, charging Gawain to meet him at the Green Chapel a year hence. Then horse and rider wheel and depart. Not surprisingly, "All who saw it say / 'Twas a wonder past compare" (ll. 465-66). Their revels now are ended. *Domaine* #1 is shaken, troubled to its depths by this apparition. How can anyone explain, much less defeat, such an opponent?

Part II tolls the passing seasons: green spring, then summer, followed by harvest and autumn gales. But the days grow short when you reach September; all too soon it is time for Gawain to leave Camelot. He departs after a long description of his armor, especially the five-pointed star or pentangle (an ancient sign with magical and religious connotations) on his shield. The five points stand for his five virtues, among other things. He rides northeast through the Welsh wilderness, which the poet wants us to feel in winter. It is hard travel through mountain and forest in cold, wet weather; overnighting in his armor ("Near slain by the sleet he sleeps in his irons": l. 729); fighting with "wild men of the woods" (721), beasts (including bulls, bears, and boars: this is alliterative verse), and serpents – probably dragons. He asks anyone he meets about the Green Chapel, without success, but on Christmas Eve and Christmas Day he prays, crosses himself, and sees "a wondrous dwelling" on a mound within a moat (764): the comely castle that will be *domaine* #2.

Initially all is propitious. He is welcomed by the lord, whose knights, squires, and servants seem delighted by his arrival. At the feast that evening Gawain identifies himself, which pleases the lord, and meets his beautiful lady. Well entertained, he rests until the third day, when he says that he must find the Green Chapel by New Year's. The lord laughs. It is only two miles from here: you can stay three more days and still make it easily! He proposes to hunt each day with his men while Gawain relaxes at the castle; then each evening they will exchange whatever they gained that day. Gawain agrees. If he thinks the lord's idea of sport strange or has any reservations, he hides them as "the two laughed together" (l. 1113). Thus ends Part II.

Part III covers the rest of Gawain's sojourn there. The hunting party leave early on Day One, the latch of his bedroom door is lifted soon after, and the lady enters. Still abed, Gawain feigns sleep. She sits on his bed, he pretends to wake, and the verbal jousting begins. I'd like to rise and dress, he says. What, quoth she, I have captured the knight "Whom all the world worships" and I should just let him go? (l. 1227). We are alone, the others have gone out or are asleep, and "My body is here at hand, / Your each wish to fulfill..." (1237-38). The dialogue is sexy and teasing on her side, courteous and defensive on his: 'I don't know what you've heard about me', 'I am not worth your attention', etc. She protests that he *cannot* be the famous Gawain, for "Had he lain so long at a lady's side," he "Would have claimed a kiss" (1299-1300). Oh, he replies, "I shall kiss at your command" (1303). And "...she turns toward him, takes him in her arms, / Leans down her lovely head, and lo! he is kissed" (1305-06). Some believe "the *Pearl* poet" was a woman. Once the lady departs, Gawain dresses and goes to mass. His host returns late with several deer they killed. After helping his liegemen dress one, he presents the venison to Gawain. The knight responds by kissing his host, who asks where he won this boon. Gawain replies, "That was no part of the pact" (1395). This is well received, and they renew the agreement for the morrow.

The poet chooses not to reveal Gawain's feelings here, but the knight must know by now that this *domaine* has an agenda and rules of its own. In the late Middle Ages and early Renaissance, hunting and fishing were common metaphors for courtship and seduction. The first of Sir Thomas Wyatt's *Ten Sonnets* begins, "Whoso list [wishes] to hunt, I know where is an hind," while the most famous of his *Songs and Lyrics* is "They flee from me that sometime did me seek" ("I have seen them gentle, tame, and meek, / That now are wild..."). That was written almost two centuries after *Sir Gawain*, but the *Pearl* poet's Gawain lives in such a world.

Day Two has a similar structure: fun and games at home and abroad. Once the lord sallies out with his men to hunt the boar, his spouse, the *chatelaine*, begins her own pursuit.

The lady, with guile in heart,
Came early where he lay;
She was at him with all her art
To turn his mind her way. (ll. 1472-75)

Warm and apparently willing, she again chides him for not behaving as "courteous knights" do (1491). Returning serve, Gawain says that he fears to offend. But you are strong, you can take whatever you want, she says. I would never threaten force, he replies, nor accept "any gift not freely given," but "I am yours to command, to kiss when you please" (1500-01). She kisses him, but then complains: Two days, and I have yet to hear "the language of love" from you (1524). Where are your manners? Do you think I don't want to hear what other women do?

In hope of pastimes new
I have come where none can spy;
Instruct me a little, do,
While my husband is not nearby. (1531-34)

Gawain pleads his obligations under the code of hospitality: "my aim is to please, / As in honor behooves me" (1546-47). And though she "tried many a time, / ...to entice him to sin, / ...so fair was his defense that no fault appeared" (1549-51). Kissing him again, she withdraws. When the lord returns and presents Gawain with a slain boar, the knight kisses him twice. He plans to leave tomorrow, he says, but his host insists that he stay another night, promising to have him at the Green Chapel on New Year's Day. Gawain agrees.

The next day the hunters depart early and the lady breezes through Gawain's door in minimal battle array, "Her face and her fair throat freely displayed; / Her bosom all but bare, and her back as well," and kisses him (ll. 1740-41). She "Made so plain her meaning" that Gawain is torn between the code of courtly love, his status as a guest, and desire for this "high-born beauty" (1771, 1770). He plays dumb and laughs a lot. Then she proposes an exchange of gifts. Gawain protests that he has none, and will not accept her ring. Then take my girdle (belt), she says: it protects the wearer ("...no hand under heaven...could hew him down": 1853). That sounds useful, so he accepts. Just don't tell my husband, she adds, and he promises. That evening when the lord returns and gives him a "foul fox pelt" (1944), Gawain kisses him three times, but does not mention the belt. Mediaeval readers, fond of bestiaries, would notice the pattern of the three hunts, from deer (associated with royalty) down to the wild boar (ugly, fierce) and the fox (low cunning, "foul" smell); and might also have seen a parallel to the human drama: the lady's increasingly foxy seductions, Gawain's weakening defence, and his moral error: the unreported gift.

Part IV begins on New Year's Day: dark, stormy, and alliterative.

> *The clouds in the cold sky cast down their snow*
> *With great gusts from the north, grievous to bear.*
> *Sleet showered aslant upon shivering beasts;*
> *The wind warbled wild as it whipped from aloft... (ll. 2001-04)*

Gawain's dressing and arming – including "his love-gift, the lady's girdle" (2030) – are recounted sombrely. Then he mounts and follows the guide lent him by his host (not in evidence this morning) out into the snow. The sun has not yet risen. They ride silently toward the Green Chapel, "Under bare boughs" and "Over high cliffs," until the guide halts on a hilltop (2077-78) and tries to dissuade Gawain from proceeding: You have no idea what you are up against; the "villain in yon valley" strikes down everyone who goes there, being "heedless of right" (2106). Your death is certain. Turn aside, find "some other land" (2198, 2120). I won't tell! This is the kind of temptation that Gawain is trained to resist, however. He thanks the man, but, he says, *I* would know that I was a coward. I have to do this. It is Gawain's most heroic moment, in the classical sense. The escort turns back, and the knight rides down a slope into the valley to meet his destiny.

But where is the Green Chapel? There is only a snowy mound by a stream and cataract. Dismounting, he sees that the mound *is* the Green Chapel, buried under a snowdrift. Then he hears a clattering noise, "As if someone on a grindstone ground a great scythe" (l. 2202). His shout is answered by the Green Knight, who is sharpening his axe. Understanding intimidation, he continues whetting for a few minutes; then bursts from a cave, "Hurtling out of hiding with a hateful weapon," and vaults the creek, using his axe (2232). Now the pace quickens. The Green Knight compliments Gawain on his fidelity ("It seems your word holds good!...you have followed me faithfully and found me betimes") before telling him to remove his helmet and bare his neck (2238, 2241). Gawain complies, but as the axe descends, he "glanced up aside...And his shoulders shrank a little from the sharp iron" (2265, 2267). If he were not an Arthurian, we might say that he flinched. The Green Knight remarks that this cannot be "Gawain the glorious" (2270). After all, *he* "moved not a muscle" a year ago (2274). Gawain's reply is splendid; after all the tiptoeing around with milady, he shows himself quite willing and able to speak his mind:

> "Strike once more;
> I shall neither flinch nor flee;
> But if my head falls to the floor
> There is no mending me!" (2280-83)

The second swing is just "a mighty feint" (2290). This infuriates Gawain, who defies the green man: "thrash away, tyrant, I tire of your threats" (2300). The Green Knight obliges. This time

> He hammered down hard, yet harmed him no whit
> Save a scratch on one side, that severed the skin;
> The end of the hooked edge entered the flesh,
> And a little blood lightly leapt to the earth. (2311-14)

The graphic "hooked edge" reminds us of the stakes. Gawain is up in a flash, feet well apart, repossessed of helmet, shield, and sword. The one stroke granted has been taken; anything else is a fight. The axeman laughs and says that their contract has been fulfilled. He explains that the first two strokes were for your first two mornings *with my wife*: he is the lord of the castle. The cut on the third chop punished Gawain's failure to exchange *all* gifts, "For that is my belt about you" (2358). Still, he says, on the whole you have been admirable; my wife "made trial of a man most faultless by far / Of all that ever walked over the wide earth" (2362-63).

Scholars have praised the poem's acute psychological analyses, and the subtle play of emotion is equally interesting. Gawain, long fearful and beset, now suddenly excused, does not feel relief or gratitude, but stands "in a study...a long while, /...gripped with grim rage" at himself (2369-70). Then "he shrank back in shame" (2372). His host may pardon him, but Gawain condemns his own conduct. "Cursed be a cowardly and covetous heart!" he snaps, handing the girdle back; "Now am I faulty and false" (2382). The hitherto stern giant now laughs, excuses all, says keep the girdle, and invites him home to a feast. Gawain, however, is inconsolable. I have been here long enough, he says, but please commend me to your wife and the other "honourable ladies, / That have trapped their true knight in their trammels so quaint" (2411-12). What "ladies"? Gawain delivers a tirade against women; mediaeval misogyny, never far below the surface, erupts.

> ...*if a dullard should dote, deem it no wonder,*
> *And through the wiles of a woman be wooed into sorrow,*
> *For so was Adam by one, when the world began,*
> *And Solomon by many more, and Samson the mighty*
> — (2414-17)

Biblical examples of women's perfidy from Eve onwards were often cited (and contested). Gawain ignores his host's claim that this was his own scheme. He does accept the gift of the girdle – not as a token of knightly achievement, but as a reminder of his failure.

Before departing he asks the name of his host. "Bertilak de Hautdesert," replies the green man, Hautdesert being his barony and castle. ("Desert" could mean "hermitage," or have the older sense of "a deserted place.") He explains that his magical powers come from Morgan le Fay, the great sorceress of Arthurian legend, who lodges at his castle, appearing as an "old withered lady," companion to his wife (2463). Half-sister to Arthur (and Gawain's aunt), once the lover of Merlin, she stage-managed everything in order to test "the surfeit of pride / That is rumored of the retinue of the Round Table," says Bertilak (2457-58): the sole motive and authority given for *domaine* #2 to test *domaine* #1 so profoundly. Certainly the role ascribed to Morgan le Fay will intensify Gawain's anti-feminism. When Bertilak re-issues his invitation to "come feast with your aunt," Gawain repeats his refusal and leaves immediately.

Gawain's mood does not lighten during the ride home or at Camelot. Welcomed as a hero, he rejects that title, but "Confessed all his cares and discomfitures," showing the scar on his neck "That he got in his disgrace at the Green Knight's hands" (ll. 2495, 2499).

> *With rage in heart he speaks,*
> *And grieves with many a groan;*
> *The blood burns in his cheeks*
> *For shame at what must be shown. (2501-04)*

Clearly his trauma at Hautdesert affected Gawain deeply, nor is he shown as recovering. Still blaming himself, he displays the belt as a "sign of sore loss" suffered because of his "cowardice and coveting," a "badge of [his] false faith" (2507-09). He wears it aslant (over one shoulder, tied under the other) to confess his sin to all Camelot, but many Arthurians reject his interpretation, and "with gay laughter" decide to wear "A belt borne oblique, of a bright green" themselves (2514-16). Ironically, Gawain will now be reminded of his shame by everyone he meets.

I HAVE DISCUSSED *SIR GAWAIN* in some detail because it represents a marked advance in the literary deployment of the castle-*domaine*. Camelot and Hautdesert have enough similarities to support our definition, and enough differences to round the concept. Both are imposing seats of the high-born powerful, places of privilege, chivalry, and *courtesy*. They are exclusive, and not apologetic about it, but there is also a sense of *noblesse oblige*. Tests may occur at any time. Camelot is enjoying its New Year's feast as the poem begins, but when the Green Knight rides into the hall and demands an exchange of strokes, someone has to respond. Gawain does, and the rest of the poem is his. Of the two *domaines*, this is the more conventional. Arthur is the Good King: rational, fair, without supernatural powers, and a magnet for high-minded knights. Camelot is a locus of chivalry; Chrétien had a young Greek warrior travel there to be stamped "knight." It provides the bookends for the poem, receiving the Green Knight, dispatching Gawain, and welcoming him home.

Hautdesert – remote, unsung, and under dubious governance – is quite another matter, though it too offers a throng of good company who can welcome a knight and hold a feast. Its magic is literal, strong, and conspicuous; indeed, it is difficult to say whether Bertilak or Morgan le Fay is in charge. He is the front man, but she decides to test Camelot and empowers the Green Knight to do so. This is our best example yet of the devious *domaine*, with its hidden agenda for visitors: a place designed to take you off guard. Not the direct challenge, but the sneak attack must be feared. Gawain's chivalric code has not prepared him for this, only for open threats. In devious *domaines* there are two trials: the one you know about, and the other one. Gawain thinks that his physical courage is to be tried at the Green Chapel, whereas the real test is in the castle; the Green Chapel only delivers the verdict. When Bertilak finally explains, Gawain sees that he has been judged on his morals, not on his bravery, and is thunderstruck. It is the kind of *domaine* that John Fowles would develop in *The Magus* and *The Ebony Tower*. He pointed readers toward his French debts, but *Sir Gawain and the Green Knight* is fully as relevant.

Elizabethan Estate Masques

The reign of Queen Elizabeth provided some interesting cases of life imitating art, blurring the arbitrary, even tenuous boundaries between real and literary *domaines*. (Estate masques also foreshadow John Fowles's managed, tendentious *domaines*.) Two points of historical context are useful. The type of theatre known as masques offered spectacular entertainments in which allegorical or mythical characters wearing disguises or masks enacted plots, often classical with a moral dimension, using music, dance, and dialogue. They were popular at court and among landed aristocrats in the late sixteenth century (not yet at the popular theatres where Shakespeare mostly worked). The other point is that the Queen liked to make "progresses" with her courtiers through large tracts of England, on which they would visit favoured nobles' estates and be guests in their manors. This was both an honour and a burden for the host: how was Her Majesty to be diverted during her stay, which might last days or even weeks? In the 1570s, one of the answers was to "stage" a masque, in some cases one composed for the occasion, making use of natural venues on the estate. Some scripts for and accounts of these shows have survived and are printed in Stephen Orgel's *The Jonsonian Masque* (1965), to which I am deeply indebted in this section.

In 1575 one such progress stopped at the Earl of Leicester's Kenilworth Castle for nineteen days. Leicester, at the time a suitor of the queen, spared neither trouble nor expense to entertain her, arranging concerts, dances, and drama – separately, or in a masque. He employed four men, including the leading poet of the day, George Gascoigne, to compose and stage the masques. Evidently some of these entertainments were announced and spectators invited to attend, but others just seemed to occur as the guests strolled the extensive grounds of the estate. We have two records of what transpired when "The Deliverie of the Ladie of the Lake" by William Hunnis, Master of the Chapel, was presented on July 18th. One is in Gascoigne's *The Princelye pleasures at the Courte at Kenelwoorth* (1576), which prints the texts, and the other is a letter by Robert Laneham, a courtier, to

a friend, describing the performance; Orgel quotes at length from both. Together
they provide valuable clues to what the royal entourage saw and heard that afternoon. Laneham describes the scene (I have modernized his quaint but distracting
Elizabethan orthography):

> *about five o'clock her Majesty in the chase hunted the hart.... Well,*
> *the game was gotten: and her Highness returning, came there upon*
> *a swimming mermaid...Triton, Neptune's blaster: who, with his*
> *trumpet...as her Majesty was in sight, gave sound very shrill and sono-*
> *rous, in sign he had an embassy to pronounce.* (quoted Orgel 39)

Obviously something was afoot. When the Queen and Triton – life and myth –
met at the bridge over a lake, he told her a tale both classical and British. One Sir
Bruse Sauns Pittie, he said, is harassing The Lady of the Lake because she imprisoned his cousin Merlin the magician to punish his lusts. Neptune has given her
this lake as her refuge, but she is trapped there. Merlin has prophesied that only
"the presence of a better maide then hir selfe" can release her. Neptune has sent
him to request that Elizabeth "would no more but shew her selfe, and it should
be sufficient to make sir *Bruse* withdrawe his forces" (quoted Orgel 40). Triton
blows his trumpet and commands winds, waters, and animals to be still until the
evil has been exorcised and the Lady released. This was accomplished wordlessly
(Elizabeth's mere presence sufficing), but Laneham narrates the sequel:

> *At which petition her highness staying, it appeared straight how Sir*
> *Bruse became unseen* [presumably he had been seen until then],
> *...and the Lady by and by, with her two Nymphs, floating upon her*
> *movable islands...approached toward her highness on the bridge.*
> (Quoted Orgel 41; spelling modernized)

The Lady of the Lake thanked the Queen not only for herself, but on behalf of
all women threatened by bruisers. The spectators knew that they had witnessed
a morality play in which maidenly virtue triumphs over male force, but the show
was not yet over. A large raft was rowed toward them, bearing a semblance of a
dolphin whose fins were the boat's oars. On its back sat Proteus, and within it
was hidden a consort of six instrumentalists, accompanying Proteus as he sang
the Queen's praises to conclude the masque. Laneham found this music deeply
stirring, and evoked for his friend the "delectable ditty of a song...so deliciously

delivered," the "melodious noise" of the unseen instruments with their "parts so sweetly sorted,"

> *...and this in the evening of the day, resounding from the calm waters: where presence of her Majesty, & longing to listen, had utterly damped all noise and din; the whole harmony conveyed in time, tune, & temper, thus incomparably melodious: with what pleasure..., with what sharpness of conceit, with what lively delight, this might pierce into the hearers' hearts, I pray you imagine.... As for me, surely I was lulled in such liking, & so loth to leave off, that much ado, a good while after, had I, to find me where I was.* (Orgel 43; spelling modernized)

The impressionable and articulate courtier had stumbled upon a *domaine* from which only the royal wishes and nightfall could draw him. The troupe's preparations had been impressively thorough. Leicester must have been delighted with the outcome.

Those who created and produced "The Deliverie of the Ladie of the Lake" (the "most famous of the Elizabethan entertainments," says Orgel) had constructed a pleasing form that was capable of further development (38). Though planned and scripted, it looked like a "happening" and nearly achieved "interactive theatre." But because it did not offer a real choice, it seems rather static. The Queen is not asked to say or do anything but "show herself" (as she was already doing); her presence alone made sense of all subsequent action. She could have just turned her back and walked away, but the committee knew that Elizabeth would not waste an opportunity to play the heroine. A "static" monarch can still be "impressive" and "dignified."

But the estate entertainment that Orgel considers "the finest," Sir Philip Sidney's "The Lady of May" (1578), is fully interactive (38). "The Lady of May" (aka 'the masque at Wanstead Castle') dares to offer royalty a choice. While we do not have a spectator's report on it, the 1598 folio of Sidney's works describes the scene and narrates the actions of participants, as well as giving the speeches. Orgel quotes it from *The Complete Works of Sir Philip Sydney* (Cambridge, 1922).

> *Her most excellent Majesty walking in Wanstead garden, as she passed down into the grove, there came suddenly among the train*

[her retinue], *one appareled like an honest man's wife of the country,*
where crying out for justice, and desiring all the Lords and gentle-
men to speak a good word for her, she was brought to the presence
of her Majesty, to whom upon her knees she offered a supplication....
(Quoted Orgel 44; spelling modernized)

At this point, what reality pertained? Was this a real-life supplicant – not uncommon, though this is bold – or an actor? Did she come out of a social frame, or a dramatic one? There would have been a moment of uncertainty. The woman explains that her daughter, the May Lady, has two suitors, a shepherd and a woodsman, whose addresses "encomber her" (quoted Orgel 45). Her neighbours are divided in their opinions of the suitors' merits, so would the Queen adjudicate? She hands Elizabeth a paper, asks her to continue on this path until she meets the protagonists, and runs off. In order to refuse, the Queen would have had to turn back from her intended walk. And why should she? This is entertainment.

Read aloud, the "Supplication" proves to be a graceful piece of complimentary verse, worthy of Sir Philip ("the flower of chivalry"). It expresses both awe of Elizabeth's high station, and a willingness to appeal to her warmer, milder qualities: a mixture of emotions typical of Maryolatry. Almost at once "there was heard in the woods a confused noyse," which proves to be half a dozen shepherds and as many foresters, each band trying to pull the Lady of May to their side (quoted Orgel 47). The mere sight of the Queen quiets them, however. Now the real talking begins, which proves messy; it takes time for a clear theme to emerge from their argument.

First up are two rustics who try to present the case to the Queen, but both are disasters. Lalus, a "substantial" shepherd, is so "euphuistic" (fancy), and the schoolmaster, Rombus, so pedantic, that the May Lady dismisses them as tedious fools. She describes the suitors herself: Espilus, a rich shepherd, mild-mannered but dull; and Therion, a lively but ill-tempered forester. She sums up the question pithily: "whether the many deserts and many faults of *Therion*, or the verie small deserts and no faults of *Espilus* be to be preferred" (quoted Orgel 49) – a formulation worth remembering when the verdict is rendered.

Now the two suitors appear and agree to state their cases in a formal "singing" contest: a staple of classical pastoral poetry. They recite alternate six-line stanzas of iambic pentameter. Espilus leads off, so Therion rebuts – considered the stronger position in debate – which is one reason why Orgel believes that Sidney favoured Therion's suit. Not that the outcome matters to us, or mattered to the courtiers, any more than it matters that Espilus has two thousand sheep and Therion two thousand deer in the wildwood: these are still diverting developments as you stroll anyone's *domaine*.

When the suitors conclude, two more debaters come forward: Dorcas, an older shepherd, and Rixus, a young forester. The plot seems cluttered here, or stalled. How long is the speakers' list? Sidney seems to want to explore what the suitors' occupations had traditionally represented: contemplative shepherds, active foresters. Dorcas does advocate contemplation, but Rixus is a very relaxed "man of action"; his idea of work is "to see the long life of the hurtless trees...they hinder not their fellows..." (quoted Orgel 52; spelling modernized). He is really a park ranger, watching over the forest and drawing moral lessons from it. The contemplation vs. action theme dissolves – there is some of each in each way of life – leaving us two examples of on-the-job contemplation. Again the forester is given the position of rebuttal, and Orgel states that there is "no question" that the rebutter has triumphed (53).

The contest being ended, the Lady of May asks the Queen for her verdict. And her choice is...Espilus, the shepherd. Orgel is amazed: "Since the case is so clear, we may find it amusing enough that Elizabeth should have picked wrongly, but astonishing that no one since then should have noticed the error" (53). We may. Also amusing is his consternation that Elizabeth, who *heard* the speeches once, delivered an immediate verdict different from that of a modern scholar of the pastoral *reading* them in tranquillity. He points out that the final song seems to assume that Therion won, and speculates that she chose Espilus "because shepherds are the heroes of pastoral" and this was a pastoral (Orgel 54). But she could have been moved less by the suitors' speeches than by the May Lady's summation of their merits: "many deserts and many faults" versus "small deserts and no faults." Thinking of her own court, the Queen might have decided that "no faults" sounded good, or that Therion seemed a bit sharp; the duller Espilus might be easier to live with, or manipulate. Musing on "this fiasco," Orgel notes that the text we have may be the "original script" that was altered for "the actual performance" (54-55). True: what the Queen heard may not have been exactly what we now read in a text published years after the author's death.

That text does portray the setting and conduct of a "*domaine* experience" we have not seen before. The Garden of Eden was managed, but supernaturally; the romances of Marie and Chrétien narrate wondrous events at unreal castles. Only *Sir Gawain and the Green Knight* approaches the effect of the Elizabethan castle-masques, where performances are not announced as such: they just occur, like a deer glimpsed in the forest. Orgel notes that the masques ignore "theatrical conventions," presenting an action as if it had "the same kind of reality as everything else," and "the same sort of immediacy" (39, 44). The play's the thing, but if it is not *called* a play, we must infer the nature of the thing. That inference is not difficult when newcomers speak in verse or impersonate Triton, yet there is still a new set of possibilities. What do these unforeseen characters want? How should we respond? Nothing was asked of the Queen at Kenilworth except to stay there and exude moral authority, but at Wanstead she judged a debate and made a choice, i.e. played a role. Probably the attending courtiers had their own views on the masque and were drawn into the drama. In any case, Sidney's masque suggested how a *domaine* might be used for purposes of instruction as well as delight: *utile et dulce.*

Building on Sand

The father of modern literary *domaines* is Henri Alain-Fournier, whose novel *Le Grand Meaulnes* (1913) impressed John Fowles deeply. In "A Personal Note" in *The Ebony Tower*, Fowles writes that after studying French at Oxford, he "learned to value what [he] couldn't over the years, forget" (1974, 110). That was Alain-Fournier, between whose work and Fowles's *The Magus* (and "The Ebony Tower") stretches an "umbilical cord." *Le Grand Meaulnes* is a powerful, flawed, dark, conflicted book, intwined with the author's life and central to my topic. Linking Arthurian romance and Fowles, it delineates the modern *domaine*. The book is magical in either French or English, and the titles of its translations point to what has been seen in it: *Le Grand Meaulnes* (Augustin Meaulnes, the protagonist), *The Wanderer* (he is happiest on the road), *The Lost Estate* (the *domaine perdu* that he finds), *The End of Youth* (its coming-of-age aspect). Robin Buss's *The Lost Estate* is the most faithful translation. There are two related stories here: the novel, and

Alain-Fournier's own life, as revealed in his letters from England (*Towards the Lost Domain*). We *should* read them synoptically – in parallel columns – but since that is not feasible I begin with the novel; the biography's relevance and poignancy are seen and felt only when you know that.

Le Grand Meaulnes opens on a November day in the 1890s in provincial France: villages and small towns among extensive fields, long hedgerows, and belts of forest. The narrator, François Seurel, a boy of 15, attends a school run by his father, M Seurel. One Sunday a new pupil arrives, a "*grand garçon*" of 17 named Augustin Meaulnes (pronounced "mown"). François says his "new life" started then. Bigger and bolder than other boys, who dub him "*le grand Meaulnes*," he is indifferent to rules. One day, hearing that M Seurel's parents are coming for Christmas and will arrive at the railway station at Vierzon, he commandeers a horse and buggy and sets off alone to meet them. But he does *not* pick them up, and the horse and buggy return without him that night. Not until the fourth day does he reappear, exhausted and tattered. Clearly something has happened, but "LGM" does not blurt out his story, nor is the author in a hurry to tell it.

That night, however, in the garret room they share, François sees, when Meaulnes doffs his school clothes, that underneath is

> ...a strange, silk waistcoat,...which fastened at the bottom with a tight row of little mother-of-pearl buttons....a delightfully quaint garment, of a kind that might have been worn by the young men who danced with our grandmothers at a ball around 1830. (Alain-Fournier 2007, 32)

It is not a garment that he possessed before. He has been...Somewhere, and (like Wells's time traveller) has a relic as proof that he was *there*. François begs for the story, in vain. For weeks LGM looks agitated and paces the floor at night, wishing he were *there*. In February, François, convinced that "he must have met a girl..., like the hero of a novel," promises to help him find the place that summer (34). Meaulnes agrees, and tells him what happened. His account forges a bond between them and describes the *domaine*. All we know is what François reports of LGM's story.

> ...it was to remain the great secret of our adolescent years. But today, now it is all over, now that nothing is left but dust

of so much ill, of so much good,
I can describe his strange adventure. (36)

This narrator sounds much older than 15, and his tone is portentous. The adventure to be revealed is set in the frame of 'it's all finished'; *"il ne reste plus que poussière"* [nothing left but dust] (Alain-Fournier 1971, 56). If ever an early warning was issued about an unknown *domaine*, it is here.

Meaulnes set out on a cold afternoon, a blanket around his legs. After the first village there was an unsigned crossroads. No one was there, he guessed wrong, and the road soon deteriorated. He shouted to one driver, could not hear the answer, but drove on through a stark scene: "All around him...the vast, frosty plain, featureless and lifeless" (Alain-Fournier 2007, 37). He fell asleep in the cart, and when he awoke "the landscape had changed. No longer were there the distant horizons..., but little fields, still green, with high fences" (37): from Siberia to the *Midi*! Meaulnes saw that he had missed the Vierzon station and was lost. The horse started limping, and as he pried a pebble from her shoe, dusk came on. He considered going back, but the village was far behind now, he had lost the way while he slept, and he felt a "desire to achieve something" (38). Proceeding along a narrow rough road, "he felt anger, then pride – and a profound sense of joy at having, unwittingly, broken free [*évadé*]." A stream running across the lane stopped him, but he saw a light. Leaving the horse in a meadow, he crossed fields and a stream to a cottage, where an old couple fed him and invited him to stay. Meaulnes wanted to fetch the horse, though night had fallen. Unable to find the mare and buggy, or relocate the cottage, Meaulnes spent a cold night in a sheepfold. There he recalled a childhood dream of waking up in a "long green room with tapestries like forest greenery" in an "enchanted mansion," where a girl sat sewing with her back to him (45).

At dawn he was off, limping on a sore knee through "the most desolate region of the Sologne" (2007, 46). The whole morning he saw only one person, "a shepherdess in the distance" with her flock – Arcadia? – but when hailed "she vanished." He saw no one else, nor any house, and heard no birds as he walked. The sun shone on a "perfect wilderness, clear and cold." Antarctica? In mid-afternoon he finally sighted "a grey turret rising above some fir trees, perhaps a deserted manor house. He kept on, and between white posts at the corner of a wood he found an avenue and started down it.

> *After a few steps, he paused, astonished, overcome by a feeling that*
> *he could not explain....an extraordinary feeling of contentment raised*
> *his spirits, a feeling of perfect, almost intoxicating tranquillity: the*
> *certainty that he had reached his goal and that henceforth only hap-*
> *piness awaited him.* (46)

This was the place he had not known he was seeking, "*Le Domaine mystérieux.*" If Meaulnes 'stumbled' on it, as some translations say, it was a long, arduous, complex stumble.

The avenue had been freshly swept. When Meaulnes heard voices, he hid in the trees. Some children passed by. "Aren't we allowed to do just as we like?" asked one, and a girl said, "we're allowed to organize the festivities just as we want" (47). A third mentioned "Frantz" and his fiancée, so it must be a wedding. "But are the children in charge here? What a peculiar place!" thought Meaulnes (48). He went through trees toward a building, before which was a courtyard full of old carriages. Climbing on top of one, he crawled through a half-open window into a huge room crammed with antiques: "old swords," "old books," "lutes with broken strings" (49). In an alcove was a bed that he cleared of things so that he could lie down and rest in "the half-dark of the winter evening." He drifted off to sleep hearing wafts of distant music, remembering how in his childhood his mother would play the piano and he "would listen to her until night fell."

He awoke after dark. A lantern had been lit, and he heard footsteps, voices. Two men came in saying it was time to wake up: people were arriving. One, who seemed to be in charge, was fat; the other, called "gypsy," was tall, thin, and "pathetic" (51). As they left, the gypsy said that "Mr. Lie-abed" should dress as a marquis, adding that *he* would play Pierrot, a pantomime character. They "had laid out everything needed" for a costume party; in boxes Meaulnes found "young men's clothes from long ago" (53). So he dressed, stepped out, and followed a young dandy into the main building. Inside, "he was surrounded by laughter, singing, shouts and the sounds of pursuit" (55). The place was *en fête*, but he was lost and "afraid of being discovered" or "mistaken for a thief." When he asked two dressed-up peasant boys about dinner, though, they took his hands and led him to a big dining hall with a blazing fire, trestle tables and white tablecloths. Chapters XIII and XIV are titled "The Strange Fete" (*La Fête Étrange*). "*Étrange*" connotes "foreign," yet Meaulnes felt comfortable as he ate. The diners were mostly old peasants who said little and did not all know each other; they seemed like "all-forgiving grandparents" (58). It was a scene with roots in the Middle Ages: serfs invited to a feast in the manor house or castle on a special occasion.

He heard that these festivities were all about Frantz de Galais, the scion of the owners' family, much loved and indulged. He was a student, or a sailor, and had gone to Bourges to bring his fiancée here to be married. Teenagers danced through the room, followed by children running from "Pierrot": the tall gypsy. In the corridors were other dancers and sounds of distant music. Meaulnes "felt he was someone else," and "began to chase the great pierrot...as though in...a theatre where the performance has spread off the stage": characteristic emotions on *domaine* visits (59). He saw magic lantern shows and "mingled with a happy throng" (60), swimming in what Freud called "the oceanic feeling." Tiring eventually, he found a quiet room where younger children sat reading. In the next room, a young woman with her back to him was softly playing the piano. After the noisy dining hall, he was now "in the midst of the most tranquil happiness imaginable"(60): *"plongé dans le bonheur le plus calme du monde"* (Alain-Fournier 1971, 90). As he sat listening, two children came over and sat on his knees to look at a book.

> *Then it was a dream like the one he used to have. For a long time,*
> *he could imagine that he was in his own house, married, one fine*
> *evening. And that the charming stranger playing the piano, close by,*
> *was his wife...* (Alain-Fournier 2007, 61).

The next morning he rose early and put on a venerable black suit and top hat, as someone had recommended. Outside he found another weather shift, "as though he had been transported into a spring day": frost was melting, birds were singing, and the breeze felt warm (62). With no one else in sight, he wandered through courtyards and gardens, once seeing his reflection in a fishpond:

> *And he thought he saw another Meaulnes, no longer the schoolboy*
> *who had run away in a peasant's cart, but a charming, fabled being,*
> *from the pages of the sort of books given as end-of-term prizes....* (63)

A boat excursion was planned for that day, so he looked for the landing. Behind the chateau, instead of woods, he saw "reed beds, extending as far as the eye could see," and a lake that came right to the walls (63). As he walked he heard footsteps: "...two women, one very old and bent, the other a young woman, blonde, slender," blue-eyed and tall, whose simple attire made her seem "an eccentric..., perhaps an actress," or the chatelaine's daughter (64). Meaulnes could not take his eyes off her as pleasure boats and other guests arrived. He followed the young woman, who sometimes glanced at him, onto one of the boats. The weather kept changing: even with "the winter sun, it felt cold," and the wind came up, yet out on the water "It was like being at the heart of summer," until "an icy gust of wind reminded the guests at this strange party that it was December" (65).

After a while the passengers were landed to stroll on woodland paths, where

> ...everything happened as in a dream.... Meaulnes walked along an avenue with the young woman ten paces ahead of him. Before he had time to think, he was beside her, and said simply, "You are beautiful." (65)

She took a side path without a word. Meaulnes walked on, regretting his clumsiness. When she approached again, he risked an apology. She forgave him, but as he babbled on she remarked, "I don't even know who you are." He said, "I don't know your name, either" (66). They came to a house where other guests were gathering, which she said was Frantz's house, and gave her name as Mlle Yvonne de Galais. So she *was* the chatelaine's daughter, and Frantz's sister.

After lunch Meaulnes told her his name and occupation: student. Yvonne trembled, looked anxious, and whenever he "suggested anything" would say cryptically, "What's the use?" (67). When he asked if he might return some day, she replied, "I'll be expecting you," but later, as changeable as the weather, she said, "We're two children. We've been foolish. This time we mustn't get into the same boat. Farewell, don't follow me." And when he did start to follow her she turned and stared at him. He froze, wondering what to do, and she was gone.

Now pony races were on offer, but the guests were growing uneasy: where were Frantz and his fiancée? Everyone returned to the house. In his room, Meaulnes prepared to depart, listened to the wind, watched raindrops streak the window, and felt unaccountably exultant.

> More at peace now..., the boy felt entirely happy. He was there, mysterious, a stranger, in the midst of this strange world.... What he had

far exceeded his expectations. Now it was enough, to lift his heart, for
him to recall that young woman's face.... (69-70)

Seeing a light in the adjoining room, he peeped in. A young man in a traveller's cape was pacing, whistling a sea chanty and reading some papers. Seeing Meaulnes he came over, grabbed his lapels and insisted that he must explain something. He "appeared totally distraught"(70).

The party's over. You can go down and tell them. I've returned alone.
My fiancée won't be coming. Whether from principle, or fear, or lack
of trust....I'm going to get ready to go away again. (71)

It was Frantz, of course. Meaulnes went downstairs, but his message was not needed: the guests were saying goodbye and heading for the carriages. There was "nothing left except to go. And he would soon be back, this time not under false pretences....," he thought (71). Lights were going out, and some unruly guests "who may have been drinking" were singing about libertines (72). Disgraceful! The place "had contained so much elegance and so many wonders. And this was where disorder and devastation began." Caution: Author Demolishing a *Domaine*.

On the way up to his room he ran into Frantz, who slipped past with a "Farewell, Monsieur," and vanished. He had, however, left a written message in his room:

My fiancée has disappeared, letting me know that she could not be
my wife, that she was a dressmaker and not a princess. I do not know
what will become of me. I am going away. I do not wish to live any
longer. May Yvonne forgive me.... (73)

Meaulnes exchanged the borrowed clothes (forgetting the silk waistcoat) for his own and "left that mysterious place, which he would surely never see again" (73). Two pages earlier he had told himself he would soon return. We understand that he is disturbed.

It was hard to find a ride going his way, the drivers being among merrymakers. At last a peasant with "an old berlin" (carriage) agreed to take him (75). While driving through the forest, they swerved to avoid a gypsy caravan left in the road. He saw a bright flash in the trees and heard a loud noise. A few moments later he glimpsed "a white shape running": the "tall pierrot," still in costume, "carrying... a human body" (76). There was no stop, no explanation. Throughout the night the carriage drove at a gallop (unlikely or impossible). Eventually he fell asleep, until the driver roused him at dawn. So sleep begins and ends the adventure; as Prospero says in *The Tempest*, "our little life / Is rounded with a sleep" (IV.i.157-58). The driver put him down an hour's walk from Saint-Agathe. "Swaying like a drunken man" in the wind, he set off as "the old berlin, a last link with the mysterious festivities," disappeared (77).

Thus ends Part One: the discovery of the *domaine*. Alain-Fournier's is as uncanny as Chrétien's, without resort to the supernatural. First he distances the action by filtering it through François, who recalls it years later. Second, the *domaine* does not have "a local habitation and a name"; at this point it cannot be verified. Because Meaulnes slept both going and coming, the chateau exists in a dream world. Though what he sees is never *super*natural, it is sometimes *preter*natural, outside or beyond nature, e.g. the odd shifts of weather. And the goings-on at the chateau – children in charge, the Pierrot, the flash-bang in the dark as he leaves, etc. – while peculiar, are not inexplicable or miraculous. The protagonist has much to learn, and we learn along with him. Then there is Yvonne. For Meaulnes, hopelessly smitten, it is like being run over: life will never be the same. Yet his euphoria predates her; just approaching the place gave him "an extraordinary feeling of contentment...of perfect, almost intoxicating tranquillity" (46). He has "reached his goal" and "only happiness" awaits him! These emotions heighten the wonder of the *domaine*, which is extraordinary and unforgettable but not unrealistic.

Having created this seductive artifact, Alain-Fournier spends much of Parts Two and Three undercutting it. We endure trivial schoolboy politics, the winter weather is terrible, Meaulnes and François are discouraged and isolated: other students resent their secrecy and are sceptical about the lost estate. One night some of them lure the two into a chase, ambush them in town, rough them up, and steal a map that "LGM" has drafted of the way to the estate. Directing them is a stranger with a bandaged head called *"le bohémien"* (gypsy). The next day he comes to school and becomes a hero, his satchel being full of curios that he shares. At recess he introduces a new game, a "tournament in which the horses were the big boys, carrying the younger ones on their shoulders," each team trying to unhorse the others – a schoolboy version of the jousts of Chrétien's knights (92). Irritated, Meaulnes hoists François on his shoulders and charges into the fray. Most boys scatter, and when only the gypsy is left, his "horse" throws him rather than encounter LGM. "Well done!" exclaims the stranger, regarding Meaulnes with "astonishment and immense admiration" (94). The gypsy says that he and his partner drive around in their caravan giving shows, but the cold weather has stopped them for now, so he goes to school while Ganache looks after the animals. François recalls that another stranger, a big fellow, knocked Meaulnes down last night.

But the great adventure, the *Domaine Mystérieux*? When Meaulnes and François corner the gypsy after school to repossess the stolen map, LGM says, "Your bandage is red with blood and your clothes are torn" (97). His response disarms them completely: "They tried to take your map away from me...they realized that I was going to make peace with you.... But I did save it...," and he hands the map to Meaulnes, who apologizes and shakes his hand. Then this:

> Meaulnes, I have to tell you something. I, too, went where you did. I
> was there for the extraordinary festivities. I thought, when the boys at
> the school told me about your mysterious adventure, that it must be
> the old lost estate [Domaine perdu]. To make sure, I stole your map.
> But...I don't know the name of the chateau, or how to get back there.
> I'm not sure of the whole way.... (98)

This is not a full disclosure, but it is a major development, confirming Meaulnes's story. The "gypsy" has also "added a few details" to the map. He says that "Three months ago I tried to put a bullet through my head...": the bloody bandage (98). "I wanted to die. And since I didn't succeed, I shall only go on living in order to amuse myself.... I've given everything up" (99). Something ought to click into place for LGM here, but he and François are busy swearing an oath of friendship with the visitor, vowing to "answer when I call – ...like this..." (99). He hoots an owl call, they swear, and he gives them an address in Paris where "the girl from the chateau used to spend" holidays and part of the winter. Then Ganache hoots outside, and he leaves.

Now they have (in Davison's translation) "A Link with the Mysterious Domain," but a tenuous one, and town affairs take over. Poultry is being stolen. The thief wore rope-soled sandals, like Ganache's. Jasmin Delouche, another pupil, says he saw Ganache in the square at 3 AM. Ganache says he was fetching a nurse to look at his partner's head wound. Delouche snaps, "Oh, they're clever! ...It's a good thing [my uncle] didn't meet Ganache...he could easily have shot him. They're all the same, according to him," i.e. sly thieves (2007, 103). The bandaged gypsy said he hated Delouche, who heads the anti-LGM faction. Delouche's rise in importance tends to undermine the *domaine*, of which he is dismissive (*louche* means "shady" or "dubious"). Ganache's caravan sits in the square until early March brings warm, scented breezes and birdsong. François recalls how it "aroused some long-buried excitement in" himself and Meaulnes that the map might lead them to the *domaine*: "O, my brother, my friend! O, wanderer! How certain we were... that happiness was close by and that we only had to start out down the road to find it!" (104).

The visitors give a night performance in the square. Many, including schoolboys, turn out to watch performing animals, directed by the bandaged "gypsy." During intermission, he has a loud argument with Delouche, then a louder one behind the curtain with Ganache, whom he seems to be "rebuking"; Ganache is heard "explaining and justifying" (108). But the show must go on. The finale is a pantomime. Ganache's miming as Pierrot is described in detail (a valuable record of such shows). As he finishes, a bench breaks under laughing, applauding spectators, and the penny finally drops for LGM, who has been silent and thoughtful throughout. He grabs François' arm and shouts, "Look at the gypsy! ...I know who he is!" (110) At the caravan, by a lantern, the visitor has undone his bandage, donned a cloak, and is standing "in the smoky light, as he once had been in the candlelight in the room at the chateau...just as Meaulnes had minutely described him...". He is, of course, Frantz de Galais, and Ganache was the Pierrot at the estate.

Now LGM's quest looks hopeful: he has found Yvonne's brother (who concealed his name and feigned ignorance of the chateau's name). A way to the *domaine* seems open, but Alain-Fournier soon closes it. Ganache turns off the lights and retreats with Frantz into the caravan. When Meaulnes reaches it and knocks, everything is shut and dark. Already asleep?! Very odd. The author has dangled a tempting morsel and then snatched it away. For the rest of Part Two, he will find new ways to crush LGM's chances of recovering his *domaine perdu*.

They left the performance, François recalls, feeling that "Now we understood everything" (112). The man that Meaulnes saw running through the woods was Ganache, carrying the wounded Frantz. LGM is optimistic: in the morning they will set off for the estate, "and the wonderful adventure would start again." But by morning the square is empty; the players have left. It becomes clear why when the police "alerted by Delouche" arrive, looking for "Ganache, the chicken thief" (113). Delouche must have accused Frantz, who, realizing how they had been living, confronted Ganache. So now they understand more, but have lost Frantz.

With spring comes new hope. In Chapter IX, "*A la recherche du sentier perdu*" (1971), a free day and fine weather send the schoolboys off "to the woods and meadows," and allow LGM "to try out the partial itinerary" that Frantz added to his map (2007, 115). He believes "...it may perhaps not be as far as we think...." from the end of the local woods (*Bois des Communaux*), which a fast walker can reach in a morning, so off he goes. François, given a solo task, finds himself "alone in the countryside for the first time in my life," and has a feeling "close to that mysterious happiness that Meaulnes apprehended [*entrevu*] one day" (117). In a remarkable development, he, the beta male, has his own *domaine* experience. A shift into the present tense signals his excitement: "The morning is mine, to explore the out-skirts of the wood, ...while my big brother is also away on a journey of discovery.... I am walking beneath...trees that I do not know.... Just now, I jumped over a stile... and here I am, in this broad avenue of grass flowing beneath the leaves..." (118). This is the present of immediacy, the lyrical present. When a bird (he wishes it were a nightingale) repeats a phrase, he hears "a delicious invitation to a journey" (118). He has found a natural *domaine*.

> For the first time, I too am on the road to adventure. ... I am looking
> for something...mysterious. I'm looking for the passage they write
> about in books, the one with the entrance that the prince, weary with
> travelling, cannot find. ... And suddenly, as you part the branches,
> ...you see something like a long, dark avenue leading to a tiny circle
> of light.... (118)

He has read romances and knows LGM, but is still a novitiate in these matters. While he is thus "intoxicating" himself (*m'enivre*), he enters a clearing that is "nothing more than a field. ...I have reached the end of the Bois des Communaux, which I had always imagined to be an infinite distance away" (118). Why, there is the keeper's house, with stockings drying on a window sill! For years, when we came to the *entrance* to the wood, we would point to the light at the end of the avenue and say, 'That's the keeper Baladier's house,' but we never *walked* there.

To say that someone "went as far as the keeper's house" meant an "extraordinary expedition," but now "I've gone as far as Baladier's house – and found nothing..." (119). François, old enough to cast off childish things and face reality, traverses a segment of Meaulnes's longer curve from enchantment to disillusion. Starting to feel the heat and a pain in his leg, he returns to the past tense.

As the boys troop home, they find LGM sitting on a bridge abutment, looking weary. When François questions him, he "whispered back, shaking his head in disappointment, 'No, nothing! Nothing like it!'" (120). That evening he wrote to his mother, says François, and "that is all I remember of that dreary end to a great day of disappointments." The weather turns rainy and cold. A few days later Meaulnes says that he is going to study in Paris; his mother is coming to collect him. The Seurels are stunned: the LGM era is over! He has given up on the school, but not on the quest; he will write François if he finds Yvonne in Paris. He leaves his young friend feeling that "my adolescence had just vanished for evermore" (124). *The End of Youth....*

The chapter "Betrayal" shows Delouche becoming the new leader and co-opting François. LGM has just left town when the grocer's cart comes along with three boys on it, and Delouche calls for François to join them. And, he admits, I "climbed aboard," feeling liberated from Meaulnes's obsession (126). They go to the Delouches' grocery, hide in the back of the shop, eat biscuits and drink liqueur. This grubby venue even rates the present tense.

> *A sort of unwholesome intimacy has been established between us.*
> *From now on, I can see that Jasmin [Delouche] and Boujardon are*
> *to be my friends. The course of my life has suddenly changed.* (126)

The nature of this change is made clear. François tries to ingratiate himself by telling the boys about LGM's adventure, but the story falls flat; they are neither surprised nor impressed. 'So it was a wedding,' they say. 'Betcha somebody around here knows that chateau...Meaulnes will marry the girl in a few years.' The romance that he radiated did not stir them. He should have told *us* about it, shown *us* his map. Frantz is to blame for alienating LGM from them. "You know," says Delouche, "I did just the right thing reporting him to the police" (127). François could "almost" agree. Then there is a noise in the shop. The boys hide their spoils and run to a hayloft; a woman shouts that they are good-for-nothings. "I fled with them," says François (127). "Only now do I see that we were doing something unlawful..., stealing cakes and liqueur," writes the older narrator, having come to understand these friends better. He spent a grim evening, going home in the rain, eating his burnt pancake, and bedding down in the garret by himself.

Three letters from Meaulnes end Part Two and write *finis* to the *domaine*. The first arrives soon after his departure. At the Paris address Frantz gave them he "saw nothing. There was no one. There will never be anyone" (129). The next letter comes in June; it begins, "Now all hope is lost" (130). A girl he saw on a bench near the house before was there again, so he questioned her. She said, "at one time, a brother and sister came to spend their holidays in that house," but "the brother ran away....And the girl got married" (130-31). He is "in great distress." In November, he reports that he still walks by the house, but "without the slightest hope." Even if Yvonne appeared, "I now have nothing left to tell her" (132). His mood is valedictory: "Our adventure is over.... Perhaps...death alone will give us the key, ...and the end of this failed adventure." François should forget him, "forget everything." When snow falls, François thinks of it as "forever burying our romantic adventure.... And I tried...to forget it all."

But the remains and effects of a *domaine* do not dissipate so quickly; there is more to be borne. The pieces of a puzzle are lying around and at times seem to form an image. The denouement begins with Delouche, still seeking leadership. On a summertime trip in a donkey cart (after telling "salacious stories" about a girl they see but declining to approach her), he reminisces about places he has visited, especially "a half-abandoned estate near Le Vieux-Nançay, called Le Domaine des Sablonnières," which had a tombstone inscribed "Here lies the knight Galois" (138). He saw its "old grey turret" above the trees, and a guardian gave him a tour of "a whole maze of ruined buildings...in the middle of the woods" (139). "But since then," he says, "everything had been pulled down" except "the farm and a little summerhouse," where an old officer lives with his daughter (139). It is a detailed account, based on more than one visit. Delouche's next remark seems studiedly casual, but François takes it at face value.

> *Why, do you know what? I've just thought.... That must be where Meaulnes went – you know. The Great Meaulnes?...the guardian*

mentioned the son of the family, an eccentric lad who had some extraordinary notions. (139)

To have this dragging of the chateau from romance into reality done by Delouche is a telling stroke. François sees that this information is useful, however: a road to the 'lost' estate exists. It is near a known town, and is called *Le Domaine des Sablonnières*. A *sablonnière* is a sand-pit. It should not surprise us that Meaulnes's *domaine* was built on sand.

These connections soon ramify. The Seurels have relatives in Le Vieux-Nançay, the *commune* in which the Sand-Pit Domaine lies, and often visit them during school holidays. In the "*Chez Florentin*" chapter, Alain-Fournier introduces material from his childhood, integrating it with the plot. The "Mysterious Domaine" is well known there. Uncle Florentin says that M de Galais used to give parties for Frantz, including the *fête* that LGM attended. He confirms Delouche's account:

> *It's not a proper estate any more.... They sold everything, and the purchasers...had the old buildings pulled down to increase their hunting ground. ...The former owners just kept a little, one-storey house and the farm.* (142)

François asks if they are wealthy. Florentin says they *were*, but even when "All of Les Sablonnières was in ruins, ...they still tried to entertain" grandly. You're sure to meet Yvonne de Galais, he adds: she comes here for groceries! No, she's not married. And at dusk the next day a farm wagon draws up, bearing "perhaps the most beautiful young woman that ever there was in this world," with charm, dignity, a slender waist, a mass of blonde hair, and a "finely moulded face" (144). François is struck dumb; even when she addresses him, he cannot produce a word. So she delivers a pointed monologue. If I were to teach little boys, she says, "I wouldn't give them an urge to go travelling all around the place [*courir le monde*] as I expect you will, Monsieur Seurel" (he is earning his teaching credential); "I would teach them how to find the happiness that is right beside them. ...there may be some tall, crazy young man looking for me at the furthest corner of the world, while I am here in Madame Florentin's shop..." (145).

That (smiling) remark finally opens the visitor's mouth: "And perhaps I know that tall, crazy young man?" (146). Yvonne looks at him sharply. Then Florentin issues invitations to a *fête* by the River Cher to which M de Galais has agreed:

guests can bathe, fish, hunt, dance! Mlle de Galais can come, and François can bring his friend Meaulnes. Yvonne rises, "the colour suddenly draining from her face": the prospect of seeing Meaulnes again blanches her. She offers François her hand at parting. He senses "a secret understanding" between them "that only death would break and a friendhip more poignant than a great love." That is saying a great deal more than has been shown, but if he feels this, then the *domaine* has touched him, too.

François knows that Meaulnes is at his mother's house, only a day's bicycle ride away. Once he knows how close he is to Yvonne, surely he will come! Aunt Moinel lives in that same village, so François can spend the night *chez elle*. A widow now, she was always fond of him, though her ghost stories scared him. This time she tells one that she has never told anyone. She and her late husband, returning from the *Domaine des Sablonnières*, where a rich friend's son was to get married, were driving in their carriage at sunrise in mid-winter when they saw a figure with a white face standing in the road ahead, ghostlike. It was a dishevelled young woman, who said, "I've run away and I can't go on" (151). She was Frantz de Galais's fianceé, Valentine, the daughter of a poor weaver. Realizing that Frantz was "too young for her, and that all the wonderful things he had told her about were imaginary," she had run off, and sent Frantz a letter saying that "she was going to be with a young man that she loved" (152). She spent the winter with them, then went to Paris, where she was a dressmaker. Aunt Moinel has her address.

Having found another piece of the puzzle, François wonders what to do with it. He too swore loyalty to Frantz: should he search for him? Tell Meaulnes? But wouldn't he go looking for Frantz and neglect Yvonne? François decides not to mention Valentine to his friend until after he has married Yvonne! At the former town hall where the Meaulnes live, he finds Mme Meaulnes preparing for her son's departure. He is in the old council chambers, writing. Surprised by his friend's visit, he seems embarrassed, keeping "his hands behind him"; "a mist had settled over the enthusiasm of earlier times" (156). François asks about his journey. Meaulnes is vague: it will be long, has to do with that "strange adventure" at the school, the *domaine* is lost but I can't live like other people, etc. (157). François presses: Are you trying to keep a promise? Make amends? Yes, says Meaulnes: the promise I made to Frantz. "And perhaps something to make amends for."

Relieved because he thinks he can help, François is about to deliver his news when Meaulnes goes on. It would have been nice to see Yvonne once more, he says, but

> *...now I'm sure that when I discovered the Estate Without a Name, I reached a height, a degree of perfection and purity that I shall never achieve again. In death alone, as I once wrote to you, I may perhaps recapture the beauty of that time...* (158)

For him, the *domaine's* beauty cannot be recovered in this life, but this journey will be "the continuation of my old adventure" (158). Feeling that he must speak now, François blurts, "Suppose I were to tell you that all hope is not lost?" The blood rushes to Meaulnes's face. François tells all he knows. It is almost as if Yvonne sent him! The great one seems bewildered, shaken. If the old estate has really been demolished, though, "there is nothing left," he asserts (159)! Yes, there's a picnic, insists François. "Do I really have to go?" asks Meaulnes. Still dazed, he reluctantly agrees to cycle back to Le Vieux-Nançay on the morrow.

Next day The Great Meaulnes seems to be back, tearing on ahead like a bicycle racer, and looking impatient that night at Florentin's. In the morning they drive a "trap" to the rendezvous: a farm near the Cher only two kilometres from the chateau. The scale of the countryside, which Meaulnes once thought vast, is quite manageable. Others arrive, including Delouche, who tries to be agreeable. Meaulnes still dislikes him: he "had the key to everything while we went looking as far away as Paris" (160). François "felt sorry for him. But, then, for whom would I not feel sorry before that day was done?"(161). It is like hearing low notes begin to rumble in the bass when the symphony was sounding hopeful. The early chapters of Part Three repaired much of the damage done to the *domaine* in Part Two and appeared to turn toward the Final Assembly of comedy: the lovers' reunion. But François can never recall the picnic without "vague...regret. ...Everything seemed perfectly coordinated for happiness, yet there was so little happiness to be had." The riverside is beautiful, and the heroine arrives with her father on horseback, yet Meaulnes, too nervous to wait, has walked off, so it is François who runs to meet her. Yvonne looks anxious, too, but when he escorts her to the group of young men in which the hero is hiding, she goes up to him, holds out her hand, and says, "I recognize you, Augustin Meaulnes" (164).

But as at their first meeting, they "were separated" and "By ill luck" not placed at the same lunch table (165): very formal seating for a picnic, and Meaulnes is amazingly passive. Not until late in the day are they together again, and then only because Yvonne comes to his group to ask why they are not boating. He says, "What we need is a motor boat or a steam boat, like the one you used to have." Embarrassed, Yvonne replies, "We don't have it any longer. We sold it." This turns out to be thematic, and highlights Meaulnes's *idée fixe*.

> *...with a persistence of which he was surely not aware, Meaulnes kept returning to all the wonders of the past, and each time, the girl, miserably, had to repeat that it had all vanished: the old mansion...had been pulled down; the great lake had been dried up and filled in; the children...had gone their own ways....* (166)

Meaulnes is very slow to grasp this point. Fixated on the physical *domaine*, he cannot see that Yvonne is the *domaine* incarnate. He keeps yielding to "his obsession, asking for information about everything that he had seen there": old carriages, their drivers, horses, furniture! His eagerness is both pathetic and painful; at last Yvonne sees that he must be disabused beyond any doubt.

> *You'll never see again the fine château that Monsieur Galais and I got ready for poor Frantz. We spent our lives doing what he asked. ...But everything vanished with him on the evening of his failed betrothal. Monsieur de Galais was already ruined without us knowing. Frantz had run up debts, and his former friends, when they found out that he had gone, immediately turned to us for payment. We became poor. Madame de Galais died and we lost all our friends in a matter of days.* (167)

"Nobody wants you when you're down and out." Yvonne describes the fall of the House of Galais clearly and frankly: Frantz's unpayable debts brought his family down – our first clue that he might be the villain of the piece. But then, trying to mitigate his offence, she weakens and suggests that someday Frantz could reappear, the postponed wedding take place, and "everything might go back to what it was before." Or "can one return to the past?" she asks (167). It is a resonant question, central to the book, and it seems to stun Meaulnes. He retreats into himself, becoming so catatonic that François takes notice. "Why was the Great Meaulnes behaving like a stranger, like a person who had not found what he was looking for...? ...where had he found this emptiness, this distance, this inability to experience happiness...?" That too is a good question, which the novel will leave to us.

As Meaulnes walks away, Yvonne looks "thoughtful and dejected," telling François, "He is not happy. And perhaps there is nothing that I can do for him..." (168). Then shouts are heard. The de Galais' horse has become tangled in his tether, and in struggling has hurt his leg. Meaulnes is reproving Delouche and even M de Galais: the horse was tethered improperly, and is too old for work. Yvonne, on the verge of tears, leads the horse away, and her father follows, limping. The "party of pleasure" breaks up; everyone heads home. But Meaulnes asks Florentin to stop, jumps out of the wagon and runs back, down the same avenue to the *domaine* that he used that first time. "And that evening, sobbing," he asks Yvonne to marry him (171). Alain-Fournier does not narrate that scene, but evidently she accepts. Improbable as that may seem, a husband and protector for her and her father might well seem a good idea at this juncture, whatever her reservations.

Their five-month engagement is a halcyon interval. Twice a week Meaulnes visits Yvonne in the one house left on the property, and (says François) "Happiness seems to have quieted his strange anguish" (172). Their wedding takes place on a cold February day in the chapel at the estate, and the few friends and family who attend soon leave. As François and Delouche (a surprise guest) walk by the wood behind the cottage in mist and wind, they hear a piano, as in Meaulnes's dream. François thinks, "At last they are happy" (174). It is the goal of comedy: the lovers joined at last in fruitful union. If only the curtain could drop now! Instead, a faint "*Whoo, whoo*" is heard.

> ...*it was the cry of the tall actor hailing his young friend from the school gate. It was the cry to which Frantz had made us promise to respond, anywhere and at any time. But what did he want of us here, today?* (175)

Delouche says, "They're both here, in the village.... I caught Ganache...keeping watch...near the chapel. He took off as soon as he saw me" (175). He insists, "... we've got to chase them off. ...Or else all the madness will start again" (175). They spread out, François hailing Frantz. A young man approaches through the trees. Where has he been? Why pop up now?

This return of the once-pampered hope of the *de Galais* family is made ugly. He looks thinner, "seemed to have been crying," and is in a foul temper: "What do you want?" he snaps (176). But François is firm, asking home questions: "What are you doing here? Why have you come to disturb people who are happy?" Frantz blushes, stammers, "I'm so unhappy," and begins to sob. A nervous breakdown? When François offers to lead him to the newlyweds, who will welcome him "and it will all be over," he retorts, "So Meaulnes doesn't care about me any more? Why doesn't he answer when I call him?" (176-77). François replies much as Delouche would: "Come on, Frantz. The time for childish make-believe is over. Don't let some folly spoil the happiness of those you love..." (177). But all Frantz can see is his own injuries:

> ...*he alone can save me.... Only he is able to find the trail I've lost. For almost three years, Ganache and I have been hunting all over France.... [Meaulnes] was the only one I still trusted. And now he's not answering.... He has found his love. So why doesn't he think of me, now? ... Yvonne will let him go. She has never refused me anything.* (177)

He is irrational as well as selfish. How can Meaulnes find Valentine if he and Ganache cannot? Though shocked by his appearance – "the face of an exhausted, defeated old child" – François judges him coldly: "...he was more a child than ever: imperious, capricious," yet "already showing signs of age" (177). He pities Frantz, but resents his "playing the ridiculous part of the young romantic hero," and he and Ganache have probably been "stealing to survive." Then *he* suggests that Meaulnes could join the hunt in a few days, or if Frantz returns in a year he might find Valentine there! Here François seems childish, too. Why not just go to Aunt Moinel and get Valentine's address in Paris: not romantic enough? Frantz withdraws after an outburst clarifying the role he wanted to play: "We thought that we would arrive in time before the wedding to take Meaulnes and look for my fiancée..." (178). The heir apparent to the *domaine* is a disaster.

In the next chapter (ironically titled "The Happy People"), Meaulnes hears Frantz's call, sees François, runs to the wood and learns what has happened. He is distraught, feeling that he cannot stay at the cottage until he has fulfilled his oath to Frantz. So, "for the sake of some childish promise..., you are destroying your happiness," says François. "Oh, if that promise were the only thing," exclaims Meaulnes. He says that there is "some other bond between the two young men," but does not explain (182). Then Yvonne appears, "dishevelled, wild-eyed," her forehead bloody: in running after Meaulnes, she fell. She takes his arm, glad that "this time, at least, he would not abandon her," and he wipes the blood from her hair, all tender concern for the moment. "We must go back now," he says, and they return to the cottage, he helping her over the rough places, she smiling (183). They seem to have survived their first trial.

Married life has many tests, however, and the last part of *Le Grand Meaulnes* is painful to read. When François next calls, he learns that Yvonne is abed with a fever and Meaulnes "had to leave that Friday morning on a long journey" (185; the wedding had been on Thursday). He sees that "the secret regret that Meaulnes had been harbouring since his trip to Paris had proved too strong, and eventually my friend had fled the tight embrace of happiness...." *Eventually?* The morning after the wedding night! When Yvonne is better, she tells François, "I don't know when he'll come back." He visits her as often as his nearby teaching duties allow, and they walk and talk. She shows him "Frantz's house," a cottage that M de Galais provided to grant the boy's wish for a place of his own; it keeps memories of him alive. And she would "confide in me all that great, unspoken sorrow and her regret at losing her brother – so crazy, so charming, and so much admired" (188). François is a friend, not a suitor, but his feelings are ardent, and she encourages his visits and takes his arm. Yet even this closeness withers as Meaulnes's silent absence stretches on:

> *Weeks and months went by. Time past! Lost happiness! She had been the fairy, the princess and the mysterious love of all our adolescence, and it fell to me,...to take her arm and say the words that would assuage her grief.* (188)

They seldom talk about Meaulnes – the absent centre – but rather around him, and François is happy to be her confidante. He says that what she is to Meaulnes, she is to him as well. "I remained her faithful friend – her companion in an unspoken vigil – for a whole spring and summer, the like of which will never come again" (189). Yvonne, the *domaine* that remains, is his love.

François spends the summer holiday at home in Sainte-Agathe, "filled with memories of our adolescence" and regrets for *le temps perdu*: "our youth was ended and happiness had passed us by" (190). Yvonne is expecting in October, and he returns a few days early to visit her. At dusk the first evening, he walks to the cottage and sits on a garden bench, "happy at simply being there, close to what absorbed and preoccupied me most of anything in the world" (191). Yvonne emerges. Meaulnes has not returned. François muses, "So much folly in such a noble head," but she objects:

> *Only I am at fault. Think what we did... We said to him, "Here's happiness, this is what you have been searching for...and here is the girl who was at the end of all your dreams! ... What else could he do, ...except be seized with uncertainty, then dread, then terror? How could he do otherwise than give in to the temptation to escape?* (192-93)

François protests that she *is* the girl of his dreams, but she insists on taking the blame. "How could I for a moment have had such an arrogant thought? That thought was the whole trouble" (193). Seeing Meaulnes's "feverish unease" and "sense of remorse," hearing him say "I am not worthy of you" at daybreak, she realized that she could not help him. So she said, "If you must go, ...so that afterwards you can come back to me at peace, then I am the one asking you to go" (193). We may feel that she is too good for him, or empathetic to a fault. François wonders how to respond. She acted "out of generosity, in a spirit of self-sacrifice": how could he condemn "so much goodness and love"? (193) He remains silent. Meaulnes has still not written; they suppose he is searching in France or Germany. All they can do now is trade memories and speak kindly "of the one who had abandoned us" (194).

In Chapter XII, "The Burden," a messenger informs François that Yvonne has borne a daughter, but the birth was difficult: the doctor had to use forceps, the baby was hurt, and Yvonne is "very weak" (195). Meaulnes should have been there. Impregnate your bride on the first night and then leave on a "mission of conscience"?! He replaces Frantz as top villain. François rushes to the cottage and has a few words with the limp mother, but when he returns the next day the doctor says that "The little girl almost died last night, and the mother is very ill" (196). He may be able to save the baby, but Yvonne has pulmonary congestion. François is stunned, M de Galais looks terrible, and Yvonne, gasping for air, eyes rolling, unable to speak, just holds out a hand to him. François leaves, daring to hope, but when he appears at school the next morning, a student informs him that "the young lady from Les Sablonnières died yesterday at nightfall" (198).

He is crushed. "Everything is painful, everything bitter, now that she is dead. The world is empty.... ...the mysterious fête is over... Everything has reverted to the misery it was before" (198). The wanderers, Frantz and the not-so-great Meaulnes, have done something irrevocable. François dismisses his pupils and walks to the cottage with a "bitter feeling of outrage" (199).

> We had found the beautiful girl; we had conquered her. She was the wife of my friend and I loved her with that deep, secret love that is never spoken. When I looked at her, I was happy as a little child. (199)

Despite the dubious note of "we had conquered her," this is clearly a declaration of love for Yvonne, his *domaine*. At the house, he is spared nothing. Her body must be brought downstairs, and M de Galais is too weak to help, so François carries Yvonne's corpse by himself, "Slowly, step by step, ...down the long, steep staircase," his head bent over hers so that "her blonde hair is sucked into my mouth – dead hair with a taste of earth." This and her "weight on my heart are all that remain for me of the great adventure, and of you, Yvonne de Galais, a woman so long sought and so much loved" (200). What we are left with, then – absent the wanderers – is François' verbal love letter to Mlle de Galais as he carries her ("The Burden") to the coffin.

M de Galais, "whose indulgence and whimsy" were central to Meaulnes's adventure, dies the next winter (201). The will makes François his heir, pending Meaulnes's return. François moves into the cottage, walking to the village to teach; that way, with the help of servants, he can "keep the child with me" (201). Rummaging through dusty boxes of family papers and photographs, he discovers Meaulnes's "school trunk," in which is a "Monthly Composition Book," started at Saint-Agathe and continued in Paris. François devours these pages that "explained so much" (especially "Oh, if that promise were the only thing"), and transcribes the lines "exactly as I found them" (203). Almost as he found them (see 209).

Three chapters of Meaulnes's journal, titled "The Secret" (XIV-XVI), describe his relationship with Valentine Blondeau, the young woman who haunts the de

Galais house in Paris. She says he reminds her of a "young man who once paid court to me in Bourges. We were even engaged" (204). He takes her (and her sister) to the theatre, and finds that "close to her, I feel almost happy"; her connection to the *domaine* soothes him (205). Attentive readers may find some of this familiar before Meaulnes does – but then we visited Aunt Moinel. Meaulnes keeps company with Valentine, who seems unstable. She disappears for a few days; then returns looking like "a guilty Pierrot" (another faint echo) to say that he should go away, yet they keep walking together. Valentine talks more about her fiancé, whom she calls "my love."

> *I drove my fiancé to desperation. I abandoned him because he admired me too much. He could only see me in his imagination and not as I was. And I am full of faults. We should have been very unhappy.* (208)

Then she turns to him and asks, "What do you want, in the end? Do you love me, too? Are you, too, going to ask for my hand?" Meaulnes, as startled as we are, "stammered something. I don't know what.... I may have said, 'Yes'" (208). *Don't know? May have said*?! Here the diary stops, but François gives the gist of some "rough copies of unreadable, shapeless letters": "What a precarious engagement! At Meaulnes' request, the girl had left her job...he took charge of the preparations for the wedding" (209). So he *did* say yes, but, still trying to find Yvonne, he goes off several times, absences that Valentine demands he explain. Now he is emotionally involved with *two* young women linked to the *domaine*.

In the second "Secret" chapter, François keeps trying to make sense of scribbled, fragmentary letters. On a trip into the country, the couple stayed in adjacent rooms at an inn and passed for man and wife. Noting Valentine's practicality, François remarks, "This was the companion that Meaulnes, the hunter and peasant, must have wished for before his mysterious adventure" (211). But both are shy, and Meaulnes remains troubled and quiet. Valentine rambles on about her fiancé's extravagant promises, his imaginings of a rural cottage where children would jump out from behind bushes and shout, "'Long live the bride!' What madness, isn't it"? (212) But "Meaulnes listened to her uneasily.... ...he felt something like the echo of a voice already heard," as well he might (213).

Sensing his unease, Valentine offers him something "more precious than anything else to me!": her fiancé's letters. It is a generous but disastrous gesture (213).

> *Oh, he recognized the fine writing at once. Why hadn't he realized*
> *it earlier? It was the writing of Frantz, the gypsy, which he had*
> *seen previously on the desperate note left behind in the room at the*
> *chateau.* (213)

Such remarkable recall of handwriting glimpsed once some time ago is rare, but perhaps no more far-fetched than that Meaulnes should, in a nation of tens of millions of people, have fallen in with Frantz's fiancée. He starts reading the letters. Valentine explains that (in the one he is holding) Frantz was referring to a piece of jewelry that he gave her and "made me swear to keep it always. That was one of his crazy ideas" (213). Meaulnes snaps, "Crazy! Why keep repeating that word? Why did you never want to believe in him? I knew him: he was the most wonderful boy in the world!" (213). Valentine is of course stunned. "You knew him?" "He was my best friend, my brother in adventures – and now I've taken his fiancée...!" (214).

Affairs have still not reached their nadir; there is more pain. Furious at Valentine, Meaulnes tries to hurt her: "You are the cause of it all. ...the one who ruined everything..." (214). He has found a scapegoat for the loss of the *domaine*. "Leave me," he says. Then Valentine, "half weeping," plays her only card, delivering a piteous and powerful riposte:

> *Very well, if that's how it is, I shall leave. I'll go back to Bourges....*
> *And if you don't come to look for me, you realize...that my father is*
> *too poor to keep me. ...I'll come back to Paris, I'll walk the roads...and*
> *certainly become a lost woman....* (214)

The account ends there, with the parting of two devastated people, but there are drafts of other letters. Meaulnes *may* have written Valentine several times, seeking a way to reconnect with the *domaine*; if he could find Frantz, might she be reconciled with him? She did not reply. Clearly struggling with his guilt, Meaulnes decided to cycle to Bourges and find her.

In the third "Secret" chapter, François summarizes the last pages of Meaulnes's journal, covering that journey and "his final error" (215). In Bourges he found Valentine's house, but her mother said that she had returned to Paris; a letter to her old address would be forwarded. Meaulnes fell into self-recrimination. Her remark about becoming a "lost woman" stung deeply: "I forced her to do this.... I'm the one who ruined Frantz's fiancée!" (216). Yet the letter he eventually wrote her was accusatory: "How could you do that? How could you ruin yourself?" When some officers drinking in a cafe joked about a woman, he imagined Valentine on their knees. Brothels near the cathedral, and two prostitutes whom he followed, seemed to foretell her fate. During the long ride home he was agitated almost to madness, thinking that "the unsatisfied love that had just been so cruelly assaulted, and the girl whom he should, above all others, have protected and safeguarded, was the very one that he had just sent to her ruin" (218).

Meaulnes added a few valedictory lines, vowing to find Valentine at all costs "before it was too late" (218). From its date, François sees that this was the journey for which his friend was preparing when he brought him news of Yvonne. Thus Meaulnes was sidetracked – until Frantz recalled him to his other obligation. The last lines were written at dawn on the day he left Yvonne; they include the pledge to return only "if I can bring back with me Frantz and Valentine, married, and settle them in 'Frantz's house'" (219). Meaulnes seems daft or quixotic in this vow, which is true to the original spirit of the quest. Frantz too was a part of the *domaine*.

A short epilogue ties up that which can be tied. François, still in the cottage and teaching school, feels "dreary" and "sad" except for the child, who looks "healthy and pretty" (220). Merry and energetic, she enlivens the house. François has begun to think that "for all her wildness, she will be a little bit my child" when one day, twenty-one months after he left, Meaulnes reappears, bearded and "dressed like a huntsman" (221). They are at first speechless; then François, "overwhelmed with all the pain reawakened by this return," embraces him, sobbing. Meaulnes understands. "'Ah!' he said, curtly, 'she's dead, isn't she?'" In the room where Yvonne died he kneels by the bed, head in his arms. Then he sees his daughter, whom he picks up and holds tightly, weeping. He announces that he has "brought the other two back": Frantz and Valentine, married, are in Frantz's house (222). He has at last fulfilled his promise, at what expense we know. Watching them with "a slight sense of disappointment," François sees that "the girl had at last found the companion for whom she had unconsciously been waiting." Meaulnes would "deprive me of the only joy that he had left me"; some night he would set off "with her for some new adventure" (223).

BALANCING THE NOVEL'S ACCOUNTS IS not easy, which I believe was intentional. Alain-Fournier makes judgments difficult, leaves questions open, and maintains a distance from the action. The conclusion is a good example. Is François right to think that Meaulnes will go wandering with his daughter? If so, how do we react? That will depend on our opinion of "LGM," and of footloose young men in general. The author drops the curtain at that point, but ambiguities and uncertainties have been present from the first. Our main narrator, François, two years Meaulnes's junior, naturally looks up to the big, bold new boy who narrates the visit to the *fête étrange*. So what François knows about that is filtered through him, and what *we* know comes from an older, sadder, wiser François. It is an oblique structure such as Emily Bronte built in *Wuthering Heights*. Initially François views his new roommate as a hero who will inaugurate "a new life" (11). But a page later the narrator – who contains the whole experience of the book – renders a different verdict:

> *...someone came and swept me away from all these tranquil, childish*
> *joys – someone who snuffed out the candle that had cast its light on*
> *my mother's gentle face as she prepared our evening meal; someone*
> *who turned off the light around which we gathered as a happy family*
> *on those evenings, after my father had closed the shutters.... And that*
> *someone was Augustin Meaulnes....* (12)

This sounds condemnatory, but wait. François is fifteen: is it not time for him to supersede "childish joys," time for "The End of Youth"? The Garden of Eden hovers behind this opening, and while Satan "turned off the light" there, a considerable body of opinion holds that the consequences were necessary and desirable. Meaulnes brought François some of the worldly knowledge that Satan brought the First Couple.

Critics who have written on *Le Grand Meaulnes* present a wide range of views. John Fowles, in an Afterword to Signet's *The Wanderer* (1971), warns that the book cannot be understood discursively, i.e. via reason. That would save trouble, but it is more accurate to say that critics' discursive approaches differ: one sees an ironist, another an aesthete or a pilgrim. However, this is also the case if we react to the novel intuitively, as Fowles wants. We can learn something from every critic if we remember that each has only a few pieces of the puzzle. Fowles's warning remains useful: we must swim in subjective waters to talk about Alain-Fournier.

At the outset I said that *Le Grand Meaulnes* is both powerful and flawed. Some flaws are minor and common: a few characters seem significant for a while, but then drift away, almost unused; some autobiographical scenes are less than integral. But the ambiguity of some characters and our dubious reactions to them are more consequential. Chief among these are Frantz, whose debts ruin his family, and Meaulnes. Do they stir us, or do we find them childish? Is the book's title ironic? "LGM" could be considered the villain for his romantic excesses. He abandons Yvonne after their wedding night to keep his promise to Frantz, returning only after her death. The later Meaulnes verges on madness: he is a disaster for Yvonne, a negative for François, and what kind of a father will he be? His and Frantz's honour code and fable-driven fantasies cause undeniable harm. Alain-Fournier provides rich mixtures in these characters, but what did he want us to think of them? If he loses control of our responses and we go our own ways, this becomes a serious flaw.

Yet these ambiguities are also a strength. Like (most) real people, the characters are three-dimensional, multi-faceted, and not easily known. Some of Alain-Fournier's strategies to heighten the mystery of Meaulnes's adventure and replicate his emotions in us are potent. His visit to the chateau is preceded by one sleep – during which the landscape is transformed – and followed by another, so that he cannot know the way or the distance to the *domaine*. Except for the silk waistcoat, he could have dreamt it. There *are* many dreams: sleeping, waking, remembered, nested. The one that comforts him the night before the *fête* is a link back to his own childhood and onwards to a place run by children, where before falling asleep he hears a distant piano, or remembers his mother's playing, or both. Later, listening to "the girl" play the piano as children rest on him, he has "a dream like the one he used to have," which also points to a future wherein the pianist is his wife (61). And Yvonne plays for him on their wedding day. It becomes eerie: one of the ways in which the author creates the 'magical' atmosphere that has moved many readers.

This aura is thickest during the *fête étrange*. A resonant word, *étrange*. It can mean "strange" or "weird," and is the root of *étranger*: the noun "stranger" or "alien" and the adjective "foreign." To be *à l'étranger* is to be abroad. Fêtes like that at the chateau and in many *domaines* manifest all these qualities, being excursions into the unknown. Meaulnes does not know the chateau's location or name, and it does not observe the usual conventions. Children rule, as in mediaeval ceremonies of inversion such as the "Lord of Misrule"; the costumes are of the previous century; the banquet has an Anglo-Saxon look. His feelings there are complex: a blend of serenity, security, contentment, and happiness; fear of being exposed as an intruder; and a strong sense of loss as the fête breaks up in disorder. That feeling of loss recurs frequently and sometimes dominates the novel's mood long after the chateau is in ruins.

Unexpected encounters with alluring scenes dovetail with the idea of wandering. For the mediaeval "knight errant," wandering was an essential part of life: he *needed* to travel to show his *arete* (excellence) against villains, dragons, and rival knights. But what prompts Meaulnes to hit the road? In the *Metamorphoses*, Ovid introduces the myth of the hunter Actaeon and the goddess Diana by asking, "*Quod enim scelus error habebat?*" In Frank Justus Miller's translation (Loeb Classical Library), this is a rhetorical question: "For what crime had mere mischance?" *Scelus* is crime or sin, but *error* here is likely not modern English "error" or "mischance." Its first meaning in classical Latin is "wandering," followed by "meandering": winding. "Mistake" comes well down the list; that is usually *erratum*. 'For what crime (or sin) was there in wayward wandering?' would be a tenable translation. The myth delivers a clear answer: Actaeon's roving brings him to the pool where Diana and her nymphs are bathing naked. The offended goddess changes him into a stag, and his own hounds tear him apart. To put *Le Grand Meaulnes* in this punishing context raises the question of how Alain-Fournier regards the footloose Meaulnes and Frantz, compared to, say, the rootedness of François and Yvonne. In his novel, "error" and "errant" are profoundly ambiguous words (as they are in Chrétien's *Yvain*), and we are left with the question that Ovid posed.

Many of these issues involve *domaines*. What is Alain-Fournier's attitude toward such experiences? In Part One he presents a classic estate-*domaine*. His protagonist must struggle before chancing upon it, but then is strongly attracted by its mystery and beauty. Because they are Other, *domaines* often do require effort and travel. Wandering may be necessary but not sufficient, however; mere arrival does not guarantee entrance or success. At the estate Meaulnes feels like an intruder or imposter, though a strangely contented one. Yvonne rejects his advances, but not a future meeting. Something is wrong this time; things must be done otherwise.

The fête breaks up in disorder, for reasons that are then obscure. The *domaine* seems to expel him and others, leaving major questions open, though it is no less memorable and appealing for that.

Thereafter, Alain-Fournier both tears apart that *domaine* and expands the concept. Meaulnes learns that he witnessed the last great fête at the estate named Sandpit. Its finances are so marginal that when Frantz runs off, his debts cannot be paid. Most buildings are sold and pulled down; M de Galais retains only one cottage. Then it seems that the *domaine*'s people are central; Yvonne and Frantz are what move Meaulnes. Or is questing his ultimate, enduring *domaine*? Wanderlust brought him there, made him run after Yvonne and Frantz, and may send him off with his daughter. Are these actions to be admired or deplored? There are certainly some dark strains: Alain-Fournier shows that following your heart and imagination, trying to revisit your *domaine*, can be disastrous. The obsessed Meaulnes of Part Three hurts people as he follows his dream. Yvonne and Valentine complain, with reason, of their lovers' tendencies to view them through romantic spectacles, instead of seeing them as the women they are and settling down. And what but romance, *domainisme*, can be blamed for that?

François is not the only young man who resists the Sirens' song. Jasmin Delouche – Mr "Scented Shadiness" – plays this role, flatly. Resentful and suspicious of Meaules, he can be nasty or banal, and has a gift for turning poetry into prose with a shrug, but he also tends to be right about some matters. He figures out where the "lost estate" is, supplies its name, and joins with François to contact the people there. If only he did not take such pleasure in detonating Meaules's excitement about the *domaine*! He may even enjoy its ruin. His forte (and his weakness) is to bring everything down to his own level. Though he is not, like François, a balanced character, he makes us look at the estate through the lens of practical common sense. It is part of the whole view.

SOME PARALLELS BETWEEN ALAIN-FOURNIER'S LIFE and his novel shed light on the characters of Yvonne and Meaulnes, especially. We are fortunate to have *Towards the Lost Domain: Letters from London, 1905*, edited and translated by W.J. Strachan, which reveals some subtexts of *Le Grand Meaulnes*. Alain-Fournier, a keen student of English, spent the summer of 1905 clerking in London, going to the theatre, and corresponding with his parents, his friend Jacques Rivière, and others. We learn that he saw *Hamlet* (the novel has a "Shakespearean gravedigger"), liked Mark Twain's *Tom Sawyer* (another wanderer), and was influenced by Dickens and Hardy, etc. The origins of the *fête étrange* may be visible in his description of English meals:

> *You're continually under the impression that you're dining with grown-up children whom you've allowed to do the dinner of their choice for a day and who have more or less transformed dinners into doll's dinner-parties.* (Alain-Fournier 1986, 32)

He repeats this later. A closer approximation to the "strange fête" is his account of a garden-party on the shared grounds of a school and a church, where visitors were invited to "walk *ad libitum* in the illuminated garden until 11 pm." Of course it was all fresh and foreign, "*étrange*," to him.

> *At first all I see in a little garden are clumps of bushes decorated with 'fairy-lights', as the English call them. Then a profusion of bunches of flowers or plants right along the wall of the strange little church with its faintly glowing stained-glass windows. Next, groups of youths with the handsome girls from the office. Finally a group of nice girls, one of whom, oddly dressed with a strange little Directory* [late eighteenth century] *hat... comes towards me with her hand held out....*
> (1986, 50)

Strachan also maintains that Alain-Fournier's poem "*A travers les étés*" was the genesis or "germ" of *Le Grand Meaulnes*: "recollections of childhood, schooldays and, above all, the encounter with Yvonne de Quiévrecourt" (1986, 186, n. 1; cp. 190).

The chief interest of the letters is what they reveal about the author's feelings for the "first Yvonne," who inspired the novel's heroine. She is a remote, idealized figure whom he saw in Paris a month before sailing to England; he called her a "haughty blonde" (Letter #6) or "HER." Strachan prints the lyrical account of their first meeting that Alain-Fournier wrote for himself (Appendix II), which became the first meeting of Meaulnes and Yvonne. The author, like his hero, sees HER out walking and says, "You are beautiful" (1986, 208). Every detail of her face, dress, and movement is etched indelibly; it is Dante seeing Beatrice. Alain-Fournier follows her onto a tram and apologizes for his remark and for following her. She replies simply, "It's no matter," deflating him (1986, 209). When he follows her off the tram, she says, "...what's the good...I leave tomorrow...I don't belong to Paris." Again he asks forgiveness and she grants it. Slender, tall, elegant, she has "a body beyond all dreams" – he is not quite Dante (1986, 210). Then he writes, "We are children, we have acted foolishly," later attributed to her (in the novel Yvonne says it). His conclusion about Yvonne I, "there cannot be anyone more beautiful in the world," is François' judgment of Yvonne II (1986, 211). Alain-Fournier also gives prose-poetry impressions of the encounter as Yvonne begins to etherealize in his mind, becoming more like Beatrice.

For the next few years Alain-Fournier was studying, then serving in the military and trying to become a writer. He learned that Yvonne de Quiévrecourt married a naval surgeon in 1906, and heard in 1909 that she had borne a son. Then there is nothing until 1913, when Le Grand Mealnes was published, showing how far he was from forgetting her. In May 1913 he arranged a meeting with Yvonne, then living in Rochefort. On that visit he handed her a letter, written the previous autumn but not mailed, which Strachan prints (Appendix III). "It is now more than seven years since you were lost to me," it begins, since "You said 'We are two children...,'" and "I have never stopped searching for you" (1986, 214). He recalls their movements that day, quotes her, and describes return visits to places where he saw her, on their 'anniversary' and at other times. He paced the sidewalk beneath windows where she had appeared; once she raised the curtain, saw him and smiled. Yvonne must have seen at once that he was obsessed with her. "I have forgotten nothing. I have remembered every minute of the short time when I have seen you..., every syllable of the few words you have spoken..." (1986, 215). He feels for her "something much more than love," and she must know this "dreadful thing": "away from your presence I have no desire to live." He asks "to be no longer completely parted from you. ...command me to do what you like." Tell him to marry, or to go away; he will obey, but let him write her or see her. Do not "cast me into hell" (1986, 216).

We also have a draft of the letter he wrote her after that meeting (1986, Appendix IV): more quivering sensibility and hopeless love. He arrived and left "in despair," but close to her he was "happy" (1986, 217). Both her silences and her words were lovable, the latter being "mysterious, prudent and wise beyond those of other women." He concludes, "there is only one being in the whole world with whom I would have loved to spend my life. Once again I have seen the face of Beauty, purity and grace..." (1986, 218). We note that he did not allow Yvonne de Galais to enjoy married life, sending her husband away at once and having her die in childbirth. So there are close correlations between some people in Alain-Fournier's life and in his novel, but we do not find the original of the Sandpit estate. The chateau was invented as a literary setting for the action; the author's own *domaine* was Yvonne.

Le Grand Meaulnes was published, first serially and then in book form, in 1913. Alain-Fournier was reported missing after a patrol near the Meuse River on 22 September 1914 and presumed killed, though his body was never found.

The idea of a *domaine* that Alain-Fournier bequeathed to posterity is a place strongly attractive (at a certain time), partly because of its inhabitants, and capable of marking people for good or ill, but subject to mutability. It can both exalt and scar someone like Meaulnes who cannot let go. It spoils Frantz, who lives there. Even François, tracing a distant orbit, is strongly affected by its pull. Only Yvonne takes it in stride and keeps her balance. The physical *domaine* – chateau and grounds – is prey to natural forces (subsidence) and mismanagement. Debts must be paid; the scenery is fragile. *Domaines* behave like theatrical illusions, dependent on well-chosen materials and moments for their effects. With another owner, another time, different actors or audience, you might wonder what all the fuss was about, but those who were there That Night will never forget it. Imagine sodden Woodstock, the morning after. Say, mister, where's the *domaine*?

Bourani and Coëtminais

John Fowles emerged as a promising young English novelist in the mid-1960s, and while opinion is divided over whether that promise was fulfilled, he was successful enough for the journal *Twentieth-Century Literature* to devote a special issue to him in 1996. A student of French literature at Oxford, Fowles discovered Alain-Fournier's novel and adopted the idea of the *domaine*, but not slavishly. In *Le Grand Meaulnes*, Les Sablonnières glows warmly at first, but is weakly led and economically unsound. Fowles thought, What if the *domaine* were not only mysterious and attractive but strong, directed by a formidable man whose purposes are unknown? In *The Magus* (1965), a young English teacher goes to the Greek-island estate of enigmatic Maurice Conchis; in "The Ebony Tower" (1974), a youngish painter and teacher goes to interview the venerable but vigorous British painter Henry Breasley at his French *domaine*. Both visitors are probed deeply by older authority figures, whose estates become proving grounds, like the jousts and battles that tested mediaeval knights. In *The Magus*, these trials are part of Conchis's elaborate masque, while in "The Ebony Tower," Breasley steps back in order to let the estate and his assistants assess the visitor.

Fowles made *The Magus* more difficult to discuss by publishing a "revised version" in 1978. I resent anyone tinkering with a text that has moved me, but one summer I read the two 600-page versions in parallel, comparing them sentence by sentence. Whole pages were left unchanged, while others were revised extensively, or cut, or lengthened. Sometimes I could see why he had revised, sometimes not; sometimes it seemed an improvement, sometimes not. Paul H. Lorenz, in the *Twentieth-Century Literature* issue on Fowles, calls the revision "less sympathetic" to protagonist Nicholas Urfe than is the original (71). But in both versions Urfe can be sympathetic or unsympathetic, and sometimes seems more sinned against (by the divinely amoral "gods") than sinning. As "the author's final wishes," the revised version must be respected, and I mostly quote from that, but cannot altogether disregard the 1965 text.

The 1978 version adds a Foreword in which Fowles discusses influences on the novel and the principal changes he has made. He acknowledges three predecessors: Alain-Fournier, Richard Jefferies for his boys' adventure book *Bevis* (discussed below), and Dickens's *Great Expectations*. Of all the revisions, he rates only two as "considerable changes": the "erotic element is stronger in two scenes...the correction of a past failure of nerve"; and he altered the ending because "some readers" found it "obscure." Of this Fowles writes, "I accept that I might have declared a preferred aftermath less ambiguously...and now have done so" (1978, 7).

Omitted from the revision is the early explanation of the term "magus." Prior to the 1965 title page is a quotation from Arthur Edward Waite's *The Key to the Tarot*, which introduces "The Magus, Magician, or Juggler, the caster of the dice and mountebank in the world of vulgar trickery." Among the symbols of the Magus, it explains, are roses and lilies. Some of this is told to Urfe in the enlarged chapter 58 in 1978 (485), but readers might find this information useful earlier. Why did

Fowles drop this quote: Did he think it gave away too much? Showed Conchis in a worse light than he intended? Was unnecessary? The original, quite appropriate dedication "To Astarte" was also removed from the publication page in 1978. Dell paperbacks placed a dark satyr with a lighted candle beween his horns on the covers of both versions, although the later design is head-and-horns only, and thus lacks the phallic suggestiveness of the 1965 cover. The Magus, Maurice Conchis, does deploy a satyr in one of his masques.

The aspect of *The Magus* that mainly concerns us here, the *domaine*, is fairly consistent in the two versions. Bourani is both an estate- and an island *domaine*: a Mediterranean villa and its grounds, including a bit of coastline, on *Phraxos* ('fenced'). This gives Conchis ample scope for his masques. Mitford, Urfe's predecessor at the boys' school, warned him about "the waiting room," and sure enough, prowling around the estate's boundary (another "errant"), Urfe finds an old sign, "*SALLE D'ATTENTE*," probably from a French *gare*. He goes to the villa, uninvited, and meets Conchis, who seems to expect him: tea for two has been set out. Urfe puts his age as sixtyish, and is struck by his penetrating eyes, more simian than human, his gnomic manner, and a slight resemblance to Picasso. He seems "slightly mad, no doubt harmlessly so" (Fowles 1978, 82). His villa contains a harpsichord, a library, and mementoes that Conchis uses as teaching tools. "Come now," he says. "Prospero will show you his *domaine*" (85): a loaded remark, evoking old French romances and Shakespeare, to whom the novel makes repeated references. While *Othello* and *Twelfth Night* are mentioned, most allusions are to *The Tempest*. But if Conchis is Prospero, which character will Urfe play? When he remarks, "Prospero had a daughter," Conchis retorts, "Prospero had many things. And not all young and beautiful" (85). As Urfe leaves, the "master of his domaine" strikes a pose: both arms raised, one foot forward – like an antique statue (91). Back at school, Urfe recalls the reference to Prospero, thinks of "sinister" meanings, and shivers (92).

Why go back, then? Staying away is not a viable option for Nicholas: there is little for him to do in the village except teach his schoolboys English, and he enjoyed the good life of "swinging sixties" London. No woman in the village is available to him. And it is in the nature of *domaines* to entice: as he left Bourani, Nick found an old, elbow-length, perfumed woman's glove by the path. The same musky scent, he thinks, emanated from a towel on a beach he explored earlier.

Under the towel was a poetry anthology with poems by Eliot, Auden, and Pound bookmarked and underlined. The glove seemed "unreasonably old, something from the bottom of a long-stored trunk," like the clothes at the *fête étrange*. These are hooks, and they are well set. Whatever Conchis may be, Urfe wants to know more about him. His shiver is not only of fear, but of attraction to a mystery: the standard emotional ingredients of most *domaines*.

Nicholas Urfe, however, is not a type of protagonist we have encountered before: a noble knight, or even a *"grand Meaulnes."* He is a personable cad, a bounder of the 'love-em-and-leave-em' school, like the rake Alfie in the film of that name. *Alfie* (1966) subjects its protagonist to moral scrutiny by confronting him with an abortion that he has made necessary, and following him until he is superseded (with a rich mistress he was prepared to marry) by a younger man. Thus life teaches him something. In *The Magus*, the rake's reform is not left to chance or time, but undertaken by Conchis and a cast of actors on and off the island. He is not their first pupil: Mitford was another, and perhaps the schooling will continue. Only late in the book does Nick learn the scope of the project: the subjects selected represent the moral deficiencies of modern, educated western manhood, whose values are to be ameliorated. The reformers have chosen to work privately, improving the breed one subject at a time.

Conchis, Urfe's host and judge, is elusive, with chameleon-like alterations during the novel. At first he is attractive in his mystery – the polyglot background that he reveals in cameos – and his culture: literacy, books, music, psychiatry, experimental theatre. Later he sours on Nick, treating him more harshly as he succumbs to the temptations that Conchis contrives for him: called "entrapment" if the police do it. In the last scenes of "arrest," trial, and verdict, Conchis comes close to Gregory Peck's chilling portrayal of Dr Josef Mengele in *The Boys from Brazil* (1978). His character is unprecedented in earlier *domaine* literature; the castle-lords that Arthurian knights encountered never ran such a gamut. Yet Conchis is not judged in the novel except by the discredited Urfe, and he is defended by the temptresses' mother, Lily de Seitas, who tells Nick late in the novel that Conchis and the actors refer to their project as "the godgame" (1978, 637). That is, they "play God" with their subjects: tempting, judging, and punishing them. But who judges the judges? Who rules on the morality of *their* actions, or the soundness of their philosophy of education? The success or failure of *The Magus* with its readers

– both fervent devotees and fervid haters – depends on how they evaluate the characters of Urfe and Conchis.

The Magus keeps its *domaine* before the reader to an unusual degree, referring to it directly and developing it at length. After its first association with Prospero, the *domaine* expands to include Conchis's masques, long before his views on theatre are explained. He spends one evening telling Nick (now his guest) about the Great War. After they part, Nick is falling asleep when he hears distant men singing "Tipperary," then the quintessential British marching song. As he listens, he is hit by a "cesspool smell," "an atrocious stench..., a nauseating compound of decomposing flesh and excrement": Conchis told him about the smell of the trenches and of being with a rotting "corpse in the shell-hole" (1978, 137). The scene and chapter end with Nick's remark, "I had entered the domaine" – not the physical estate, which he has entered before, but the realm of powerful magic and mystery. It is felt deeply, though its *how* and *why* are unknown. Later Nick is so fascinated by the weekend masques that, after finishing his Monday classes, he "had to go back to Bourani. ...I had to re-enter the domaine" (248). But the windows are shuttered and the house is empty. Nick is "furious that Conchis could spirit his world away; deprive me of it, like a callous drug-ward doctor with some hooked addict." The seductive happenings and visions of the *domaine* are seen as akin to opium or heroin, whose highs can be withheld, turning heaven to hell.

But if Conchis can dissolve his masque, he can also restore it, changed, keeping Urfe off balance or teaching a new lesson. In chapter 46 Nick rises late after sleeping at Bourani, only to find himself on "an empty stage" (1978, 328). Though his breakfast has been set out, there is no sign of Conchis or the cook. Nick searches the house, walks around the estate, and goes for a swim. From out in the water he sees the "girls" – by now Bourani's chief attraction and prime conundrum – waving from the beach. Everything about them is alleged, provisional, dubious. Are their names Rose and Lily (as on the Magus tarot card), or June and Julie, or neither? Are they hirelings? Patients? Sisters, as they say, or just look-alikes? Are they with Conchis, with Nick, or out for themselves? As their identities shift, so do his attitudes toward them. A *domaine* still exists, but in a different form, and it is obviously unstable. In the following chapter, the three of them see the American Sixth Fleet on the southern horizon, bearing "thousands of gum-chewing, contraceptive-carrying men" eastward. To Nick it seems that he is

...looking into the future...; into a world where there were no more Prospero's, no private domaines, no poetries, fantasies, tender sexual promises.... I...felt acutely the fragility not only of the old man's extraordinary enterprise, but of time itself. I knew I would never have another adventure like this. I would have sacrificed all the rest of my days to have this one afternoon endless, endlessly repeated, a closed circle, instead of what it was: a brief and tiny step that could never be retraced. (359-60)

This defines a "*domaine* experience" well: a "peak moment" (such as Fowles had on his first walk around Spetsai), unforgettable, but *only* a moment – short, tenuous, unrepeatable. The importance of time, with the protagonist's conscious-ness of the *domaine's* transience, is prominent and weighty here. Spenser knew it as Mutability.

Things turn sinister in chapter 49. One phase of the "godgame" is the *deus abscon-ditus* or hidden god. By this time Conchis is so seldom seen that Urfe believes he has withdrawn, giving him a free hand with the girls; he and Julie have some aqueous sex play just offshore. Starting to walk home at midnight, Nick fantasizes about exploring a more experienced and aroused Julie, and, "when we were satiated," somehow involving her sister: "two for the price of one" (1978, 377). No improvement yet! But nearing the ridge he hears a sound and dodges behind a tree. Six men, soldiers with guns and helmets, are standing on the crest. As they pass by on the path, he sees their German uniforms. Then "...I knew. The masque had moved outside the domaine, and the old devil had not given in one bit" (379). He recognizes the "soldier" carrying a radio: a science teacher at his school who has a transmitter in his laboratory. A spy! No wonder Conchis always knows when he is coming. He starts to run away, but is tripped and surrounded by seven German-speaking, German-looking soldiers – different ones, so now there are thirteen. Imagining the cost and effort of arranging all this, Nick falls "under the spell of Conchis the magician again. Frightened, but fascinated..." (382). The number of actors grows to 21, the last being a Greek playing a captive who hisses at Nick, "*Prodotis!*" (Traitor), tries to escape, is caught and beaten. Nick is having to relive the Nazi occupation, which Conchis described. Finally the "Nazis" walk away, leaving him tied up but within reach of a knife: furious but awed, "a man in a myth" (388).

Nick understands that the *domaine* has expanded, that Conchis can reach him anywhere on the island, but has yet to grasp the full implications of his power. He thinks of going to the police or phoning his embassy in Athens, but calms himself with the thought that Conchis is just playing Prospero (who is ultimately benign to the young suitor in *The Tempest*), and Julie professed to have "intuitive trust" in Conchis. He now believes that both girls are on his side. The Nazi masque, and a subsequent note from Conchis saying stay away, you have disappointed me, must be a "last black joke" before the sun comes out (1978, 390; not in 1965).

But the godgame is not over. Conchis will receive him again at Bourani, let him stroll "round the domaine," tell him more war stories (414-15). Then he will use his formidable powers to 'arrest' and 'try' him for emotional and moral failings, find him guilty, and leave him enraged, helpless, humiliated, and unconscious. Yet once back in London, hurting and depressed, Nick cannot let go of the *domaine*. "I looked back, Adam after the fall, to the luminous landscapes" and all that happened there, "as unable to wish that they had not happened as I was to forgive Conchis for having given me the part he did" (587): he had been cast as Caliban, not Ferdinand. Even so, realizing that his mixed feelings constitute "a sort of *de facto* forgiveness" of what was done to him, he follows the faint "trail of Conchis and Lily in England" because that "kept me, however tenuously and vicariously, in the masque..." (587). If Nick is still "in the masque," he is hooked on the *domaine*. He longs for its enchantment as ardently and hopelessly as Meaulnes ever did.

Conchis likes to dramatize his main points: stories he has told or subjects that have been discussed. Eventually he shares his *avant-garde* views on theatre, but Urfe notices his thespian leanings early on. As Conchis recalls finding Bourani in 1928, feeling that he was "expected," and that what had been waiting for him there was *himself*, Nick thinks, "underlying everything he did I had come to detect an air of stage-management, of the planned and rehearsed." It was done "as a dramatist tells an anecdote...the play requires" (111). This analysis is confirmed on later visits as Conchis produces the invisible "Tipperary" chorus, masques using myths (Apollo and Diana), the Nazi patrol, and others. Through these Urfe becomes involved with the two actresses who are supposed to be central to his "cure." Reflecting on "the miracle-mystery" of Conchis's *domaine*, Nick sees the dramas as "subtle psychosexual bars that kept us chained to Bourani" (377): "us" because he thinks June and Julie are his friends. Conchis is like an "Elizabethan nobleman. We were his Earl of Leicester's troupe" (377). Leicester and other aristocrats were patrons of drama in Shakespeare's day, in London and on country estates, as described above. Nick surmises that Conchis may have incorporated Heisenberg's uncertainty principle into his work, so that its outcome would be "indeterminate" (377). The "masque of Nazis" would be an example.

That night-scene on the ridge shows the elasticity of the *domaine*, but Urfe is slow to comprehend its scope. When the "Nazis" rough up the bruised, bloody, barefoot Greek partisan who stumbles along, groaning, Nick thinks, "the masque was running out of control" (1978, 384): another underestimate of Conchis's powers. During a long scene in chapter 52 (extensively revised in 1978), the Magus describes in detail what is happening around them, but Nick is too aggrieved and arrogant (thinking June and Julie his allies) to recognize the warning. Conchis explains that he had a private theatre at Bourani before and during the war, and that he

> *conceived a new kind of drama...in which the conventional separation*
> *between actors and audience was abolished. ...the notions of prosce-*
> *nium, stage, auditorium, were completely discarded. ...the action,*
> *the narrative, was fluid...the participants invent their own drama....*
> *...Artaud and Pirandello and Brecht were all thinking...along similar*
> *lines.* (411)

Urfe smiles sceptically, so Conchis spells it out. "We are all actors here.... None of us is what we really are. We all lie some of the time, and some of us all the time" (411). He announces that Nick has "failed to gain a part" in the play, that "The comedy is over," and repeats, "All here is artifice" (412). Urfe agrees to cooperate with the scheme "within limits." His host replies that "There is no place for limits in the meta-theatre," as he calls his "new kind of drama" (413).

The Greek prefix *meta-* meant "with" or "behind," and sometimes "change," says Oxford. In today's English it often means "beyond," which, along with "change," is Conchis's sense: his theatre transcends older norms, and he uses it to change people by mirroring their conduct. "Greece is like a mirror," he tells Nick, and uses that image in describing his discovery of Bourani (1978, 101, 111). Later Nick remarks that "one sometimes cannot stand one's own face in a mirror" (579). But Conchis has given the crucial meaning of "meta-theatre": it discards the distinction between actors and audience, stage and auditorium, and has "no place for limits." Walking around the estate afterwards, Nick remarks, "The theatre seemed truly empty" (414). "Seemed": the *grounds* may be empty, but now the meta-theatre accompanies him, so long as Conchis cares to impose his will. The Magus gives him one more warning: "The object of the meta-theatre is...to allow the participants to see through their first roles," in the part of the play that "precedes the final act, or catastrophe" (415). This is plain enough in retrospect, describing Nick's last days on Phraxos, when he is overpowered, drugged, and subjected to a "trial" – the dissection of his life by the actors he has seen in other roles – whose stated purpose is to destroy his illusions and show him his own true nature. Its effect on him is deep, thorough, traumatic humiliation. The application of force by the powerful to the weak is no prettier for being billed as justice.

Fowles retains enough features of earlier *domaines* for us to recognize this as one, but shifts the tone and function significantly. Bourani is attractive in a mysterious, quasi-magical way, so that Urfe is fascinated. Even at the end, in England, he barely regrets what happened there. He feels like an intruder at first, and a later visit is "like the first day. The being uninvited, unsure..." (1978, 408). (Alain-Fournier stressed Meaulnes's sense of intrusion at his *domaine perdu*.) While Nick *feels* "uninvited," he has actually been sent for, is expected and being observed, which points us to Fowles's own take on the *domaine*. Bourani does not sit idly waiting for passersby, as castles and chateaux once did, but lures and secures its prey like a Venus Flytrap. Its subjects are chosen for defects that are to be rooted out during their stay, willy-nilly. The closest parallel in the works discussed here is Bertilak in *Sir Gawain and the Green Knight*, who wants to test a knight (Urfe is several times likened to a knight errant). Hautdesert has a temptress, and Morgan le Fay, able to make Bertilak a vegetation god, as its Magus. But *Sir Gawain* is a milder version of the "godgame"; behind the meta-theatre is the shock treatment. Bertilak is comparatively open, fair, and friendly to Gawain: at their parting he explains everything, and gives Gawain an A-minus on his performance. Though the knight is chagrined, taking his shortcoming to heart, the action does not create the outrage or emotional turbulence of Conchis's psychiatric "trial" of Nicholas.

FOWLES'S NOVELLA "THE EBONY TOWER" (1974, in the volume of that name) is closely related to *The Magus*. Katherine Tarbox considered the two so similar that she did not give "The Ebony Tower" a separate chapter in *The Art of John Fowles*

(1988); Mahmoud Salami reports that Fowles said the story elucidates the novel (136). Fowles took a dim view of critics, interviewers, and professors, however, and sometimes misled them, or gave answers only partially true. This attitude, already noted in regard to *The Magus, The French Lieutenant's Woman,* and *Daniel Martin,* also operates in "The Ebony Tower." Fowles points us toward mediaeval French literature – an epigraph from Chrétien, mentions of him and Marie in the text, a translation of *Eliduc* in the volume – and sets the story at Coëtminais, a *manoir* in the ancient forest of Paimpont or Brocéliande in Brittany, home of earlier *domaines.* Yet these are not the deepest literary roots of the story. The painter Henry Breasley, lord of this estate, shares Fowles's low estimate of academic critics like the protagonist. David Williams is also a painter, but an abstractionist, a style that Breasley contemns, an art teacher, and a critic, sent by a London publisher to interview Breasley for a book on his work. Thus he represents the whole complex that Breasley derides as "the ebony tower." Several writers have noted that the "godgame" in *The Magus* has its counterpart in Fowles's relationship with readers, and so it is here. *Caveat lector,* then: treat authorial pronouncements sceptically.

Henry Breasley is not simply a re-run of Maurice Conchis. He is less exotic: a native Englishman who lives in neighbouring France. He is less sophisticated than the suave Greek, less self-controlled, less powerful; he could not mount the elaborate plots and masques that Conchis stages. Although Breasley seems comfortable, he is not wealthy, nor as self-assured as Conchis, yet he is more productive. Conchis's metatheatrical efforts are creative, but private and ephemeral; Breasley's paintings are a substantial legacy for museums and collectors. His work is "out there" to be judged, and has been widely approved for years. The cast of the two men's minds and their styles are very different: the Greek moralist and seeker after spiritual, psychological, and dramatic truth; the periodically crude English bohemian and former "bad boy" on his way to becoming a legend, still totally devoted to painting. Yet for all these differences, each is master of a *domaine* that reflects his essence, and is surrounded by compatible souls. Each receives a visitor from the outside world, a younger man seen as deficient in some way, and works on him, making his *domaine* a school and a mirror. Breasley's approach to David is more honest and open than Conchis's treatment of Nick, but in both cases the magus and his entourage overwhelm the visitor and leave him traumatized. Each of the victims refers to his host as an "old devil."

Nor are the targeted young men interchangeable. Urfe is a callow lad just out of college, footloose enough to take a post in Greece, and a libertine. Williams is 31, married with children, and paid to teach and write about art, besides being a painter. Little or nothing can be said against his morals; his wife is the only woman mentioned in his biographical sketch. He is "rather fond of being liked," and seasons his honesty with tact (Fowles 1974, 14). That his paintings exhibit "technical precision" and "went well on walls that had to be lived with," that he works on a "smaller scale than most nonfigurative painters," may be gentle digs, and he is complacent about his career: "things in general were shaping up well" (14-15). In retrospect, his stop to paint while driving through France foreshadows trouble: "stripes of watercolor" record "pleasing conjunctions of tone and depth," with notes ("in his neat hand") on the date, time of day, and weather, yet "he drew nothing" (3). David is a bit of a precisian ("rigidly precise or punctilious": Oxford). Still, Fowles presents him as "a young man who was above all tolerant, fair-minded and inquisitive" (16). We will see how far those qualities will take him at Coët, and so will he. (There is no corresponding passage about Urfe, *The Magus* being a first-person narrative.)

Fowles treats David almost as roughly as he did Nick, and in both cases the *domaine* delivers the assessment. Coëtminais – the old *manoir* and the surrounding forest, Chrétien's *Brocéliande* – has its charm, and is felt to be magical. It is deeply satisfying to those who belong there, but can be unsettling to the outsider. Like Bourani, it is a mirror with the power to reflect home truths about the viewer (as in most *domaines*, its inhabitants share this power). David is braced for the famously difficult Breasley, but he first meets the two young women, the painter's "assistants." Arriving early, he intrudes (as did Meaulnes), climbing over an apparently locked gate. Then, finding the front door open, and seeing no knocker or bell, he walks in, crosses the entrance hall and looks out to the back lawn, where, "in a close pool of heat, two naked girls lay side by side on the grass" (1974, 6). Having heard about "the wicked old faun and his famous afternoons," David lingers. "For a brief few seconds he registered the warm tones of the two indolent female figures, the catalpa-shade green and the grass green, the intense carmine of the hat-sash, the pink wall beyond...". Oh good, it is just an abstract painter using stripes of watercolour to record "pleasing conjunctions of tone and depth," not a voyeur! Returning to the front door, he sees a handbell, missed before, and rings.

Soon one of the girls (wearing a galabiya) appears. She says that the gate is not really locked: just pull on the padlock. So he *could* have driven in, and the noise of his car would have alerted them. So sorry! As she turns to go back to the garden, "the galabiya momentarily lost its opacity against the sunlight beyond; a fleeting naked shadow" (8).

David is *not* entering the lion's den because he has to: "his journey was not really necessary" (1974, 10). He has sketched his introduction, knows what he wants to say, *might* settle some biographical details (which he could do by mail), but will not make "artistic queries" because Breasley has been "cryptic, maliciously misleading or just downright rude" to previous interviewers. Why has he come, then? To meet a man he has studied, whose work he admires (up to a point), and "for the fun of it, to say one had met him." This is not quite the "wayward wandering" of Actaeon – though he has just seen Diana naked. Just why a famous painter with a well-known aversion to abstract painting agreed to this intrusion by a young abstractionist (the offer to David was made with his approval) is a pertinent question. Breasley did not acknowledge the copy of one of David's articles sent to him. (The rather lofty, pretentious tone of the biography of Breasley could be a take-off on Williams's style, or a general satire on art criticism.)

Yet the first meeting with Breasley is friendly, and David begins to hope that his host is "a paper tiger." At dinner that night, however, as the *vin rouge* begins to flow, Breasley attacks: the *veritas* in this *vino* is harsh and personal. "Obstructs" for abstracts is just the warning shot (1974, 35). After the third bottle Williams stops, but Breasley, eyes glazed, keeps drinking. Abstraction is the "Greatest betrayal in the history of art," the "Triumph of the bloody eunuch" (38-39): the genital theme is heard. David's open-mindedness just increases his fury against "piddling little theorems and pansy colors" (39). Pansy? "How many women you slept with, Williams?" – and, told that is none of his business, "Castrate. That's your game. Destroy." Rattled, David wonders if he was invited precisely for this. Breasley then denounces all "you people" as traitors, liberals: advocates of tolerance and "*Le fairplay*. Sheer yellowbelly" (40). David, described by Fowles as "fair-minded and inquisitive," is now quiet, embarrassed by "this monstrous bohemian travesty" (41). His host, however, wants to argue. Am I disappointing you? he asks. "Just overstating your case," replies David. "You really a painter, Williams? Or just a gutless bloody word-twister?" That might seem enough, but no. Does David know what "turning the cheek" means? "Bumboy. You a bumboy, Wilson? [sic]" (42). "On your knees and trousers down. Solves all, does it?" But there the limit of outrage has been reached; Breasley allows himself to be placated by the girls and escorted off to bed, with one final remark: "Ebony tower. That's what I call it" (44).

The aftermath is relatively benign. After helping move Breasley to his bedroom, David chats with each "gel," learning that the one Breasley calls "the Freak" is Anne, and "the Mouse" is Diana of the diaphanous *galabiya*, whose managing of and interpreting for Breasley impressed him. He "would have liked to talk a little longer." She reminds him of

> *The old teaching world — students you fancied, who fancied you a little, in some way the atmosphere of Coët reminded him of the days before Beth had entered his life; not that he had ever gone in much for having it off with students. He was a crypto-husband long before he married.* (1974, 47)

Breasley's "How many women you slept with?" was prescient, then. But the next morning he is "un*speak*ably sorry about last night. Gels tell me most ap*pall*ingly rude" (1974, 48). They shake hands, become "David" and "Henry," and after breakfast "stroll around the domain," chatting about gardens and rural life. David respects this Breasley, who "regretted nothing," was "a standing challenge to the monogamous" and "enormously selfish," yet "had come through to this": reputation, Coët, women, freedom (49-50). Compared to his own style, though, "it seemed not quite fair": you tried hard, did all the system demanded, and when you looked up the mountain, "on the summit stood a smirking old satyr in carpet slippers" (50). Soon, though, the four of them are strolling through the woods with picnic baskets, the girls wanting "a little *déjeuner sur l'herbe*" (48). Henry hails the forest and notes its theatrical aspect ("the quality of empty stage"); David basks "in the old man's...good graces" and plans to use this in his introduction (50-51).

He is off guard, then, believing that "his baptism of fire" the night before "had been a blessing in disguise" (1974, 51). That is, he thinks his troubles are over. Breasley's assault was the "ordeal" that knights errant endured in old romances, and "evidently he had passed the test" (55). But those ordeals rarely came singly; Arthurian heroes are usually tested at least twice. In *Sir Gawain and the Green*

Knight, Gawain thinks that his trial will be the return stroke, but it is his corner-cutting pact with Bertilak's wife that causes the only bloodshed he suffers. Later David realizes all this, but only after falling into a worse predicament. During the halcyon second day, he finds himself eying Diana (particularly after they strip to swim in the lake, then come ashore for lunch without dressing) and desiring her. Impossible, of course, or improbable, he thinks: "just that one was tempted" (57). This is where the parallels with Ovid's myth become striking. Actaeon, straying into a sacred grove (*errans / pervenit in lucum*), saw the goddess Diana bathing in a pool with her nymphs. Coëtminais is "the monks' forest": another sacred grove. David's craving for her will be punished in more than one way, but for the moment he is "all eyes," "head over heels," and other clichés denoting a tumble into Cupid's realm.

The entire estate acts on its denizens. Anne and Diana say that it has its own magic, which David senses the first day: a "faintly gamy ambiguity that permeated the place after predictable old Beth and the kids at home" (1974, 28). At the end he will feel that "Coët had been a mirror" (101). Diana too feels "under a spell" there (83). When she and David, mutually smitten, try to rationalize their feelings, she suggests, "It's just Coët" (90). Anne has a slant on this, telling David, "It's this place. You think, fantastic. When you first come. Then you realize it's the original bad trip" (97). That could apply to many a *domaine,* starting with the Garden of Eden. David uses the term "domain" (in its English form) on his first-morning stroll, and soon feels its growing power. Talking with the girls while Breasley sleeps during the picnic, David

> *felt drawn on into a closer and closer mesh with these three unknown lives, as if he had known them much longer, or the lives he did know had somehow mysteriously faded and receded in the last twenty-four hours. Now was acutely itself; yesterday and tomorrow became the myths. There was a sense of privilege too....* (66)

This is how it feels to enter a *domaine.* That evening, sitting across from a dressed-up Diana ("just a tiny air that she was out to kill") at dinner, David "felt a little bewitched, possessed; ...one had forgotten what the old male freedom was like..." (68). It is not only her, he thinks: it is Coët and "the whole day. He had enjoyed it enormously.... It had been so densely woven and yet simple; so crowded with new experience and at the same time primitive, atavistic, time-escaped." "Atavistic" denotes a "Resemblance to remote ancestors, reversion to earlier type," but can also mean a "recurrence of disease after intermission..." (Oxford). If Fowles had that sense in mind, what disease might this be? Promiscuity? "The old male freedom"?

Fowles's general intentions with David are clear, though. Like Nick, he has a design flaw to be exposed. Nick is mostly attacked from the outside; he does not seem to change or learn much about himself. David's correction moves from outer to inner: Breasley's insults the first night, Diana's rejection, and his own acceptance of their verdicts as he drives to Paris. Everything the old man said – yellowbelly, eunuch, traitor, obstructs – rings true. His whole career has been wrong, and somehow the fiasco with Diana proves this. The painter showed him why he calls her the Mouse. She is his Muse: M( )USE. In the space he sketches an O-shaped vulva. So, "if one wanted signs as to the nature of the rejection..." (1974, 101). The Greek Diana was goddess of the hunt, the moon, and the night, but also a muse and the mother of muses, the "White Goddess." Now, like intruding Actaeon, David is torn apart by his own property: not hounds but self-doubts. He acknowledges the strength of the case against him, the justice of the sentence. Language failed him with Diana, and his draft introduction now looks "hopeless" (104). In retrospect, he had "sailed past" the "preposterously obvious reef" of Henry's rant, had thought the ordeal behind him, and then his blindness and "love of being liked did the rest. The real rock of truth had lain well past the blue lagoon" (100-01). Fowles even makes David see that "he would not change; he would go on painting as before, he would forget this day," or re-interpret it in his favour (104). At the end, meeting his wife, he "surrenders...to abstraction," saying "I survived" (106).

Why was Fowles so hard on the male leads of two of his own own popular fictions? A sympathetic response to feminism makes sense for *The Magus*, but not for "The Ebony Tower": Williams has been "behaving himself" (which Breasley sees as a fault). David, however, teaches and presumes to be a critic: Fowles's most detested occupation. Daniel Martin, in the novel of that name, says, "No creator can like critics. There is too much difference between the two activities. One is begetting, the other is surgery. However justified the criticism, it is always inflicted by someone who hasn't, a eunuch, on someone who has, a generator..." (Fowles

1977, 99). There is the eunuch again: Breasley's insult to David. In a later inter-view Fowles complained that English critics treat authors as schoolmasters treat backward pupils. "And there's this weird feeling," he added, "that the true basis of authority must lie in the analyzing academic. Now that I hate; that I hate" (Tarbox 180). So Fowles agreed with Breasley on this point, which explains their savag-ing of the teacher-critic-obstruct painter David Williams. In fact he is made to savage himself, cry "*Mea maxima culpa!*" and kiss the rod. At Coët, David is given a revelation of "what he was born, still was, and always would be: a decent man and eternal also-ran" (Fowles 1974, 105). The flaw, being of the essence, cannot be changed or lived down; like 'Brighton Rock', it goes all the way through. He has *posed* as an artist – an offence against the Muse, who, Robert Graves warns, "demands full-time service or none at all" – and must serve a life sentence.

In the 1984 film version of "The Ebony Tower," John Mortimer (screenplay) and Robert Knights (director) made the Fowles / Breasley view of David visible. Casting Sir Laurence Olivier as Breasley gave gravitas to the role, making it the moral centre, and Mortimer wrote several new speeches to buttress his position. Pale, slender, 40-year-old Roger Rees played David as a tense, uptight fellow: Breasley's sense of him. The opening scene shows a close-up of one of his abstracts being created en route to Coët: horizontal stripes of colour, applied *using a ruler* that also makes black verticals. Then the camera retreats to show that he is paint-ing a row of tall poplars across a broad river: a much richer scene. When David leaves his car at the gate and walks in to Coët, he pauses to *put on a tie*, and dons a foppish white suit for dinner. He even wears a tie on his romantic night walk with Diana. If anything, he is *less* amiable, more buttoned-down, than in the book, and no match for Olivier's Breasley, before whom he looks frightened and defen-sive. Mortimer does not write new speeches to fortify *him*. Breasley's contempt seems well-founded.

We may wonder more broadly why any author would take the time and trouble to create an enticing *domaine* and then use it so destructively. Why create plot, setting, characters, dialogue, only to drop the whole mass on your blunderering protagonist? This is not the last time the question will arise, and answers are rarely provided (though they may be implicit) in literary texts. We can see why Milton devoted so much effort to describing the Garden of Eden: readers are drawn into sympathy with the place so that they will later feel the magnitude of its loss. At a guess, Conchis might say that he did not use his *domaine* to destroy, but rather to cauterize the base, unhealthy parts of Nick and thus ultimately to help him. (I doubt that Breasley would offer a serious justification.) But there is a broader answer to the general question: interesting but flawed young people are attracted to *domaines* as bears to honey, and that can be the beginning of an absorbing tale. Build it and they will come – and never be the same, nor ever forget.

SEVERAL OTHER PROMINENT ESTATE-*DOMAINES* COULD be treated at this point. Fonthill Splendens, the mansion where wealthy William Beckford, Junior gave a notorious Christmas party in 1781, is tempting, despite the paucity of reliable information. Jay Gatsby's rented mansion (itself quite Splendens) in *The Great Gatsby* is also an obvious candidate for inclusion here. But both of these places are so famous for the *parties* once thrown there that they achieve *domaine* status chiefly or entirely because of them, so they appear in the festive section of Chapter 9. In any case, the estates discussed above are sufficiently representative of the main types: benign, malignant, amorous, indeterminate, or tutti frutti.

CHAPTER 6:

Domaines of Childhood and Youth

ANCIENT MIDDLE EASTERNERS NATURALLY SAW gardens – oases in the surrounding deserts – as *domaines*, and mediaeval Europeans used castles and manors, the centres of their social lives, in the same way. But some later authors found their *domaines* in the earlier stages of life, wherever lived – i.e. in the fourth dimension rather than the first three. That is not a firm dichotomy, of course. All time is lived in some space, remembered as it was at a certain time or times. Several of the authors in this chapter appear to make a *domaine* of rural or of collegiate life, for example, but their nostalgia can be seen to stem from the fact that *they were young* then, and are not so now. In the works I treat below, youth and its evanescence seem to be the deepest substratum of feeling.

But whence comes the urge to idealize or hallow those early, long-ago times? Not everyone does this: if you had an unhappy childhood or schooldays those will not be *domaines*, though they may be anti-*domaines*. Yet for many people their early experiences *were* iconic, and they worship them in some way. In part, this is a manifestation of the phenomenon discussed in Part I: our sensitivity to time's passage and the changes it brings, our dread of its irreversibility, its one-way street. Some of the oldest extant literature frames the first stage(s) of human *history* as the best, which may have begotten the idea that childhood is the most favoured part of the individual life. The pristine Garden of Eden is the best known, but near the beginning of "western" writing, the Greek poet Hesiod (8th century BCE?) gave in his *Works and Days* a mythic history of humanity in which the first phase was the highest. A "golden race" of god-created men (there were no women yet) lived in peace, justice, and innocence, healthy and happy, simply eating the fruits of the earth in a perpetual spring. Even then this idea may have been borrowed from farther east, probably India. Hesiod's five "races" were the Golden, Silver, Bronze, Heroic, and Iron. Each was worse than the preceding – except the Heroic (the Trojan War): a brief uptick. Hesiod's idea passed to Empedocles, other Greek poets, and the Romans, especially Vergil and Ovid.

Hesiod's "Heroic anomaly" had been excised by then: there are only Four Ages (not "races"), all metallic, each worse than the last, in Ovid's *Metamorphoses*, the most popular account of the idea; those ages are the first metamorphoses. His Golden Age builds on Hesiod's: no laws, judges, punishments, wars, walled towns, tree-cutting, or farming. Men gathered fruits, nuts, and cereals, drank from rivers of milk or honey, and took nectar from the trees (still no mention of women). The Silver Age began as a coup: the god Saturn (identified with Greece's Chronos) was deposed by Jove (Zeus), who invented seasonal extremes of weather, which necessitated houses and agriculture. So Jove was a sort of stepfather who introduced a harsher regime: a pattern subsequently found in many a folk tale and novel. The Golden Age was a kind of *domaine* in classical myth, though it lacked the literary characteristics that we have come to associate with the idea.

The idea of a Golden Age evolved further during the Renaissance (which knew Ovid well, Latin being its *lingua franca*). In the 1570s Michel de Montaigne wrote one of his first essays "On Cannibals," which introduced the idea of the "noble savage." Reading accounts of voyages to Brazil, he rejected the idea that its natives are "barbarous or savage" ("we call barbarous anything that is contrary to our own habits": Montaigne 108). Truly, "These people are wild in the same way...that fruits are wild, when nature has produced them by herself" (109). He argues that the productions of nature are superior to those of art, i.e. civilization. Montaigne adduces Plato in support of this view, a reversal of prevailing European thought. These South American natives, he continues,

> ...are still very close to their original simplicity. They are still governed
> by natural laws and very little corrupted by our own. They are still
> in ...a state of purity.... I think that what we have seen of these people
> with our own eyes surpasses not only the pictures with which poets

have illustrated the golden age,...but the ideas and the very aspira-
tions of philosophers as well. (109-10)

Montaigne had not studied Brazilians himself, and there are notes of ignorance
and condescension here, yet with the publication of the *Essais* (1580) the intellectual framework was in place for childhood to be recognized as a Golden Age
that each of us might remember. The *classical* one was long gone, but Montaigne
had located a contemporary descendant of it, and if the Brazilian native, representing the childhood of the species, could "surpass" the Golden Age, why not the
individual child? Was infancy not a time of peace, innocence, and absence of work
as well?

That step was taken, though not quickly; attitudes towards children needed
to change first. They might be pampered in well-off families, but childhood was
regimented, not celebrated or idealized, in the sixteenth century. Renaissance
paintings often depict children as dwarfish adults; in lower-class families, they
joined the work force early. In later seventeeth-century Europe, however, the emotional bonds that we now believe (should) unite family members were being discussed, encouraged, and sometimes observed. Lawrence Stone's *The Family, Sex
and Marriage in England 1500-1800* (1977) argues that during that period ties of
affection within middle-class families were strengthening. After 1640, he writes,
the growth of "Affective Individualism" produced the "Closed Domesticated
Nuclear Family," with its "strong affective ties" (7). Parents became more devoted
to their children (the spread of contraceptives may have helped), who enjoyed
"greater freedom" and were identified as a "special status group" (8, 221). In family
portraits they were painted in a more natural way. Parent-child relations became
more "child-oriented, affectionate and permissive" (405). For guidance in child-
rearing, bourgeois parents turned from Calvinism to John Locke's treatise on
education (1693), which saw each child as a *tabula rasa* (blank slate) to be written
on, rather than as an inheritor of original sin. There was more home-schooling,
recommended by Locke. We even hear complaints about "excessive permissive-
ness" (435ff.)! Still, "Childhood came to be regarded as the best years of one's
life," writes Stone: a veritable "Golden Age" (449).

By the end of the eighteenth century, creative writers were reflecting these
changes. Jean-Jacques Rousseau's treatise on education, *Emile* (1762), gave

extended treatment to a subject whose importance was one of his tenets. Locating evil in society, not in human nature, Rousseau seconded much of Locke; the sinless child was not to be stamped with society's wisdom, but to be allowed to seek truth where intelligent curiosity led. One of the pioneers of permissive education, he was duly persecuted. In England, William Blake attracted notice in 1789 with *Songs of Innocence*, in whose "Introduction" a child on a cloud asks him for a song about a lamb. So he writes "happy songs" for "Every child" (ll. 19-20), including "The Lamb," "Cradle Song," and "Laughing Song." He also produced engravings and mottoes "For Children: The Gates of Paradise" (1793). Later he darkened the picture, tempering innocence with experience, but this is still a high level of attention from a major poet. Blake anticipated Wordsworth in seeing the artist as a grown child.

The social-exposé novels of Charles Dickens prove that this transformation was far from complete in his time; in fact, Stone found that the improved treatment of children went into reverse as Victorian England industrialized. Yet Dickens could assume that many readers shared his belief that "Gradgrind" educators and child labour were aberrations from a desired norm and *ought not to be*. Their perpetrators were throwbacks to a lower stage. And Dickens's audience was likely to be familiar with some literary *domaines* built around childhood and youth by then.

Mighty Prophet! Seer Blest!

That is how William Wordsworth hails *you* in his "Intimations Ode." Yourself as a child, that is, when you were also "Nature's Priest" and "best Philosopher." The tougher strains of sixteenth- and seventeenth-century social and political thought – Machiavelli, Hobbes, La Rochefoucauld – gave way to softer, even sentimental tones in Locke and the Third Earl of Shaftesbury during the eighteenth. Moral feeling and altruistic sympathy came to be prized as uniquely human. Wordsworth's contribution to this shift was to place the purest, highest form of these feelings in the child. In "Intimations of Immortality from Recollections of Early Childhood," we come "trailing clouds of glory... / From God, who is our home" (Wordsworth 1936, ll. 64-65). Like the sun and the light of revelation, we arise in the east, but glorious dawn fades to ordinary daylight as we travel west, and "Shades of the prison-house begin to close" upon us (67). For Wordsworth, childhood was everyone's *domaine*, for the loss of which we seek compensation. That is the subject of the ode, which begins with the *domaine*, goes on to admit its loss, and concludes with the consolations he finds in the remnants of our "primal sympathy" with Nature: faith, philosophy, and fellow-feeling. That is the familiar shape of a *domaine*: it was wonderful, it is unforgettable, and it is gone forever. Just one of those things. ("A trip to the moon on gossamer wings.")

Some of Wordsworth's best-known short poems clarify his outlook. "My Heart Leaps Up" (written 1802) describes his exultation on seeing rainbows, and identifies it with his feelings as a child. There is no suggestion that time has dimmed his response; this natural *domaine* still delights him whenever sunshine strikes aerial moisture at the right angle. His conclusion about the importance of that continuity became the epigraph of the Immortality Ode:

> *The Child is father of the Man;*
> *And I could wish my days to be*
> *Bound each to each by natural piety. (Wordsworth 1936)*

"Piety" was originally reverence for parents; Vergil calls Aeneas *pius* because he honours his father. Wordsworth is pious toward his own child-father, and hopes that rapport will last. "I Wandered Lonely as a Cloud" (1804) is a simpler instance of connecting with nature and the past. The sight of thousands of wild daffodils blooming beside a lake once brought him "wealth," and often, even now, lying "on my couch," he can relive that vision: "They flash upon that inward eye" we all have, filling his heart with such pleasure that it "dances with the daffodils." "The Solitary Reaper" (1805) is another record of such continuity. The "Highland Lass" singing a plaintive air as she reaps not only pleases him deeply at the time, but "The music in my heart I bore, / Long after it was heard no more." This moment too, with the feelings it aroused, has stayed with him. Each of these is a small *domaine* that moved him once and, preserved in memory, retains its force.

But these are mere chips on the great stream of *The Prelude*, begun in 1799. Equal to a healthy novel in bulk, *The Prelude* is one of the longest poems in English: longer than *Paradise Lost*. Wordsworth revered Milton, and wanted to revive the true bardic voice that seemed to have died with him. His chosen subject – secular, but touched with gleams of divinity – is "The Growth of a Poet's Mind." The purity that Milton located in the beginning of human history and Montaigne in the New World, Wordsworth placed in every infancy: a deist recasting of Judaeo-Christian myth. Though he refers to "God," his religion is rarely Biblical. "Eden" changes meaning as it is relived in each person's life. "Deity" is a shadowy power behind Nature, through which we sense it. *The Prelude* is a time machine that recreates a lost *domaine*, but not Milton's. The poem implies that we all had this, though only poets can bring it back.

Wordsworth left us two versions: the original, written by 1805 but not published, and the revision published in 1850. Both deserve to be consulted, which can most conveniently be done in *The Prelude. A Parallel Text*, edited by J.C. Maxwell (Penguin 1986). My quotations are from the 1850 text in that edition unless otherwise indicated.

The first book ("Childhood and School-Time") evokes Wordsworth's pastoral, outdoor boyhood. "Fair seed-time had my soul": a time in which he found both "beauty" and "fear" in nature, as when he hung on steep cliffs in the wind, seeking birds' nests (I: 301-02). Philosophical passages ("Dust as we are, the immortal spirit grows": 340) alternate with narratives that generate morals. One evening he filches a rowboat from a cave on a lake shore and rows out ("an act of stealth / And troubled pleasure": 361-62). To row straight, he keeps his eyes fixed on a rocky ridge, but as the boat moves farther out,

> ...*from behind the craggy steep till then*
> *The horizon's bound, a huge peak, black and huge,*
> *As if with voluntary power instinct*
> *Upreared its head. (377-80)*

A teacher of geometry or art might diagram this scene to explain angles or perspective, but the boy's only teacher is Nature – and conscience, which decides to make a point. As he rows,

> ...*growing still in stature the grim shape*
> *Towered up between me and the stars, and still,*
> *For so it seemed, with purpose of its own*
> *And measured motion like a living thing*
> *Strode after me. (381-85)*

Turning around, he hastens back to shore and returns the rowboat to its cave.

This was his first encounter with what he calls "Powers." Wordsworth repeat-edly tried to recreate what he felt on the occasions when he half-glimpsed, half-intuited mysterious forces. Ice-skating with friends on winter evenings was "a time of rapture!" (430). "We hissed along the polished ice in games / Confederate" (434-35) as precipices echoed their shouts and icy crags tinkled above. But did other children notice that "distant hills / Into the tumult sent an alien sound / Of melancholy" (442-44)? One may doubt that Nature *intended* this education, but not his claim that these scenes stayed with him:

> *- Unfading recollections! At this hour*
> *The heart is almost mine with which I felt*
> *From some hill-top on sunny afternoons,*
> *The paper kite high among fleecy clouds*
> *Pull at her rein like an impetuous courser (491-95)*

"Almost." The vividness enhances the validity of the claim, though "Almost" resembles the tortured wrestling of the "Intimations Ode."

Book II presents the teen-age Wordsworth, whose rural upbringing apparently kept the "shades of the prison house" at bay. He recalls other scenes: rowing to an island and patronizing a tavern, "a splendid place" for strawberries and cream, and bowling on the green (II: 142). He was still impressionable – "the sky, / Never before so beautiful, sank down / Into my heart," and "Thus were my sympathies enlarged" (172-75) – and consciously sought nature "For her own sake" (203). A central passage (232-44) hails infancy's blissful sense of closeness to a mother indistinguishable from Mother Nature. (Northrop Frye wrote that poesy tries to "recapture" a "lost sense of identity with our surroundings": 1963, 9.) Wordsworth insists that the nursing babe both receives and creates: "the first / Poetic spirit of our human life" (1986 II: 258, 260-61). Most lose this spirit, but poets develop it. As in "My Heart Leaps Up," the child fathers the man, who feels "natural piety." The artist / child became a Romantic cliché partly because Wordsworth described communing with nature in "solitude / More active even than 'best society'" (294-95). Loss and longing exist, but the soul recalls "how she felt," if not "what she felt" (316-17). The *domaine* does not vanish.

Wordsworth believes that he developed both "religious love / In which I walked with Nature" and a "creative sensibility," which shed an "auxiliar light" on the data of his senses (II: 357-58, 360, 368). At seventeen, he still communed with and paid homage to Nature, having lost neither his "sense of identity" with Her nor a unified sensibility; "all my thoughts / Were steeped in feeling," he writes (398-99). If he has lived close to Nature, it is the gift of mountains, lakes, cataracts, mists and winds; if he has retained confidence in human nature "in these times of fear," it is the gift of Nature (432; the passage is the same in 1805). This is the conviction of which "I Wandered Lonely" and "The Solitary Reaper" provide examples, the recollected natural *domaine* giving comfort in later years and thus still existing. It resembles Marcel Proust's perception that *le temps perdu* is not really lost, but lives on deep in memory, from which it may be recalled, or may arise spontaneously. The first two books of *The Prelude* are much of a piece, then: the rural *domaine* of his childhood, the spiritual and emotional responses that made him the poet he is.

But Book III brings radical changes. Hitherto he has lived in rural western England; now he goes up to Cambridge, which is shockingly different. At first he roams "Delighted through the motley spectacle" – gowns, gateways, courtyards, towers – as if in a dream: "Migration strange for a stripling of the hills" (III: 31, 34), yet touched by a "Fairy's wand" (36). Perhaps he has just exchanged one *domaine* for another? But soon we hear of alienation. Within days he is wondering how he can live there, "a strangeness in the mind, / A feeling that I was not for that hour, / Not for that place" (80-82). As "the dazzling show" of the university pales, he begins taking long solitary walks in the country (90). The Cambridgeshire fens lack the sublimity of the western hills, yet have their own beauty. He sees that the earth is "nowhere unimbellished by some trace / Of that first Paradise" (111-12). His own beliefs sound more pantheistic; he attributes "a moral life" to the stones on the road (132). In regard to Nature, he finds himself "as sensitive as waters are / To the sky's influence," as "a lute [an Aeolian harp] / That waits upon the touches of the wind" (139-42). Yet Cambridge threatens to divide his soul: he loves Nature, but his "heart / Was social," and "if a throng was near," he went to it (234-36). He feels that he wasted much time there.

A large rhythm of *The Prelude* is this cycling between communion and alienation. In Book IV, "Summer Vacation," he returns to the pastoral scenes of his youth. An inspired image describes leaning over "the side / Of a slow-moving boat, upon the breast / Of a still water" and gazing down into the lake (IV: 256-58). "Beneath him in the bottom of the deep" are many beauties, yet he "often is perplexed and cannot part / The shadow from the substance" (260-64). Reflections confuse him; his field of vision "now is crossed by gleam / Of his own image, by a sunbeam now" (267-68). Then he pounces: "Such pleasant office have we long pursued / Incumbent o'er the surface of past time" (271-72). It is a neat closure of an extended simile (rowing-writing). Anyone who has meditated on past events will see the metaphor's aptness: the reflections of self, the "wavering motions sent he knows not whence" (269). The poem / rowboat floating on the past is a Proustian image, yet "There was an inner falling off" (278). His list of diversions – feasts, dances, games – indicts socializing again: "all conspired / To lure my mind from firm habitual quest" (286-87). Such "trivial pleasures" were a "poor exchange" for nature and books, to which he should have been truer (298). He now dedicates himself to poetry.

Wordsworth stops narrating in Book V to reiterate the importance of nature and childhood to him; "the speaking face of earth and heaven" was his "prime teacher," so "This verse is dedicate to Nature's self" (V: 13-14, 230). What he values in childhood is spelled out later: children should be "not too wise" (or learned, or good), "but wanton, fresh..." (411-12. The first meaning of "wanton" in England was "sportive, playful, wild"). Let them live simply, and "May books and Nature be their early joy!" (423). Help them to knowledge, but "not purchased by the loss of power!" – a term of growing importance (425). One power is the appeal of romantic fiction, legends, "adventures endless," and the psychological role that products of the imagination play, for "Dumb yearnings, hidden appetites, are ours" (500, 506). Then, crucially, "Our childhood sits / ...upon a throne / That hath more power than all the elements" (507-09): our identification with the natural world, which, Frye warns, we generally lose. Yet even as "we learn to live / In reconcilement with our stinted powers" and become "yoke-fellows / To custom," we know that our real friends are imagination and its offspring, including literary *domaines* (517, 520-21).

Wordsworth does not deny that some powers are lost over time (as in the "Intimations Ode"), and there follows another cry for the *domaine perdu* of childhood freshness:

> *I am sad*
> *At thought of raptures now for ever flown;*
> *Almost to tears I sometimes could be sad*

To think of, to read over, many a page,
Poems withal of name, which at that time
Did never fail to entrance me, and are now
Dead in my eyes, dead as a theatre
Fresh emptied of spectators. (V: 545-52)

He will produce a theatrical *domaine* in Book VII, but an *empty* theatre is also a strong image: a *domaine* stripped of its magic. (Alain-Fournier and Fowles also have empty theatres.) Wordsworth considers the world of imagination no less powerful when untrue, because its source is our "most noble attribute": a "wish for something loftier" than reality (V: 573, 575). An "intimate" acquaintance with nature during youth prepares us for the "great Nature" of "mighty poets," for the same "Visionary power" lives in them, in childhood, and in nature: all part of one economy (588-95).

In Book VI he returns to college, "not so prompt / Or eager" as before, keeping more to himself, reading randomly (VI: 6-7). Wordsworth skims over two years en route to "the third summer," when he and a friend head for France, the Alps – a new *domaine* – and rejuvenation (322-23). France wakes him from his alienated mood, and he recovers some of his childhood joy: one of a series of such recoveries. The Grande Chartreuse monastery moves him by the "awful" ('full of awe') and "soul-affecting *solitude*" of its setting (419, 421). Anti-clerical mobs want to eject the monks and despoil the place, but Wordsworth heeds another voice. "'Stay, stay your sacrilegious hands!' – The voice / Was Nature's, uttered from her Alpine throne" (430-31). Nature speaks for the spirit: "Let this one temple last, be this one spot / Of earth devoted to eternity!" (434-35). The place's transcendental qualities, the "imaginative impulse sent / From...yon shining cliffs," appeal strongly to the poet (462-63). When they cross the Alps, he is "grieved" that there is no more to climb, and eulogizes the imagination (586; cp. 525-26). Its "awful Power" hints at the "invisible world" beyond our senses, the "something evermore about to be" that is our true home (594, 602, 608). It is a thoroughly spiritual reading of the Alps.

Imagination is also central to his tribute to the theatre in Book VII ("Yet was the theatre my dear delight," VII: 407). He can show that his themes operate everywhere. Sketching several character types of Georgian drama – the "beauteous dame," the "romping girl," the "mumbling sire" – he notes how effective their broad acting is on the "common man," even at "a country playhouse, some rude barn / Tricked out for that proud use" (449-50), where you might see daylight through a chink in the wall at a summer performance, and suddenly realize where you were. Theatre "Gladdened [him] more" than any "dazzling cavern of romance" (454-55), but both are *domaines*. Late in Book VII, Wordsworth evokes London's "blank confusion," its "perpetual whirl / Of trivial objects," and suggests that only someone raised in the country could feel "The Spirit of Nature" there (722, 725-26, 765-66). That also holds for nomadic peoples, the "roving Indian" and "sun-burnt Arab," brought in as examples of 'noble (or fortunate) savages' (747, 749).

The importance of a country upbringing for city-dwellers is developed in Book VIII. Again recreating his own childhood, Wordsworth celebrates the cult of the shepherd, almost as idealized as in pastorals. "Smooth life had flock and shepherd in old time," it begins, "Smooth life had herdsman" (VIII: 173, 177). This romantic homage claims that, for a sensitive boy, a shepherd seen on a skyline was "A solitary object and sublime" (272), rather like the cross on a rocky spire above the Grande Chartreuse. And "Thus was man / Ennobled outwardly before my sight," and "purified," inspiring "reverence of human nature" (275-76, 304, 278-79). This extension of his own love of nature to humanity worked to heal the split between city and country hitherto prominent in his thought. As his own inner resources grew, he could feel "what in the Great City had been done / And suffered," which helped him to appreciate its "majesty and power," as in "the Wilds" (626-27, 631, 633). And since that was congenial to his imagination, he could take "more elevated views / Of human nature," including a "trust / In what we *may* become" (644-45, 649-50). This is no mean achievement for the youth who arrived at Cambridge inclined to see himself as a nature boy, well apart from the madding crowd.

When not too oppressed by the "sad scenes" of London, he has a revelation: "Lo! every thing that was indeed divine / Retained its purity inviolate" (VIII: 654-56). Perhaps such an idea "aroused / The mind of Adam, yet in Paradise / Though fallen..." (658-60). Wordsworth can conceive of a time, however brief, when the fallen existed inside the unfallen, and *knew* that. So both Adam and he lived in *domaines* that were fragile and mixed, yet still wondrous and pure, "with something heavenly fraught" (664). For Wordsworth, London is both a place, and a time downstream from the (unfallen) Eden of a childhood in nature.

Book IX returns to the "powers" that link humanity and nature. Visiting Paris, Wordsworth finds that the Bastille, whose fall marked the start of the Revolution, has the same aura of living history that he felt in London. "History" is an illusion ("all men are deceived, / Reading of nations and their works," IX: 170-71), yet *being there* so soon afterwards, he senses "powers, / Like earthquakes," thrusting up events (178-79). Sympathy with egalitarian ideas, and the "mountain liberty" experienced in his youth (238), made him a Republican in France, seeing more links, giving more instances of "natural piety." Nature, you could say, taught him politics.

Domaines are conspicuously absent from Book X; Wordsworth saw none. France was in the throes of revolution, and when he returned to England, he could not "glide / Into communion with her sylvan shades," preferring to live in London: a radical shift in his outlook (X: 242-43). The Engish mood was reactionary. Wordsworth was shocked by Britain's siding with European regimes opposed to France's revolution. The feelings he reports – "pity and shame," a "shock" to his "moral nature" – resemble those of many Americans during the Vietnam War (265, 268-69, 272). He asserts that such reactions were widespread, and that there occurred "in the minds of all ingenuous youth / Change and subversion from that hour" (267-68):

> *Oh! Much have they to account for, who could tear,*
> *By violence, at one decisive rent,*
> *From the best youth in England their dear pride,*
> *Their joy, in England.... (300-03)*

Then came a second powerful shock: the Revolution turned violent. Seeing little that he could affirm, Wordsworth felt like one of the "ancient Prophets" who "denounced, / On towns and cities" their "punishment to come" (437, 441-43).

Yet in Book XI Wordsworth regains a *domaine* and (some) faith as he recalls the French Revolution. For an idealist ("I had approached, like other youths, the shield / Of human nature from the golden side": XI, 79-80) it was a taste of paradise: "Bliss was it in that dawn to be alive, / But to be young was very Heaven!" (108-09). Those old enemies Romance and Reason called a truce. Prelapsarian Eden was revived, enlarged:

...the whole Earth,
The beauty wore of promise – that which sets
(As at some moments might not be unfelt
Among the bowers of Paradise itself)
The budding rose above the rose full blown. (117-21)

Not a myth, "But in the very world," *this* one, "where, in the end, / We find our happiness, or not at all" (142-44). This is a bold assertion by one raised in a Christian country, and he adds that he remains "a child of nature, as at first" (168). But his distress over England's conduct and events in France increases, bringing about a sort of nervous breakdown. Wavering between belief and disbelief, "endlessly perplexed," desperately seeking proof of anything, he "lost / All feeling of conviction," and so, "Sick, wearied out with contrarieties, / Yielded up moral questions in despair" (298, 302-05). He found some solace in studying science, and in his sister Dorothy. The book that begins by celebrating the Revolution moves on to a tribute to her.

In Book XII Wordsworth tackles his problems. His solution is again Nature, which acts as a restorative in bad times. It helped him overcome his weaknesses: a spirit of criticism and excessive reliance on sense impressions, especially from his eyes, "The most despotic of our senses" (XII: 129). They "often held my mind / In absolute dominion," he admits (130-31). This may seem a minor flaw, but for one who possessed "imaginative power" in childhood, it was intolerable, and he "shook the habit off" (203-04). This rejection of 'sensationalist' philosophy has personal implications. The famous "spots of time" passage (208 ff.) is another example of how nature's ministry operates, giving the literary time machine a basis in psychology: "...diversity of strength / Attends us, if but once we have been strong" (270-71). A "spot of time" may become a *domaine*. Among accounts of his own 'spots' is one summarizing the whole process throughout the poem. Now it is "man" whom he apostrophizes, for the poet can "see / In simple childhood something of the base / On which thy greatness stands" (272-75). This he has known "almost from the dawn / Of life" (278-79), but his powers are failing. "I see by glimpses now; when age comes on, / May scarcely see at all," but he "would give" his present feelings "Substance and life," capturing "the spirit of the Past / For future restoration" (281-86). Memorials, then, and time capsules.

This mood continues in Book XIII. Nature gives us what cities cannot, chiefly the "calmness" that genius needs to thrive (XIII: 2). Wordsworth wants to study "Man," and the root of his thoughts on human development is the notion of a childhood *domaine*. Asking why so few reach their full potential, he examines "the basis of the social pile," the rural folk he knew best (94). In the country, he questioned people he met on roads and paths, which generated several short poems, including "The Leech-Gatherer." Thus he did "reverence / To Nature, and the power of human minds," especially the mind and "very heart" of these folk (224-25, 241). He also describes a visit to Stonehenge and Sarum plain's other ancient remains, where he had an epiphany: "I saw / Our dim ancestral Past in vision clear" (319-20). In this "waking dream" of Druid times he "Beheld long-bearded teachers, with white wands" expound the mysteries of the heavens and the stone circles (343, 345), suggesting a link between the Druidic prophet-bard and his own mission. If this is a *domaine* experience, as his language suggests, it is also a time machine.

The final book turns from thought to action, opening with a vivid account of a night ascent of Mt Snowden. His party are trudging uphill in cloud or fog, silent and scattered, when "at my feet the ground appeared to brighten," and

> *...instantly a light upon the turf*
> *Fell like a flash, and lo! as I looked up,*
> *The Moon hung naked in a firmament*
> *Of azure without cloud, and at my feet*
> *Rested a silent sea of hoary mist. (XIV: 35, 38-42)*

The view is capacious, almost unbounded: all around, hilltops poke through clouds, which stretch west to the Atlantic beneath a clear sky. The passage was revised in 1850, but in both versions Wordsworth takes the moment very seriously. It is both a *domaine* – magical, mysterious, fleeting, unforgettable, remote from the world – and a vision, being "the type / Of a majestic intellect" and "emblem of a mind / That feeds upon infinity" (66-67, 70-71). This is another epiphany: in a Platonic thought-world he has seen the Divine Mind behind nature. But he quickly returns to earth, where "higher minds" send out "kindred mutations" (90, 94). These are artists, creative people, perhaps philosophers, whose "minds are truly from the Deity" (112).

A closing self-examination includes a summary of his views on love, imagination, and reason. Wordsworth was almost mystical in his desire to fuse separate entities: himself and you, his childhood and yours, the human mind and the Divine Mind. Not every reader will grant him all of that, but his final destination is predictable. Wordsworth and Coleridge, "Prophets of Nature," will try to inspire a nation (falling into "idolatry" and "servitude") to seek "solace" in reason, faith, and love (444, 434-35, 438, 446). The mood at the end is Neoplatonic, moving from Nature to Mind and Idea, as "the mind of man becomes / A thousand times more beautiful than the earth" by virtue of its links to divine intellect and thus to infinity (448-49).

The ultimate shape of *The Prelude* is not quite what we might have guessed in its first books. Nature, where Wordsworth had his first *domaine*, continues to be important, but he finally moves into a realm of Mind and Idea that childhood cannot understand, though it intuits the transcendental. While that original *domaine* is never rejected, in the last book it is sublimed: there is a progression, and the initiate can no more relive stage one and be content than an adult can feel a child's joy in nature. Yet is that not very nearly what Wordsworth did in the early books of *The Prelude*? Having glimpsed the Divine Mind, sensed a higher realm of human Mind, and dared to hope that his is one of those "truly from the Deity," he has devoted years to revisiting the earthly realm of sense, recreating its charms, hints, fears, and contradictions. He has shown us a *domaine* of childhood and youth, one we may have known if we were fortunate, but that we lose as we grow, and suggests some possible consolations. It is the program of the "Intimations Ode" – losing "splendour in the grass," retaining a "primal sympathy," living the "years that bring the philosophic mind" – spelled out at the length of an autobiography. By the end we know more about his philosophy: a Platonic transcendance of sensual pleasure, seen as belonging to a lower stage of being. We cannot go back to those pleasures, any more than to Eden or another *domaine perdu*, but we are assured that we would not enjoy them so fully if we could. Revere, but regret not.

The New Sea

William Wordsworth's reputation and literary production exist on a different plane from those of the Victorian journalist Richard Jefferies, who struggled with ill health and poverty. Several novels were unsuccessful, but his 1872 letter to *The Times* about life on the Wiltshire Downs of his youth brought him recognition as a writer on rural culture, and he wisely followed that star, describing his boyhood in *Wood Magic* (1881) and *Bevis* (1882). Guy Pocock, in the introduction to the Everyman *Bevis* (1930), denies that it is a novel, an autobiography, or a series of stories, yet it is "fine literature," a "little prose epic" by a "genius," dealing with two subjects that (he innocently thought) do not change over time: boyhood and nature (Jefferies 1930, xi-xii). He notes that Wordsworth and Jefferies shared a reverence for a youth steeped in nature. Their ideas and styles are quite differ- ent – Wordsworth a Neoplatonist, Jefferies a Boy Scout instructor – yet both treat "natural childhood" as a *domaine* apart from the world, possessing its own magic, and never forgotten, as they proved by their loving reconstructions of it as adults. The title *Wood Magic* (which depicts Bevis's earlier boyhood) suggests the dominant mood in both of his quasi-autobiographical sketches, largely concerned with recreating *domaines*. Jefferies wrote and published several more books about country life before he died in 1887, not yet forty.

If read as a novel, *Bevis* is doomed to disdain. Most readers find it too long, owing to Jefferies' love of boys' outdoor adventures and his pedantic streak. If Bevis and Mark build a boat or fix up a cave, if Bevis's father teaches them how to swim or shoot safely, we must learn along with them; long stretches of *Bevis* are instruction manuals. And a novel would develop the hints about interesting females, like the country girl whose "unhooked" blouse shows the "graceful con- tours" and "soft roundness of the swelling plum," and whose "large, black eyes" are "loving and untaught" (Jefferies 93). Mark's older sister Frances and Bevis notice and approve each other's love of adventure, but she likely married Big Jack. The boys are young for that game anyway: around ten or twelve. These are prob- ably girls that Jefferies adored as a boy and remembered fondly, but since nothing came of it in life, he feels bound to that. *Bevis* is also quite episodic: sketches of "what I did last summer." Yet it has qualities, chiefly power over the imagination, that elicited Pocock's praise and a tribute from John Fowles. In his Foreword to *The Magus* (1978), Fowles lists among the major influences on his novel "Bevis's farm, perhaps" (Fowles 9). This acknowledgement of a debt to a much different, much simpler writer is qualified, but it is a nod.

The most Wordsworthian aspects of the book are its emphasis on youth, nature, and imagination. The latter is introduced in the first chapter when Bevis pulls a worn volume from a bookcase; his "fingers went direct to the rhyme he had read so often, and in an instant everything around him disappeared...he forgot himself..." (Jefferies 7). He "put himself so into" *The Ballad of King Estmere* "that he did it all" – played a harp, drew a sword – for "these were no words to him, it was a living picture in which he himself acted." In the garret is an old bedstead on which he hoists sail and voyages to any port at all. He and Mark are adepts in the realms of imagined bold travels. They pole the raft that Bevis makes from a packing case along a stream called the Mississippi, then "discover" the local body of water, Longpond – a large reservoir where cattle drink – and name it the New Sea. Never having been around it, they set off on foot, naming places and map-making. After hiking to the old quarry ("Put it down in the diary, thirty days' journey"), they reach a point with a general view of the landscape and name Fir-Tree Gulf (34). Mark says they are "a long way...from other people" and Bevis agrees: "Thousands of miles" (35). A creek flowing into the New Sea proves to be the Nile. And so it goes: a whole summer of classic boy-play, enlivened by unbridled imaginations nurtured on books of legends and derring-do.

Most of *Bevis* is a series of outdoor rambles and games. Jefferies' Wiltshire was quite a different environment from Wordsworth's late-eighteenth-century Cumberland: downs, not mountains; settlement, development, farming, and cattle-raising, not "wilderness." Longpond may have been partly artificial. Yet the fact that their playground is managed – a quarry, "plantations," posts and rails stuck into Longpond where the cattle drink – has little effect on the boys' play. They work with what they have: the quarry is part of a "battlefield," a plantation is an African jungle, posts and rails are useful holds as you learn to swim. Jefferies does not treat the landscape as "spoiled." At any moment a natural *domaine* may coalesce. Bevis, tired of cutting the willow saplings impeding the Mississippi, lies in the grass among buttercups, listens to a bee, inhales the "sweet scent of green things growing," and hears Indians in the forest (15). He sits on a hill, "lost in his dreamy mood," while Jefferies writes a long description – in effect a cinematic "pan" – of farms, valleys, meadows, "a limitless forest," the distant gleam of the New Sea, swallows up in "the vast aerial space, and the golden circle of the sun. He did not think, he felt, and listened to it" (172). It is one of the self-annihilating moments that childen can have in their play, when nature subsumes self. Wordsworth rendered them more eloquently, but we recognize the genus.

Bevis offers a series of *domaines*, most of them aspects of nature as experienced by two boys. The book is full of paeans to summer's beneficent effects on human beings. For Bevis and Mark, bushwhacking through Central Africa on the *tour de Longpond*, "the sky was blue and clear, and the sunlight fell brightly on the open space by the streamlet." But also

> *The long, long summer days seem gradually to dispose the mind to expect something unusual. Out of such an expanse of light, when the earth is tangibly in the midst of a vast illuminated space, what may not come?—perhaps more than is common to the senses. The mind opens with the enlarging day.* (48)

In Jefferies, the obvious often glides into the unexpected, sometimes to the edge of metaphysics, as in Wordsworth's "Powers." Such times quiet the boys' animal spirits for reasons they do not articulate. Playing around the big old sycamores by the quarry and running down into a hollow, they sit at the bottom "so that they could see nothing but the sky," lie back on the grass, silent for a moment under the sun, drifting clouds, and blue sky, savouring "the delicious sense of growing strong in drowsy luxury" (82). Soon they are up and running again, but a few pages later are back at the same spot, playing, shouting, and chasing each other – just as they should, says the author: "they bathed in air and sunbeam, and gathered years of health like flowers from the field" (91). This is Jefferies the scoutmaster, heartily recommending that children roam and play in the outdoors for the good it does them, now and in the future.

Many of the *domaines* are variations on this theme. A luminous still day among the islands of the New Sea – clear air and clear water – may be common in summer, but it is still marvellous, Jefferies insists. "It's magic," says Bevis; "Enchantment," adds Mark, wondering if "the old magician" does it: shades of Burnett's *The Secret Garden* (264). Such moments abound while they play Robinson Crusoe in a cave on "New Formosa" island. The chapter on "Bevis's Zodiac" adds the night sky to the *domaine*; the spatial dimension is equally important for him.

> *The heavens were as much a part of life as the elms.... They were neither above nor beneath, they were in the same place...so he felt the constellations and the sun on a plane with him...he was moving among them as the earth rolled on, like them, ...in the stream of space.* (289)

Jefferies presents Bevis's experience as mystical: "he could feel the oak in his mind" as "he felt the stars"; he was "moving through, among, and between the stars"; "he lived out and felt out to the sky," "living, not thinking"; and "There was magic in everything" (289). Bevis finds the self-annihilation that mediaeval monks and nuns sought: "he himself went away; his mind joined itself, and was linked up through ethereal space to its beauty" (290). Here little difference exists between Jefferies's program for the natural child and Wordsworth's or Burnett's. Bevis's sensation of total fusion recalls the babe on the maternal bosom in *The Prelude* (1850, 2: 234-44, 252-65), and resembles Freud's "oceanic feeling" in *Civilization and Its Discontents* (1930; 1961, 11).

The "Battle of Pharsalia" on the plain behind the quarry – the summer's largest gathering – is another *domaine*, spurring the boys to emulate ancient models. Ted, leading the attackers, "fought that day like a hero" who "feared no mortal being," while Bevis's party were equally determined: "Like knights with their backs to the tree, the four received them" (137). Bevis escapes capture by tumbling down to the shore and launching a punt in a "hurricane"; among "immense" waves "a wild delight possessed him," so he shouts and sings the Ballad of King Estmere (153-54). The waves bring him close enough to Unknown Island to allow him to jump ashore at sunset as the punt sinks. Moving inland and onto the bluff, he "began to enjoy his position": "Only think, I'm really shipwrecked. It's splendid!" (156). Finding some matches in his pocket, he gathers wood, makes a fire, dances around it, and sings the old ballad as night falls. Later, when the *Pinta* is built, they love sailing her in fresh winds. "This is the best sail we've had," says Mark. (192). With "No land in sight," he wonders how far they are from shore: "Six thousand miles," says Bevis (193). Mark is sure "It's the first time that anybody has ever sailed out of sight of land in our time." They expect to "be made a great deal of when we get home," and then, of course, "put in prison afterwards. That's the proper way." Obviously these *domaines* differ from castles and estates, but they are magical, formative times, lived apart from the world, and they occur on later sails, too.

Chapter XXXIX, "The Story of the Other Side," introduces a mythical *domaine*. While camping on New Formosa, Bevis tells Mark one of his grandfather's tales, about a great traveller who sailed, walked, and climbed all over the world, but grew discouraged. Wherever you went, "there was always an end to it," and he tired of "always coming to the other side," which made it "all no good" (313). Then an old man whispered a secret to the traveller, who went to Tibet, was taken to a wall across a narrow valley, allowed to look through a "little narrow bronze door" in it, and thus glimpsed "the country which had no other side" (315). Everything about it was wondrous: air so clear that he could see for a hundred miles, but no sun (though he could feel sunshine on his back), and he heard celestial music from the "starry organ" (316). He saw people wandering around happily and yearned to join them, but was dragged back and the bronze door shut, nor could he ever find it again. They said that only one person was admitted every thousand years. His only memento was his right hand, which he had put through the door into that country; it remained "always white and soft" as he grew older (319). This is the perfect fable for two boys who have run off to sleep on an island; they decide to go to Tibet, find the bronze door, *blast* it open, and explore the land where "there is no other side." It is resonant, to say the least – an imaginative *domaine* well attuned to their age and outlook – and the most exotic chapter in the book.

Soon they find another natural *domaine*. At the end of the New Sea is a plantation through which a creek enters. They pole their raft into reedbeds, then up a narrow channel between sedges, flags, and willows, until the "sea" disappears. They hear falling water. "Niagara!" exclaims Mark. But there are houses at Niagara, so this is probably the Zambesi! The channel widens to a pool into which a "little stream fell down," producing enough spray to support moss and "long cool hart's-tongue ferns" (328). Beech tree branches meet overhead. They can see only a few yards farther through dark firs. This is "Sweet River," which "comes out of the jungle" (329). Jefferies develops the place as a sort of "Green Mansions." The foliage is so thick above that they cannot see the sky, but "the turquoise studs of forget-me-nots, with golden centres" are bright in the shade. They like the place, although the birds are silent, listening to the "song...of the waterfall," which rises and falls, tinkles or laughs, as the volume and pace of its flow vary. Jefferies leaves no doubt as to the nature of their find.

> *The forget-me-knots and the hart's-tongue, the beeches and the firs, listened to the singing. Something that had gone by, and something that was to come, came out of the music and made this moment sweeter. This moment of the singing held a thousand years that had gone by, and the thousand years that are to come.* (329)

The vegetable life *listens*, but cannot *think* this; it is simply "there *now*," and the boys exist on the same plane: "Bevis and Mark were there now, listening to the singing, that was all in all."

Bevis sketches a map as they walk around the New Sea, and Jefferies prefaces his book with a full map. It helps us follow their travels, and is typical of one kind of *domaine* literature, where the author's imagined world is sufficiently vivid, complex, or extended as to call for cartography (Eudora Welty and C.S. Lewis provide other examples). Jefferies' map of "the Bevis Country" also reveals the size of the boys' "playground." The Straits of Mozambique, narrowest part of the New Sea, are a hundred yards across. This gives us a scale by which to measure the Sea's longer axis – just over 600 yards – and greatest width: about 340. Camped on New Formosa, the boys are about 500 yards from Bevis's house. Yet the sea, its islands and shores, with their quarry, streams, plantations, a forest, and "the Waste" occupy the boys for a whole summer (plus a brief winter coda). The map shows how little real estate our imaginations require for their work.

Jefferies' variations on his theme outlast the summer. After dozens of chapters in which time seems to stand still, we finally hear a tick-tock. In Chapter XLIII, the summer "rested before it went on to autumn" (347). Natural signs are noted – reed-tips browning, birch leaves speckling, acorns swelling – and the boys enjoy this season, too. Hunting wakes them from "drowsy joy," sending them out into the countryside to hunt game (to give to a poor family). Bevis's "senses gradually became more acute" (388). One quiet dawn he "looked up and became conscious of the beauty of the morning," which gives a feeling of Oneness (390). "Bevis, the lover of the sky, gazed and forgot": forgot everything except "the earth's surpassing beauty" at sunrise (391). While "the mind has no time" at such moments, they are transient, "only a second or two," Jefferies admits. He does not let his young self go far down this path; a slight movement claims Bevis's attention and he shoots an otter. Hunting dominates the later chapters, two of which offer instruction in styles of shooting. Does Jefferies lose the thread here? Is this really where he wants to go? But it would be silly to pretend that shooting was *not* part of a rural upbringing in Victorian England.

In the final chapter, "The Antarctic Expedition," Jefferies vaults over the (doubtless boring) fall school term into winter. January is cold enough to freeze most of the New Sea, which bears a crowd of skaters, some playing ice hockey. A strong wind allows them to spread their coats and glide before it. Bevis works on an ice-raft with runners, but a thaw begins breaking up the ice, and a north wind pushes the floes south, jamming them around the islands. This frees up the sailboat *Pinta*. The boys plan "an arctic expedition": popular fare in magazines around 1850 because of Franklin. But they will sail *south*, so it must be *Antarctica*. Two boards lashed to the prow in a "V" make the *Pinta* an icebreaker. As they are casting off, Frances appears, "wrapped up in sealskin and muff," eager to join them (420). There is no objection: she boards and away they go, running before the wind. Jefferies casts off restraint as they enter the widest, most exposed part of the New Sea: "the black north roared and rushed at them.... ...waves hissed as their crests blew off in cold foam and spray...". It does sound Antarctic when they reach "ice jammed in the channel between the two islands," some fragments "almost perpendicular, like a sheet of glass standing upright" (421). Lurid engravings of similar (Arctic) scenes appeared in the *Illustrated London News* and elsewhere; there were also a few paintings by 1882. As the north wind howls and the waves break, "the ice heaved," splintering and grinding. "Oh!" cries well-read Frances, "It is Dante!"

Our mariners drive the *Pinta* into the ice-field between the islands. Following waves break over them, the mainsail must be struck, and the noise is terrific, but "the boat acted like a battering-ram" and "the mass gave way" (421). They sweep down the narrow channel beside chunks of ice, shouting "Hurrah!" Beyond it the floes spread out and they reach New Formosa. Bevis helps Frances ashore, saying suavely, "You are wet." Laughing, she replies, "But it's jolly! ... Only think what a fright *he* would have been in if he had known!" (422). When they escort her up to the height to show her the stockade, cave, and sundial where they camped, though, they see a figure atop a hill onshore: Big Jack, watching. He knows. Descending, they bail out the boat, row up the channel, and hoist the sails for the "roughest voyage" ever, at dusk. "The wind was dead against them, and...every wave sent its spray...over the bows," yet "Frances laughed and sang" (423). Jack waves for them to land where he is, but Frances wants to complete the voyage, so they sail through the Straits into "harbour" at the north end. Jack walks around to meet them and hands Frances ashore. "How *could* you?" he asks indignantly. He does not speak to the boys. "Why it was splendid!" says Frances as they walk off together. Jefferies does not belabour his or Bevis's admiration for her; the account of the voyage and her response, written years afterward, suffices. He cannot pair her up with Bevis, but we may wonder if she and Jack are well matched.

Jefferies does not let the Frances question dominate his ending. The boys furl the sails, make the *Pinta* shipshape, and walk home in the dark, pausing at the big oak tree to survey the scene of their adventures: i.e. review the book's setting and themes. "The whole south burned with stars. There was a roar in the oak like the thunder of the sea" as the windstorm continues (423). "The sky was...black as velvet, ...and the stars shone" as if the wind were fanning their flames: Sirius, Orion, and myriad others. More is happening, outside and inside. "A scintillation rushed across from the zenith to the southern horizon," and the roar in the oak fills them with "the strength of the north wind." Will they emigrate, or wander abroad? "I should like to go straight to the real great sea like the wind," says Mark, starting to outgrow Longpond. Bevis agrees: "We *must* go to the great sea." It is their final *domaine* moment, and Jeffries joins them in his last sentence, trying to enlarge the scope of their adventures and his canvas: "The wind went seawards, and the stars are always over the ocean." Had they lived in the age of orbiting space telescopes, and learned that many of the faint points of light in the black sky were not just stars but entire *galaxies*, far beyond our Milky Way, their delight would have known no bounds, rating at least an "Hurrah!"

The Low Door in the Wall

Evelyn's Waugh's *Brideshead Revisited* (1945) strengthened my suspicion that Alain-Fournier and Fowles were onto something rich but not rare, that a yearning after lost *domaines* was one of the most persistent impulses underlying literary composition. Seeing the Granada film of it (1981) sent me back to the text, and the nostalgic voiceovers by Jeremy Irons proved to be the authorial narratives of the original. Adaptor John Mortimer, directors Charles Sturridge and Michael Lindsay-Hogg, and composer Geoffrey Burgon seemed alert to the novel's *domaines*. The television series delighted the novel's admirers and made new friends for it.

Set beside *The Prelude* and *Bevis*, *Brideshead* demonstrates how disparately authors can treat the "lost Eden" theme; the treatments could hardly be more different. Waugh's subject is not childhood but youth: Charles and Sebastian meet as first-year collegians. Wordsworth and Jeffries give their protagonists a series of *domaines*: several peaks with dips between them, like a long ridge with bumps. Waugh confines the lyrical moments to the first few chapters; after that, his principals outgrow the lyrical and look back in sorrow. That Charles Ryder is pushing forty as he recalls Brideshead and Oxford does not explain the differences. Jeffries was 33 when he wrote *Bevis*, but he allowed his boy leads to play and dream. Charles and Sebastian are sickened even as they taste the nectar of youth. (Later Waugh complicates his narrative by suggesting a second *domaine*, whose values are difficult to square with the first's.)

When Capt. Ryder chances on Brideshead in 1944, the very sound of its name has the "ancient power" to stir him, producing first a great silence, and then "a multitude of sweet and...long forgotten sounds" (Waugh 21). The "sequestered place" has its own music, which Burgon's stately Albinoni-like theme captures well. The slope opposite the camp is "still unravished." (Keats calls the Grecian urn a "still unravish'd bride of quietness," a classic example of art resisting the ravages of time.) Between the two slopes flows a stream named Bride, which rises at Bridesprings, i.e. Brideshead. In the film, Castle Howard, its temple, artificial lakes, "mighty beeches" and oaks represent the Marchmain estate. Gazing upon it, Ryder, playing the melancholy pastoralist, asks rhetorically, "Did the fallow deer graze here still?" We understand that this place meant a great deal to him at one time, and that it moves him to see it now. The frame has been established, and the rest (until the Epilogue) is flashback: another *"recherche d'un temps perdu."*

No writer I have read introduces a *domaine* earlier, or dismantles it sooner, than Waugh. Book One, Chapter One presents two of them on its first page, where Ryder, seeing Brideshead in wartime, recalls his first visit with romantic nostalgia. It was

> *...with Sebastian more than twenty years ago on a cloudless day in June, when the ditches were creamy with meadowsweet and the air heavy with all the scents of summer; ...a day of peculiar splendour...it was to that first visit that my heart returned....* (23)

They had come, Ryder recalls, from an Oxford "now...obliterated, irrecoverable," but "in those days...still a city of aquatint" in whose "quiet streets men walked and spoke as they had done in Newman's day" – introducing a lost *domaine* and the Catholic motif. That day, when "the chestnut was in flower and the bells rang out

high and clear over her gables and cupolas," she "exhaled the soft airs of centuries of youth." Oxford is gendered female, yet here, "discordantly, in Eights Week
[annual rowing races], came a rabble of womankind, ...twittering and fluttering."
Discordantly? A *rabble* of women? They have been invited to Oxford by young
men, but not by Charles or Sebastian, who decamp. The title of Book One is *Et in
Arcadia Ego*, the old warning from the pastoral tradition that "I, Death, am also in
Arcadia": in the *domaine*. There are enough danger signs among the enticements
on this page for any reasonable reader.

The flashback continues with Sebastian entering Charles's digs. A dandy
("dove-grey flannel, white *crêpe de Chine*, a Charvet tie"), he asks what *is* going on
(24). Last night Oxford was "pullulating with women" and today is "*most* peculiar" (24-25). *Pullulate*: to sprout, as seeds and buds do; its Latin root is *pullus*,
the young of animals (OED). He proposes a trip to Brideshead in a borrowed car,
with strawberries and Chateau Peyraguey, a wine that is "heaven with strawberries" (25). This draught of rank and privilege intoxicates middle-class Charles.
That Sebastian is carrying Aloysius, a large teddy bear he takes everywhere, seems
part of his charm. They drive through verdant countryside until Sebastian turns
up a track and parks in a glade. Lying on the grass under trees, they eat strawberries, drink wine, and smoke Turkish cigarettes, "Sebastian's eyes on the leaves
above him, mine on his profile" (26). As the scents of tobacco and wildflowers
mingle, "the fumes of the sweet, golden wine seemed to lift us a finger's breadth
above the turf and hold us suspended": a *domaine* moment. Sebastian wishes for
a "crock of gold." He likes to "bury something precious in every place where I've
been happy": then, when he is "old and ugly and miserable, ...dig it up and remember." Drinking, smoking, and being adored, he is happy *now*.

Then the first, outer flashback opens to an inner one describing how they met
the previous term. One night Sebastian and some drunken cronies staggered into
the quadrangle of Ryder's college, where he occupied ground-floor rooms. Charles
was hosting a serious discussion group and his window was open. As the group
approached, laughing, he recognized Sebastian, "the most conspicuous man of his
year by reason of his beauty, which was arresting, and his eccentricities," who left
the others, saying he was "unwell," came to the window, "looked at me...with unfo-
cused eyes and then, leaning forward well into the room, he was sick" (30, 31).
Lunt, Charles's "scout" (servant), was left to clean up in the morning, but when

Charles returned, the room was filled with flowers, a contrite note from Sebastian invited him to lunch, and Lunt appeared charmed: "A most amusing gentleman. I'm sure it's quite a pleasure to clean up after him" (32). And Charles was easily seduced by the "luncheon party" on "foreign ground."

> *I was in search of love in those days, and I went full of curiosity and the faint, unrecognized apprehension that here, at last, I should find that low door in the wall, which others, I knew, had found before me, which opened on an enclosed and enchanted garden, which was somewhere, not overlooked by any window, in the heart of that grey city. (32)*

This comes from the 39-year-old Ryder, still spellbound by the idea of finding a secret garden. Some who had found it before him were Guillaume de Lorris, Frances H. Burnett, and H.G. Wells (chapter 4). Oxonians, including Lewis Carroll and C.S. Lewis, seem particularly susceptible.

In this "enchanted garden, ...the beginning of a new epoch in my life," his host was counting plovers' eggs that "Mummy" had sent from Brideshead (32). Charles thought him "entrancing, with that epicene [androgynous] beauty which in extreme youth sings aloud for love and withers at the first cold wind" (33). Then came three unremarkable Etonians. The last guest, however, was "tall, slim, rather swarthy, with large saucy eyes" and a stutter, wearing a "loud" outfit, who addressed Sebastian as "My dear" (34). He looked "part Gallic, part Yankee, part, perhaps, Jew; wholly exotic." Anthony Blanche, "the 'aesthete' *par excellence*," had been pointed out to Charles "as he pranced along with his high peacock tread," and "I found myself enjoying him voraciously." Blanche did not hide his sexual preferences, coming-on to each guest. But he was also diverting, going out on the balcony with a megaphone to recite passages from *The Waste Land* to some sturdy lads heading off to row. They sipped Cointreau until 4 PM, and when the others left, Sebastian offered Charles more Cointreau, "so I stayed" (35). Sebastian proposed a walk in the Botanical Gardens, and took his arm as they strolled there. By the time Charles returned to his rooms they looked "jejune," and he began discarding. That "was the beginning of my friendship with Sebastian," Ryder explains. Again the seeds of trouble in paradise are visible.

The inner flashback ends; we return to his first visit to Brideshead. They drive through gates between "classical lodges," down an avenue, across a park, around a turn and "suddenly a new and secret landscape opened before us": half a mile away, "grey and gold amid a screen of boskage, shone the dome and columns of an old house" (36). "What a place to live in!" exclaims Charles. "It's where my family live," replies Sebastian. Charles "felt, momentarily, an ominous chill at the words he used." And something about this "vision" of a country estate is wrong. Charles, interested in architecture, notes that "The dome was false." The only person they see is old Nanny Hawkins, after which Sebastian rushes him away. If my "madly charming" family got hold of you, he warns, "they'd make you *their* friend not mine" (38-39). They leave as sister Julia arrives, and wave but do not stop. So this *domaine*, too, has a problematical aura.

The Oxford scene darkens for Charles with his older cousin Jasper's "Grand Remonstrance." The advice that he offered Charles on arrival was not taken, Jasper notes, and now he has fallen in with the *"very worst set in the University,"* for which *he* is mocked at his club (42). He sees "evidence of profligacy" in Charles's room: costly, useless objects, including a skull from the School of Medicine with *Et in Arcadia ego* written on its forehead (43). His clothes are showy, and he is said to drink too much. As usual, Charles responds minimally: "I happen to *like* this bad set. I *like* getting drunk at luncheon" (44). The passivity of Charles, much spoken to but usually taciturn, is a weakness for some readers. In subsequent interior reflections we hear his side of things: that with Sebastian he is enjoying the "happy childhood" he never had; that he learned a "more ancient lore" than was in his texts that term; and that "to know and love one other human being is the root of all wisdom" (45-46). All of this refers to Sebastian, and would not reassure Jasper.

The appeal of the Oxford and Brideshead *domaines* to Charles is understood when he returns to his father's house in Bayswater for the summer with no plans. Having overspent his allowance, he will have no income until October, nor does he seem to possess alternative resources. An only child whose mother died during the war, he is stuck there with his wickedly playful father, an amateur antiquarian. When Charles admits that he has "run rather short," his father replies, "I'm the worst person to come to for advice" (63). Mr Ryder recalls, gleefully, that your cousin Melchior was "imprudent" and "got into a very queer street. *He* went to Australia." It is looking like a *very* Long Vacation when a telegram arrives from Brideshead: *Gravely injured come at once Sebastian.* Charles (somehow) departs immediately. He is met at the station by Lady Julia, who has her brother's voice and manner, and resembles him physically. She explains that while playing croquet Sebastian "cracked a bone in his ankle so small that it hasn't a name" (73). Charles is at once attracted to her: so like Sebastian, yet gendered otherwise. "I felt her to be especially female, as I had felt of no woman before" (74). And when she has him light a cigarette and place it between her lips, "I caught a thin bat's squeak of sexuality."

Brideshead begins to work its magic. At dusk it "seemed painted in *grisaille*, save for the central golden square at the open doors" (75). Sebastian is in a wheel-chair, and Charles is only slightly vexed to find his injury so trivial. Julia soon disappears, Sebastian predicts "We'll have a heavenly time alone," and Charles feels "a sense of liberation and peace" (76). After dinner, they retire to the library, "where we sat...nearly every night of the ensuing month." Its windows overlook the lakes and are "open to the stars and the scented air, ...to the...moonlit landscape of the valley and the sound of water falling in the fountain." The attractions are idleness and privilege. Chapter Four hails "The languor of Youth." Capt. Ryder testifies that while other "attributes" of youth "come and go" later on, "languor...belongs to Youth alone and dies with it" (77). "I, at any rate, believed myself very near heaven, during those languid days at Brideshead." As self-justifications go, this is slight; he sounds like Tennyson's Lotus-Eaters. But this is a powerful memory for Ryder: "It is thus I like to remember Sebastian, as he was that summer, when we wandered alone together through that enchanted palace." Perhaps *alone together* is the key to this enchantment.

Other interests include the great house, an "aesthetic education" for Charles, who undergoes a "conversion to the Baroque" and paints murals (78-79). He has started to dabble in art, and this is part of his stimulus. "I felt a whole new system of nerves alive within me," he recalls, so his time was not wasted (79). Alcohol also figures prominently; the cellars are full of well-aged vintages. They study a book on wine-tasting, and compare three bottles each night. Their verdicts remind us that Waugh was a satirist (here, of wine reviews). "It is a little, shy wine like a gazelle." "Like a leprechaun." "Dappled, in a tapestry meadow." "Like a flute by still water" (81-82). Memories of those nights still warm Capt. Ryder: "...we would leave the golden candlelight of the dining-room for the starlight outside and sit on the edge of the fountain, cooling our hands in the water, and listening drunkenly to its splash and gurgle" (82). They are living, as country folks say, high on the hog. One morning Sebastian asks, "Ought we to be drunk *every* night?" Both answer in the affirmative. Their nude sunbathing sessions on the roof end when Sebastian's siblings arrive for the weekend; his younger sister Cordelia almost surprises them. The elder brother, Brideshead ('Bridey'), a sober, serious man, appears too, and there is much talk of religion. This is what Sebastian feared: that his family would take Charles over. Their *domaine* has been invaded, and altered.

Sebastian proposes a trip to Venice, where his father resides, and "live on" him (91). For the price of the first-class sleeper the lawyers will give him, they can both travel third class. Venice, with its art, architecture, and Mediterranean light, is a new *domaine* for Charles, and good for Sebastian, too; Lord Marchmain, a lapsed Catholic with "a Byronic aura" and an Italian mistress, Cara, is his favourite relative (94). Capt. Ryder recalls that he was then "completely ignorant of women" and could not even "recognize a prostitute" (96-97). Charles calls her "a middle-aged, well-preserved, well-dressed, well-mannered woman," and not a social outcast. She is the most important person he meets there, as a guide and commentator on *mores*. He is overwhelmed by the place: "The fortnight at Venice passed quickly and sweetly – perhaps too sweetly; I was drowning in honey, stingless" (97). One day when father and son are out, leaving him and Cara together, she remarks, "I think you are very fond of Sebastian" (98). Silence. She continues, "I know of these romantic friendships of the English and the Germans. ...I think they are very good if they do not go on too long." Clearly she has something on her mind, and Charles listens. "It is a kind of love that comes to children before they know its meaning. In England it comes when you are almost men; I think I like that. It is better to have that kind of love for another boy than for a girl."

No one has talked to Charles the Silent like this before. Cara offers frank appraisals of Lord and Lady Marchmain as well as of Sebastian. Waugh risks making her seem simply a *raisonneur*, and perhaps he felt in need of one; Cara is as important for us as for Charles. "Sebastian is in love with his own childhood. That will make him very unhappy. His teddy-bear, his nanny...and he is nineteen years old" (100). This is exactly what Waugh has shown us, but Charles would not say it. She adds, "Sebastian drinks too much." Charles's instinct is to defend Sebastian by sharing the blame: "I suppose we both do." Cara will have none of it.

With you it does not matter. I have watched you together. With Sebastian it is different. He will be a drunkard if someone does not come to stop him.... Alex [Lord Marchmain] was nearly a drunkard when he met me; it is in the blood. I see it in the way Sebastian drinks. It is not your way. (100)

Waugh could easily have undercut Cara's observations, but the rest of the novel bears her out in every detail. Sebastian is a case of arrested development, and his family-fuelled depression is making him a dipsomaniac. Remember how he and Charles met.

Readers who like their *domaines* pristine should stop here, for the theme of the rest is "The Good Times Are All Gone." Oxford that September is wet and misty. Damp fallen leaves smoulder, and "The autumnal mood possessed us both" (101). Sebastian feels "precisely one hundred years old." He has just had four "talkings-to" by his tutor, a dean, and two family contacts, Mgr Bell, and Mr Samgrass of All Souls, "someone of mummy's. They all say that I made a very bad start last year, ...and that if I don't mend my ways I shall get sent down": expelled. Charles replies, "I believe we have had all the fun we can expect here" (102). Anthony Blanche has gone to Munich (where he lives with a policeman), taking with him the theatricality that graced their first year and dissolving their circle. Now they are just two, and *they* have changed. "We had lost the sense of discovery which had infused the anarchy of our first year," is Capt. Ryder's verdict; he "had begun to settle down." He even missed Jasper, who had graduated, so "the college seemed to lack solidity." And the boys are divided: Charles, "glutted"and "chastened" by the follies of their first year, will try to reform, but for Sebastian, last year's "anarchy...filled a deep, interior need," and restrictions make him "listless and morose" (103). Same place, different time: no *domaine*, or an anti-*domaine*.

Brideshead and its values become more powerful, intruding on academe, making Charles's view of Oxford more like Sebastian's. Lady Marchmain comes to urge him to help Sebastian – as if *he* were now "someone of mummy's." Julia stops by with her Canadian boyfriend Rex Mottram, MP. He is not Catholic, or even religious, guaranteeing trouble in the family. Sebastian runs afoul of the law by driving drunk and is rescued by Rex and Mr Samgrass, conferring obligations. The Christmas holiday, which Charles spends at Brideshead, is disastrous. Sebastian drinks heavily (a subheading proclaims "*Sebastian contra mundum*") and religion is ubiquitous. "We must make a Catholic of Charles," says his hostess (121). Charles sees that Sebastian's "days in Arcadia were numbered," alluding to Book One's title (123). Sebastian looks "like a deer suddenly lifting his head" at the sound of distant hunters, and Charles realizes that, as his friend feared, he himself will be among "the bonds which held him" as his intimacy with the family grows.

Oxford is no refuge. Sebastian looks sad and sullen, "sick at heart" and obviously "a drunkard" (124). He would sit up "late and alone, soaking." In the ensuing "succession of disasters," Charles finally recognizes that Sebastian is "in deep trouble" (124-25). Easter at Brideshead is even worse than Christmas: more depression, inebriation, and "scenes." Caught in the middle, Charles tries to conceal the drinking, yet Sebastian accuses him of spying for his mother. After a big row with his family, Sebastian, weeping and trembling, decamps for London. When Charles says farewell to Lady Marchmain, she – despite having "been through it all before" with her husband – exhibits no understanding of Sebastian, and tries again to make Charles her ally (132). She gives him a book about their family that reveals a scarcity of male heirs, threatening the "continuity" of their "line" (134). Sebastian, out of control, is "sent down" after being found wandering drunkenly in Tom Quad after midnight. It is the end of Oxford for Charles, too: his father agrees to his studying art abroad. A note signed "Teresa Marchmain" informs him that Sebastian has gone to Venice, whence he will tour the Levant with Mr Samgrass.

Book Two ("Brideshead Deserted") begins with another family gathering, certain to drive Sebastian deeper into drink. Alcohol is now restricted there. Charles, who has been studying art in Paris, attends, as does Mr Samgrass, who gives an illustrated lecture on the eastern tour, punctuated by snide comments from Sebastian. Charles later asks him what really happened. Sebastian – "paler, thinner, pouchy under the eyes," "jumpy," "unkempt," tippling in his room – explains (147). He and Mr Samgrass met Anthony Blanche (with a "boy") in Istanbul, and in Athens Sebastian broke away, took a boat to Istanbul and stayed with Blanche until he "drifted south" and met Samgrass in Syria (153). They were to return for Christmas, but Sebastian pawned his watch and cigarette case to fund a separate, "happy" Christmas, though "I don't remember it much" (152, 154). He asks to go on a fox hunt, surprising the family, but tells Charles that he will spend the day at a pub: "If they treat me like a dipsomaniac, they can bloody well have a dipsomaniac," which, of course, is what he is (151-52). His bank account being frozen, however, he needs some money. Knowing that this will infuriate the family, Charles initially refuses, but the next morning he relents, giving him two pounds so that he can "spend the entire day quietly soaking" (151).

What to Do About Sebastian is now the question "everywhere in the house like a fire deep in the hold of a ship" (158). When Sebastian is fetched home from a pub with "clouded eye and groping movements,...his thickened voice breaking in, ineptly, after long brutish silences" is like a "blow...falling on a bruise" (161). Charles asks him if he should stay, but Sebastian says he cannot help. When Charles takes leave of Lady Marchmain, she asks if he gave Sebastian money, and he admits it. She wonders "how anyone can be so callously wicked. ...how you can have been so nice..., and then do something so wantonly cruel.... Did you hate us all the time? I don't understand how we deserved it" (163). Her lack of understanding is a problem, yet she has a point, and amoral Charles is far from blameless. Driving away, he feels that he is "leaving part of myself behind" and will "search for it hopelessly, as ghosts are said to do." Abandoned and sinking *domaines* can still hurt. "A door had shut, the low door in the wall I had sought and found in Oxford; open it now and I should find no enchanted garden." But he also feels released from "long captivity," and has outgrown...well, what? Youth? Romance? Illusion? He vows to live henceforth in a world of "three dimensions" and "five senses" – if there is one (164).

This is a serious fracture: Charles and Sebastian have been part of each other's *domaines*. The parting is a sad loss for both, and the novel will miss Sebastian, too. Saturnine Charles returns to Paris, where a note from Cordelia reaches him. She is in disgrace for giving whisky to Sebastian, whom Rex is taking to a doctor in Zurich for a "cure." Soon Rex himself appears. Sebastian has disappeared after stealing his winnings at cards, "nearly three hundred quid" (165). With that, he can reach the Levant or North Africa, where Europeans with alternative tastes and inconvenient habits can be accommodated. Rex also reports that Lady Marchmain is ill and may not last long. The family is in debt and weak financially; his courtship of Julia is hindered by her mother's opposition and the lawyers' bickering over the marriage settlement. He will seek Lord Marchmain's support. Rex is no substitute for Sebastian, but he does live in the "real" world that Charles says he covets. Later he sees their engagement notice in a newspaper, but they were "married very quietly at the Savoy Chapel" – a Protestant church – with none of Julia's family present: "a 'hole-in-the-corner' affair," evidently (171-72). The full story requires Waugh to back up several years.

He describes Julia as she was in 1923 when Charles met her, "just eighteen and fresh from her first London season," the grandest social scene since the war (172). Yet the chapter's topics – Julia and Rex's engagement, her family's resistance, their financial and religious strains – are all vexatious. Those who had *domaines* have lost them, or seen them darken. Oxford soured for Charles and Sebastian, while Brideshead (like Alain-Fournier's *domaine perdu*) has debts. Julia's hope that Rex will lead *her* to an enchanted garden is dashed: he has a divorced wife in Montréal (hence no Catholic wedding), and, after a year of marriage, she realizes that "He wasn't a complete human being" (193). Anthony Blanche and Charles are doing all right, in much different ways, but Anthony reports that when he and Sebastian were in Marseilles and Tangiers, Sebastian would "sip, sip like a dowager all day long. And so *sly*" (196). He has now gone to Morocco with a German. Julia invites Charles to Marchmain House, the family's London seat; her mother is ill and asking for him. She proves to be too ill for a visit, but Julia says that she wished to apologize for being "so beastly to you last time you met" (200). She also wants to see Sebastian, said to be in Fez but not responding to cables. Would Charles fetch him home? He tries, flying to Casablanca, busing to Fez, finding the house in the native quarter, and meeting Kurt, the German, who says, "Sebastian's sick. The brothers took him away to the Infirmary" (204).

The doctor at the Franciscan hospital says that Sebastian is very weak and "quite unfit to travel," but "what could one expect" from "an alcoholic"? (205). Sebastian, "more than ever emaciated," mildly surprised to see Charles, receives the news of his mother's illness calmly. "She really was a *femme fatale*," he says. "She killed at a touch" (206). Charles wires Julia that Sebastian cannot come, and stays on. The doctor reports that Sebastian is drinking again – cognac that "Arab boys" bring him – which makes him happier but weaker (207). On Charles's last day they learn of Lady Marchmain's death. Will this make England more attractive to Sebastian? Perhaps, he says, but would Kurt like it? "For God's sake," exclaims Charles, but Sebastian insists, "it's rather a pleasant change when all your life you've had people looking after you, to have someone to look after yourself." A Marxist would say that this unhappy son of Privilege and Idleness needed a niche where he could be useful. That Kurt, a leech with syphilis and an infected foot, *needs* Sebastian is enough. Charles arranges to keep some money flowing to Sebastian (not to Kurt), escorts him home, and leaves them there. "There was nothing more I could do for Sebastian," says Charles, as he did when leaving Brideshead (208). They will not meet again.

Returning to England, Charles becomes an "architectural painter." His first commission is from Bridey: four oils of Marchmain House, which is to be sold (a necessary economy, says Rex) and demolished. The paintings are well received, confirming Charles's choice of a vocation. Cordelia, now a novitiate in a convent, comes to visit. She waxes elegiac about family affairs: "Things have all come to an end very quickly" (211). The chapel at Brideshead was deconsecrated after her mother's requiem mass. She thinks of a chant in the vespers service, *Tenebrae* ('Shadows'): "*Quomodo sedet sola civitas*" (212). In the Vulgate Bible it refers to Jerusalem; a standard translation is, "How doth the city stand forsaken," but St Augustine applied it to the whole Catholic community. In Cordelia's family, only she and Bridey remain faithful. Her father left the fold long ago, Sebastian is a pagan, and Julia married a divorced agnostic. They are all "gone. But God won't let them go for long" (212). Charles is impatient with her "convent chatter," but Catholicism becomes increasingly important from here on; it will reel in the strays "with a twitch upon the thread" (213, 212). Waugh himself was received into the Roman Catholic church in 1930.

As Book Three, "A Twitch Upon the Thread," opens, Capt. Ryder (still gazing at Brideshead in 1944) declares, "My theme is memory" (215). Lost in his own remembrance of things past, he sees that memories of the estate have never left him, that those recollections *are* his life (as Augustine had written), and bows to their power:

> For nearly ten dead years after that evening with Cordelia I was borne along a road outwardly full of change and incident, but never during that time, except sometimes in my painting – and that at longer and longer intervals – did I come alive as I had been during the time of my friendship with Sebastian. I took it to be youth, not life, that I was losing. My work upheld me.... (215)

It is a testimonial to what *domaines* mean: Sebastian made the difference between life and death (it was "life, that I was losing"). As those ten years are sketched, we see how empty the Sebastian-substitutes proved. The "work" that "upheld" him was painting: the houses of England, then the temples of Meso-America. These brought recognition, but when he exhibited the latter in London, Anthony Blanche appeared to expose his work as "all t-t-terrible t-t-tripe" (257). He reviewed Charles's career, from "charming" English houses (as "a dean's daughter in flowered muslin" might render them) to the tropical canvases: "charm again, my dear, simple, creamy English charm, playing tigers" (258-60). Charles could only say, "You're quite right."

Other *domaines* might have coalesced. Charles married Celia, the sister of a silly Oxford friend, and they have two children. But she had an affair just before his last expedition, and when they meet in New York to sail home he is cold, hard, and nasty, by turns indifferent to her or annoyed by her bubbly, superficial personality. They grate on each other. Days of bad weather confine Celia to her bed, but Julia is also aboard, and she and Charles finally have an affair. Reaching England, they want only each other; Charles refuses to go home with Celia to see the children. His marriage has become an anti-*domaine*, then. Julia is still married to Rex, but he "isn't anybody at all," she declares; "he just doesn't exist" (261). Their marriages drag on, with token appearances alongside their spouses at Christmas, but the truth is plain and stark.

For two years Julia and Charles live together, mostly at Brideshead, where Rex also lives (!). Charles is enamoured of her beauty: "I never tired of painting her, forever finding in her' new wealth and delicacy" (263). Seeing her by the fountain at sunset, a gold tunic over her white gown, he is as lyrical as when he and Sebastian cavorted there. This suggests a love-*domaine*, but like most it is fragile and cautionary. Julia sits with "one hand in the water idly turning an emerald ring to catch the fire of the sunset": a scene of privilege and idleness also redolent of that earlier summer (264). And their situation is unstable. Julia wants to marry Charles, but for that they need two divorces, and Charles is cool to the idea. Then Bridey arrives with news: he is engaged to a widow, Beryl Musspratt. They congratulate him; you must bring her here so we can meet her, says Julia. "I couldn't do that," he says, "as things are. It wouldn't be suitable" (271). Beryl is "a woman of strict Catholic principle," he explains, and "whether you choose to live in sin with Rex or Charles or both...in no case would Beryl consent to be your guest"

(272). Julia exits in tears. Charles finds her at the fountain, having (she says) "a fit of hysteria" (275). He tells her not to mind the "old humbug" (273). But "He's quite right," she says. "'Living in sin,' not just doing wrong." The world of Catholic guilt rises, and Julia responds from the depths of her soul.

Charles is stunned: "What had happened...? What shadow had fallen...?" (273) They are divided; he cannot follow where she has gone. "Two rough sentences and a trite phrase. She was beside herself...". Julia raves at length about her transgression: "Mummy carrying my sin with her to church," "Mummy dying with it; Christ dying with it..." (274). Clearly this has all been inside, awaiting a summons. Charles, "far from her in spirit," is powerless. Earlier they reviewed their relationship complacently: seldom parted, "not a day's coldness or mistrust or disappointment" (265). Now they are estranged for the first time, by religion. Later, after Bridey and Julia discuss new domestic arrangements, Charles reads her Ruskin's description of Holman Hunt's painting "The Awakened Conscience," and Julia admits, "That's exactly what I did feel" (276). Then he asks, "You do know at heart that it's all bosh, don't you?" Julia exclaims, "How I wish it was!" Long ago he described Catholicism as "nonsense" and Sebastian replied, "I wish it were" (84). Julia says that Sebastian has "gone back to the Church" (276). As Charles keeps criticizing the church, Julia suddenly cuts him across the face with a reed switch she has made. Her two proposals that they marry elicit only languid indifference from him.

Both divorces proceed, however, against the background of 1938: Chamberlain in Munich. Suddenly Cordelia reappears. Tiring of the convent, she served with an ambulance unit in Spain's civil war, and has seen Sebastian. He and Kurt went to Athens, whence Kurt was taken to Germany by Nazis and trained to serve the Third Reich. Sebastian found him. Kurt admitted that he detested Nazis, but was caught trying to escape and put in a concentration camp, where he hung himself. It was "the end of Europe for Sebastian" (292). He went to Morocco, then Tunis, asking to become a lay-brother in a monastery. His drinking made that impossible, but put him in their infirmary. He looked so weak that she did not suggest coming home. His alcoholism is well known, she says, but everyone loves him. "How will it end?" asks Charles (293). Cordelia predicts that he will become a hanger-on at a monastery, tolerated and treated affectionately.

War being imminent, Lord Marchmain comes home, causing consternation.

Bridey and Beryl (whom Marchmain dislikes) were planning to make Brideshead their "seat," and now its rightful lord is nigh. He looks very weak, and stairs are a problem, so he has his room made up on the first floor. The "Queen's bed, …a vast velvet tent like the *baldachino* at St Peter's," is placed there for him (301). Servants and doctors cater to his heart condition. When his room is ready, he suggests that Charles paint the scene "and call it the *Death Bed*" (303). He has some lucid times, but the overall trend is downward, and Cara confirms that "he has come home to die." One evening he announces that he may leave Brideshead to Julia and Charles, not to Bridey. To Charles's surprise, Julia says that she would accept: she cares more for it than Bridey does, and "you and I could be very happy here" (306). Suddenly Charles likes the idea, too: he could be happy with Julia there, and with the view of the house from "the turn of the avenue, as I had first seen it with Sebastian, …the rest of the world abandoned and forgotten…" (306). It is a vista such "as a high pinnacle of the temple afforded after the hungry days in the desert": an image of the Israelites in the Promised Land. And "sometimes I was taken by the vision," Capt. Ryder admits in 1944.

The state of, and battle for, Marchmain's soul dominate the last chapter. Will he die an apostate, or a believer? Bridey says that "Papa must see a priest" and Cordelia agrees (308). Julia warns Charles, "I see great Church trouble ahead"; he asks, "Can't they even let him die in peace?" (309). He thinks that the man's views are well known and should be respected. If they try for a deathbed conversion, he will know that Catholicism is "all superstition and trickery." Julia is silent. "Don't you agree?" Silence. He repeats the question. "I don't know, Charles." Now *he* can see a "little cloud…that was going to swell into a storm among us." His abrasive words and intrusions irritate Julia. Charles repeats an earlier image: "the snow was beginning to shift on the high slopes" (310). Bridey brings Father Mackay to Marchmain, who waves them away. Charles's response ("I had been right, every-one else had been wrong, truth had prevailed") is hubristic and premature (312). The issue remains open, and he cannot keep out of it, asking what "you Catholics" believe (314). Julia accuses him of starting arguments. A new breach opens between them: Charles's divorce decree is final, and hers is just months away, yet "The nearer our marriage got, the more wistfully…Julia spoke of it" (315). There are flashes of hatred in her words.

As Marchmain weakens, Julia steps in: "I'm going for Father Mackay" (319). "We must stop this nonsense," Charles tells the doctor, who declines to intervene. Julia returns with the priest, who is low-key and inoffensive, but "a wall of fire" separates Julia and Charles (321). Cara describes Marchmain as unresponsive, perhaps unconscious. Julia then brings in the priest. The nurse says, "you won't disturb him...he's past noticing anything." Is consent possible, then? Julia and Cara kneel. Father Mackay blesses the still, silent man and asks him to make a sign that he is sorry for his sins. And *Charles kneels*, praying, "O God, if there is a God, forgive him his sins," and "longing for a sign, ...if only for the sake of the woman I loved" (322). Then "Lord Marchmain made the sign of the cross," for Charles "not a little thing." He recalls a phrase from childhood, "the veil of the temple being rent from top to bottom" – associating this death with Christ's. To call this unexpected is an understatement. Waugh makes a bold move, asking us to accept that a lapsed, agnostic character suddenly accepts Church doctrine. Perhaps this is meant as a mystery; it is not prepared psychologically. A few pages earlier Charles was denouncing deathbed conversions as trickery and nonsense. Now the veil is rent.

Yet Charles must still pay for the role he has played. Julia bids him a brief farewell after her father dies some hours later. "I can't marry you, Charles; I can't be with you ever again" (324). She has "always been bad" – apparently referring to Rex and Charles – "But the worse I am, the more I need God. I can't shut myself out from his mercy" by "starting a life with you.... I'm not quite bad enough... to set up a rival good to God's." This may be "a private bargain between me and God" that if she gives up her lover "[H]e won't quite despair of me in the end." For Charles, the avalanche has finally come down from the high slopes. For me, the theological coup here is another aesthetic problem, along with Sebastian's early dismissal and Charles's quietism.

Here Waugh seems to put forward Catholicism as a viable *domaine*, providing the magic, mystery, otherworldliness, capacity to test, and ability to restore a "lost sense of identity" (Frye) associated with that concept. In the Epilogue, Ryder learns that Brideshead is now Julia's, and that the chapel has been reconsecrated. Nanny Hawkins tells him that Julia and Cordelia are working in Palestine, "where Bridey's yeomanry is, so that's very nice for them" (329): three pilgrims in the Holy Land. Ryder visits the chapel, says "a prayer, an ancient, newly-learned form of words" (330), and remembers *Quomodo sedet sola civitas*. But that, he thinks ("stepping out more briskly"), "is a dead word from ten years back," i.e. from his lost years (331). More importantly, a flame has been re-lit in a lamp in the chapel. Feeling renewed, Ryder hears from his second-in-command that he is "looking unusually cheerful today."

Apparently we are to read this as evidence that God's grace has reached even Doubting Charles, and to that end Waugh risks making *Brideshead Revisited* a devotional tract and reducing its coherence. An institution that has been present (and sometimes mocked) from the first gathers strength and inexplicably catches up a character who resisted or criticized it for years, without adequate reasons for this sea-change. Waugh would probably pounce on *inexplicably* ("he loved Julia!"), but to me the book becomes pietistic here. It offers classic *domaines* – bewitching, flawed, outgrown – at first: youth, Oxford, Brideshead. The one proffered in the Epilogue, however, is sectarian. If the Garden of Eden were proposed at the end of Genesis or *Paradise Lost* as a place of refuge after all, or if Fowles finally sent Nicholas Urfe to live in Villa Bourani in *The Magus*, it would be jarring, unworkable, unconvincing. Yet that is very nearly what Waugh does with Charles at the end of *Brideshead Revisited*. A *domaine* can fail, disappoint, or be satirized only so often before becoming tarnished and losing its credibility.

Brideshead Revisited also differs from other works treated in this chapter in the age of its protagonists. When we meet them, Charles and Sebastian are already university students, whom Waugh follows into manhood, though the "*domaine* moments" belong to their first year at Oxford. While Charles and Sebastian *are* older than Bevis, Sebastian is "in love with his own childhood" and still carrying his teddy bear, which narrows the difference. In all cases, of course, we have older authors reflecting on youthful personae.

The central role given Catholicism is more of a departure. Wordsworth was a religious man whose views became less orthodox as he grew; his is a "broad church" whose doors are open. Jefferies was also pious, with a Christian world view, but not an exclusionary one. Proper worship of nature is his portfolio. In neither do we need clergy, tradition, rules of conduct, or Latin: they preach "natural theology." The religious narrowing in *Brideshead Revisited* is the opposite of the movement in *The Prelude* and *Bevis*. The end of the novel makes Catholicism the answer. The deathbed conversion of the patriarch draws the family together, and Charles's prayer ultimately seems to better him. The non-believer is left outside the wall of the garden.

A Perfect and Limpid Remembrance

James Agee's *A Death in the Family* (1957) bears little resemblance to *any* other writer's work, being virtually unique. A painfully intense and psychologically acute account of how a father's death in an automobile accident affected his family, particularly his six-year-old son, it is unhurried: each fact, aspect, nuance, and response is explored thoroughly. It has four *domaine* scenes (in which men recall childhood's modes of feeling) besides the psychic trauma of the accident. *A Death in the Family* won the Pulitzer Prize for fiction in 1958 and the editors call it "a novel," but it is highly autobiographical. Agee's own father died in a car crash when he was six; the son in the book is called Rufus: Agee's middle name. Honouring it as fiction was a tribute to the quality of novelistic devices such as invented dialogue and internal monologue, but it lives in a borderland, and could equally well have received the prize for Non-Fiction.

The editors preface the book with a "Note" describing the dilemmas they faced. In 1955, when Agee died of a heart attack at age 45, "he had been working [on the book] for many years," but was not ready to publish it (Agee vii). They say that it "is presented here exactly as he wrote it. There has been no re-writing," though they did eliminate "a few cases of first-draft material which he later reworked at greater length," and a section of seven-odd pages that they "were unable...to fit into the body of the novel." There were also some "scenes outside the time span of the basic story," which they printed in italics and placed after Parts I and II. And they added "*Knoxville Summer of 1915*" as a prologue; "It was not a part of the manuscript which Agee left, but the editors would certainly have urged him to include it in the final draft" (vii-viii). This is a significant qualification of "presented...exactly as he wrote it." Two of the passages that I call *domaines* are italicized, so if Agee had lived, they might have appeared elsewhere or not at all. Still, the editors believed the final book to be "a near-perfect work of art" (viii).

"Knoxville: Summer, 1915" sets the book's reverent, elegiac key; it would be difficult to fault the editors' judgment here. Agee's subject is "summer evenings in Knoxville, Tennessee, in the time that I lived there so successfully disguised to myself as a child" – an example of the author's penchant for transcendental leaps (3). More specifically, his subject is "the fathers of families, each in his space of lawn," watering the grass (4). These fathers are seen and heard, remembered and vividly rendered. From each hose "there was a long sweet stream of spray, ...the water whishing out a long loose and low-curved cone, and so gentle a sound." At first the nozzle emits "an insane noise of violence" as the water arrives, but then comes "the smoothing into steadiness and a pitch as accurately tuned to the size and style of the stream as any violin," his alliteration smoothing and steadying the sentence. Agee reveres this memory: a *domaine* of wholeness, albeit fragile. "[T]he hoses were set much alike, in a compromise between distance and tenderness of spray," in which he senses both "art" and "a quiet deep joy too real to recognize itself" (4-5). And the hoses being set much alike, "the sounds therefore were pitched much alike," near enough to qualify as "unison": a 'making one,' as the prologue tries to do (5). Agee sings it all – the "sweet pale streamings in the light," the "mothers hushing their children," the men "gentle and silent" – before introducing a non-human element: "the locusts carry on this noise of hoses on their much higher and sharper key."

Agee extends descriptions farther than we expect, and then shows us that it was time well spent. Have we noticed that the "noise of each locust is pitched in some classic locust range out of which none of them varies more than two full tones"? (5) Have we heard "the long, slow pulse in their noise, like the scarcely defined arch of a long and high set bridge"? Their sound seems to "come from nowhere and everywhere at once." It is "habitual to summer nights, and is of the great order of noises," like the sea. He also hails "the regular yet spaced noises of the crickets, each a sweet cold silver noise three-noted, like the slipping each time of three matched links of a small chain." Agee takes observation into a new dimension, as he did with his portrait of the black singers in *Let Us Now Praise Famous Men* (1939; "Early Sunday Morning").

The men put their hoses away. It is the "time of evening when people sit on their porches, rocking gently and talking gently," watching the street: a horse and buggy, a couple of autos, human couples, and a "street car raising its iron moan... the bleak spark crackling and cursing above it like a small malignant spirit" (6). Slipping into free verse, Agee admits that "The dry and exalted noise of the locusts...enchants my eardrums" (7). *Exalt, enchant*: we recognize this diction by now, and the *domaine* becomes cosmic after his parents spread quilts in the back yard. They lie there looking at the stars, which are "wide and alive" and "seem very near." No one says much, and that little, quietly. He lies there with his family, reflecting that both parents are "good to me."

It might stop here, in this benign moment of familial intimacy, but does not. The boy wonders "who shall ever tell the sorrow of being on this earth, lying on quilts, on the grass, in a summer evening, among the sounds of night" (7). *What* sorrow? The one that the narrator, the grown-up boy, knows will come; being implicit in *domaines*, it always comes. Keats wrote that deep sadness lives in "Beauty that must die," that Joy is ever "Bidding adieu," and that pleasure turns "to Poison while the bee-mouth sips": thus Melancholy's shrine sits in the "temple of Delight" ("Ode on Melancholy," ll. 21-26). Rufus prays, "May god bless my people, my uncle, my aunt, my mother, my good father"; Agee adds, "remember them kindly in their time of trouble; and in the hour of their taking away." Once put to bed, Rufus thinks of those who treat him "as one familiar and well-beloved in that home: but will not, oh, will not, not now, not ever; but will not ever tell me who I am." In childhood he cannot know his identity; for that he must find his vocation as a writer and tell of the year he turned six and there was a death in the family. So Yeats's golden mechanical bird, both above and within time, sang to mortals of "What is past, and passing, and to come." Knoxville 1915 was still part of Agee when he died, and through art outlives him.

Part One pays tribute to Rufus's night walks with his father. They might go to a silent movie or a "market bar," or just walk, stopping to sit on a rock for a paternal smoke; that his mother would disapprove reinforced the father-son bond. These recurrent events at one point become specific: "Usually" his father smoked, "But this time he did not," nor say that Rufus must need a rest, so "his father stopped as much because he wanted to, as on Rufus' account. He was just not in a hurry to get home" (18). So "he liked to spend these few minutes with Rufus," who felt "a particular kind of contentment" then, and believed that his father did too, "and that their kinds of contentment were much alike." Most of his pleasure "lay in the feeling that...there was really no division" between them, no flaw in their "unity." This 'oceanic feeling' (Freud) is often part of a *domaine* experience, but Agee also points to shadows: "although his father loved...them, he was more lonely than the contentment of this family love could help," yet "here, he was not lonely" or "felt on good terms with the loneliness" (18-19). Rufus's "well-being" and his father's almost merge: "each of them knew of the other's well-being," he is sure, "and the best of this well-being lay in this mutual knowledge" (19). They look up to "the trembling lanterns of the universe" or over to city lights, speaking few words, "for silence was even more pleasurable." Things are perfect.

On this special night they walk more slowly, and his father's eyes are "more calm and grave...than Rufus had ever seen" (20). He reaches over to tousle the boy's hair and draw his head against him: a brief, manly hug. After that his eyes look "still more clear and grave," and "the deep lines around his mouth were satisfied." They look up at leaves and stars until his father sighs and says, "*Well...*" (21); then walk home in silence and Rufus is put to bed. Later that night he hears lowered voices, one saying, "I'll probably be back before they're asleep," footsteps creaking downstairs, and the Ford starting and driving away. He had not heard the telephone ring: Uncle Ralph calling his brother Jay to their father's bedside because "hit looks like the end" (23). Ralph is a drunkard, but Jay cannot be sure he is wrong, and so he goes. It is a long, dark way on bad roads and a ferry crossing, but he reaches Ralph's place safely, only to find that Pa is not *that* near the end. So he starts back, but along the way loses control, runs off the road down an embankment into a ditch, overturns, and dies in the crash. The next morning, "his mother explained to [Rufus and his sister] why his father was not at breakfast" (21). The story is incomplete, and has to be pieced together over many pages, as reports from various sources trickle in, supplemented by interpretation and speculation. It *was* a special night, then: the last on which Rufus had a father.

The third *domaine* occurs in one of the scenes that the editors inserted on the author's behalf: passages that Agee had not positioned in the final manuscript. The one in question here – from the 26 italicized pages added after Part One – is clearly relevant to the sections just discussed. It shows Jay kneeling at a younger Rufus' bedside in the dark, having come to calm him after he screamed for his father. He has been speaking and singing to him softly, and stroking his forehead. By now Rufus is quiet, so Jay's mind is free to range. He is thinking of the past: "*...his mother's face, her ridged hand mild on his forehead:* Don't you fret, Jay" (87; italics in original). Once evoked, though, the past shows many levels. "*And before his time, ...she must have lain under the hand of her mother or her father and they in their childhood under other hands, ...away on back through the years, ...right on back to Adam, only no one did it for him; or maybe did God?*" From its source, the meditation broadens like a river flooding a prairie. "*How far we all come away from ourselves,*" so far that "*you can never go home again.*" You may try, but "*you never really get all* *the way home again in your life. And what's it all for?"* This illuminates the loneliness that Rufus sensed in his father during their night walks, and "the sorrow of being on this earth" that the narrator of *"Knoxville: Summer 1915"* expresses.

Then Jay thinks of *"one way, you do get back home. You have a boy or a girl of your own and now and then you remember, ...and it's almost the same as if you were your own self again, as young as you could remember"* (87). His pendulum swings. In many ways he's been lucky, for which he's grateful. *"Everything was good and better than he could have hoped for, better than he ever deserved; only, whatever it was and however good it was, it wasn't what you once had been, and had lost, and could never have again."* Jay may not have read Wordsworth, but Agee had. You could not relive that bliss, Jay knows, but every *"once in a while...you remembered, and knew how far you were away, and it hit you hard enough, that little while it lasted, to break your heart."* This is the psychological and emotional aftermath of a lost *domaine*. Dark urges course through him, including drink and suicide. He fights them off, yet his *"pleasurable sense of firmness contended against the perfect and limpid remembrance he had for a moment experienced, and he tried sadly, vainly, to recapture it. But now all that he remembered...no longer moved his heart"* (88). Then the door opens behind him: his wife coming to see why he has been so long. Jay feels *"a spasm of rage and alarm,"* then shame. It bears out Rufus' perception that his father "was just not in a hurry to get home"– not to the home he lives in now, and the other one is unattainable.

At this point we cannot fully understand why he feels this way, but in Part Two, as Jay's death becomes known and the family gathers, hints begin to help us. Jay was a controversial choice as a husband for Mary; she went against her family's wishes in marrying him. They liked him, even considered him promising – except for his drinking problem. Jay tries to control this and does not drink at home, but on his walks with Rufus he has a whisky or two, or smokes a cigarette, which Mary does not like. So he has to mask those smells on his breath; when they go to bed he pleads fatigue and turns away from her: the price of his "control." And his "promise" is unfulfilled: for her relatives, he is an underachiever who can hardly provide for his family. Mary's father Joel thinks, "After all that struggle, ...all that courage and ambition, he was getting nowhere. Jude the Obscure" (129). That is not shown as a problem for the couple, just for her family. There is also a religious difference: Mary is a devout Catholic, while Jay "wasn't a *Christian*" (Andrew, 136) or "wasn't--a religious man" (Mary, 137). Again we do not see the couple clash about this; it is an issue that divides her family after he dies. Religion – particularly Catholicism – looms almost as large toward the end of *A Death in the Family* as it does in *Brideshead Revisited*.

The caller who informs Mary of the accident requests that a male relative come to the scene. She calls her brother Andrew, who brings her Aunt Hannah before starting. Mary finds his eyes "hard and bright," conveying "cold and bitter incredulity," as if asking whether she "can still believe in that idiotic God of yours" (108). Hannah is an interesting character, comparable to Waugh's Cara: a fellow Catholic, but more experienced, in touch with the secular world (she reads *The Nation*, for which Agee wrote). Aware that Mary's piety is simplistic, she tries to comfort her, and does not criticize her naive remarks. Mary's request that they kneel in prayer makes her feel desperate, but she complies. As Mary prays for strength, Hannah thinks "God is not here" – then crosses herself for blasphemy (121). But listening to Mary, she senses "something mistaken, unbearably piteous, infinitely malign... within that faithfulness." And "Suddenly within her there opened a chasm of infinite depth and...eternal darkness." She thinks, "I believe nothing," yet joins Mary in the Lord's Prayer, and "her moment of terrifying unbelief became a remembrance, a temptation successfully resisted through God's grace" (122). Then she reflects, "But the malign was still there, as well as the mercifulness." And when Joel thinks about Mary, "her damned piety" grates on him (129). That "whole stinking morass of churchiness" has estranged them.

Mary's faith, then, divides her from some blood kin as well as from Jay. She questions Andrew about the accident; he stresses that Jay died instantly of a concussion. To him that means, "He felt no pain," but Mary says, "He never knew he was dying" – so had no time to confess his sins (136). Andrew reminds her that Jay, an unbeliever, "didn't have to make his peace with God." Thus his quick death is "the one thing we can thank God for!" When Mary's parents arrive, the mood is at first benign: let's all help Mary and make allowances. Joel does say, "I imagine you're thinking about your religion" (141). If so, "more power to you...you've got a kind of help I could never have." But he warns her to be careful: "don't just – crawl into it like a hole and hide in it." She takes this well, but the mellowness does not last. The whole story now has to be told, *fff*, for her nearly-deaf parents. Andrew conveys the doctor's opinion that Jay's head hit the steering wheel (a bruise on his chin is the only mark on his body) and the concussion killed him instantly. "He says it was just a chance in a million" (149). This is taken as an attack on Mary's faith. Even Joel says, "Good God, Andrew," who then adds, "If it had been even half an inch to one side, he'd be alive this minute" (150). Joel tells him to shut up as Mary breaks down.

This is a test on the family. Andrew apologizes without changing his mind. Mary sobs, "Just—have a little *mercy*," then moans, "O God, *forgive* me, ...It's just more than I can bear!" (150). Joel, "his mouth fallen open, wheeled upon his sister and stared at her; and she avoided his eyes, saying to herself, *No, No.*" Andrew, "his face locked in a murderer's grimace..., groaned within himself, *God, if you exist, come here and let me spit in Your face. Forgive her, indeed!*" He has the scoffing role of Charles in *Brideshead Revisited*, but does not back down. Hannah assures Mary that "There's nothing to ask forgiveness for. ...What you're doing is absolutely natural." But Mary shakes her head: "It isn't what you think. I spoke to Him as if He had no mercy!.... That's what I asked forgiveness for," she explains (151). Hannah notes that Christ on the Cross did not ask forgiveness for having asked God why He had forsaken him. Mary calms down, absolves Andrew of any ill intent, and asks for another whisky! A few minutes later, however, as Andrew continues his report of what the doctor said about "a chance in a million," it is Joel's turn.

> "It does—beat—all—hell," Joel said. He thought of Thomas Hardy. *There's a man, he thought, who knows what it's about. (And she asks God to forgive her!) He snorted.* (155)

Mary, noticing the snort, asks, "What is it, Papa?" "Nothing," he replies, "just the way things go. As flies to wanton boys." She wants to know what he means, and Joel (a Shakespeare-and-Hardy man) elucidates: "As flies to wanton boys are we to the gods; they kill us for their sport." Mary cannot let that pass. "No, Papa. It's not that way." This is thin ice. Joel

> ...felt within him a surge of boiling acid; he contained himself. If she tries to tell me it's God's inscrutable mercy, he said to himself, I'll have to leave the room. "Ignore it, Poll," he said. "None of us knows one damned thing about it. Myself least of all. So I'll keep my trap shut." (155)

This sounds conciliatory, but Mary wants more: "I can't bear to have you even *think* such things, Papa." Andrew's mouth tightens, and Hannah says, "Mary." Joel replies, "I'm afraid that's something none of us can ask—or change," which Hannah ratifies: "Yes, Mary."

There ends the exchange of opinions, fuller and less orthodox than in Waugh. Andrew resumes his detailed, sometimes insensitive summary of what the doctor said: that if an accident had to happen, a quick, painless death was the best possible outcome. He *might* have been left "An idiot, or a cripple, or a paralytic" (157). Mary decides that "In his strength" will be Jay's epitaph. Andrew does not think he "can stand this," but keeps quiet (158). Listening to Mary ramble after her second whisky, Joel says, "None of us know what we're doing, any given moment" (159). Hannah thinks, "How you manage not to have religious faith...is beyond me" – an interesting motive for belief. Joel adds, "A tale told by an idiot...signifying nothing."

So far the religious debate seems balanced, with perhaps a slight edge to the doubters, but then Hannah whispers, "Hark!" and "There's something" (169). Andrew hears nothing, but she insists: "Hear it or feel it. There's *something*." All listen, and it seems to Mary "that there was someone in the house other than themselves." This divides the family along known fault lines until Andrew, of all people, whispers, "There *is* something." The narrator says "it was never for an instant at rest," moving from room to room. Then deaf Catherine asks, "Has somebody come into the house?" Andrew shivers. Mary says that it is in the room and addresses it as "Jay," then that it is in the children's room; she goes there to say goodbye. Hannah agrees: it is Jay. Andrew admits there was "something," as does Catherine. Only Joel remains sceptical.

This event tilts the balance of argumentative power. Joel concedes that "everything of any importance leaves the body" at death (176). Mary finds it "believable that for a little while..., this force, this life, stays on." Joel considers that "highly unlikely" but "conceivable." Mary thinks it more likely in the case of a strong young person taken suddenly, like Jay. Andrew and Hannah concur: some souls may wander for a time. Agnostic Joel admits, "I *just—don't—know*," adding "If you're right, and I'm wrong, then chances are you're right about the whole business, God, and the whole crew" (177). Still, "if I can't trust my common sense..., what in hell can I trust!" He knows they will say, "*God*," but for him that's "out of the question." Hannah asks why, and he retorts, "It doesn't seem to embarrass your idea of common sense.... But how you can reconcile the two, I can't see." When Mary replies, "It takes faith," Joel pounces. "That's the word. ...makes a mess of everything.... Solves everything." He sounds sarcastic or bitter. "Well, it doesn't solve anything for me." For those who have faith, "all right.... Might be glad if I could myself. But I can't" (178). He denies that he is an atheist: without any evidence for or against God, he won't "jump either way," but, he adds, "I hope you're wrong." Andrew comments that he doesn't know either, but "I hope it's so." Joel is isolated now.

Finally the tired mourners say goodnight. Andrew walks his parents home: the setting for the book's fourth *domaine*. The most subtle, complex, and problematical of them, it resembles Rufus and Jay's night walks, when they would stargaze, but now at a tense, troubled moment. It is very late, dark between streetlamps and in houses, no one else out. The air is "pure, aloof and tender"; the stars are "secret and majestic" (188). As they walk slowly, a line pops into Andrew's head, "How still we see thee lie," and then, "above thy deep and dreamless sleep, the silent stars go by" (189). Andrew is receptive: "all these things entered him calmly and thoroughly"; he feels "involved at least as deeply in the loveliness and unconcern of the spring night, as in the death." "Unconcern" sounds like Lucretius' idea of distant, aloof gods in *De Rerum natura*, but Andrew feels "gratitude towards the night." The lines from "O Little Town of Bethlehem" are now heard in a child's voice, his own, singing in his head. He is moved, partly because it has been years since his last late-night walk outdoors; he must have been "about sixteen, when he still thought he was Shelley" (known in his time as "the atheist Shelley"). But those words "had always touched him," bringing back Christmas – often a *domaine* for Christians – vividly, and now they seem "as beautiful as any poetry he had ever known." Those stars, though: "how tired they look!"

This is the beginning of a nervous crisis for him. "*The silent stars go by*," he says aloud, but his parents do not hear (190). Tears run down his cheeks and "a deep sob" tightens his throat.

> *Yet in thy dark street shineth, he sang loudly...within himself: the everlasting light! And upon these words a sob leapt up through him which he could not subdue but could only hope to conceal.*

The narration is demanding here: how do you sing loudly within yourself?

Andrew knows *"This is crazy"*: what has he to do with everlasting light? *"The hopes and fears,* a calm and implacable voice continued within him; he spoke quietly: *Of all the years."*

> *Are met in thee tonight, he whispered: and in the middle of a wide plain, the middle of the dark and silent city, ...he saw the dead man, and struck his thigh with his fists with all his strength.*

They complete their walk, crossing "the space of bitter light" under a streetlamp, in silence, and enter the house (showing the one light on the block) by the back door, as "quietly as burglars."

What has happened? A religious experience for Andrew? If so, of what nature? In *Brideshead Revisited*, Lord Marchmain's death sounds a call to faith that Charles hears. Is something similar proposed here: Andrew touched by the grace of God? Or are these minutes just a weary response to hours of nervous strain and a walk that evokes his favourite carol? Where did this "wide plain" come from? (In "Dover Beach," Matthew Arnold envisions humanity on a "darkling plain," "swept with confused alarms of struggle and flight, / Where ignorant armies clash by night.") But Knoxville is a hill and valley town, not a plain.

These are questions for debate; they are not answered within the passage. Andrew's beliefs, like Charles's, must await their test. Waugh clearly tilts his book toward Catholicism, offered as a *domaine* to those who will accept it. The children are crucial to Agee's approach. First, their father's absence has to be explained. Mary's attempt only perplexes them, so Hannah must try. What follows is a satire with tragicomic aesthetics – dark comedy – on how children hear adults' euphemistic and periphrastic "explanations." Rufus first summarizes what Mary told them: "he got hurt so bad God put him to sleep" (234). So who hurt him? Hannah is shocked; "he was hurt, but nobody hurt him," she replies. Four-year-old Catherine wonders how that could be. Hannah says, "He was driving...and he had an accident." Rufus looks warningly at his sister, who is staring at Hannah "with astonishment and disbelief that she could say such a thing about her father. Not in his *pants*, you dern fool," he thinks: for them, 'have an accident' is potty talk. "A *fatal* accident," she adds. They do not know *fatal*, but "they knew she meant something very bad." For five pages she confuses or alarms them with her elevated language and Catholic interpretation of the crash. Finally she and Rufus agree that the concussion from hitting his head on the steering wheel killed Jay. "Then it was that, that put him to sleep," he concludes (238). Yes, says Hannah. "*Not* God," says Rufus, triumphant theologian and Agee's alter ego.

Though he does not have to go to school that day, Rufus goes outside and stands where those who do will pass. Older boys have often ridiculed him, and he wants to impress them. But some boys, or their fathers, have read the morning newspaper's story on the accident, so his narrative has to compete with that. One says that when Jay was thrown out of the car, it ran up an embankment, "fell back and...landed right on top of him *whomph* and mashed every bone in his body" (246). Another boy's father remarked, "What you get for driving a auto when you're drunk." Rufus's version, that Jay had only "a little tiny blue mark right on the end of the chin and another on his lip," falls flat (248). "Heck," says one, "how can *that* kill anybody?" Rufus sees that he is "not believed, or that they did not think very well of his father for being killed so easily." Surely they are wrong! Yet their story seemed "more exciting than his own, and more creditable to his father...; so he didn't try to contradict" (249). But *do* they have it wrong? Agee does not narrate the accident or Jay's laying-out; all we know is what Andrew reports to the family, which he has the means, motive, and opportunity to sanitize, not wanting to shock Mary more than necessary. (It occurs to her that Jay might have been drinking.) Agee lets the ambiguities stand, but the family's neatly-packaged version of the accident has been partially unwrapped.

Chapter 17 introduces Father Jackson, summoned to officiate at the funeral. He bears no resemblance to Waugh's amiable, easy-going Father Mackay. Father Jackson is first a voice on the other end of a phone call that Hannah answers. Her part is mostly "yes...yes, Father...yes"; when she hangs up, Rufus hears her "let out a long, tired, angry breath" (258). The focus is again on the children; he is seen mostly through them. Hearing "loud feet on the porch" and a ringing doorbell, they open the door. A man almost as tall as *their* father, wearing a black collar, purple vest and long hat, and carrying a black suitcase, frowns at them, standing there in his way. "May I come in?" he asks, and, without waiting, "strode forward, parting them with firm hands" (265). Hannah comes to welcome him and present the children formally. "Yes, we've already introduced ourselves," he says, "as if he thought it was funny. That's a lie, Rufus reflected," and wonders why he has to take his hat, when "The hat rack was in plain sight" (265-66). The children stay in the sitting room with him while Hannah prepares Mary for the visit. He sits, frowning, in *their* father's chair. A framed picture of Jesus as a boy talking to the wise men at the temple elicits a faint, fleeting smile, but he frowns again. The children wish that "if he was displeased with them he would tell them why," and that he would sit in another chair (267). The omniscient narrator explains:

> *He looked at both of them, feeling that their rude staring was undermining his gaze and his silence, by which he had intended to impress them into a sufficiently solemn and receptive state for the things he intended to say to them; and wondering whether or not he should reprimand them.* (267)

That is soon decided. "Children must not stare at their elders. That is ill-bred," he informs them. "Huh?" they say, wondering what "stare," "elders," and "ill-bred" mean. He continues telling them to mend their manners and to address him correctly until Hannah reappears.

She and the priest go up to Mary's room. The children creep partway up the stairs to listen: a remarkable scene in which they derive meaning from tones, as pet animals must do. "They could hear no words, only the tilt and shape of voices," as in "the man's voice rang very strongly with the knowledge that it was right and that no other voice could be quite as right"; and "their mother's way of questioning" sounds "as if she wondered whether something could be fair, could possibly be true, could be so cruel" (268-69). Then "the man's voice became still more ringing and overbearing" (269). Hannah's voice has "a kind of sweetness" as she seems to "add her voice to his, though much more kindly, in this overpowering of their mother." She questions "almost as their mother questioned, but with more spirit, with an edge almost of bitterness." Father Jackson, however, beats them down into acquiescence. Rufus "could not conceive of what was being done to their mother," but, "sure that it was something evil, to which she was submitting...and by which she was deceived," he wants to go in there with a stone and tell the man to "stop hurting my mother" (270). Catherine understands that a man "whom she hated and feared, had broken into the house," sat in her father's chair, and was "doing secret and cruel things to her mother." She is sure that her daddy would "kill him and she wanted to see it." But the priest's voice goes on, "even more strongly in charge," and "the voice loved its own sound" (270-71). Rufus guesses that he is praying. The women join him, their voices sounding "more tender," but also

> more inhuman, than they had ever heard them before; and this
> remoteness from humanity troubled them. They realized that there
> was something to which their mother and their great-aunt were
> devoted,... which was beyond and outside any love that was felt for
> them; and they felt that this meant even more to [Mary and Hannah]
> than they did.... (272)

This is the unkindest cut, as when, lost in the forest, you find a house, the witch's house. They intuit the "inhuman" dimension of Christianity that diverts some portion of human love to another realm (Jesus said that a man must "hate" his family in order to become a disciple: Lk 14:26, KJV). The children feel this, and know that while it was not the priest that their mother loved, "he was altogether too deeply involved." They also sense that Mary is calmer now, which *ought* to be better, but was "worse in one way. For before, she had at least been questioning, however gently. But now she was wholly defeated and entranced." The prayer is "her surrender."

The doorbell rings, and they scramble back to the sitting-room as Hannah comes to the door. It is Walter Starr, the benign, self-effacing family friend who drove Andrew to the crash site and also saw Jay's body. A down-home humanist, he provides a foil to the "inhuman" part of the priest, Mary, and Hannah. The children have always known him, and there is mutual affection. In the sitting room, they note that he "walked straight for their father's chair, veered unhappily, and sat on a chair next the wall" (273). Starr, who will look after them during the ceremonies, arouses their interest in the gramophone at his house. He is sensitive to their feelings without abdicating the authority of an elder, gently reproving Rufus for "lording it" over Catherine. Starr tells them how good a man Jay was, brave, kind, and generous, how hard he struggled to raise himself: altogether "one of the finest men that ever lived" (277). Then he tears up and the children move closer, "whether to comfort him or themselves they did not [k]now." Later, after the viewing of the casket and the funeral, but before taking the children to his house, he drives them to where they can watch from a distance as the casket is carried to the hearse, because "I think you'll be glad later on" (293). Once in front of his house, he says, "Maybe you'd better not say anything about this"; then adds, "No, you do as you think best," gets out, opens their door, and holds out his hands to Catherine, saying, "Up she goes" (296). The author's love for him is almost tangible.

Meanwhile Mary, in her room before the viewing, starts out the door, groans, and doubles over, her knees buckling. Hannah catches her, snapping *"Close that door"* to Father Jackson (279). Then Agee looks ahead and reports, "It would be a long time before either of the women realized their resentment of the priest and their contempt for him" (279-80). When Mary is able to walk, he takes her arm and she leans on him, though "she tried not to" (280). After the viewing of Jay's body and the words said over him by the family and Father Jackson, Mary sends the children to their aunt in another room while she and the priest remain. But in crossing the corridor Rufus and Catherine

> *...became aware that they were not alone in the dark hall. Andrew stood by the hat rack, holding to the banister, and his rigid, weeping eyes, shining with fury, struck to the roots of their souls like ice, so that they hastened into the room where their great-aunt sat....* (287)

We do not understand Andrew's fury at this point; we have to wait. The children hear Andrew tell his father that Mary is still with Father Jackson, and Joel growls.

The full story comes out in the last chapter, which begins with more religious alienation. Mary and her children are at Joel's house. She "looked as if she had traveled a great distance," and the children sense "that everything had changed" and will not change back; "they loved her, but it made no difference" (297). They realize that she is "silently praying," and "instead of love for her they felt sadness, and politely waited for her to finish." Rufus moves closer, but Catherine pulls away, hurt. Thus Andrew finds "the deceived mother, the false son, the fatally wounded daughter" ("It beats the Holy Family," he thinks), and invites Rufus to go for a walk (298). Catherine roams the house alone, crying, hearing Hannah and Mary praying in Hannah's room: long prayers that Agee quotes in full. Catherine goes into her grandparents' room and hides under their bed, ignoring the frightened voices calling her. She "wanted never to be seen by anybody again" (303).

Rufus, taking his first walk with Andrew, hopes for some great disclosure, maybe a secret, but Andrew is frowning. After a silence he says, "If anything ever makes me believe in God" (305). Rufus is all ears. "Or life after death." They are climbing a hill and a bit winded, so his sentences are short. "It'll be what happened this afternoon." We remember Andrew's emotional walk after the sensing of a ghost: is this another twitch upon the thread? But Andrew just describes the natural scene at the burial: fast-scudding clouds, shadows alternating with bursts of sunshine. As Jay's casket was being lowered there came "a shadow..., and a perfectly magnificent butterfly settled on the—coffin, ...and stayed there, just barely making his wings breathe, like a heart." Rufus does not know that butterflies are one of our oldest symbols of transformative rebirth, but Agee does. Then Andrew stops and stares at the boy.

> *He stayed there all the way down, Rufus.... He never stirred, except just to move his wings..., until it grated against the bottom.... And just when it did the sun came out just dazzling bright and he flew up out of that—hole in the ground, straight up into the sky, so high I couldn't even see him any more.* (306)

Andrew, perhaps minded of Shelley's skylark ("blithe spirit"), asks, "Don't you think that's wonderful?" Rufus says Yes. "If there are such things as miracles," says Andrew, "then *that's* surely miraculous." Many have seen God in nature: it is called "natural religion."

Rufus does not understand "miraculous" or "magnificent," but Andrew moves on. "...*that* son of a bitch!" (307). Rufus knows that is really bad. "That Jackson," says Andrew. "'*Father*' Jackson," he snarls. "He said he couldn't read...the complete burial service over your father because your father had never been baptized." We remember how Andrew's eyes frightened the children in the corridor. He is still too angry to control himself, mimicking the priest as he explains, "He said he was deeply sorry, but it was simply a rule of the Church" (308). Rufus is "glad his uncle did not like Father Jackson," but senses that there is more. "Some church," snaps Andrew, and his bile overflows.

> *And they call themselves Christians. Bury a man who's a hundred times the man he'll ever be, in his stinking, swishing black petticoats, and a hundred times as good a man too.... Genuflecting, and ducking and bowing and scraping, and basting themselves with signs of the Cross, and all that disgusting hocus-pocus, and you come to one*

simple, single act of Christian charity and what happens? The rules of
the Church forbid it. He's not a member of our little club. (308)

Andrew cannot stop. "I tell you, Rufus, it's enough to make a man puke up his soul." Pause. "That—that butterfly has got more of God in him than Jackson will ever see for the rest of eternity." Natural religion again. "Priggish, mealy-mouthed son of a bitch," he concludes.

The possibility of establishing a religious *domaine* at the book's end has by now been exploded. Father Jackson's brand of Catholicism has made him several enemies and no friends. Mary is living in her faith, which is alienating her children, which she does not know. Hannah is a believer, with some reservations. Joel remains sceptical. But Agee is also concerned with the way Andrew lets himself go before his nephew, who can read the nuances of adults' speech. Rufus' unspoken thoughts constitute a critique on Andrew's tirade. A little earlier, after the butterfly story, everything seemed "nearly all right" to Rufus, but "now it was changed and confused" (308). Uncle Andrew "had said so much"!

> *His uncle had talked about God, and Christians, and faith, with as*
> *much hatred as he had seemed, a minute before, to talk with rever-*
> *ence or even with love. But it was worse than that. ...he was talking*
> *not just about Father Jackson but about all of them. He hates Mother,*
> *...Aunt Hannah, too.* (308-09)

This confuses and disturbs him. They don't hate Andrew, but he hates them. Yet he is nice to them, so he must love them, "But he hates them, too" (309). Or when he's with them he loves them, but when he isn't and thinks about "their prayers and things" he hates them. Or maybe when he's with them "he just acts as if he likes them," but really hates them "all the time."

At the end of this reconstruction of his great childhood trauma, Agee turns the screw again. Andrew told Rufus about the butterfly but "wouldn't tell them because he hates them, but I don't hate them, I love them, and...he told me a secret he wouldn't tell them as if I hated them too" (309). Ah, they saw the butterfly! *That's* why he would tell me and not them: "he thought I would want to know and I do. But not if he hates them. And he does." But he doesn't say so because it would hurt their feelings, so he must *love* them. "But how can he love them if he hates them so? How can he hate them if he loves them?" Lost in his own oxymoron,

Rufus cannot bring the situation into focus. They walk home in silence and the book ends. For a few minutes Rufus seemed to have a second father, but then Agee darkens that prospect. Catholicism is the irritant here: it works for some in the family but not for others. What we, Rufus, and Agee are left with is the *domaine* of "*Knoxville: Summer, 1915*" and Part One, Chapter 1: memories of a father who went away. Again the earliest memories prove the most potent; the world Rufus knew and loved blows up on p. 21, never to be restored except in the world of this book. The later candidates for an alternative *domaine* are brought forward, judged, and found wanting.

THESE FOUR WRITERS RUN THE gamut of *domaines* of childhood and youth, as their experiences and natures dictated. For Wordsworth, the babe at the breast, basking in maternal love, has the purest *domaine*. During childhood something is lost, yet he dares to track the child into manhood, showing what compensations may be found for the loss of infant bliss, especially if the soul has known wild nature. Jefferies takes on a much more limited subject: the outdoor adventures of some pre-teen boys over a few months. He is as autobiographical as Wordsworth, and again nature provides a crucial context. Waugh stands apart in beginning his story so late – the college years – and largely ignoring nature. He follows his main characters for decades after the *domaine* of their first year at Oxford, eventually proposing another kind of fulfillment, Catholicism, at the end. His trajectory is like Eliot's in *The Waste Land* (which Anthony Blanche quotes): from waste to faith. Agee is very autobiographical, focusing on his childhood self and presenting the *domaine* of his closeness to his family. His originality is the early annihilation of this harmony at Jay's sudden death, and his rejection of a religious *domaine*. The only aspect of nature important in Agee's book is the stars, which can move Rufus, his father, and Andrew. All four of these authors were middle-aged men looking back on their youth, recalling its best times, and considering what compensation may be found for what has been lost.

INTERLUDE:

The C.S. Lewis File

WHEN I FIRST UNDERTOOK TO explain this book to my (grown) daughter, she quickly spotted an obvious omission in my list of examples. "What about Narnia?" I had read her *The Lion, the Witch and the Wardrobe* in our salad days. Probably many parents of my generation, and their children, would have the same reaction: Where is the famous series of tales by a major modern author? There is a *domaine* in every book, so it could be useful as well as expected. Why then had I *not* thought of including it? That was the question.

C.S. Lewis was a formidable writer in several fields, possibly the twentieth century's most versatile. I encountered his literary criticism and history first. *The Allegory of Love* (1936), on mediaeval poetry, and his volume on the sixteenth century in the *Oxford History of English Literature* were highly learned, readable, and witty; Lewis was admirable both as scholar and as stylist. His *Preface to Paradise Lost* (1942), defending Milton's epic poetry, caught my attention in another way. In Chapter II Lewis differs with T.S. Eliot on the credentials of a critic, but asserts that he and Eliot agree "about matters of such moment [Christian faith] that all literary questions are, in comparison, trivial" (Lewis 1960, 9). Including this one? I assumed this was a professional courtesy, but later Lewis insists that modern epic poets must follow Virgil's lead: "The explicitly religious subject for any future epic has been dictated by Virgil; it is the only further development left" (39). The leap from outgrowing the heroic to "explicitly religious" was long and not obvious. Did critics have a right to issue orders to future poets? Later Lewis writes, "I should warn the reader that I myself am a Christian" (65). Why "warn" us of that, when "for the student of Milton my Christianity is an advantage. What would you not give to have a real, live Epicurean at your elbow while reading Lucretius?" Did

Lewis see no difference between the demands that Epicureans and Christians make on us? And how would a non-Christian student fare in his Milton course?

Lewis answers that question himself in his chapter on the First Couple. "The whole point about Adam and Eve" is that "They were created full-grown and perfect" (116). In support of this proposition, he quotes several church Fathers and saints (but no literary critics), who describe Adam as a "heavenly being" whose mind surpassed that of "the most brilliant philosopher," so we should not laugh if he seems awkward with angels (117). Then comes what I was dreading: "If such a being had existed – *and we must assume that he did before we can read the poem*" – we would have been as tongue-tied as "stammering boys" in his presence (my italics). So if I am not a Christian (of Mr Lewis's stripe); if I think, for example, that Adam was the *adama*, 'red clay,' used by the potter-god, then I cannot "read the poem" or, presumably, study it with him, because I do not assume what he says we "must assume." Would an Epicurean tell me that I could not read Lucretius until I accepted his beliefs? These concerns would affect my subsequent reading of Lewis, who also excelled in Christian apologetics. *The Screwtape Letters*, perhaps his best-known work in that genre, shows what an imaginative writer, skilled debater, and committed Christian he was. A small industry is devoted to republishing his religious books in handsome church imprints.

His children's books reflect the views sketched above; Lewis's religious commitment includes instructing the young. In the Narnia series, children are quick to see that Aslan is God, or Jesus, or both, but only reading the seven Narnia books in sequence shows how far Lewis's beliefs carried him, and how extreme they were. I did so in *The Complete Chronicles of Narnia* (1998; henceforth *CCN*), which prints the books in Lewis's preferred reading order: the chronology of events in Narnia, not the order of publication in Britain. Only *The Last Battle*, published last, occupies the same position in both orders. The illustrations and maps by Pauline Baynes are reproduced there. The maps – one sign of a fully visualized *domaine* – remind us that Narnia has moors and "Wild Lands" to the North; Archenland, Calormen and a desert to its south; and an ocean to the east. Some of the action in several books takes place in one or more of those locales, not only in Narnia. I concentrate on the first two books and the last, which clarify Lewis's theology.

The Magician's Nephew (*MN*, 1955), published next-to-last, explains the origins of Narnia and thus leads off in *CCN*. Two children, Polly and Digory, exploring an attic tunnel in their Victorian row-house, happen on his Uncle Andrew's study. He is an odd, scary figure, dabbling in real magic: when he offers Polly a humming yellow ring, she touches it and promptly disappears. Made of Atlantis-dust, it was given him by his fairy godmother, Mrs Lefay (as in Morgan). The setting suggests Sherlock Holmes and Jack the Ripper, but Lewis makes it a fantasy world where such things may happen. Andrew tells Digory to put two green (return) rings in his pocket, wear a yellow one and follow Polly. He does. The study vanishes, he is by a pool among trees, and there is Polly, though they scarcely recognize each other in The Wood Between the Worlds. It is "a *rich* place," a drowsy grove in which you feel as if you "had always been in that place" and do not want to do anything or go elsewhere (*CCN*, 19): Lotusland. Noticing their rings alerts them, and they make a brief trial of the green rings; then put on the yellow again and return to the pool. Digory, "the sort of person who wants to know everything," is not ready to go home; he persuades Polly to try another pool, which might lead to another world (21). They hold hands and jump into one chosen at random. The yellow rings do not work (Uncle Andrew misunderstood them), but the green ones do.

Now they are in a ruined, deserted city whose light glows dull red, like Milton's Hell. In a room full of still, seated, crowned figures, they find a table on which are a gold bell and hammer. An inscription invites them to "*Strike the bell and bide the danger,*" or live on, wondering what you missed (26). Digory feels that he *must* do it, which Polly thinks is crazy. They struggle when she reaches for her yellow ring; whereupon Digory gives the bell a tap (and "was very sorry for it afterward"). The sound grows, reverberates, and becomes an earthquake; masonry falls; and one of the figures, a tall, beautiful queen, awakens and rises. Though ominous and unfriendly ("a terrible woman," thinks Polly: 28), she leads them out of the collapsing palace to a view of the ruins of Charn (as in "charnel") and a red, dying sun (see the end of Wells's *Time Machine*). She calls herself "Jadis [French, 'of a bygone age'], the last Queen, but the Queen of the World" (29). She destroyed Charn and its people by speaking the Deplorable Word. The scale of Digory's error now becomes clear: she wants to come and rule *their* world! They try to escape, but Jadis grabs Polly's hair and thus comes to the Wood Between the Worlds with them. She is paler and weaker there, and Digory, feeling sorry for her, hesitates long enough for Jadis to grab his ear as the children jump into the "home pool." Thus she reaches London with them, frightening Uncle Andrew.

The Witch (as she is henceforth called) goes out and stops a horse-drawn hansom cab. Digory and Polly, desperate to undo their blunder, use their rings to send Jadis, Andrew, the cabby, his horse, and themselves to the Wood Between the Worlds, then on to blackness. What now? Where are they? The Witch knows: "This is an empty world. This is Nothing" (*CCN* 41). It is a starless universe, without form and void. Then the cabby starts the old thanksgiving hymn "Harvest Home," the children join in, and a beautiful deep Voice begins a wordless song that seems to come from all around. It is joined by higher voices, and thousands of stars come out, as if to join the choir. At length the stars and voices begin to fade; the sun rises, revealing a river valley, distant mountains, and a Lion, who is The Voice. All except Jadis and Andrew think it wonderful. The Lion sings grass, flowers, and trees into existence. Jadis throws an iron bar at Him, which has no effect, and she runs off. Animals sprout from the earth, and pairs of them gather around Him. The stars sing again, and the Lion says, "Narnia, awake. ...Be walking trees. Be talking beasts" (48). He calls forth fauns, satyrs, naiads, and others, who hail Him as *Aslan*. He gives them Narnia, the animals begin to speak, and Aslan chooses a council to safeguard Narnia, for "an evil has already entered it" (49). Narnia's marvels make it a *domaine*, but like the others it is not flawless. "Every brightly lit eminence has its dark shadow attached," wrote Freud.

His Creation complete, Lewis must deal with humanity and evil. Digory, Polly, the cabby and his horse (who can now speak) gladly follow Aslan; Andrew understands nothing and becomes a figure of fun. Some puzzled animals try planting him as a tree. At the first council meeting, Aslan pressures Digory into admitting his responsibility for the presence of the Witch; then tells the council: "You see, friends, ...before the new, clean world I gave you is seven hours old, a force of evil has already entered it; waked and brought hither by this Son of Adam" (55). Andrew's role is not mentioned. But Aslan promises centuries of merriment before the Witch's evil falls upon them. He will take the worst of it on himself, and (as in Christianity) since "Adam's race has done the harm, Adam's race shall help to heal it" (55). Though Digory's offense parallels Adam and Eve's, there is no Expulsion. Aslan sings the cabby's wife in from London and appoints them King and Queen of Narnia. Polly is made to forgive Digory. They are ordered to pluck an apple from a tree in a garden in the Western Wild and bring it back; from its seed will grow a tree beyond the Witch's power, which can afford Narnia some protection: a clever twist on the Eden story, employing the principle of foreshadowing. That garden is distant, though, so they travel on the cabby's nag – now a flying horse whom Aslan names Fledge. They depart at once and fly far the first day, but at their rough camp that night all sense the Witch's presence.

In the morning they fly on to a lake and a green hill on whose top is a walled and gated garden: the topography of Milton's Eden. Digory enters the gate, finds the tree at its centre, takes one of the silver apples, and, despite his hunger, pockets it for Aslan. But *Et in Arcadia ego*: the Witch appears, playing Satan. She has just eaten "the apple of life," and says she will never age or die (64). Why doesn't Digory eat one, become immortal, and be king to her queen? Or take it to his sick, dying mother (for whom he has asked Aslan's help) and make her well? Digory is tempted, but refuses. The children mount Fledge and fly east as the Witch turns north to her new home. At sunset they land in Narnia and Digory hands the apple to Aslan, who says, "Well done, Son of Adam" (knowing what happened, of course), and allows him to plant it: i.e. toss it into riverbank mud where it will sprout (65). Aslan has the dwarfs make robes and crowns for King Frank (the cabby) and Queen Helen, whom he crowns and blesses. A tree with silver apples has already grown from the mud; it will shield Narnia from the Witch while it lives. Aslan lets Digory have one of its apples for his mother; then whisks the earthlings back to the Wood Between the Worlds, where he issues a warning. Their world must heed the fate of Charn (whose pool is now dry), for it could be their fate as well. And, he says, get rid of those rings! Bury them where they will not be found and used again: Narnia needs no more blundering Adamites.

Then the humans are back in London, where no time at all has passed. The apple cures Digory's Mum; Polly collects all the rings; Andrew retires with a bottle. Digory plants the apple's core in the back yard, and the next day it is up and sprouting. The children bury the rings in a circle around it. Digory's life improves greatly: his father writes from India that his wealthy uncle has died, so he is now rich and can afford to come home. He does, and they (with Andrew) go to live in the big family house in the country: stables, kennels, a river, woods, hills! Polly visits on holidays, and learns to ride and swim and climb. Narnia, we are told, had centuries of peace and joy; its king and queen and their children lived happily, the boys marrying nymphs, the girls marrying nature-gods. The apple tree in London stands until Digory is middle-aged, and then falls in a storm. Rather than chop it up for firewood, "he had part of the timber made into a wardrobe," which sits in the country house (72). Readers of the next book will understand *that*. It all hangs together quite ingeniously.

Narnia is a *domaine*, with the mystery, magic, and dark side of the archetype, but *MN* also offers theological puzzles. From what tree did Digory pluck the fruit, for example? Its produce is called the Apple of Life, which would make it the Tree of Life. But in Genesis, after Adam and Eve eat the forbidden fruit, God says, "and now, lest he put forth his hand, and take also of the tree of life, and eat, and live forever," they must be expelled from Eden (Gen. 3:22, KJV). No Tree of Life for them. *MN* also raises one of the most difficult issues in Judaeo-Christian theology: the origin of evil. If Aslan can foresee, create material existence out of nothing, and know people's minds and actions at a distance, he has divine power. Could he not have prevented Jadis from coming to Narnia and becoming its Satan? Were Andrew's rings and Digory's folly not foreseeable and preventable? Is "free will" a sufficient justification for the Witch's damage? Or is Aslan *not* omniscient and omnipotent? There are problems associated with this concept of the Godhead; Lewis, a sophisticated apologist, knew that. Did he just decide not to tackle these difficulties in a children's book? Or is their presence an admission of the problem's intractability?

Problems of a different kind arise in *The Lion, the Witch and the Wardrobe* (*LWW*, 1950), the second in chronology but the first to be published. If *MN* was Lewis's Creation story, this is his Crucifixion. It is a daunting book to read to a sensitive child whom Lewis has taught to love and revere Aslan. We pass, then, from theological conundrum to aesthetic challenge.

As it begins, four English children – Susan, Edmund, Lucy, and Peter (SELP) – are sent from London to a big old country house to avoid the Blitz, so it is the early 1940s. The old professor who lives there with his servants must be Digory (*MN* told us that he became a professor, had a country house, and brought a wardrobe there.) Exploring the rooms, Lucy (the youngest) enters the old wardrobe and finds herself in a snowy wood at a lighted lamppost (which grew from the iron bar that the Witch flung at Aslan). Soon she meets a faun named Tumnus. He takes her home to his comfy cave for tea, but confesses that he must hand her over to the White Witch, who will pay for her. Then he bursts into tears and escorts her back to the lamppost, whence she regains the wardrobe. The others have not even missed her, so we know that time operates differently in Narnia and in England; several Narnian hours are only moments in the UK. And fifty years (say) in England may have been several centuries in Narnia, because the grace period that Aslan gave the Narnians has expired. The Witch is back, now called the *White* Witch.

Since the wardrobe looks normal inside, the other children do not believe Lucy's tale, but a few days later she runs into it to hide, and when Edmund follows he finds himself in Narnia. The White Witch sees him, stops her sleigh, and plies him with a hot drink, Turkish Delight, and questions. Ordering him to come back with his siblings for more of the same, she then rides off. Walking back to the lamppost he meets Lucy, but does not mention the Witch, whom he quite liked, and when they reach the house again, he denies Narnia to Peter and Susan. Lucy runs off in tears, and Peter rounds on Edmund for being "beastly" to her. Peter and Susan consult the professor about Lucy's tall tale, but when they tell him the story, he replies that since they say that she does not tell lies, "we must assume that she is telling the truth" (*CCN* 90). This confounds them, but he answers all their questions and objections. Then one day, trying to avoid visitors touring the old house, all four run into the wardrobe and emerge in wintry Narnia (they don overcoats from the wardrobe). Peter apologizes to Lucy, tells off Edmund for lying, and asks Lucy to be their leader. She conducts them to the cave of Tumnus the faun, where matters take a sinister turn: he is gone, the furniture is wrecked, and a note states that he has been arrested for "High Treason against her Imperial Majesty Jadis, Queen of Narnia, ...and fraternizing with Humans" (93). The centuries of peace the Tree of Life provided are over. Narnia is now a police state.

Now the story shifts into high gear: the SELP quartet is in Narnia, the Witch is again a queen, and the children decide to stay and help Tumnus. They follow a robin – the first bird they have seen in Narnia – who seems to understand what they want, and leads them on from tree to tree (as a robin does in *The Secret Garden*). When the bird flies off, a beaver appears and beckons them into the woods. He shows them the handkerchief that Lucy gave Tumnus, says "Hush" (talking animals), and leads them through the woods to his lodge (Edmund sees that it is near the Witch's castle). Mr and Mrs Beaver serve dinner and mention Aslan, a name that horrifies Edmund. The Beavers think Tumnus is in the Witch's castle, where she turns captives into stone: this is a fairy tale. She is said to be the offspring of a giant and Lilith (an Assyrian demon-vampire, in Rabbinical literature Adam's first wife); Aslan is their best hope against her, and there is a prophecy that four humans enthroned at Cair Paravel (a castle on the coast) will end the Witch's rule. But now they notice that Edmund has disappeared. Beaver is sure he has gone to the Witch, so they must leave, too. We are told that Edmund slipped out after hearing the others plan to meet Aslan. He makes a long night walk through snow to the palace, where he reports to the Witch on the plan to find Aslan. "Aslan!" she cries, and orders her sledge: the bellless, silent one.

The Beavers and the children, all carrying loads, follow the riverbank by moonlight. The snow has stopped. After some hours, they crawl into a burrow to sleep. In the morning, they have a surprise visit that Mr Beaver sees as "a nasty knock for the Witch! It looks as if her power is already crumbling" (*CCN* 108). She "made it always winter and never Christmas," but this is no less than Father Christmas, whose belled reindeer are pulling a sledge with a pile of presents. He announces that she "kept me out for a long time, but I have got in at last. Aslan is on the move. The Witch's magic is weakening." (My daughter wanted to know why Aslan went away.) He distributes presents, including a sword and shield for Peter, and a bow and arrows, plus an ivory horn, for Susan. Lucy receives a vial of the medicinal juice of the mountain fire-flower, and a small dagger for self-defence. A rather martial array, presaging what is to come, but he also produces an entire tea service, piping hot, with sugar lumps and cream. Then he is gone, and they have a fairly high tea, with ham sandwiches. It is, after all, an *English* children's book.

Edmund is treated shabbily at the Witch's castle. Her soldiers, sent to kill everyone chez Beaver, find no one home. She takes Edmund in her sleigh, and the dwarf drives her white reindeer through the snowy night. At dawn she changes the animals at a Christmas party into stone, and slaps the sadder but wiser Edmund for daring to say, "Please don't" (*CCN* 111). As they drive on, the air warms, streams flow, snow melts, and grass appears. They have to walk, which does not improve her disposition; she has the dwarf tie Edmund's hands and whip him if he lags. The sun comes out, flowers push up, birds sing. "This is *Spring*," warns the dwarf (113). The Beavers and the children march all day and reach the ancient Stone Table at dusk. There they find a mediaeval-style pavilion; Aslan, looking both "good and terrible"; and mythical creatures – Dryads, Naiads, centaurs, a unicorn, etc. – as well as real animals (114). Aslan shows Peter a vision of Cair Paravel and the sea.

Then a huge wolf sent by the Witch attacks the gathering, Peter kills it with his new sword, and Aslan knights him. This is a restoration of the righteous kingdom, but questions will persist: Where *has* Aslan been? Why did he not prevent the inversion of his *domaine*?

Evil arises to challenge good in chapter *thirteen*. Jadis and her dwarf are about to execute Edmund when centaurs and unicorns intervene and take him to the Stone Table. After a talk with Aslan, Edmund is reconciled with his siblings, but then the Witch appears and claims Edmund's blood under the code of "Deep Magic from the Dawn of Time" (the chapter title), which she explains. It is "the Magic which the Emperor put into Narnia at the very beginning" and engraved on the Table of Stone, according to which "every traitor belongs to me as my lawful prey" (*CCN* 118). Everyone knows who the traitor is. And "unless I have blood as the Law says all Narnia will...perish in fire and water," to which Aslan responds, "It is very true. I do not deny it" (119). It is clear that the Emperor stands for the God, and the Deep Magic (or Law) for the moral code, of the Pentateuch, whose Ten Commandments were engraved on the stone tablets that Moses brought down from Mt Sinai (Exodus 20, Deuteronomy 5). The Witch insists that this code be honoured. She talks with Aslan apart from the others, and after negotiating for some time, Aslan announces, "I have settled the matter. She has renounced the claim...". But the Witch, after a cryptic reference to keeping a promise, leaves with "a look of fierce joy on her face," so we are forewarned, and the next chapter is titled "The Triumph of the Witch."

Aslan leads the way to camp and advises Peter on how to fight the Witch, but seems sad and distracted (as the Gospels depict Jesus on the eve of the Crucifixion). In the middle of the night Aslan leaves the camp (Lucy and Susan following) and returns to the Stone Table, where the Witch is waiting with ogres, wolves, and hags. They put the passive Lion on his back, bind him tightly, cut his mane (Samson), muzzle him, and drag him onto the Stone Table. This is strong stuff for a children's book, the aesthetic equivalent of Mel Gibson's *The Passion of the Christ*. As the Witch approaches Aslan with her long knife, gloating that he has given her Narnia forever and vowing to kill Edmund, Susan and Lucy look away, and Lewis does likewise. When the killers leave, the girls weep over Aslan (the two Marys at the Cross) and remove the muzzle; mice chew through his bonds. At dawn the Stone Table cracks (the veil in the Temple was rent when Jesus died;

the Old Law is giving way to the New) and Aslan is seen alive and larger than ever. The chapter title is "Deeper Magic from Before the Dawn of Time." Aslan takes the girls on his back for a wild ride across the vernal countryside, "perhaps the most wonderful thing that happened to them in Narnia," clear to the Witch's palace (126). There he breathes life into the stone statues, including Tumnus and a Giant, who knocks down gate and walls for them. After a joyful celebration, Aslan calls on everyone to find the Witch and help his army defeat her forces.

Following a hound, they all run or ride up the valley – larger, faster animals carrying smaller, slower ones – and join the fight: Peter's small band (and his sword) against the Witch's ugly hordes. The battle ends when Peter fells the Witch, but he tells Aslan that Edmund deserves credit for breaking the Witch's wand, which had been turning her enemies to stone. He was badly wounded by her ogres, however, so Lucy gives him a few drops of her Christmas cordial. She lingers by him until Aslan observes that others are badly wounded, too. "Must *more* people die for Edmund?" (CCN 130). She goes to help others, and when she returns, Edmund is up and looking better than at any time since he went off to "that horrid school...where he had begun to go wrong." A bad education! (More of this later.) Aslan knights him. The next day they all march to Cair Paravel, and the children are crowned kings and queens of Narnia. Then Aslan slips away, for "he has other countries to attend to" (132). Does that mean that Narnia will be left unprotected again, or can Aslan be ubiquitous, everywhere at once?

The four reign well for years, even learning to speak the "royalese" of bad English historical novels. One day they go in quest of the White Stag (said to have the power to grant wishes when caught), but lose it in a thicket, and while searching see...the lamppost! Pressing forward, they find themselves in the wardrobe, and discover that no time has passed since they left. When they report to Digory, he predicts that they will return to Narnia sometime, but not in the same way. Don't *try* to go there, he says: just let it happen. Thus end the two books that are the foundation of Aslan's Gospel: Creation, Crucifixion, Resurrection. We are left wondering how Narnia will fare without its royal family and its Creator. Has Evil been slain?

The Later History of Narnia

Not all books in the series are so epochal and weighty as to repay detailed examination. Narnia figures in every one, though not always as a principal setting; it may be over the horizon, a place to be remembered, yearned for, or rescued and restored. Aslan appears in each book, inspiring awe and love, or fear. Sometimes his role is to comfort the afflicted and afflict the comfortable: helpful, but comprehensible as a natural phenomenon. *The Horse and His Boy* (1954), third in the sequence, offers several lions, one of whom attacks and injures the heroine Aravis. In the next chapter Aslan assists the young hero, Shasta, through some dark moments, revealing that he has always been with him, that he was in fact all the lions (including the one that wounded Aravis?). He supports deserving characters, and eventually deals with the villainous Prince Rabadash of Calormen, who courted Queen Susan of Narnia. Calormen is the desert country south of Archenland and Narnia; the names of its people and places often have an Arabic ring.

The fourth book, *Prince Caspian* (1951), portrays a later, darker Narnia; a usurper, Miraz, is making it a militaristic regime. The SELP four, awaiting their train back to school, are whisked off to a wood near an island beach. Nearby they find a ruined castle that proves to be Cair Paravel. They rescue Trumpkin, a dwarf, from being executed by soldiers. He tells them about Prince Caspian, an orphan who lives with his uncle – Miraz – and aunt; *he* is the true King of Narnia, though his Telmarine ancestors overthrew Old Narnia. Caspian, appalled to learn this, says Trumpkin, fled from Miraz's castle to join a band of rebels. The children make a long, difficult journey to find them. Aslan guides them to Caspian and roars to awaken Narnia from its subjugation. The very trees rally to him; Bacchus and Silenus appear; human and vegetable mingle. Peter challenges Miraz to single combat and kills him; his forces also win the general battle. Aslan leads a cross-country progress of fertility and liberation, crowns Caspian, and makes a magic door to re-distribute the population: the Telmarines can stay, or go back to Earth, where they lived before Narnia.

In *The Voyage of the* Dawn Treader (1952), Aslan is everywhere. He intervenes to change Eustace, SELP's feckless cousin, from a dragon back to himself, by baptising him in a magic well; ends a quarrel; introduces Lucy to a magician; and helps the *Dawn Treader* escape from the Dark Island. From chapter 14 on we are taken Somewhere Else. On World's End Island, a silver-haired father and his daughter sing the sun up. Once he was Ramandu, a star in the heavens. As *Dawn Treader* sails east over the calm Last Sea, the sun grows larger, everyone needs less food and sleep, and they can see cities and seahorse people underwater. The sea, fresh and tasty, serves for food, and they can look at the sun. *Dawn Treader* drives on, day after day, with the older people feeling younger. A growing whiteness on the eastern horizon proves to be lilies. Eventually this Silver Sea shallows out. Edmund, Lucy, Eustace, and Reepicheep, the mighty mouse who fought against Miraz, go on in the rowboat. Caspian wants to go too, but Aslan says he must stay with his ship and return to Narnia. On the third day, the rowers see a high standing wave, and, *through it*, the mountains of Aslan's country: Heaven, and the End of the World. They run aground. Reepicheep goes on in a tiny coracle, disappearing over the wave.

The children wade through lilies onto sand, then grass, and then a plain where a white lamb gives them fish to eat and turns into Aslan. He tells Lucy and Edmund that they are now too old for Narnia. They must go home and learn to call him by another name, which is "why you were brought to Narnia, that by knowing me here..., you may know me better there" (*CCN* 370). They zip away into the sky. *Dawn Treader* sails to Ramandu's island. Caspian marries Ramandu's daughter and returns to Narnia. In England, "everyone soon started saying how Eustace had improved": one motive for these adventures (370). *The Voyage of the Dawn Treader* is the most theological book since *The Lion, the Witch and the Wardrobe*.

It also makes passing reference to the essence of what I call a *domaine*. In chapter one, Edmund and Lucy, who are passing a dull summer with their aunt and uncle, spend a few minutes

> ...*talking about Narnia, which was the name of their own private and secret country. Most of us, I suppose, have a secret country, but for most of us it is only an imaginary country. Edmund and Lucy were luckier than other people in that respect. Their secret country was real. They had already visited it twice; not in a game or a dream but in reality.* (*CCN* 293)

Though we do not use the same vocabulary, Professor Lewis and I are talking about nearly the same thing: wondrous places that change us and that we never forget.

He and I might want to have a civil chat about "reality" and fiction. *Domaines* can be real – the island where John Fowles taught – or imaginary: the island where Nicholas Urfe was tested. Narnia, of course, is the latter.

The Silver Chair (1953) mostly subordinates theology and *domaines* to adventure, plus one of Lewis's pet peeves: permissive schools (such as Summerhill) that think "boys and girls should be allowed to do what they liked" – a distortion of the Summerhill philosophy (*CCN* 376). Jill Pole (JP) is unhappy at Experiment House, whose "freedoms" include license to bully (specifically forbidden at Summerhill). She is befriended by a classmate, the "improved" Eustace (ECS). Perhaps they could go to a magic place he visited last summer! He calls on Aslan, a door opens in a stone wall, and there is a sunny forest park with bright birds. They walk to the edge of a cliff, over which ECS falls. Aslan appears and blows him away into the distance; then tells JP that he has sent him to Narnia. After having her memorize a list of tasks and "signs," Aslan launches her on a gentle ride to join him. They see Cair Paravel and a tall ship. An old man, King Caspian X, boards, and the ship sails. Then the children make a long, perilous journey, facilitated by owls, Trumpkin the Dwarf, Puddleglum their guide, and Aslan, to find the rightful heir, Prince Rilian, who has disappeared in the north. They meet a woman in green, who directs them to the Giants' palace, Harfang. Humans are on the menu there, but they escape into the underground. Down below they find Rilian, enchanted by the queen, alias the White Witch and the woman in green. They manage to kill her, ending her tyranny over the subterranean world, and find paths that lead to the Narnian *domaine*. Rilian succeeds his father, Caspian X. Aslan then appears, puffs the children away to His Mountain, and gives a drop of his blood to resurrect and rejuvenate Caspian X.

We are not surprised by the reappearance of religion at this point – the children saw heaven in the previous book, too – but what happens next *is* surprising. Caspian is curious about our world, and Aslan agrees to let him see England with them, briefly. He turns a switch into a riding crop for Jill, and bids the others draw their swords, but use only the flats. They all go to Experiment House, where Aslan roars. Part of the wall around the school falls over (Joshua at Jericho), the team rush in, bullies come running, and Aslan lies down in the gap with his "hinder parts" toward the school (cf. Exodus 33:23, Moses and YHWH). The terrified bullies are beaten: the girls by JP, the boys by ECS and Caspian. Then "the Head (who was, by the way, a woman) came running," but seeing Aslan, the broken wall, and the attackers "she had hysterics" and called the police (*CCN* 452). The police find no lion, no broken wall (Aslan has spoken), and no fight, just an hysterical woman. An inquiry unearths "all sorts of things" about the school. The Head is dismissed, but her friends find her a post as Inspector ("to interfere with other Heads"), and when she fails at that, too, a seat in Parliament, "where she lived happily ever after." It is quite a descent from the preceding scenes of Heaven, and shows Lewis's reactionary side: he could not resist a crack at modern education (and women in authority, and Parliament). Then he resumes the Narnia narrative, assuring us that Caspian X returned to Heaven, and that Rilian, after burying his father, ruled the land well.

In the Last Days

The final Narnia book – in chronology and publication date – begins, "In the last days of Narnia" (*CCN* 456). Having seen the Creation, Crucifixion, and Heaven, we will witness the End of Days: Lewis's Armageddon and Day of Wrath (*dies irae*). *The Magician's Nephew* was his Genesis; *The Last Battle* (1956) is his Apocalypse (Catholic) or Revelation (Protestant: "The Revelation of St John the Divine"), which ends Christian Bibles. Revelation, giving the signs and events preceding the Last Judgment, using vivid metaphors and details, is a favourite of fundamentalists who await the Rapture: the Second Coming, ending life on earth, and the ascent of virtuous souls to Heaven. Lewis uses Milton's methods throughout the Narnia series, writing scenes and plots that echo the Bible and prefigure events in ecclesiastical or secular history. Some of these amount to veiled or "dark" prophesies, whose drift is uncertain. As in Revelation and Milton's religious poetry, the meaning of events and the identity of some characters are conjectural.

One of Revelation's themes is fakery: lying apostles, false gods, and fake Jews will blot the End Times. In *The Last Battle*, Shift, a wily old ape, and Puzzle the donkey find a bit of yellow flotsam in Caldron Pool: a lion's skin that has come down from the Western Wild. Puzzle wants to bury it, but Shift sews it into a winter coat, telling him to put it on and pretend he's Aslan. Puzzle is aghast; Shift says that Aslan is never seen now. Thunder and an earthquake knock them both down, which the ape insists *confirms* what he has said.

At a hunting lodge near Lantern Waste, King Tirian of Narnia and his best friend, Jewel the Unicorn, are discussing reports of Aslan's return when Roonwit the Centaur arrives with a message. Skilled in astral lore, he has never seen such disastrous portents as are now in the stars. They do *not* announce Aslan, or anything good; rather "some great evil hangs over Narnia" (*CCN* 461). Rumors about Aslan's reappearance are false. Tirian asks who would lie about such a matter. Roonwit answers, "I know there are liars on earth; there are none among the stars." It is the world of Revelation, filled with deceit and imposters. They are interrupted by the arrival of a Dryad crying woe: ancient trees are being cut in Lantern Waste! Then she shudders, expires, and vanishes: her tree has fallen. Furious, Tirian sends Roonwit to Cair Paravel for reinforcements. He and Jewel head for Lantern Waste, despite the centaur's warning that it may be dangerous.

En route, a water rat on a raft of recently cut logs says that trees are being felled *on Aslan's orders*. He is taking these to sell to Calormenes. Tirian and Jewel rush to the cut, an ugly gash through old-growth trees that grew up around the Tree of Protection that Edmund planted. The loggers are all Calormene, two of whom are abusing a talking horse they have harnessed to a log. Enraged, Tirian and Jewel kill them both. They escape, Tirian on Jewel's back, as Calormenes come running like guards in the *Arabian Nights*, brandishing scimitars. But soon Tirian calls a halt: he feels like a murderer, and if this cutting *is* by Aslan's order.... He will go back and surrender. Jewel says he will be going to his death. Who wants to live in a world where *Aslan* would do such a thing? replies the king. Jewel, who also feels ashamed, agrees, for "This is the end of all things" (*CCN* 465). They walk back, weeping, to the cut. "Then the dark men came around them in a thick crowd, smelling of garlic and onions, their white eyes flashing dreadfully in their brown faces": stereotypical Middle Eastern villains. They put a halter on Jewel, bind the king's hands, take his sword and crown, and march them to a clearing in which is a small thatched-roof hut. Shift the Ape ("Lord Shift") is sitting on the grass, clad in gaudy, ill-fitting clothes that he has commandeered somewhere: their first glimpse of the New Dispensation in Narnia.

Shift drapes the king's swordbelt around his own neck. Chewing nuts, spitting shells, and talking like a Chicago *capo* ("Where's that Head Squirrel got to?"), he demands enough nuts to ruin the squirrels' hoard (*CCN* 466). Some animals ask to talk to Aslan, as of old. Shift retorts that "times have changed": they may see Aslan briefly tonight, but all questions must pass through *him*. And "another thing you got to learn," I'm not an ape but a wise man who is Aslan's spokesman. Oh, and all able-bodied workers will go to Calormen to work in the mines. You'll be paid, and your wages will go into Aslan's treasury to be used for the common good. A Lamb asks, "What have we to do with the Calormenes? We belong to Aslan. They belong to Tash" (467). Shift calls him a "Silly little bleater" for not knowing that "Tash is only another name for Aslan." At that Tirian roars, "You lie like a Calormene. You lie like an Ape" (468). Guards knock him down and cart him off, unconscious. He awakes tied to an ash tree. Small animals bring wine and cheese, and bathe his face, but dare not untie him. That night, Shift exhibits "Aslan" by the low light of a bonfire. Later, in the darkness, Tirian calls on Aslan and on "helpers from beyond the world": "Friends of Narnia!" (471). He has a vision of "the seven friends of Narnia," sitting around a table. They see him, ghostlike, but he cannot speak, and awakes alone and cold.

Narnia's *domaine* is desecrated and its natives are enslaved by the desecrators. Soon after Tirian awakes, however, the youngest of The Seven – Jill (JP) and Eustace (ECS) – materialize to cut his bonds. They flee together, pausing at dawn to break their fast, then exchange stories while marching to a watch-tower. After seeing Tirian during their banquet, JP and ECS meant to use the Rings to reach Narnia, but while they were on a train with Peter, Edmund, Lucy, Polly, and the Professor, "suddenly there came a most frightful jerk and a noise," and they were in Narnia (474). Reaching the tower, they find biscuits, arms, and armor. All "disguise" themselves as Calormenes (by rubbing a brown juice on their hands and faces), collect wood, cook, eat, and drill with Calormene weapons. They rise before dawn and march to Stable Hill, where Tirian overpowers a guard and frees Jewel while JP liberates Puzzle and the lion-skin. Heading west, they meet some Dwarfs guarded by Calormene soldiers. Tirian shows the Dwarfs "Aslan"; then he and ECS kill two of the guards, and the Dwarfs the other two; Lewis does not shrink from righteous violence. The attempt to start an uprising fails, however: the Dwarfs will *not* join Tirian. Sick of higher authorities, they live for themselves. Off they go, but one, Poggin, returns, swearing belief in Aslan and fealty to Tirian. The party, now six, returns to the tower.

In the morning Poggin explains the new regime to them; Ginger the Cat and the Calormene captain Rishda are guiding Shift. Suddenly the day darkens and chills as a grey bird-man glides past. It is the Calormene god Tash, entering Narnia because Shift "called" him (*CCN* 486). We are deep in Revelation's End Times: strange beast-gods, anti-Christs. Washing off their brown-skin disguises, they start walking to Cair Paravel, hopeful of meeting the Centaur's force. Then Farsight the Eagle drops down to report that Calormenes came last night by sea, took Cair Paravel and killed Roonwit, whose last message was "all worlds draw to an end" and "noble death is a treasure" (489). Tirian declares the end of Aslan's realm: "Narnia is no more." He wants JP and ECS out of harm's way, but they will not leave, so all march to Stable Hill and hide in the woods. Their plan to produce "Aslan" at the bonfire and start a revolt is undercut when Shift announces that "Tashlan" is angry because a beast in a lion-skin is impersonating Aslan. There is one good result, for Puzzle: Jill cuts the lion-skin off him. He never liked it.

Now the narrative accelerates: small, quick actions, short intervals, less coherence. Shift says that "Tashlan" will not appear any more, but any of you may go into the stable – one at a time. All hang back except Ginger the Cat, who enters the dark doorway, but a second later comes shooting out, screeching, runs up a tree, every hair on end, making cat noises but unable to *speak*, then disappears. The animals are shocked (speech was a gift of Aslan, contingent on good behaviour). Then a young Calormene officer, Emeth, goes in. The man who shortly runs out and falls dead, however, is not Emeth, but another soldier. Tirian and his party urge the Narnians to rise before the invaders kill them all, one by one.

Chapter Eleven's title, "The Pace Quickens," prefaces a long, messy, inconclusive, back-and-forth struggle: Lewis's Armageddon. Narnians drive Calormene soldiers back. Dwarfs jeer Calormenes, but do not help the king. Tirian throws Shift into the stable, causing light, noise, and a small tremor. Calormene drummers call for reinforcements. Talking horses arrive to aid Tirian, but the Dwarfs shoot them all! Narnian forces kill some of their enemies, yet Calormene numbers grow as others arrive. A Calormene soldier flings ECS into the hut; Dwarfs shoot arrows at Calormenes, who throw some of *them* to Tash. It is a general melee: "the last battle of the last King of Narnia" (*CCN* 504). Calormenes surround Tirian, who sees Jill taken as he is backed to the door of the stable. Meeting Rishda in single combat, Tirian drops his sword, grabs Rishda's belt with both hands, and jumps backward into the hut, pulling Rishda with him.

There is more noise, another tremor, and bright light, but this time *we* enter the stable. Tash, a huge four-armed vulture with terrible talons, seizes Rishda under one arm and turns on Tirian. But suddenly a voice says from behind Tash, "Begone, Monster, and take your lawful prey to your own place: in the name of Aslan...": a Second Coming (*CCN* 505). Tash and Rishda vanish. Then Tirian sees seven kings and queens, crowned and beautifully dressed. The youngest queen he recognizes: Jill, last seen a minute ago dirty, tearful, and dishevelled, but now looking as if she has just stepped from her bath into royal robes. The youngest king is Eustace, similarly changed. Tirian feels awkward about his dirty battle clothes, but finds that he has also been cleaned up and regally clad. Jill presents him to Peter, who introduces him to the rest: Polly and Digory – the pioneers – and his siblings Edmund and Lucy. But where is Queen Susan? Ah, she grew up and got silly ("nylons and lipstick and invitations") and "is no longer a friend of Narnia" (506). Luckily Peter, who is even older, did not get silly, being one of those serious, stable adolescent *boys* we hear about.

Then they are outside, standing on grass. It feels summery, and the trees all bear exotic fruit, which surely they may eat, and do. The Friends of Narnia discuss how this mission began: some were on a train, others on a platform awaiting the train, something happened, and then...this. A stable door opened – and there it is, just standing on the grass, but if you look through its planks you see Stable Hill by night! Very odd: it seems to be two different things, depending on whether you are looking in or looking out. Digory says, "Its inside is bigger than its outside" (*CCN* 508). This prods Lucy (the youngest, closest to Aslan): "In our world too, a stable once had something inside it that was bigger than our whole world." She recounts how the night's events looked from inside the stable: Ginger the cat terrified by Tash; the Calormene who killed the sentry; Shift the Ape eaten by Tash; and so on. The Dwarfs are still there, sitting in a circle facing inward, in total darkness, as intractable as ever. All efforts to help them are spurned. Aslan appears in a great light, and all except the Dwarfs kneel in worship. Not even He can reach them. "They will not let us help," he remarks. "They have chosen cunning instead of belief. Their prison is only in their own minds..." (511). They may be unbelievers in general, or a specific group, but Aslan has seen enough. Walking to The Door, he roars, "TIME," and the portal flies open.

"Night Falls on Narnia" in the next chapter, and more than night. The stars fall until the sky is black: another echo of the Book of Revelation. Beasts – giant lizards, dragons from the moors – invade Narnia and adjacent lands as their inhabitants flee to The Door. There stands Aslan: it is the Last Judgment. Sinners who hate the Lion swerve to his left and disappear into his huge shadow. Those who love Aslan pass to his right through The Door; they include some departed friends: Jewel, Roonwit, Farsight, Poggin. Time speeds up or is compressed, perhaps destroyed. Giants strip Narnia bare, eating everything; then die and rot. A tsunami rolls in from the east, inundating Narnia and its environs as far as the stable door. A map of Narnia is now a nautical chart. The sun eats the moon, and Father Time puts out the sun. All of these events have counterparts in the eschatological chapters of Revelation (5-20). Aslan then has Peter shut and lock the door on that world, that history, whereupon they find themselves in a flowery mead on a warm day, as they were before Aslan appeared. Now he disappears. Walking west, they meet Emeth, the pleasant and noble young Calormene who braved the hut, and sit down to hear his story.

Emeth says that disillusion with Rishda, Shift, and the invasion caused him to enter the stable, where he found...sunlight! He had to kill the sentry, but then walked through pleasant country until Aslan appeared, absolved him ('all good deeds serve me, so go in peace'), then vanished, leaving him a convert. Emeth is a "virtuous pagan," like Virgil in Dante's *Inferno*. Now Puzzle – no longer an ersatz lion but a beautiful donkey – joins the party marching "Further up and further in," towards Aslan. The country looks like Narnia, and they realize that it *is* Narnia, only more colourful and spacious. Digory (looking younger now) explains that the Narnia they knew was a dream, "a shadow or a copy of the real Narnia" that they are now seeing (*CCN* 519). He wonders what they teach in schools these days. "It's all in Plato." Indeed: as the series ends, Lewis gives us a hefty dose of neo-Platonism and the world-despising strain of Christianity. He says it is the difference between looking out a window at a beautiful landscape, or turning to look into a mirror reflecting that scene. The Centaur is ecstatic: "I have come home...! ...This is the land I have been looking for all my life..." (520). He gallops off and the others follow, amazed that they can keep up with him at the speed of a car, then of an express train. They are participating in the Rapture: the taking up or Assumption of the saved souls into Heaven. Good Platonists now, they are saying – as the title of the last chapter puts it – "Farewell to Shadowlands."

That chapter recapitulates places and people from all the Narnia books. The high-speed distance runners reach Caldron Pool, where Puzzle and Shift found the lionskin; run *up* the Great Waterfall; then into the Western Wild and down a valley to the hill topped by a green wall and trees bearing golden fruit, where Aslan sent Digory and Polly in *The Magician's Nephew*. They meet Reepicheep, the martial mouse from *Prince Caspian* and *Voyage of the Dawn Treader*, and Tirian's father Erlian. They visit beautiful meadows where many Narnian characters live now, from King Frank and Queen Helen to Mr and Mrs Beaver and Tumnus the Faun, who helped the children in *The Lion, the Witch and the Wardrobe*. The garden, like the stable, is bigger inside; looking outward they see not the waterworld but the true Narnia, "more real and more beautiful" (*CCN* 523). Tumnus compares their journey to peeling an onion, except that "as you...go in..., each circle is larger than the last." It is all seen clearly, as through a telescope or on a map. The vista also includes "the real England," where good things are preserved: the old house with the wardrobe is still standing. SELP's parents are waving at them from a ridge across the valley, which is accessible, because all the *real* countries are "spurs jutting from the great mountains of Aslan" (524).

All walk up the connecting ridge toward towering yet verdant mountains and growing light. At length Aslan appears, bounding down the cliffs like a cataract. He asks the humans why they do not look happy. "We're so afraid of being sent away," Lucy answers; "you have sent us back into our own world so often" (*CCN* 524). Not this time, he assures them. Haven't they guessed? In his final speech of the entire series, he explains. Brace yourself:

> *There was a real railway accident.... Your father and mother and all of you are – as you used to call it in the Shadowlands – dead. The term is over: the holidays have begun. The dream is ended: this is the morning.* (524)

(Surely "real" is a misstep here: Lewis has been reserving it for the Platonic or *celestial* realm.) A parental reader or listening child may well be shocked at this news. Having wiped out his Narnian *domaine* (but not its Platonic Idea), Aslan announces that the children – Friends of Narnia, and of us – and a set of parents died (as we say in Shadowlands) in a train wreck that killed – how many? Were his characters the only passengers on the train or greeters on the platform? Does any other children's book have such an ending? What did the author think he was doing?

Actually the last is clear. Lewis tries to palliate Aslan's disclosure by assuring us that "they all lived happily ever after" death (i.e. their souls did), that the accident was just "the beginning of the real story" (but the train crash was "real," he said). Their earthly lives were "the cover and title page" of the book of their heavenly adventures, "the Great Story which no one on earth has read," but which Lewis says "goes on for ever," and "every chapter is better than the one before." Readers who do not share his belief in resurrection are left with a drowned Narnia, a pile of mangled bodies, and some metaphors: a holiday, or waking from a dream. Lewis follows his extreme *contemptus mundi* faith to its logical conclusion: "all flesh is as grass" and "grass withereth," while "the word of the Lord endureth forever" (1 Peter 1:24-25, KJV), so "love not the world," for "the world passeth away" (1 John 2:15, 17, KJV). If transience rules *here*, we should rejoice to die and rise to eternity. Do not love the world we know, but embrace the heavenly hypothesis. This is, technically, propaganda, which has not always been a pejorative term; in churchly circles, *de propaganda fide* was just 'spreading the faith.' And the most effective way to disseminate your faith is to teach it to children. If you have come to love Aslan and his followers, you are less likely to reject the heaven he proclaims, and if you are a parent reading to a child, you have strong inducement to explain the Christian concept of the afterlife in a sympathetic way.

For secular social activists like Joe Hill, the "heavenly hypothesis" was a distraction from the actual problems of this world. Hill adapted the old gospel favourite "The Sweet By and By" to explain his objection to the way Christianity was used in the here and now:

> *Long-haired preachers come out ev'ry night*
> *And they tell you what's wrong and what's right,*
> *When you ask them for something to eat,*
> *They will answer in voices so sweet*
> *'You will eat, by and by,*
> *In that glorious land above the sky,*
> *Work and pray, live on hay,*
> *You'll get pie in the sky when you die.'*

The level of invention and creativity in Lewis's Narnia books is impressive. His attention to detail, the quasi-epic sweep of the plots, and the interweaving of action from book to book compel admiration. It is obviously a different mountain from his well-respected scholarly work, but not an inconsiderable one. His books of Christian apologetic display argumentative ingenuity and have long been popular. Problems arise when the attitudes and stance appropriate to the apologetics spill over into other genres, however. That occurs as early as *A Preface to Paradise Lost* (1942), when he steps forward as a *Christian* commentator on Milton and represents that as a benefit to the reader. In the Narnia series, the Creation story in *The Magician's Nephew* does not create difficulties, being constructive and peaceful, non-violent; nor, being rooted in Genesis, is it specifically Christian. The same cannot be said of the graphic, Gospel-based Crucifixion of Aslan in *The Lion, the Witch and the Wardrobe*. And the denouement of *The Last Battle* does, I think, raise questions about the author's state of mind. Was his literary judgment still sound? Did his own religious convictions overcome his taste and sense of decorum? Readers will decide that for themselves.

Among the observant Christians at Oxford in the 1930s and after was another don, mediaevalist, and creative writer: J.R.R. Tolkien, author of *The Hobbits* (1937) and *The Lord of the Rings* (parts 1 and 2, 1954; part 3, 1955). The Bible and Catholicism were strong influences on Tolkien's work; he reportedly told a Jesuit friend that his principal themes were theological. Lewis was probably familiar with the main outlines of Tolkien's fictional world from an early date: the struggle between Good and Evil in Hobbiton, The Shire, and Middle-earth generally several millennia before Christ; the Valar pantheon, Gandolf, Frodo, Elves, and human allies against Sauron, Gollum, Orcs, Dragons, and human slaves; the Three Ages, etc. Tolkien's mythology reflects pagan mediaeval Europe and its literature. His admirers understand Middle-earth as a *domaine* – flawed and unstable, as usual – and Peter Jackson's films of the trilogy (shot in rural New Zealand) support that reading, as do the maps of Middle-earth that Tolkien published. I believe that the Narnia books, which were appearing as *The Lord of the Rings* was being published, can be understood as a "Christianization" of Middle-earth. The only distance between the two men as believers was the Protestant-Catholic divide, but as authors, they were quite different. I see no attempt on Tolkien's part to weave Christian history, cosmology, or eschatology into his fabric as Lewis does. Tolkien does not come forward as a Christian author and try to align the meaning and reception of his work with his faith. I never feel proselytized.

CHAPTER 7:

Domaines of Nature

THIS CATEGORY REQUIRES THAT I make some distinctions and admit a degree of structural contingency. Yes, some "Nature" does exist in the gardens and at the estates discussed earlier, but only in limited, managed slices. The subject of this chapter is large tracts of wild, or at least wild*er*, nature. These are not always "wilderness," however; there is some settlement or habitation in the main texts treated here, but the authors emphasize and admire chiefly the "natural" state of the unsettled parts. Some of my *domaines* of childhood and youth – notably Wordsworth's – meet this chapter's standard of "nature," but I placed them in chapter 6 because their focus on the *young* experience of nature is central. Similarly, while parts of estate and castle literature take place in forest wilderness, those parts are usually subordinated to actions set in and around the seats of royalty or nobility. Finally, the books treated in this chapter often present the *cultures* living in or near wild nature, and thus could appear in chapter 8. The choice to use them here is based on my assessment of where their priorities lie. The categories are not mutually exclusive; there is partial overlap. Some works can be viewed from more than one perspective, and so come up more than once.

Setting aside the pastoral (whose landscapes are highly artificial), *domaines* of wild nature appeared about midway between European literature's first *domaines* and our own; they have achieved moderate popularity since. Like childhood, raw nature had to await certain developments, including photography and the burgeoning of intercontinental travel, before it came to be felt and celebrated in this way. More people needed to wander farther afield, and be pleased by wilder scenes than most of Europe afforded, in order for this type of *domaine* to be recognized.

Slavery in Eden

Among the earliest nature *domaines* in English is the novella *Oroonoko* (1688) by Aphra Behn. So little is known of her youth that any biographical source *not* filled with expressions such as "may have," "probably," "supposed," and "No evidence" is suspect. "Much conjecture and little tangible knowledge" is a fair summary. She *may have* been born in 1640, and her family name *may have* been Amis (or Cooper, or Johnson). She *may have* sailed with her family to Surinam (later Dutch Guiana) on the northeast coast of South America, her father dying en route, and stayed for some months, but *no documentary evidence* of this exists, nor of Oroonoko, the "royal slave" of her novella, nor of the slave revolt she describes. She is *supposed* to have returned to England ca 1664, married a Dutch merchant (Mr Behn), and been a Catholic. By 1666 she was *probably* widowed or separated from him, and *may have* then been a spy in Antwerp. When she returned to England (unpaid?), she *may have* been imprisoned for debt, but survived to become its first known professional female writer. She is certainly a landmark in the history of women's writing, long before Jane Austen, George Eliot, or Virginia Woolf, who paid her a handsome tribute. By 1667 she was known in London literary circles, and her life emerges from the shadows. She published verse, prose fiction, and drama; a dozen of her plays were performed in London, beginning in 1670. Her friends included major authors and playwrights of the period: Dryden, Otway, and Thomas Southerne, who turned *Oroonoko* into a popular tragedy. She was labeled "the incomparable Aphra."

Behn, like Montaigne in the previous century and Rousseau in the next, took an interest in "the noble savage," but Oroonoko, an African prince betrayed to slavery in Surinam (where Behn says she met him), is not a "pure" example of the type. A tribal military leader at seventeen, he had a French tutor, and met English merchants and a Spanish slave trader, all of whose languages he learned, so Europe contributed to his make-up. Though he did some slave-trading himself before he was taken, Oroonoko and his wife Imoinda are treated as "noble," with high praise of their physical beauty, mental qualities, and moral standards. Nor is it only African "savages" who are approved: the native *indios* of Surinam are initially innocent, happy, and good neighbours to the Europeans. They bring to the author's mind Adam and Eve, being handsome, as well as "modest and bashful," quite "like our first Parents before the Fall" (Behn 2-3). *Paradise Lost,* published a decade earlier, was already considered a great poem, and Milton's influence is strong. As is Montaigne's: he likened the Brazilian natives to the happy, simple people of the classical Golden Age, whose lives were above civilized artifice. Behn followed the Edenic model of innocent happiness: her *indios* wear bead-and-flower aprons, "as Adam and Eve did the Fig-leaves" (2).

> ...*these People represented to me an absolute Idea of the first State of Innocence, before Man knew how to sin:...simple Nature is the most harmless, inoffensive and vertuous Mistress. 'Tis she alone...that better instructs the World, than all the Inventions of Man: Religion wou'd here but destroy that Tranquillity they possess by Ignorance; and Laws wou'd but teach 'em to know Offence, of which now they have no Notion.* (3-4)

Like the virtuous horses in Swift's *Gulliver's Travels,* they have justice without fraud, and no vices except what Europeans bring them. They are polygamous, which Behn defends as a system that works for them. They are not vegetarians like Adam and Eve, but their hunting and fishing skills are helpful to the British settlers, and they are industrious, weaving clothes and baskets, and working metal. Overall it is a very favourable portrait of a "savage," "natural" life.

"Noble (or happy) savages" are not quite the issue here, although their mood and "lifestyle" are not irrelevant, either. Behn establishes at the outset that Surinam is a Land of Plenty; its cornucopia – birds, fish, animals – provides the natives with food, adornment, and items to trade with the whites. Representing it as a Utopia full of wonders, including "Buffalo skins" and snakeskins sixty yards long, she regrets that England allowed the Dutch to appropriate that "vast and charming World," which

> ...*affords all things both for Beauty and Use; 'tis there eternal Spring, always the very months of April, May, and June* [as they are in England]; *the Shades are perpetual, the Trees bearing at once all degrees of Leaves and Fruit, from blooming Buds to ripe Autumn: Groves of Oranges, Lemons, Citrons, Figs, Nutmegs, and noble Aromaticks, continually bearing their Fragrancies.* (Behn 48-49).

Behn far exceeds the basic requirements for describing nature in Surinam, reiterating that the trees bear "at the same time ripe Fruit, and blooming Young." Trees provide no "common Timber," but please the eye with "different Colours, glorious to behold," and soothe the nose with "rich Balm, and Gums," made into candles that "cast their Perfumes all about" as they burn (49). She claims that "The very Meat we eat...perfumes the whole Room." Behn stops only because "it were endless to give an account of all the divers wonderful and strange Things that Country affords, and which we took a very great delight to go in search of...," but not before she has comprehensively established her South American *domaine* (confusingly called the West Indies).

Behn was not an adroit stylist. Wanting to make Surinam a *domaine*, she simply lists its attributes – abundant flora and fauna, pleasant climate, happy people – and declares them wonders. She does not create a sense of place that helps us imagine how it *felt* to be there, as some later writers were able to do. But Behn was very good at showing how evil enters a place, and in what forms. In *Oroonoko* it begins in Africa, which should have provided a good life for Prince Oroonoko. His problems started when the chief, his aged grandfather, conceived a passion for the prince's beloved Imoinda, and sent her the Royal Veil, calling her to his bed. He is the *senex amans* (old fool in love) of many a comedy, but this is a tragedy: no one stops him, and "Court-Flatterers" egg him on, though "he could but innocently play" with the maiden (Behn 11). The Court is the original source of evil in the book. Behn came to London during the Restoration, and lived through the reign of the Merry Monarch, Charles II: a fount of immoral behaviour who caused a strong moral backlash. Courtiers play a diabolical role in Behn's tale, telling the dotard that he may take Imoinda because the prince does not care. The sexual intrigues depicted would have been seen to resemble those common under Charles II. *Oroonoko* was not published until 1688, after his death.

Darkness also comes from outside in the form of an English ship captain, a man of some breeding who is welcome at Court. That *should* ring alarm bells for Oroonoko – by then avoiding the Court – but the captain is a smooth operator whose professions of friendship are believed by the prince. He is also a slave trader to whom Oroonoko has sold many prisoners of war, it being their custom to enslave captives. The captain invites Oroonoko and a number of young courtiers aboard for a feast, plies them with wine punch, then suddenly claps irons on them and sets sail; they are all "betray'd to Slavery" (Behn 33). The prisoners rage and go on a hunger strike. To prevent "the loss of so many brave [and valuable] Slaves," he feigns repentance, promising to "set [them] a-shore on the next Land they should touch at" (34). This he does – but that is South America. In one of our earliest anti-slavery texts, Behn shows how, besides its obvious evils, slavery poisons every human relationship. The captain, who *seemed* to like Oroonoko, dissembles during the voyage to keep the peace, and the prince, who *did* like the captain and judges others by his own values, trusts him until he understands hypocrisy. He leaves the ship crying, "*'tis worth my Sufferings, to gain so true a Knowledge both of you, and of your Gods by whom you swear*" (37).

Likewise, in Surinam the prince and Trefry may like and esteem each other, but they are slave and master. Though Trefry is kind, plantations run on slavery; planters must keep the slaves in their place, so the prince's charisma may be dangerous. When he learns that Imoinda – whom he was led to think had been killed – is also a slave and lives nearby, he is delighted. They make so much of each other that Behn gives stage directions for their "Extasies of Joy" (44). *Caesar* and *Clemene*, as they are called, are married, "to the general Joy of all people," and she is soon with child. Fruitful union! This starts to look like a comedy and a happy ending, but they remain slaves, and their nobility cannot accept that. Imoinda, marriage, and impending fatherhood increase Oroonoko's discontent: their child will be born a slave! That makes him "more impatient of Liberty," and he took to "treating with *Trefry* for his and *Clemene's* Liberty" (45). The planters "fed him from day to day with Promises" until "he began to suspect them of Falshood," as well he might. He grows sullen, and the slaveowners, fearing a mutiny, send Behn to sound out the couple: an interesting development, implicating the narrator in the slavers' duplicity. She warns Oroonoko that resisting the owners "might occasion his Confinement," which he resents, but assures her that he would not hurt the whites on his plantation (46). Still he is seen as a threat.

At this point Behn reviews her own (alleged) experiences in Surinam. The "Edenic" paragraphs quoted earlier preface a description of her house, which sat "on a vast Rock of white Marble" amid lush rainforest (Behn 49). Her shady, fragrant "Walk" of citrus trees was a personal *domaine*: "the whole Globe of the World cannot shew so delightful a Place" (49-50). She also narrates the sorties that they made into the jungle. On hunts and fishing excursions, "Caesar" was their guard, required to slay the occasional "Tyger" (jaguar) with his sword. Once, picking up a "Cub" whose mother he had killed, he "laid the Whelp at my feet" (51). Oroonoko exhibited a distinct partiality for the author, his "*Great Mistress*" (46). The main incident is a visit to a native village and the radical revaluation of their *domaine.* The planters, after some disputes, have developed "mortal Fears" of the *indios;* only with Caesar as their guard will a party travel to a village eight days' barging upriver (54). Behn reports that later, when the Dutch controlled Surinam, the natives fell upon them, cut them into pieces, and hung or nailed body parts in trees. This is a Fall indeed for people who, at the beginnng of the book, brought to mind Adam and Eve in Eden; the emphasis in "noble savage" shifts to the noun.

Back in the present, her party enters a village. Naked natives cry out in alarm or wonder at well-dressed Europeans, whom they paw over ("feeling our Breasts... taking up one Petticoat": Behn 55). Then they spread a large leaf on the ground for a tablecloth, and set out a feast of venison and "buffalo." The author notes their "extreme Ignorance and Simplicity," childish love of shiny things, "superstitious" natures, and gullibility about the medicine man's "legerdemain Tricks, and sleight of hand" (56-57). Then she dwells on the frightful appearance of their "War-Captains," some of whom "wanted [lacked] their Noses, some their Lips, some both Noses and Lips, some their Ears, and others cut through each Cheek, with long Slashes, through which their Teeth appear'd..." (57). They say that before a war, those who seek to lead must show their indifference to pain by serial self-mutilation: one cuts off his nose, the other his lips or an eye, and "so they slash on until one gives out..." (58). This is "a sort of Courage too brutal to be applauded by" Oroonoko, who does express esteem. There Behn ends her long digression, intended, she says, to exhibit the sterling qualities of Oroonoko. It does that, but also destroys the image of peaceful savages. Surinam's nature is still wondrous, but its inhabitants are slaveowning colonial planters, savages without nobility, and black African slaves.

Eventually Oroonoko, mistrusting the English more as Imoinda's delivery approaches, assembles several hundred blacks for a feast and delivers a fiery oration. He does not want to attack the whites, only to withdraw services, walk to the coast, found a colony, and find a ship that can reach Africa. The men kiss his feet and vow "to follow him to death" (Behn 62). They leave that night, but (with families) cannot march fast, and are missed early the next morning. The planters summon their militia, and the narrator reveals her allegiance: "*we* had by Noon about 600 Men...to assist *us* in the pursuit of the Fugitives" (63; my italics). There is some sympathy for Oroonoko among "the better sort" in the colony, but the shoddy Deputy Governor, Byam, very "violent...against him," rallies the *other* sort. Following the track that the slaves have cut, the pursuers catch them. Oroonoko's forces fight for their liberty, "all promising to die or conquer" (64). They fell "pell-mell upon the *English*, and killed some, and wounded a great many...". The weapons used are primitive, the militiamen mainly using their whips and calling, "*Yield, and be pardoned!*" The women and children, "being of fearful cowardly Dispositions," beg the men to yield, and "the Slaves abandon'd *Caesar*." Only Oroonoko, his friend Tuscan, and Imoinda fight on. She wounds Byam, but he survives, and offers to free her and Oroonoko if they surrender.

Oroonoko retorts that there is "no Faith" in white men: "honest Men could not live amongst them," and he would "never...credit one Word they spoke" (Behn 66). But he is also "ashamed" of trying to free fellow Africans "who were by Nature Slaves, ...treacherous and cowardly...the vilest of all creeping things." At last he lets Byam and Trefry talk him into surrendering, for Imoinda's sake. They sign an agreement to meet his demands. As soon as the party reaches Trefry's planta-tion, however, Oroonoko and Tuscan are seized, bound to stakes, and whipped. Even his followers are ordered to whip him, and do so. He is then clapped in irons, hot pepper is rubbed in his wounds, and he is tied down. Imoinda is imprisoned. Meanwhile the Englishwomen had fled downriver, and "while we were away, they acted this Cruelty; for I suppose I had Authority and Interest enough...to have prevented it..." (68). This supposition cannot be tested, but none of the men of "good will" has any effect on Byam. "The worst are full of a passionate intensity." The women proclaim their "Abhorrence of such Cruelties; making a thousand Professions..." to Oroonoko (68; he told Byam, "though no People profess'd so much, none performed so little": 66). He accepts that the women had no hand in his whipping, but he can never forgive Byam, and will live only for vengeance. The women arrange a soothing bath, medical attention, and comfortable quarters.

Convoking some "notorious Villains" as a council, Byam obtains a unanimous vote to hang "Caesar," but Trefry challenges their authority and ejects them from the plantation (Behn 69). Behn says that "we set a Guard" to keep out all but "Friends to us and *Caesar*" (70). Oddly, Byam, recovering from his wound, walks, hunts, and fishes with the prince, who lusts for revenge but struggles with the Love vs Honour dilemma popular in Restoration tragedies. Honour bids him kill Byam, yet what then becomes of Imoinda? For the English will then kill *him*, and who will protect her from slavery and rape? No: he must kill her first, then Byam, then himself. Trefry lets him walk with Imoinda into a wood, where he produces a knife and explains his plan. She approves, and begs him to proceed. After an emotional farewell, she lies down, Oroonoko cuts her throat, decapitates her, and lays her on a bed of leaves and flowers, strewing more on top. Now to murder Byam! "But when he found she was dead, ...his Grief swell'd up to rage; he tore, he raved, he roar'd like some Monster of the Wood" – or a thwarted hero in melodrama (72). Yet "however bent...on his intended Slaughter, he had not power to stir..." (73). When he finally does rise after two days, he is so weak and breathless that all he can do is lie down again. Thus he remains for six days, until found by a colonists' search party.

Oroonoko has more to suffer. When some searchers speak of "taking him alive," he pulls his knife, cuts "a piece of Flesh from his own Throat," throws it at them, slashes open his stomach, pulls out his entrails, stabs an Englishman who rushes at him, and wounds Tuscan, trying to intervene (Behn 75). Then he weakens, and is carried to the big house. A doctor says that he cannot live, but they sustain him for a week, until he can recount his story. By then "the earthy Smell about him" is strong, and Behn withdraws (76). The women take a boat downriver, and Byam sends Trefry upriver on an errand, "having communicated his Design to one *Banister*, a wild *Irish* Man." Banister has Caesar tied to the whipping post. The executioner "cut off his Members," then his ears and nose, then one arm, while Oroonoko smoked a pipe (77). But when they cut off the other arm "he gave up the Ghost, without a Groan." His body is quartered, and pieces are sent to large plantations. Behn writes, "Thus died this great Man..." (78). There are no other reflections, no critique, no real conclusion. As for the other people involved, Behn says that the witnesses to the execution "paid dearly enough for their Insolence" (77). Perhaps this was under the Dutch, who are said to have hung some of Byam's councillors and arrested others.

What can we make of this grotesque shambles? Did it actually happen, or did Behn invent it? If so, to what purpose? We do not know what she saw and did in Surinam, *if* she was there; she wrote *Oroonoko* years later: remembering or imagining. This was the situation of many other writers treated here, especially those who created *domaines* of childhood and youth. But Behn was above all a professional writer trying to live by her pen. What models there were for that taught that to sell books she had to interest, entertain, and fascinate. She could learn from pamphleteers, travel-writers, and proto-novelists: the forerunners of Daniel Defoe. Hers is a travel book, deploying the Lurid Exotic, though like many fablers she advertises "A True History." Behn crosses the Garden of Eden story with Montaigne's essay on "noble savages" (available in English since 1580). She first shows readers a South American jungle *domaine* with happy savages as a modern counterpart of Adam and Eve, but then dulls the gloss: they *are* savage. But British settlers dependent on slavery do most of Satan's work here, bringing evil to a hitherto stable, self-sustaining natural place. The jungle remains intact at the end, but the colonists are tainted, either as conscious agents of evil, or as ineffectual, hand-wringing bystanders.

We know little of Aphra Behn's early life apart from what her writings suggest. *Oroonoko* reveals an impulse to sketch Surinam and its indigenous population as a *domaine*; then an urge to use a different lens and expose both natives and settlers. Like many a predecessor in exposé, she looks closer and closer until the flaws are revealed, staining the original picture. Behn ranks as a moderate on this axis; she does not, like C.S. Lewis, annihilate the natural along with the human *domaine*. Yet she is one of the hardest on her characters. Her initially Edenic *indios* are shown as ignorant, self-mutilating, and ignoble; the whites are slaves of their slavery; and the Africans are condemned by Oroonoko as treacherous and cowardly. He himself murders his wife. Behn gives us little to enjoy or admire. Poisoned by slavery, this *domaine* is made known for what it is; botanical bounty cannot mask the human ugliness. We have seen other writers exploring the weaknesses in their principal performers – from Gilgamesh to Nicholas Urfe – and in the *domaines* themselves, but none has gone farther than Mrs Behn in meting out punishment.

Dispossession; or, Irony in Arcadia

In sharp contrast to Behn's case, what we know of W.H. Hudson's early life, from his own writings and external sources, aids us in understanding the content and feeling of his books. He provided both facts, and interpretations of them. "My life ended when I left the pampas" at age 33, he wrote, which literary historian Samuel

Chew amended to, "it became a *recherche du temps perdu*." The titles of the books he wrote in his dreary London flat are elegiac: *The Purple Land That England Lost, Idle Days in Patagonia, Green Mansions, Far Away and Long Ago* (a memoir of his youth). He subtitled *Green Mansions,* his most successful book, a "Romance of the Tropical Forest," preparing readers for a work of the imagination, but his "romance"gains poignancy and coherence when we realize how much a sense of disconnection haunted his life.

Born to American parents on a sheep ranch near Buenos Aires, Hudson grew up on the pampas: riding a horse, watching birds, climbing into great *umbú* trees. Surviving early bouts of typhus and rheumatic fever with a weakened heart, he had tutors but no formal schooling. *Far Away and Long Ago* describes his animist religion: a sense of something in nature that eludes civilized man, a projection of his own intelligence onto nature. It breaks off in 1859, his eighteenth year, when his mother died and he read Darwin. It does not cover the years when he collected bird skins for museums in Buenos Aires, Washington, and London; later he co-founded the Society for the Protection of Birds, perhaps in expiation. After his father died he stayed on for a few years, observing and writing about birds, before sailing away – not to his parents' homeland, but to England, where his work on Argentinian birds had been published, and henceforth his home. Hudson's adjustment to life in England was not easy, however. He (and later his uncongenial wife) lived in genteel poverty for years. His early books looked back or forward, not at the present. *The Purple Land That England Lost* was Uruguay (he thought Britain should have colonized it). *A Crystal Age* (1887) is utopian, but mostly he drew on his past: *Argentine Ornithology* (1888), *Naturalist in La Plata* (1892), and *Idle Days in Patagonia* (1893), a nostalgic re-creation of his wanderings on the South American plains and a discourse on the appeal of that terrain.

Not until 1895 did Hudson write about his adoptive home, publishing *British Birds* (which he worked to protect through his Society). In 1900 he became a British subject and was awarded a pension. Still, he turned back to South America for the subject of his next book, *Green Mansions* (1904). He published several other books on nature in England, but only the American success of *Green Mansions* in 1914 finally ended his financial worries. He began his memoir while ill in 1916; *Far Away and Long Ago* was published in 1918. He continued to write about birds, and when he died in 1922, left his estate to the Society for the Protection of Birds.

In his literary returns to South America, Hudson created two *domaines*: one that he knew well, the other imaginary. The first was *Idle Days'* memorial to Patagonia, whose vast tracts of unspoiled land gave him quasi-religious feelings. His first glimpse of a "solitary wilderness, resting far off in its primitive and desolate peace, untouched by man," moved him (Hudson 1979, 4). Words that usually connote deprivation – *solitary, primitive, desolate* – are affirmative here; Hudson was an instinctive minimalist. He celebrates the power of "a desert that had been a desert always, and for that very reason sweet beyond all scenes" (6). He attests that "... there is nothing in life so delightful as that feeling of relief, of escape, and absolute freedom which one experiences in a vast solitude, where man has perhaps never been..." (7). Yes, he is misanthropic; his "freedom" arises from the absence of men. Forest, ocean, and mountain may be "beautiful and sublime," inspiring "admiration," but this "gray, monotonous solitude woke other and deeper feelings" (204). The Patagonian plains stretch "into infinitude": metaphysical territory (205). He would willingly die there, unseen, unfound. He goes out onto these plains every day in poor weather, as if to "a festival." One attraction is that the wind- and rainswept ground can reveal "old ocean-polished pebbles," hinting at the abyss of geological time that excited Darwin (206). The "reversion to the primitive" there gives him a "feeling of elation": the happiest he ever sounds (210, 215).

Green Mansions provides a *domaine* that Hudson imagined. The "Green Mansions" whose loss is mourned by his principal narrator, Abel, are Hudson's dream of luxuriant South American forests: in effect the opposite of Patagonia's empty plains. The magical grove is situated in a vague, remote region of southwest Venezuela, near its borders with Colombia and Brazil: an area that Hudson had only read about. (The narrative's earlier place-names appear on maps, but I have not found the later ones – a kind of verisimilitude at least as old as Daniel Defoe.) Abel's anguish over the fate of bird-woman Rima is Hudson's guilt about shooting birds and selling their skins; their laments for a lost paradise are close parallels.

The five phases into which the novel's plot falls crop up in fictional *domaines* from *Sir Gawain* to *The Magus*, but the paradigm is perhaps clearest here. The first phase comprises the initial sighting of, entry to, and sense of wonder at the place (Hudson 1989, 20-51). The second phase reveals the ironies of Arcadia (or Eden): a sense of threat, sometimes with biblical allusions, here a serpent and a fall (60-103). The third contains the charmed moments of love and happiness that will fuel the nostalgia of the visitor for a lost paradise (130-95). In the fourth, outside knowledge is brought to bear on Arcadia, with ambiguous or inconclusive results (209-28). The last phase consists of the destruction, disfigurement, or loss of the *domaine* (at least for the visitor), sin, and real or metaphorical death (253-80). Henceforth the protagonist and the *domaine* are parted, inaccessible to each other – except via literary re-creation.

In *Green Mansions*, an "outer narrator" tells the story given him by Abel, the "inner narrator": a structure that Joseph Conrad (a friend who admired Hudson's work) also used. As Abel moves toward Rima's grove, we are shown the *impurity* of his motives. Having participated in a failed insurrection, he had to flee Caracas, but still hopes to return and use family connections to win political office. His jungle wanderings are also prompted by a desire for gold, of which he sees many traces. He spent months "searching with eager, feverish eyes in every village," stream, and ravine for "glittering yellow dust" (Hudson 1989, 19). He is not interested in natural beauty, yet late one afternoon when the sky clears and the sun comes out after a "day of despair" in which he has exhausted his last lead and realized that "there was no gold," a vision is granted (18, 19). As wet trees glitter in the sunset, the "rare loveliness of the scene touched...my heart," and the light on the Parahuari hills gives them "strange glory" and "mystic beauty" (20). Bell birds fly over, uttering their clear tones like a heavenly benison, and "into the turbid tarn of my heart some sacred drops" fall; he feels "purified" by the "spirituality in nature," conferring "unexpected peace" (21). It is an epiphany of redemption, expressed in the language of religion and *domaines*. Cleansed by his response to natural beauty, he is ready for the green mansions.

Here Abel ends his wanderings and begins his encounter with a *domaine*. Having felt the magic of the place, he decides to "rest for a season" (Hudson 1989, 21). After plying the natives with gifts and fair words, impressing them with his martial character (fencing and firing his pistol), and habituating them to both his presence and his absences, he crosses the ridge on his western horizon and sees in the next basin "a very inviting patch of woodland covering five or six square miles" (31). Venturing there, he enters a "wild paradise" of old-growth rainforest, whose layers of vegetation are "much more delightful" than any jungle he has seen previously, or the bare savanna around the village (32). His first sight of the "leafy cloudland," with its "exquisite greenish-golden tints" and abundance of birds, generates the feeling of wonder that visitors to most *domaines* express (33). He is surprised that the locals, who hunt anything edible, do not hunt there; when he reports his find, they say that "something bad" lives in it (35). Putting this down to superstition, he returns, and is fascinated by a particular birdcall, sweet and almost human, that seems to follow him. Once he brings along a young hunter, who soon flees in terror, after which the bird-voice sounds resentful; then, Ariel-like, it leads him to a quiet spot deep in the forest, where he is treated to a deafening concert of howler monkeys.

The simian performance ends the first phase of the plot: the luring of the narrator to the mystery. The *forte* of the 1959 film with Audrey Hepburn and Tony Perkins was its ability to *show* us what enchants Abel. The second phase begins in Chapter 5 with Abel's crowing that the glade is "truly and absolutely...mine with all its products...its wild animals that man would never persecute...my new domain" (Hudson 1989, 60). He kneels and thanks God for *giving* him "those green mansions" (61). A day later he has his first glimpse of Rima, the bird-woman or woodspirit: a slim, girlish figure about four and a half feet tall. She looks strange, metahuman, with her off-white dress, hair and skin of indeterminate colour, "a kind of mistiness in the figure," giving an impression of "greenish grey," and an ability to disappear in the trees (66). Yet he allows himself to be drawn into the hunter Kua-kó's jokes about Abel's archery: "Soon you will be able to hit...a bird as big as a small woman": he has seen Rima, too (69). When Abel admits that he saw her, the tribesmen expect him to kill the *Didi* (malicious spirit) who spoils their hunting. To them, Rima is "the evil being I was asked to slay with poisoned arrows!" (72). Abel, always the slave of his temper, rages and flourishes his pistol, but they still want him to kill her, and their distrust of him deepens. So this *domaine*, too, is menaced, and its defender does not inspire confidence.

Returning to the glade, Abel sees a beautiful serpent. We should not be surprised: *Et in Arcadia ego*. He casts the first stone towards it, occasioning a burst of vocables from Rima, who comes forward to calm the serpent. But she and Abel do not understand one another, and he is so fascinated by her that he moves nearer, regardless of the serpent, slips his arm around her waist, and is bitten on the ankle. "O cursed reptile!" he exclaims melodramatically, "I must go away into the cursed blackness of death" (Hudson 1989, 84, 85). He runs off through the forest as a thunderstorm darkens the grove, becomes disoriented (the topography is vague here in Hudson's imagined jungle), jumps off a cliff, hoping to land in a treetop, and loses consciousness. It is a Fortunate Fall, however, ending his misguided dash and allowing his friends to find and care for him. Friends? Yes: Abel wakes up in the hovel inhabited by Nuflo, Rima's guardian and titular "grandfather." The final twist of phase two is that he proves to be a man of the world who smokes tobacco and eats meat.

Once Abel and Rima have daily contact, they begin to develop a bond. Abel falls in love with her and decides to stay. Later Rima says that she loves him, too (though she did not know the word). He adopts her religion – nature-worship plus Catholicism – and enjoys happy moments. Returning to the glade after days in the village produces "a strangely delightful [and Wordsworthian] sensation": "I likened myself to a child" going back to his mother, for "Mother and Nature seemed one and the same thing" (Hudson 1989, 195). But this love-*domaine* is threatened by the natives' hostility, and by Rima's wish to leave the glade and seek her ancestral home. Hoping to dissuade her, Abel takes her to a hilltop to show her "the world" (as Satan did for Jesus), but his tactic backfires. She asks what is over the horizon, so he draws a map in the dirt, and in naming the places on it, mentions "Riolama." She reacts immediately. "That is the place I am seeking! There was my mother found...! Therefore was I called Riolama...!" (163). Rima is a nickname. This disclosure troubles their *dulce domum* and the plot. Both have angry arguments with Nuflo. She blames him for keeping the secret of her birth, and he blames Abel for disclosing the secret and alienating her. As in Genesis, tasting the fruit of knowledge has immediate consequences. They decide to undertake a long journey – Nuflo to guide Rima to Riolama, and Abel to support them – which will leave the glade without its guardian. Abel's ability to protect them (and himself) has been compromised, however: the villagers have managed to steal his pistol.

The fourth phase – their arduous journey and what they learn – is the only one whose action occurs away from the glade and the village, yet what it brings to light profoundly affects the green mansions. The knowledge of Rima's mother and her people that they acquire is ambivalent, both liberating and destructive. Other *domaines* offer a number of rough analogues to this stage: Adam and Eve leaving Eden and starting a family; Sir Gawain going to Bertilak's chopping-block to learn more about the castle and himself; *le grand Meaulnes* abandoning his bride to fulfill a promise; Nicholas Urfe leaving Bourani to learn more about its people. However brilliant the *domaine* may appear, full knowledge of it often requires a departure in search of context or perspective. Afterwards the visitor *may* be allowed to return or, if not, may emerge a more complete person for the search. "Sadder but wiser" pretty well covers it.

At first they travel only by night; later Rima ranges on ahead in daytime, often up in the trees. Once, when she is with them, they meet three *indios* from their district, returning from a visit to relatives. Nuflo fears that they will report the meeting at home, so the natives will know that the glade is unprotected. When Rima is away, Nuflo explains how he became her guardian. Seventeen years earlier, he led a band of fugitives from Venezuelan justice (like Abel) through the jungle, raiding villages for food and women. While camped at a mountain cave they saw Rima's mother, who looked as strange to them as Rima had to Abel. Nuflo knelt and crossed himself, thinking her angelic, but the younger men chased her, and she dove down a steep ravine. Uneasy now, they left the mountain to camp elsewhere. Sick of them, Nuflo stole away that night, returned to the cave-camp and found the woman at the bottom of the ravine with a badly injured foot. He carried her up to the cave, cared for her, and later helped her to the closest Christian village. He saw that she was pregnant. When the girl was born, the local priest baptised both. The mother never learned a local language and was not understood, but Rima learned her language and Spanish. Seven years later the mother sickened and died. Nuflo, having sworn to care for Rima and take her to healthier air, chose the Parahuari village. Rima disliked the natives, so they moved to the glade, where the *indios*' hunting of the "animals she loved" brought them into conflict (Hudson 1989, 217).

Thus far Nuflo has been Abel's and our informant. What follows is centred on Rima. After an eighteen-day walk they reach a sphinx-shaped mountain; Nuflo leads them up to the plateau and cave where he first saw Rima's mother. Rima, "apparently expecting great things," is not satisfied (Hudson 1989, 220). That night she leaves the cave and starts climbing by moonlight, followed by Abel. He asks why she is ascending at night. "Why should I wait?" she replies. "Perhaps from the summit I shall see my people's country" (223). For her, this is a "roots" quest to find others who speak her language and look like her. Abel objects: "Rima, never, never, never would you find your people, for they exist not. ...this hope to find your people...is a mirage" (224). And Nuflo can offer no more help, because "of your mother's people he knows nothing" (225). Rima retorts that he has lied before. Abel is telling her what Nuflo said, not what he himself knows, and he has also found Nuflo untrustworthy. When she persists, he swears that "there is no mountain, no forest, in whose shadow your people dwell" (227). But where are they? What happened? she keeps asking. All he has to offer are Nuflo's words ("she showed no wish to return to her people") and hypotheses: a "great calamity" (disease?) fell on them, or "hostile tribes" killed them (228). This insensitive presentation of mere conjecture causes Rima to faint.

Abel carries her to the cave, wondering why he had "told her that sad tragedy *I had imagined,*" as well he might (Hudson 1989, 230; my italics). Nuflo, who thinks she is dying, kneels and begs her to speak well of him in heaven. But she begins to revive in Abel's arms, and Nuflo goes to sleep. Despite his presence, Abel, still holding her, thinks,

> I could not have felt more alone with Rima – alone amid those remote mountains, in that secret cavern.... In that profound silence and solitude the mysterious loveliness of the still face I continued to gaze on...produced a strange feeling in me, hard, perhaps impossible, to describe. (233)

Here begin the couple's central moments of union: in effect, a brief love-*domaine*, their only one, found far from the glade. Rima is still unconscious. Abel compares her to the white Hata flower, of which there is said to be only one at a time. It possesses "a different kind of life. Unconscious, but higher; perhaps immortal," and a "sacred purity" (234). This he holds in his arms! We are at the heart of the "Romance of the Tropical Forest," in a fairy tale. Abel kisses her. She blushes, he kisses again, her eyes open, and, he thinks, "we were united in perfect love" (237). He tells her that their "anguish" will be replaced by love; her people are lost, but "I am with you," and feels certain that she understands (237-38). She puts her arms around his neck and sits on his knee.

Calling him "Abel" for the first time, Rima struggles to express her feelings in his language: "all I wished to know was there – in you" (Hudson 1989, 239). She recalls her mother crying for someone ("she and another were like one, always... the other was lost for ever, and she was alone"); now she understands (243). She even voices an aubade, the lover's wish that the night go on: "Not yet, dear light; a little while longer..." (239). Abel replies, "a greater love than this...we could never feel...love will make us happy..." (242). But at this moment of "delicious languor that was partly passionate," of "tender assured happiness," she drops a bombshell (244). "I must go back alone," she says. "Before day comes I must leave you" (245). Abel is stunned: dismantle the *domaine* at this moment of perfection? She must travel quickly, prepare the glade to receive them, make herself a white dress like her mother's! He cannot stop her ecstasy. Then she hears the first bird of morning, embraces Abel, slips from his arms, and leaves. Fatally slow to react, he goes outside, but the only reply to his shouts is distant bird calls. So in *Paradise Lost*, Adam and Eve argue about whether to work together or alone, eventually separating, which gives Satan unfettered access to Eve.

But Abel's first reaction to Rima's flight is quick compared to his and Nuflo's pursuit of her. Having sat up with her all night, Abel sleeps that day, and Nuflo likes the cave. Two full days are lost. Then bad weather slows their return, so almost four weeks elapse between her departure and their arrival at the glade. Searching for the house, they find only a pile of ashes. Nuflo understands: "the children of hell have been here, and have destroyed everything!" (Hudson 1989, 252). The fifth and final phase – destruction of the physical *domaine* – has begun. Its magic is gone: "A strange melancholy rested on the forest, ...seldom broken by a distant bird's cry" (253). Nuflo sits on the ground, catatonic; Abel wanders. His calls for Rima attract several *indios* with weapons, happy to hunt in the forest now. Weak with fatigue and hunger, and under a cloud for having left without permission, he is told that the "daughter of the Didi" they once feared "is not there now" (257). In the village, the chief, Runi, questions him. Abel says that he went to Riolama to investigate a report of gold, which proved false. That eases the tension, but does not assuage his own "black and terrible suspicion" and growing "fury" (264). When Kua-kó returns from a hunt (wearing *his* revolver), Abel asks about Rima, and learns that the *indios* they met on the trail did indeed report having seen her heading away from the glade, so then they felt free to hunt there. Yes, says Abel, she went away to the mountains.

"But she came back!" exults Kua-kó (Hudson 1989, 268). A week ago they saw her in the wood, chased her into a great tree, and built a bonfire at its base! When the flames reached the top she cried, "Abel!" and fell to her death: "burnt to ashes like a moth in the flames" as the villagers shouted, "Burn, burn, daughter of the

Didi!" (270). The scene in *Avatar* (2009) where the huge sacred tree is incinerated may suggest Abel's feelings. He lies down, cloak over his face, and feigns sleep, but when all are quiet he steals outside; if he can reach the village of Managa, Runi's great enemy, he may find allies. Kua-kó, however, follows him and throws a spear, wounding his left arm. Abel turns to face him. They fight with their knives and Abel kills him with "a feeling of savage joy" (274). Now, thinking of Rima, Abel curses a Manichean god, from whom come "love and hate, good and evil" (276). At Managa's village he is fed and nursed. For two months, a "period of moral insanity," he incites the villagers against Runi, so they join him in the "hellish enterprise" of revenge (279, 280). The entire population of Runi's village is massacred, "old and young, all who had lighted the fire round that great green tree." It will be the stuff of nightmares. Revulsion comes quickly: he faints and falls asleep.

Here Hudson moves into a new mode. From Genesis to John Fowles, survivors have faced the question: After the *domaine*, what? Abel wants to be alone and live off the land. He returns to the scarred glade in search of peace and a natural existence. He gathers food – roots, berries, birds' eggs, grubs – and learns how to make fire. There are painful memories: at the site of Nuflo's hut he finds the old man's skeleton; he too was killed by the *indios*. He discovers Nuflo's secret cache, which contains tobacco, vegetables, bread, utensils and a hatchet: the equivalent of the shipwreck general store in *Robinson Crusoe*. In fact, Abel begins to play Crusoe. He imagines a new *domaine* there in which he would have "luxuries added to necessaries; a healthful, fruitful life of thought and action...; ...a peaceful, contemplative old age" (Hudson 1989, 285). Building a hut "where Rima's separate bower had been," he feels "almost triumphant," taking pride in his fire and "dry bed," clasping "a visionary Rima" in his arms (286). He imagines being with her again: "my lost Rima recovered...mine at last!" (287). In this mood he can kill no animal, so the hut fills with spiders, crickets, beetles, centipedes, etc. One night a moth flies in and settles on the thatch above the fire. Abel is ecstatic, but while he is apostrophizing it ("O night-wanderer of the pale, beautiful wings, go forth") it suddenly drops into the fire (289).

He shrieks, forced to see how Rima died, and at once begins to deteriorate. Eating and sleeping less, he becomes thin, weak, a "ragged man" with a tangle of shoulder-length hair who argues with himself and is "evidently going mad" (Hudson 1989, 290). He tries to revive the *domaine*, the "sweet old days," fantasizing about being "alone together in the wood" with Rima (293). That ends when he discovers the spot where she died: a fire-blackened tree surrounded by an ash-heap containing her skeleton. Gathering her calcined bones and ashes ("sacred relics"), Abel puts them in one of Nuflo's earthen jars, which he decorates with a serpent in token of their first meeting (295). And then he sits with his ashes, "dwelling alone on a vast stony plain in everlasting twilight," in "a universe where *she* was not, and God was not" (297).

Eventually his dwindling supplies, inability to find food, hallucinations of Rima, "remorse and insanity" drive Abel to start walking, east toward the coast (302). Neither Abel nor Hudson seems to know what to do now. Abel's description of his long, hellish walk is vague about where he went, how long it took, and whether natives helped or hindered him, but he is sure that only the "talisman" of Rima's ashes saved him from the "phantom arrows" of "phantom savages" (310). The landscape becomes more allegorical, including "Sloughs of Despond," and is troubled by "many serpent fancies": another bow to our oldest symbol of trouble in Eden (311). At last he staggers into Georgetown, British Guiana, with his "sacred ashes" (314).

The main story – enchantment, love, murder, revenge – ended many pages earlier, but the novel persists. Its final section leaves Abel "in rags, half-starved and penniless," seeing himself as a pilgrim with his reliquary, rather as the author treasured his South American memories and fantasies in London (Hudson 1989, 313). There is no closure of the inner story or return to the narrative frame, as in most of Conrad's tales. Abel's Miltonic sense of catharsis at the end ("in calm of mind, all passion spent") appears to be Hudson's, too; he has little to add. We are never told how Rima should be regarded. Was she a dryad or avian wood-spirit? Is she mythical, symbolic, or a being created to express his conception of nature? Did she belong to our space-time dimension? No clues are offered there, but Hudson does give Rima a moral of sorts. In one of her appearances to Abel, his "Rima of the mind" – a relic of the *domaine* – tells him that "if I [Abel] forgave myself Heaven would say no word, nor would she." That becomes his philosophy: "outside of the soul there is no forgiveness in heaven or earth for sin" (314). And, he tells us, "In that way I have walked...self-forgiven and self-absolved..." (315). It does sound as if he has made his peace, which resembles Hudson's own mood toward the end of his valedictory *Far Away and Long Ago*.

Ex Patria

We have now seen *domaines* in a variety of styles and types serving different functions: origin myths (the Garden of Eden, the Golden Age), legends of adventurous quest (Chrétien, Marie, *Sir Gawain*), social/moral drama (Elizabethan estate masques), trials of flawed characters (Fowles), love bowers, secret gardens. We have examined reminiscences or sublimations of childhood experiences (Wordsworth, Jefferies), of precious times with departed parents (Agee), of college days and great mansions (Waugh), of lost love (Alain-Fournier). There are also fantasies and spiritiual instruction for children (Lewis), exotic novels of escape (Behn, Hudson), and allegorical poetry for mediaeval courtiers (the *Roman de la Rose*). A full range of exemplars stretches along the spectrum from fiction to non-fiction, from reportage to imaginative literature. My emphasis so far has been on the last, but this subsection includes writers whose love of nature engages them strongly with the world as it is, was, or will be. They use their imaginations on real-world issues. Nor can we always find the border between imagination and reported experience; "imaginative literature" has its own spectrum. Behind many or most literary *domaines* lurks a remembered one.

Out of Africa by 'Isak Dinesen' (one of Karen Blixen's pen names) stands near the factual end of the spectrum. Whatever liberties she took with chronology and dialogue, whatever discretion she used in respect to her private life, she offers a generally realistic, occasionally surrealistic or impressionistic account of her years in Africa, not a fable or romance. Her elegant style heightens her experiences, but she never ceases to be the observant reporter, trying to convey how it felt to live in Kenya in the early twentieth century as an expatriate, distanced both from the patriarchal, mainly British, colonial society, and the local labour on which she depended. A Dane, she became Baroness Blixen when she married her cousin Bror Blixen-Finecke. They went to Nairobi before the First World War and bought a coffee plantation in the Ngong Hills nearby. The baron preferred to stay in Nairobi – more women there – so most of the work fell to his wife. He gave her venereal disease (she had to seek treatment in Denmark), and they divorced in 1921. The farm survived until 1931, when the collapse of world coffee prices killed it: the bank foreclosed on her mortgage, and she became another victim of the Great Depression. Returning to Denmark, she turned to writing, mostly under the name of Isak Dinesen. Like Behn, Hudson, and Fowles, she found that her thoughts ran on youthful experiences in exotic places; thus *Out of Africa* (1937) and *Shadows on the Grass* (1960) came to be. She died in her birthplace in 1962.

Blixen's writings about Africa have many moods. She is pragmatic in economic and agricultural matters, cutting about social life in the colony, nostalgic for some natives, and discerning about their culture. But with landscape she is almost always lyrical, from the first lines, "I had a farm in Africa, at the foot of the Ngong Hills" – voiced by Meryl Streep in Sidney Pollack's film (1985) – to the last, saying adieu to those hills (Blixen 1985, 15). She portrays Kenya as a *domaine*: magical, unique, set apart. Though only a hundred miles from the Equator, her farm lay at six thousand feet, so mornings and evenings were fresh, nights chilly. It was "a landscape that had not its like in all the world," with "no fat" or "luxuriance," a distillation or "strong and refined essence" of Africa. The trees' structure differs from that of European trees; their "horizontal layers" have "a heroic and romantic air like full-rigged ships with their sails furled." A grove of such trees *vibrates*, she says, and the wild grass of the plains was perfumed and "spiced" with thyme and myrtle. She is not talking about her farm here, but about the whole district where the "white highlands" abutted the Great Rift Valley. Spaciousness is its charm and keynote: "The views were immensely wide. Everything that you saw made for greatness and freedom." Pollack's camera never tires of roaming over this expansive landscape, but its "chief feature," the "blue vigour" of the high air that paints the land its own colour, shining and scintillating, it cannot convey.

All this is on the first page, and Blixen often restates her theme with variations. On a "lovely morning," cold but "clear and serene," the sunrise is a series of blushes, grading from "delicate gold" to copper (Blixen, 60-61). At the foot of glowing hills, she has the illusion of "walking along the bottom of the sea" and "gazing up towards the surface of the ocean" (61). Of course "plains always have a maritime air, the open horizon recalls the sea" (200). Flying with Denys Finch-Hatton in his biplane gave her "the most transporting pleasure of my life on the farm": "tremendous views" and "the full freedom of the three dimensions" (167). For "When you have flown over the Rift Valley and the volcanoes of Suswa and Longonot, you have...been to the lands on the other side of the moon." It was extraterrestrial pleasure, as well as psychic healing: "the homesick heart throws itself into the arms of space." Blixen's wartime safari with a supply caravan to a

British camp on the border of German Tanganyika was another high; they rode through new country, camping under the great vault of stars undimmed by light pollution. "The air of the African highlands went to my head like wine...the joy of these months was indescribable" (188). Fewer readers will share her love of lion-hunting: "the roof of my own life" (in *Shadows*, 307-08). She came to see the ugliness of killing other animals on the "game plains" – but not of killing a lion.

Blixen shows early on that this *domaine* is subject to Time; she is describing a place at a stage in its history that has ended. Come, see a bygone Kenya – as we observe stars that may have exploded years ago. Most literary *domaines* are about the past, but not all are equally anguished by the changes that time brings. Milton does not suggest that Eden declined after the Fall; the nostalgia is muted in Marie and Chrétien. It swells from the Romantics onward, though, especially with Wordsworth, Alain-Fournier, Waugh – and Blixen, grieving for a departed past. "When I first came to Africa, there were no cars in the country," but by the time she left, the servants were driving (Blixen, 20). Her mourning is urgent, full of *carpe diem*. In those days, "Nairobi said to you: 'Make the most of me and of time. *Wir kommen nie wieder so jung* – so undisciplined and rapacious – *zusammen*'" ("We will never again meet so young"). Blixen acknowledges that "The colony...has already changed since I lived there," but her memoir "may have a sort of historical interest," she adds (27). Her favourite European men, Berkeley Cole and Finch-Hatton, were "outcasts": not cast out by society, "but time had done it, they did not belong to their century" (151). And "When Berkeley died, the country changed": losing class, becoming "a business proposition" (158). Her own departure may have had a similar effect.

Here every *domaine* comes with a contingency clause. The author describes "Lulu," a bushbuck who would come to the farm looking for handouts. But in Blixen's last years she seldom saw Lulu, and in her final year not at all, for

> *Things had changed; south of my farm land had been given out to farmers and the forest had been cleared here, and houses built. Tractors were heaving up and down where the glades had been. Many of the new settlers were keen sportsmen...the game withdrew to the west....* (64)

It is a familiar story now: population pressures, development, losses not understood or even noticed by new settlers. The Ngong farm was becoming a suburb of Nairobi. This overwhelming of a former *domaine* is the theme of *Out of Africa*'s last chapters. Serial disasters – crashing coffee prices, a ruinous fire, a "blizzard" of grasshoppers that devour the crop – make the farm untenable by ruining its owner (232).

> *When I had no more money, and could not make things pay, I had to sell the farm. A big company in Nairobi bought it. ...they were not going in for farming. ...they meant to take up all the coffee-trees, to divide up the land and lay out roads, and...to sell the land for building-plots.* (233)

"...had to sell the farm." The plague of insects is followed by the plagues of bankers and developers, rapacious but not undisciplined. The farm no longer being hers, "the attitude of the landscape" seemed to change: "the country disengaged itself from me" (234).

Her companion in the bad years as in the good ones, Denys Finch-Hatton, saw what was happening in Kenya and what that was doing to her. Perhaps she would be happier in Europe now, he said, "well out of the sort of civilization that we were going to get in Africa" (Blixen, 243). For him this was home; he could be happy with "a tent in the Masai Reserve," or in his house on the coast, set amid "divine, clean, barren marine greatness": another *domaine*. But, fearing what the future held, he urged her to come and see wild Africa before it was spoiled, settled, gone. One may object that progress is inevitable, that new settlers have as much (or as little) right as they to be here, but Blixen insists on showing us what is sacrificed in the process. Loss and leave-taking dominate the final chapters: "Hard Times," "Death of Kianjui," "The Grave in the Hills," "Farah and I Sell Out," "Farewell." The grave is Finch-Hatton's, dug near the farm after his plane crashes – his great passion finally exacting its toll. His resting place on a ridge in the Ngong Hills has "an infinitely great view," north to Mt Kenya, south to Kilimanjaro; Blixen also hoped to lie there (248). Farah was her Somali servant, dignified and loyal to the end: the first and last African man in her life. Whatever measure of success Blixen has in casting the spell of her Kenyan adventure on us, in that measure will we feel her loss at the end. For that is the nature of *domaines*: "a sometime thing."

More than two decades after publishing *Out of Africa*, Blixen revisited that *domaine*, still magical, but shaded. *Shadows in the Grass* (1960), which provides some updates on characters in the first book, exhibits few shifts of attitude or perspective, despite all the changes in Africa. There is the same nostalgia for that time and place, the same sense that they were charmed but doomed. Her feelings seem not to have altered, and perhaps she was loath to disappoint admirers of *Out of Africa* by repudiating or undermining it. The history and sociology of British Kenya move into the foreground. When she arrived, "the Highlands were still in very truth the happy hunting grounds," where (she avers) "white pioneers lived in guileless harmony" with natives, preferred Africa to Europe, were "country-bred" people comfortable in the outdoors, and meant to stay in Africa (Blixen 285-86). After the war, however, England's "energetic advertising" brought "a new class of settlers, ...strangely provincial." Land was also given to military officers, mostly "city people." She thought it "a sad programme," and "from the point of view of the country itself, the 'true home of my heart', a closer white settlement was a dubious benefit." Her stance is 'moderation in all things,' including white immigration to third-world countries.

Those notes are sounded early in *Shadows*. Then she moves on to what attracted her to the old East Africa, which is no less appealing in retrospect. The spaciousness of the landscape, *Out of Africa*'s first theme (especially during airplane rides), is reborn in *Shadows* as a prominent feature of her dreams. Second only to a sense of familiarity, of belonging to that place, is her dreams' "vastness, their quality of infinite space. I move in mighty landscapes" – and this is said of her life in Denmark, decades after leaving Kenya (Blixen 334). "Long perspectives stretch before me, distance is the password of the scenery," and it is not surprising to hear that in dreams she often flies, "to any altitude," though no airplane is mentioned (Finch-Hatton had her sit in the front seat, with an unobstructed view). So the deep psychic appeal of her Kenya years is an enduring boon, still accessible via her unconscious. Wordsworth and Proust would understand that.

Those are occasional graces, however; the prevalent mood of *Shadows* is elegiac. She calls the roll of European friends who died in Kenya and now lie "safe in the mould of Africa, slowly being turned into African mould themselves" (336). As she walks Danish paths and seashores, "the plains" of her old farm are "being cut up into residential plots for Nairobi business people, and the lawns, across which I had seen the zebras galloping, were laid out into tennis courts." This seems a falling-off, but then "What business had I had ever to set my heart on Africa?" She tries to avoid bitterness when people she knew in Kenya report on what is happening there. During one "sad little talk about the changes," she realizes that *Out of Africa* has "become history, a document of the past. ...as much out of date as a papyrus from a pyramid" (347). Her old house is now a "club-house" in "the residential district of Karen," named for her (348). She still corresponds with the literate among her former servants, who remember her fondly but are getting on, going blind, dying. Blixen is openly sentimental about them, quoting their letters, and about her recollections of "the time that once had been": all that remains of a *domaine* now irrevocably vanished (349).

THE PORTRAITS OF NATURAL *DOMAINES* by these three writers form a curve related to their historical eras. In the seventeenth century, Aphra Behn makes South American jungles an integral part of the Edenic existences that the colonists initially perceive the natives as leading. Though the narrator ceases to regard them as Adams and Eves after closer contact, she does not revise her view of their environment. The jungle remains largely intact – planters' clearances are relatively minor – and it is not cursed or belittled. Two centuries later, Hudson's natives destroy some of Rima's grove by fire: human malice has natural repercussions. The grove is desecrated, scarred and burnt in places. This was Hudson's invention; *Green Mansions* is a work of fiction. Blixen extends this curve into the twentieth century, describing – from her own observation and what she was told later – the effects of government programs, a surfeit of settlers, bank foreclosures, and aggressive development on wild or rural Kenya after the Great War. Her report is a memoir, not a novel. It is clear, thorough, and persuasive, being empirically verifiable, and has many parallels today (the extensive rainforest clearances in modern Brazil for roads, mining, and farms, for example). Many millions around the world now know that natural tracts of land cannot be taken for granted; if unprotected, they will be lost. Market value trumps "*domaine* value" in most cases.

Adding William Wordsworth's prose writings on nature to the mix would roughen this steady curve of rising concern for the loss of natural spaces. A century or so before Blixen and Hudson, his early poetic love of unspoiled nature grew into a pragmatic, almost polemical argument for protection of it. In 1810, he published *A Guide through the District of the Lakes in the North of England*, whose fifth edition

(1835) expresses ambiguity about the region's increasing popularity with visitors. Though he gives "Directions and Information for the Tourist," he also treats the problems of 'developing' the Lake District ("The Country disfigured") and lists the "Causes of false Taste." Wordsworth wondered how all these "New Settlers" would affect the lakes he loved ("Changes, and Rules of Taste for Preventing their Bad Effects"). Would they know to leave well enough alone, or would they want to import their urban comforts? The *Guide* is included in *The Prose Works of William Wordsworth* (Oxford, 1974).

And two letters that he sent to *The Morning Post* in 1844 opposing the extension of a railway to the head of Windermere attack "tourism" on conservationist grounds; both appear in *Prose Works of William Wordsworth* (Macmillan, 1896). The district's "staple" products, he maintains, are "beauty...seclusion and retirement," not mines or manufacturing, and the "intrusion" of the railroad would "sacrifice" much of its "quiet and beauty" (Wordsworth 1896, 2: 386, 393). In several aesthetic passages that draw on his own climbing experiences in the Alps and on Snowden (narrated in *The Prelude*), he points out that apprehending mountain scenery as sublime is a culturally and recently acquired taste, and that the railroad will deliver to the region large numbers of people who lack that taste. The second letter goes even farther. While "Utilitarianism" generally despises higher thought and finer feeling, the Lake District *ought to be* one of those "temples of Nature" that we hold sacred (Wordsworth 1896, 2: 400). This was throwing down the gauntlet with a vengeance; at 74, the poet probably saw no reason to hold back.

If Wordsworth's advocacy for the environment in the 1830s and 1840s complicates the curve of increasing disquiet about threats to wild nature drawn by the other authors, his whole career recapitulates that general development. The long movement is from Behn's Paradise-inflected memories of South American jungles and Hudson's fantasy about an Edenic grove to Blixen's lamentation for a once-pristine Kenyan *domaine* that has now been spoiled by bankers, realtors, and unfit settlers. Wordsworth's career has a similar shape. Beginning as a fervent worshipper of nature whose main concern was the gradual loss of youthful freshness and sensitivity, he lived to see the danger of larger, exoteric threats to natural landscapes, and came to believe that caring individuals have an obligation to take up whatever cudgels are available in defence of Mother Nature, lest there be no more natural *domaines* to teach and delight.

CHAPTER 8:

Domaines of Culture

IN PASSING FROM DOMAINES SET in gardens, estates, wild nature, or an author's youth to those expressing a distinct culture, we encounter more ambiguity and overlap. The *Roman de la Rose* and mediaeval romance generally are cultural arti-facts, not just stories about gardens and castles; Aphra Behn and Karen Blixen depict societies (exotic for their readers) as well as untamed nature. Wordsworth, Jefferies, and Waugh arguably sketch "youth cultures." The Woodstock festival and Joni Mitchell's "Woodstock" visit several types of *domaine*: youth, parties, gardens, nature worship, and cultural values. F. Scott Fitzgerald's parties are also commentaries on the culture that generated them. Which category best hosts a given work depends on its main emphasis or salient feature, so its placement requires an arbitrary judgment. That *domaines* can possess a variety of styles or subjects is, of course, part of their interest, and their challenge.

As I use it here, a *"domaine of culture"* means a work in which a well-defined social structure that can motivate characters and move them (and us) out of quo-tidian existence is a prominent feature. Within the work, attitudes toward that culture may vary considerably, from lyrical rhapsody to a critical, 'warts-and-all' appraisal; and readers' opinions may range just as widely, independent of the main narrative view. A number of the best examples occur in North American film and literature, issuing especially from 'the heartlands', where popular culture tends to be homogeneous and coherent (urban settings being more likely to produce anti-*domaines*). Generally, the artists of any 'heartland culture' will produce some *domaines* of this kind.

Field of Dreams, the 1989 film based on W.P. Kinsella's *Shoeless Joe Jackson Comes to Iowa* (1980) and *Shoeless Joe* (1982), exemplifies the type. The books and the film are works of 'magic realism' about cornfields, baseball, and the Homeric search for a lost father. The film gives a stronger sense of a *domaine* owing to the power of the visual medium and the collaboration between director Phil Alden Robinson – who also wrote the screenplay and the first ('temp') score – composer James Horner, and actors Kevin Costner as Ray Kinsella, James Earl Jones as novelist Terence Mann, Ray Liotta as Jackson, and Burt Lancaster as Archibald Graham. Briefly, a young farmer (Kinsella) starts hearing a disembodied voice in his cornfield intoning "If you build it, he will come," and "Ease his pain." Puzzled but obedient, he plows his corn under, lays out a baseball field, and puts up night lights. This endangers his family's financial health, and, as in Blixen, the bankers close in. But eventually magic realism works: one night a ball player walks out of the corn into the arclights. It is Joe Jackson of the notorious "Black Sox," who threw the 1919 World Series. Add Horner and Robinson's eerie music and we are in a *domaine* where a farmer can pitch to or play catch with Shoeless Joe, and invite him to bring the rest of his team next time.

The aftermath is equally wondrous. Joe returns with the spectral Black Sox (more weird music); later they field two full teams and play day games. But only those who *believe* can see them: to most people it is just an empty, cornless field, an offence against Iowa's *raison d'être*. There are wider concerns, though: we can't watch the Boys of Yesteryear play ball indefinitely, and the messages keep coming. If "he" is not Joe Jackson, who *is* he? And what pain wants easing? In the novel, Ray becomes convinced that "he" is J.D. Salinger, then a recluse in the Northeast, and sets out on a long journey to find and help him. Salinger was outraged by Kinsella's use of him in *Shoeless Joe*, and warned that he would sue if it was repeated in any other medium. In the film, Terence Mann, a black writer of the '60s now living in Boston, disillusioned and silent, replaces Salinger. Far from Iowa, Ray and Mann see a message about "Archie 'Moonlight' Graham" (who appeared in one game in 1922) on the scoreboard at Fenway Park, and hear the voice: "Go the distance." They drive to Chisholm, Minnesota, where Dr Graham settled, hoping to find him, but learn that he died in 1972. However, Ray takes a nighttime stroll there, sees a Nixon campaign poster, a licence plate sticker saying "1972," and an old doctor shuffling along, carrying his medical bag, as the uncanny music kicks in. Another *domaine*, plus time travel.

It seems to be a dead end, though. Graham, who has had a long, satisfying life in Chisholm, says that he left baseball behind long ago, declines to visit Iowa, and shuffles off. Sure that he has wasted his time, Ray heads for Iowa, where, his wife reports, the vultures are circling. Mann, now hooked, goes with him. They stop to pick up a young hitchhiker who is looking for small towns with semi-pro baseball teams; his name is...Archie Graham! The situation he describes *once* existed in the Midwest, but not now: another time-warp. Ray drives them to the farm. They can both see the phantom ball players, and Archie is accepted as a rookie; he even drives in a run with a sacrifice fly. Then Ray's daughter falls off the miniature bleachers and lies unconscious on the ground. The game stops. Archie comes forward, and as he steps off the Field of Dreams becomes old Doc Graham with his medical bag. He saves the girl by extracting the bite of hot dog that was choking her, but there is no going back. He strolls off through the players, basking in their plaudits, and disappears into the high corn – a fitting last exit from Lancaster's long career.

Suddenly Ray's brother-in-law – a banker – can see the players, and urges Ray *not* to sell or plant the field. Mann agrees, predicting that "People will come," and their admission fees could save the Kinsellas' farm. As the players begin leaving, they invite Mann to come along. He is delighted to accept, and disappears into the corn, chuckling, but Ray is annoyed: Hey, what about me! You have a family and work to do *here*, Joe replies, and points to the catcher, who is removing his mask. It is John Kinsella, Ray's father, in his youth a promising baseball player, from whom Ray was estranged at 17. He has come; "Ease his pain." As they start the game of catch that Ray once refused because he could not respect a man whose hero (Shoeless Joe) was a criminal, the camera draws back to show long lines of cars, headlights glowing in the prairie dusk, winding toward the Field of Dreams. *They* – paying customers – have come. It *is* sentimental (as *Rotten Tomatoes* said), but so magical that disbelief may be suspended.

There are several ways of regarding the story that Kinsella and Robinson created. It is a paean to the hallowed place that baseball occupies in North American hearts, and to the enduring value of rural cultures that foster the sport and feed the nation. It also follows a young family's struggle to survive without relinquishing their moral values or ignoring their promptings. It is one more exculpation of Joe Jackson, and another tale about the search for a lost father: the "Telemachan theme" in Homer. And it shows baseball and (irrational) belief rescuing a jaded writer from a sense of failure and a bitter old age. Along the way, it generates several *domaines*. The Field of Dreams, with its resurrected, quasi-mythic players, is the most obvious and pervasive. Early on, Joe asks Ray, "Is this heaven?" No, Ray replies, "This is Iowa," which at that moment seems heavenly. But this magic is far-reaching. In Boston, Ray and Mann are (apparently) the only fans who see the message about 'Moonlight' Graham and hear the voice urging, "Go the distance." Chisholm, MN, provides a time machine that carries Ray seventeen years into the past to meet Doc Graham. And on the road to Iowa, their act of stopping for a hitchhiker introduces them to young Archie Graham. The *domaine*-creating power seems to follow Ray wherever he goes.

Field of Dreams must be one of the sunniest *domaines* ever created, with almost no downside. The ballplayers of yore keep returning (from wherever they exist) to play before appreciative crowds in the heartland that most of them probably came from, and thereby keep the appealing young family that hosts them from losing the farm. They also provide an opportunity to close the rift between John and Ray Kinsella. Doc Graham has one productive at-bat with the storied old-timers, and then both he and Mann are admitted to the Heavenly Cornfield: an Ascension of sorts. No one is hurt or left out of the goodies, with the possible exception of a few offstage bankers and developers. It is, in the end, a 'feel-good' film, and, yes, sentimental – which we have seen is *not* the ruling paradigm of *domaines* – but it is also magical in the way it frees several of its characters from the constraints of mortality and unidirectional time.

There was an unlikely but fascinating coda as the film's optimism overflowed into reality. *Field of Dreams* used two farms for its Iowa scenes. After the shoot was over, one of the farmers went back to raising corn, but the other, Don Lansing, heard a different drummer, left his spread as it had been transformed for the film, and opened it to tourists. (He did not charge admission or parking fees, making his money from the souvenir shop.) By 2009, twenty years downstream, it was receiving 65,000 visits annually. "If you build it...". In 2011 the property was sold to Go the Distance Baseball, LLC, for a reported $5.4 million, which is a lot of sentiment. In this case, at least, life has followed art into a sunny place, and there seems to be no downside.

Past Glories, Lost Forever

To pass from *Field of Dreams* to *Gone With the Wind* (1936) is to leave the brightest of *domaines* for one of the darkest, though at first the darkness is covered by a veneer of chivalrous men, pretty women, and lush plantations. Margaret Mitchell was born and raised in Atlanta, and eventually her Confederate sympathies emerge in the novel, but the first time I read it, ignorant of her background, I took the first few hundred pages as an *exposé* of the Old South. From a mid-twentieth-century (northern) perspective – Jim Crow, segregation, civil rights protests – her antebellum South seemed an overripe plum for The Few, ready to fall and split. It was as dependent on slavery as the English colony in *Oroonoko*. In its glory days, the O'Haras' plantation had a hundred slaves; when Scarlett returns after the Yankees have swept through, it has three, and "Nobody can run a big plantation without the darkies" (M. Mitchell, 564, 688). Emancipate the slave labour and brute economics kicks in: plantations can no longer support a gracious lifestyle for beautiful people. It is significant, and symptomatic, that Scarlett's father Gerald came from Ireland, another glittering but troubled culture, bearing his "family tradition of past glories, lost forever" on his back, like Aeneas carrying his father from burning Troy (59). He named his place "Tara," evoking the great days of Irish kings, celebrated in song and story ("The harp that once through Tara's halls," by Thomas Moore), and cast himself as a latter-day Irish-American monarch of all he surveyed. The Irish historical experience rumbles along beneath that of Dixie, forming a rough, sinister parallel.

While her heart sided with the defeated, occupied Southerners, Mitchell has some of her leading men give candid appraisals of the South's prospects as hostilities commence. One function of Rhett Butler and Ashley Wilkes, who live at opposite ends of the book's moral spectrum, is to question the Confederacy's ability to win a war or maintain its way of life. At the outset, she shows us the gracious prewar scene – a prosperous, cotton-rich white elite served by obedient slaves – but during the all-day barbecue at the Wilkes's plantation, arguments begin. Should the southern states (having fired on Fort Sumter) leave the Union peaceably or by force of arms? Gerald O'Hara and the young bucks clamour for war, while John Wilkes and his son Ashley favour a civil exit. Rhett Butler observes that "there's not a cannon factory south of the Mason Dixon Line": in fact, few factories of any kind, or foundries, or mills (M. Mitchell, 154). And no warships, so they will not be able to trade with Europe. Southerners don't travel enough, he says, or learn from their travels. He has seen the North's mines and industries, and many immigrants willing to earn money fighting: "all the things we haven't got" (155). He speaks like an historian – the underdeveloped, pastoral-agricultural South vs the developed, capitalistic North – but adds, "all we have is cotton and slaves and arrogance. They'd lick us in a month." Then he strolls off to examine his host's library, leaving the testosterone crowd to mutter, seethe, and spoil for a fight.

In the first year the South did well, winning several battles. But at the patriotic ball in Chapter Nine, the *narrator* declares that "the Cause" (the rebels' "states' rights") has crested. "It was high tide of devotion and pride in their hearts, high tide of the Confederacy" (M. Mitchell, 237-38). This is about one-sixth of the way through *Gone With the Wind*, leaving a long time for the tide to ebb. Ashley, off at war, writes to his wife Melanie that he is "fighting for the old days, ...which, I fear, are now gone forever" (293). He predicts that "we will never get back to the old times" he loved (294). Rhett Butler, who keeps well-informed as he runs the Yankee blockade, tells Scarlett the facts of the war: Southern zealots are stupid and will lose everything; England "never bets on the underdog" and will not help the South, nor will anyone else; so "The Confederacy is doomed" (330-31). Its "system" will be "smashed," as it should be (332). Their *domaine* is coming apart. His report is wasted on Scarlett, who has "never heard of any system," but she is said to feel the truth of his predictions. She stops going to church, which does not "seem so sinful now": "For some time she had felt that God was not watching out for her, the Confederates or the South," and Scarlett does not pay for undelivered goods (465). Her religion and Old Dixie have gone, raked by the "mighty storm" of the Union army "sweeping away her world" (550).

From here on, *Gone* and its variants constitute a *Leitmotif*. When Scarlett returns to Tara from burnt Atlanta and has to scrabble for vegetables among the old slave cabins, she is felled by an attack of nausea, and lies in the dirt remembering "a way of living that was gone forever" (M. Mitchell, 592). Her mother Ellen, once a tower of strength, taught Scarlett that she was "responsible for the moral as well as the physical welfare of the darkies God has intrusted to your care. ...they are like children," but "Ellen's ordered world was gone" (655, 602). When the men reappear she hears the same dirge. Frank Kennedy, a good, solid man and a suitor of Suellen O'Hara, tells Scarlett as the fighting winds down, "It sure looks like the end of the world to me" (672). And with the surrender in 1865 comes the bitter realization that (for Southern whites) "It was all over, the bright beautiful dream they had loved and hoped for.... The Cause they had thought could never fall had fallen forever" (679). *Lost, dead, fallen, the end, all over.* Ashley limps home from a Yankee prison camp, his mood apocalyptic: "My home is gone.... ...the world I belonged in has gone," and he feels "helpless...to cope with" the new one (733). Scarlett agrees that "The South is dead," but asks him to leave Melanie and run away with *her* (738)!

When Ashley and Melanie return to Atlanta, Scarlett follows, desperate enough to marry Frank Kennedy (stolen from her sister) just to have access to Ashley. Atlanta society has resumed its diversions, but "Something had gone out of them" (M. Mitchell, 845). It's the old "feeling of security," Scarlett decides: "Now it was gone and with it...the old thrill, ...the old glamor of their way of living." Rhett Butler reappears, interested in Scarlett; he gives her money and bulletins on the new state of affairs. Why does she think upper-class people look unhappy? Because they have lost their money, she says. No, he laughs, it's because they are "losing their world – the world they were raised in" (1075). He wants her to stop pursuing Ashley (and giving him Rhett's money) because he esteems Melanie, and believes that Ashley's "breed is of no use or value in an upside-down world like ours" (1077). Later, after Kennedy dies and Scarlett marries Rhett, she denounces the "new people" pouring into Atlanta, trying to take over (1207): "Scallawag" Republicans and Yankee "Carpetbaggers," the *bêtes noirs* of old Southern society, and, along with freed slaves and their white agents, the chief artificers of its post-*domaine* hell. At the end, after Melanie dies, Rhett repeats his verdict on Ashley as "a gentleman caught in a world he doesn't belong in," still playing by "the rules of the world that's gone" (1435).

Ashley and Scarlett differ radically on the relative values of the Old South and the New. A nearly-flat character, a walking fossil, he identifies hopelessly with pre-war society. "I want the old days back again," he admits, "and they'll never come back" (M. Mitchell, 1288). Scarlett, however, has "set her face against the past" and is determined to make good in the ugly present, with help from Rhett. "I like these days better," she tells Ashley. "The old days were so dull." He insists that they "had a charm, a beauty, a slow-paced glamor." Scarlett admits that beauty to herself, but not to him: that was then and this is now, the only reality. "Don't look back!" is her motto (1289). Still, mutual thoughts of "the sunny lost youth that they had so unthinkingly shared" make for closeness (1290). The memories hurt, but the pain brings on her tears and a warm, lingering hug – which happens to be observed by others. They are both compromised.

It is time to deal with "the Scarlett question." Ask any reader or moveigoer who the heroine of *Gone With the Wind* is: she will be named without hesitation. Who else stands before us, striving to recover, from first to last? Scarlett is a tough, stubborn fighter and survivor in wartime and afterwards. If she becomes as hard as nails, that is what circumstances required. She is the Unsinkable Molly Brown of her time. We may deplore her obsession with happily-married Ashley, but must admire her endurance. After her pre-war *domaine* – slave-owning white plantation society – crumbles, she tries to construct a more modest one at her birthplace, Tara. Leaving Atlanta (again),

> It seemed that if she could only get back to the stillness and the green cotton fields of home, all her troubles would fall away and she would somehow be able to mold her shattered thoughts into something she could live by. (M. Mitchell, 1349)

This is clearly a fantasized *domaine*, not a realistic program: we have been told that big plantations require many slaves. Riding through the boot-trampled countryside, Scarlett sees "plantation after plantation...going back to the forest.... It was like moving through a dead land" (1358). Her overseer, Will, is blunt: "Tara's the best farm in the County, ...but it's a farm, a two-mule farm, not a plantation." Scarlett soldiers on anyway, refusing to crawl back to Atlanta. The ancestral estate will not die on *her* watch, even if it *is* now just a two-mule farm; she will keep it alive somehow, for her will is cast iron.

Thus say her defenders. The prosecution, while not denying the strengths that the defence sees in Scarlett O'Hara Hamilton Kennedy Butler, asks the court to remember the other side, to complete the portrait. Its two witnesses portray the defendant, despite the literary appeal of her spirited *agon*, as often foolish, childish, amoral, cold, and heartless; as inarticulate to a fault and of limited intelligence; and as a bad mother. In their testimony she seems far from admirable. The leading female protagonist, yes, but the "heroine"? Hardly. Mrs Butler is a mixture of disparate qualities, the prosecution argues, and they must all be considered.

Its first witness, the American novelist Pat Conroy, wrote the preface to the Pocket Books edition of *Gone With the Wind* (1996). His own mother "modeled her whole life on that of Scarlett O'Hara," he admits (M. Mitchell, xii, xv). She did this well, being a "willful, emotional beauty with just the right touch of treachery and flirtation" herself, says her son (xiii). His mother's love of Scarlett dominates his preface: he refers to "my mother" at least thirty times. Conroy likens Mrs Butler to Shakespeare's Juliet, yet he is conflicted about this "most irresistible, spiderous, seditious and wonderful of American heroines," at once "lovely" and "Machiavellian" (vii). He grants her "uncontrollable self-centeredness," but finds it "charming" (ix). When not representing his mother's views on Scarlett, Conroy is less complimentary, calling the character on whom his mother "modeled herself" both "immoral" and "unscrupulous" (xv).

The prosecution's second witness is Scarlett's creator, who provided the materials for all opinions of her. For many chapters Margaret Mitchell presents her protagonist's actions, words, and thoughts, and some assessments by other characters, with little or no comment. In the last ten chapters, however, she herself renders several judgments on Scarlett's mind and morals. Discussing Rhett with Ashley, Scarlett asks, "[W]hen will you stop seeing both sides of questions? No one ever gets anywhere seeing both sides" (M. Mitchell, 1287). Ashley asks her, "just where do you want to get?" She thinks, "Where did she want to get? That was a silly question. Money and security, of course. And yet – Her mind fumbled." Readers who have been wondering about her mind will welcome this acknowledgement of a problem. Scarlett's limited capacity for ratiocination is often painfully evident; she makes decisions by deliberately narrowing the range of her consideration. Her catchphrase throughout is "I won't think about that now." With a small store of information, she relies mainly on intuition, so her judgments can be ludicrous ("there isn't going to be any war. ...It's all just talk"), and she often misjudges people, starting with Ashley and Melanie (6). Rhett accuses her of "lusting in [her] heart after Ashley Wilkes," adding, "That's a good phrase, isn't it? There are a number of good phrases in that Book, aren't there?" (1306) Scarlett is confused: "'What book? What book?' Her mind ran on, foolishly, irrelevantly...".

But Mitchell lays worse than feeble-mindedness to Scarlett's account: she is generally indifferent to her children, who react by finding surrogate parents. And when a riding accident takes away Bonny, one she *does* care about, she lashes out at a surviving daughter. The doctor's advice – have another child right away – makes Scarlett reflect:

> *Oh, for another girl, pretty and gay and willful and full of laughter, not like the giddy-brained Ella. Why...couldn't God have taken Ella if He had to take one of her children? Ella was no comfort to her, now that Bonnie was gone.* (M. Mitchell, 1399)

That thought might cross a mother's mind at such a time, but most would disavow it at once; Scarlett does not, and she wishes her son Wade were like Ashley and Melanie's son. True, Melanie is not working and has more time for child-raising, she tells herself, but "honesty forced her to admit that Melanie loved children" – and that Bonny "infinitely preferred Rhett to her" (1334-35). Single-minded devotion to prospering and rebuilding the *domaine* at Tara comes at a price. The women at Bonnie's funeral understand and pity Rhett, not Scarlett, for "Everybody knew how cold and heartless she was" (1400). Scarlett has few friends and "no cronies" left: "somehow, these people had slipped away. She realized that it was her own fault" (1402).

Scarlett also tends to become inarticulate, almost catatonic, in emotional crises, hurting her own cause. After Melanie dies, Rhett predicts that she will divorce him and marry Ashley. Scarlett is horrified – "I don't want a divorce" – then stops, "for she could find no other words" (M. Mitchell, 1433). "[S]he tried to speak. But she could marshal no words...". Scarlett is too conflicted to explain her view of their complex history. It is a serious failure; the scene ends with his famous "My dear, I don't give a damn" (1446). While we may dismiss Rhett's denunciations of Scarlett ("brutal," "hard and greedy and unscrupulous," etc.) as a bitter husband's bile, Mitchell's own critique of her cannot be set aside so readily (1437-38). The final chapters compile an indictment on several fronts. Yet Scarlett's ability to shrug off failure and opprobrium remains impressive: at the end she is back at Tara, scheming to bring Rhett to heel. That is a long shot, though by this time only a very reckless gambler would bet against her. She seems to have learned little or nothing, but her will is unbroken and her drive to succeed as strong as ever.

How are we to understand this schizoid character, both model and Machiavel, heroine and tramp? I suggest that Mrs Conroy's devotion to *Gone With the Wind* as a powerful presentation of enduring Southern anguish over the Civil War did not require her to identify with its protagonist. Scarlett is perhaps best regarded as flawed and damaged goods, one of the war's and the Cause's walking wounded. That she is still walking at the end is an achievement, but her deep emotional and spiritual injuries should be acknowledged, not minimized. Those scars were earned in the War and Reconstruction and poverty, owing to her identification with the damage to Tara and the devastation of the Old South. All her energies are funneled into addressing those losses and building a new *domaine* on what remains of the old. Pat Conroy writes that the novel portrays "the Confederacy as Paradise, as the ruined garden looked back upon by a stricken and exiled Eve" (M. Mitchell, vii). This Eve is both Scarlett O'Hara and Margaret Mitchell, trying to make sense, or at least a go, of life after the irrevocable loss of their Eden.

The Golden Persuasions of the Fairchilds

There are some obvious similarities between *Gone With the Wind* and Eudora Welty's *Delta Wedding* (1945), two novels about life in the American South by Southern women, published within a decade of each other (Welty even includes a mother named Ellen and a sister named India). Beyond that they diverge considerably, however. *Gone With the Wind* is a long historical / political novel, often sad and bitter, about events that occurred in Georgia some seventy years before Mitchell wrote, events of which she had heard or read, or which she imagined. *Delta Wedding* is a compact memoir of life in the Mississippi Delta as Welty remembered it, fondly for the most part, from her girlhood. Instead of years it covers a week or so; there is no slavery as such, no war, no political agenda, and seemingly no bitterness.

Yet these differences must not be overstated. Welty's scene is also dominated by large plantations worked by poor blacks, the descendants of slaves, who are themselves indentured servants trying to stay afloat in an economic backwater. We are rarely let into *their* feelings. *Delta Wedding* was published on the cusp of the civil rights movement, just before the soldiers returned from the war and the Brooklyn Dodgers signed Jackie Robinson. The Signet paperback edition of 1963 has a stunning prefatory page, promising readers an entree to "the charmed life of Shellmound [a plantation house]...a fairy world long gone...the gracious world of the Mississippi Delta in the 1920s." *Charmed*! *Fairy*! *Gracious*! Did anyone at Signet actually know the Delta? This blurb emanates from some other plane; it is unlikely that any African-American had a say in it. But the two novels and this starry-eyed summary remind us that a love of mythical *domaines* is rooted in American history. It has taken the forms of pastoral idylls, millenialism, and utopianism (Samuel Coleridge and Robert Southey considered joining a Pantisocratic commune on the Susquehanna River in their youth), a willingness to turn a blind eye to the social costs of such ventures, and a strong preference for myth over reality.

Delta Wedding itself is a lyrical, occasionally rhapsodic pastoral novel evoking the old / new South. It describes a few days before and after the wedding of Dabney Fairchild to the plantation overseer, Troy. The Fairchilds are an old family who still own three fine old houses, while Troy is a poor boy from the hill country: a hillbilly. Sociologically, the book resembles eighteenth-century English novels showing marriages between different classes as safety valves for social tensions and examples of upward mobility. Battle and Ellen Fairchild are the patriarch and matriarch, Shelley and India are Dabney's older and younger sisters, and their cousin Laura McRaven is a "little motherless girl" who lives with her father in the state capital, Jackson, and has come for the wedding (Welty 11). She can sound like the author's own childhood sensibility and provide us with a point of view (though Welty's own mother was long-lived). At other times Shelley, who is "literary," sounds like Welty: the young woman interested in writing (we are given a few pages of her diary). Now and then Ellen or Robbie Reid seems to have the microphone. The Fairchilds' relationship to "their" Negroes is close but paternalistic, and can be thoughtless. The macro-*domaine* here is that version of ante bellum Southern society that survived the war, Emancipation, Reconstruction, reaction, and (by the 1920s) the Dred Scott decision, poll taxes, Jim Crow, etc., to live an attenuated life in this patch of rich Delta farmland, carrying the ghosts of the nineteenth century into the twentieth.

Delta Wedding is as pure a *domaine* novel as one will find, due to its feeling for Southern rural culture, its responsiveness to wide sweeps of nature (planted here, almost a huge garden, but still appreciated), the freshness of childhood and youth, the charm of old estates, and the magic of a memorable party: the wedding. The book signals its nature with a prefatory sketch-map depicting a small slice of "The Delta country." There is the little world that we will inhabit for a few hundred pages, lovingly detailed: the patronymic village of Fairchilds, Mississippi, on the Yazoo River, just across from the railroad, the cotton gin, Brunswick (the Negro quarter), and the cemetery. In an arc around the northern quadrant are the three Fairchild homes: Marmion (a homage to Walter Scott) west of the river, The Grove and Shellmound east of it. Several of the fields are named (Moon, Mound, Deadening), and two of the lakes or ponds are equipped with alligators. It is a sufficiently small area to know well before the book's end, but rather large to walk over in the heat, so most people ride on a horse or in a car whenever they can. (If a character does walk for any distance, there is likely a problem; someone has blundered.)

Laura is driven to Shellmound – the book's Tara – as soon as she arrives, and her recollection of seeing it for the first time in a year, almost at dusk, is breathless, rapt:

> *Facing James's Bayou, back under the planted pecan grove, it was gently glowing in the late summer light, the brightest thing in the evening – the tall, white, wide frame house with a porch all around, its bayed tower on one side, its tinted windows open and its curtains stirring, and even from here plainly to be heard a song coming out of the music room, played on the piano by a stranger....* (Welty, 15)

Welty's prose makes love to the scene, or to its memory. Shellmound may or may not outshine the sun, the pianist may or may not be a "stranger": the aesthetic, here and often, is impressionism. Occasionally we are shown the Fairchilds as Laura might see them. Like the author she is half-alienated from this scene, a city cousin who visits occasionally, trying to understand the goings-on, devouring the eccentricities. At bedtime, the older girls dress up and dance around the dining-room table as Laura watches them "from the upper landing cavorting below, like marvelous mermaids down a transparent sea" (18). The hounds would bark at night, and cousin Roy "believed when you heard dogs bay, a convict had got out... and they were after him in the swamp," but they bayed "every night of the world," and Roy would lie "shaking in his bed." Recollected moments of beauty and fear, and the novel that enshrines them, are the *domaines* here. As Dabney and India ride at dusk, India is our perceiver. "Dabney could not help it if she rode beautifully then and felt beautiful"; "Through parted lips her engaged sister breathed the soft blue air of seven o'clock in the evening on the Delta" (62-63). It is easy to fall in with this mood, or to disengage from it – if you have never felt a subtropical evening on your skin.

Laura's sense of semi-alienation, of her difference, is acute. Although she lives in the state capital with 25,000 other people, she "felt like a little country cousin when she arrived, appreciating that she had come to where everything was dressy, splendid, and over her head" (Welty, 69). So she does not put on big-town airs, but accepts her outsider status and observes the scene closely and respectfully. It is not just Shellmound that stirs Laura; her family's entire orbit is wondrous. Even the general store in the village seems a marvel: "square glass jars with gold-topped stoppers...fishing boxes all packed, ...buckets marked like a mackerel sky, dippers, churns, bins, ...popcorn poppers, ...mouse traps, all these things held the purest enchantment for her" (162). Once she even embraces the pickle barrel. Besides the Thingness of hardware, "The air was a kind of radiant haze, which disappeared into a dim blue among hanging boots above – a fragrant store dust that looked like gold dust...". The author explains this as the dust of crackers, flour, and brown sugar, but Laura thinks, "in the Delta, all the air everywhere is filled with things – it's the shining dust that makes it look so bright." Every sense is pleased: "All was warm and fragrant.... The cats smelled like ginger when you rubbed their blond foreheads," and the odors of bananas, medicine, rope, rubber, bread, cheese, tobacco, and chicory mingled amicably with "the smells of the old cane chairs... creaking where the old fellows slept" (162-63). For Laura, it might be the Xanadu General Store.

The Fairchilds' Marmion is "a wonderful house in the woods...twice as big as Shellmound," but "quiet, and unlived in," with the dark Yazoo River "going in front of it, not a road" (Welty, 202). But Laura finds much more there: Aunt Studney comes walking along, carrying a big sack. Unlike the other aunts – Tempe, Primrose, Jim Allen – she is "coal-black, old as the hills, with her foot always in the road"; if you speak to her, she says, "Ain't studyin' you." Laura asks where she lives. Roy replies, "Oh, back on our place somewhere. Back of the Deadening": that is, the field (203). She is often seen walking the railroad track with her sack.

Laura asks if he is scared of her. "No. Yes, I am," he says, but so is Papa. Roy says the sack is "where Mama gets all her babies" – black children Ellen cares for and in effect adopts. Stamping along "like an old wasp over the rough, waggling her burden," Aunt Studley is a serious irruption of black folkways into the sheltered white lives at the centre of the book. She surprises them by "going in Dabney's house" (Marmion will be Dabney and Troy's wedding present). They follow her up the drive, shaded by old trees and vines, into "a vast room, the inside of a tower" whose ceiling is barely visible (204). Two stairways spiral up to galleries on two levels. Aunt Studley drops her sack with a thud as if to say, "This is the place!" Looking up, Laura has "a moment of dizziness," wonders if this could really be "*Dabney's* house," the mortal girl that she knows, and asks, "Is it still the Delta in here?" (205). A sudden rush of bees heightens the uncanniness of Marmion, and hastens their exit back into the "green rank world" (207).

The Delta *domaine* exists not only for Laura, but, at least in its natural aspect, for some other characters. Ellen, perhaps because she is an outsider (a transplanted Virginian), is open to the aesthetic appeal of the countryside, although Welty is cautious about making her *conscious* of these feelings. The line between author and character is indistinct as Ellen looks down the road for Dabney's return at the end of the day.

> *Stretching away, the cotton fields, slowly emptying, were becoming the color of the sky, a deepening blue that was so intense that it was like darkness itself. There was a feeling in the infinity of the Delta that even the bounded things, waiting, for instance, could go on forever. Over and over from the bayou woods came the one high note, then the three low notes of the dove.* (Welty, 95)

"Infinity" and "forever" are powerful concepts to deploy here. At times we are told what Ellen "thought," but most of this pastoral could be either hers or the author's. The same is true of Dabney's rapture as she rides her red filly out into the idyll of a warm, clear Delta dawn:

> *Flocks of birds flew up from the fields, the little filly went delightedly through the wet paths, breasting and breaking the dewy nets of spider webs. Opening morning-glories were turned like eyes on her pretty feet. The occasional fences smelled sweet, their darkened wood swollen*

with night dew like sap, and following her progress the bayou rustled
within, ticked and cried. The sky was softly blue all over, the last rim
of sunrise cloud melting into it like the foam on fresh milk. (143)

The intense language and focus on physical details tell us that Dabney is in a *domaine*, but not whether she was conscious of it. (Welty might respond that Dabney's awareness is not the point, or that any adult writing (fiction) about her youth crosses ambiguous territory.)

Late in the novel, as wedding festivities begin, Robbie Reid, the runaway young wife, reappears. She has a number of readjustment problems, but family warmth and dancing please her. "Oh, there's always...so *much* happening here!" she cries (Welty 222). She "put her hand up to her head" while dancing "against the whirl" of her in-laws. "Indeed the Fairchilds took you in circles, whirling delightedly about, she thought, stirring up confusions.... But they did not really want anything...". Dancing with her husband, the beloved Uncle George, she ponders the complexity of family ties. The Fairchilds take "comfort...in him," but they do not know him as she does. They see him by the "gusty lamp...of their own indulgence," whereas she has a steadier light: "his own fire." Seeing him basking in their adoration, she foresees that "when all the golden persuasions of the Fairchilds focused upon him, he would vaunt himself again, if she did not watch him. He would drive her to vaunt herself too" (223). "Vaunting" is what she fled, but now the threat is clearer: "He looked out at the world, ...sometimes, with that...remote, proud, over-innocent Fairchild look...as if an old story had taken hold of him.... And she did not know the story." She is an outsider, but is firmly resolved that "whatever threatened to waste his life, to lead him away, *even if he liked it,* she was going to go up against if it killed her." It is a crucial moment for any visitor to any *domaine*: seeing "golden persuasions" for what they are, bewaring of the Midas touch, remembering Adam and Eve, and finding a way forward with acquired knowledge, as *they* had to do.

It is Laura who flies highest in the aura of familial and nuptial warmth, though. On "picnic night," which includes a sort of hayride in Uncle George's wagon,

...she felt part of her cousins' life – part of it all. She was familiar
at last with that wonderful, special anticipation that belonged to
the Fairchilds, only to the Fairchilds in the whole world. A kind of

wild cousinly happiness surged through her and went out again....
(Welty, 281)

This going out does not leave her bereft, just asleep. She wakes up for the celestial display on the last page, however, and is instantly exalted as "One great golden star went through the night falling" (287). "Oh!" she cries. "It was beautiful, that star!" Others see it too, and snuggle closer together. It is like the "fair augury" of the ancients, a sign to be observed and appreciated. "Laura lifted on her knees and took her Aunt Ellen around the neck. She held her till they swayed together. ...She touched Aunt Ellen's cheek with three anxious, repaying kisses." We understand what this means to the motherless girl, and the heavens promptly endorse the healing on earth: "Another star fell in the sky." Laura lets go and steps forward, saying, "'I saw that one too...I saw where it fell',...bragging and in reassurance." In harmony with her family and the cosmos, "She turned again to them, both arms held out to the radiant night." There the novel ends, with as pure and unadulterated a *domaine* moment as we are likely to find anywhere. Others may judge the experience, put it in perspective, but Laura is completely in the moment, and her creator, who is somewhat farther along the line, chooses to ratify her ecstasy and leave her there.

One theme of the novel is time and its human cousin, memory. In a general sense this is true of most novels, and of all writing about the past; we understand or assume that the author is recalling something, and reviving parts of it according to an artistic design. This recall is managed in various ways. *Delta Wedding* gives a great deal of physical detail about the characters' environments, often as seen by Laura, the visitor who naturally notices what others take for granted. When the author wants to describe Shelley's room, she has Laura's eyes record the "medallions on the wallpaper," "curling irons hung like a telephone," snapshots of a western trip stuck on the mirror, a "square silk screen painted by Aunt Tempe" in front of the fireplace, and much more, all seen by the dim glow of "a long, naked, but weak light bulb" as she "stood in the door watching" (Welty, 100-02). Shelley herself has almost total recall of a near railway accident she witnessed: "The scene on the trestle was so familiar as to be almost indelible in Shelley's head, for her memory arrested the action and let her see it again and again..." (106). Clearly it was "indelible" in Welty's, too.

Other passages have different emphases. Ellen, an aging gardener, feels time as seasonal cycles of vegetation, one of the earliest bases of religious worship. In the last part of the novel, which covers the wedding – an ancient fertility symbol in literature, the usual goal of comedy – Ellen notes early signs of autumn: crape myrtle shedding its bark, cypress leaves reddening in the bayou. They prompt her to examine the die-back in her garden, and inventory its needs.

> *Her chrysanthemums looked silver and ragged, their few flowers tarnished and all their lower leaves hanging down black...dead iris foliage curled and floated wraith-like over everything. ...tall grass in her beds, as if it knew she could no longer bend over and reach it. What would happen if she were not here to watch it.... Of all the things she would leave undone, she hated leaving the garden untended....* (Welty, 263)

Dying plants in the garden suggest her own mortality: dead foliage is "wraith-like," ghostly. As a Christian, she *could* think of resurrection – those iris bulbs contain new life – but she does not. Untended gardens have long stood for certain emotional states in well-known English classics. In his first soliloquy, Hamlet expresses disgust with "this world" horticulturally: "...fie! 'Tis an unweeded garden, / That grows to seed, things rank and gross in nature / Possess it merely" (I.ii.135-37). In *Great Expectations*, Dickens has Pip walk through Miss Havisham's garden: first "rank," then "ruined," finally "old" and ivy-covered (60, 228, 387, 467, 469). It can remind him of giddy days with Estella – once his hopeless *domaine* – but later it mirrors the sadness of their lives. At the end of *Delta Wedding*, the nuptials, shooting stars, and Laura's affection will comfort Ellen, but Welty lets the darker outlook stand unrelieved for now. It has its own legitimacy, its own place in the cycle. Comedy is not shallow: these things happen there, too.

In one remarkable passage Laura has a vivid recollection of when her mother was alive. It happens in a moving car, driving to Shellmound from the village. Lying on the seat, she presses Marmion, her stocking doll, against her cheek. Its smell (a frequent trigger of memories) revives the fragrance of "a certain day... in Jackson," as the taste of a *madelaine* biscuit took Proust back to his childhood (Welty, 268). And suddenly she is *there*, not here: "absent-minded." She and her parents have just returned from a summer trip, a thunderstorm is coming, her father is winding the big clock, her mother opening windows in the hot house, and Laura, at this "most inconvenient" time," calls out, "Mother, make me a doll – I want a doll!" (269). Her mother smiles, asks "Would you like a stocking doll?" and pulls materials out of her sewing basket. Laura gazes at her mother – "excited, smiling, young" – as she works at the sewing machine, sews on the head by hand as Laura leans on her knee, and draws on the face. It is "like magic to watch" (270). Laura asks its name. "[H]e can be Marmion," says her mother. Of course: they have just come back from the Delta and Marmion! It all makes sense now, and she can recall, even smell, the fresher air, the sweet moisture. She runs to the corner, shows Marmion to a friend, and runs home just as the heavens open. Laura and her mother stand at a window and watch it pour. That *was* her *domaine*, but now she is back in the car, and "Never more would she have...the instant answer to a wish, for her mother was dead" (272). Laura may not know Poe's "The Raven," but Welty does. Rarely does she go inside Laura and reveal her feelings as she does here. Shellmound is Laura's secondary *domaine*, then, the one she can still have, being forever cut off from the primary one. "Quoth the raven, 'Nevermore.'"

THE WOODSTOCK MUSIC FESTIVAL, CITED earlier as an example of a multi-faceted *domaine*, is useful here in a different way. In its first form, the refrain of Joni Mitchell's song about the event celebrates the magical ("stardust") aura of the "golden" young participants, whose passion is obvious to her as she watches on television in a distant hotel room. Yet the refrain also yearns for something they do not entirely possess: "we've got to get ourselves / Back to the garden." The lyrics of "Woodstock" darken toward the end, voicing a need to honour the *full* truth of her generation's experience. In the final stanza, the singer can see bombers in the sky, and though her imagination can turn them into butterflies, they seem to affect the last reprise of the refrain, adding new levels of science and political turmoil:

> We are stardust
> Billion year old carbon
> We are golden
> Caught in the devil's bargain
> And we've got to get ourselves
> Back to the garden

The added lines (2 and 4) move us away from any starry-eyed, stoned-out, "it's all good" acceptance of things as they are, toward the mood prevalent among anguished youth in the musical *Hair*, a big success in that same year of 1969. They acknowledge that you cannot *simply* have a "summer of love" when the Vietnam war is raging. A cultural *domaine* must at least acknowledge the darkness, and find some way either to lighten or to live with it.

CHAPTER 9:

Domaines of Many Colours

CHAPTERS 4 THROUGH 8 TREATED the major kinds of *domaine* literature: "major" in that they appeared relatively early in literature and became influential, serving later authors as models. But there are other types whose practitioners have been fewer, yet which exhibit interesting variations on the core idea of the charmed place and occasion that impresses visitors as extraordinary and remains unforgettable, playing a role in their subsequent lives. In this chapter I discuss three of these – Islands, Parties, and Love/Sex – more briefly as examples of how these genres have been used. The three are not unrelated; as we have seen, works brought forward as instances of one type may have other aspects, and could be discussed under a different heading.

Islands in the Sea

An island mystique has long existed in the literature of various cultures. Islands are a natural fit with the idea of the *domaine*: set apart from the world, a place where you could start over, a *tabula rasa* in regard to rules and manners. They are oases in the desert of the sea, but aside from providing a solid place for swimmers or sailors to rest, they are unpredictable. In *The Magus*, Spetsai, the Greek island on which John Fowles had taught, became Maurice Conchis's Phraxos, a suitable arena for meta-theatre and moral re-engineering, or for Nazis to terrorize. Daniel Defoe's Robinson Crusoe went from half-mad castaway to comfortable proprietor of his deserted Pacific island. Being a capitalist entrepreneur, he struck a deal with visiting pirates, who would stay and remit annual tribute to finance his retirement in England: he had somehow become the island's "owner." The sombre

Victorian Matthew Arnold had a different use for islands. Whereas John Donne had preached that "no man is an island" – i.e. we are all part of a spiritual continent – Arnold wrote that each of us is an island in the "unplumb'd, salt, estranging sea" ("To Marguerite – Continued," 1852). That is, being "islanded" is *la condition humaine*. We live *isolated*, *insulated*, and

> *...in the sea of life enisled,*
> *With echoing straits between us thrown,*
> *Dotting the shoreless watery wild,*
> *We mortal millions live alone.*

On Arnold's metaphorical islands there are no *domaines*, only solipsistic souls. Real islands, though, are mirrors in which we recognize our own "islandness."

Not every island is in the "salt, estranging sea," of course. One of W.B. Yeats's best-known early lyrics meditates on the sort of existence he might have on "The Lake Isle of Innisfree."

> *I will arise and go now, and go to Innisfree,*
> *And a small cabin build there, of clay and wattles made*
> *Nine bean-rows will I have there, a hive for the honeybee,*
> *And live alone in the bee-loud glade.*
>
> *And I shall have some peace there, for peace comes dropping slow,*
> *Dropping from the veils of morning to where the cricket sings;*
> *There midnight's all a glimmer, and noon a purple glow,*
> *And evening full of the linnet's wings.*
>
> *I will arise and go now, for always night and day*
> *I hear lake water lapping with low sounds by the shore;*
> *While I stand on the roadway, or on the pavements grey,*
> *I hear it in the deep heart's core.*

When Yeats looks at the lake isle, he sees neither a possible investment nor a metaphor of self, and certainly not a reform school, but a place where he could return to nature, find peace, even drop out: Henry David Thoreau channeling Robinson Crusoe. It is also a very Wordsworthian poem, which made it sound rather old-fashioned in 1893.

These few titles suggest the range of literary uses to which islands have been put; they can be what you want them to be. The ancient Sumerians' paradise was an island: Dilmun. A text of 2050 BCE, well before Isaiah, describes a place where the lion and the wolf do not kill the weak, nor does old age burden the elderly (Campbell 1976, 53). Imagined islands exist toward the other end of the moral spectrum, too. In *Timaeus* (ca. 360 BCE), Plato tells of Atlantis, once a huge island ("larger than Libya and Asia put together") in the North Atlantic Ocean (Plato 1949, 9). He calls it a "great and wonderful empire" that ruled other islands and "parts of the continent" after conquering North Africa and much of Europe, but does not explain "great and wonderful." Athens defeated it, liberating the Mediterranean basin. After that, "violent earthquakes and floods" obliterated Atlantis "in a single day." Whatever historical truth may underlie Plato's account, it uses an island as *carte blanche* for the imagination. So in *Gulliver's Travels*, when Jonathan Swift wants a metaphor for oppressive government, he invents the flying island of Laputa ("the whore"), which cruises above its subject terrain, maneuvering by magnetic attraction and repulsion. Courtiers sample public opinion by lowering fish hooks to which citizens attach petitions. Laputa's base is forty feet of solid adamantine, conventionally the hardest rock. If subjects resist, the magnets are realigned and the island simply "crushes the rebellion."

Not all of these examples are *domaines*. Dilmun is, as much so as Elysium or Eden or Innisfree; as imagined or remembered, they are magical for visitors or residents. Swift's Laputa, however, is a dystopia. Most islands are mixtures, or change over time. Crusoe's island seems a hostile wasteland at first, but as he learns and works it improves, and before the end he is lord (then absentee landlord) of a seignorial *domaine*. Arnold's symbolic islands are powerful images of existence, but they are grim and lonely. Their truth may set you free, but then you are on your own. Plato's Atlantis may have been a "great and wonderful empire" from some perspective, but was probably judged more harshly by its conquered subjects. In William Golding's *Pincher Martin* (1956), Rockall – an actual rock in the North Atlantic – is where his hero (apparently) lands when his ship is torpedoed by a Nazi submarine. Rockall could mean survival, but his efforts give way to long, vivid reviews of his chequered life. At the end, his body washes up on the Irish coast, where the finder notes that he did not even have time to remove his seaboots. The survival scenario was an hallucination: he may have died on the first page, and certainly by the fourth ("Both boots had left him"). The island was the courtroom in which his life was tried: his Purgatory.

Ambiguity also pervades the presentation of Phraxos in *The Magus*. The island's natural beauty charms Nick (as Spetsai's did Fowles), while Conchis, Villa Bourani, and the masques provide increasing excitement. But later events become confusing, and Nick begins to wonder about the motives and agenda of his host and other guests. Conchis clearly has a lot of money and influence; his reach extends at least across the island. By the end Nick learns just how potent he is, and understands one of his allusions better. In chapter 13, Conchis offers him a tour of the villa: "Come now. Prospero will show you his domaine" (Fowles 1965, 79; 1978, 80). Nick says, "Prospero had a daughter," to which Conchis retorts, "Prospero had many things...not all young and beautiful...." This exchange (identical in the two versions) acquires more weight as the plot moves to Nick's humiliation and its aftermath in England. The morality of Conchis's "godgame" is questionable and sharply divisive, depending on one's values. Our assessment of the two men governs our view of *The Magus*.

"THE PROSPERO ISSUE" BEGAN IN *The Tempest* itself. Shakespeare's island *domaine* is another indefinite place whose meaning oscillates from scene to scene. The isle means one thing to Prospero and Miranda, something slightly different to his indentured spirit Ariel, much different to his angry slave Caliban, and wholly different to the stunned, wandering castaways. *The Tempest* (1611), probably the last play entirely by Shakespeare, shows his powers at their height after two decades in the theatre. He read widely, and borrowed many of his plots, characters, and themes from others; Elizabethan audiences did not demand originality. *The Tempest* is actually one of his most nearly original plays, no source having been found for the plot, but it was not wholly invented. The Signet Classic edition prints some primary materials that show he used accounts of storms and shipwrecks in the Caribbean. William Strachey's *True Repertory of the Wrack* (1610) described a tempest and wreck on Bermuda, the noises made by the "sea-owl" there, and dissension among the castaways. Sylvester Jourdain's *A Discovery of the Barmudas* (1610) told of the *domaine* that the survivors found there: "the air so temperate and the country so abundantly fruitful" that they sailed away with excess food (Shakespeare 1964, 134-35). Altogether "it is...the richest, healthfulest, and pleasing [sic] land...and merely [utterly] natural, as ever man set foot upon."

What did Shakespeare (who also used Montaigne and Ovid) want to do with his materials? The isle's de facto ruler, Prospero, may hold the answer. Twelve years earlier he was the Duke of Milan, but so rapt in "secret studies" as not to see that his brother Antonio was plotting a coup (I.ii.77). Helped by Alonso, King of Naples, Antonio overthrew Prospero, took his crown, and set him adrift in a small boat with his infant daughter Miranda. Prospero's loyal counsellor Gonzalo had food, water, Prospero's wand, conjuring robes, and books on magic placed in the boat, saving them. They drifted safely to a Mediterranean island. The deposed duke, a magician, vengeful and powerful in conjuration, watches over his now fourteen-year-old daughter – the age of Romeo's Juliet. The island also has a history. It once sheltered Sycorax, a wicked witch who was banished, pregnant, from Algiers. Ariel was her slave. Before she died, Sycorax imprisoned him in a tree and gave birth to Caliban, now Prospero's slave and critic. While Prospero's magic gives him control of the isle, Caliban maintains a counterclaim: "This island's mine by Sycorax my mother, / Which thou tak'st from me" (I.ii.331-32). Only corporal punishment (cramps) keeps him in line as a ship containing Prospero's enemies approaches the island.

"The tempest" rages only in the first scene; in the second, Prospero (who raised it) calms the waves, and the rest of the play moves jerkily toward the "calm seas" and "auspicious gales" of the last speech. The incoming ship has escaped harm and been hid "Safely in harbor" by Ariel (aerial spirit and stage manager), who frightened the royal party into abandoning ship and left the mariners asleep (I.ii.226). Shakespeare's travel reading figures in the early scenes – the storminess of "the still-vexed Bermoothes" and their odd sounds – as men wash ashore and react to what they see (I.ii.229). Ariel has "dispersed them 'bout the isle" in sorted groups (I.ii.220). Ferdinand, prince of Naples, wanders in dazedly, following the music of Ariel and his choir, all invisible. The "strange hollow and harsh howling" of sea-owls in Strachey's account is transmuted into eerie pieces played and sung, apparently, by Nobody (Shakespeare 1964, 131). "Where should this music be?" wonders Ferdinand, "...sure it waits upon / Some god o' th' island": the usual reaction of an entrant to a *domaine* (I.ii.388-90). A second song follows. "Full fathom five thy father lies," sings Ariel (untruly), but softens that with the play's central metaphor, the "sea change":

> *Nothing of him that doth fade*
> *But doth suffer a sea change*
> *Into something rich and strange. (I.ii.397, 401-02)*

His bones are coral, his eyes, pearls. "This is no mortal business," says Ferdinand (I.ii.407). He is granted a first sight of Miranda ('to be admired'), who is, "sure, the goddess / On whom these airs attend" (I.ii.422-23). Miranda perceives *him* as "A thing divine," and Prospero murmurs approval (I.ii.419). It is a good start – if this is to be a comedy.

Ferdinand is young, handsome, and innocent, but another high-ranking party on the island includes some villains. There are Prospero's enemies, Alonso (grieving for the supposed death of his son) and Antonio; Alonso's shoddy brother Sebastian; Gonzalo, Prospero's benefactor; and two lords, Adrian and Francisco. Adrian pronounces the isle good, and "of subtle, tender, and delicate temperance" (climate), for "The air breathes upon us here most sweetly" (II.i.37, 44-45, 49). "Here is everything advantageous to life," adds Gonzalo, "How lush and lusty the grass looks!" (II.i.52, 55). Both are mocked (*aside*) by Antonio and Sebastian. Gonzalo describes the utopian colony he would plant here, a natural commonwealth with no officers, trade, learning, property, inequality, or crime; it would "excel the Golden Age" (II.i.148-73; all from Montaigne's "Of the Cannibals"). Ariel enters to "solemn music," puts to sleep all but Antonio and Sebastian, then exits. Antonio, who promised to "guard [Alonso's] person" while he slept, now urges Sebastian to kill the king (II.i.201). With Ferdinand thought dead and Alonzo's married daughter in Tunis, the crown will be Sebastian's. He quickly agrees: "As thou got'st Milan, / I'll come by Naples" (II.i.295-96). Ariel returns in time to wake the others, averting the murder, but this *domaine* is riven, and subject to violence.

Meanwhile the churlish Caliban, cursing Prospero as he totes firewood, meets Trinculo, a court jester, and Stephano, a butler who rescued a "butt of sack" and has a bottle of it. Dazzled, Caliban kneels and swears fealty to him as the sack goes around, so we have a drunk scene, which, with Trinculo's wit, pleased the groundlings. This "lowest" of the ship's trios does not enjoy the island's natural beauty, which they find odd. With his allies, Caliban poses a threat to Prospero's *domaine*; he swears to rebel against him and "follow thee, / Thou wondrous man"

(II.ii.171-72). Singing woozy verses – "Caliban / Has a new master. Get a new man!" – he howls for "Freedom" (II.ii.192-94). This does not look dangerous yet, only inconvenient: Prospero told Miranda, "We cannot miss [do without] him. He does make our fire, / Fetch in our wood, and serves in offices / That profit us" (I.ii.311-12). Prospero's economy, then – like the plantations in *Oroonoko* and *Gone With the Wind* – depends on slavery. One might think that a magician who can command the winds and spirits, conjure up masques, and befuddle distant minds could tele-transport a few logs, but the play's premises rule otherwise.

Shakespeare then shows Ferdinand doing what Caliban has just sworn off: "bearing a log." His mood is mellow, for "some kinds of baseness / Are nobly undergone," and though Prospero seems "composed of harshness," still "The mistress which I serve.../ makes my labors pleasures" (III.i.3-4, 9, 6-7). Prospero has wisely made the courtship "uneasy..., lest too light winning / Make the prize light" (I.ii.452-53). The chore puts the prince in a flattering light, and allows Miranda full scope for her sympathy. In short order they proclaim their love and plight their troth; henceforth their *domaine* is love. But that mood gives way to a return of the "low trio," now more than half-seas over, and (*in vino veritas*) plotting murder. Caliban calls for a *coup* (as happened in Milan and is planned for Naples). If they kill Prospero, the isle will be theirs. They must seize his magic books, "Batter his skull" with a log, stab him in the belly, or cut his throat (III.ii.91-98). A further incentive is "The beauty of his daughter," he tells Stephano. "She will become thy bed" (III.ii.103, 108). When Prospero said that Caliban "didst seek to violate / The honor of my child," the slave chortled, "Would't had been done" and I had "peopled... / This isle with Calibans" (I.ii.347-51). Stephano pledges, "Monster, I will kill this man" and begins to gloat. Caliban warns him to save *that* for "When Prospero is destroyed" (III.ii.110, 151). *The Tempest* is a comedy with a very dark middle.

As darkness exits stage left, the weary "high group" enter stage right. Antonio and Sebastian, who intend to kill Alonso, are shown a spectacle by Prospero and Ariel: "strange Shapes" setting out a banquet and dancing to "Solemn and strange music" (III.iii.17 s.d.). But when they approach the table, lightning flashes, thunder peals, the food vanishes, and Ariel appears (as a harpy) to deliver Prospero's judgment, beginning, "You are three men of sin" (III.iii.53). Their drawn swords elicit another tongue-lashing: they would stab the wind with swords they cannot even lift (another spell). Ariel charges them formally – "you three / From Milan did supplant good Prospero; / Exposed unto the sea," etc. – and sentences them to "Ling'ring perdition" (III.iii.69-71, 77). Prospero exults that his enemies are in his power. This is the testing phase of the *domaine*, trying the visitors to their depths (as Fowles brought his "man of sin" to the lord of another island). Alonso, deeply moved, says that the elements "pronounced / The name of Prospero" and made his "trespass" plain; he exits in distress (III.iii.98-99). Sebastian and Antonio, though, harder cases, vow to fight on. When they exit, Gonzalo calls them "desperate" men whose "great guilt" has begun to "bite [their] spirits" (III.iii.104-06). Act III – almost always pivotal in Shakespeare – ends with this clarification of the moral accounts, and at least a distant glimpse of a possible resolution.

Further vicissitudes trouble Act IV. Prospero explains his conduct to Ferdinand, says that he has passed all tests, approves his union with Miranda, and has Ariel produce a wedding masque for them. (Masques were popular by 1611, owing largely to the talents of Ben Jonson and Inigo Jones.) This one features Iris, goddess of the rainbow; Juno, a *dea ex machina*; and Ceres, a fertility goddess. Ferdinand, enchanted by the show, wishes to live in this "paradise" forever. There is music, there are nymphs and reapers dancing – but suddenly Prospero starts and speaks: "I had forgot that foul conspiracy / Of the beast Caliban and his confederates / Against my life" (IV.i.139-41). That is unlikely, but again the spectre of violence threatens the comic mood. The spirits vanish. Prospero recovers to give one of Shakespeare's most famous speeches, beginning "Our revels now are ended," and rising to "We are such stuff / As dreams are made on, and our little life / Is rounded with a sleep," often taken as Shakespeare's farewell to the stage (IV.i.148, 156-58). Fowles's Conchis, who also staged masques, had good reason to identify with Prospero, but Nicholas Urfe, who hoped to be the Ferdinand of Bourani, found himself cast as Caliban.

Prospero and Ariel prepare for the "low" conspirators, looking bedraggled after being misled into a muddy pool. Caliban is still bent on the murder, but Stephano and Trinculo are distracted by fancy clothes left for them. Prospero and Ariel, invisible, watch this knave and two fools. Caliban, now the brains of the gang, tries to keep them focused ("What do you mean / To dote thus on such luggage? Let't alone, / And do the murder first"), but they are hopeless: magically addled (IV.i.230-32). Caliban sees how it will be: "We shall lose our time / And all be turned to barnacles, or to apes" (IV.i.247-48). The isle remains in Prospero's power, without which the outcome would be a drunken murder. He and Ariel send spirit canines to stampede them. Prospero, promising to free Ariel, dons his "magic robes" for the final scene. Ariel's report on the royal party – "distracted," "mourning," so full of "sorrow and dismay" that "if you now beheld them, your affections / Would become tender" – touches Prospero (V.i.7-19). If Ariel can feel human afflictions, should not he? His mood has altered: "with my nobler reason 'gainst my fury / Do I take part," he says; "The rarer action is / In virtue than in vengeance" (V.i.26-28). Their penitence is what he wanted, and having that, he need go no farther. He will undo his charms. Ariel goes to release them.

Prospero's soliloquy on his career builds to renunciation: "this rough magic / I here abjure"; to celestial music "I'll break my staff" and "drown my book" (V.i.50-57). Ariel ushers in the "high" party, who stand dazed in a "charmed circle." Prospero recounts their sins, but forgives them. Attired now as Duke of Milan, he welcomes his guests, embracing Alonso – who returns his dukedom with an apology – and Gonzalo. Aside, he tells Sebastian and Antonio that he will not expose their plot "At this time"; then calls Antonio "most wicked sir" and demands that he "restore" his dukedom (V.i.128, 130, 134). All must now be exposed and settled; Prospero is reassembling his broken *domaine*. Alonso mentioning the lost Ferdinand, Prospero says, "I / Have lost my daughter," and Alonso exclaims, "O heavens, that they were living both in Naples, / The King and Queen there!" (V.i.147-50). Prospero then opens the curtain hiding the upstage recess, revealing Ferdinand and Miranda – who have lost only their hearts – playing chess. Father and son are reunited, and a general reconciliation occurs. Miranda's remark upon seeing the crowd is both naive and ironic: "O brave new world / That has such people in't!" Her father replies drily, "'Tis new to thee" (V.i.183-84). All this makes Gonzalo wonder whether Prospero was driven from Milan *in order that* Miranda should become Queen of Naples. In one voyage Ferdinand has found a wife, "Prospero his dukedom / ...and all of us ourselves / When no man was his own" (V.i.211-13).

Be that as it may, the others fall in with his mood. Alonso blesses the lovers, Ariel leads in some dazed mariners to join the final assembly; then *drives in* Caliban, Stephano, and Trinculo to be ridiculed, but not otherwise punished for their plot. Caliban admits he was a fool to think these companions deserved worship. Too rude for polite society, they are sent off into the "cell." Prospero dominates the final speeches, inviting the royal party to spend the night – in the cell! – where he will tell them "the story of my life" (V.i.305). In the morning they will embark and sail to Naples for the wedding of Ferdinand and Miranda, "And thence retire me to Milan, where / Every third thought shall be my grave" (V.i.311-12). Although he is again Duke, Prospero still does not want an active role in the exercise of power. But he promises winds so favourable that they "shall catch / Your royal fleet far off" (before it can deliver false bad news), so he retains some of his old magic. That is his last command to Ariel, thenceforth a free spirit.

The Tempest is finally a mellow play; even Caliban is treated leniently at last. Shakespeare's Providence resolves human problems and reconciles enemies. Compare the first scene – a storm, class conflict, natural and social tumult – with the last: a marriage restoring political order and healing rifts, the tempest replaced by favourable winds. The benignity is remarkable, considering the materials. Where else in Shakespeare are two lovers from hostile families brought together? What other play has a mighty storm and a ruler who sets aside his powers? Yet neither *Romeo and Juliet* nor *King Lear* comes close to being a comedy. Comedy and tragedy are not total opposites; their plot-lines may start together, then diverge. The longer they are parallel, the "darker" the comedy. Older critics – E.M.W. Tillyard and Dover Wilson – explored "The Tragic Pattern" in *The Tempest* (Shakespeare 1964, 154-62). Here we are repeatedly given pleasant surprises: a tempest that harms no one; plots that fail; Prospero liking Ferdinand; Ariel working Prospero's will. We see evil intent foiled every time. The mellowness comes from Shakespeare's will, and Prospero's, maturing to forgiveness. When Prospero warns Caliban to "trim it handsomely" and "have my pardon," Caliban promises to "be wise hereafter, / And seek for grace" (V.i.294-96). Yet Prospero, who is leaving the next morning, says nothing about coming back, or taking Caliban to Naples. What happens to him, then? Will the isle finally be his, without a murder?

Prospero, the most complicated and divisive character in the play, has some control over the four traditional elements of nature (earth, air, fire, and water), at least in his vicinity, and over human behaviour, too – thanks to "secret studies" in the magical arts (I.ii.77). If this magus proves benign, all may be well, and Elizabethan audiences (who were suspicious of anyone dabbling in the dark arts) would welcome his answer to Miranda's question, "How came we ashore?": "By providence divine," he replies (I.ii.158-59). This confession of a Higher Power is the equivalent of the Semitic provisional, "God willing." Though Prospero acknowledges Gonzalo's aid (food, water, clothing, books), he is also shown as pious, the earthly agent of Providence.

That is one way of seeing him: a man who defeats violent plots, gives up his revenge, effects reconciliation, and blesses the young lovers. But Shakespeare has been treated by every school of analysis – Freudian, Marxist, exegetical, deconstruction, feminist, post-colonial, etc. – several of which radically reassess Prospero. In modern performances of *The Tempest*, some directors have seen the play as a study of imperialism with Prospero as colonial master. A few productions made him very nearly the villain, lording it over Caliban and others. At the end of Paul Mazursky's film *Tempest* (1982), Prospero apologizes for all the trouble he caused, basically conceding that his *domaine* was an inverted or anti-*domaine* for others. Sometimes it is now taught that way.

Shakespeare is rarely simple, however, and that approach to *The Tempest* creates problems. Does the *text* present Prospero's power as malign? Can we take Caliban's part without reading against the text, excusing a would-be rapist and murderer? Does Shakespeare show the island as an anti-*domaine*, or does he share Prospero's view of that and most events, characters, and values? Elevating Caliban to 'aggrieved' status means rejecting *The Tempest* we inherited, and viewing its author as a victim of ignorance or imperial propaganda. And what would that profit us? Yet all critiques of literature tell us something about the society that produces them, and what we learn about our age in this case is that we have come to distrust authority, rank, and the exercise of power, even (or especially) when we are officially assured that it is just.

The Tempest has a strong cultural / aesthetic dimension. Prospero is an artist, often paralleled with Shakespeare himself; certainly they have similar gifts. Their artistic material is Nature: the tempest, the isle, the wedding masque. Nature / art was a common polarity in the Renaissance, but in *The Tempest* they sometimes work together. Both men are "magicians" who use words to produce marvels: a storm, invisible servants, disdembodied music. Squalls, banquets, confusion and clarity come and go via the power of the Word, the divine *Logos* ordering Chaos into Cosmos. In *The Tempest*, the symbol of that power is the sea, which surrounds the island and the plot. In the second scene, "Full fathom five" introduces the idea of the "sea change / Into something rich and strange." Reuben Brower writes convincingly that the song "presents...the main lines of the metaphorical design" of *The Tempest* (Shakespeare 1964, 184).

With Shakespeare we do not expect, nor have we found, a *domaine* fitting neatly into existing categories. At the beginning, the isle seems a classic case: an out-of-the-way place, crackling with magic, replete with visual and aural wonders, testing visitors, transforming lives. But soon variants and epicycles begin to appear. Ferdinand and Miranda develop their own love-*domaine*, which is independent of the island, and finally leaves it. For many of the visitors, especially Prospero's enemies, the island is an anti-*domaine*, weird and hostile. Some of them are plotting new crimes: murder and insurrection. They are prevented and exposed, but only lightly punished. Despite abundant evidence that not all evil is in the past, Shakespeare writes a final reckoning in which everyone gathers, plots and plotters are neutralized, and would-be malefactors are forgiven or tolerated, being included in a general amnesty. Accounts are squared, but not every debt is collected. Comedy's central tendency – inclusion – is more evident here than in almost any other Shakespeare play. The humans will sail to Naples for the wedding; the *domaine* will reconfigure as marriage and fruitful union. Ariel is set free, and Caliban may possess the isle after all. Will it still be magical? Not necessarily. It is a place where a *domaine* once crystallized, but is not the *Ding an sich*.

COULD ISLANDS HAVE BEEN THE *Ur-domaine*, the archetype of the idea? An island – remote from the workaday world, a blank slate – has a head start. Billions have been and still are drawn to islands by the possibilities there; millions more who have merely seen them offshore can attest to their imaginative power and aura of mystery. Early Middle Eastern sources provide examples of insularity, from the Sumerian paradise, Dilmun, and Eden, effectively 'islanded' by the surrounding blankness, to the tale of *Hayy ibn Yaqzan*, first told in the eleventh century in Avicenna's philosophical fable. It was taken up in the next century by Ibn Tufayl, whose literary version achieved wide popularity. In his novel, Hayy ibn Yaqzan ("Alive, Son of Awake") is a foundling raised by a gazelle on a subtropical island. That is his *domaine* for seven years. When the gazelle dies he dissects her, beginning his quest for knowledge, which carries him from anatomy to physics, mathematics, astronomy, and religion. He lives on a nearby island for a time, but the ignorance and narrowness of its priests drive him back home. The book awoke echoes in eastern and western literature and philosophy, reaching Europe (in Latin) in 1671. There were English translations by 1674, well before Hayy's descendant, *Robinson Crusoe*, appeared (1719). In 1721, Cotton Mather, the New England Puritan preacher, made reference to *Hayy*. The idea of islands as vehicles for imaginative speculation appeared early, then, and had many variations. Among those I pass over are Thomas More's *Utopia*, Francis Bacon's *New Atlantis*, and Voltaire's *Zadig*. In Rousseau's *Emile: or, of Education*, the only book that Emile is given to read at first is *Hayy ibn Yaqzan*, the author's lodestar being a 'rational' and 'natural' education.

The Aid of the Party

If an island was not the first *domaine*, perhaps a really good party was. "Party" is used broadly here, covering everything from private social gatherings to large-scale celebrations – "festive occasions" in general. Any student of anthropology can cite a long list of examples: the seasonal agricultural festivals of European and Asian antiquity; fertility rites; the religious feasts that tamed or replaced them; well-oiled banquets such as those where *The Iliad* and *Beowulf* were first chanted; mediaeval holidays of social inversion in which rulers let the have-nots run things for a day; *Mardi Gras* observances in Catholic countries where masked people ran amok (see Marcel Camus's film *Orfeo Negro*, 1959); the office Christmas party. After any such occasion, participants wonder just what happened during that time out of time. Did we exchange our real selves and usual roles for something exotic, or did we discover our true selves? (Answer: define "real" and "true.") But did I really do that? Did s/he really say that? And will it happen again?

Histories of the Mediterranean world in classical times often trace connections between its religious observances and Graeco-Roman literature. The *Bacchanalia*, for example, orgies of the god Dionysus (Roman Bacchus), spread from Greece to Italy; their excesses were suppressed in 186 BC. Euripedes' tragedy *Bacchae* (405 BC) – a favourite citation for pagan religious rites – gives some idea of these excesses. Sir James Frazer's *The Golden Bough* is useful on the Bacchanals, though his language is cautious. The "ecstatic worship" of Dionysus, god of the grape, wine, and nature, involved "wild dances," "mystic doctrines and extravagant rites" (Frazer 449). Dionysus, often depicted as a bull, was seasonal, like agriculture; he died and was resurrected annually. Honouring his death, frenzied devotees on Crete "tore a live bull to pieces with their teeth and roamed the woods with frantic shouts," then devoured the bull, believing that it was the god and that they were "eating his flesh, and drinking his blood" (Frazer 452-53). *Dionysia* festivals were more restrained and artistic. Besides wine-tasting, dramatic performances took place in Athens and elsewhere: the beginnings of tragedy and comedy. H.D.F. Kitto notes that the Greeks balanced the worship of Apollo, god of order, with that of unruly Dionysus; when Order took his annual holiday from the shrine at Delphi, his replacement was Disorder (104, 176).

Bacchanalia and *Dionysia* might be witnessed by outsiders from a discreet distance, but the rituals of "mystery cults" were for initiates only, and carefully guarded. What little we know of them suggests that many a later secret society, from Freemasons to fraternities, is in their debt. The best-known cult was that of Demeter, goddess of plentiful harvests, at Eleusis, not far from Athens. Dionysus, as a kindred deity of agrarian bounty, also came to be celebrated there. Aeschylus, the great tragic poet, was from Eleusis, and probably an initiate, for he is said to have been threatened with punishment for divulging cult secrets, which could have been a serious matter. If true, the story shows how powerful the priests of Eleusis were. Given the nature of Demeter and Dionysus, it is likely that the "mysteries" celebrated the cycles of life, sexual reproduction, death, and possibly an afterlife. Robert Graves's *The White Goddess* and Joseph Campbell's *The Masks of God: Occidental Mythology* speculate on the content of the rituals and suggest connections with other cults and gods (Graves 1961, 327, 395, 404; Campbell [1964] 1976, 14, 43, 268). Stanley Kubrick's last film, *Eyes Wide Shut* (1999; based on Arthur Schnitzler's 1926 novel *Traumnovelle*), imagines how such a cult might look in modern times – if run by wealthy sensualists devoted not to the fertility principle itself but to the varieties of sexual experience.

As temporal power shifted west to Rome, the Greek gods (often under aliases) and their rites came along. Romans enjoyed attending *Ludi* (games) that were "closely associated with religion" and included plays (Harvey [1937] 1974, 249). There were half a dozen different *ludi*, honouring various deities. Two springtime festivals are of particular interest: the *Ludi Cereales* on behalf of Ceres (Demeter) in mid-April, and the *Ludi Florales* for Flora, goddess of blossoms, in April-May, "a time of general merriment" (Harvey, 250). The *Saturnalia* in mid-December began as festivals marking the sowing of the next year's crops, but lost their agricultural character later and became "a period of general festivity," including "licence for slaves" (Harvey, 384). Graves describes the *Saturnalia* as a time when "all social restraints were temporarily abandoned"; Vestal Virgins might couple with courtiers (or priests, or shepherds), from whose issue a king could be chosen (1961, 67, 357). He also mentions "Egyptian Saturnalia" during which "bodily lusts" were "given full rein" (290). If the *Saturnalia*, with their candles and gifts at the winter solstice, underlie our Yuletide observances, they may have inspired those office Christmas parties, too.

Some Graeco-Roman writers drew on this material, rich in religious and social meanings. Apuleius was from North Africa, part of the Roman Empire in the second century. His most famous work, *Metamorphoses* or *The Golden Ass*, is about transformations both comical and serious. It is mostly a picaresque novel, with many adventures on the road and abundant farce stemming from the narrator, Lucius, having become an ass, but chapter 17 aims higher. Inspired by the full moon rising from the sea, Lucius takes a purifying bath therein and prays to the "Queen of Heaven" – whether called Ceres, Venus, Artemis, or Proserpine – to "have mercy" on his plight and "make [him] Lucius once more" (Apuleius, 236-37). Graves's White Goddess promptly appears in his dream. She is known by many names, she says, but her "true name" is "Queen Isis" of Egypt (239). She grants his prayer, and Apuleius then describes a solemn yet joyous procession whose celebrants sing and play music, carry flowers, and show symbolic objects figuring "the sublime and ineffable mysteries of the Goddess, never...divulged" (244). The ass turns into a human being again, "reborn" as a devotee of Isis (247). It may be as close as we can come to observing an ancient mystery cult at work, and Apuleius (a student of both natural science and magic) makes it clear that these mysteries could transform.

Early on, before his metamorphosis, Lucius stumbles into a predicament in the town of Hypata: he is suddenly arrested and dragged to the theatre to be tried for murder before most of the population. The evidence of witnesses is against him, and matters are carried pretty far before the spectators start laughing. The local dignitaries then explain to Lucius that they "annually hold a solemn festival in honour of Laughter, the best of all gods, which must always be celebrated with some new practical joke" on a stranger (Apuleius, 56). It is a sort of jovial *domaine* – for those who are in on the joke and have all year to look forward to the next one. Lucius is embarrassed and indignant, but he will not forget Hypata. Even this one-sided prank, which requires an ignorant victim, is dressed as a religious festival honouring "the best of all gods."

This was extraordinary, but some accounts of more typical festivities do survive from that era. Two of them are titled *Symposium* ('Banquet'): one by Plato, from the fourth century BCE, the other by Xenophon. Socrates appears in both works, discoursing on love. Plato's is the more famous, and likely the more accurate in representing the views of Socrates, his mentor, who introduces his famous progression from (young) carnal love to a philosophic adoration of the Beautiful, the Idea or Form of Beauty: i.e. "Platonic love." Alcibiades arrives late, tipsy, and babbles a long, indiscreet eulogy of Socrates, admitting his vain pursuit of him as a lover. At the end, some revellers burst in, calling for wine, and the banquet breaks up. Often the drinking was regulated at such gatherings, the ratio of wine to water being set according to the kind of evening desired. Here the guests just agree "not to drink too much" (Plato 1956, 75). Xenophon's narrative of a banquet during a festival in 421 BCE also depicts Socrates as espousing a metaphysical kind of love. It is considered less reliable than Plato's because Xenophon would have been only about nine at the time, yet its depiction of an Athenian social occasion is entertaining (Harvey 412). This one included dancers, whereas the guests in Plato's evening vote to send away "the piping girl."

For a less demanding social evening, try Petronius, author of the *Satyricon* (first century CE). His identity is uncertain, more than one Petronius being known in the period. The *Satyricon* mixes prose, poetry, ribaldry, lyric passages, mock-epic, and satire; later Europeans thought it a picaresque novel. The best known of its many episodes is "The Banquet of Trimalchio," a comedy of (bad) manners. Trimalchio is that reliable butt the *parvenu*: a vulgar, ostentatious upstart. Fashionably late and wearing many trinkets, he is carried into his salon to music and deposited on pillow-cushions ("A laugh escaped the unwary": Grant [1958] 1967, 320). Trimalchio's account of his rise, meant to impress, reveals his shallowness and poor taste. He anticipated conspicuous consumption: a silver dish that falls on the floor is swept up with other rubbish; the fingerbowls contain wine. His wife Fortunata also rose from the gutter, but is much sharper and is now said to rule him. In their conversations, the guests broaden the satire by dissecting contemporary Naples: corrupt magistrates, famine, expensive food, neglect of the gods. "It is a Symposium far removed from Plato's" (Grant, 318). After describing his palace – four dining rooms, twenty bedrooms, etc. – Trimalchio concludes, "So your friend who was once a worm is now a king" (328). He enjoys Swift's "happy state of being well deceived," while his guests enjoy watching and ridiculing him, but the fullest *domaine* is ours. Alexander Pope saw in Petronius "the scholar's learning, with the courtier's ease."

The Goings-On at Fonthill

Speaking of ease, consider William Beckford, Junior. His father, "Alderman Beckford" – MP, Mayor of London, reputedly the richest man in England (with income from slave-based West Indian estates) – died when his son was 9, so at 21 Junior would be the richest man in England and master of Fonthill Splendens, a Palladian mansion west of Salisbury. Educated by tutors, he may have been coached in music by the nine-year-old Mozart when he was five. Beckford proved an avid reader and student of languages, but some of his tastes were *outré*. As he entered his teens, his godfather, the Earl of Chatham, warned that he was "inordinately fond of Arabian tales," which would be dangerous if carried too far (Oliver 10). The warning was futile: Beckford was already an orientalist by then, and that taste grew. J.W. Oliver, his most moral biographer, sounds like a concerned relative or a therapist: Beckford "was drawn by an irresistible attraction to all that was exotic, irregular, and high fantastical...his abilities seemed every day further and further from finding an outlet in normal social directions" (10). In 1779, he met eleven-year old William Courtenay, and soon there was gossip about their relationship. During Beckford's Grand Tour in 1780 he became involved with a Venetian youth, and in Naples discussed homosexuality with Lady Hamilton, a famous beauty, wife of England's ambassador to Italy Sir William, both family friends (Jack 15-16).

Back in England, he had an affair with his cousin Peter's beautiful wife, Louisa

Pitt-Rivers Beckford, and his attraction to Courtenay flared up again. One might expect him to welcome his 21st birthday in 1781, freeing him from lawyers, tutors, and restrictions, but he was depressed by the need to assume the responsibilities of public life, i.e. "accept" a seat in Parliament. He considered returning to Italy, but Lady Hamilton advised against it, so he started planning his birthday party: tents, bonfires, singers, beef and beer aplenty. On September 28th, three hundred guests dined in the Grecian Hall, danced until 1 AM, then had supper and danced till dawn. The next day the gates were opened and ten to twelve thousand local people came to be fed, serenaded, and regaled with fireworks. Beckford was saluted with a pastoral cantata composed and performed by Italian musicians brought from London. He sent a full account to Lady Hamilton, evincing distaste for "the crowds that...pressed in upon me, the swilling of punch, the cramming of venison," "fulsome compliments and begging epistles," but also pride that he had produced a "scene [so] nearly allied to enchantment" that "I could not believe myself at Fonthill" (Oliver 85-86). It was quite a party, but it felt *required*, and his mixed feelings limited its impact. He was now an adult, however, his mother moved out (to Bath), and he began designing a Christmas party for a few young guests that would have no such deficiencies. Much of the fall went to arranging it.

Exactly what transpired during those few days is a mystery; the participants, belatedly acquiring discretion, kept their peace for decades, frustrating biographers. Malcolm Jack (*William Beckford: an English Fidalgo*) writes, "We cannot be certain of what actually took place at the bizarre Christmas celebration...rumors of satanic rites became widespread..." (19). Christopher Thacker in *The Wildness Pleases* admits, "What happened at Beckford's party we do not know," but thinks that the "exotic" and "sultry" parts of his novel *Caliph Vathek*, written soon after, may have been inspired by the party (187-89). Robert J. Gemmett's *William Beckford* borrows Beckford's own phrase "voluptuous festival" (84-85). The few known facts are titillating. Both Louisa Beckford and William Courtenay attended: an interesting triangle. Beckford had hired Philippe Jacques de Loutherburg – the famous scene designer, a master of sound effects, lighting, and depth illusions, whom David Garrick had brought from France to Drury Lane – to "orientalize" Fonthill Splendens in accordance with its new owner's tastes. Yet we can say that the party achieved *domaine* status only because Beckford himself finally broke the silence – up to a point. In 1838, at the age of 78, he appended a long note to his copy of a letter he had written to Louisa in 1782. It contains most of what we know about the revels, as recollected by their host 57 years later, and testify to the effect they still had on him. Believe it or not, I have edited for brevity.

> *Immured we were...for three days... – doors and windows so strictly closed that neither common day light nor common place visitors could get in or even peep in – care worn visages were ordered to keep aloof – no sunk-in mouths or furroughed foreheads were permitted.... Our société was extremely youthful and lovely to look upon... not only Louisa...but her intimate friend...Sophia...perhaps the most beautiful woman in England, threw over it a fascinating charm. Throughout the arched Halls and vast apartments...prevailed a soft and tempered radiance – distributed with much skill under the direction of Loutherbourg.... The solid Egyptian Hall looked as if hewn out of a living rock...apartments and apparently endless passages... were all vaulted...suites of stately apartments gleaming with marble pavements....steps led to another world of decorated chambers and a gallery.... Through all these suites – through all these galleries – did we roam and wander – too often hand in hand – strains of music swelling forth at intervals – sometimes the organ – sometimes concerted pieces – in which three of the greatest singers then in Europe – ...most amicably joined...and melted the most beloved the most susceptible of my fair companions into tears. Delightful indeed were these romantic wanderings – delightful the straying about this little interior world of exclusive happiness surrounded by lovely beings, in all the freshness of their early bloom, so fitted to enjoy it. Here, nothing was dull or vapid – here, nothing resembled in the least the common forms and usages, the...routine of fashionable existence – all was essence.... Even the uniform splendour of gilded roofs – was partially obscured by the vapour of wood aloes ascending in wreaths from cassolettes [perfume-boxes] placed low on the silken carpets in porcelain salvers of the richest japan [Japanese style]. The delirium of delight into which our young and fervid bosoms were cast by such a combination of seductive influences may be conceived but too easily. Even at this long, sad*

distance from these days and nights of exquisite refinements, chilled by age, still more by the coarse unpoetic tenor of the present disenchanting period – I still feel warmed and irradiated by the recollections of that strange, necromantic light which Loutherbourg had thrown over what absolutely appeared a realm of Fairy, or rather, perhaps, a Demon Temple deep beneath the earth set apart for tremendous mysteries – and yet how soft, how genial, was this quiet light. Whilst the wretched world without lay dark, and bleak, and howling, whilst the storm was raging against our massive walls and the snow drifting in clouds, the very air of summer seemed playing around us – the choir of low-toned melodious voices continued to sooth our ear, and...tables covered with delicious viands and fragrant flowers – glided forth, by the aid of mechanism at stated intervals, from the richly draped, and amply curtained recesses of the enchanted precincts. The glowing haze investing every object, the mystic look, the vastness, the intricacy of this vaulted labyrinth occasioned so bewildering an effect that it became impossible for anyone to define...where he stood, where he had been, or to whither he was wandering – such was the confusion – the perplexity so many illuminated storys of infinitely varied apartments gave rise to. It was, in short, the realization of romance in its most extravagant intensity. (Oliver 89-91).

A socio-political reading of this passage could compare Beckford's account of the luxuries of the rich ("this little interior world of exclusive happiness") with others, such as *Brideshead Revisited,* while a scholar of the eighteenth century would see another specimen of mediaevalist aesthetics. The late Edward Saïd might deplore one more pairing of "oriental" trappings with sensual licence. Literary historians point out parallels between the Yuletide orgy and the plot, characters, and scenery of *Caliph Vathek,* with Beckford as Vathek and Louisa as Nouronihar. Biographers have traced the party's consequences: Beckford's agitation and depression afterwards; the persistence of the love triangle; society's suspicions and rumours, especially about Courtenay; the family pressures on Beckford to go abroad and to marry, which he did in 1783, shattering Louisa. What strikes me is that Beckford gives in his appended note nearly the Platonic Idea of a *domaine,* emphasizing

separation from the world and a generous indulgence of the protagonist's fantasies. This was a real-life *domaine perdu* whose celebration of youthfulness foreshadows Alain-Fournier. It was also an estate-based sex party, which had received
scant literary expression, apart from *Vathek*.

Beckford's fascination with *domaines* did not pass. In Paris in 1784, he wrote
Louisa about a strange house. A friend, the architect Le Doux, arranged the visit
and imposed conditions: ride there in a shuttered cab and do not speak. Beckford
agreed. They stopped in a dark, seedy *quartier* and walked through a walled
lumberyard where a hidden door opened to allow access to a series of rooms,
humble at first, then magnificent. Le Doux was silent and unsmiling. They saw
a strange old man and a huge porphyry cistern whose clear water heaved up as
they approached; in the waves Beckford saw agonized human forms. The old man
now looked malign, but the waters calmed. Hearing choral music in an adjacent
chapel, Beckford knelt there and prayed for deliverance from evil. When he finished, Le Doux said that he was not the person they had thought him and would
not be enlightened further. Evidently he had failed the test of a secret society – by
praying? They retraced their steps, Beckford noting the absence of the old man, the
cistern, and other objects seen before (Oliver 175-80). We have only Beckford's
word for all this. It *could* be the story of his encounter with someone's dark magic,
or a fiction without any basis in reality.

Coming home in 1791 after years abroad, Beckford recovered his "old delight
in Fonthill," and "began to think that he might...create in his ample domains a
little world of his own" (Oliver 210). He consulted an architect, James Wyatt,
about a new "mediaeval" building there, like Horace Walpole's Strawberry Hill,
but grander. This vision became Fonthill Abbey, one of the century's great Gothic
follies. It took years, and was still incomplete when Beckford hosted Admiral
Nelson, no less, in December 1800, but enough had been done for the Abbey to
house the big banquet on the 23rd. Beckford went all out: a torchlit procession
from the old place to the new, led by a band, with hundreds of escorts and spectators, a *faux*-mediaeval dining hall, hidden musicians playing, a theatrical performance, and then a quiet walk back to their beds (Oliver 241-43). It was a memorable occasion, a time warp to the Middle Ages. Among other roles, Beckford
was a producer of histrionic spectacles. Work continued on the Abbey until
1809, Fonthill Splendens being serially dismantled to supply building materials.

Descriptions and illustrations give some idea of how imposing and exotic it was, but Beckford had to sell out and move to Bath in 1822: taxes, building expenses, and lower income from his plantations in the post-slavery era had sapped his fortune. And finally the Abbey's central tower collapsed in 1825, ruining much of the rest. Like *Les Sablonnières* and many another *domaine*, it was unstable and, ultimately, unsustainable.

The Death of the Party

F. Scott Fitzgerald's penchant for *domaines* rivalled Beckford's. Lacking a fortune and thus the means to produce real-life extravaganzas, however, Fitzgerald created them in stories and novels. They come in several types, enough of them being social occasions to earn a place in Christopher Ames's *The Life of the Party. Festive Vision in Modern Fiction* (1991). Its section on "The Party Between the Wars" reminds us that the decade after the Great War was a time of wild optimism and prosperity in parts of America, a period, for some, of careless excess, conspicuous consumption of alcohol and other stimulants, and epic parties, memorable though hazily recalled. Fitzgerald lived through and wrote of all this; Ames's "Charioted by Bacchus" chapter is about him. The quotation is from Keats's "Ode to a Nightingale," but the poet wanted to fly "on the viewless wings of Poesy," *not* charioted by Bacchus (ll. 32-33) – fuelled by alcohol – as Fitzgerald and some of his characters were. Ames notes that these parties often do not achieve the host's purpose. This pattern in Fitzgerald's fiction is the dark side of would-be *domaines*, which have an inherent tendency to disappoint, haunt, or turn on their creators in the long run. Many a slip 'twixt cup and lip, says the proverb, or, as Eliot's "Hollow Men" sing, "Between the conception / And the creation / Between the emotion / And the response / Falls the Shadow."

We should not be surprised when festive *domaines* fall apart. Anyone who has arranged a birthday party for children knows the expectations, the wonder, and the Shadow, when sassy Becky makes the birthday girl cry, or Tommy pins the tail on the young master. Recall that when the Great Meaulnes first stumbled on the *domaine perdu* it was *en fête*: an engagement party for teen-agers. That was why the place was beautifully illuminated, why children in antique costumes were running the chateau, why actors had been brought to entertain them, why there was music, why Meaulnes was bewitched. But the *fiancée* got cold feet and did not show, the jilted scion ran off, leaving unpaid debts, the party broke up in disorder, debtors foreclosed, and *Les Sablonnières* started to slide into its own sandpit. We have been warned. These things happen.

Fitzgerald's ill-starred *domaines* appear not only in his later career, after his loss of popularity, his "crack-up," and his wife's nervous breakdown(s), but from the beginning. Even in 1920 (when the publication of his first novel prompted Zelda Sayre, the Southern belle who had once rejected him, to say yes) his short stories have dark patches. In "The Cut-Glass Bowl," Evelyn, whose beauty is fading in her thirties, sees that the good times are over and feels angry nostalgia: "...life had once been the sum of her current love-affairs. It was now the sum of her current problems" (Fitzgerald 1962, 25). Evidently "life was a thing for youth. What a happy youth she must have had!" (26). Her *domaine*, taken for granted at the time, is appreciated only after its demise. In "The Lees of Happiness," widowed Roxanne and divorced Harry accept reality and decide to stay apart: "To these two life had come quickly and gone, leaving not bitterness, but pity; not disillusion, but only pain" (238). It is a fine, sad, autumnal story – written when Fitzgerald was 23. "The Ice Palace" has a *domaine* of sorts: for Sally Carrol, "the Confederate dead... died for the most beautiful thing in the world – the dead South" (Fitzgerald 1986, 66). When a dance band plays "Dixie," Sally feels stronger – the closest approach to a party *domaine* in the early stories.

Fitzgerald's first novel made up for lost time: *This Side of Paradise* abounds in parties. Amory Baines enjoys many social occasions in his youth. His cultured mother, Beatrice (a heavy drinker who has breakdowns), "fed him sections of the 'Fêtes Galantes' [music or poetry about courtship picnics] before he was ten" (Fitzgerald 1996, 2). The family estate at Lake Geneva, Wisconsin, "dotted with old and new summer houses...fountains and white benches...came suddenly into sight from foliage-hung hiding-places," like Brideshead (14). His prep school in the east is close to New York: "a picture of splendor that rivalled the dream cities in the Arabian Nights," while "romance gleamed from...the women's eyes," and the theatre "enchanted him" (21). His Princeton years abound in parties and *domaines*. "Long afterward Amory thought of sophomore spring as the happiest time of his life," though its series of alcoholic binges ended in the death of a friend in a car crash (53). The parties in *Paradise* are often *manqués* or disastrous. At one, after they rush into a café "like Dionysian revellers," Amory sees the Devil, who reappears later at another debauch (81). Yet he has good times, too. Like Fitzgerald, he acts in the Triangle Club's plays, but women are his chief *domaine*. Isabelle, Clara, Rosalind, Eleanor: each offers a vision of happiness. Amory is highly susceptible, yet for various reasons none of these relationships lasts.

A partly-fictionalized autobiographical pastiche written in college, later revised and expanded, *This Side of Paradise* does not meet Fitzgerald's mature standards; his account of campus trivia grows tedious, and his pontifications can be cringe-worthy. But later in the book, beyond the debutante parties, bull sessions, and bar-hopping, there is more substance. As seniors, Amory and his roommate Tom develop a sense of time that brings tears, and Amory's prose poem begs sleep to "*press from the petals of the lotus flower / something of this to keep, the essence of an hour*" (Fitzgerald 1996, 114). This mood prevails when he is with charismatic, literate Eleanor. They read Swinburne's "Triumph of Time" together, and Amory sees that "it was only the past that ever seemed strange and unbelievable" (173, 175). This is important: what seems ordinary as the present may become a weird *domaine* as the past. Time hurts again when he meets an old Princeton friend in Atlantic City, where they had an extreme binge years before. Several participants have since died, so the meeting depresses Amory, who "longed for death to roll over his generation.... His youth seemed never so vanished as now..." (184). The joy of that "party...had flown," leaving only memories of "his love for Rosalind...as payment for the loss of his youth" (184-85). Of course we all lose our youth if we live on, but for Amory this means that "life had rejected him"(185).

His stories in the early 'twenties have more heft. "The Diamond as Big as the Ritz" (1922) is as exemplary of *domaines* as Alain-Fournier's *domaine perdu*, and exhibits Fitzgerald's fascination with the wealthy, treated mythically here. The protagonist, John Unger from Hades on the Mississippi, attends St Midas's School near Boston, "the most expensive and...exclusive boys' preparatory school in the world" (Fitzgerald 1962, 93). A fellow student, Percy Washington, invites him to spend the summer at his home out West. On the train Percy tells him that his father "is by far the richest man in the world," with "a diamond bigger than the Ritz-Carlton Hotel," which sounds like hyperbole, to say the least (94-95). When they reach the Rocky Mountains in northern Montana, have been escorted by uniformed blacks with southern accents on a long drive by buggy and car, then lifted over a pinnacle by cables, deposited on a private road, and driven another five miles, they attain a view suggestive of Lake Louise.

> *Full in the light of the stars, an exquisite chateau rose from the borders of the lake, climbed in marble radiance half the height of the adjoining mountain, then melted in grace, in perfect symmetry, in translucent feminine languor, into the massed darkness of a forest of pine.* (100)

Towers, parapets, and a thousand glowing windows create "a chord of music." John, so tired that he falls asleep at dinner, awakes in a quiet room to be told that "The mountain the chateau rests on" is a "solid diamond...one cubic mile without a flaw" (103).

So the title actually understates the case: their diamond is significantly larger than the Ritz. They can dig in their back yard and chip off a large enough diamond to cover their expenses for the next year – but "without a flaw" is heavily ironic. Percy makes some massively indiscreet disclosures. Their property is "the only five square miles of land in the country that's never been surveyed" (Fitzgerald 1962, 99). Airplanes can see them, though, so they have "half-a-dozen anti-aircraft guns and we've arranged it so far – but there've been a few deaths and a great many prisoners," which "upsets mother and the girls." Touring the chateau, John is shown a room "like a platonic conception of the ultimate prison": ceiling, floor, and walls are lined with "an unbroken mass of diamonds," dazzling in their brilliance (101). Where the surfaces are not diamond, they are marble, ivory, emerald, crystal, or fur. There are aquaria beneath transparent floors, piped music in the corridors, and feathered chairs. The diamond mountain and the chateau are a *domaine* that is – as Derrida says – 'always already' deeply flawed, but we know to expect that.

Fitzgerald presents this as the Washingtons' *domaine*, not his or John's. The family were Virginians, but near the end of the Civil War, Fitz-Norman Culpepper Washington left the plantation to his younger brother and headed west with some "faithful blacks" (Fitzgerald 1962, 105). One day, riding alone in the Rockies, he chanced upon the diamond mountain, which is likened to the legend of Eldorado. He learned how many diamonds of what size to sell, and where, without attracting attention. He imported his brother to manage the blacks, "who had never realized that slavery was abolished" (he told them the South had won), and married a Virginia lady who bore him a son, Braddock (107). Fitz-Norman had to dispose of his brother, who drank and talked too freely, but "few other murders stained these happy years of progress and expansion" (108). When he died, Braddock converted their wealth into radium (a billion dollars' worth fit into a cigar box), and sealed the mine: they had enough. John meets Percy's sisters, Jasmine and Kismine, and falls for the latter. Braddock, who has a "vacuous face," shows him the slave quarters, the golf course ("all a green...no rough, no hazards"), and the prison: a huge sunken glass bowl containing about two dozen aviators (113, 114). One prisoner whom Braddock allowed to tutor the girls escaped. Fourteen agents have reported killing a man of his description in different towns.

Kismine reveals that all visiting friends are killed when their time is up, and offers to elope with John. That night the executioners appear, but while chasing him they are suddenly recalled by an alarm. Running to Kismine, John learns that they are under aerial attack: "it's that Italian who got away" (Fitzgerald 1962, 127). With Jasmine, they take a path up the mountain and watch as airplanes silence the anti-aircraft guns. At first light, John follows Braddock and slaves carrying a huge diamond up to a ledge, where the heir offers God a bribe. His hair turns white as he speaks. The bribe is evidently refused; the airplanes land and an assault begins. The Braddock family and two slaves enter a trap-door into the mountain. Kismine sobs, "The mountain is wired!" (136). Within seconds the whole slope turns a "dazzling burning yellow" that leaves a smoking "black waste," and a huge explosion destroys the chateau. Too bad about slaves and aviators. When the escapees reach the edge of the enclave and sit down to eat their last food, John asks to see the diamonds he told Kismine to bring. Oh, she brought rhinestones instead: they will "have to live in Hades" (137). Jasmine will take in laundry to support them: "I have always washed my own handkerchiefs." So much for a love *domaine*! What remains is the image of the blood-stained diamond mountain, burned and torn, killing more as it goes. So much for the estate *domaine*!

Neither "Diamond" nor the other stories of those years provide much material for Ames's "festive vision." Most concern the evanescence of love. "Winter Dreams" (1922) laments a lost *domaine* of young love with its intense feelings. In "Absolution" (1924), Rudoph, caught in religious and family coils, makes a *domaine* of his "inner life" (Fitzgerald 1986, 167). But *The Great Gatsby* (1925) repays the deficit, describing Gatsby's lavish parties for hordes of boozers whom he may or may not even know. Ames rejects this boon, calling the parties "thematically insignificant" because they are unimportant to Gatsby (139). He has a *goal* in giving them (to lure Daisy to his estate) that "obviates the purposelessness" of the "true festive spirit" (145, 148). To rule purposive parties irrelevant is to define "true" parties narrowly. Let them be false or impure occasions! They will have lots of company. From my perspective, Gatsby's *fêtes* are glittering *domaines* where revellers' lives are touched with magic and lifted above the ordinary. Ames fixes on their emptiness for the host, but we have seen *domaines* recognized and partly defined by outsiders before. That is what happens here: Nick Carraway, a young Midwestern bond agent renting the bungalow next door, marvels at the spectacle *chez* Gatsby, and we see it through his eyes.

> *There was music from my neighbor's house through the summer nights. In his blue gardens men and girls came and went like moths among the whisperings and the champagne and the stars. ...in the afternoon I watched his guests diving from the tower of his raft...* (Fitzgerald 1945, 47)

Music, blue gardens, whispering, and champagne under the stars: Nick has stumbled upon a *domaine* as wondrous as Meaulnes found at the "lost estate."

Gatsby's upscale rental is within easy reach of New York. Crates of citrus fruit arrive every Friday, caterers put up tents and tables, string coloured lights in the garden, set out food and a bar; an orchestra appears. Private cars come from the city, Gatsby's Rolls-Royce shuttles guests back and forth day and night, and his station wagon meets the trains. Gatsby is less a host than a destination. Nick is "one of the few guests who had actually been invited. People were not invited – they went there" (Fitzgerald 1945, 49). A chauffeur brings Nick a handwritten note signed "Jay Gatsby" (we learn that he was born Jimmy Gatz). Nick even meets Gatsby that night; most guests do not. His background and how he made his money are obscure, which fuels his guests' gossip, but *domaines* usually have their mysteries. When Nick departs with the last guests and glances back across the lawn, the nature of the place becomes clear: "A sudden emptiness seemed to flow now from the windows and the great doors, endowing with complete isolation the figure of the host, who stood on the porch, his hand up in a formal gesture of farewell" (64). The *domaine* is suspended.

And for Gatsby, that *domaine* is incomplete. Also on Long Island are the

Buchanans: Tom, an athletic, wealthy racist whom he knew at Yale; and Daisy, Nick's cousin from Louisville. Jordan Baker, an old friend of Daisy's he meets there, tells him that Gatsby and Daisy had a past, which Gatsby confirms. The possibility of reviving it in the present drives the plot. Gatsby says that she was "the first 'nice' girl he had known," and "excitingly desirable" (Fitzgerald 1945, 158). This was when he was in basic training at Camp Taylor, Kentucky, in 1917 (the author drawing on his own experiences). Visiting her home, Gatsby felt that "he had never been in such a beautiful house before." Even remembering it years later makes him lyrical. It had

> a ripe mystery about it, a hint of bedrooms upstairs more beautiful and cool than other bedrooms, of gay and radiant activities taking place..., of romances that were not musty...of this year's shining motor-cars and of dances whose flowers were scarcely withered. It excited him, too, that many men had already loved Daisy – it increased her value in his eyes. (158)

He could sense the "echoes of still vibrant emotions." That was Gatsby's *domaine*, whose resurrection he seeks, but he has an original sin to expiate. He deceived Daisy, letting her "believe that he was...from much the same stratum as herself" and "able to take care of her" (159). This was untrue but useful: "he made the most of his time. He took what he could get, ravenously and unscrupulously – eventually he took Daisy one still October night."

But now he must deal with Tom, who married Daisy while Gatsby was overseas. Desperate to see her alone, he has Nick arrange a meeting at his bungalow. Afterwards they walk over to the mansion, where Daisy weeps over his beautiful shirts (as Gatsby emoted over her house). After a slow start they warm to each other, and by the time Nick leaves they are holding hands, having "forgotten me," existing "remotely, possessed by intense life" (Fitzgerald 1945, 104). This is their love-*domaine*, as fragile and transient as any we have seen. When the Buchanans finally come to a *soireé*, Daisy is entranced ("in the very casualness of Gatsby's party there were romantic possibilities":117), but Tom is not. "Who is this Gatsby anyhow?" he demands (116). A bootlegger? He vows to find out "who he is and what he does." But Tom has a secret, too: a married mistress, Myrtle Wilson, living at an automobile garage in an industrial wasteland along the New York road, "a valley of ashes" where grey men stir up sooty clouds with their spades beneath the gigantic signboard eyes of Dr Eckleburg, Oculist (31). This is the anti-*domaine*, visually and structurally. Once when Gatsby and Daisy are returning from the city in Tom's car, Myrtle runs out to hail them; Daisy runs over her and keeps going. Myrtle dies, and Tom tells Mr Wilson that Gatsby was driving. Wilson kills Gatsby, then himself. This is a classic turn: ugliness brings down flawed beauty. Gatsby was a mere shell by then, the Buchanans having made up and gone west.

So Gatsby (who parried Nick's warning "You can't repeat the past" with "of course you can!") loses everything: his love-*domaine*, his reputation (ruined by rumours and Tom), and his life (Fitzgerald 1945, 118). Yet that is not quite the end of the story. Not one of Gatsby's many guests comes to his funeral; only Nick Carraway attends, faithful to his memory. On his last night in the cottage Nick has a vision. It is late summer; most of the big houses, including Gatsby's, are closed and dark. Under these conditions, in the moonlight,

> *I became aware of the old island here that flowered once for Dutch sailors' eyes – a fresh, green breast of the new world. Its vanished trees...once pandered in whispers to the last and greatest of all human dreams; for a transitory enchanted moment man must have held his breath in the presence of this continent, compelled into an aesthetic contemplation he neither understood nor desired....* (190-91)

"*Green* breast" (my italics), "vanished trees," "pandered," and "transitory enchanted moment" alert us to a lost pastoral *domaine*. Gatsby could not accept that his dream "was already behind him," believing in the "future that...recedes before us" as we are "borne back ceaselessly into the past" (191). This is not a philosophy of time, but it makes a resonant ending to the novel. Fitzgerald had come a long way since *This Side of Paradise*. Too bad he did not know that Long Island is the terminal moraine of an Ice Age glacier: he could have made a good thing of that.

Fitzgerald's mid-career stories present other *domaines*: love, theatre, dances, New York. Two are important here. "The Last of the Belles" (1929; filmed 1974) revisits Fitzgerald's southern courtship. A tale of love in the shadow of war, it is haunted by lost time. The narrator recalls a dance when the orchestra played "*After You've Gone*, in a poignant incomplete way that I can hear yet, as if each bar were trickling off a precious minute," while couples "in organdie and olive drab" kept time on the dance floor (Fitzgerald 1986, 243). "It was a time of youth and war, and there was never so much love around": young lovers sent to the trenches. The soldiers' last night has both "the universal nostalgia of the departing summer" and the "bewitched impermanence" of a magic carpet (248). "The South sang to us," says the narrator: "I wonder if they remember. I remember...," and it hurts. Years later he returns, looking for "the lost midsummer world of my early twenties," and finds all changed (251). Ailie is still there, but no longer has the power to enchant – or he his power to be enchanted. Where the army camp stood is now underbrush; a "place that had once been so full of life and effort was gone, as if it had never existed" (253). Once Ailie left, "the South would be empty for me forever." The narrator's nostalgia is the author's.

The other crucial story is "Babylon Revisited" (1931), "Babylon" being Paris, revisited after Black Friday 1929 sent most of its Americans home. Charlie, a party boy back then, has been chastened by financial losses and a stint in a sanitarium. He hopes to regain custody of his daughter Honoria, living with Aunt Marion, who blames Charlie for the death of her sister Helen (drunk, he locked her out of their apartment on a snowy night; she died soon after). Her husband Lincoln, who never got rich, sympathizes with Charlie, but "the big party's over...those crazy years," he reminds us (Fitzgerald 1986, 398). Charlie walks on eggshells – just one drink a day – but running into two friends from '29 spoils everything: enter karma. Duncan and Lorraine want to pick up where they left off with good old Charlie. She pens him a note ("We *did* have such good times that crazy spring") suggesting a get-together. He shies away, but they find him at Marion and Lincoln's, barging in tipsily while negotiations are in progress. Charlie's credibility is destroyed, Marion stalks out, and Lincoln says that the deal is off. Charlie goes to the half-empty Ritz bar, orders whisky, and "the memory of those days swept over him like a nightmare...": women, drunk or stoned, carried away screaming, men locking wives out in the snow (401). But "the snow of twenty-nine wasn't real snow. If you didn't want it to be snow, you just paid some money" (402). Well, "they couldn't make him pay forever," he hopes, but the *domaine* is past: an old ruin, a present "nightmare."

Tender Is the Night (1933) has Fitzgerald's last important party *domaines*. The title, from Keats's "Ode to a Nightingale," is ironic; a more accurate clue comes later in the poem (quoted in the epigraph): "But here there is no light." It is a sad novel, reflecting the Fitzgeralds' own fortunes. Scott's career had declined, he was drinking heavily in Hollywood, and Zelda's depressions were worse. The book depicts American expats on the French Riviera, chiefly Dr Dick and Nicole Diver: first in their salad days, then in trouble. Dick is a prominent psychiatrist who lectures, publishes, and had a clinic in Switzerland; Nicole was one of his patients (she had been sexually abused by her father). In a long flashback we see them come together despite her instability. He married her over the strenuous objections of his colleagues. It worked for a while (six good years, she says) and they have two children – but then he falls for Rosemary Hoyt, a young American actress, and they have an affair (as Fitzgerald did in Hollywood). Life darkens: Dick turns to binge drinking and moral decline. The novel traces his fall, including an *imbroglio* with Italian police, while Nicole gains strength. Eventually she has an affair with their old friend Tommy Barban and leaves Dick, who returns to the United States, practices in Buffalo, then does general medicine in small towns. He becomes a non-person to the author, reduced to what Nicole hears of him.

Rosemary first sees the Divers as gatekeepers of a *domaine*. Dick, "kind and charming...would open up whole new worlds for her, unroll an endless succession of magnificent possibilities" (Fitzgerald 1933, 16). They invite her to a party at their villa, and "to be included in Dick Diver's world...was a remarkable experience" (27). He is so confident that he plans "to give a really *bad* party. ...where there's a brawl and seductions and people going home with their feelings hurt and women passed out in the cabinet de toilette." This hubris is treated as it deserves. Though Rosemary thinks Villa Diana "the centre of the world," during the party one woman sees *something* in the bathroom but won't say what; Barban, a soldier of fortune, a mercenary, is up in arms; Diver is in damage-control mode; and a duel is demanded (29). That indeed sounds like a bad party, yet years later, Dick bumps into one of that night's guests, who says,

> *I've never forgotten that evening in your garden – how nice you and your wife were. To me it's one of the finest memories of my life, one of the happiest ones. I've always thought of it as the most civilized gathering of people that I have ever known.* (246)

Yes, *domaines* are subjective. How was the party? Depends on whom you ask.

Later, at a luncheon in a Paris restaurant, Dick makes their group "bright," and gives the train ride back from a war cemetery "a faint resemblance to one of his own parties" (52, 59). He could do that, then.

Nor does he lose his power all at once, escorting Rosemary to a *soirée* at a strange old house in Paris that gives her "an electric-like shock, a definite nervous experience": the "false-and-exalted feeling of being on a set" (Fitzgerald 1933, 71). They are falling in love, and Dick – "Organizer of private gaiety, curator of a richly-encrusted happiness" – can do no wrong (76). His "Odyssey over Paris" for sixteen people in cars is a party moving "with the speed of a slapstick comedy"; people join "as if by magic." After he departs, Rosemary thinks, "At last I've been on a wild party...but it's no fun when Dick isn't there" (79). They are in a love-*domaine*. All these examples come from the first quarter of the novel, however; later ones are hard to find. Once, Rosemary being away, Dick "felt her absence" when a cafe orchestra played a "Carnival Song," which "started the little dance that went on all about her" (164). There are no *domaines* after that, and few parties, the Divers losing their popularity as Dick's drinking problem worsens. Its toxic effect on his judgment disrupts the party on a yacht; he insults a young Englishwoman, who takes offence, and they tangle crudely. Nicole is furious. It is as needless as his run-in with Italian police, and inebriation is again to blame. This is the last party we attend with the Divers: one not likely to be remembered by anyone as a "civilized gathering." So *Tender Is the Night* has its *domaine* moments and parties, but the moments end early and the parties go on too long.

Fitzgerald, then, wrote of *domaines* and parties from early in his career until near its end. Some of them, especially Gatsby's, are wondrous affairs, but others are disappointing or catastrophic, often due to alcohol abuse. In "Babylon Revisited," "the party's over" stands for the end of a festive epoch as the roaring 'twenties give way to the dirty 'thirties, and the emphasis falls on the aftermath: hangovers, wreckage, death. Dick Diver's self-destructive arc curves from his own parties, which enthralled some, to his last tipsy incursion on another man's party, making a fool of himself. Nor are these only late, burnt-out developments: in *This Side of Paradise*, a party in New York ends with an overturned car and the death of one of Amory's friends. The "devil" who appears several times after that haunts Fitzgerald's binges: *he* represents "the death of the party."

Domaines of Love and Sex

By this time readers are well aware that love affairs can create those separate, charmed adventures that I call *domaines*. In western literature, the primal example is in the Book of Genesis, where Adam and Eve, created in chapter 1 (or 1 and 2), enjoy the Garden of Eden for a time before being seduced by Satan (chapter 3) and ejected from paradise. Chapter 4 begins, "And Adam knew Eve his wife; and she conceived" – the first mention of carnal knowledge. Does this mean that sexual intercourse had not occurred while they were in the Garden, but was post-lapsarian? The Hebrew sources admitted into Scripture do not settle this interesting point. At the other end of the moral spectrum, Petronius' *Satyricon* talks freely about sexual love and sex without love. Behind Sir Paul Harvey's Oxford euphemisms ("disreputable adventures," "gross indecency") lie some vivid, unbuttoned stories about classical couplings.

European mediaeval romances furnished many examples. Marie de France gave her leading men and ladies love *domaines* in *Guigemar* and *Yonec*. Marvels and wonders abound, but we see loving relationships, too. Lanval falls in love with a beautiful lady who carries him off to the Land of Avalon. The Welsh knight Milun sires a love-child and achieves a "happily-ever-after" style *domaine* at the end. Chrétien de Troyes treated almost every court and castle as a *domaine* of bravery, beauty, chivalry, and courtesy. The hero and heroine of *Cligés* enjoy a long honeymoon in a tower and garden, and the knight Yvain marries Laudine for love (then leaves her). Neither author shows the course of love as smooth – towers are not impregnable, and dalliances in secret gardens may be overseen – but true lovers do exist. And the great mediaeval best-seller, *The Romance of the Rose*, is almost completely concerned with the conduct of courtly love affairs and the possibility of sex in those circles. When Sir Gawain is (apparently) offered sex by Bertilak's wife, his refusal saves his neck. Love-*domaines* tempt and test.

As we saw, the English Renaissance also treated this topic. In Shakespeare's *The Tempest*, Ferdinand and Miranda are true lovers who survive hostility and are ultimately rewarded; at the end they sail off to their nuptials. Later in the century, John Milton, converting the Genesis Garden of Eden story into *Paradise Lost*, took an interest in the First Couple as lovers, and in whether angels might enjoy a heavenly counterpart of sexual union, though his Biblical sources gave him scant basis for speculation. Aphra Behn's *Oroonoko* has at its centre the star-crossed fortunes of a noble African couple, Prince Oroonoko and Imoinda.

A century later, love-*domaines* tended to be sinful. Jean-Jacques Rousseau's novel *Julie, Letters of Two Lovers,* updated Abelard and Eloise's mediaeval *jeux interdits*. Here the obstacle to young love is the class system: Julie's father, a proud baron, will not let her marry her middle-class tutor, Saint-Preux. Their love-*domaine* is fleeting and guilty; in Part One he seduces Julie, and they spend the rest of the novel atoning for their sin. Class pride may have been the villain, but bourgeois morality finally rules the plot: Julie must die young. And in the twilight of the *ancien régime*, wealthy William Beckford Jr created and lived an illicit (adulterous and bisexual) love-*domaine* in the family mansion. The feelings and decor of that Christmas party were preserved in his "oriental" novel *Vathek,* and in an account written years afterward.

The *domaines* in W.H. Hudson's *Green Mansions* are double and doomed: an enchanted glade, and the brief love of Abel and Rima. Alain-Fournier's *Le Grand Meaulnes* adds a third layer. There is the lost estate itself, with its cast of dress-ups; then the love that grows between Augustin and Yvonne de Galais. Both are ill-fated, by impoverishment and dismantling, abandonment and death. The author's hopeless, distant, obsessive love for Yvonne de Quiévrecourt suggested a potential, extra-textual third *domaine,* but this was doomed by his sensibility, given to idealistic flights rather than action. In John Fowles's estate-*domaines* (*The Magus* and *The Ebony Tower*), love is imperfect, an illusion or transient idea not pursued. In fact, twentieth-century love-*domaines* are apt to be tenuous. Scarlett's *domaine* in *Gone With the Wind* is Tara; despite her three husbands, it would be difficult to argue that she loves anyone except herself and Ashley, a married man. And in Waugh's *Brideshead Revisited,* the late-blooming love of Charles and Julia lives marginally, illicitly, for some years, and is finally destroyed by their religious differences.

Love has been such a potent generator of *domaines* that to name *all* the lovers, classical and modern, tragic and comic, who have found their (often dangerous) world in each other is a Sisyphean task. A line of heroes and heroines of plays, operas, novels, stories, gossip magazines and Harlequin romances would stretch to the crack o' doom; I have only scratched the surface. A fresh example, of the third millenium, seems appropriate.

DURING HER LONG CAREER, DORIS Lessing created fiction, non-fiction, poetry, drama, and two operas (with Philip Glass). *The Golden Notebook* impressed many readers with her intensity and frankness, especially about sexual relations. A mature work, *The Grandmothers. Four Short Novels* (2003), shows that Lessing knew what *domaines* are and how they act on the mind and nervous system. In "Victoria and the Staveneys," a poor, orphaned black girl in London is taken to the home of the wealthy, white-liberal Staveney family overnight as a nine-year-old (her aunt being ill, she is stranded at school and needs a refuge). To her wondering eyes it is "a big place...like a shop," radiating "Colour, light and warmth" in a neighbourhood she has never seen; its kitchen alone is "so big all of her aunt's flat would fit into it" (Lessing 63-64). Since this is *her first visit to a house,* she can hardly grasp that this is not the entire domicile: "Where are all the other people?" (69). Led upstairs, "flight after flight," to a bedroom, she still cannot believe that this "great empty house" contains only one family (70-71). The next morning she realizes that "the night had been like a door opening into prospects and places she had not even known were there" (73). And she feels a new desire: "I want my own room. I want my own *place*" (74). That wish "she brought into her own life from that night, which had been like a wonderland": that is, a *domaine.* Her life, though it will continue in the old way for a time, will never seem the same.

Years later, as a teenager, she "took a wrong turning" down a vaguely familiar street and there it was again, shocking because *that house* lived "in a part of her mind that corresponded to her dreams of it, floating in another dimension, nothing to do with the quotidian" (Lessing 75). But "the most extraordinary thing was that the house... was so close – only a short walk away" (76). Its dreamlike quality attests to the impact it had on her imagination as a *domaine perdu*: it once was lost, but now is found. While nursing her aunt through her final illness, Victoria would go look at the Staveney house when things were too depressing at home, and think "about what was inside. Space, room for everyone" (78). And still only one family! Amazing! Then the house shifts roles. At 19 Victoria is seduced there, not by Edward, the older boy who rescued her at school and took her home, but by his younger brother, Thomas, who fancies black girls. She goes through with it, though he seems "a stranger" and the house a "deception," smaller, colder, and shabbier than the image in her dreams and memory (90). Returnees to any *domaine* beware: you *may* go home again, but you risk disillusion. Ask *le grand Meaulnes.*

Another boyfriend takes her to a stage musical, which she later recalls "as she did the Staveney house, a vision into another world, beautiful," but one to which she did not belong (Lessing 100). The process of coming to terms with reality, of understanding the nature of her link to the *domaine*, has begun. "She had lived for years in a dream, she knew that now, thinking about that house...golden lights and warmth and kindness" (103). Clearly the Staveneys' world is not hers, but Victoria gradually realizes that caramel-coloured Mary, the love-child she conceived with Thomas, *can* cross over to "that other land"; once introduced, the Staveneys adore her (113). Over time Victoria half-consciously, half-willingly finds herself "losing Mary to the Staveneys" and the wider opportunities they offer: better schools, higher society (116). How could she not want all that for her sweet daughter? The rest is foreseeable: "Victoria would say yes" to a boarding school "and that would be that" (128). It will be a richer life for Mary than *she* could provide. Of course it will be hard on Mary for awhile, caught "in the middle" between the maternal and paternal worlds; she will feel that tension, will "want to be a Staveney. ...That is what will happen" (129). So "What sort of luck had [it] been" that Edward brought her home, or that Thomas seduced her? (103) It had given her Mary, and then (gently) taken her away. Had her stumble into their world been "lucky or unlucky," then? That is not a question that Lessing will answer.

"Victoria and the Staveneys," then, is another ambiguous, multi-faceted *domaine*, with aspects of the estate, culture, and love subtypes. In the same volume, "A Love Child" also works this last vein, tracing a sensitive English soldier's years-long obsession with finding the child he thinks he begot during a wartime stopover in Cape Town, and with the mother, remembered as the great love of his life. But the fullest, most extreme love-*domaine* in the book is the title story, "The Grandmothers." Lessing's camera-eye narration initially discloses two middle-aged grandmothers, Roz and Lil; their sons, respectively Tom and Ian; and their granddaughters, Shirley and Alice, picnicking at a table outside a cliff-top restaurant overlooking the ocean. All six are fair-haired and handsome. The two mothers, who arrive at the end of the scene, troubled or angry, brandishing a packet of letters and reclaiming the girls, are dark-haired. We do not fully understand that scene until the end of the story, most of which is a long flashback.

Roz and Lil grew up as neighbours, bonded as schoolgirls, married in a double wedding, bore sons in the same week, and soon had marital troubles. Roz's Harold felt excluded by the women's close friendship; Lil's Theo liked having affairs. Roz and Harold separated, he moving to another town. Lil and Theo divorced, and he died in a car crash. So the boys grew up mostly fatherless, and lived in a close-knit quartet. By the time they reached their mid-teens they were as handsome as "young gods," with a "poetic aura," and their mothers were still wearing bikinis (Lessing 20). One day the "good-looking women" (raising boys "so beautiful" that Roz and Lil would "look at each other, sharing incredulity") found a photo album with old pictures of themselves. When the boys saw it, they pronounced their present mothers "better" (22). Ian blushed to say that. He had been "disturbed" since his father's death, and would seek out Roz (on whom he had "a crush") when he had crying fits. Tom – a joker, a regular guy – was untroubled. So the physical attraction was acknowledged, they were all old friends living opposite each other, and soon after, without discussion, Roz awoke to find that Ian had "blundered" into her bed, and the next night Tom followed Lil home (25). This is classic – older women instructing young men – and not *really* incest, but since each of the boys was used to thinking of his new-found lover as a "second mother," it was close enough to produce a *frisson* of guilt-tinged excitement.

This arrangement worked for a while. The boys improved: Roz was "quietly proud" of having "made a man of" Ian, Tom grew more "thoughtful," and both were "protective" of the women (Lessing 32). All loved their *domaine*, but Lil was "so happy it made her afraid. 'How could anything possibly be as wonderful?' she whispered." Roz knew that she meant "such an intense happiness must have its punishment," for this love "dare not speak its name." Interested girls began to hang around, and surely the boys would "soon get bored with the old women and go after girls their own age." As "Time passed," Lil had a serious suitor, whom she put off until he married elsewhere. The women discussed what to do "when the boys get tired of us" (36). They were working now, Ian in his mother's sports shop, Tom in the theatre. He was still "charming with Lil, and as often in her bed as he could, considering," but she saw it as "a beginning" of neglect. Tom went to the town where Harold lived, directed a play, and met a girl, Mary, but soon felt "imprisoned," "restless, ...moody," and took long walks in the desert at night, alone (40). On one of them he realized why "I'm so unhappy" (41). He told Mary to leave him alone, walked deeper into the desert, and lay on a rock murmuring "Lil... he was missing Lil, that was the trouble." He wrote letters to her, then came home, but Mary followed him, wanting clarification.

Roz and Lil saw that their cosy arrangement was over. Mary announced her engagement to Tom. The mothers told the boys that they really *must* stop. Ian was furious: just like that?! Tom married Mary, who was soon pregnant. Ian, disconsolate, surfed recklessly, smashed on the rocks, damaged his spine and was left with a limp. This might be a moral judgment, or karma. Then Hannah, a friend of Mary, came to nurse Ian. They also married, and conceived. The couples took over the two homes; Roz and Lil bought a beach house together and wept for the beauty that had flown. When Roz said, "It has turned out all right," Lil replied, "I suppose so" (Lessing 49). "What more could we expect?" asked Roz.

> *"I didn't expect to feel the way I do," said Lil. "I feel..."*
> *"All right," said Roz quickly." Let it go. I know. But look at it this*
> *way, we've had..."*
> *"The best," said Lil. "Now all that time seems to me like a dream. I*
> *can't believe it, such happiness, Roz"... (49)*

"I know," cried Roz, tears trickling from under her sunglasses. "Well – that's it." But will regret and personal sadness expiate the liberties they have taken? In short, No. Ian blames the women for rejecting them, and unsettles the others. Hannah and Mary, finding their family life unfulfilling, decide to start a business. They go off with their babies for a weekend, allowing the quartet to assemble for the first time in a good while. It is tense, confrontational, with the women crying, Ian insisting that "nothing has changed" and Roz saying that "It's finished" (51-52). Clearly it is *not* finished and everything *has* changed. The strains show. Mary becomes suspicious: "There's something *there*" (55). Hannah has heard Ian call Roz's name in his sleep.

Hannah accepts Ian's innocence, but Mary is not so sure. Why is she uneasy? "I have everything," she assures herself (Lessing 56). "But then, a voice from her depths – I have nothing," and "waves of emptiness swept over her. In the deep centre of her life – nothing, an absence." Now living in Tom and Roz's old house, Mary finds a "bundle of letters" written while Tom was away. Those from Lil to Tom look harmless, but an unposted one from Tom to Lil gushes, "I think of you all the time, oh my God, Lil, I love you so much, I dream of you...I love you I love you..." and pages more. Lil's letters look less innocent now, and Mary "understood everything." Those are the letters she brandishes when she arrives at the cafe in the first scene, reducing the lovers to silence. Mary takes the little girls' hands, tells the four that they will never see them again, and descends to where Hannah is waiting. The four make no defence; they can only bicker. "It's all your fault this has happened," Ian tells Roz, and she laughs ("hard angry bitter") as tears roll down her cheeks (10). But down the path Mary and Hannah hear it as "hard... triumphant laughter,...harsh loud...cruel," and Mary says "Evil." This does sound like a moral judgment. The quartet dared to enter the *domaine* of forbidden sexual freedom, *des jeux interdits*, and enjoyed them to the full. Now Mephistopheles has come for them.

Or did the quartet really *want* the young mothers and children out of the way so that they could resume their *ménage á quatre*? While Lessing does not rule out that possibility, I do not think that "The Grandmothers" encourages it. The ending's punitive content may have surprised some devotees of Lessing's early, apparently permissive work – but one can argue with that reading of *The Golden Notebook*. An early reviewer wrote that Anna Wulf "tries to live with the freedom of a man" – foreshadowing *Sex and the City* – but how "free" *are* her "Free Women"? Does that repeated label not become ironic? In any case, authors grow and change. Lessing seems to take a pragmatic line here, acknowledging that some laws do govern human relationships. "The fundamental things apply...." Mary, Hannah, and their daughters are not guilty, yet they will be punished, too. "Victoria and the Staveneys" and "A Love Child" also exhibit biological and psychological realism: action A leads inexorably to outcome B. You may go with the flow, but there is no guarantee about what lies downstream.

THIS CHAPTER PRESENTS EXAMPLES OF *domaines* somewhat less travelled-by on the spectrum of (mainly western) literature. Each has venerable antecedents that with world enough and time could be explored at greater length. But *domaines* are quite individual, even unique, and may be peculiar to cultures and communities (see Chapter 10), so the number of variant types is unwieldy. Though I have confined myself to the "main" avatars here for practical reasons, the reader is under no such constraint. Once equipped with the definition, you will find your own examples – some of which may modify the definition I have suggested.

PART THREE:

BROADENING

CHAPTER 10:

Testing the Archetype

Notes on World Literature

In the Introduction, I described the time machines and *domaines* that may help explain why we write and read literature as "archetypal," "global," and "universal." *Universe* has a daunting scale, especially these days, with gravitational waves from black-hole collisions arriving from billions of light-years away and ago, but even earthly terms must submit their credentials, and will lack credibility until illustrated or qualified. There has been little testing of my thesis on "non-western" texts thus far. (The "literary world" in which I grew up was western. "Literature" usually connoted the Anglo-American variety; "World literature" meant adding Europe and the Levant. As late as 1980 the popular *Norton Anthology of World Masterpieces* went no farther east than Homer and the Bible: beyond that you were referred to *Masterpieces of the Orient*.) While my acquaintance with "world literature" is modest, I present here some tentative excursions into that much wider field. The emphasis is on whether literary *domaines* and time "machines" do occur on a global scale, and if so in what forms and colours, rather than on what other roles, functions, and uses of literature appear there. Yet when unexpected guests show up on such occasions, they are to be welcomed. Sometimes they turn out to be relatives.

The temporal and geographical scope of non-western literature is at least as extensive and intimidating as that of the traditions on which I have been drawing. Its origins are most likely in the Sanskrit *Ramayana* and *Mahabharata* from the Indian subcontinent. Romesh C. Dutt, who translated parts of both (still quoted by Salman Rushdie), called them the *Odyssey* and *Iliad* respectively of ancient India and Hindu epic (154). We grasp at familiarity: these long poems about ancient heroes or demigods impressed their first important English interpreter as the eastern equivalent of Greek epics; both transmitted the real or imagined actions of distinguished ancestors to (initially) their descendants, then to their culture and the world. Thus they preserved the past for the future: i.e. they acted as literary time machines. Tradition credits Valmiki (3rd-4th century BCE, who appears in the *Ramayana*) as the poet, but his role is as provisional as that of "Homer." Valmiki probably compiled his poems from various materials dating back to ca 1000 BCE, describing still earlier events (156). As for the nature of his epics, they are "recollections of the golden age," says Dutt – that is, they preserve a shining *domaine* from the cultural past, when time was young and things were better, or at least bigger.

But that is to oversimplify the ancient Indian epics, which are more like the shadowed *domaines* of Alain-Fournier, Fowles, and other moderns. *Ramayana. Epic of Rama, Prince of India*, does open with a *domaine* of glorious ancient times, just and happy, albeit with polygamy and castes. In Book I (Dutt's "book structure" being a bow to Graeco-Roman epic), Ayodhya is an eminently righteous city. At Mithila, Rama wins Sita's hand by stringing the bow of Rudra as demanded by her father King Janak (much as Odysseus does on his return to Ithaka). Valmiki's accounts of wedding preparations and festivities describe superb royal courts, elevated manners, and due ceremony as four noble marriages are celebrated. Thus far we have an idealized world and characters, but the idealization is transitory. Already in Book II, joy yields to grief as "dark intrigues" at court cause Rama to be banished for fourteen years. This darkness (arising from an old promise too rigidly honoured) reveals that the *domaine* of Book I was only an appearance: a splendid moment, not the whole story. Book III follows Rama and Sita into exile in the forest, where they meet St Valmiki. Rama's father, King Dasa-Ratha, dies, and Rama's brother Bharat comes to ask Rama to return as king. No, says the prince: my sentence has not expired! He chooses a personal code of honour as his *domaine*. Rama goes deeper into the jungle, wandering in South India with Sita and another brother, Lakshman, often reminiscing nostalgically about home. Eventually, after Rama rejects the advances of a demon-princess from Ceylon, her demon-brother King Ravan has Sita abducted.

Now action scenes become prominent. South Indian allies help Rama recover Sita from Ravan's palace on Ceylon. Ravan declares war on Rama, but with Vishnu's help (Ravan is an enemy of the gods), Rama's forces invade Ceylon, defeat Ravan, and kill him. Then Sita is required to prove her chastity during her imprisonment by undergoing the ordeal of fire! It is difficult to ascertain whether that episode appeared in the original, or was a later addition (a problem with which Biblical scholars are familiar). Sita and Rama return to Ayodhya in an aerial car lent by the gods (an episode used by some to argue that ancient peoples mastered levitation). Dutt's Book XII, considered a "supplement," is another blot. The people again murmur against Sita, and Rama sends her away, pregnant, into the forest, where she is again sheltered by Valmiki, and bears twins. Years later, they come to a festival and recite the *Ramayana*, which Valmiki has written for them. Rama is moved, recognizes them as his sons, and sends for Sita – to come and prove her purity again! She does come, but is so heartbroken by the demand that she asks Earth to take her back. It yawns opens and does so. This scene may be another gloss by later patriarchal moralists, but it is still a sad decline from the *domaine* of Book I and Rama's "code of honour." At the end, descendants of his family found the great Indian cities.

Dutt's epilogue calls this a "domestic" poem. What he meant becomes clear when we read its martial companion-piece in Hindu / Sanskrit antiquity, the *Mahabharata* (Epic of the Bharatas): a gigantic work compiled from legends about a great war. It dwarfs the *Ramayana*, and is about ten times the length of the *Iliad* and the *Odyssey* combined. Written in roughly the same period as Valmiki's epic, it may recount much earlier events. The *Mahabharata* was a popular ("of the people") poem, transmitted orally by bards for centuries; it probably evolved in the manner of folk songs, acquiring various layers in successive periods, so that the original poem became encrusted with additions from later poets with different agendas. The earliest written version is attributed to Vyasa, like Valmiki also a character in the poem. This huge compilation struck early western readers as chaotic. In outline, it traces the struggle between the Kaurava and Pandava families for the throne of Hastinapura, culminating in the Kuruksetra War and the Pandavas' victory (all of questionable historicity.) Although the heroes, like Homer's, have links to the gods, the tone differs from either Greek epic or the *Ramayana*. It is a very political poem, whose characters (said to be based on real people) are clearly not idealized in most cases. It ends with the death of Krishna and the onset of the Fourth Age of Man: a period of decline from noble characters to sobering examples of moral decay. The *Mahabharata* preserves the past, as epics generally do, in this case by chronicling the *loss* of a golden age, an earlier (mainly implied) *domaine*.

Considered more closely, the contents support this view. Initially we are introduced to some principal characters at a tournament, so a competitive edge exists from the beginning, albeit governed by rules here. Then, as early as (Dutt's) Book II, we begin to encounter jealousy, anger, and attempted murder. Books III and IV disclose many a "dark scheme": treachery, cheating, gambling, and banishment. There is some relief in Book V – gods appear; many Hindu tales and legends are retold – but Book VI features cattle-stealing, Books VIII and IX describe war and fighting, and Book X narrates single combats. Finally the war ends, so Book XI focuses on funeral rites. Dutt's Book XII is a didactic supplement to the epic, no longer concerned with the fates of individuals but rather with law-giving, death, and heaven; it bears the marks of a later insertion, perhaps by a priestly author or authors. In his epilogue, Dutt hailed the *Mahabharata* as not only "an encyclopedia" of ancient India treasured by millions of Hindus, but as Asia's "greatest work of imagination" (324). Scholars of Indian epics often liken their influence to that of the Bible, Shakespeare, Homer, and the *Quran*.

Rooted in Africa

It is instructive to set these ancient Indian examples beside a much later entry in the "oral heroic epic" category produced by a totally distinct culture in West Africa. We are fortunate to have two recitals of the Malinke legend of Sunjata or Sundiata (d. 1255), founder of the Mali empire, as chanted by modern bards, Bamba Suso and Banna Kanute. Its historicity, like that of the old Indian epics, is unclear; it has been transmitted orally since the thirteenth century, evidently with the usual epic intention of preserving the heroic deeds of the past for the future. In 1970 Gordon Innes began recording and transcribing the two Gambian *griots* (bards) performing the story, which eventually led to *Sunjata. Gambian Versions of the Mande Epic*, edited by Lucy Durán and Graham Furniss. The editors describe the Sunjata material as "one of the world's major oral epic traditions" (xxiii). In Mande culture, middle-class *jalis* (itinerant bards) sing the stories and lineages of free-born nobility. These bards, like the Greek tragedians, could assume their audiences' familiarity with the plot and characters of the saga, which evokes the "glorious past, heroic behaviour, and moral values" of Mande culture (xxix): a *domaine*, then, as time goes by.

Bamba Suso gives the shorter, bare-bones version, beginning with a recitation of the principal names and families. Sunjata's father, S.M. Konte, married Sukrelung the Ugly because a soothsayer said, "She's the one." After a seven-year pregnancy, Sunjata was born (heroes from Hercules to John Henry have had extraordinary beginnings), but he was far from precocious, crawling until he was 7. Finally Sukrelung helped him to stand; then he was circumsized and put on (altered) royal trousers. When his father died, the only asset Sunjata kept was his *griots*. Anticipating trouble, his brothers had sorcerers persuade Sunjata to go into exile. First he passed a major test, pulling a ring from hot wax; other marvels followed. After he went away most of his brothers were killed, but once Sukrelung died, the youngest came to summon him back (as Bharat did Rama) to be king of Manding. Sunjata complied, cutting off a piece of his own calf to feed his starving companions en route. Back in Manding, Sunjata summoned the leading tribesmen to battle, but avoided fighting his arch-enemy Susu Sumanguru until his friend Tira Makhong arrived. Meanwhile Sunjata's beautiful sister went privately to Susu to discover his secrets, such as how to kill his father, a *jinn* or evil spirit; then escaped and reported to her brother. When battle was eventually joined – Sunjata and Tira against Susu – the friends killed the *jinn* and Susu, took the town, and Sunjata was made king.

Banna Kanute's *Sunjata* also opens with genealogy, but is longer, more circumstantial, and some of its details differ from Bamba Suso's. Here Sunjata's mother was quite old, had lost forty sons in one war, and had not lived with Sunjata's father for twelve years, but after her great losses God made her "as 14" again and she conceived Sunjata. The father died in the seventh month of her pregnancy, leaving the widow destitute. A prophecy about a dangerous baby led King Susu to imprison all women of child-bearing age for seven years and have all male infants slain (as King Herod ordered the murder of infants in the New Testament). Sunjata's mother responded by remaining pregnant for fourteen years. In this version, Sunjata's sister slept with the spirit king. A ram belonging to the (unborn) Sunjata defeated King Susu's ram in a contest. When at last Sunjata was born, his mother dug a hole and put him in it with a "steamer" on top so he could breathe.

At age 12, Sunjata was still sitting in a hole in the back yard, yet at 13 he was seen by the king as a threat, and at 14 he demanded to be circumcised. His mother went to King Susu for help! He ordered iron staffs made (presumably to help Sunjata rise), but they buckled. The king's diviners warned that Sunjata was dangerous. When his mother needed a baobab leaf for his circumcision couscous, Sunjata pulled himself up, reached into a tree and laid a leaf of it at his mother's door. Susu visited him, declared his enmity, and decided to kill him, but Sunjata's sister's spirit-king lover warned her, and flew Sunjata to the king's wash-place with a sword. Sunjata had a *griot* sing there; then the spirit-king returned Sunjata and his sister to the circumcision area. People were now saying, "Sunjata has come," so Susu attacked the family and captured Sunjata, who escaped and raided the king. A *hajji* brought Sunjata a spear, bow, and arrow. His sister asked Sunjata to join with her spirit king, but Sunjata instead tried to kill him for his xylophone! The spirit king disarmed him and gave him the xylophone. Sunjata cut the tendons of Susu's emissary. His sister went to Susu and offered to marry him, but, she said, there will be no sex until you tell me how to kill you. Susu complied! She then escaped and told Sunjata the secret. He had a crocodile and a black catskin brought to Manding, and fought the king. Their weapons shattered on each other's. Susu fled, Sunjata shot him with a cock's spur, and the king fell. *Griots* sang Sunjata's praise. He went on to rebuild Manding and reigned for seven years.

The editors call this a "major oral epic," but it is too often incoherent, jerky in its movements, and menial in its concerns to survive serious comparison with European epics, at least in translation (though we do not know how "Homer" would have sounded in its oral form). The narrative frequently appears to lack internal logic or comprehensible motivation, but allowance must be made for what outsiders cannot understand: the roles played by magic numbers and charms, the context of tribal traditions, etc. The *domaine* is nascent and marginal here, living in the magical aspects of Sunjata's youth, and in the listeners, who are assumed to know that he became a great king. And *Sunjata* discharges a prime function of epic, the overcoming of time, by preserving the story of an ancestor's heroic deeds for the admiration and edification of posterity. Of that role we have a well-known example. Alex Haley's *Roots. The Saga of an American Family* (1974) was first a best-selling, award-winning book, then a successful miniseries on public television, making it one of the most celebrated literary phenomena of the late twentieth century (and boosting the popularity of American genealogical studies). As it happens, Haley's own African roots were in Sunjata's territory, now (The) Gambia, to which his research led him. He and Sunjata might have been related. Haley's enslaved ancestor was named Kunta Kinte. Sunjata's father was S.M. Konte.

Readers familiar with the Sunjata epic will at times be rewarded in reading *Roots*. It makes references to the Mandinka hero himself – "the crippled, brilliant slave general" – as a "forefather," celebrated by *griots* and praised by Kunta Kinte's father (Haley 70). The deeds of Sundiata (Haley's preferred form) were a part of his village's education of young men. Later, enslaved in America, Kunta tries to escape, and thinks of Sundiata while spending the night hidden beneath a bush. Later still, hearing stories of Toussaint, the famous leader of a slave rebellion in Haiti, Kunta ranks him "second in stature only to" Sundiata (465). *Griots* are as important in *Roots* as in *Sunjata*, where they were the one part of his patrimony that Sunjata kept. Haley acknowledges his "immense debt to the griots of Africa," the oral libraries of the people (viii). In Kunta Kinte's time, they moved from village to village, reciting the central stories of the tribe; that was how Kunta first heard of Sundiata. In manhood training, they learned that "no harm to griots" was a rule of war (130). One of the greatest of them, bearing "The history of our people" in his gray head, came to Juffure, their village (133). Haley found that *griots* still existed in Gambia, "living, walking archives of oral history" (870). One of them, in reciting the history of Juffure, "remembers" when Kunta Kinte was taken by slavers: Haley's peak moment (876). In time he realized that his own relatives, who recited family traditions about its origins, had acted as his *griots* in America.

Griots are central to Haley's thoughts about time and history. Kunta Kinte was born in 1750 and lived into the early nineteenth century. Surprised alone in the forest and torn from the world he knew, transported to plantation slavery in the American south, illiterate, how could he and his story survive the ravages of time and enslavement? The African answer was the *griot*, in whose head the chronicle of his people was "carried to the future," and the *griot* would teach it to whole villages and to his son, who would teach his son, and so on, "so that the events of the distant past would forever live," without writing, until Alex Haley came to provide the written, American half of the equation (133-34). *Griots* are, then, time machines, discharging the preservative function that literature has had in lettered societies.

In the early chapters of *Roots*, where Haley is more creative writer than historian, young Kinta thrives in a warm, nourishing environment: parental and grandparental love, unspoilt nature in the nearby marshes, rich in birds, fish, and rice paddies. The surrounding country is fecund, especially after the rains, and provides grains, nuts, antelope, and berries to keep hunger at bay. The social fabric is intact; adults and children treat each other with respect. Thus Haley imagines a mostly happy, unalienated childhood for Kunta, but does not idealize it; eighteenth-century Gambia was no pastoral paradise. Nature did not always favour Juffure: the long rains could be a time of hunger bordering on starvation, and of illness, which superstition attributed to evil spirits. When people were dying and nought else availed, the village might resort to hiring an exorcist. And even as a child, Kunta Kinte heard stories about slavers – "hairy, red-faced...white men" – bogeymen who skulked in the jungle, hoping to carry off bad boys in their "big canoes" (Haley 27). In retrospect, though, the enslaved, shackled Kunta "thought of all of Juffure, ...he had never realized...how very deeply he loved his village" (280). "Don't it always seem to go," sang Joni Mitchell in *Big Yellow Taxi*, "That you don't know what you've got / Till it's gone" (1970).

Some Early Chinese Lyrics

Lyric poems – their topics and how they are treated – often provide insight into the authors' values and concerns. In a culture as old as China's, they can also be ancient. That *The Complete Works of Tao Yuanming* (365-427) even exist in the twenty-first century is fortuitous. Though Wang Rongpei's 2003 translation, mostly in heroic couplets, can be awkward and simplistic, it is quite intelligible. Tao was above all obsessed by the inexorably destructive passage of time. In "Matching a Poem by Secretary Guo" (so there was a community of poets), he professes to "yearn sincerely for the bygone day," implying that there had been some good times for him, apparently in his youth (Tao 19). Similarly, "The Course of Nature" laments, "Gone forever are the days of old" (41). We encounter more of this oppression in "Secretary Dai," "The Flesh, the Shadow & the Spirit," and "Back to My Former House": "Time flies.../...my life begins to pine" (129). In "On Restrained Passion," the speaker says, "I grieve that the prime of my life is vanishing" (221), again suggesting a happier past. Within "Four Miscellaneous Poems," #I and II agonize over that most intractable of problems: the unstoppable march of time. So in "Eight Miscellaneous Poems," #I counsels us to seize the day – snatch it away from time!

The pattern or design of what we have looks incomplete, and of course it is likely that over that span of time some poems were lost. There are passing mentions in Tao's lyrics of the "good old days," but good for whom, when, and in what way? Apparently before he began to write poems: he never evokes, let alone dwells on, his "prime." "A Letter to My Sons" (in prose) is telling: Born poor, he informs them, "I have led a wretched life since my childhood" (271). Was there, then, never a *domaine* for Tao Yuanming? No blissful memories of his youth with parents or friends, no discovery of self or other, no peak experience or lost Eden? Seemingly not, though some Sinologists describe him as a recluse who latterly found peace in nature (and wine). Many a western poet saddened by adult life has reminisced wistfully about a golden *temps perdu*, but that is only a distant, flickering idea in Tao. He is subjected to the gloomy reign of Time the Destroyer, and not consoled by what he once had – at least not in the poems that Wang has translated.

The Poetry of Li He (N.p.: n.pub., n.d., no pagination) initially seems to reinforce Tao's dominant mood. John Warden's introduction (he and Dai Daqi did the translation) says that little is known of Li He (790-816) apart from his 240 surviving poems, which reveal a man "obsessed with death" and the "shortness of life" (if we have his dates right, he lived as briefly as John Keats). #2 ("A song of silk threads") is already autumnal: "The leaves grow old on the willows..."; "Fallen petals dance in the rising wind." In #4 ("Two Poems of Reflection"), section ii bumps into mortality: "What's this? A white hair on the page?/.../so much for dreams of old age." By #12 the poet is "just an old man grubbing about for words and phrases./.../All a poet can do is grieve as the Fall winds blow." "Drums on Government Street" (#26) is an *ubi sunt* poem about the lover of a long-dead Emperor: "Cypress surrounds the tomb where Fei Yan's sweet bones are laid." Of two other emperors obsessed with immortality, Li He writes, "Like anyone else, their gleaming hair turned to dead rushes./.../Time and again up in Heaven the gods are laid to rest./But the dripping of the water clock goes on for ever." And #39,

"Chang Gu," describes some nearby ruins thus: "The spice walls crumble on the ancient palace./.../Worms chew the wood where there used to be singing; / there are wisps of colour where the dancers danced." As in Arnold Bennett, Time rules.

But Li also "takes us outside time," and is "attuned to natural beauty," says Warden. In #1 ("Li Ping plays the Harp"), the speaker is alive to the beauty of the scene *now*: "The light is clear on the mountains"/.../"Here at the heart of the country." His pages are dotted with fleeting *domaines*. "A Dream of Heaven" (#8) is not a dream, but flashes of union with the world, as in *haiku*: "Cloud towers gape, shafted by walls of white. /Jade wagon wheels in the dew, liquid light pooling." In #9 ("Up in Heaven"), "On the cassia trees in the jade palace the blossoms last forever" – "outside time" – and "a little green phoenix stands in a tong tree's shade." "Poems from my Southern Garden" evokes an orchard *domaine*: "Sturdy long-limbed girls clamber up the arching branches,/to feed the super silkworms of the King of Wu." Later, "Walking in the fields in the Southern Mountains" (#16), Li finds that the "woods and fields are radiant,/.../water in the pools is clear and deep...". #28 recalls "The Pleasures of Youth": drinking wine as "Willow branches brush the river with silken gold." In #36, "A Beautiful Woman Combing her Hair" walks "Down the steps to break off a sprig of flowering cherry." The focus of #37 is sharp: four lines, a lotus flower, and "A single mandarin duck / lands on the pond with a splash." And in "Chang Gu," Li observes "pale green light on the face of the brimming water. / Far off the mountains climb each other's backs"; at dusk "a lone crane stands dozing like a slender tower." These are moments that repay his subjection to time, which both gives and takes.

Lyrical poetry, like other forms of imaginative literature, often raises the question of the author's motivation. Besides lamenting time's passage and revisiting *domaines*, why do poets bare their souls? What moves authors to generate poesy? Vanity, ego? I have heard a published poet admit as much. But vanity is a lust for fame, a secular form of immortality, and thus another attempt to counter the wasting effects of time. An effort to make sense of the writer's own life? (John Cheever once confessed something like that to a university audience.) An antidote to misery, an endeavor to "write your way out" of emotional problems? This often seems to describe Li He (#18, "Give me a drink!"), and perhaps most poets have such moments. The trouble with that impulse is that it may strike readers as mere whining (Li's #23, 29, 30, etc.); at times Li can sound more pitiful than sensitive. He also tries to revive some historical figures (#35, "Song for General Lu"): another attempt at a time machine. Despite the difficulties of finding a clear answer, this is a question that we ought to keep asking.

Japanese Court Prose

Diaries occupy a unique niche in the history of literature. Though they are supposedly personal records of actions, thoughts, and feelings, not works of the imagination, most historians of the novel in western culture have asserted a connection between the two forms. Both evince an interest in preserving the surface details of daily life and exploring what lies beneath them. Every diary is a potential novel; many a novel germinated from a diary. Historically – in France, England, and America, at least – the rise of the novel was preceded by a period of increased interest in journal-keeping, as if proto-novelists were homing in on prose fiction. And who can say finally that a diary is *not* (partly) a work of the imagination – in some cases, a fevered one? Only the author, whom we often cannot trust to know or tell the truth on that point. Nor, in the case of Sei Shōnagon, who wrote at the end of the tenth century, can we request an interview. Nevertheless, I feel justified in discussing her diary as a preface to early East Asian novels.

Her entries were ostensibly not intended for an audience; they leaked out, to her professed regret (Sei #184-85) – not that accidental disclosure has ever diminished interest in private papers. Hers circulated first at court, and later found their way into print, first appearing in English in 1889. *The Pillow Book of Sei Shōnagon*, translated and edited by Ivan Morris (1967), is most convenient for English readers (a "pillow book" because her writing paper was supposedly intended for a pillow). It consists of notes on society and nature by a lady-in-waiting at the imperial court of Japan for a decade or so after the early 990s. Morris reports that Japanese readers prize the book for the purity of its style, and notes that its author (like most ladies-in-waiting) was of "the leisured class" (Sei 13-14; 102, n. 16). Japan was a rank-ridden society at that time, and Sei did not transcend this. She devotes pages to her pet peeves (40-50), and often comes across as spoiled. The first sentence of #39, for example: "Nothing can be worse than allowing the driver of one's ox-carriage to be poorly dressed" (78). Yes, a slovenly chauffeur can ruin your whole day, but "Nothing worse"? She grouches about *seeing* people of "low station" or "humble rank" (109-10), for "One needs a few companions of one's own class with whom one can chat congenially" (143, #77). By current western standards, Sei was a snob.

What then makes her worth reading for those without Japanese? The usual interest of a diary: preserving the writer's mind and time and place, like curios encased in glass. "We were overwhelmed by the whole delightful scene," she writes after walking with the Royals among blossoming cherry trees on a fine day. "Deeply impressed, I wished that all this might indeed continue for a thousand years" (Sei 35). Occasionally she laments the swift passage of time, as in "autumn's stolen up" (#140, 212, and n. 465). These are conventional responses, but her keen eye and ear for "*domaine* moments" is remarkable. These occurred daily at the imperial court, whose rituals were evidently constructed to create them. Sei was often moved by beauty, poetry, Royal strolls, trees in bloom, even a sliding screen. The moment might be musical: two flutes being played, one by His Majesty, and "as I observed..., I felt that I had never in my life been unhappy" (50). That might well be. In Sei's *domaines*, high-born, well-dressed, literate courtiers live ritualized days, have impeccable manners, appreciate natural beauty (a sunny morning after a night of rain; dew dripping from flowers and spider webs: #84, 148), and make appropriate literary allusions, quoting the right poem at the right time (#115, 185). Sei was initially awed by the Empress ("I did not understand how a being like this could possibly exist in our world": #116) and by the court (186, 188). She is a document in the history of Japanese emperor-worship and respect for hierarchy.

Sei was primarily an aesthete, which her position at court enabled her to be. On many occasions she responds sensitively to attractive dress (#121, 196) or natural beauty (#125, 200). Moonlight falling on bedclothes struck her as a literary stimulus ("on such occasions...people write poems": #141, 213). Her "pillow book" resembles what the Renaissance called a "conduct book," instructing courtiers in right behaviour and right feeling (e.g. #145). It has other facets as well, showing, for example, how superstitious the Japanese of that age were, obsessed with avoiding unlucky times, directions, etc. And though Sei was quite discreet, we may wonder how promiscuous the court actually was: all those flimsy screens, easily pushed or slid aside.... Were love affairs common, or were all those nocturnal comings-and-goings innocent?

One answer or set of answers exists in Murasaki Shikibu's *The Tale of Genji*, which depicts the intrigues of the Japanese court in the same period (ca. 1000). It is a problematical text in authorship, and has a frustrating reticence about naming its characters, yet Edward G. Seidensticker, who translated it, says that it is considered the apex of Japanese prose. The author, another court lady, apparently wrote only the first 41 chapters; chapters 42-44 are considered spurious, and the last ten may be by another hand. Perhaps this explains its wavering structure; at any rate, the last thirteen chapters tend to be disregarded or taken more lightly. But the entire work is addicted to periphrasis when it comes to the *dramatis personae*. Titles or offices may be used to identify them – the crown prince, the bishop, the nun – and women are often named for where Genji first encounters them or some association: the Rokujo lady, the Hitachi princess, the orange blossom lady, and so on, as if protocol or authorial discretion precluded naming them.

On top of these difficulties is the manner in which the story is told. *Wikipedia* states that *The Tale of Genji* "does not make use of a plot" – then provides an eight-paragraph summary under "Plot." "Plotless" would be a startling description of any novel, but is *Genji* a novel? In Augustan England, a "tale" was a free, loose narrative, lacking the shape and craftsmanship later demanded of a novel. Often *Genji* seems a "tale" in that sense, or perhaps a diary, recording the intrigues of the upper crust. We do not expect a diary to have a shape other than self-absorption, let alone a moral arc bending toward anything. Still, readers not familiar with classic Japanese texts may want to know what happens, or seems to happen, in the book.

Once the Emperor of Japan loved a "lady not of the first rank," a concubine resented by his other ladies; when she bore him the most beautiful of all his sons they resented her more (Murasaki 5). However, she died when Genji was only 3. The Emperor's grief annoyed his women, especially Kokiden, mother of his eldest son and hostile to Genji. Her son was made crown prince. The Emperor brought Genji to court (where foreign tutors praised his learning), but raised him as a commoner. Later the Emperor married Princess Fujitsubo, who resembled Genji's mother. Genji fell in love with her, but at 12 he married Aoi, a minister's daughter. Neither she nor many other lovers slaked his lust; he spent more time at court than at home. In north Kyoto he found Murasaki, who at ten resembled her aunt Fujitsubo. Later Genji took Murasaki to his palace to be raised as his ideal woman. He also slept with Fujitsubo, who bore him a son, Reizei (accepted as the

Emperor's). Reizei became crown prince and Fujitsubo empress. Aoi also bore Genji a son, then died, and Genji married Murasaki. When the Emperor died, his and Kokiden's son Suzaku took the throne. Kokiden took power, though, learned that Genji was sleeping with her sister, and had him exiled to remote Sama. There Genji slept with the Akashi lady, who bore him a girl. Suzaku, troubled by dreams, pardoned Genji, who returned to Kyoto. Reizei became emperor, learned that Genji was his father, and promoted him; turning 40, Genji declined the promotion. He took another wife, the Third Princess, whom his nephew Kashiwagi raped. She bore Kaoru, who was accepted as Genji's. Murasaki became a nun, but soon died, mourned by all.

That is a bare outline of the part of *The Tale of Genji* attributed to Murasaki Shikibu (a pen name). Its ambiguous trysts and serial affairs do not need the additions of later contributors, which mostly present the destructive philanderings of the next generation of Gengi's relations. What we could have used is more examination by the original author of her story. Genji's erotic pursuits – particularly of his stepmother Fujitsubo, who looked like his mother, and later of ten-year-old Murasaki, who resembled Fujitsubo – beg for psychosexual analysis. Why did the author give Genji's "ideal woman" her own (pen) name? And what do Genji's restless prowlings mean? He appears to have been bisexual (in one episode, failing to bed the woman of the house, he "pulls the boy down"), but he rarely seems to find satisfaction. And what are we to make of the book's social scene: high-born men roaming in search of unprotected or unresisting women? There is no overt critique. Does the mere narrative of a lopsided power structure and rampant fornication constitute an authorial judgment? She does not stand apart and deliver a verdict. Nor did the writer(s) who "finished" *Genji* help us there: they no more evaluated the society than she did.

So the "tale" could have given us more, but what it does give is interesting. Seidensticker notes that "a vaguely nostalgic air hangs over the narrative and... the setting is vaguely antiquarian. One of the things *Genji* means is that the good days are in the past" (x). Its wistful yearning for the bygone may have had autobiographical origins: Murasaki Shikibu came from a great family, her branch of which had fallen on hard times. The text also supports Seidensticker's feeling. In chapter 10, Fujitsubo's waiting women weep for the old days they shared; in chapter 35, Genji and the "Akashi nun" reminisce sadly about their youth. Back

at court, Genji helps arrange the Emperor's grand "fiftieth year" celebration, fea-
turing music. The principal concert, involving many of Genji's favourite ladies, is
described minutely and each performer appraised; Genji or his son Yugiri taught
them all. Yet Genji chooses that evening, with its rich gifts and overnight guests, to
lament the "decline" (three times on p. 605) of "the Good Law" and of musician-
ship. "Ours is a day of very sad decline," he says, which will continue. We recognize
this structure: the *domaine* of the unrecoverable past, when life was wonderful, or
at least better. What is odd is that the speaker's present seems as splendid as his
remembered past. Is not this well-planned, well-attended, harmonious celebration itself a *domaine* for which people will weep someday? Evidently good times
can still occur. Here Genji seems merely sentimental, mourning his lost youth.

The *Tale of Genji* does include *domaines* that are not specifically undercut or
denigrated. In chapter 23, the New Year observances at Genji's are superb. All are
in their finery, and the host basks complacently among "his ladies": Reikiden,
Tamakazura, the Safflower Princess, the Lady of the Locust Shell, and the Akashi
lady, who spends the night (in the morning Murasaki ignores his excuses). Genji
feels good about how he has treated each of them! Carolers arrive at dawn and sing
in the snow: a memory to be treasured. In the following chapter, when Murasaki's
spring garden peaks, she and Genji host a floral fest at Rokujo. Pleasure boats move
on the lake, musicians play, poetry is recited amid the blossoms. After dark, by
flarelight, more music is performed, including "How Grand the Day" and "Joy of
Spring." Guests are entranced, for "all seemed better here," and "a perpetual spring
radiance seemed to hang over" Rokujo (420). It is clearly a *domaine*, and thus
inherently brief. Transience rules; Genji's *domaines*, like Gatsby's, are parties, not
ways of life. In chapter 33 he is given new honours. The current and past emperors
pay a "grand" state visit to Rokujo, with arrangements of "unprecedented...com-
plexity" and "brilliant detail" (531-34). From brocaded galleries guests observe
military reviews, autumn colors, cormorants fishing, and dances; then listen to
music as they dine. Kotos are brought for the emperors and Genji to play. Earlier
festivities are recalled: a series of transient *domaines*.

Chapter 40 could be titled "The Last Party." Murasaki, weak and wasted by
disease, has wanted to take holy vows for some time, but Genji has said No. So
she has a thousand copies of the Lotus Sutra made; then arranges a "dedication"
to which many priests, royals, nobles, and friends contribute. The weather is fair,

cherry trees are in bloom, priests chant, and flutes play for dancing, but Murasaki is never up for long, and once the guests leave, Nijo House becomes a place of prayer and recitals of scripture. As Murasaki fails, empress Akikonomu visits with her children to say goodbye. Autumn is cooler, more comfortable, and Murasaki is lovely but thin. The empress comes to take her leave. Genji wishes they could live a thousand years, but knows that they are governed by time's "great, sad truth" (717). At dawn Murasaki dies. Mourners send poems or arrive to pay respects as she ascends to heaven in smoke. Her women are inconsolable. Genji, recalling her fondly, missing her already, speaks of taking vows himself, but holds back.

Complaints against time's tyranny are rare in *Genji*, but references to the concept of *karma* permeate most works written under Buddhist or Taoist influence – i.e. most classic East Asian literature. Part of the doctrine of reincarnation, karma affects how one thinks of time. In most western thought, a soul knows only one life; for some believers, our conduct will be rewarded in heaven or punished in hell. In the eastern system, rebirth (transmigration) of souls allows a plurality of lives, but it is pay-as-you-go. Karma is what our souls bring over from one existence to the next: a moral lift or burden, depending on how we behaved. It may even determine whether we are reborn as humans or as animals. Suffering is intelligible, and perhaps more tolerable, within a cyclical framework; it is a consequence of action, a cause-effect relationship (Eliade 98-100). *We* do not remember what we did in earlier lives, but something does, and reacts accordingly. That something is karma, whose influences we can infer if we observe closely. In *Genji*, when his mother bears the emperor his most beautiful son, it is taken as the work of karma: souls are being rewarded for merit in a prior life. This colours your sense of time and time's meaning. A Christian who lives a good life may hope for a heavenly hereafter. Buddhists and Taoists exist on a long sliding scale, influenced by deeds done in earlier lives, aware that today's choices shape the soul's future. For them, one must look both forward *and* into the deep past.

Karma permeates *The Tale of Genji*. In chapter 4 he has a shadowy amour with a calm, quiet, lower-class married woman whom he always meets in the dark, incognito. Obsessed with her, Genji wonders if karma is at work. He takes her to a strange, neglected villa where a demon-woman appears and frightens her – to death. Distraught, Genji summons his friend Lord Koremitsu, who (with the dead woman's assistant Ukon) takes the body to a mountain nunnery. Genji goes there to view the body one night and falls ill for three weeks. He interrogates Ukon about the (still unnamed) woman's background. (Learning that she had a young daughter, Genji wants to take her in.) This *could* be a case of bad karma – perhaps *she* did *him* wrong in a previous life, and the demon-woman was a karmic agent – but this cannot be known for certain.

This proof that clandestine love can be fatal does not deter Genji's rovings, however. Soon after, he contracts malaria, and while convalescing in the mountains peeps through a fence and sees a beautiful girl resembling Fujitsubo. His host, a bishop, says that her father is Fujitsubo's brother, Prince Hyobu. Genji requests custody of her! The bishop and his sister, a nun, say no; he must wait some years. Returning home, he writes to them all and sends Koremitsu to her nurse, Shonagon, but receives no encouragement. Fujitsubo is staying with her family; a meeting is arranged, during which she and Genji make love. He visits the nun in the city; gravely ill, she still opposes his suit. When she dies, the girl returns to the city. Genji visits Shonagon, talks to the girl, follows her to her bedroom and stays the night. The next day Prince Hyobu calls, wanting his daughter; he will come for her tomorrow. Genji goes there first, pushes his way in and *takes* the girl, despite objections. Shonagon comes along and stays with her. Murasaki – for it is she – weeps at first, but Genji, convinced of their "karmic connection," wins her over.

It would be difficult to argue from these two episodes that a belief in karma acts as a check on immoral or imprudent behaviour; Genji tends to use it for his own ends. Time brings him a darker perspective, however. In chapter 12, undergoing "reverses and afflictions," Genji considers retiring to remote Suma (219). This is often described as "exile," and Genji *is* out of favour at court, but his departure is represented as voluntary. He orders his affairs and says farewells, including a visit to his father-in-law and little son by Aoi. Genji has many regrets and strong feelings of karma – i.e. a belief that he is being punished – but this mood is transient. He tells Murasaki that he may send for her sometime, but does not ask her to come now. He also visits Fujitsubo before leaving for Suma and later Akashi, where he will impregnate "the Akashi lady."

There is a sustained example of karmic action toward the end of the author's original text (chapters 34-37). With Murasaki's health failing, Genji marries the beautiful but immature young Third Princess, which hurts his long-suffering wife: the original sin of this subplot. His nephew Kashiwagi marries the Second Princess, but lusts for the Third Princess. He persuades a maid to take him to her when everyone else is away. "And was that not a little extreme?" asks the narrator (613). The princess is "appalled" and "speechless." Finding her "gentle and unresisting," he stays the night (614). Both then come unhinged; she barely speaks as Kashiwagi blathers. He returns to his father's house, frightened by what he has done. The Third Princess tells her women that she is sick, which brings Genji – until word arrives that Murasaki has died. He hastens home to find confusion and wailing. But Murasaki is not dead, only possessed: a "malign spirit" is observed to jump from her to a little girl, called the "medium" (617). When she speaks to Genji, it sounds like his first wife, the neglected Aoi, evidently still angry post mortem. This would be an instance of domestic karma, doling out short- to medium-term punishment.

Kashiwagi, hearing that Genji has found a letter he wrote to the princess, is miserable. He has no self-confidence and cannot face the public, has "no wish to live" but ought not to kill himself, and it is too late to become a monk. "His own deeds were working themselves out" is a fair description of karma at work (636). In due time the Third Princess delivers a son about whom Genji has doubts; he allows some elaborate ceremonies, but "no music" (640). Seeing his coolness, the Third Princess wants to become a nun. Her father (the "old emperor") visits her and lets a priest cut her hair. That morning the "malignant spirit" emerges and says, You were too happy with Murasaki, so I stayed to see what I could do; now I'll go (644). Genji is horrified; Kashiwagi declines further. He hints to Yugiri about a problem between himself and Genji, and asks Yugiri to apologize for him. Kashiwagi dies soon after, shattering his family. Genji dutifully attends to the Third Princess and his new son's fiftieth-day celebration. Most guests seem innocent of the situation, but Genji squirms: the baby resembles his nephew. Who else sees this and is laughing at him? Yugiri, grieving, recalls what Kashiwagi said during their last visit.

Aftershocks continue. Yugiri mourns his friend, and becomes very attentive to his widow, the Second Princess. Genji tries to curb his anger, mourn, and be nice to his wife, but is obsessed by the boy's resemblance to Kashiwagi. Doubtless it had all "been predestined," yet that does not make it "more acceptable," and her "transgression" is "hard to excuse" (660). Predestination, or karma? Visiting the

Second Princess, Yugiri plays one of Kashiwagi's favourite pieces on the koto, and her mother gives him Kashiwagi's best flute. Back home, Yugiri dreams that Kashiwagi says of the flute, "I did not mean it for you" (663). A child screams and vomits; women scatter rice to placate spirits; his wife says he has brought home devils. Yugiri, seeing that the boy resembles Kashiwagi, tells Genji of his visit to the Second Princess, the gift of the flute, and his dream. Genji says "there are reasons why I should have the flute" (666). Yugiri tells him that Kashiwagi's last wish was to apologize to him. Genji sees that Yugiri suspects the truth, but holds back.

While we can infer that the rape of his wife contributed to Genji's depression and wish to retire, the author leaves the matter there. Yet further reverberations trouble her last chapters. Yugiri's obsession with the Second Princess hurts his wife Kumoinokari. She intercepts a letter from her to him, which she hides, but Yugiri finds it, writes an answer, and sends it to her at Ono. Her mother reproves the princess for this business, and wonders what she did in a past life to bring this on. Suddenly in great pain, the mother becomes comatose and chill. She dies quickly, troubled in mind. Her daughter clings to her; condolences pour in. Yugiri rides to Ono, arriving at the "worst possible moment," realizes that he tormented both women, and retreats (692). But the princess stays at Ono, silent, grieving, and Yugiri soon returns. Her reputation is ruined, he thinks, so "he might as well...have his way with her" (695). She will "pull herself together," he reasons, since "I am all she has left" (697). Sulking at home, he realizes that he is losing his senses. Genji hears of the affair, so like many of his own. Yugiri worries about his reputation but turns the local governor against the princess, forces her out of Ono, installs her in Ichijo house and demands entrance to her quarters, pushing through her maids. She locks herself in a closet, he retreats in tears – and so on, through a series of demeaning episodes, all stemming from Genji's genes and Kashiwagi's sin.

Two other themes come up even more often than *domaines*, time, or karma. They form a polar pair: Sacred and Profane. Eros – men lusting for women immured behind screens or glimpsed through gauze – figures in over half of Murasaki's chapters. Early on, virile young Genji, already married, hangs out with his married brother-in-law To No Chojo at the palace. In chapter 2 they have a long talk with two young courtiers about women and amours. At home, Genji finds Aoi cool, so he spends the night at the governor of Kii's house, pursuing a boy and a woman. When she resists, Genji "pulls the boy down." His treatment of Tamakazura, the beautiful lost daughter of To No Chojo, is symptomatic. Her mother is dead and she wants to see her father, so Genji brings her to his own mansion, where he hovers between paternal and romantic. He advises her on her suitors, but maybe "she was too good to let go" (425). Tamakazura is uncomfortable, sensing Genji's ambiguity, and keeps asking for To No Chojo. Murasaki is not fooled either, remembering other cases. Eventually he confesses to Tamakazura and takes her hand. She is confused – until he throws off his robe and pulls *her* down. Stunned, she weeps. Knowing that he is wrong, Genji accepts the rejection and withdraws, but writes to her. His keeping her from her father (his friend) and her suitors is indefensible, and he keeps flirting with other women – though by then Kashiwagi and Yugiri are even worse.

The contrary wish, to rise above carnal desires and take holy vows, is felt almost entirely by women. It surfaces when the "Rokujo lady," despondent over Genji's neglect, decides to go to the Ise shrine with her daughter, its new high priestess (ch. 10). Soon after, Fujitsubo, who wants Genji to protect her son but fears his passion, becomes a nun. This shocks the court, but similar desires (some acted on, some not) are voiced in about a quarter of Murasaki's chapters. Buddhism itself is discussed (ch. 13), and Genji is identified as a Buddhist. Toward the end this yearning spreads; chapters 34 to 40 have many examples. The past ("Suzaku") emperor's wish to retire and become a monk, yet not leave his daughters unprotected, prompts Genji to marry the Third Princess. Then Murasaki, Genji's wife, wants to become a nun. (He objects whenever she brings it up.) The Third Princess – Genji's other living wife – longs for a nunnery after she bears Kashiwagi's son. Genji can hardly fail to see a pattern here, and again says No, but her father is sympathetic, and the princess has her way, renovating her bedroom as a chapel. Ten of her serving women also take their vows. Genji deplores "this flight to religion" (671). He visits her often, expressing regrets and hinting that "he knew of her misdeeds." And she became a nun to escape him!

Reikeiden's daughter Akikonomu, whom Genji sponsored at court, also chooses to renounce the world. Sought by the Suzaku emperor, she was "awarded" to the new emperor (Fujitsubo's son by Genji), who "distributed his nights impartially" between her and another lady (309). She became the leader of the Plum Pavilion arts faction at court. Genji tries to talk her out of retiring, but believing that her "mother died carrying a heavy burden of sin," she feels obliged to pray and arrange prayers for her (675). Genji predictably deplores this action, too. As we saw, the widowed Second Princess, pursued by Yugiri, asked to stay at Ono as a nun, but he had her evicted and taken to Ichijo house, prevented her from cutting her hair, and forced his attentions on her. And when Gengi opposed Murasaki's desire to take vows, she had the Lotus Sutra copied and held a religious dedication as her farewell to society. Afterwards there were prayers and Buddhist readings. Not until she died did Genji finally let the priests cut her hair. The Lotus Sutra was read over her.

Clearly Murasaki (the author) meant for this contest of eros and spirituality to dominate her book; it outlasts the treatments of all other themes. Those who extended *The Tale of Genji* used this duality about as often as she does, yet the continuation does not show pious renunciation besting the pursuit of carnal pleasure, as Murasaki finally does. The added chapters follow the testosterone-driven assaults by Kaoru, Kashiwagi's son, and Niou, Akikonomu's son (a protégé of Genji), on the daughters of the Eighth Prince. In chapters 45-47 and 55-56 those women do seek nunneries, but only as a refuge from aggressive suitors. We are shown how much trouble the Eighth Prince caused by retiring early, leaving his daughters vulnerable. The results constitute a warning against fathers embracing monkhood, which Murasaki did not consider.

Confucius or Buddha?

Cao Xueqin's *The Story of the Stone* (aka *The Dream of the Red Chamber*) is another Asian blockbuster, one of "the four classics" of the Chinese novel. It is the longest novel I have read, 2480 pages in the Penguin edition – *War and Peace* plus *Gone With the Wind* – with dozens of major characters and hundreds of minor ones. The nearest approach to a plot summary is *The Dream of the Red Chamber* as retold by Wang Guozhen (N.p.: China International Press, n.d.), which reduces 120 chapters to just 31. Unfortunately it is short on coherence and transitions, as if Wang had just summarized selected paragraphs, and marred by English errors. A 1958 translation with the same title by Florence and Isabel McHugh (from the German of Franz Kuhn) is of more interest, particularly for Kuhn's introduction. He identifies the Confucian "core" story as the "self-destruction" of a noble, wealthy house

(Kuhn, xv): actually the two houses of a powerful clan. And why did they fall? He answers (giving textual support), because of weakness in the male line: Bao-yu, the only promising grandson, cannot be relied upon. This translation encourages the view that the parklike grounds of the estate constituted a *domaine* for its residents (*Dream* 27, 42).

But modern readers will want *The Story of the Stone* in five volumes (Penguin, 1973-86). David Hawkes translated the first three volumes, and his introduction to the first sketches the overall shape of the work. He also explains its nightmarish tangle of authors, texts, and titles, concluding that manuscripts of eighty chapters circulated for decades after Cao Xueqin's death in 1763. Yet the first printed edition (1792), edited by Gao E and Cheng Weiyuan, has 120 chapters, the last forty being "a supplement by an anonymous author" – probably the editors (Cao 1.18). It is not feasible to disregard the later additions this time: Cao's text was clearly unfinished; the final one-third is required to complete the plot.

Hawkes then attempts to make sense of the whole text. Volume 1 is titled "The Golden Days"; like Kuhn, he sees the subject as the apex and fall of the Jia clan. He calls it "a sort of Chinese *Remembrance of Things Past*" that is at least semi-autobiographical (22). Cao was poor in old age, he notes, and believes that a "vanished splendour" furnished "material for his 'Dream of Golden Days'" (23-24). Cao was 13 years old when his family fell on hard times; that was clearly traumatic. For Hawkes "There is no doubt" that Cao made "the history of his own family's decline and fall the general background of the novel," and that its characters are partly imaginary and partly the "real companions of his golden youth" (31, 45). Thus Hawkes's translation, like McHugh-Kuhn's, sees this as a lost-*domaine* novel.

There are two drawbacks to the Kuhn-Hawkes view. First, the novel is not *just* a decline-and-fall story: its shape is high – far down – reviving. Neither translator mentions that after the Jias tumble, they are restored to imperial favour, and repair most of their losses. True, the recovery narrative was not written by Cao, appearing only in the forty added chapters, but the translators accept those as integral to the novel. The force of the late recovery is somewhat weakened by the fact that while the Jias' fall is adumbrated by numerous premonitions over hundreds of pages – financial sloppiness, misconduct, murmurs of discontent, "The Warning Voice" – the reparation occurs suddenly, with almost no preparation. Virtually "out of the blue," the Emperor, reminded of the Jia clan's long, faithful service, decides to reopen their case. Given his quasi-divine status, it is a *deus ex machina* resolution, easy to contrive and insert.

It is also misleading to call the novel simply "Confucian," ignoring the super-natural frame around the social and domestic activity. Kuhn's formulation is cautious: the *Confucian* "core" is the Jia's "self-destruction"; the Buddhist, Taoist, and western perspectives would be different (xv-xvi). Confucius, the pragmatic, worldly-wise rulegiver for family and society, would agree with Kuhn that the fortunes of the Jia clan are the book's "core." But *The Story of the Stone* also presents many Buddhists, Taoists, priests, monks, and pious itinerants: transcendentalists with their eyes on a higher prize. The novel opens in Legendland. To repair the sky, the goddess Nü-wa melted rock and formed 36,501 blocks, each 72 by 144 feet. The extra one was left in the mountains, able to move and shape-shift, but ashamed not to have been used. One day a Buddhist monk and a Taoist came by. The rock shrank to a small lustrous stone, which the monk picked up, vowing to take it away and inscribe it. The stone was delighted to be used. Eons later the Taoist Vanitas found the stone, large again and inscribed, in the same place. Reading, he learned that it had once been a mortal, and found its life interest-ing. Vanitas copied it out and took it to a publisher, titling it *The Tale of Brother Amor* (his pen-name). Subsequent hands changed the title: Wu Yu-feng called it *A Dream of Golden Days* and Cao Xueqin *The Twelve Beauties of Jinling*, but one Red Inkstone "restored the original title when he recopied the book" (Cao 1973, 1.51).

The transition to our world occurs after an asterisk, where "The Story of the Stone" begins. At first it sounds like *Pilgrim's Progress*: in Carnal Lane off Worldly Way in old Suchow lived Zhen Shi-yin, a quiet man over 50, his wife Feng-shi, and their daughter. One day while reading he dozed off and dreamt of a monk and a Taoist talking about what to do with a stone. The monk wants to give it "a taste of human life" (Cao 1.52). Stone has already wandered to the Land of Disenchantment, fallen for Crimson Pearl Flower, and watered her with dew, allowing her to become a girl. The fairy Disenchantment will send her and other "amorous young souls" to our world, where the monk is sending Stone (1.53). He and the Taoist will go, too. They show Zhen a beautiful jade. He starts to read its inscription, but they cry "Here we are!" and disappear into The Land of Illusion with Stone (1.55). Waking, Zhen takes his baby daughter outside. Down the street come...a monk and a Taoist. The monk asks why he is holding "that ill-fated creature" who will bring him bad luck. He offers to take her, but Zhen refuses. The monk intones cryptic, sinister verses, and they depart. A poor student from the temple next door, Jia Yu-cun, whom Zhen supports, appears and is invited to tea, but Mr Yan arrives and Zhen has to see him. Left alone, Jia notices Zhen's attractive young maid in the garden, and she him. Yan stays, so Jia leaves, as the mystic gives way to the worldly.

All of these characters reappear, hundreds or thousands of pages later; the novel's towering structure forgets no one and uses everything. The Stone becomes Bao-Yu, our chief protagonist; Crimson Pearl Flower is his beautiful cousin and *inamorata* Dai-Yu; the baby daughter is lost, and found much later. Jia Yu-cun is a link to *the* Jia family, the Buddhist and Taoist recur at intervals, and so on. Most of the book transpires in the Jia mansions in the capital, but it occasionally jumps to another plane of existence or receives extra-worldly characters. Near the end the frame reappears: Bao-Yu, his "earthly karma...complete," strides off in the snow with the Buddhist and Taoist, all singing of "the Cosmic Void," watched helplessly by his earthly father (Cao 1986, 5.359-60). The Jias' disgrace is cleansed, and various sages impart wisdom, especially Zhen Shi-yin, who turns up as a Taoist hermit in chapter 120 to inform his old protégé Jia Yu-cun that "The Land of Illusion and the Paradise of Truth are one and the same" (5.371). Kuhn was right: the Buddhist and Taoist perspectives on the novel's action differ sharply from the Confucian.

To press farther into the "core" plot is to enter a jungle. Its various themes come and go from book to book, giving the work its shape. The first volume supports the McHugh-Kuhn thesis, echoed by Hawkes, that the work traces the decline of a great family owing to a lack of male talent. En route to the capital, Jia Yu-cun runs into Leng Zi-xing, an antique dealer whom he knew in Beijing, and asks for news. Leng reports an "unusual event" in your clan, the Jias (Cao 1973, 1.72). Imagine, a baby born with a jadestone in his mouth! Jia says we have no connection with that "exalted" branch, but Leng replies that they are now "greatly reduced" (1.73-74). Then in a dream-scene (chapter 5), the Fairy Disenchantment reveals that the dukes of both Jia houses have asked her to help their family by tutoring Bao-yu, the jade-born boy; she will show him the illusory nature of fleshly pleasures. Singers and dancers perform "A Dream of Golden Days," whose songs have titles like "Mistaken Marriage," "Hope Betrayed," and "Mutability" (1.140); their themes include parting, grief, an abusive spouse, and the transience of earthly glory. Several describe the Jias' case: "The ruin of a mighty house," "weakness in the line" (1.144). Thus are the main themes of the novel introduced: a family ripe for decline, danger signs visible to the observant, and a supernatural level of being, accessible to some through dreams or spiritual practice.

The second volume continues these concerns, concentrating on Bao-yu as he passes from infancy through boyhood and his character and personality emerge. Is he the "worthy young male" that the family clearly needs? Those are high expectations, not easily met. There is dramatic irony in the situation: we know, and his family does not, that Bao-yu is the incarnation of a magic stone intended for the heavens. The Jias are dedicated Confucians, prizing social conformity and success in practical studies. We, like Taoists, possess higher knowledge and can see farther. Bao-yu is pampered (as are all the young people in both mansions, with their maids and a wealth of food, goods, and games). Some relatives worry that he is effeminate: spending his time with the girls, interested in their clothes and cosmetics, weeping easily, and preferring their pursuits. His cosmic origins were neuter, so a bipolar gender is likely enough, nor are there many boys to play with. His worst problem is his father, Jia Zheng, a strict, classically-trained Confucian, a government official and harsh disciplinarian. The two clash often, with Jia Zheng always demanding too much. The worst incident is a false accusation of rape made against Bao-yu by his half-brother. Jia Zheng, believing it, flogs him into unconsciousness. Only the intervention of his mother saves him. Behind Jia Zheng's rage are the fears about the weakness of the male line and the family's future.

Time and *domaines* are also subjects of significant interest in volume two; they bear on the family and its decline. These are not philosophical discussions of time, and there are few laments over its relentless passage (we are mostly among the young). Dai-yu's song rejoices that spring finally came, yet "grieved it so soon was spent" (Cao 1977, 2.39). What we *are* given is detailed lists of things, trivia, whose only purpose can be to preserve the physical surface of eighteenth-century China for future generations: another time machine. Why else go on and on about "two little boxes of lacquer and bamboo bastketwork" in which the maid puts "foxnuts and caltrops in one and a saucerful of chestnut fudge (made of chestnut purée steam-cooked with cassia-flavoured sugar) in the other" (2.230)? A recipe! Why else devote a page to what Xiang-yun was wearing when she arrived, or a paragraph to what Bao-yu put on the next day: the "elegant rain-hat" that the prince of Beijing gave him and his "pear-wood pattens" (2.479, 481)? *The Story of the Stone* is an historical novel; it takes us back, and it acknowledges karma. When Bao-yu and Dai-yu quarrel, Granny Jia grumbles, "It must be my punishment for something I did wrong in a past life" (2.91). And if Charmante releases a caged bird, it will be an "act of merit" that "will help [her] in the next life" (2.209). Other such remarks, serious or casual, are sprinkled through that volume.

Domaines figure variously in that volume. Bao-Yu, reaching adolescence, already misses his idyllic childhood. He and Dai-yu were close then: "I was your faithful companion.... We slept in the same bed" (Cao 2.43). Those were the days! But now she has "grown more touchy.... You spend all your time brooding." In Bao-qin's poem "The Land of Ebenash," the "foreigner" is nostalgic for a lost island with "marble halls" and "mists about its mountain forests": "...still my heart yearns for that distant South, / Where time is lost in one eternal spring" – blending the themes of a charmed time and a wondrous place (2.541). Ironically (and typically), the settling of young people in the Garden, each in a distinctive cottage, becomes a *domaine*, not clearly recognized as such until they have to leave it. In its heyday, the Garden is a high-end commune in which well-born youth, educated in Confucian culture, attended by maids, play games testing each others' minds. They pose one another riddles whose answer may require minute knowledge of Chinese literature (2.508 ff). A favourite reference is *The Western Chamber Romance*, of which more later. They also read, recite, and compose poems, often adapting classical themes or forms. The name of this volume, "The Crab-flower Club," is that of their poetry society. So they live at a high cultural level, as if trying to justify their privilege. The rituals associated with ancestor worship and the New Year are described in detail; they too constitute *domaines* for young and old alike in the Jia clan.

In the third volume the balance shifts. Time, karma, and weak males are still mentioned, but danger signs proliferate. "The Warning Voice" is an apt title, though "Warning Voices" would be more accurate. The pragmatic Wang Xi-feng, a daughter-in-law and the family's business manager, tells a maid that it's "like riding a tiger," for despite the economies she has introduced, "our expenditure is still far above our income": the volume's Dickensian theme (Cao 1981, 3.62). Bao-chai, another of Bao-yu's cousins (eventually his wife), knows that "we are less well off than we used to be" (3.109). Even celestial, unworldly Dai-yu has "made a few calculations" and discovered that "We are all *much* too extravagant. ...our expenditure is vastly in excess of our income" (3.206). The lavish funeral for Jia Jing further strains the family's resources, and authority figures are not alert. When Jia Zheng returns from a distant posting as an education officer, he is "determined to relax," and refuses "even to think about money" (3.394). Some Jias are already cash-poor, and the long celebration of Granny Jia's eightieth birthday prompts Xi-feng to repeat her mantra: expenses exceed income! The steward says that "too big a staff" is one of their problems (3.431). Now the Jias seem a house of cards, threatened by money-wrangles, servant disorder, borrowing, stealing, hocking and redeeming, even food strictures. One sign of decadence is gambling parties with cross-dressing male prostitutes.

By the time the supernatural element enters, three-quarters of the way through the volume, it may seem superfluous or belated, but is nevertheless a show-stopper. During a Mid-Autumn Festival celebration, "suddenly a long-drawn-out sigh was heard from the foot of one of the garden walls" (Cao 1981, 3.498). Hackles rise around the tables. All hear it, followed by the sound of a door opening and closing inside the empty Hall of the Ancestors. Though that is all the "warning voice" has to convey, it is eloquent: the party is over. Melancholy flute music and poetry accompany the next night's family gathering, which Granny Jia pronounces sadly shrunken – another symbol of their attenuation. The few remaining chapters of this pivotal volume are in the same key: the society that made the Garden a *domaine* is beginning to break down, and Bao-yu, a teenager now, is increasingly depressed by the gradual loss of his youthful delights.

The warnings continue in the fourth volume. During a scare over the health of Yuan-chun, the Jias' prized "Imperial Concubine," Granny Jia has a dream about her in which she says, "Prosperity may all too soon be spent; draw back, draw back before it is too late" (Cao 1982, 4.147). And there are more signs of decline. The two sides of the family – Rong-guo and Nin-guo – are now feuding, not cooperating. Disorder grows: fighting among servants and humbler members of the clan. Money troubles worsen. Xi-feng knows that "behind our magnificent façade things are going from bad to worse" (4.83). Jia Zheng tells his wife that Bao-yu (their son) is loafing and *must* shape up. "If *he* should fall by the wayside, the whole future of the family could be threatened" (4.44). They still do not know that he is other-worldly. Several family members fall ill or die unexpectedly. Then Xue Pan, the loosest cannon in the clan, kills a man in a tavern brawl and is arrested. By bribing the judge, his clerk, witnesses, and the victim's family, and by lying, the Jias get his charge reduced to manslaughter, but that can be appealed, and the litigation is expensive. There are reports of hauntings, visitations, and "terrors of the night" (4.194). Jia She, Zheng's elder brother, admits that we are not "the great and glorious house we once were, ...Nothing but a hollow facade," and Jia Zheng bemoans their "lack of ability and positive achievement. We are living on borrowed time...." (4.258, 260). Bao-yu loses his jade birthstone and seems to sink into idiocy, along with Dai-yu. About all the Jias have left is some residual favour at the palace.

The final volume delivers a logical conclusion – the fall – and then an epilogue of sorts. Its early pages disclose further proofs of financial strain, another ghostly warning, and more family misconduct. Jia Zheng, no less, a model of rectitude and hard work within the system, is impeached for mismanagement and extortion at his provincial post. Recalled to the capital, he is questioned by His Majesty, not about those charges, but about other members of his family. At the end, He makes "a sound of disapproval" (Cao 1986, 5.104). Soon after, the axe descends. An Imperial Commissioner and a detachment of Embroidered Jackets (secret police) appear during a reception in the Hall of Exalted Felicity, followed by a stern prince who dismisses the guests. Officials begin cataloguing the contents of both mansions for confiscation, and detain some Jias, including Jia She, for questioning. Everyone is traumatized; women wail as chests and cupboards are ransacked. (An interesting inventory occupies two pages.) Jia Zheng is in shock: "We are finished! I never thought we should be brought so low!" and "This is truly the end!" (5.124-25). Though he gets off lightly, he blames himself for neglecting the family's problems, especially its finances. Bao-yu, wailing with the women, treasures his "memories of past happiness, of the golden days of the poetry club in the Garden" (5.135). This is classic: after the Fall, the *domaine* shines more brightly.

The family's woes multiply. Jia Zheng discovers how badly, how unsustainably, its affairs have been managed; his mother, the matriarch Granny Jia, dies; Xi-feng the manager dies, and her maid Faithful commits suicide. There are more reports of hauntings in the derelict Garden, and a shameful plot against young Qiao-jie's innocence surfaces. One of Zheng's literary friends tells him how venal servants have hurt the family. But in other areas the Jias are holding on, and even rising a bit. Jia Zheng's promotion was negated when he was impeached, but the Prince of Beijing remains friendly and helpful. A relative from Nanking who had been fired for misconduct, undergone confiscation, and "been reinstated by Imperial favour" comes to call, suggesting that matters might yet improve (Cao 5.263-64). Bao-yu and Jia Lan are progressing in their studies, so Jia Zheng urges them to excel on the state examination and "help to redeem the family" (5.298). They do so, and the Emperor, seeing two Jias on the pass list, orders the Jia case reopened. Pardon of prisoners, restoration of hereditary rank, reinstatement of Jia Zheng, and the return of confiscated property follow quickly. Jia Zheng lectures the household on good behaviour henceforth. Bao-yu has disappeared, but the Emperor, intrigued by his story and impressed by his essays, gives him the title of *Magister Verbi Profundi*: Master of the Profound Word (5.366). He has left behind not only the world but his wife Bao-chai, who is pregnant: perhaps the most profound word.

CAO XUEQIN'S HUGE LITERARY WAREHOUSE supports the view that it is "about" the trajectory of a great family's fortunes. There are more discussions of the Jias' glory and decline than of Bao-yu's conduct, the warnings, karma, or the weaknesses of the family's males. Fewer still are references to time, *domaines*, corruption, and signs of the family's incipient recovery. But karma is inseparable from time, the medium in which it operates, and those two topics together are second only to the Jias' fortunes as a concern of the authors. Time is most conspicuous in the second volume, where it underpins the effort to preserve the surface of eighteenth-century Chinese life; and the fourth, where it is tinged with sadness for the loss of happy days. Karma appears mainly in the last two books as characters wonder why things fall apart. When Jia Yun, seeking a job, is rebuffed by Xi-feng, he pronounces her a tyrant, nor did it help that her little girl wept when he praised her, "as if we had some feud from a past life" (Cao 4.190). Karma often resembles fate; most characters confuse or conflate the two. Did she cry because of karma, or was it decreed by higher powers? Do I have free will, or was I predestined to miss out on this job?

The nostalgic treatment of old *domaines* in the final books naturally differs from that in volume two, when one still existed. Bao-chai's letter to Dai-yu in chapter 87 sets the tone, mourning departed happiness: "...you shared the joy of that golden autumn, when harmony and conviviality prevailed," when, "united beneath the aegis of the Crab-flower Club, we tasted crustacean delicacies and contemplated chrysantheums" (Cao 4.158). She asks, "...are not you and I late blooms, that tremble at the approaching chill?", and attaches a desolate autumnal poem. It is easy to dismiss this as precious daintiness, but it must be agonizing to realize that you were once privileged to exist on an exalted plane, and now you are not. Dai-yu also daydreams about her happy youth in the South, making a *domaine* of that. And we have seen how Bao-yu idealized the "golden days of the poetry club in the Garden" (5.135). A few chapters on, when family and maids are playing games reminiscent of those days, he drifts off into a reverie about all that has been lost: "...of my fair cousins, most have been scattered to the four winds. Why have so few been spared?" (5. 165). Bao-yu, with his cosmic origins in the Unchanging, is profoundly troubled by the changes that time insists on ringing in mortal lives.

John Minford, who took over as translator of Penguin's *The Story of the Stone* after the third volume, went to Beijing to look for the mansion that a Chinese scholar believed was the original of Cao's Rong-guo House. It was a strange day: Beijing, a northern desert city that should have been cold in January, had a spring-like warmth. After a long, frustrating search, a firecracker salesman helped him find the place behind a gateway and a screen-wall. Formerly a prince's palace, it was by then the Chinese Academy of Music. Minford was dubious, and the gateman was loath to admit him, but once inside he was soon convinced: stone lions couchant on either side, the raised stone walk, and surely this was Granny Jia's courtyard! Everything was "exactly where it should be," "exactly what one would have expected" from reading the novel, and the students living there were the "same kind of people – musicians, artists, dreamers – as those...in *The Stone*" (Cao 4.17). It was decidedly eerie. To reach the Garden, Minford had to go back out to the street, follow the wall to another gateway and talk his way inside, but he persevered, and was rewarded.

> *In mid-winter, the prince's garden has a desolate charm. Entering it,*
> *I felt, even more than with the palace, that I was entering a world of*
> *vanished romance, a lost domain.The past, the world of illusion and*
> *dreams, hung heavily...in the air* (4.18).

Unless Minford had read Alain-Fournier, this passage is an entirely independent corroboration of the kind of magic that may at times inhabit such a place. Again everything was "exactly where it should be": the artificial mountain, "dilapidated courtyard," small pavilion, drained pond, and "miniature... buildings" (4.18-19). The children playing there, and their mothers and aunts, were well aware that this was the famous novel's setting. The Garden and the mansion had been repopulated in the fullness of time, and appropriately.

Three Chinese Dramas

In chapter 26 of *The Story of the Stone*, Bao-yu goes to visit Dai-yu. Nearing the cottage, he hears her recite a line of poetry – "Each day in a drowsy waking dream of love" – that he recognizes as taken from "his beloved *Western Chamber*." Entering, he quotes another line, "in somewhat dubious taste," alluding to marriage and a "bridal bed"; Dai-yu, offended, runs off in tears (Cao 1.516-17). It is one of ten or so mentions of this work in Cao's novel – more than to any other literary title. Not all exploit its *risqué* content; it provides lines to be used in the poetry club's word games, and its description of a lonely courtyard reminds Dai-yu that she is an orphan far from home. Nearly all of the young people are familiar with it. The allusions cluster in the second volume, when the literary bent of the Garden is flourishing. Grandmother Jia knows the story too, but she voices her low opinion of the content and moral influence of such romances.

The *Western Chamber* probably circulated orally from the eleventh century in various versions; our earliest texts date from the late twelfth and early thirteenth centuries. Stephen H. West and Wilt L. Idema translated Wang Shifu's *The Story of the Western Wing* (1995), "China's most popular love comedy," a "tremendous influence" in all periods except 1966-78: the Cultural Revolution (Wang 3, 10, 12). They call it a "ballad opera," using assorted musical measures (43). Their introduction traces the interplay of *yin* and *yang* throughout. *Yang* (male, Confucian, patriarchal) dominated "mediaeval" Chinese culture; Chang, the hero, is a student of Confucius. However, they argue, the drama is suffused with *Yin* forces – female, dark, lunar, the heroine Ying-ying – despite its "fear of female sexuality" (52, 66). I use *Master Tung's Western Chamber Romance. A Chinese Chantefable*, translated by Li-Li Ch'en (1976), whose introduction and footnotes are excellent. She uses the French term for its genre, meaning a 'sung story' – here told alternately in song, spoken poetry, and prose – and distinguishes "four voices": the narrator's, the characters' dialogue, interior monologues, and addresses to the audience (Tung xxv). Tung Chieh-yüan (fl. 1189-1208) had not yet hit upon the style of later operatic dramas, in which characters stroll on and introduce themselves casually to the audience; here the narrator tells the story, quoting the characters. The story is known to have circulated in French, Arabic, Persian, Japanese, Korean, and Chinese.

Chancing on *Master Tung's Western Chamber Romance* in my reading, I was surprised that a mediaeval Asian folk drama provided so much data for a topic rooted in modern European novels. The plot is classic: true love between suitable partners, long thwarted (by maternal opposition, civil unrest, academic study, and a rival) but ultimately triumphant. En route to the happy ending (replacing an earlier tragic version) we hear a good deal about time, *domaines*, and karma. The narrator's prologue evokes the passing seasons for three pages exhibiting a strong sense of time either flying or oppressing. Its beauty "can't buy" spring "permanence," for it yields to hot weather, and "how can one pass the interminable summer days?" (Tung 2, 3). Here time stretches out bleakly, as in *Ecclesiastes, The Sun Also Rises*, and James Taylor's "Oh, I've seen fire and I've seen rain / Seen sunny days that I thought would never end." But all seasons pass. "Furtively, time carries our years away," says the narrator, "Man's century passes like the morning dew," before telling his "story of secret love" (4, 2). Ying-ying finds her long wait for Chang's return a trial. "Waning autumn further abets [her] gloom," and "Time flies quickly like shuttles on a loom," where we might expect the opposite (184). But her letter to him insists: "Time flies..." (201).

Karma, the enduring consequence of actions, is everywhere in the story. When Chang first sees Ying-ying he stands "transfixed" and "almost deranged," says the narrator, "face to face with his predestined lover who had come to avenge herself for the wrong he had done her five hundred years before" (Tung 14). What?! Though never clarified, this could explain his long, frustrating delay. Her mother quickly calls her in, but "suffering of this nature can't be avoided; / It's caused by evil karma" from an earlier life (27). Chang recognizes this kind of causation repeatedly. It's simple, really: "Once I hurt you, / Now you hurt me" (32). The rule applies to everyone: if bandits attack a monastery, maybe its abbot "did evil" to them in another life, so it is "natural that they should seek revenge now" (67-68).

Later Ying-ying grants karma's power, wondering if *she* is "paying a debt / Incurred in my last incarnation" (186). The financial metaphor is pursued: there is a "ruthless creditor / Exacting payment for a debt" carried down through the ages (190). The kinship of karma and destiny is asserted; no sooner does Ying-ying discern karma than she says, "My suffering is predestined." In this system, she is "predestined" by her own soul's previous actions, not by a deity. As late as Li-li Ch'en's final "chapter," Chang (on the eve of success) bemoans his "abominable luck and / A loathsome karma" before the omniscient narrator and omnipotent author grant a full discharge of his debt (215).

The obvious goal toward which the romance moves is a love-*domaine* for Chang and Ying-ying, but other possible ideals and outcomes exist. Before meeting Ying-ying, Chang is torn between nostalgia for better days (his family's fortune has dwindled), and the life of an itinerant student: visiting wise men, "Delighting in solitude. / Free, unbridled" (Tung 7). Either one *could* become his *domaine*. Likewise, the magnificent temple that he is visiting is perceived as magical, a veritable "heaven on earth," "unsullied by worldly dust and mire," a place that "Dispelled all vulgar thoughts," and as a scholar he would be welcome to stay there indefinitely (13). But then he is mesmerized by his first glimpse of the heroine (staying there with her mother), and forgets the monastic ideal. That night he chants his poem about "the lunar goddess" in a courtyard within her hearing, and is rewarded by her presence (24). She resembles Ch'ang-o, the moon goddess ("the spring Beauty / Has flown from the lunar palace"), but is even more beautiful (25). "Her low-cut lapels reveal her charm," her tiny dancer's waist and *bound feet* are irresistible, and her "tight-fitting jacket / Set her shapely figure to advantage" (25-26). When she responds with her own poem in the same rhyme scheme he is "mad with joy," but her mother's intervention cuts their meeting short (26). They will have to live on that first lyrical encounter for a good while.

Their next high is musical. As Chang intones intricate poems, accompanying himself on the zither, his little study acquires "an unworldly charm" (Tung 103). A model is thus established for special places: "unworldly charm" vs "worldly dust" (a *domaine* is set apart from the workaday world). Using "Classic techniques," Chang plays an "ancient air" with "orthodox purity"; then modulates into a "modern tune" expressing "exquisite sentiments" (103). The maid Hung-niang, an advocate for him, calls Ying-ying's attention to the music, and – mother being asleep – they tiptoe nearer to Chang's room in the monastery's guest house. Outside his window "Ying-ying listens attentively / To the lofty, unworldly sound," like "a pure, glorious wind vibrating on the strings": an Aeolian harp (104). When Hung-niang's cough alerts Chang to the presence of an audience, he puts on more incense and prays for "divine inspiration," knowing that this performance "Must so move Ying-ying that she'll want to marry me" (105). He retunes the zither to produce both "a masculine and a feminine voice," which "reveals his love" so deeply that "Tears roll down her cheeks" (105). Hearing Ying-ying sob, he senses his success, rushes outside, embraces the girl he sees there and propositions her, invoking their destiny to be together tonight. But it is Hung-niang, the maid: Ying-ying has departed. Master Tung has pulled a fast one, shifting into comedy, or farce. More time must pass, more pain be endured, before fruition is granted.

Not as much time as her mother wishes, however. Ying-ying is torn between love and filial obedience, but when her mother reneges on a promise to let Ying-ying marry whoever can save the monastery from bandits (which Chang does, via his friend General Tu), love triumphs. She sends Chang a promissory note: "... propriety I set aside: / I send this poem as a matchmaker. / There will be clouds and rain [sexual intercourse] this eventide" (Tung 141). Chang snaps out of his despondency, devouring three meals that Hung-niang prepares. And Ying-ying is as good as her word, allowing herself to be led to his room with the sweet, reluctant, am'rous delay of Milton's Eve: "Feigning shyness," looking away, adopting "a posture of cool hauteur" (147). But not for long, both being "passionate romantics." Chang is appropriately ardent: "He caresses and cuddles her," "fondles her fragrant body ecstatically," etc. In short, "They make love all night" (148). Li-li Ch'en describes their love-making as mutual, "tender and pleasant," and reports that Tung's "unabashed treatment of sex" is "quite unlike the self-conscious, euphemistic approach elsewhere" (xix, xiii). Only the pre-dawn "morning bell" ends the "dream-like visit"; they part reluctantly (149). Yet she is back the next night for more talk, clouds, and rain, and "They know they'll rediscover this joy again and again" (157). Which they do nightly for six months, until Madam Ts'ui decides that her daughter looks so happy that she must have a lover, and bullies Hung-niang into confessing.

Hung-niang is no pushover, though: in a turn that must have delighted plebeian audiences, she speaks truth to power. Come on, she says, they're young, attractive, unmarried: "When they meet late at night, / Madam, need one ask questions?" (Tung 161) Yes, "For the past half year, / They've slept together every night," but is it wise to make a fuss about that? You blame me, yet "is Madam herself blameless?" (162) You have failed to govern your household or to reward Mr Chang adequately for helping against the bandits, Madam. Do you want to be laughed at for ruining your daughter's reputation as well? We await a retort, but no: "What should I do?" asks Madam Ts'ui. Chang is "a perfect gentleman," says the maid; let them marry! Madam finds this "most sagacious," and after conferring with her daughter, consents (163). She invites Chang to a betrothal banquet where the agreement is sealed with wine and his present of gold (for which he had to borrow money from a friend). The love-*domaine* is formally approved.

In a western drama observing the conventions of European comedy, the story would probably end here, but this one is eastern. Ying-ying is still in mourning for her late father and "cannot be married right away," says her mother (Tung 170). That's all right, replies Chang: I'm off to the capital and will take the civil service examination; next year will be fine. Only Ying-ying looks "heartbroken." His departure occasions much weeping, and this turns into a major separation: a fall-to-spring school year of study and tests, plus Chang's ensuing illness, give the lovers a large dose of lonely suffering. And a rival turns up: her uncouth cousin Cheng Heng, to whom she was affianced in childhood. His lies (that Chang has married) fool Madam, but are exposed by General (now Governor) Tu and by Chang when he returns. Totally discredited, Cheng commits suicide. Only then do the lovers complete their penance for whatever they may have done to each other in a previous incarnation and earn their happy ending. It turns out that Chang has placed third nationally in the big state examination, and is thus assured of an exalted position as a mandarin. Mother and daughter are delighted: all is as it should be. "From time of old," the narrator declaims, "The suitable match for a ravishing beauty / Has always been a talented scholar. / Ying-ying is now a Lady, / Her husband being an Academician" (234-35). If we needed a reminder that this text comes to us from long ago and far away, this will do nicely.

THE PEONY PAVILION (1598), BY Tang Xianzu (1550-1616), was very successful, perhaps the most popular play of the Ming Dynasty. Cyril Birch, the translator of a fine edition (1981), reports that its heroine, Bridal Du, was much admired by

Chinese audiences, who compared her to Ying-ying in *Western Chamber* (mentioned several times in the play). Birch's introduction describes the genre as "a play, or rather opera," specifically a "Southern-style opera" (Tang ix, xii). By then, Chinese playwrights had moved from Tung's bardic narrative-with-quotation to fully dramatic style: characters come before the audience to speak and sing for themselves. Set in the dying days of the Song Dynasty, *The Peony Pavilion* is to some degree a story of dynastic fall and thus a history play, one that also presents intense personal struggles (Tang's contemporary William Shakespeare, then working on his 'Henry histories' and *Julius Caesar*, would have recognized the form). If you want to know the plot, the Prologue (scene 1) provides a quick overview of the whole story; Tang was more interested in dramatic irony than in suspense or surprise. His way of interweaving the public and private strands of the plot is clever, and informs what he has to say about time and *domaines*.

Tang does not discuss time as such, and karma is hardly mentioned, but he juxtaposes scenes and perspectives that raise questions about how time operates and what is possible. In scene 2, Liu Mengmei, our hero, enters and introduces himself. He comes of an old family, he says, now much fallen, and lost both parents early. Forced to make his own way, he wants to succeed on the state examinations and become an official (cp. *The Western Chamber* and *The Story of the Stone*). He then reports a dream he had about a beautiful girl who said that she is his destined bride. The next few scenes ramify. Du Bao and Madam Du fear that their teenage daughter Bridal is too dreamy: she needs a tutor. In scene 4, Mr Chen applies for the post. Du, Bridal, and her saucy maid Spring Fragrance accept him. Next, Liu meets an old friend, Han Zicai; they bemoan the plight of unemployed scholars (themselves). Han urges Liu to apply to Secretary Miao, a sympathetic official. Scene 8 is a pastoral idyll in which Prefect Du visits villages and farms of his district in spring: a natural and political ideal, a *domaine*. While he is away, Spring Fragrance persuades Bridal to walk in their garden and Chen takes a holiday, setting up scene 10, "The Interrupted Dream," central to the play and one of the most notable dream sequences in dramatic literature.

As Bridal walks among vernal blossoms and pairs of songbirds, she reflects that her own spring is passing without a lover, not like romances such as *The Western Chamber*, and feels "secret discontent," i.e. spring fever (Tang 46-47). Back in the house, she falls asleep and dreams of...Liu Mengmei, who is searching for "the

Peach Blossom Source of [his] desire" (alluding to a mythical Chinese paradise). He finds her, *wants* her, speaks warmly and directly (47). They sing of having met in the past, and he carries her off. A "Flower Spirit" says that the couple's "marriage affinity" will make this a "joyous experience" (49). They re-enter and again sing of a previous meeting, which could be his dream of her, or karma. Liu then leaves and Bridal awakes, saying that "our bliss was accomplished" (52). But Madam Du rebukes Spring Fragrance for letting Bridal walk in the garden, a "vast and lonely place" (54). Bridal, fasting, sleepless, and sad, wanders in the garden alone, recalling the joys of love and longing for her "bygone dream" (57). But does Liu belong to her future or to her past? The time sequence is vague here. Did Liu dream of her before, or as, she dreamed of him? Are the scenes in chronological order?

Now the focus, hitherto fairly tight, splays out into an historical chronicle, whose justification seems to be "it happened that way." The real-life Liu, tired of studying at home, gifts the family orchard to its gardener, Camel Guo, and leaves to seek a patron. Bridal, still pining, paints a self-portrait before her beauty deteriorates. The barbarian prince Dignai exults over his victories near Beijing and predicts more, foreshadowing civil war. Back home, Mrs Du weeps over Bridal's decline, and learns of the erotic dream from Spring Fragrance. Du summons Sister Stone, a nun with a "rock-hard hymen," who recounts her one attempt at marriage and withdrawal to a convent (Tang 80). She and Chen are useless; Bridal weakens further. After another military interlude – bandit leaders Li Quan and his wife plot to bring down the Song Dynasty – Bridal dies. One might think that would end the young-love plot and leave a dream as Bridal's only *domaine*. As she requested, Spring Fragrance asks Du to take a young scholar named Mei or Liu (Apricot or Willow) into the family. Du receives orders to join the fight against the bandits. Chen and Sister Stone will help Madam Du manage domestic affairs in his absence.

The plot proliferates. In scene 21, the Imperial Commissioner of Gems, Miao Shunbin (recommended to Liu as a possible patron), receives the young man and gives him funds for his journey to Chang'an. In the next scene, however, Liu – lightly clad, ill, traveling hard – falls while crossing a stream. His cries for help produce...Tutor Chen, offering a refuge! Perhaps China is smaller than we thought. Then we are in the afterlife, a version of hell in which Judge Hu of the Infernal Tribunal sentences four men to be reborn as birds (one hopes to be "Miss

Oriole": Ying-ying in *Western Chamber*), but returns Bridal to life and her destined marriage. Liu, recovering at the Dus' Apricot Shrine (an allusion to his name), finds a portrait of, apparently, the "bodhisattva Guanyin" in the garden (Tang 138). By scene 25 it has been three years since Bridal's death; Spring Fragrance and Mrs Du hold a Buddhist rite for her. Chez Du, Liu sees that the portrait is not of a saint but of a mortal beauty, and the poem with it suggests a future with him. After a mass for Bridal is celebrated, her ghost appears, hears Liu moan, and strews apricot blossoms (seen and wondered at by several). In scene 28, Liu yearns for the girl in the portrait, invokes her, then lies down. It is enough: Bridal appears, assuring him "This is no dream, it is real" (163). Sister Stone hears a female voice in Liu's room and is suspicious enough to mention *Western Chamber*. She interrupts Bridal's next visit; the ghost slips away.

From then on, romance and political/military history alternate more quickly. Du's involvement in the defence of the realm increases, but the love plot continues. Bridal has (understandable) difficulty in explaining, and Liu in grasping, her status – ghost or mortal? – yet they plight their troth. From Sister Stone, Liu learns that the Apricot Shrine is Bridal's, and calls her his wife. In scene 35, Sister Stone, Liu, and a gravedigger exhume her body, dazed but living, from her grave. This spectacular turning back of the clock seems to reunite her soul or spirit with her corporeal form, and Sister Stone tries to help her re-adapt to life. When Liu proposes to marry Bridal right away she puts him off, but Chen invites Liu to picnic with him at the tomb tomorrow, which will reveal the grave-robbing. Feeling cornered, the couple elope to Hangzhou by boat that night. Chen finds the empty grave the next day and vows to report the outrage to Du, but it is now wartime: Li Quan and Dame Li plan to attack a town in Du's district. Liu and Bridal have been married; she confides her garden dream to him. But their love-*domaine* is brief: he will risk a trip to the capital to take the examinations that could make his career.

Now Tang begins to gather the many strands of his plot. Miao, grading examinations, allows Liu to present his late "essay" verbally and is impressed, but says the war must take precedence. Du and his wife lament the sorrows of war and Bridal's death as messengers update them on the fighting. They must part: she stays, he leads an army to Huaian, where they break through Li Quan's forces into the city. Du is received as a hero. Liu returns to Bridal, reports that his exam results will be delayed, and sets off to find her parents. Chen arrives at Huaian (to tell

Du about the empty grave), but is captured and taken to Li Quan, who shows him the severed heads of two women, said to be Mrs Du and Spring Fragrance; then allows him into the city. Chen reports this to Du, and is sent back to Li with a message offering princely rank if they lay down their arms and submit to Song rule. They accept and march away. In Hangzhou, Mrs Du and Spring Fragrance meet Sister Stone, and are shocked to see Bridal with her. Liu limps into Huaian, lamenting his poverty. Spurned for that offence at the inn, he sleeps out. The next day he tries to gain entrance to Du's patriotic victory banquet and tell him about Bridal, but is arrested as a vagrant and an imposter. Du is summoned to court, thenceforth the focus of the action.

The ending delivers a denouement different from any that a European drama-tist would have been likely to contemplate. Chen presents Li Quan's submission to the imperial court, earning a promotion to chamberlain, and Miao announces that Top Prize in the examinations goes to Liu Mengmei. Searchers sent out to find him include Camel Guo, Liu's gardener. Then matters take a dark turn: Liu, jailed for *posing* as Du's son-in-law, is beaten, and when brought to Du is beaten again and condemned to death for grave-robbing. Camel Guo identifies Liu, and Miao declares him Top Candidate. Du is a minority of one in rejecting Liu's story and exculpation. Liu goes to the banquet for successful candidates in his scholar's robes. Chen confirms Liu's story, but Du still denies it, so they will submit the question to the Emperor. Two officers locate Bridal and inform her of Liu's prize and Du's protest. She is brought to court, where Camel Guo backs up the officers' account. At this point, western audiences would anticipate the "final assembly" of classic comedy, in which most of the characters gather to clarify everything and reconcile everybody, and the "heavy father" lightens up, producing harmony.

The long final scene is dominated by the Imperial Audience. Decorum dictates that the Sovereign be only an offstage Voice: mysterious, impressive, leaving much to the imagination, as in *The Wizard of Oz*. Chen summarizes the case for the court; Du and Liu argue and even scuffle. Then Bridal enters. The Voice: "Do you recognize her?" Liu: "Yes." Du: "No." The Voice commands two tests. Her image appears in a mirror and she casts a shadow, so she is not a ghost. Bridal is then told to narrate her dream, death, and rebirth. Liu confirms all he can, but Du again mocks him and rejects her. Madam Du vouches for Bridal's reality, which has no effect on Du, but The Voice believes her. He asks Bridal to explain how punishments work in hell, which she does (a sure crowd-pleaser). The Voice then accepts her story and commands family reconciliation. Du, however, still rejects Liu's account of the grave robbery and Bridal's claim to be his daughter. She deals with this by one of drama's oldest devices: a faint. Immediately Du cries out, "Bridal, my daughter!" (Tang 336). Yet even when Sister Stone and Spring Fragrance confirm the identities of the couple, Du cannot accept Liu. A courier reads the Imperial Verdict, promoting almost everyone and blessing the family. The actors circle the stage, marveling and giving thanks, but Du and Liu never make up, nor is Du heard to accept the Imperial Will and the marriage.

As in Shakespeare's "problem plays," Tang leaves us with a difficulty. His image of union and reunion does *not* deal with the unresolved antipathy of Du to his son-in-law. What sort of marriage can the couple expect? The kind where you move far away from your parents? Can we assume that Du will come to take a mellower view of Liu? Tang could have endorsed this hope with a few words or a gesture; he did not do so. Bridal and Liu had their dream-*domaine*, then their brief honeymoon, but their future looks problematical. Cyril Birch characterizes Du as a decent and respected though blinkered man (Tang xi). Does the play bear this out? Du is isolated mainly because he refuses to accept that time can be reversed and the dead rise again. Remember, he saw Bridal buried: now comes this young stranger, a known grave-robber, with a Bridal look-alike and a far-fetched story. Du maintains that in reality mortals are granted only one life, whatever "Judge Hu of the tenth Infernal Tribunal" is alleged to have said. What kind of "Destiny" would let Liu's "destined" wife die, then fold back on itself? Du is the only character prepared to say that the plot has become absurd. Is he "blinkered," or a pragmatist, insisting on nature and time as we have known them? Past, present, and future are strangely interwoven in Bridal and Liu's relationship, and at the end the nature of time is still a mystery, open to question.

CYRIL BIRCH ALSO CONTRIBUTED TO the excellent edition of *The Peach Blossom Fan* (1699) by K'ung Shang-jen (1648-1718); the translation is by Chen Shih-hsiang and Harold Acton, "with Cyril Birch." Acton's preface describes the drama as "...a highly poetic chronicle play...by a distinguished scholar," and "a vivid evocation of the downfall of the Ming Dynasty" (K'ung vii). It is very "historical," many of its scenes being dated to a year and a month. A witches' brew of weak rulers, corruption, factionalism, bankruptcy, famine, brigandage, and rebellion, says Acton, drove China from Ming to Manchu rule. Birch's introduction calls the play a South China-style opera, full of nostalgia for the Ming heyday. For him it is the most interesting and authentic of "southern" plays, detailing "the breakdown of a long-cherished order" (xvii). K'ung, looking back past the Ming breakdown to its long summer of glory days (it had begun in 1368), saw a *domaine* that could be wished for, but revisited only in history or literature.

In the Prologue (dated 1684), the former Master of Ceremonies at the Imperial Temple reviews his 97 years. He has seen both "rise and fall," but the current omens are good (K'ung 1). Last night he watched the first half of *The Peach Blossom Fan*, and he proceeds to sing us an outline of its plot (he also appears as a character in the play). Mainly because of its devotion to history, K'ung's story-line is much more complicated than those of the earlier dramas discussed; the young love vs obstacles component is often buried under military history and partisan plotting, or set aside while the great national issues are addressed. The details of the plot are often hardly worth following if your interests are literary rather than historical (the playwright had both), but the first few scenes and the ending are crucial to my concerns.

In Part I, scene 1 (dated 1643, historical-events time now), the young scholar Hou Fang-yu introduces himself in song and speech. Two friends, Wu and Ch'en, join him. Keen on current events, they persuade him that minstrel Liu is politically sound, and they all go to see him. Surprised by their visit, he offers to comment on...Confucius' reforms of music. This seems irrelevant, but Liu explains that Confucius did politics too, exposing the crimes of three powerful clans. As a result, four great singing-masters (minstrels) realized their errors, left their usurping patrons, and went to find employment elsewhere. Some of them sought Peach Blossom Spring, a utopia in Chinese folklore, and "a metaphor for a place of retirement" far away (K'ung 13, n. 10). They also sang of the Sea God's marvelous palace. Taken literally or metaphorically, these sound like *domaines*: distant but aspirational ideals. At the end of the scene, Liu and the three young men are united in amity and song as they exit.

Then Li Chen-li comes on to present herself as a matronly, high-class courtesan. She hopes that a friend and go-between will find a wealthy patron to deflower (and perhaps "keep") her adopted daughter. Enter her friend Yang, and then our young heroine, who is complimented on her beauty. Yang sketches some orchids for her, names her Fragrant Princess, and asks about her training. Music is her specialty, and Su K'un-sheng, her teacher, comes on to show her off. They sing a nature lyric together, and he makes some corrections to demonstrate his credentials. Yang then proposes Hou Fang-yu as a mate for Fragrant Princess. From what we have seen he hardly qualifies as a "wealthy patron," but all approve the proposal and sing in celebration of it.

This is not a romantic comedy, however; henceforth amiable singing will be rare or undercut. Scene 3 depicts a Confucian rite at the Imperial Academy in Nanjing. The Master of Ceremonies, Wu (who spoke the Prologue), and some scholars are the celebrants, but the bearded Juan Ta-ch'eng butts in. When the ritual ends, Wu denounces Juan as a villain and "an insult to the Sage" (K'ung 27). Though Juan says he is a wronged man, everyone else censures him and cheers his hasty exit. The main objection seems to be his dubious character; later we see his Machiavellian politics and hostility to the lovers. Juan is also a playwright, a right-wing dramatist who maintains a troupe of actors to hide his true purposes. In scene 4, he lends his thespians to some gentlemen who wish to see his new play, sending along a spy to report their reactions. When Yang arrives to visit his "old crony," they read some of the play aloud (32). The spying servant returns periodically to report on its reception: first praise, then blame for Juan's politics and personal conduct. Juan is furious; he must find a way to neutralize his enemies. Yang suggests that he provide the dowry for Hou (a member of the opposition) to marry Fragrant Princess. Juan agrees to send money and gifts. Thus K'ung joins his personal and political plotlines.

For a time Juan's plan works. In scene 5, Hou enters singing, en route to Madam Li's. He meets minstrel Liu, and they walk to the "hamper party": a picnic (K'ung 39). Go-between Yang (a "friend" in both plots) and singing teacher Su are there, music is heard, and courtship flourishes: Hou tosses his fan pendant up to a second-floor window, and cherries are dropped to him. Madam Li and Fragrant Princess appear with a teapot and flowers, but when Liu suggests that the couple exchange vows, the maiden runs off. Yang offers to pay the dowry for the penurious Hou, and Madam Li proposes an auspicious date. In the next scene she sings of the "union banquet," after which Yang sings about peach blossoms and hands out clothes and (Juan's) money (47). Hou enters, thanks Yang, and dons a graduate's gown. Three "poet-singers" and three "singing-girls" arrive (49-50). Fragrant Princess is led to Hou for the "celebration wine," which supposedly signals not marriage but engagement: "an expression of intention" (51n). Hou writes a poem about peach blossoms on his fan, explaining the title. Hou and Fragrant Princess sing a love-duet, after which they are escorted to the bridal chamber, which sounds like more than "intention." The guests joke and sing, as in western comedies' closing saturnalia.

In fact, our comedies usually stop there, with the achievement of a lawful love-*domaine*, but this play has just begun. In scene 7, Yang arrives the next morning to congratulate the newlyweds. They appear, singing of their joy and fulfilled desire. But then Fragrant Princess steps out of her previous meekness into personhood, asking Yang why he is being so generous to them; Hou seconds the question. Yang says (indiscreetly) that Juan wants to be friends with Hou, and may need his help. Fragrant Princess surprises us again, saying that Juan is a traitor to be spat on, and tears at the finery he has sent them. Yang and Madam Li deplore this, but Hou supports her. Yang exits abruptly. Though the bride and groom are in accord here, they have lit a months'-long fuse to a bomb that will blow them apart. In the next scene, Juan avoids a festival simply because his enemies are there: the newlyweds and their friends.

More emphasis begins to fall on politics and war. Tso Liang-yu, a proud general hurt by protests from his starving army, plans to march on Nanjing and *take* food. By scene 10 our friends are embroiled in the strife: Liu offers to help Ming loyalists, among them Hou. Yang reports on Gen. Tso's actions. Hou's father was once Tso's patron: could he write the general a letter on his father's behalf? He complies. Liu volunteers to deliver it, and departs with the letter. He finds the general at Wuhang, and though arrested as a spy, soon charms him. Tso asks him to stay; Liu begs *him* not to advance on Nanjing. Scene 12 (still 1643) is critical for the lovers. Yang and Juan attend a meeting about Gen. Tso. Yang listens as Juan makes proposals and names traitors. Two local governors, Shih and Ma, join them. Yang tells them not to worry about Tso, but Juan claims that Tso has a collaborator in the city: Hou Fang-yu! Shih and Yang disagree, but Ma believes Juan and will have Hou arrested. Yang hastens to warn Hou and Fragrant Princess. Hou must flee *now*. The couple are parted for the foreseeable future, their love-*domaine* on hold.

Political and military scenes predominate now. In scene 13 (1644), Gen. Tso has captured Wuhang, but bandits have reportedly entered Peking, killing and burning, and the Emperor has hung himself. All present wail and change into mourning white: it seems the end of the Ming dynasty. Then Hou describes conditions "south of the river," a region divided over the succession. Minister Shih says the country is leaderless, though there is a rumour that the Emperor and Heir Apparent escaped Peking. Gov. Ma supports Prince Fu as the new emperor, but Hou opposes this, citing his three vices and five other disqualifications, all of which he writes down. Juan, backing Fu, tries to win over Shih, who rejects him. Juan is furious. Hou writes to Ma. In scene 15, Ma and Juan discuss support for Fu; Ma makes Juan a minor official. A month later, Fu dons imperial robes, but when Shih, Ma, and others urge him to ascend the throne, Fu says he prefers to "act as regent" (K'ung 114). He makes Ma his Prime Minister. Juan asks for recognition and is made Ma's private secretary. Darknss deepens in scene 17. A friend bribes Yang to buy him a "lovely singing-girl" (K'ung 119); Fragrant Princess would be perfect! Three poet-musicians and three courtesans call, asking exemption from Imperial service. Yang promises – *if* they can persuade Fragrant Princess to become his friend's concubine. They try, but she refuses. Loyalist generals are shown quarrelling, the opposition is impotent, and the empire is tottering.

At this point comes an "Interlude." Three travellers meet on the road to Nanking – Lan, a young painter; Chang, a former Imperial Guard; and Ts'ai, a merchant – and trade war stories, broadening the scope. Chang, who was in Peking when the bandits came, says the Imperial Couple committed suicide, but the Heir Apparent escaped by sea. As a storm rages, all do homage, burn incense, kowtow, and wail. Chang gives Ts'ai the names of martyred officials, and traitors, for his bookshop to publish. That night, Chang sees the ghosts of fallen soldiers march past, then the royal procession to the east and heaven: K'ung genuflecting to the royalist cause. In the morning Chang tells the others of his vision. They agree to look for each other in Nanking.

This concludes Part I. In the Prologue to Part II, the Master of Ceremonies, again a member of the audience, returns to watch the second part of *Peach Blossom Fan*. "Time whizzes like an arrow," he reflects; "...the soul drifts from the sleeper's pillow" (K'ung 151). Though time is omnipresent in this chronicle, it has not been discussed per se. The soul itself is timeless, he says, but art and life also concern him: "Writing is not reality; acts are vain. / He only is wise to know the very instant / When he should raise the wine-cup to his lips" (153). Then he adds, "In bygone years, reality was the play; / The play becomes reality today." He and Calderon de la Barca ("Life is a Dream") might have an interesting conversation about that, but the old MC's thoughts here will be modified by other ideas and attitudes in the rest of the play.

As Part II opens, Prime Minister Ma holds "the greatest power in the land"; Emperor Fu is in effect his ward (K'ung 154). Ma, Yang, and Juan discuss singing-girls, of whom Fragrant Princess is considered the star. Ma has her brought; then, angry that she refused to become a concubine and insulted Juan, orders her dragged away. Juan "would gladly put her to death" (160). Yang tries to buy Fragrant Princess, but she and Madam Li refuse: she is married! A struggle ensues. Fragrant Princess falls, hitting her head, faints, and lies bleeding. Yang suggests that Li take her place: only *he* knows them apart! Li agrees, dresses as a bride, and departs. Fragrant Princess, left alone, bemoans her lot. When Yang and Su arrive, they find the Peach Blossom fan (Hou's gift) spotted with her blood. Yang paints twigs and leaves around it, making a semblance of peach blossoms: the symbol of her love. Su has heard that Hou is somewhere along the Yellow River, and volunteers to search for him. Could he take a message? Fragrant Princess says, Just take the fan.

Months later, Juan gloats that he now belongs to the Inner Court and is a friend of the Emperor *and* the Prime Minister. His job is to seek out musicians and singing girls, i.e. to pimp. This search turns up some earlier characters – but courtesan Pien is to become a Taoist nun, and musician Ting a Taoist monk. This will prove thematic. Fragrant Princess limps onstage, having been dragged from her domicile. But she is defiant, and will denounce the "shameless flatterer" and "cruel tyrant" as before (K'ung 180). Enter Ma, Juan, and Yang. Ma remarks that "Actors can be dangerous" (181). Flattery is often the villain, he says as they flatter him. Guards lead in singing girls, but detain only Fragrant Princess (whom they confuse with Madam Li). She sings her accusations of Ma as "Pandering to the Emperor's lust" and Juan as one of the "upstart foster sons of eunuchs" (183). She pushes over a steward, Juan kicks her, and she is taken away; he says that she should be beheaded. Left alone, Yang decides to have painter Lan house-sit the Tower of Enchanting Fragrance (Li's house) until Fragrant Princess returns to it.

In the Hall of Balmy Breezes, Juan sends for "Madam Li" (really Fragrant

Princess). Enter Emperor Fu and eunuchs. It is a year since his coronation and he is searching for good actors to perform at the Lantern Festival. Juan has five of them (including "Li") brought in. Fu asks if they know Juan's play *The Swallow Letter*. All do except "Li," so Juan says that she can play the clown. They rehearse a scene, which pleases Fu, but, struck by the clown's beauty, he asks what plays she *does* know. She sings an aria from *The Peony Pavilion* so movingly that he insists on her playing the heroine. "Li" will be given a copy of the part and three days to learn it. After they all exit, Fragrant Princess weeps, fearing that she may never escape.

Beside the Yellow River, Hou is at his wit's end. Gen. Kao, to whom he is an aide, makes enemies by his foul temper, even abusing Commander Hsu to his face. Hou urges him to be more friendly, but Kao says that Hsu is a failure and will be sacked. Hou obtains permission to visit his family, and leaves. That evening Gen. Kao and his guards ride into the city, where an officer of Hsu's invites them to a banquet. Kao and some others go in; the rest stay outside. They eat, drink, and toast; then firecrackers explode, and Hsu's men set on Kao's party. His guards are slaughtered and he is beheaded. Hsu intends to show Kao's head to the "northern leaders," gain their support, defeat Kao's troops, and conquer the south.

Coincidence rules in scene 27. Su, searching for Hou along the river, is thrown into it by soldiers who want his donkey, but pulled out by...Madam Li's boatman! While tied up that night they trade stories, overheard by...Hou in the next boat! Again China seems small. They confer, Su gives Hou the peach-blossom fan, and they proceed to Nanking on Hou's boat to search for Fragrant Princess. In the next scene Hou reaches Madam Li's house, which Lan is tending. Yang arrives and, knowing the situation at court, warns Hou to "find some other beauty" to replace Fragrant Princess (K'ung 210). Lan paints a picture of the Peach Blossom Fountain (likely the Peach Blossom Spring of scene 1), spoken of with the reverence associated with *domaines*. Yang tells Hou to avoid the house: his connection with Fragrant Princess is well known to Juan and Ma.

A month later, Hou, obsessed with finding Fragrant Princess, and Su, alarmed by "the political situation...going from bad to worse," visit Ts'ai (from the Interlude), enjoying the success of his bookshop (K'ung 213). Su recommends that they all flee to the hills, but Ts'ai is hosting a resistance group and promoting new works by Ch'en and Wu, who appear from the back of the shop. They are catching up – Hou mentions "three wasted years" in the field (215) – when

Juan enters, exulting in his high office, python robe, jade belt, etc. He arrests and removes Ch'en, Wu, and Hou. Ts'ai and Wu lament that "Ma and Juan are now omnipotent. / Woe to the world" (219). The prisoners are taken to a jail run by Chang Wei, once a court official. Knowing the regime's corruption and longing to retire, he sees that these men are innocent, but newly revised rules require that he detain them. He counsels patience and withdraws to his pavilion, where a guard brings him yet another prisoner: Ts'ai. Chang tells the guard to take his horse and symbols of office back to town; then persuades Ts'ai to head for the hills with him. Chang will become a religious recluse: the second time this has happened, to a total of three characters. We have a pattern.

But the Resistance continues. Su obtains an audience with Commander Tso, Yuan, and Huang at army headquarters. He describes the mess in Nanking, and others update the charges against Ma and Juan. Yuan drafts articles of impeachment, Huang proclaims them, and Liu volunteers to deliver them. In the next scene, the Master of Ceremonies, Ma, Yang, and Shih observe the first anniversary of the Emperor's death with kowtows, burnt offerings, and an elegy. Juan arrives late, "crying aloud" his "crocodile tears" (K'ung 239). Shih exits in disgust, followed by Yang. Ma and Juan stay to plot how to crown Fu Emperor and become ministers. The Heir Apparent is in prison; the troublesome First Consort will be controlled, dissidents executed. Then messengers arrive with the impeachment declaration. Sending their army against Tso's would expose them to "northerners," which is dangerous; alternatives are discussed (242). Juan orders two rebels executed, then changes the penalty to detention in case Tso wins. In the jail, Hou, Ch'en, and Wu are joined by Liu, who provides a list of other arrested officials and "eminent men of letters" (247).

It is not yet clear how K'ung means to use all this personal, historical, and military material; like *War and Peace*, the play's quotient of war history can feel excessive. China has been cut into three zones, armies are in the field, and rebel forces are split. Ma and Juan's man, Gen. Huang, is blocking Tso's army, and one of Tso's generals has defected. When word comes that forces commanded by Tso's rogue son are sacking a city, Tso vomits blood, collapses, and dies (a famous incident). That front is hopeless now. Shih despairs: they are losing battles, northern troops are advancing, only 3000 men are left, and *they* want plunder. His attempt to rouse them falls flat – until he weeps "Tears of blood": another legend (K'ung

256). Inspired, the generals accept his orders and depart with war-cries. But there is anarchy in Nanking: armies approach, rioters riot, losers hide or try to flee. They include great ones like Hung-kuang, the last Ming emperor; near-greats such as Ma and Juan (beaten and robbed); and lesser figures, including Lan, who escapes with Fragrant Princess and Su. Lan reveals their goal: "No strife disturbs the realm of Peach Blossom Cave," where Fragrant Princess hopes to rest (266). Every mention of "Peach Blossom" – spring, fountain, fan, cave – is redolent of a *domaine* of some kind. That now seems the likely goal.

Yet military and political issues still preoccupy the dramatist. Gen. Huang learns that northern forces are threatening Nanking. When the Emperor arrives, Huang welcomes Him reverently, but cannot provide and will not promise the protection He wants. That night two generals advise Huang to deliver Him to the northern court. Infuriated, he beats them, but his aide T'ien wounds him, then turns over the last Ming ruler to the generals himself. In despair, Huang cuts his own throat. Gov. Shih, fleeing Yangchow, meets the Master of Ceremonies, and hearing that the Emperor has fled Nanking, doffs his robes of office and jumps into the river, not to resurface. Liu and Hou, then Ch'en and Wu, all fleeing, praise Shih and lament his loss.

Then the play does finally change course. Liu, Hou, and the Master of Ceremonies decide to head for remote Cloud's Roost Mountain; Ch'en and Wu will go there via a different route. The theme of withdrawal from chaos takes over. Henceforth the setting is a mountain wilderness dotted with temples, monks, and nuns. In scene 39 the principals reach Cloud's Roost. Lan brings Fragrant Princess and Su to Foster Purity Temple, where Abbess (formerly singing-girl) Pien welcomes them. Su goes to gather firewood, and Fragrant Princess starts sewing a prayer-banner. When Hou, Liu, and the Master of Ceremonies arrive, asking shelter, it is refused: this is a nunnery, nor are they recognized! On the mountainside the men encounter Ting, once a poet-musician, now a Taoist and herbalist. *He* recognizes them, and recommends Gather Purity Temple. The Master of Ceremonies prefers White Cloud Temple; the others row across the river to Gather Purity. Hou sings, "within the gate, the alchemist's crucible," and "As in a dream we enter fairyland" (K'ung 285). This sounds like the long-sought *domaine*, the magical abode of peace and retirement evoked in the first scene, although that has always been a Peach Blossom (something) before.

The 40th and last scene is dated 1645, 7th month: over two years since the action began. Chang, the former Imperial Guard, now abbot at White Cloud Temple; merchant/bookseller Ts'ai; and painter Lan – all from the Interlude, all Taoists now – prepare the altar for a ritual. The Master of Ceremonies and villagers carry out "rites of purification" and offerings to the Emperor and other victims of the war (K'ung 288). Chang recounts his visions of good and evil spirits, importing that "virtue reaps reward" and "evil meets retribution" (292-93). He calls them a "karmic mirror" showing the "karmic circle" in which justice will be done (K'ung's first invocation of karma). There follows what writers on comedy call a "general assembly" of characters, whose usual agenda is also justice: eject villains and celebrate the union of lovers. Pien and Fragrant Princess enter on one side, Ting and Hou on the other. The lovers have not met for almost two years. Chang is preaching against "dusty desires" and "lingering mortal passion." Then Hou sees Fragrant Princess, rushes to her, and presents the fan, spotted with drops of her blood: the emblem of their love and trials. Surely some resolution is at hand.

They gaze on the fan for a moment; then Pien and Ting part them. Chang seizes the fan and flings it to the ground. He acknowledges their relationship and debts, but when Hou mentions "man and wife," Chang denounces this as "meaningless chatter" and "piteous passion-clinging" (K'ung 296). Rather than protesting, the couple submit: Hou salutes Ting as his tutor and Fragrant Princess takes Pien as hers. They don Taoist robes and *prostrate* themselves before Chang. Ting and Pien sing, "Root out passion /.../ Life is brief as bubble of foam" (297). Chang tells Hou to go south and Fragrant Princess north: no temptation must arise from proximity. They agree. "All is illusion," says Fragrant Princess. "I know not that man before me" (298). Chang laughs and sings, happy that he shredded the Peach Blossom Fan, symbol of the couple's desire for a love-*domaine*. So much for comedy's "fruitful union"! Renunciation rules. It resembles our last glimpse of Bao Yu, walking out on his pregnant wife and disappearing into falling snow with his otherworldly friends in *The Story of the Stone*. Both works redefine an earthly *domaine* and assign it to another plane of existence.

K'ung added an Epilogue, dated 1648: about three years later. Su is gathering wood and Liu is fishing when the Master of Ceremonies arrives with a jar of wine to share. He sings a song he has written. Titled "Questions to Heaven," it reflects the experiences of his long life and what they have all endured. "Is it the Creator's will / That the poor stay poor, / The rich continue rich?" he asks (K'ung 301). The song is praised. Liu responds with a ballad, "Nanking Autumn," lamenting the fall of the Mings. Su describes his recent visit to Nanking: once a great city, now a place of death and ruin. Who could foresee that "all would vanish" (309)? Then a stranger appears: a "magistrate's runner," i.e. a spy for the new regime. Feigning sleep, he hears their incriminating talk of resistance; then rises to say that you "loyalist recluses" must come with him (311). The trio immediately decamp in three directions, scrambling "up cliffs and over gullies" faster than he can follow. Offstage voices sing an elegy for "Dreams that did not last" and "Praise for the painted fan" (312) – the one that Chang tore and threw in the dirt. Our friends are on the run, but at least they are still free.

There it ends, with the survivors scattered, fleeing or hiding, and the Hou/ Fragrant Princess plot cut off, a non-story under Taoist auspices. The impulse that most western dramatists would feel toward a "happy ending" is absent, though a Taoist would say that "happy" has been redefined. All the "offstage voices" can give is an elegy. K'ung's apparent path to a conventional comic conclusion for the lovers is *only* apparent: he was not headed there after all. Everything, including the Good in life, has changed and, we are told, risen to the realm of spiritual self-knowledge, far above mortals' "dusty desires." If that is not what we came for, perhaps we were misinformed; if we are disappointed by the Taoist idea of happiness, we are evidently not ready. K'ung has finished: the play is already long enough, taking several days to perform, and he has given us what he wanted to give. We are free to use our imaginations, or follow the Way ourselves, or ignore the play.

OBVIOUSLY THESE THREE WORKS DIFFER sharply. *The Western Chamber Romance* is a dramatic narrative (not a play) and a romantic comedy, with a degree of frankness about premarital sex that made it notorious (and popular) in Chinese culture. Treating of both time and karma, it hints at other possible *domaines* before settling on a love-match for Chang and Yin-Yin. *The Peony Pavilion* is clearly drama, a type of opera, but a comedy only with reservations. The early death of the heroine delays her union with the hero; it takes a judgment in hell and a grave robbery to make her eligible for marriage, and the cloud of her father's rejection of the match is not dispelled at the end, so its "comedy" and love-*domaine* are dark and qualified. The play's structure raises questions about the workings of time, whose alleged healing powers seem the best hope for the principals at the end. *The Peach Blossom Fan* is also an operatic drama, but finally neither "romantic" nor comic. Its lovers achieve conjugal bliss early, but are soon parted by political chaos and civil war. When finally reunited, they defer to their Taoist friends and renounce each other. It is finally an anti-comedy, then, and ultimately its only *domaine* is spiritual. A history or chronicle play, it has a strong, insistent concern with time. If *The Peony Pavilion* plays with the idea that time's arrow can in rare cases be recalled, *The Peach Blossom Fan* shows it as inexorable and destructive of both political and amatory *domaines*.

The Asian works considered are not as obsessed with time as is Proust, nor with *domaines* as are Fowles and Alain-Fournier, but those entities form part of their fabrics. The two later plays develop themes familiar from *The Story of the Stone*: the rise and fall of dynasties and families, declines from past glories leading to nostalgia for rosier times. (The *Western Chamber Romance* stands apart in being devoid of such nostalgia.) Cyril Birch wrote that *The Peony Pavilion* and *The Peach Blossom Fan* look back longingly to the salad days of great dynasties. His descriptions of their wistfulness resemble those given of other *domaines*; and such comparisons of past and present conditions naturally generate meditations on the effects of time. The latter scenes of *The Peach Blossom Fan* also present the phenomenon of lay men and woman turning away from secular life to become monks or nuns, as in *The Tale of Genji* and *The Story of the Stone*. This kind of renunciation amounts to redefining what qualifies as a *domaine*, and locating it on a higher, more spiritual level, well clear of the world of mortal desires and ticking clocks.

Miscellaneous Prose: Philosophical, Fictive, Legendary

Hayy Ibn Yaqzan, mentioned in Chapter 9 as an island *domaine*, was also a non-western text. Ibn Tufayl (or Tufail or Tafayl), its author, came from southern Spain, which in the twelfth century was part of a 'Moorish' empire stretching west from Arabia. A Muslim Arab, he spent most of his life in Morocco, where he served two caliphs as secretary, later physician, and wrote the "first Arabic novel." His sources and settings were Middle Eastern. He took his title (but not his plot) from Ibn Sina (Avicenna), a Persian polymath (c. 980-1037) best known for works on medicine and astronomy, not for his 'philosophical romance'. Ibn Tufayl thinks more like a novelist than had Ibn Sina. How did Hayy come to *be* on the island? Well, he could have fallen from the legendary *waqwaq* tree (whose fruit fell crying "Waqwaq!"), or have floated over in an ark launched by the sister of the king of a nearby island (she having married without his permission). Hayy's island is called Waqwaq, which some scholars identify with Ceylon / Sri Lanka (Verde 3). In the *Ramayana*, that is the island from which Rama had to rescue Sita. After the death of his gazelle foster mother, Hayy seeks scientific and philosophical truths. His life falls into seven periods of seven years each, seven being a powerful number in eastern thought, ranging from its use in Moorish architecture to the seven-day week. The book's reputation spread throughout the east, influencing Arabic and Persian writers and Islamic philosphers; then, when it was translated into European languages in the seventeenth century, touched the west's literature and philosophy in several places.

The classic example of an eastern work with western popularity, though, is *The Arabian Nights* (*The Thousand and One Nights*). Joseph Campbell's introduction to the Viking edition (1952) is an excellent guide, providing information and interpretations. The book's sources were Persian and Arab, mainly Arab in its final form (Campbell 3-5). The tales range widely in date (eighth century to seventeenth) and place (across the Muslim empire), with a core in fourteenth-century Iraq (6, 9-10, 22). Its central figure is Caliph Haroun al Rashid (Rachid, Raschid), who lived ca 800 CE: the last ruler of a huge caliphate when Baghdad was at its zenith. Campbell calls *The Arabian Nights* a "brilliant revival of a golden age," which can be done only by literature's time machine (1). The caliph can roam the city incognito by night, but he must also face enchantments in that wondrous environment: a *domaine*. The wide world of Sindbad the Sailor is as charmed a place as Baghdad, where a girl drawing water at a well may meet the caliph, and marry him. But the greatest wonder of *The Nights* is Sheherazade (Shahrazad), the Grand Vizier's daughter who enters the royal harem, but escapes the usual fate of its members – execution the next morning – by spinning the tales of *The Arabian Nights*, pausing in mid-tale each evening, to be continued. A gifted tease, queen of "the hook" and narrator *sans pareil*, she tells the king and us about Haroun al Rashid, Sindbad, Aladdin, Ali Baba and the rest in well-measured doses: 1a tonight, 1b and 2a tomorrow night, etc. Finally the king surrenders and marries her. The tales' meta-story ends happily.

AMONG THE WORKS OUTSIDE MAINSTREAM western literature that can test my core hypothesis are the oral traditions of peoples about where they originated and how they lived, such as indigenous myths of the Americas. These have the merit of bringing in some previously neglected areas, but they also pose special difficulties. They are not "literature" until written down, which inevitably alters the pre-literary material – yet that is the only way most of us will know them. The "imaginative" aspect of literature is also problematical. Those within these traditions regard them as religion, history, or both, not as works of the imagination, which in general usage connotes stories that may not have happened, but were created by authors for their own purposes, not to preserve a people's beliefs. In Platonic terms, they regard these legends as the Real, the highest reality, not the earthly copy that human fiction is, so the politics of discussing them is tortuous. If they are tribal credos emanating from a community to which I do not belong, how can I understand them? Do I have any right to discuss them? My credibility, competence, and good will are going to be suspect. The same objection can be made to this whole chapter: Chinese, Japanese, East Indian, African. These are not charges that I can simply dismiss by pleading that my best efforts, and my apologies, should suffice. Not having found any truthful answer that satisfies those who feel this way, I have chosen to discuss them anyway, as carefully as possible, and risk the censure.

Frank Waters faced some of these same difficulties in publishing *Book of the Hopi* (1963), but his was a less politicized age, and he had other advantages. His father was part Cheyenne, and growing up in the American Southwest, Frank lived among Utes and Navajos; in manhood he spent considerable time with Hopi and Taos Pueblo natives. So he was partly "of the blood," with some experience of native life. His collaborator on the book, Oswald White Bear Fredericks, recorded the testimony of thirty Hopi elders about their creation and "emergences"; they spoke "out of the depths of an archaic America we have never known, out of immeasurable time" and an archetypal unconscious (Waters ix). On the basis of that testimony, collected over three years, Waters sketches their pre-history, whose serial creations have parallels elsewhere in the Americas.

The legendary *First World*, a beautiful and happy place where healthy people enjoyed a Golden Age, was simply "good" (3, 6-7, 11): i.e. a *domaine*, like prelapsarian Eden. But as these first humans multiplied and spread, some forgot the gods, and tribal differences caused them to divide and fight. The gods decided to destroy the First World, but saved a Chosen Few by putting them in an ant kiva (house) – an anthill – to learn cooperation. The First World was then destroyed by fire, and when it cooled, the *Second World* was created, somewhat less beautiful. People and animals separated from each other then, and trade led to greed, unbelief, and war. The Second World was destroyed by ice after the Chosen were sent back to the ants. The *Third World*, an age of cities, civilization, corruption, and aerial warfare on flying shields, had to be destroyed too, by a great flood, but again a righteous remnant was saved, this time in (and by) reedbeds.

Round Four is different from the start. The survivors float east in reed boats and pause on some islands that they agree are *not* the Fourth World. (Clues point to a voyage from East Asia or a Pacific island toward the Americas.) Sailing on, they do reach the *Fourth World*, where their god-guide Sótuknang, nephew of the Creator, appears and says, Look back. Facing west, they see their island "stepping-stones" – the mountain summits of the Third World – disappear under the Pacific (Waters 20). He has sunk the "footprints of your Emergence," which (if they keep the faith) will re-emerge when needed. Sótuknang announces that this place is called "Túwaqachi, World Complete"; it is "not all beautiful and easy," but "it has everything" (21). They are apparently on the west coast of Central or North America. He tells them to "separate and go different ways," i.e. begin their migrations. The tribes roam for many years, following the stars and instructions from the gods, leaving petroglyphs as records of their travels. These migrations are understood as purifying tests of the various bands. The elders say that we are still in the Fourth World, though much later we hear that "The Emergence to the future Fifth World has begun" among "the humble people of little nations, tribes, and racial minorities" (334). (This is among the Hopi prophecies, which include World War III, started by Asian and African nations, and the destruction of the United States by nuclear war.)

All this is in Part One, "The Myths." The other sections ("Legends," "The Mystery Plays," and "History") are full of division, conflict, invasion, and violence. Some of them have historical interest, such as the "Mysterious Red City of the South," where Kachinas ("spirits of the invisible forces of life") taught history; and the arrivals of Asians from the north and whites from the east and south (Waters 67-68, 112). Other chapters are simply grim, describing civil war, and how the Bow Clan flouted the will of the gods and brought "the power of evil" from the Third World to the Fourth (90). But the founding of the clifftop village of Oraibi on religious principles and according to prophecy seems to produce a *domaine* – at least in hindsight, which is how "the good old days" tend to be seen most reverently:

> *Every year the kachinas came to help the people, bringing blessings from other stars, worlds, and planets. Grass grew knee-high on the vast plain. Herds of antelope grazed within sight of all villages. Bighorn sheep were numerous on the farther mesas. Game of all kinds was abundant everywhere.* (111)

Domaines also occur in the Hopi spiritual beliefs recounted by Waters and dramatized in the mystery plays, especially the representation of previous emergences. These ideas are developed in "The Kachina Night Dances" (III.4), which reenact a series of once and future *domaines* of pure emergence followed by corruption and destruction (165). It is said that there will be three more worlds to emerge into, and (by the way) there are six universes besides our own. Some of the kachina songs repeat the promise of returning rains in terms of a spiritual *domaine*: blessings, happiness, joy, "oneness," and "harmony with the one Creator" (172).

Most of Part Four, "The History," however, is dystopic, an anti-*domaine*. The "Castillas," Spanish soldiers and friars, arrived from the south in 1598. Pressured by missionaries, "many Hopis were converted" in some villages (Waters 253). Forced labour was used to build churches and supply the needs of the priests. "The *padres'* illicit relations with young Hopi girls were common in all villages," Waters reports. The priests also made the Hopi give up their 'pagan' ceremonies, whereupon "the rains stopped," "the crops failed and famine spread over the land," so they covertly resumed 'paganism.' Their grievances swelled into the Pueblo Revolt (1680), which expelled the Castillas, but they returned twelve years later and converted the village of Awatovi, tearing the fabric of Hopi rituals. Warriors from other villages attacked Awatovi, killing the inhabitants and burning the village. The elders called this "ruthless massacre" a "mass murder" and a "tragic defeat of the Hopi spirit" (266). In the same period "Navajos, an Athabascan people," came through "the Back Door to the north": Canada (255; a Canadian Dené and an Arizona Navajo confirmed this connection to me). They were "barbarians" with "no legends to tell" and "never stopped eating until everything was gone." The Hopi taught them to plant, but the Navajos became their worst native enemies. And in the nineteenth century came Americans from the east, bringing army rule, more missionaries, "Indian agents," tribal division, and disintegration (270ff.).

In his last chapter, Waters reviews this bleak modern history, concluding that the Hopi are in "ethnic eclipse"; they need to transcend tribalism and "integrate as a social whole," accept outside help, and free themselves from witchcraft (Waters 335). But he also channels the Hopi perspective with obvious sympathy. Despite their "immemorial tenure" in the southwest, they have been "ruthlessly dispossessed" by invaders who value property above all else: a victory of "armed might over moral right." Governments have broken treaties with them, hypocritical churches have betrayed professed principles, and "the juggernaut march of the dollar" tramples all. It is an ugly picture, and he sees little room for hope. Yet Waters places the Hopi among the oppressed peoples of the world who are finding their voices. In the fullness of time, they believe, the wheel will come round. Their conception of time is crucial.

> Hopi time, unlike our own, is not a shallow horizontal stream. It does not flow out of a conveniently forgotten past...into a future we are hurrying to reach. All Indian time has a vertical dimension that cups past and future in a timeless present that forgets no injustices and anticipates all possible compensations. (335)

This view resembles some of the "time machines" of Part I, and karma, but it is communal, not individual. Whether the Hopi can maintain their identity amidst racism, materialism, and a strong, hostile culture is the question. Waters does not undertake to give a definitive answer, but hopes that the elders' voices will be heard. He has done what he can to that end.

THE MAYAN SACRED BOOK, *POPOL VUH*, is formidable to approach but too important to avoid. After a long existence as oral legends, it was written: first in hieroglyphic characters, later as an alphabetic text. It has a strange feel if your idea of a holy book is the Bible. Its account of Creation is lively, but considerably less august than that of Genesis, and includes a good deal of (seemingly gratuitous) horseplay and violence (the Bible has some of the latter, too). Fortunately there are helpful scholars to guide us. In *The Maya*, Michael D. Coe provides an admirably compressed summary of this "great epic of the Quiché Maya" (42). It recounts how the gods

> brought forth the earth from a watery void, and endowed it with
> animals and plants. Anxious for praise..., the divine progenitors fash
> ioned manlike creatures from mud, but to mud they returned. Next
> a race of wooden figures appeared, but the mindless manikins were
> destroyed by the gods, to be replaced by men made from flesh. These,
> however, turned to wickedness and were annihilated as black rains
> fell and a great flood swept the earth. Finally true men...were created
> from maize dough.

Writing in the 1960s, Coe seemed to feel that there was little he could confidently add to this Mayan account of their origins.

We also have Dennis Tedlock, who revised his earlier translation in 1996 (the edition I cite) because of changes in the scholarly community's understanding of some Mayan hieroglyphics. Like Frank Waters, he worked closely with a native informant. Tedlock makes several points that are central to my purposes. After noting the rise-and-fall trajectory of Mayan history – a shape found in several Asian texts – he argues that the authors of the alphabetic sixteenth-century *Popol Vuh*, descendants of the families who ruled the Mayan capital Quiché, acted from a desire to preserve the 'back-story' of Quiché's ruins (Tedlock 22-23, 25, 27): the preservative function of literature discussed in Part I. Equipped with *Popol Vuh*, the early Quiché leaders were said to know *everything*, including the future. They had the "clear sight" attributed to the first humans; readers could "see and move beyond the present" (29). At the end of his Introduction Tedlock repeats that *Popol Vuh* provided a means of seeing into different eras, making it in effect a time machine. He also warns that the Mayans' seemingly obscure mythic plots hide astral / calendrical meanings. Their strong, sustained interest in astronomy, astrology, and calendar-making attests to their seriousness about the measurement of time, which is one of the themes of *Popol Vuh*.

Tedlock summarizes its contents in some detail. In the beginning there was sky and sea; then the gods created earth and the celestial bodies (except for the sun). The first three attempts to make humans were unsatisfactory, as the Hopi believed

– one of many parallels among native American creation myths. The "defeats" of the gods Zipacna and Earthquake remind us that the Mayans were polytheists, and that not all of their gods were benign (the volcanic "spine" of Central America makes Earthquake a recurrent menace). The narrative then backs up a generation to the Hunahpu twins: a lively section of origin myths, astronomical lore, and abundant word-play. After more exploits with (at least) double meanings, there was a fourth try at making humans, which (like the fourth Hopi Emergence) was successful. Wives, tribes, and cities followed – yet there was still no sun. En route to Copán, a great Mayan centre, the Jaguar lords and others saw the first sunrise. Then we begin to hear of Quiché lords – in historical time now – three of whom travel far and win a great victory. In the next generation, three other Quiché lords representing three important lineages make a pilgrimage east to a large body of water, returning to widespread acclaim and leadership roles in governing and migrating. Plumed Serpent, a "lord of genius," appears as both a god and a king (Tedlock 216, n. 63). Other rulers of Quiché are mentioned as well.

Moving from such summaries into *Popol Vuh* itself is like leaving a plantation for the deep forest: one is often lost or confused, but also delighted at times. The Mayan gods are less august than the Hebrews' YHWH, more nearly human – specifically a human committee, bumbling along, sharing our puzzlement. Early in Part 1, they "worry" about the project of creating us (Tedlock 65, 66). Animals are made first, but since they do not speak, man is created to praise the gods. Initially unsatisfactory, they need revision. The second draft is manikins and carvings (the first, silent humans are destroyed by a flood). Then comes a Trumplike figure of uncertain genre named 7 Macaw who magnifies himself, saying, "I am great...I am their sun" (73). But aspiring to grandeur, it is said, he puffed himself up. Two boy-gods vow to destroy him in Part 2. They shoot an arrow that breaks his jaw, and direct their grandparents to pull his teeth and pluck out his eyes. 7 Macaw and his wife die, but when the Four Hundred Boys (Tedlock's "booze gods") go to kill his son Zipacna, he kills them instead. The boy-gods then lure him into a cave where he is turned to stone.

Part 3 has entertaining moments, but is long, violent, and often baffling. This version of humans – idle, noisy, irritating – displeases the gods. There are also several demi-gods: human forms with higher powers. Venturing to Xibalba (the underworld), the twins 1 and 7 Hunapu are "defeated" several times (Tedlock

94-96). They fail a test in the Dark House and are sacrificed, but 1 Hunapu's head, placed in a tree, causes it to bear calabashes (an origin myth). The head spits in Blood Moon's palm, impregnating her; she gives birth to Hunahpu and Xbalanque. Their grandmother and half-brothers put them on an anthill and in brambles, but they trick the half-brothers into the trees and turn *them* into monkeys. The twins become gardeners, but animals devour the plants at night. However, a rat announces that their *real* job is the ball game: the ancient Mayans' top sport, played on special courts. The rat brings proper equipment, so they clean the court and play. The "Lords of Xibalba" send a message to Granny proposing a match. She commits the message to a louse, which is eaten by a toad, which is eaten by a snake, which is eaten by a falcon, which the boys shoot. The sequence is then reversed, and the louse delivers the message. The boys accept the challenge, but first plant corn, a staple and a symbol.

Hunahpu and Xbalanque walk to Xibalba, sending a mosquito ahead to bite its lords and bring back their names (having an enemy's name confers power). Entering the Dark House, they receive a torch and cigars with instructions not to use them up; they substitute a macaw tail and fireflies. In The Game, the lords' ball is a skull with a knife inside. The boys lose, and owe the lords flowers as a prize. In Razor House they appease the knives by giving them animal flesh; then ants gather the flowers. They survive other houses, but in Bat House a bat decapitates Hunahpu. A coatimundi brings a squash: his new head. The real head is used in the next ball game. They recover it, but foreseeing their deaths, the boys tell seers to grind their bones and toss them in the river. When this is done they revive as catfish, work wonders and become famous. Invited to dance before the lords, they sing, perform magic, kill and revive others and themselves. 1 and 7 Death ask to be sacrificed, too. They are killed, but not revived! The boys reveal their identities, then threaten the Xibalbans with death. They beg for mercy, so their sentence is reduced to a low standard of living and denunciation as "masters of stupidity" (Tedlock 139). The boys reconstruct their father, leave him at the ball court to receive prayers, and ascend to the sky.

All this predates humans; not until Part IV do Plumed Serpent and others create them out of corn. These "mother-fathers" can walk, talk, understand all "perfectly," and are good, so the Mayans, too, once had a *domaine* – but not for long. This is "no good," say the Makers, they'll be "as great as gods," and "take them apart just a little," limiting their foresight and knowledge (Tedlock 145-48; cp. Genesis 1:22-24). Women are created as wives and mothers. All pray to the Makers for dawn. At Citadel Tulan, the clans receive their different gods and languages, but lose the common one. Tormented by hunger and alienation, they burn incense as sun, moon, and stars appear. Then the clans disperse and things fall apart. The gods regulate worship: some will sacrifice less and defeat "the [other] tribes." Some killing is done by Cauec Quichés. "The tribes" send maidens to seduce the gods' "spirit familiars" (168), but the gods are not fooled. The tribes march on the Quiché gods and "mother-fathers," but falling asleep en route, have their beards plucked and their metal taken. They attack the citadel anyway, are routed by wasps and yellowjackets, and made to pay tribute. The four lords (three Jaguars and Not Right Now) depart, leaving instructions in a Bundle of Flames.

In Part V, three of their sons (named or titled Noble) marry women from other tribes, journey to meet Lord Naxit, receive tokens of Lordship over the Quiché, and return with the knowledge of writing. Here *Popol Vuh* passes from oral tradition to history and literature. The Nobles' reign is happy. After that generation's mothers die, the Quiché move onto four mountaintops, and the next generation relocates again. They are attacked by the Ilocs, who are defeated and enslaved or sacrificed. The three main houses of the Quiché intermarry. In the fifth generation they move again, quarrel, and divide into nine lineages. Now there are four clans and 24 lords with great houses and vassals. Plumed Serpent (named for the god) becomes sole leader, but the sixth generation's leaders have to fight the tribes again, install "sentries" and "lookouts," take "spoils and prisoners" (Tedlock 187-90). The lords can see all times, places, and events clearly because their time machine, the Council Book (*Popol Vuh*), assists them. Rich tributes flow in. This has the making of a *domaine*, but lists of the Lordships' generations and the lineages of great houses tell a different story. The Quiché become tributaries in the ninth generation, and in the twelfth the Spanish appear. Quiché leaders are tortured; those of the 14th generation have Spanish names.

Conquistadores, tribute, and torture were only the beginning of the cultural destruction that was coming to the Mayans; its effects can be seen and felt in Latin America today. The later pages of *Popol Vuh* depict the kind of anti-*domaine* found in Waters's final comments on the Hopi: decline and disorder under oppressive occupations by alien invaders. Both of these indigenous peoples created and preserve myths or legends that have two functions with which we are familiar. They reach well back in time, reciting their earliest and subsequent traditions of how they came to be, of what and where they were 'in the beginning'. Using *Popol Vuh*, it was said, rulers could see along the flight of time's arrow and thus guide their people – until the *conquista*, where its limitations were revealed. Both peoples assert that there was a Golden Age at or soon after the creation or Emergence: life was good and people were united. This *domaine* did not last, but it was a far better era than those that followed, and memories of it are important to heal the wounded spirits of descendants. Waters's accounts of Hopi ceremonies show that they aspire to re-create that pristine state – while the ritual lasts – and the tribe's collective memory is crucial to that. In this case at least, the temporal and *domaine* functions of the imaginative / historical performance are intimately related.

OF THE OTHER WORKS DISCUSSED in this subchapter, *Hayy ibn Yaqzan* is the more complex. Hayy is raised on an island by his gazelle foster mother – a *domaine* and a "natural" upbringing that Rousseau and Wordsworth would approve. After her death, his quest for knowledge becomes a *domaine* of learning, possessing its own magic. It takes him to another island for a while, but that disappoints him and he returns to his natal island for the rest of his life, as Wordsworth kept returning to wild England in various ways. *The Arabian Nights* is simpler, a classic *domaine* book (re)creating "golden age" Baghdad as a time and place where anything might happen and often did; where a benign caliph, eager to know and able to delight his subjects, roamed incognito, and the world's prize storyteller spun lifesaving tales. *Hayy* is temporally symmetrical, with its seven seven-year segments. *The Arabian Nights* is more casual about time, and may often seem timeless, though its component tales were for the most part historical short stories, the productions of earlier ages when things were different and often uncanny.

THIS CHAPTER ASKS WHETHER THE ideas I propose about the springs of western literature are really "archetypes" that operate in other literatures as well. We have seen that the evidence is mixed. It is not difficult to find *domaines* and time machines – or some concern with time – in non-western literature; whether they are as plenteous and of the same nature as those in the west is the question. Epic, lyric poetry, and drama give equivocal answers, and my sample may be too small to settle the issue. East Indian epics preserve ancient heroics for the present, and record brilliant court life; in *Sunjata*, it is hard to find any *domaine* for the characters, although the editors think that it constitutes one for modern readers, and Alex Haley makes Kunta Kinte's village a natural and cultural idyll early in *Roots*. Asian lyric poems contain familiar laments about Time the Destroyer, but they may or may not evoke wondrous places. While Japanese and Chinese literature contains fleeting *domaines*, their treatment of time is guided by the concept of karma, a special kind of "time machine," with a strong moral dimension inside a system of reincarnation. These remarks also apply to the Chinese dramas discussed, which tend to avoid the love-conquers-all resolution of our comedies, qualifying it and / or redefining happiness as spiritual instead of emotional and carnal; this is true of *The Story of the Stone* as well. The origin myths of native Americans present early Edenic *domaines*, but subsequent time is apprehended mainly as a destroyer. Their legends and rituals reenact the myths and preserve the collective memory of a halcyon era, as do the Asian books and plays discussed, which hark back to a recollected ideal existence. And naturally the eastern works have their own set of preoccupations: the rise and fall of great families; proper education; right religion; corruption; and the perennial workings of karma. In short, they modify my "archetypes."

EPILOGUE:

The Time Machine
and the Domaine

IF IT HAS OCCURRED TO you that time machines and *domaines* – the two fundamental generators and functions of literature that I have proposed – are related,
you are not alone. I have pointed out several instances of their kinship along the
way. But does this affinity justify a synthesis: "The two are one"? Are they reduc-
ible to a unity, or is this a useful way to think of them? To compare small things
with great, Albert Einstein's concept of spacetime, still largely intact as it enters
its second century, posits that time and space are interdependent, that they affect
each other and "warp" together. In Brian Greene's formulation, "by knitting
space and time together into the unified structure of spacetime, special relativity
declares, 'What's true for space is true for time'" (66). Does "unified structure"
mean that they are identical, however? The same can be asked of time (machines)
and *domaines*. While theoretically or philosophically time may pass or be considered without reference to a spatial location, we mortals live each moment of our
lives in *some place*, while every *domaine* occurs at *some time* and not at others. At
the beginning of the western world's fascination with time machines, H.G. Wells's
Victorian contraption had to occupy a particular patch of London's real estate as
the centuries whizzed by – except when it endured the consequences of being
dragged for a short distance.

So while time (theoretically) *may* not require location or even space to exist,
a *domaine* has both temporal and geographic coordinates, joined and interact-
ing, like spacetime. Change either the position or the period and the *domaine*
evaporates, subtilizing into ordinary air. Take the classic modern paradigm,

Alain-Fournier's 'lost domain' of *Les Sablonnières*. When Meaulnes first arrives, it is a magical *domaine* for him – not for everyone, not for Franz, nor for the comedians, for whom it is just a gig – but "as time goes by" it becomes merely a troubled property, a set of problems without the power or magic to move anything other than concern, regret, and nostalgia. And the same applies all up and down the line, from Eden to Tara and Lessing's grandmothers: that was then and this is now. Ay, there's the rub. A *domaine* exists only at a certain period in a special place.

The difficulty is reconciling those characteristics with our experience of time. Again, the kind that can be discussed without regard to space is philosophical or theological – i.e. inhuman – time (several treatments of which are mentioned in my first chapter). Yet while time as a concept *may* be considered without reference to location, in most *literary* treatments we have to do with human time, and (bating a few exceptions in science fiction) we are always *somewhere* as well as *somewhen*. *Where* and *when* occasionally come together in a certain way and achieve the critical mass I call a *domaine*. But they are rare, enhancing their value; the vast majority of our time is lived outside of *domaines*, though some of that time will be spent remembering and perhaps trying to revive them in our imaginations or in literature. A "time *machine*" may be used to transport our consciousness back to a *domaine*, but time and *domaines* do appear to be two distinguishable entities.

IN THE INTRODUCTION TO PART II, I suggested that Mircea Eliade's "Myth of the Eternal Return" provides a communal analogy to the (mostly) individual revelations characteristic of the *domaine*. In my subsequent chapters, especially Chapter 10 on world literature, that analogy has continued to resonate, which is not surprising, given the global reach of Eliade's research. His work is so deeply germane to mine that I need to return to him here and discuss his findings in more detail. Their relevance will, I hope, be more obvious now.

Eliade asserts that archaic man's recurrent rituals were meant to emulate the actions of "gods, ancestors, or heroes," which constituted a "transcendant reality" imitating a "celestial archetype" (4-5). These rituals were understood as having come down from the beginning of the world. It follows that "every ritual has...an archetype": the original supernatural act being imitated (21). Eliade believes that such rites abolished or suspended ordinary time, transporting the participants to a "mythical moment" at "the beginning of time" (35) – an idea he develops later in connection with Fijian rituals that "annul past time" to return to the beginning (80-81). In that sense, the ritual functioned as a time machine, and, viewed sacrally, the celebrant was transformed into the imitated archetype. In like manner, individuals who encounter a powerful *domaine*, such as Alain-Fournier's Augustin Meaulnes and Fowles's Nicholas Urfe, feel that they have reached an extraordinary place where they are in contact with ancient traditions or a society more real, more fundamental to their existence, than life as they have previously known it.

Eliade argues that ancient societies' solar, lunar, and agricultural rites, besides marking the phases of the year, were designed to purify the people and regenerate life and time: to make a fresh start. "Creation" was not a long-ago event but a periodic recurrence; at the New Year, ordinary time halted, chaos recurred, and then life began anew. The fires lit at the winter solstice renewed creation; in some cases, anarchic social reversals symbolized a return to the primordial. Though primitive societies realized that history could not be changed, he says, they tried to live in "the paradise of archetypes" (Eliade 74-77). Northrop Frye would call this a regaining of their sense of identity with the world. Eliade notes that Brahmanic sacrifices aim to restore the original unity of "the *whole*," while ancient East Indian tribes enacted "a symbolic return to the atemporal instant of primordial plenitude" (78, 82). The moon's importance in archaic rituals arose from the way it measured time, encouraging a cyclical view of history, and a belief in rebirth and "eternal return." The leading ideas here – (periodic) renewal and purification – also appear in many of my discussions of *domaines* in the preceding chapters. Eliade wonders whether the "tendency toward purification" represented a "nostalgia for the lost paradise of animality" (91). With or without the last two words, that describes many *domaines*, and his assertion that archaic rituals embody "an absolute reality" not of this world applies to most of them: ask de Lorris, Yeats, or Fitzgerald (92).

The beliefs and phenomena that Eliade describes were not *only* "archaic." The myth of the eternal return lingered in Graeco-Roman thought: Plato's myth of an original paradise, Hesiod's and Ovid's golden age. Ideas of periodic returns, and the Persian-Zoroastrian notion of a great fire ending cycles of history, were common in Near and Middle Eastern cultures. In the *Zend-Avesta*, after the cosmic fire comes a renewal of the world, purged of evil, old age, and death, a perfect world of immortals living in "beatitude" (Eliade 124): Heaven, perhaps, or a new *domaine* that you must go through fire to reach. The key question for Eliade becomes, "How has man tolerated history?" (130). For him, our belief systems try to rationalize the awfulness of the past. But whether you believe in one life or cycle or many, he says, we are always in a "descending phase" in a "crepuscular world" (131). Things *always* used to be better and are getting worse. In that case the "eternal return" must not be perfectly efficient; something is lost each time. As in mechanics, and *domaines*, perpetual motion machines are illusory.

Eliade believed that a "considerable fraction" of humanity "still lives" by the "traditional" views he calls "archaic"; even western writers as central as T.S. Eliot and James Joyce struck him as "saturated with nostalgia" for the myth of the eternal return, with its "abolition of time" (152-53). The finale of his argument is interesting and controversial. Maintaining that Christian thought resists "eternal returns" and cycles, Eliade concluded that Christianity is "the religion of 'fallen man,'" that is, of *modern* man who, "identified with history and progress," has abandoned "the paradise of archetypes and repetition" – of returns to Eden – to focus on Heaven (162). This takes us some distance past *domaines* as originally defined, but then so did *The Story of the Stone* and *The Peach Blossom Fan*, which manifested the influences of Buddhism and Taoism. Like most ideas and ideals, *domaines* are subject to reinterpretation.

LET ME CLARIFY WHAT I think has been established here. I set out to ask what motives compel us to write or read imaginative literature, and to identify the abiding "uses, roles, or benefits" that it has been thought to have. I proposed that two such roles occur often enough to rank as archetypes. Part One examined how a variety of authors used literature to address "the problem of time": its intractability, inexorably unidirectional flow, destructive effects, etc. By preserving moments, reviewing the past, or imagining the future, writers made literature a kind of "time machine." Part Two discussed the evidence of unforgettable portions of a writer's or character's life where and when something momentous happened, generating a kind of nostalgic homage, whether remembered as blessed, scarifying, or some of each. Following Henri Alain-Fournier and John Fowles, I call this a *domaine*, which is both a place and a time. I submit that the examples presented in Parts One and Two show that those are powerful and widespread attractions of literature. In Chapter 10 I tested this finding on a selection of world literature, and found a version of the same results. There were certainly differences, such as what a belief in reincarnation and karma do to one's concept of time, but eastern texts were no less time-conscious for that. And if *domaines* of the positive kind seemed a bit scarcer outside western literature, they still occurred, and my small sample might not yield reliable statistics on such a point. So my premise about time and *domaines* being central concerns of literature survives global exposure modified, but mostly intact.

My confidence in this conclusion has been bolstered since I began writing as other works and passages that support it have come to my attention (or been brought to my notice). Canadian novelist Margaret Laurence's *The Diviners* (1974) has as pervasive a sense of time's many aspects as I have found. Her "River of Now and Then" is a river of time, and it "flowed both ways" (Laurence 11). Actually it flows south but the wind can blow its surface north, so we see what she means. Heraclitus (ca 500 BCE) observed that 'You cannot step twice into the same river' because its components are ever-changing. A river is a symbol of flux over time, and it flows "both ways" as our time machines – memory and imagination – take us back or forward. So the protagonist Morag immediately states her age; guesses that the river "would probably go on like this...for another million or so years" if left alone; pulls out her photograph album, puts its pictures in chronological order, and describes a series of "Snapshots": popular time-stoppers (14). This frames up the whole of the novel, which touches on time travel via literature, the losses that come with time, and the seasonal cycle. At the end Laurence returns to the River of Now and Then, and begins to write her novel about living in the stream of time.

Ursula K. Le Guin's *Always Coming Home* (1985) is a remarkable, original, even unique work of science fiction. Le Guin creates a whole world: people(s), land, language, beliefs, society, diet, myths, etc. She appears as the "Editor," an anthropologist (like her actual father) studying the Valley people, and as "Pandora," said to have brought them the gift of time (Le Guin 148, 430, 506). Her portrait of the Kesh draws on Amerindian customs, hippie communes, the Greens, Taoism, and village life in general. "Dancing the Moon" (245-50) depicts a *domaine* of love and harmony. Maps – which often signal a *domaine* – abound: "Rivers That Run into the Inland Sea" (half-drowned California); "Peoples and Places Known to the Kesh" (the Central Valley); close-ups of a village and middle-distance maps of river towns and watersheds. "Back of the book" gives information on Kesh lodges, kinship, arts, clothes, food, dances, The Train (wood and iron, pulled by a steam engine or beasts), medicine (a naturopathic *domaine*), games, love and sex, literature, and music (they did not record musical performances, considering that "a mistake concerning the nature of Time": 505). Their enemies, the Condors, sound like Arabs or Mormons (immured women), or us (tanks and warplanes). "Time in the Valley" tells the Kesh creation stories.

But this is only one level of the story. "Time and the City" alters the picture radically, describing their computer technology and "the City of Mind." Computers refer to humans as "makers" and consider them relatives, "primitive" ancestors, "divergent and retarded" (152). "Exchanges" are where humans and computers interact. The Exchange has internet and stations in deep space, but Kesh homes are not online. The post-Neolithic millennia of long ago are called "the City of Man" (152-53). One man found a "hole" to "the outside world" of backward people there, but it poisoned him (154-57). Big Man (God) made Little Man: humans with their heads on backwards. Little Man poisoned the earth and died of fear. The Kesh believe that Little Man must have ruined the world deliberately to have done so much damage; they had their "heads on wrong" (159). In my terms, the City of Man was a dystopia or anti-*domaine*, out of which the Kesh have made a better world – until or unless the Condors, or the computers, take it over.

Alice Munro, who gave us an instance and a definition of a *domaine* (Prologue to Part Two), has also described the metamorphosis of our sense of time. In the story "Child's Play" (in *Too Much Happiness*, 2009), she prefaces the narrative of a long-ago drowning with general remarks on how chronological awareness grows up. "Every year, when you're a child, you become a different person," and you feel it in the fall as you enter a different grade in school (Munro 188). For most children that happens regularly, year after year, and "For a long while the past drops away from you easily and it would seem automatically, properly" (188-89). You could be lulled by the rhythm, like a deciduous tree, but "then there's a switchback, what's been over and done with sprouting up fresh, wanting attention, even wanting you to do something about it, though it's plain there is not on this earth a thing to be done" (189). Munro knows how to move suddenly from a seemingly placid and even banal surface to a rough one: here, a shocking catapult into adulthood, and a realization that "healing all things" is not time's full job description.

Chris Adrian transplanted the idea of his novel *The Great Night* (2011) from

Shakespeare's *A Midsummer Night's Dream* to contemporary San Francisco. Midsummer night, the shortest of the year, is still wild: elaborate observances, anarchic parties, odd doings, and "magical... transformation" (Adrian 6). The "faeries" are out dancing and making things happen, for this night of abnormal and absurd rule is as much a *domaine* as in Shakespeare (15). The moon looks bigger than Will has ever seen it, he cannot orient himself in Golden Gate Park (which he knows well) tonight, or recognize its trees, though he is an arborist; all is "strange" and "weird" in a "dreamy undream" (81-82). Molly feels "suspended in a place where absolutely anything could happen": "dancing squirrels," "insomniac budgies," and "frogs lined up on the top two" steps, staring at her (97). Huff wanders there too, sensing "a different order...much stranger than anything else he'd ever lived through, and yet it didn't feel at all unreal" (113). Space is malleable; you can march for "longer than ought to have been possible, given the size of the park" (115). Will, blown away by the "wonder and horror" of the Great Night, just tries to appreciate "the extraordinary things...around him" (186). Overall, about par for novitiates stumbling into a *domaine* for the first time.

The reputation of Cixin Liu has spread from his native China and science fiction buffs to a global audience. His Tri-Solaran trilogy (*The Three-Body Problem*, *The Dark Forest*, and *Death's End*) is marketed as "The Remembrance of Earth's Past." The later chapters of the final volume are particularly interesting. In his future, Earth becomes untenable due to attacks by forces in other galaxies, and some humans flee to planets in distant systems. Their physicists and cosmologists work to "recover the original appearance of the universe before the wars...a really lovely time, when the universe itself was a Garden of Eden" (Liu, 559). But its "beauty could only be described mathematically," for "The universe of the Edenic Age was ten-dimensional...how beautiful that ten-dimensional Garden must have been." By then time has been kneaded, stretched, even altered, through long "hibernations," lightspeed travel, and manipulating the speed of light, yet the characters and the narrator still find it "the cruelest force of all" (Liu, 578, 579). Ironically, the way to send messages farthest into the future is still to carve them in stone. Liu brings his time and *domaine* interests together in the chapter "Outside of Time." The First Couple are "immersed in a time vacuum" and total darkess (582). "Time did not flow here," for "time did not exist." Then darkness pales and "time began." The sun brightens "like a song" and blue sky overarches a "pastoral":

"an unplanted field with black soil" beside "an exquisite white house," and "the peaceful scene appeared like a welcoming embrace." The house "looked brand new" – not surprisingly, "as time had just begun to flow" (583). They will want farmhands, but instead of human slaves, a row of robots awaits instructions. To follow this *domaine* farther I would have to issue a spoiler alert. Mr Liu has the most fertile imagination I have encountered in an eon or two.

But I see critics rise in the pit, hear a clamour from the gallery – What, more time machines? New *domaines*?! – so let me also stipulate to what has *not* been done. There are two main points, one already mentioned: I do not claim that time (machines) and *domaines* are the only possible archetypal foundations of imaginative literature. That would clearly be premature, and hubristic. They are rather the two roles or functions that have insistently obtruded on my consciousness during several decades of reading with this question in mind. I am convinced that they are valid answers, but I do not and cannot say that they have a monopoly, that there are no allies or alternatives. Wider reading or subtler senses than mine may discover other archetypes that are not simply subsets of these two, or devise a way to resolve my two into one, perhaps by finding a greater entity that subsumes them both. I would welcome that development, and hope to live to see it. Being corrected or trampled by succeeding generations is the way scholarship progresses.

Some readers may be disappointed that I do not discuss works that exhibit an interest neither in time nor in *domaines*, and then explain what they are doing instead. In offering what I believe to be an original account of how literature works for us, I conceived my proper role as making my own case, not rebutting it. I am aware of objections to it, however, some of which are mentioned in the Introduction. While friends and colleagues have generally been interested and supportive, some – especially creative writers – have been dubious, as in "That's not what *I'm* about!" Of course writers do not let academics tell them what they are *really* doing, so my response is to back away. Yet if pressed, a writer will often give an account that sounds to me like a version of the functions I have explored in this book; or will offer an alternative, such as "I'm a satirist." Yes, but *why* do you write satire, or we read it? A satirist is basically a disillusioned idealist who has utopian ideas about society, i.e. can imagine a *domaine*, but sees that society is actually dystopian (Swift), or fears a future dystopia (Orwell). Then we may argue about whether "classic" satire is the only kind, and whether its explanation fits other types, while the core of my subject falls astern. Or my informant says that s/he is a comedian, or a tragedian, or a wit, starting a different chain of explanations. In this book I have tried to move beyond genres, to analyze the underlying human impulses that drive us to write and / or read, whatever the form.

But my readers will be the ultimate judges of the book's shortcomings and achievements. Dr Johnson famously held that "by the common sense of readers uncorrupted with literary prejudices, after all the refinements of subtilty and the dogmatism of learning, must be finally decided all claim to poetical honours" ("Life of Gray"). Virginia Woolf's *Common Reader* implies her approval of this view, a version of which applies to critical and scholarly writing as well.

WORKS CITED

Adams, Hazard, and Leroy Searle, eds. Critical Theory Since 1965. Tallahassee: Florida State UP, 1986.

Adjustment Bureau, The. Dir. George Nolfi. Universal Pictures, 2011.

Adrian, Chris. The Great Night. 2011. New York: Picador, 2012.

Aesthetic Transgressions: Modernity, Liberalism, and the Function of Literature. Eds. Thomas Claviez, Ulla Haselstein, and Sieglinde Lemke. Heidelberg: Universitätsverlag, Winter 2006.

Agee, James. A Death in the Family. 1957. New York: Penguin, 2008.

Alain-Fournier, Henri. Le Grand Meaulnes. 1913. N.p.: Librairie Fayard, 1971.

---. Le Grand Meaulnes. Trans. Frank Davison. 1959. Harmondsworth: Penguin, 1966.

---. The Lost Estate. Trans. Robin Buss. London: Penguin Classics, 2007.

---. Towards the Lost Domain. Letters from London 1905. Trans. and ed. W.J. Strachan. Manchester and New York, 1986.

Ames, Christopher. The Life of the Party. Festive Vision in Modern Fiction. Athens: U Georgia P, 1991.

Apuleius. The Golden Ass of Apuleius. Trans. Robert Graves. 1951. New York: Pocket Books, Cardinal Ed., 1953.

Arabian Nights, The. The Portable Arabian Nights. Trans. John Payne. Ed. Joseph Campbell. New York: Viking, 1952.

Avatar. Dir. James Cameron. 20th Century Fox, 2009.

Back to the Future. Dir. Robert Zemeckis. Universal Pictures, 1985.

Baker's Pocket Bible Concordance. Grand Rapids, MI: Baker Book House, Direction Books, 1974.

Bamba Suso and Banna Kanute. See *Sunjata*.

Baugh, Albert C. *A Literary History of England*. Ed. A.C. Baugh. New York: Appleton-Century-Crofts, 1948.

Beckford, William. See Jack; Gemmitt; Oliver; and Thacker.

Behn, Aphra. *Oroonoko or the Royal Slave*. 1688. Introd. Lore Metzger. New York: W.W. Norton, 1973.

Being Erica. Television series. CBC, 2009-2011.

Bennett, Arnold. *The Old Wives' Tale*. 1908. Introd. Alan Sillitoe. London: Pan, 1964.

Bible, The Holy. King James Version. Oxford and Toronto: Oxford UP, n.d. (Preface 1897).

Big. Dir. Penny Marshall. 20th Century Fox, 1988.

Birch, Cyril. See K'ung and Tang.

Blake, William. *The Complete Writings of William Blake*. Ed. Geoffrey Keynes. London: Nonesuch; New York: Random House, 1957.

Blanchot, Maurice. See Adams and Searle.

Blixen, Karen [Isak Dinesen]. *Out of Africa*. 1937. *Out of Africa and Shadows on the Grass*. Harmondsworth: Penguin, 1985. Film version: Dir. Sidney Pollack. Universal, 1985.

Bloch, Ernst. *The Utopian Function of Art and Literature. Selected Essays*. Trans. Jack Zipes and Frank Mechlenburg. Cambridge, MA, and London: MIT Press, 1988.

Brigadoon. Alan J. Lerner and Frederic Loewe. Stage: New York, Ziegfeld Theatre, 1947. Film: Dir. Vincente Minnelli. MGM, 1954.

Burnett, Frances Hodgson. *The Secret Garden*. Lavergne, TN: n.p., 2014.

Burroughs, Edgar Rice. *The Caspak Trilogy*. Ed. Glenn Kahley. N.p.: Kahley House, 2008.

Butch Cassidy and the Sundance Kid. Dir. George Roy Hill. 20th Century Fox, 1969.

Calvino, Italo. The Uses of Literature: Essays. 1980. Trans. Patrick Creagh. New York: Harcourt, Brace Jovanovich, 1986.

Campbell, Joseph. The Hero With a Thousand Faces. 1949. 2nd ed. Princeton, NJ: Princeton UP, 1968. Paperback ed., 1972.

---. The Masks of God: Occidental Mythology. 1964. New York: Viking Penguin, 1976.

---. The Thousand and One Nights. Trans. John Payne. Introd. Joseph Campbell. New York: Viking, 1950.

Cao Xueqin. The Story of the Stone. 5 vols. Trans. David Hawkes (vv. 1-3) and John Minford (vv. 4-5). London: Penguin Books, 1973-1986. See also Dream of the Red Chamber.

---. The Story of the Stone. Vol. 3, "The Warning Voice." Trans. David Hawkes. 1980. Bloomington: Indiana UP, 1981.

Chaucer, Geoffrey. See Robinson, F.N.

Chrétien de Troyes. Arthurian Romances. Trans. D.D.R. Owen. London: Dent, 1987.

Coe, Michael D. The Maya. 1966. London: Penguin / Pelican Books, 1971.

Coleridge, Samuel T. The Selected Poetry and Prose of Samuel Taylor Coleridge. Ed. and introd. Donald A. Stauffer. New York: Random House, 1951.

Daniel, Samuel. See Rollins.

Dickens, Charles. Bleak House. 1853. Introd. Morton Dauwen Zabel. Boston: Houghton Mifflin, 1956.

---. Great Expectations. 1861. Introd. Earle Davis. 2nd ed. New York: Holt, Rinehart, Winston, 1972.

Dirda, Michael. Bound to Please. New York: Norton, 2005.

Drayton, Michael. See Rollins.

Dream of the Red Chamber, The (Cao, Story of the Stone, abr.). Trans. Florence and Isabel McHugh, from the German trans. by Franz Kuhn (1932). Introd. Franz Kuhn. 1958. New York: Grosset and Dunlap, 1968.

---. Trans. and "retold" by Wang Guozhen. N.p.: China International Press, n.d.

Dunne, J[ohn] W[illiam]. An Experiment with Time. 1927. New ed. London: Faber, 1939, 1958.

Durant, Will. Our Oriental Heritage. The Story of Civilization: Part I. New York: Simon and Schuster, 1935.

---. The Life of Greece. New York: Simon and Schuster, 1939.

Dutt, Romesh. See Ramayana.

Eliade, Mircea. The Myth of the Eternal Return. 1949. Trans. Willard R. Trask. Bollingin Ser. XLVI. New York: Random House, Pantheon, 1954.

Etherege, George. See Pinto, V.

Eyes Wide Shut. Dir. Stanley Kubrick. Warner Bros., 1999.

Felski, Rita. Uses of Literature. Malden, MA, and Oxford: Blackwell, 2008.

Field of Dreams. Dir. Phil Alden Robinson. Universal Pictures, 1989.

Final Countdown, The. Dir. Don Taylor. United Artists, 1980.

Fitzgerald, F. Scott. The Diamond as Big as the Ritz and Other Stories. Harmondsworth: Penguin, 1962.

---. The Great Gatsby. 1925. New York: Bantam, 1945.

---. The Stories of F. Scott Fitzgerald. 1951. New York: Collier / MacMillan, 1986.

---. Tender Is the Night. New York: Scribner's, 1933.

---. This Side of Paradise. 1920. New York: Dover, 1996.

Fowles, John. "Behind The Magus". 1994; emended 1995. Rpt. In Twentieth Century Literature 42, no. 1, 1996, 58-68.

---. Daniel Martin. Boston: Little, Brown, 1977.

---. Ebony Tower, The. 1974. Scarborough, ON: NAL of Canada, 1975.

---. Magus, The. 1965. New York: Dell, 1973.

---. Magus, The. A Revised Version. 1978. New York: Dell, 1979.

Fraser, J.T. The Genesis and Evolution of Time. Amherst: U Massachusetts P, 1982.

Frazer, James G. The Golden Bough. 1922. 1 vol., abridged ed. New York: Macmillan, 1960.

Freud, Sigmund. Civilization and Its Discontents. 1930. The Standard Edition. Trans. and ed. James Strachey. New York: Norton, 1961.

Gadamer, Hans-Georg. See Adams and Searle.

Gautier, Théophile. Poésies Complètes de Théophile Gautier. V. 3. Paris: Firmin-Didot, n.d. (1932?)

Geertz, Clifford, ed. Myth, Symbol, and Culture. New York: Norton, 1971.

Gemmett, Robert J. William Beckford. Boston: G.K. Hall, 1977.

Gilgamesh, The Epic of. Trans. and introd. N.K. Sandars. Harmondsworth: Penguin, 1964.

Golding, William. Pincher Martin. 1956. Harmondsworth: Penguin, 1962.

Good, Graham. "The Hegemony of Theory." Univ. of Toronto Quarterly 65.3 (Summer 1996): 534-55.

Grant, Michael, ed. Roman Readings. Harmondsworth: Penguin, 1958, rev. 1967.

Graves, Robert. Some Speculations on Literature, History, and Religion. Ed. Patrick Quinn. Manchester: Carcanet, 2000.

---. The White Goddess. Amended and enlarged ed. London: Faber & Faber, 1961.

---. See also Apuleius.

Greene, Brian. The Elegant Universe. Superstrings, Hidden Dimensions, and the Quest for the Ultimate Theory. 1999. New York: Random House Vintage, 2000, 2003.

Groundhog Day. Dir. Harold Ramis. Columbia Pictures, 1993.

Gunn, J. Alexander. The Problem of Time. An Historical and Critical Study. London: Allen and Unwin, 1929.

Haley, Alex. Roots. The Saga of an American Family. 1974. Thirtieth Anniversary Ed. Da Capo: n.p., 2014.

Harrison, G.B., ed. Shakespeare. The Complete Works. New York: Harcourt, Brace, 1948, 1952.

Harvey, Sir Paul, comp. and ed. The Oxford Companion to Classical Literature. Oxford: Clarendon, 1937. Rpt. with corrections, 1940-1974.

Hayy Ibn Yaqzan. See Verde, Tom.

Heidegger, Martin. See Adams and Searle.

Herodotus. The Histories. Trans. Aubrey de Sélincourt. Baltimore: Penguin, 1954.

Herrick, Robert. See White, Helen.

Hesiod. See Durant, Will, The Life of Greece.

Howe, Susan. The Winter Sun. Notes on a Vocation. Rev. in The Nation (6 Apr. 2009) by Ange Mlinko: 34-36.

Hudson, W.H. Far Away and Long Ago. London: Dent, 1918.

---. Green Mansions. A Romance of the Tropical Forest. 1904. Mineola, NY: Dover, 1989.

---. Idle Days in Patagonia. 1893. Berkeley: Creative Arts, 1979.

Hughes, Peter. Spots of Time. Toronto: CBC, 1969.

Huxley, Aldous. "Usually Destroyed." 1955. In Collected Essays by Aldous Huxley. London: Chatto and Windus, 1959.

Ibn Tufayl. See Verde, Tom.

Iser, Wolfgang. "Changing Functions of Literature." In Prospecting. From Reader Response to Literary Anthropology. Baltimore and London: Johns Hopkins P, 1989.

Jack, Malcolm. William Beckford: an English Fidalgo. New York: AMS, 1996.

Jeffries, Richard. Bevis. The Story of a Boy. 1882. Everyman ed. London: Dent, 1930.

Johnson, Samuel. Samuel Johnson. Rasselas, Poems, and Selected Prose. Ed. and Introd. Bertrand H. Bronson. 1958. 3rd ed. New York: Holt, Rinehart and Winston, 1971.

Keats, John. See Thorpe, Clarence D., ed.

Kinsella, W.P. See <u>Field of Dreams</u>.

Kitto, H.D.F. <u>The Greeks</u>. Baltimore: Penguin Books, 1951. Rpt. with rev., 1957.

Kuhn, Franz. See <u>Dream of the Red Chamber</u>.

K'ung Shang-jen. <u>The Peach Blossom Fan</u>. Trans. Chen Shih-hsiang and Harold Acton, with Cyril Birch. Berkeley: U California P, 1976.

Laurence, Margaret. <u>The Diviners</u>. Toronto: McClelland and Stewart, 1974.

Le Guin, Ursula K. <u>Always Coming Home</u>. New York: Harper and Row, 1985.

Lessing, Doris. <u>The Grandmothers</u>. <u>Four Short Novels</u>. New York: HarperCollins, 2003.

Lewis, C.S. <u>The Allegory of Love</u>. 1936. New York: Oxford UP (Galaxy), 1958.

---. <u>The Complete Chronicles of Narnia</u>. New York: HarperCollins, 1998.

---. <u>A Preface to Paradise Lost</u>. 1942. London: Oxford UP Paperbacks, 1960.

Li He. <u>The Poetry of Li He</u>. Trans. and introd. John Warden, with Dai Daqi. N.p.: n.p., n.d.

Liu, Cixin. <u>Death's End</u>. 2010. Trans. Ken Liu. A Tor Book. New York: Macmillan, 2016.

<u>Lost Horizon</u>. Dir. Frank Capra. Columbia Pictures, 1937.

Lukács, Georg. See Adams and Searle.

MacIver, R.M. <u>The Challenge of the Passing Years. My Encounter with Time</u>. New York: Simon and Schuster, 1962.

Mackenzie, John L. <u>Dictionary of the Bible</u>. 1964. New York: MacMillan, 1965.

<u>Mahabharata</u>. See <u>Ramayana</u>.

de Man, Paul. "The Rhetoric of Temporality." 1969. In <u>Blindness and Insight</u>. 1971. 2nd ed. rev. Minneapolis: U Minnesota P, 1983.

Margolies, David N. <u>The Function of Literature</u>. <u>A Study of Christopher Caudwell's Aesthetics</u>. New York: International Publishers, 1969.

Marie de France. <u>The Lais of Marie de France</u>. Trans. Robert Hanning and Joan Ferrante. 1978. Durham, NC: Labyrinth P, 1982.

Marvell, Andrew. See White, Helen.

Maxwell, J.C. See Wordsworth 1972.

Meerloo, Joost A.M. Along the Fourth Dimension. New York: Day, 1970.

Meyerhoff, Hans. Time in Literature. Berkeley and Los Angeles: U California P, 1955.

Midnight in Paris. Dir. Woody Allen. Sony Pictures, 2011.

Millennium. Dir. Michael Anderson. 20th Century Fox, 1989.

Miller, J. Hillis. On Literature. London and New York. Routledge, 2002.

Milton, John. John Milton. Paradise Lost. A New Edition. Ed. Merritt Hughes. Indianapolis: Odyssey Press, Bobbs-Merrill, 1962.

Mitchell, Joni. "Woodstock". Perf. 1969. Released 1970 as B-side of "Big Yellow Taxi" single. Hollywood: A & M Studios. Pub. Sony / ATV Music.

Mitchell, Margaret. Gone with the Wind. 1936. Pref. Pat Conroy (1996). New York: Simon & Schuster, Pocket Books, 2008.

Mlinko, Ange. See Howe, Susan.

Montaigne, Michel de. Essays. Trans. and Introd. J.M. Cohen. Harmondsworth: Penguin, 1958.

Mooij, J.J.A. Fictional Realities. The Uses of Literary Imagination. Amsterdam and Philadelphia: John Benjamins Publishing, 1993.

Munro, Alice. Too Much Happiness. Toronto: Penguin Canada, 2009.

Murasaki Shikibu. The Tale of Genji. Trans. and Introd. Edward G. Seidensticker. New York: Knopf, 1987.

Nahin, Paul J. Time Machines. Time Travel in Physics, Metaphysics, and Science Fiction. New York: American Institute of Physics, 1993.

Nordmann, Charles. The Tyranny of Time. Einstein or Bergson?. Trans. E.E. Fournier D'Albe. London: T. Fisher Unwin, 1925.

Norris, Christopher. What's Wrong with Postmodernism. Critical Theory and the Ends of Philosophy. Baltimore: Johns Hopkins UP, 1990.

Oliver, J.W. The Life of William Beckford. London: Oxford UP, 1932.

Orfeo Negro. Dir. Marcel Camus. Lopert Pictures, 1959.

Orgel, Stephen. The Jonsonian Masque. 1965. New York: Columbia UP, 1981.

Out of Africa. See Blixen, Karen.

Ovid. Metamorphoses. Trans. Frank Justus Miller. Loeb Classical Library. 2 vols. Vol. 1, 1916. 2nd ed. Cambridge, MA: Harvard UP; London: Heinemann, 1921.

Oxford Companion to English Literature, The. Ed. Sir Paul Harvey. 1932. 3rd ed. Oxford: Clarendon Press, 1946.

Peggy Sue Got Married. Dir. Francis F. Coppola. TriStar Pictures, 1986.

Petronius. See Grant, Michael.

The Philadelphia Experiment. Dir. Stewart Raffill. New World Pictures, 1984.

Pinto, Vivian de Sola, ed. Poetry of the Restoration. London: Heinemann, 1966.

Planet of the Apes. Dir. Franklin J. Schaffner. 20th Century Fox, 1968.

Plato. Symposium. In Great Dialogues of Plato. Trans. W.H.D. Rouse. New York: NAL Mentor, 1956.

---. Timaeus. Trans. Benjamin Jowett. 3rd ed. Intro. Glenn R. Morrow. Indianapolis: Bobbs-Merrill, 1949.

Popol Vuh. See Tedlock, Dennis, trans.

Proust, Marcel. The Past Recaptured. Trans. Frederick A. Blossom. New York: Random House, 1932.

---. Swann's Way. Trans. C.K. Scott Moncrieff. Intro. Lewis Galantiere. New York: Random House, 1928.

Quantum Leap. NBC Universal Television, 1989-93.

Ramayana, The, and the Mahabharata. Trans. Romesh C. Dutt. London: Dent, 1910.

River Runs Through It, A. Dir. Robert Redford. Columbia Pictures, 1992.

Robinson, F.N. The Works of Geoffrey Chaucer. 1933. 2nd ed. Boston: Houghton Mifflin; Cambridge: Riverside Press, 1957.

Rochester, Earl of. See Pinto, Vivian.

Rollins, Hyder E., and Herschel Baker, eds. The Renaissance in England. Boston: D.D. Heath, 1954.

Roman (or Romaunt) de la Rose. See Robinson, F.N.

Rousseau, Jean-Jacques. Julie; or the New Eloise. Trans. Philip Stewart and Jean Vaché. Hanover, NH: UP of New England, 1997.

Said, Edward. The World, the Text, and the Critic. Cambridge, MA: Harvard UP, 1983.

Salami, Mahmoud. John Fowles's Fiction and the Poetics of Postmodernism. London and Toronto: Associated UP, 1992.

Sartre, Jean-Paul. Qu'est-ce que la littérature? 1949. What Is Literature? Trans. Bernard Frechtman. New York: Harper and Row, 1965.

Sei Shōnagon. The Pillow Book of Sei Shōnagon. Trans. Ivan Morris. 1967. Harmondsworth: Penguin, 1971.

Shakespeare, William. Shakespeare. The Complete Works. Ed. G. B. Harrison. 1948. New York: Harcourt, Brace, 1952.

---. The Tempest. Ed. Robert Langbaum. New York: NAL Signet Classics, 1964.

Sidney, Sir Philip. See Rollins, Hyder E., and Orgel, Stephen.

Sir Gawain and the Green Knight. Trans. Marie Borroff. New York: Norton, 1967.

Sliders. Fox (seasons 1-3); Sci Fi Channel (seasons 4-5). Distrib. NBCUniversal. 1995-2000.

Somewhere in Time. Dir. Jeannot Szwarc. Universal Pictures, 1980.

Source Code. Dir. Duncan Jones. Summit Entertainment, 2011.

Spenser, Edmund. Spenser. Poetical Works. Ed. J.C. Smith and E. de Selincourt. Intro. E. de Selincourt. 1912. New York: Oxford UP, 1970.

Stargate. Dir. Roland Emmerich. Distrib. MGM / UA (US) and AMLF (France), 1994. TV series, "Stargate SG-1," 1997-2007.

Star Trek. (The Original Series) CTV, NBC, 1966-69. (Film) Star Trek: The Motion Picture. Dir. Robert Wise. Paramount, 1979.

Stillinger, Jack. See Wordsworth, Willam, 1965.

Stone, Lawrence. The Family, Sex, and Marriage in England 1500-1800. London: Weidenfeld and Nicolson, 1977.

Strelka, Joseph P., ed. Literary Theory and Criticism. Festschrift Presented to René Wellek in Honor of His Eightieth Birthday. New York: Peter Lang, 1984.

Sunjata. Gambian Versions of the Mande Epic. (By Bamba Suso and Banna Kanute.) Ed. Lucy Durán and Graham Furniss. London: Penguin Classics, 1999.

Sypher, Wylie. Four Stages of Renaissance Style. Transformations in Art and Literature 1400-1700. New York: Doubleday Anchor, 1955.

Tang Xianzu. The Peony Pavilion. Trans. and intro. Cyril Birch. Bloomington: Indiana UP, 1981.

Tao Yuanming. The Complete Works of Tao Yuanming. Trans. Wang Rongpei. Hunan: Hunan People's Publishing House, 2003.

Tarbox, Katherine. The Art of John Fowles. Athens, GA: U Georgia P, 1988.

Tedlock, Dennis, trans. Popol Vuh. Rev. ed. New York: Simon and Schuster / Touchstone, 1996.

Tempest. Dir. Paul Mazursky. Columbia Pictures, 1982.

Thacker, Christopher. The Wildness Pleases. The Origins of Romanticism. London: Croon Helm; New York: St. Martin's P, 1983.

Thorpe, Clarence Dewitt, ed. John Keats. Complete Poems and Selected Letters. New York: Odyssey, 1935.

Time After Time. Dir. Nicholas Meyer. Warner Bros., 1979.

Timecop. Dir. Peter Hyams. Universal Pictures, 1994. (TV) ABC, 1997-98. Distrib. NBCUniversal.

Time Machine, The. Dir. George Pal. Loew's, 1960.

Time Trackers. Dir. Howard R. Cohen. Concorde Pictures, 1989.

Time Travelers, The. Dir. Ib Melchior. American International Pictures, 1964.

Time Traveler's Wife, The. Dir. Robert Schwentke. Warner Bros., 2009.

Toulmin, Stephen, and June Goodfield. The Discovery of Time. New York, Harper and Row, 1965.

Tung, Chieh-yüan. Master Tung's Western Chamber Romance. Trans. and introd. Li-li Ch'en. New York: Columbia UP, 1976.

Twilight Zone, The. CBS, 1959-64, 1985-89, 2019-2020; UPN, 2002-03.

Verde, Tom. "Hayy Was Here, Robinson Crusoe." Aramco World v. 65, #3 (May-June 2014): 2-11.

Verne, Jules. Journey to the Center of the Earth. 1864. London and New York: Penguin, 2009.

Wagon Train. NBC, 1957-62; ABC, 1962-65. (Inspired by Wagon Master. Dir. John Ford. RKO-Radio Pictures, 1950.) "The Princess of a Lost Tribe." Dir. Richard Whorf. NBC, 1960.

Wang Shifu. The Story of the Western Wing. 13th century. Trans. Stephen H. West and Wilt L. Idema. Berkeley: U California P, 1995.

Waugh, Evelyn. Brideshead Revisited. 1945. Rev. ed. London: Penguin, 1962.

Way We Were, The. Dir. Sydney Pollack. Music: Marvin Hamlisch. Columbia Pictures, 1973.

Wells, H.G. "The Door in the Wall." In The Door in the Wall and Other Stories. 1911. E-book, Project Gutenberg Online Catalog, n.d.

---. The Time Machine. 1895. The War of the Worlds and The Time Machine. New York: Doubleday Dolphin, 1961.

Welty, Eudora. Delta Wedding. 1945. Signet ed. New York: NAL, 1963.

Western Chamber Romance. See Tung.

White, Helen C., Ruth C. Wallerstein, and Ricardo Quintana, ed. Seventeenth-Century Verse and Prose. New York: MacMillan, 1951.

Wilmot, John. See Pinto, Vivian.

"Woodstock." CBC Retrospective, "Woodstock Remembered." August 1989. See also Mitchell, Joni.

Wordsworth, William. Poetical Works of Wordsworth, The. Ed. Thomas Hutchinson. 1904. New Ed., rev. Ernest de Selincourt. London: Oxford UP, 1936.

---. William Wordsworth. The Prelude. A Parallel Text. Ed. J.C. Maxwell. London: Penguin, 1972.

---. The Prose Works of William Wordsworth. N.p.: Macmillan, 1896.

---. The Prose Works of William Wordsworth. Ed. W.J.B. Owen and Jane Worthington Smyser. Oxford: Clarendon P, 1974.

---. William Wordsworth. Selected Poems and Prefaces. Ed. Jack Stillinger. Boston: Houghton Mifflin, 1965.

World Without End. Dir. Edward Bernds. Allied Artists Pictures, 1956.

Yeats, William Butler. The Collected Poems of W.B. Yeats. The Definitive Edition, With the Author's Final Revisions. New York: Macmillan, 1960.

CPSIA information can be obtained
at www.ICGtesting.com
Printed in the USA
LVHW052117010422
715014LV00006B/109